DevOps with Windows Server 2016

Obtain enterprise agility and continuous delivery by implementing DevOps with Windows Server 2016

Ritesh Modi

Packt>

BIRMINGHAM - MUMBAI

DevOps with Windows Server 2016

Copyright © 2017 Packt Publishing

First published: March 2017

Production reference: 1210317

Published by Packt Publishing Ltd.
Livery Place
35 Livery Street
Birmingham
B3 2PB, UK.
ISBN 978-1-78646-855-0

www.packtpub.com

Credits

Author
Ritesh Modi

Reviewer
Satya Srinivas Gogula

Commissioning Editor
Pratik Shah

Acquisition Editor
Nitin Dasan

Content Development Editor
Juliana Nair

Technical Editor
Aditya Khadye

Copy Editor
Dipti Mankame

Project Coordinator
Judie Jose

Proofreader
Safis Editing

Indexer
Pratik Shirodkar

Graphics
Kirk D'Penha

Production Coordinator
Shantanu Zagade

About the Author

Ritesh Modi is currently working as Senior Technology Evangelist at Microsoft, where he ensures that developers, startups, and companies are successful in their endeavors using technology. Prior to that, he was an Architect with Microsoft Services and Accenture. He is passionate about technology and his interest lies in both Microsoft as well as open source technologies. He believes optimal technology should be employed to solve business challenges. He is very active in communities and has spoken at national and international conferences.

He is a known industry leader and already a published author. He is a technology mentor for T-Hub and IIIT Hyderabad startup incubators. He has more than 20 certifications and is a Microsoft certified trainer. He's an expert on Azure, DevOps, Bots, Cognitive, IOT, PowerShell, SharePoint, SQL Server, and System Center. He has co-authored a book titled *Introducing Windows Server 2016 Technical Preview* with the Windows Server team. He has spoken at multiple conferences, including TechEd and PowerShell Asia conference, does lots of internal training and is a published author for MSDN magazine. He has more than a decade of experience in building and deploying enterprise solutions for customers. He blogs at `https://automationnext.wordpress.com/` and can be followed on Twitter `@automationnext`. His linked profile is available at `https://www.linkedin.com/in/rite sh-modi/`.

Ritesh currently lives in Hyderabad, India.

Acknowledgments

Writing this book has been a fantastic experience. I personally have gained as a person who has more patience, perseverance, and tenacity than before. I owe a lot to the people who pushed me through their encouragement and motivation. I would like to thank the Almighty and my parents for their blessings. I would like to thank many people for making this book happen.

I must start with the people who mean the world to me, who inspire me to push myself and who ultimately make everything worthwhile. I am talking about my mother Bimla Modi, wife Sangeeta Modi, and daughter Avni Modi, the three wonderful ladies in my life.

Thanks of course must go to the PacktPub team. I would like to thank my editors Rashmi Suvarna and Juliana Nair for taking this project and helping me through it. I would like to thank the acquisition editor, Kirk D'costa, for finding me for this book. I would also like to thank my technical editor, Aditya Khadye, who walked through the book multiple times and gave incredibly useful feedback.

Last but not the least, I would like to thank my team at Microsoft, Manoj Damodaran, Michael Hopmere, and Ravi Mallela with whom I had several discussions to make this book better.

About the Reviewer

Satya works as a DevOps consultant at Microsoft. He enables teams to adopt best DevOps practices across different delivery domains which leads to better agility, reliability, and consistency.

In the past 18 years, he has gathered diverse experience in product planning, development, testing, and release management areas that helps him define DevOps strategy for various software projects.

He delivered multiple product releases in engineering domains such as Geographic Information System, Software Delivery, Unified Communications, Modern Engineering, and Application Lifecycle Management while working at Intergraph, Computer Associates, and Microsoft.

Satya has also contributed to Release Management service, which is an integral part of Visual Studio Team Services (VSTS) and Team Foundation Server (TFS).

Acknowledgments

I would like to thank my son, Kaushal, and my daughter, Srikari, for being patient when I spent most of my personal time during technical review. They are awesome. I would like to thank my wife, Swati, for her constant support. It would not be possible without her.
I would like to thank my mother, Surya Parvathamma, and my father, Krishna Rao, for their blessings. They are foundation of what I am. I would like to thank the author, Ritesh Modi, for asking me to be a part of this wonderful project. I am sure this book will make the implementation of best DevOps practices real. I would like to thank my manager, Manoj Damodaran, and leadership at Microsoft for allowing me to undertake this.

www.PacktPub.com

For support files and downloads related to your book, please visit `www.PacktPub.com`.

Did you know that Packt offers eBook versions of every book published, with PDF and ePub files available? You can upgrade to the eBook version at `www.PacktPub.com` and as a print book customer, you are entitled to a discount on the eBook copy. Get in touch with us at `service@packtpub.com` for more details.

At `www.PacktPub.com`, you can also read a collection of free technical articles, sign up for a range of free newsletters and receive exclusive discounts and offers on Packt books and eBooks.

Mapt

`https://www.packtpub.com/mapt`

Get the most in-demand software skills with Mapt. Mapt gives you full access to all Packt books and video courses, as well as industry-leading tools to help you plan your personal development and advance your career.

Why subscribe?

- Fully searchable across every book published by Packt
- Copy and paste, print, and bookmark content
- On demand and accessible via a web browser

Customer Feedback

Thanks for purchasing this Packt book. At Packt, quality is at the heart of our editorial process. To help us improve, please leave us an honest review on this book's Amazon page at https://www.amazon.com/dp/1786468557.

If you'd like to join our team of regular reviewers, you can e-mail us at customerreviews@packtpub.com. We award our regular reviewers with free eBooks and videos in exchange for their valuable feedback. Help us be relentless in improving our products!

Table of Contents

Preface

With the adoption and popularity of cloud technology, DevOps has become the most happening buzzword in the industry. The concepts of DevOps are not new and have been implemented historically. In recent times, DevOps is getting implemented widespread in enterprise world. Companies that have not yet implemented DevOps have started discussing its potential implementation. In short, DevOps is becoming ubiquitous across both big and small organizations. Organizations are trying to reach out to their customers more often with quality deliverables. They want to achieve this while reducing the risks involved in releasing to production. DevOps helps in releasing features more frequently, faster, and better, in a risk-free manner. It is a common misconception that DevOps is either about automation or technology. Technology and automation are enablers for DevOps and help better and faster DevOps implementation. DevOps is a mindset and culture, it is about how multiple teams come together for a common cause and collaborate with each other, it is about ensuring customers can derive value from software releases, and it is about bringing consistency, predictability, and confidence to overall application life cycle processes. DevOps also has levels of maturity. The highest level of DevOps is achieved when multiple releases can be made in an automated fashion with high quality through continuous integration, continuous delivery, and deployment. It is not necessary that every company should achieve this level of DevOps maturity. It depends on the nature of the company and its projects. While fully automated deployment is a need for some companies, it could be overkill for others. DevOps is a journey and companies typically start from a basic level of maturity by implementing a few of its practices. Eventually, these companies achieve high maturity as and when they keep improving and implementing more and more DevOps practices. DevOps is not complete without appropriate infrastructure for monitoring and measuring health of both environment and application. DevOps forms a closed loop, with operations providing feedback to development teams about things that work well in production and things that do not work well.

In this book, we will explore the main motivation for using DevOps and discuss in detail the implementation of its important practices. Configuration management, source code control, continuous integration, continuous delivery and deployment, monitoring and measuring concepts and implementation will be discussed in depth with the help of a sample application. We will walk through the entire process from scratch. On this journey, we will also explore all the relevant technologies used to achieve the end goal of DevOps.

This book has relevant theory around DevOps, but is heavy on actual implementation using tools and technologies available today. There are many ways to implement DevOps and this book talks about approaches using hands-on technology implementation. There is little or no material that talks about end-to-end DevOps implementations, and this book tries to fill this gap.

I have approached this book by keeping architects, developers and operations teams in mind. I have played these roles, understand the problems they go through, and tried to solve their challenges through practical DevOps implementation.

DevOps is an evolving paradigm and there will be advancements and changes in future. Readers will find this book relevant even in those times.

What this book covers

Chapter 1, *Introducing DevOps*, introduces the motivation for implementing the DevOps paradigm in any software development endeavor. The chapter focuses on practices and principals at a high level, creating the context for other chapters in the book.

Chapter 2, *DevOps Tools and Technologies*, walks through the major technology components important from a DevOps implementation perspective. It discusses cloud technologies, build and release management services, Git, Windows Server 2016, Docker containers, and Nano servers. This chapter provides a brief introduction to each of these technologies.

Chapter 3, *DevOps Automation Primer*, walks through major automation technologies, enabling faster and better DevOps implementation. This chapter provides a brief introduction to PowerShell, Azure Resource Manager templates, Pester, and Desired State Configuration.

Chapter 4, *Nano, Containers, and Docker Primer*, focuses on new Windows Server 2016 features such as Nano servers, containers, and Docker. It provides an introduction to these technologies with examples. The chapter shows how to provision Nano servers using Azure PowerShell, containers using Azure Resource Manager template, and working with Docker and dockerfiles.

Chapter 5, *Building a Sample Application,* introduces a sample application that helps in showing and implementing DevOps practices. It is an ASP.NET MVC web application consisting of a frontend and a database. The chapter also discusses important technical components that are integral to the sample application.

Chapter 6, *Source Code Control,* discusses the importance of using a version control system and provides multiple ways to interact and work with Visual Studio Team Services using Git. It shows ways to check-in the sample application into Git, and multiple ways to interact and work with VSTS Git repositories using Visual Studio. It also provides a small primer into working with Git using commands.

Chapter 7, *Configuration Management,* introduces one of the most important DevOps practices and its implementation. It discusses the concept of Infrastructure as Code and its importance. This chapter focuses on infrastructure and application configuration management. It provides descriptions of the code, scripts, and configuration used for the sample application. The sample application will be deployed using these configuration management artifacts.

Chapter 8, *Configuration Management and Operational Validation,* continues where the last chapter ended. It shows implementation of Infrastructure as Code, along with unit testing and the operational validation of environments.

Chapter 9, *Continuous Integration,* discusses another important DevOps practice and provides details about its importance, principles, benefits, and implementation. Visual Studio Build pipelines are discussed extensively while providing details about a sample build pipeline built for the sample application.

Chapter 10, *Continuous Delivery and Deployment,* discusses two of the most important DevOps practices and provides details about their importance, principles, benefits, and implementation. Visual Studio Release pipelines are discussed extensively while providing details about a sample release pipeline consisting of multiple environments built for the sample application.

Chapter 11, *Monitoring and Measuring,* discusses at length the concepts and implementation related to monitoring and measuring the different aspects of applications and environments in the production environment for the sample application.

What you need for this book

This book assumes a basic level knowledge on Windows operating system, cloud computing and application development using a web programming language, and moderate experience with the application development life cycle. The book will go through deployment of a sample application on Azure within Windows Containers using a set of virtual machine. This requires a basic understanding of cloud storage, computing, networking, and virtualization concepts on Azure. The book implements DevOps practices using Visual Studio Team Services and basic knowledge of this is expected, although this book tries to cover its foundations. If you have experience with Azure and Visual Studio Team Services, this is a big plus.

A valid Azure subscription and Visual Studio Team Services subscription is needed to get started with this book. They are both available free of cost on a trial basis.

As all deployments are made to the cloud, you will require a development environment on a local computer, consisting of:

- CPU: 4 cores
- Memory: 8 GB RAM
- Disk space: 250 GB

This should be enough for the development environment.

In this book, you will need the following software:

- Azure subscription
- Visual Studio Team Services subscription
- Windows 10 OS build 14393 version 1607 or Windows Server 2016 build 14393
- SQL Server Management Studio version 12 or 13
- Git for Windows 64-bit 2.12.0
- Visual Studio community 2015 SP 3 version 14.0
- Docker 1.12.2-cs2-ws-beta

Internet connectivity is required to work with chapters in this book.

Who this book is for

The primary audience of this book are developers, IT professionals, enterprise architects, and software and solution architects who are shaping, implementing and designing strategies for their customers. DevOps engineers, IT operations professionals and students interested in learning and implementing DevOps will find this book extremely useful.

To make full use of the content of this book, basic prior knowledge of a programming language, scripting language, containers, and cloud computing is expected. If you feel you do not have that knowledge, it is always possible to catch up on the basic requirements by quick reading the documentation available on the Internet at `https://docs.microsoft.com/en-gb/`.

Conventions

In this book, you will find a number of text styles that distinguish between different kinds of information. Here are some examples of these styles and an explanation of their meaning.

Code words in text, database table names, folder names, filenames, file extensions, pathnames, dummy URLs, user input, and Twitter handles are shown as follows: "`Dockerfile` is a file containing instructions to create an image"

A block of code is set as follows:

```
{
        "type": "Microsoft.Storage/storageAccounts",
        "name": "[variables('vhdStorageName')]",
        "apiVersion": "2015-06-15",
        "location": "[resourceGroup().location]",
        "tags": {
          "displayName": "StorageAccount"
        },
        "properties": {
          "accountType": "[variables('vhdStorageType')]"
        }
},
```

Any command-line input or output is written as follows:

```
PS C:> docker --version
Docker version 1.12.2-cs2-ws-beta, build 050b611
```

New terms and **important words** are shown in bold. Words that you see on the screen, for example, in menus or dialog boxes, appear in the text like this: "Right-click on *.westeurope.cloudapp.azure.com | **Certificate** | **All Tasks** and then **Export**."

> Warnings or important notes appear in a box like this.

> Tips and tricks appear like this.

Reader feedback

Feedback from our readers is always welcome. Let us know what you think about this book-what you liked or disliked. Reader feedback is important for us as it helps us develop titles that you will really get the most out of. To send us general feedback, simply e-mail feedback@packtpub.com, and mention the book's title in the subject of your message. If there is a topic that you have expertise in and you are interested in either writing or contributing to a book, see our author guide at www.packtpub.com/authors.

Customer support

Now that you are the proud owner of a Packt book, we have a number of things to help you to get the most from your purchase.

Downloading the example code

You can download the example code files for this book from your account at http://www.packtpub.com. If you purchased this book elsewhere, you can visit http://www.packtpub.com/support and register to have the files e-mailed directly to you.

You can download the code files by following these steps:

1. Log in or register to our website using your e-mail address and password.
2. Hover the mouse pointer on the **SUPPORT** tab at the top.
3. Click on **Code Downloads & Errata**.
4. Enter the name of the book in the **Search** box.
5. Select the book for which you're looking to download the code files.
6. Choose from the drop-down menu where you purchased this book from.
7. Click on **Code Download**.

Once the file is downloaded, please make sure that you unzip or extract the folder using the latest version of:

* WinRAR / 7-Zip for Windows
* Zipeg / iZip / UnRarX for Mac
* 7-Zip / PeaZip for Linux

The code bundle for the book is also hosted on GitHub at `https://github.com/PacktPubl ishing/DevOps-with-Windows-Server-2016`. We also have other code bundles from our rich catalog of books and videos available at `https://github.com/PacktPublishing/`. Check them out!

Downloading the color images of this book

We also provide you with a PDF file that has color images of the screenshots/diagrams used in this book. The color images will help you better understand the changes in the output. You can download this file from `https://www.packtpub.com/sites/default/files/down loads/DevOpswithWindowsServer2016_ColorImages.pdf`.

Errata

Although we have taken every care to ensure the accuracy of our content, mistakes do happen. If you find a mistake in one of our books-maybe a mistake in the text or the code-we would be grateful if you could report this to us. By doing so, you can save other readers from frustration and help us improve subsequent versions of this book. If you find any errata, please report them by visiting `http://www.packtpub.com/submit-errata`, selecting your book, clicking on the **Errata Submission Form** link, and entering the details of your errata. Once your errata are verified, your submission will be accepted and the errata will be uploaded to our website or added to any list of existing errata under the Errata section of that title.

To view the previously submitted errata, go to `https://www.packtpub.com/books/content/support` and enter the name of the book in the search field. The required information will appear under the **Errata** section.

Piracy

Piracy of copyrighted material on the Internet is an ongoing problem across all media. At Packt, we take the protection of our copyright and licenses very seriously. If you come across any illegal copies of our works in any form on the Internet, please provide us with the location address or website name immediately so that we can pursue a remedy.

Please contact us at `copyright@packtpub.com` with a link to the suspected pirated material.

We appreciate your help in protecting our authors and our ability to bring you valuable content.

Questions

If you have a problem with any aspect of this book, you can contact us at `questions@packtpub.com`, and we will do our best to address the problem.

1
Introducing DevOps

Change is the only constant in life is something I have been hearing since I was a child. I never understood the saying; school remained the same, the curriculum was the same for years, home was the same, and friends were the same. However, once I joined my first software company, it immediately struck me that yes, *Change is the only constant!* Change is inevitable for any product or service, and this is amplified many times over when related to a software product, system, or service.

Software development is a complex undertaking comprising multiple processes and tools, and involves people from different departments. They all need to come together and work in a cohesive manner. With so much variability, the risks are high when delivering to the end customer. One small omission or misconfiguration and the application might come crashing down. This book is about adopting and implementing practices that reduce this risk considerably and ensure that high-quality software can be delivered to the customer again and again. This chapter is about explaining how **DevOps** brings people, processes, culture, and technology together to deliver software services to the customer effectively and efficiently. It is focused on the theory and concepts of DevOps. The remaining chapters will focus on realizing these concepts through practical examples using Microsoft Windows 2016 and Visual Studio Team Services.

This chapter will answer the following questions:

- What is DevOps?
- Why is DevOps needed?
- What problems are resolved by DevOps?
- What are its constituents, principles, and practices?

Before we get into the details of DevOps itself, let's understand some of the problems software companies face that are addressed by DevOps.

Software delivery challenges

There are inherent challenges when engaged in the activity of software delivery. It involves multiple people with different skills using different tools and technologies with multiple different processes. It is not easy to bring all these together in a cohesive manner. Some of these challenges are mentioned in this section. Later, in subsequent chapters, we will see how these challenges are addressed with the adoption of DevOps principles and practices.

Resistance to change

Organizations work within the realms of economic, political, and social backdrops, and they have to constantly adapt themselves to a continuously changing environment. Economic changes might introduce an increase in competition in terms of price, quality of products and services, changing marketing strategies, and mergers and acquisitions. The political environment introduces changes in legislation, which has an impact on the rules and regulation for enterprise. The tax system and international trade policies are also examples of areas in which change can have an impact. Society decides which products and services are acceptable or preferred and which are discarded. Customers demand change on a constant basis. Their needs and requirements change often and this manifests in the systems they are using. Organizations not adept at handling changes in their delivery processes and who resist making changes to their products and features eventually find themselves outdated and irrelevant. These organizations are not responsive to change. In short, the environment is ever changing and organizations perish if they do not change along with it.

Rigid processes

Software organizations with a traditional mindset release their products and services on a yearly or multi-year basis. Their software development life cycle is long and their operations do not have many changes to deploy and maintain. Customers demand more but they wait till the next release from the company. The organization is either not interested or does not have the capability to release changes faster. Meanwhile, if the competitor is able to provide more and better features faster, customers will soon shift their loyalty and start using them. The first organization will start losing customers, have reduced revenues, and fade away.

Isolated teams

Generally, there are multiple teams behind any system or service provided to the customer. Typically, there is a development team and an operations team. The development team is responsible for developing and testing the system, while the operations team is responsible for managing and maintaining the system on production. The operations team provides post-deployment services to the customer. These two teams have different skills, experience, mindset, and working culture. The charter of the development team is to develop newer features and upgrade existing ones. They constantly produce code and want to see it in production. However, the operations team is not comfortable with frequent changes. The stability of the existing environment is more important to them. There is a constant conflict between these two teams.

There is little or no collaboration and communication between these two teams. The development team often provides code artifacts to the operations team for deployment on production without helping them to understand the change. The operations team is not comfortable deploying the new changes since they are neither aware of the kind of changes coming in as part of a new release nor have confidence deploying the software. There is no proper hand-off between the development and operations teams. Often, the deployments fail on production and the operations team has to spend sleepless nights ensuring that the current deployment is either fixed or rolled back to a previous working release. Both the development and operations teams are working in silos. The development team does not treat the operations team as equivalent to itself. The operations team has no role to play in the software development life cycle, while the development team has no role to play in operations.

Monolithic design and deployments

Development goes on for multiple months before testing begins. The flow is linear and the approach is **Waterfall**, where the next stage in software development life cycle happens only when the prior stage is completed or nearing completion. Deployment is one giant exercise in deploying multiple artifacts on multiple servers based on documented procedures. Such practices have many inherent problems. There are a lot of features and configuration steps for large applications and everything needs to be done, in order, on multiple servers. Deploying a huge application is risky and fails when a small step is missed during deployment. It generally takes weeks to deploy a system such as this in production.

Manual execution

Software development enterprises often do not employ proper automation in their application lifecycle management. Developers tend to check-in code only after a week, the testing is manual, configuration of the environment and system is manual, and documentation is either missing or very dense, comprising hundreds of pages. The operations team follows the provided documentation to deploy the system manually on production. Often this results in a lot of downtime on production because smaller steps have been missed in deployment. Eventually, customers become dissatisfied with the services provided by the company. Also, this introduces human dependencies within the organization. If a person leaves the organization, their knowledge leaves with them and a new person has to struggle significantly to gain the same level of expertise and knowledge.

Lack of innovation

Organizations starts losing out to competition when they are not flexible to meet customer expectation with newer and upgraded products and services. The result is falling revenues and profits, eventually making them nonexistent in the marketplace. Organizations that do not innovate newer products and services consistently nor update them cannot provide exponential customer satisfaction.

What is DevOps?

Today, there is no consensus in industry regarding the definition of DevOps. Every organization has formulated their own definition of DevOps and has tried to implement it accordingly. They have their own perspective and tend to think they have implemented DevOps if they have automation in place, configuration management is enabled, they are using agile processes, or any combination thereof.

DevOps is about the delivery mechanism of software systems. It is about bringing people together, making them collaborate and communicate, working together toward a common goal and vision. It is about taking joint responsibility, accountability, and ownership. It is about implementing processes that foster a collective and service mindset. It enables a delivery mechanism that brings agility and flexibility within the organization. Contrary to popular belief, DevOps is not about tools, technology, and automation .Automation acts as an enabler to implement agile processes, induce collaboration within teams and help in delivering faster and better.

There are multiple definitions of DevOps available on the Internet and they do not provide complete definition. DevOps does not provide a framework or methodology. It is a set of principles and practices that, when employed within an organization, engagement, or project, achieve the goal and vision of both DevOps and the organization. These principles and practices do not mandate any specific process, tools and technologies, or environment. DevOps provides guidance which can be implemented through any tool, technology, and process, although some of the technology and processes might be more appropriate than others to achieve the vision of DevOps principles and practices.

Although DevOps practices can be implemented in any organization that provides services and products to customers, for the purposes of this book, we will look at DevOps from the perspective of a software development and operations department of any organization.

So, what is DevOps? DevOps is defined as follows:

- It is a set of principles and practices
- It brings both the developers and operations teams together from the start of the software system
- It provides faster and more efficient end-to-end delivery of a value to the end customer again and again in a consistent and predictable manner
- It reduces time to market, thereby providing a competitive advantage

If you look closely at this definition of DevOps, it does not indicate or refer to any specific processes, tools, or technology. It does not prescribe any particular methodology or environment.

The goal of implementing DevOps principles and practices in any organization is to ensure that stakeholders' (including customers') demands and expectations are met efficiently and effectively.

Customers' demands and expectations are met when:

- The customer gets the features they want
- The customer gets the features they want, when they want
- The customer gets faster updates on features
- The quality of delivery is high

When an organization can meet these expectations, customers are happy and remain loyal to the organization. This in turn increases the market competitiveness of the organization, which results in bigger brand and market valuation. It has a direct impact on the top and bottom lines of the organization. The organization can invest more in innovation and customer feedback, bringing about continuous changes to its system and services in order to stay relevant.

The implementation of DevOps principles and practices in any organization is guided by its surrounding ecosystem. This ecosystem is made up of the industry and domain the organization belongs to.

Let us look in detail at these principles and practices later in this chapter.

The core principles of DevOps are as follows:

- Collaboration and communication
- Agility toward change
- Software design
- Failing fast and early
- Innovation and continuous learning
- Automating processes and tools

The core practices of DevOps are as follows:

- Continuous integration
- Configuration management
- Continuous deployment
- Continuous delivery
- Continuous learning

DevOps is not a new paradigm. However, it has gained a lot of popularity and traction in recent times. Its adoption is at its highest level so far, and more and more companies are undertaking this journey. I purposely mentioned DevOps as a journey because there are different levels of maturity within DevOps. While successfully implementing continuous deployment and delivery are considered the highest level of maturity in this journey, adopting source code control and agile software development are considered among the lowest.

One of the first things DevOps talks about is *breaking the barriers between the development and operations teams*. It brings close collaboration between multiple teams. It is about breaking the mindset that the development team is responsible only for writing code and passing it on to operations for deployment once it is tested. It is also about breaking the mindset that operations has no role to play in development activities. Operations should influence the planning of the product and should be aware of the features coming up for release. They should also continually provide feedback to development on any operational issues so that they can be fixed in subsequent releases. They should have some influence in the design of system to improve its overall functionality. Similarly, development should help the operations team with the deployment of the system and solve incidents as and when they arise.

The definition talks about *faster and more efficient end-to-end delivery of systems to stakeholders*. It does not talk about how fast or efficient the delivery should be. It should be fast enough depending on the organization's domain, industry, customer segmentation, and more. For some organizations, fast enough could be quarterly, while for others it could be weekly. Both types are valid from a DevOps point of view and they can deploy any relevant processes and technology to achieve their particular goal. DevOps does not decide what that goal is. Organizations should identify the best implementation of DevOps principles and practices based on their overall project, engagement, and vision.

The definition also talks about *end-to-end delivery*. This means that everything from the planning and delivery of the system to the services and operations should be part of the DevOps implementation. The processes should be such that they allow for greater flexibility, modularity, and agility in the application development life cycle. While organizations are free to use a best-fit process such as Waterfall, Agile, Kanban, and more, typically organizations tend to favor agile processes with an iterations-based delivery. This allows for faster delivery in smaller units, which are far more testable and manageable compared to a large delivery.

DevOps talks about delivering software systems to the end customer *again and again in a consistent and predictable manner*. This means that organizations should continually deliver newer and upgraded features to the customer using automation. We cannot achieve consistency and predictability without the use of automation. Manual work should be reduced to zero to ensure a high level of consistency and predictability. The automation should also be end-to-end, to avoid failures. This also indicates that the system design should be modular, allowing faster delivery while remaining reliable, available, and scalable. Automated testing plays an important role in consistent and predictable delivery.

The result of implementing the previously mentioned practices and principles is that organizations are able to meet the expectations and demands of their customers. Such an organization can grow faster than its competition and further increase the quality and capability of their products and services through continuous innovation and improvement.

DevOps principles

DevOps is based on a set of foundational beliefs and processes. These form the pillars on which it is built and provide a natural ecosystem for the delivery of excellence within an organization. Let's look briefly into some of these principles.

Collaboration and communication

One of the prime tenets of DevOps is collaboration. Collaboration means that different teams come together to achieve a common objective. It defines clear roles and responsibilities, overall ownership, accountability, and responsibility for the team. The team comprises both development and operations people. Together they are responsible for delivering rapid high-quality releases to the end customer.

Both teams are part of the end-to-end application life cycle process. The operations team contributes to the planning process for features, providing their feedback on overall operational readiness and issues regarding business application and services. Concurrently, the development team must play a role in operational activities. They must assist in deploying the release to production and provide support in terms of fixing any production issues that arise. This kind of environment and ecosystem fosters continuous feedback and innovation. There is a shared vision, where everyone in the team are working toward common goals.

Flexible to change

Agility refers to the flexibility and adaptability of people, processes, and technology. People should have a mindset open to accepting change, playing different roles, and taking ownership and accountability. Processes would generally refer to the following:

- Application lifecycle management
- Development methodology
- Software design

Application lifecycle management

Wikipedia defines application lifecycle management as follows:

> *Application lifecycle management (ALM) is the product lifecycle management (governance, development, and maintenance) of computer programs. It encompasses requirements management, software architecture, computer programming, software testing, software maintenance, change management, continuous integration, project management, and release management.*

Application lifecycle management (**ALM**) refers to the management of planning, gathering requirements, building and hosting code, testing code in terms of code coverage, unit tests, versioning of code, releasing code to multiple environments, tracking and reporting, functional tests, environment provisioning, deployment to production, and operations for business applications and services. The operational aspects include monitoring, reporting, and feedback activities. Overall, ALM is a huge area and comprises multiple activities, tools, and processes. Special attention should be given to crafting appropriate application lifecycle steps to induce confidence in the final deployed system. For example, processes can be implemented which mandate that code cannot be checked in the source code repository if unit tests do not pass completely. ALM comprises multiple stages such as planning, development, testing, deployment, and operations.

In short, ALM defines a process to manage an application from conception to delivery and integrates multiple teams together to achieve a common objective. The phases of a typical application lifecycle management process is shown in *Figure 1*. ALM is a continuous process that starts with the planning of an iteration, building and testing the iteration, deploying it on a production environment, and providing post-deployment services to the customer.

Feedback from customers and operations is passed on to the planning team, which eventually incorporates them into subsequent iterations, and this process loop continues.

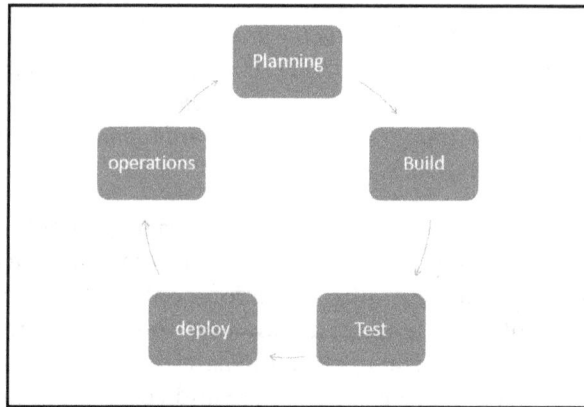

Figure 1: Application lifecycle management phases

Development methodology

Development methodology should be flexible and elastic to enable multiple smaller iterations or sprints of delivery. Each sprint and iteration must be functionally tested. Smaller iterations help in completing specific smaller features and pushing them to production. This provides the team with a clear sense of the direction and scope of the work, raising expectations and giving them a sense of ownership over the release.

Software design

Software design should implement architectural principles that foster modularity, decomposition of large functionality into smaller features, reliability, high availability, scalability, audit capabilities, and monitoring, to name a few.

Automating processes and tools

Automation plays an important role in achieving overall DevOps goals. Without automation, DevOps cannot achieve its end objectives. Automation should be implemented for the entire application lifecycle management, from building the application, to delivery and deployment to the production environment. Automation brings trust and a high level of confidence in the output from each phase of the software development life cycle.

The probability that deliverables are of high quality, robust, and relatively risk-free is quite high. Automation also helps in the rapid delivery of a business application to multiple environments because it is capable of running multiple build processes, executing thousands of unit tests, figuring out code coverage comprising millions of lines of code, provisioning environments, deploying applications, and configuring them at the desired level.

Failing fast and early

At first glance, it seems weird to talk about failure in a DevOps book that is supposed to assist with the successful delivery of software. Trust me, it is not! Failing fast and early refers to the process of finding issues and risks as early as possible within application lifecycle development. Not knowing the issues that arise toward the end of the ALM cycle is an expensive affair because a lot of work has already been done on it. Such issues might involve making design and architectural changes, which can jeopardize the viability of the entire release. If the issues can be found at the beginning of the cycle, they can be resolved without much impact to the release. Automation plays a big part in identifying the issues early and fast.

Innovation and continuous learning

DevOps fosters a culture of innovation and continuous learning. There is a constant feedback flow regarding the good and bad, and what's working and what's not working in various environments. The feedback is used to try out different things, either to fix existing issues or find better alternatives. Through this exercise, there is a constant information flow about how to make things better and that in turn provides the impetus to find alternative solutions. Eventually, there are breakthrough findings and innovation, which can be further developed and brought to production.

DevOps practices

DevOps consists of multiple practices, each providing distinct functionality to the overall process. *Figure 2* shows the relationship between them. Configuration management, continuous integration, and continuous deployment form the core practices that enable DevOps. When we deliver software services that combine these three services, we achieve continuous delivery. continuous delivery from an organization is a mature capability that depends on the maturity of its configuration management, continuous integration, and continuous deployment.

Continuous feedback at all stages forms the feedback loop that helps provide superior services to customers. It runs across all DevOps practices. Let's take a closer look at each of these capabilities and DevOps practices:

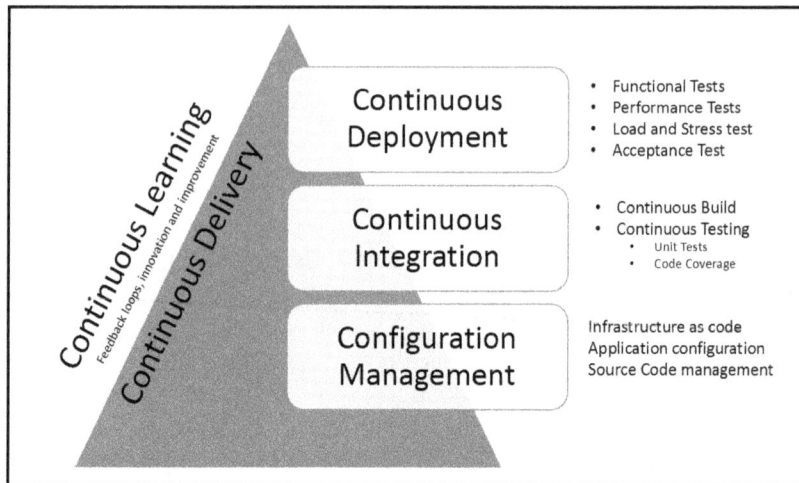

Figure 2: DevOps practices and their activities

Configuration management

Software applications and services need a physical or virtual environment on which they can be deployed. Typically, the environment is an infrastructure comprising both hardware and operating system on which software can be deployed. Software applications are decomposed into multiple services running on different servers, either on-premises or in the cloud. Each service has its own application and infrastructure configuration requirement. In short, both infrastructure and application are needed to deliver software systems to customers, and each has their own configuration. If the configuration drifts, the application might not work as expected, leading to downtime and failure. Modern ALM dictates the use of multiple stages and environments on which an application should be deployed with different configurations. For example, the application will be deployed to a development environment for developers to see the result of their work. It will also be deployed to multiple test environments, with different configurations, for executing different types of tests . It would also be deployed to a preproduction environment to conduct user acceptance tests, and finally, it will be deployed on a production environment. It is important to ensure that the application can be deployed to multiple environments without undertaking any manual changes to its configuration.

Configuration management provides a set of processes and tools which help ensure that each environment and application gets its own configuration. Configuration management tracks configuration items, and anything that changes from environment to environment should be treated as a configuration item. Configuration management also defines the relationships between configuration items and how changes in one configuration item will impact another.

Configuration management helps in the following ways:

- **Infrastructure as Code**: When the process of provisioning infrastructure and its configuration is represented through code, and the same code goes through the application lifecycle process, it is known as Infrastructure as Code. Infrastructure as Code helps automate the provisioning and configuration of infrastructure. It also represents the entire infrastructure in code that can be stored in a repository and version-controlled. This allows you to use previous environment configurations when needed. It also enables the provisioning of an environment multiple times in a consistent and predictable manner. All environments provisioned in this way are consistent and equal at all stages of the ALM process.
- **Deployment and configuration of an application**: The deployment and configuration of an application is the next step after provisioning the infrastructure. An example of application deployment and configuration is to deploy a **WebDeploy** package on a server, deploy SQL server schemas and data (bacpac) on another server, and change the SQL connection string on the web server to represent the appropriate SQL server. Configuration management stores values for the application configuration for each environment on which it is deployed.

The configuration settings applied to environments and application should also be monitored. Records for expected and desired configuration along with the differences should be maintained. Any drift from this expected and desired configuration can make the application unavailable and unreliable. Configuration management is capable of finding the drift and reconfiguring the application and environment to their desired state.

With automated configuration management in place, the team does have to manually deploy and configure the environments and applications. The operations team is not dependent on the development team for deployment activities.

Another aspect of configuration management is source code control. Software comprises code, data, and configuration. Generally, team members working on an application change the same files simultaneously. The source code should be up to date at any point in time and should only be accessible by authenticated team members. The code and other artifacts themselves are configuration. Source code control helps in increased collaboration and communication within the team, since each team member is aware of other team members activities. This ensures that conflicts are resolved at an early stage.

Continuous integration

Multiple developers write code stored and maintained in a common repository. The code is normally checked-in or pushed to the repository when a developer has finished developing a feature. This can happen in a day, or it might take days or weeks. Developers might be working together on the same feature and they might also follow the same practices of pushing/checking-in code in days or weeks. This can cause issues with code quality. One of the tenets of DevOps is to fail fast. Developers should check-in/push their code to the repository often and as soon as it makes sense to check-in. The code should be compiled frequently to check that developers have not introduced any bugs inadvertently and the complete code base can be compiled at any point of time. If a developer does not follow such practices, then there is possibility of each developer having stale code in their local workstation not integrated with other developer's code. Eventually, when such stale and large codebase is integrated from all developers, it starts failing and becomes difficult and time-consuming to fix issues arising from it.

Continuous integration solves these kinds of challenges. Continuous integration helps with the compilation and validation of any code pushed/checked-in by a developer by taking it through a series of validation steps. Continuous integration creates a process flow consisting of multiple steps and is comprised of continuous automated build and continuous automated tests. Normally, the first step is the compilation of the code. After successful compilation, each step is responsible for validating the code from a specific perspective. For example, when unit tests are executed on the compiled code, code coverage can be measured to check which code paths are covered. This could reveal whether comprehensive unit tests have been written or whether there is scope to add further unit tests. The result of continuous integration is deployment packages that can be used by continuous deployment for deployment to multiple environments.

Developers are encouraged to check-in their code multiple times a day instead of after multiple days or weeks. Continuous integration initiates the execution of the build pipeline automatically as soon as the code is checked-in or pushed. When all activities comprising the build execute successfully without any errors, the build-generated artifacts are deployed to multiple environments. Although every system demands its own configuration of continuous integration, a typical example is shown in *Figure 3*.

Continuous integration increases the productivity of developers. They do not have to manually compile their code, run multiple types of tests one after another, and then create packages out of it. It also reduces the risk of introducing bugs into the code. It also provides early feedback to the developers about the quality of their code. Overall, the quality of deliverables is high and deliverables are delivered faster by adopting a continuous integration practice:

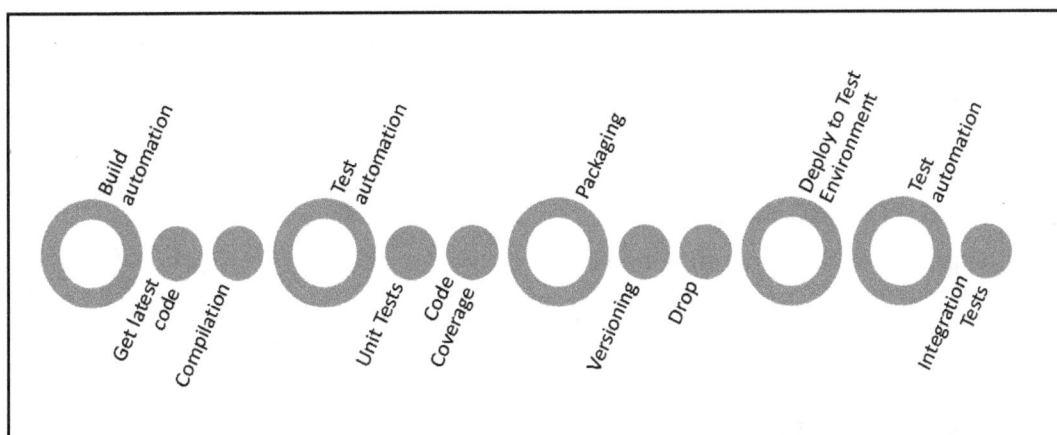

Figure 3: Sample continuous integration process

Build automation

Build automation consists of multiple tasks executing in sequence. Generally, the first task is responsible for fetching the latest source code from the repository. The source code might comprise multiple projects and files, which are compiled to generate artifacts such as executables, dynamic link libraries, assemblies, and more. Successful build automation indicates that there are no compile-time errors in the code.

There can be more steps to build automation depending on the nature and type of a project.

Test automation

Test automation consists of tasks that are responsible for validating different aspects of code. These tasks are related to testing the code from a different perspective and are executed in sequence. Generally, the first step is to run a series of unit tests on the code. Unit testing refers to the process of testing the smallest denomination of a feature to validate its behavior in isolation from other features. It can be automated or manual. However, the preference is automated unit testing.

Code coverage is another aspect of automated testing that can be executed on code to find out how much of the code is executed while running the unit tests. It is generally represented as a percentage and refers to how much of the code is testable through unit testing. If code coverage is not close to 100 percent, it is either because the developer has not written unit tests for that behavior or the uncovered code is not required at all.

There can be more steps to test automation depending on the nature and type of a project. Successful execution of test automation resulting in no significant code failure should start executing the packaging tasks.

Application packaging

Packaging is a process of generating deployable artifacts such as MSI, NuGet, web-deploy packages, and database packages, as well as versioning them and storing them at a location such that they can be consumed by other pipelines and processes.

Continuous deployment

By the time the process reaches the stage of deployment, continuous integration has ensured that there is a functional application that can now be deployed to multiple environment for further quality checks and testing. Continuous Deployment refers to the capability to deploy applications and services to preproduction and production environments through automation. For example, Continuous Deployment could provision and configure an environment, deploy and configure an application on top of it. After conducting multiple validations, such as functional tests and performance tests, on a preproduction environment, the production environment is provisioned and configured, and the application is deployed to production environments through automation. There are no manual steps in the deployment process. Every deployment task is automated.

Continuous deployment should provision new environments or update existing environments. It should then deploy applications with newer configuration on top of it.

All the environments are provisioned through automation using principle of Infrastructure as Code. This will ensure that all environments, be it development, test, preproduction, production, or any other environment, are similar. Similarly, the application is deployed through automation, ensuring that it is also deployed uniformly across all environments. The configuration across these environments could be different depending the application.

Continuous deployment is generally integrated with continuous integration. When continuous integration has done its work by generating the final deployable packages, continuous deployment kicks in and start its own pipeline. This pipeline is called the **release pipeline**. The release pipeline consists of multiple environments, each consisting of tasks responsible for the provision of the environment, configuration of the environment, deploying applications, configuring applications, executing operational validation on environments, and testing the application on multiple environments. We will look at the release pipeline in greater detail in the next chapter and also in Chapter 10, *Continuous Delivery and Deployment*.

Employing continuous deployment provides immense benefits. There is a high degree of confidence in the overall deployment process, which helps ensure faster, risk-free releases on production. The chance of anything going wrong is drastically reduced. The team will have lower stress levels and rollback to a previous working environment is possible if there are issues with the current release:

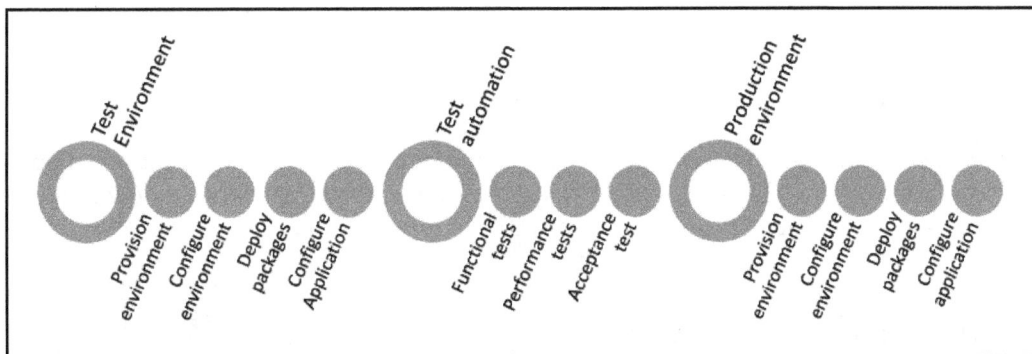

Figure 4: Sample continuous deployment/release pipeline process

Although every system demands its own configuration of a release pipeline, a typical example of is shown in *Figure 4*. It is important to note that, generally, provisioning and configuring multiple environments is part of the release pipeline and approval should be sought before moving to the next environment. The approval process might be manual or automated, depending on the maturity of the organization.

Preproduction deployment

The release pipeline starts once drop is available from Continuous Integration. The steps it should perform is to get all the artifacts from the drop, either create a new environment from scratch or use an existing environment, deploy and configure applications on top of it. This environment can then be used for all kinds of testing and validation purpose.

Test automation

After deploying an application, a series of tests can be performed on the environment. One of the tests executed here is a functional test. Functional tests are primarily aimed at validating feature completeness and functionality of the application. These tests are written from requirements gathered from the customer. Another set of tests that can be executed are related to scalability and availability of the application. This typically includes load tests, stress tests, and performance tests. It should also include operational validation of the infrastructure environment.

Staging environment deployment

This is very similar to the test environment deployment, with only difference being that the configuration values for the environment and application will be different.

Acceptance tests

Acceptance tests are generally conducted by stakeholders of the application and can be manual or automated. This step is a validation from the customer's point of view regarding the correctness and completeness of an application's functionality.

Deployment to production

Once customers provide their approval, the same steps as those of test and staging environment deployment are executed, with the only difference being that the configuration values for the environment and application are specific to the production environment. Validation is conducted after deployment to ensure that the application is running according to expectations.

Continuous delivery

Continuous delivery and continuous deployment might sound similar to many readers; however, they are not the same. While continuous deployment talks about deployment to multiple environments and finally to a production environment through automation. Continuous delivery is the ability to generate application packages in a way that they are readily deployable in any environment. To generate artifacts that are readily deployable, continuous integration should be used to generate the application artifacts. A new or existing environment should be used to deploy these artifacts, conduct functional tests, performance tests, and user acceptance tests, through automation. Once these activities are successfully executed with no errors, the application package is referred to as readily deployable. It helps get feedback faster from both operations and the end user. This feedback can then be implemented in subsequent iterations.

Continuous learning

With all the previously mentioned DevOps practices, it is possible to create stable, robust, reliable, performant business applications and deploy them automatically to a production environment. However, the benefits of DevOps will not last for long if a continuous improvement and feedback principle is not in place. It is of utmost important that real-time feedback about the application's behavior is passed on as feedback to the development team from both end users and the operations team.

Feedback should be passed to the teams, providing relevant information about what is going well and, importantly, what is not going well.

Applications should be built with monitoring, auditing, and telemetry in mind. The architecture and design should support these. The operations team should collect telemetry information from the production environment, capture any bugs and issues, and pass this information on to the development team such that they can be fixed in subsequent releases. This process is shown in *Figure 5*.

Continuous learning helps make the application robust and resilient to failures. It also helps make sure that the application is meeting consumer requirements:

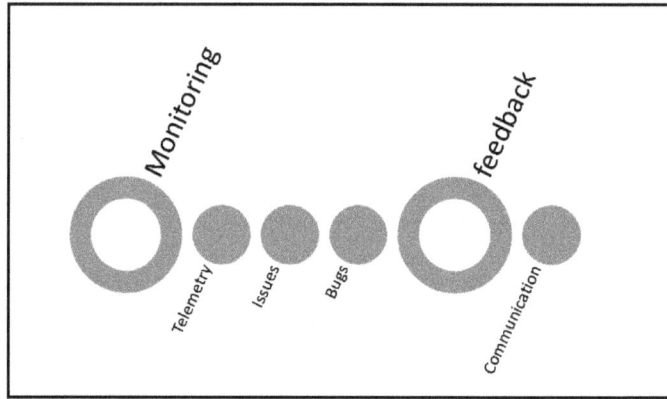

Figure 5: Sample continuous learning process

Measuring DevOps

Once DevOps practices and principles are implemented, the next step is to find out whether these DevOps practices and principles are providing any tangible benefits to the organization. To find the impact of DevOps on delivering changes to customers, appropriate monitoring, audit, and collection of metrics should be developed and deployed. This telemetry should be measured on an ongoing basis. Also, there should be regular baselining of data for effective comparisons in future. After implementing DevOps, the metrics should be captured over a period of time and then compared with the baseline. This comparison of data should uncover intelligence about effectiveness of DevOps in the organization and appropriate corrective measures should be undertaken.

Some of the important metrics that should be tracked are as follows:

Metrics	Impact
Number of deployments	If the number of deployments is higher prior to DevOps implementation, it means that continuous integration, continuous delivery, and deployments favor the overall delivery to production.

Number of daily code check-ins/pushes	If this number is comparatively high, it denotes that developers are taking advantage of continuous integration and the possibilities for code conflict and staleness are reduced.
Number of releases in a month	A higher number is testimony the fact that there is higher confidence in delivering changes to production and that DevOps is helping to do that.
Number of defects/bugs/issues on production	This number should be lower than pre-DevOps implementation numbers. However, if this number is considerable, it reflects that testing is not comprehensive within continuous integration and the continuous delivery pipeline and needs to be further strengthened. Quality of delivery is also low.
Number of failures in continuous integration	This is also known as broken build. This indicates that developers are writing improper code.
Number of failures in the release pipeline / continuous deployment	If the number is high, it indicates that code is not meeting feature requirements. Also, automation of environment provisioning might have issues.
Code coverage percentage	If this number is less, it indicates that unit tests do not cover all scenarios comprehensively. It could also mean that there are code smells with higher cyclomatic complexity.

Summary

In this chapter, we have looked at some of the problems plaguing software organizations with regard to delivery of services to its end users. We covered the definition of DevOps and how DevOps helps eliminate these problems. We also went through the principles and practices of DevOps, briefly explaining their purpose and usefulness. This chapter forms the foundation and backbone for the remaining chapters. Later chapters in the book will be a step-by-step realization of these principles and tenets. Although this chapter was heavy on theory, subsequent chapters will start delving into technology and practical steps to implement DevOps. You should by now have a good grasp of DevOps concepts. In the following chapter, we will cover automation tools, languages, and technologies that will help in implementing DevOps principles in practice.

2
DevOps Tools and Technologies

In the previous chapter, we looked at the problems faced by organizations in delivering software services to customers. We understood the meaning of DevOps and the way it addresses the challenges of software delivery. We went through the principles on which DevOps is based and discussed the practices through which DevOps achieves its end goal.

This book is about the practical implementation of DevOps through technology. Technology is an enabler for DevOps. Technology helps DevOps in the following ways:

- Enables faster collaboration and communication among teams, making them more efficient and effective.
- Helps in faster, better, and automated process implementation.
- Consistent and predictable automated delivery. Brings higher cadence and confidence in the delivery process.
- Feedback backed up by telemetry.
- Agile deployments.

This chapter and the following two chapters will introduce core platforms and technologies instrumental in enabling and implementing DevOps practices.

These include:

- Technology stack for implementing configuration management, continuous integration, continuous deployment, continuous delivery, and continuous improvement. These form the backbone for DevOps processes and include source code services, build and release service through **Visual Studio Team Services** (**VSTS**).
- Platform and technology used to create and deploy a sample web application. This includes technologies such as Microsoft .NET, ASP.NET, and SQL server databases.
- Tools and technology for configuration management, testing of code and application, authoring scripts and templates as part of Infrastructure as Code, and deployment of environments. Examples of these tools and technology are **Pester** for environment validation, environment provisioning through **Azure Resource Manager** (**ARM**) templates, **Desired State Configuration** (**DSC**) and PowerShell, application hosting on containers through **Windows Containers** and Docker, application and database deployment through web deploy packages, and SQL server BACPAC files.

Cloud technology

Cloud is ubiquitous. It is used throughout this book. Cloud is used in this book for hosting all environments, implementation of DevOps practices, and deployment of applications.

Cloud is a relatively new paradigm in infrastructure provisioning, application deployment, and hosting space. The only options prior to the advent of cloud was either self-hosted on on-premises data centers or using services from a hosting service provider. However, cloud is changing the way enterprises look at their strategy in relation to infrastructure and application development, deployment, and hosting. In fact, the change is so enormous that it has found its way into every aspect of an organization's software development processes, tools, and practices.

Cloud computing refers to the practice of deploying applications and services on the Internet with a cloud provider. A cloud provider provides multiple types of services on cloud. They are divided into three categories based on their level of abstraction and degree of control on services. These categories are as follows:

- **Infrastructure as a Service** (also popularly known as **IaaS**)
- **Platform as a Service** (also popularly known as **PaaS**)
- **Software as a Service** (also popularly known as **SaaS**)

These three categories differ based on the level of control a cloud provider exercises compared to the cloud consumer. The services provided by a cloud provider can be divided into layers, with each layer being a specific type of service. As we move higher in the stack of layers, the level of abstraction increases in line with the cloud provider's control over services. In other words, the cloud consumer starts to lose control over services as you move higher in each column:

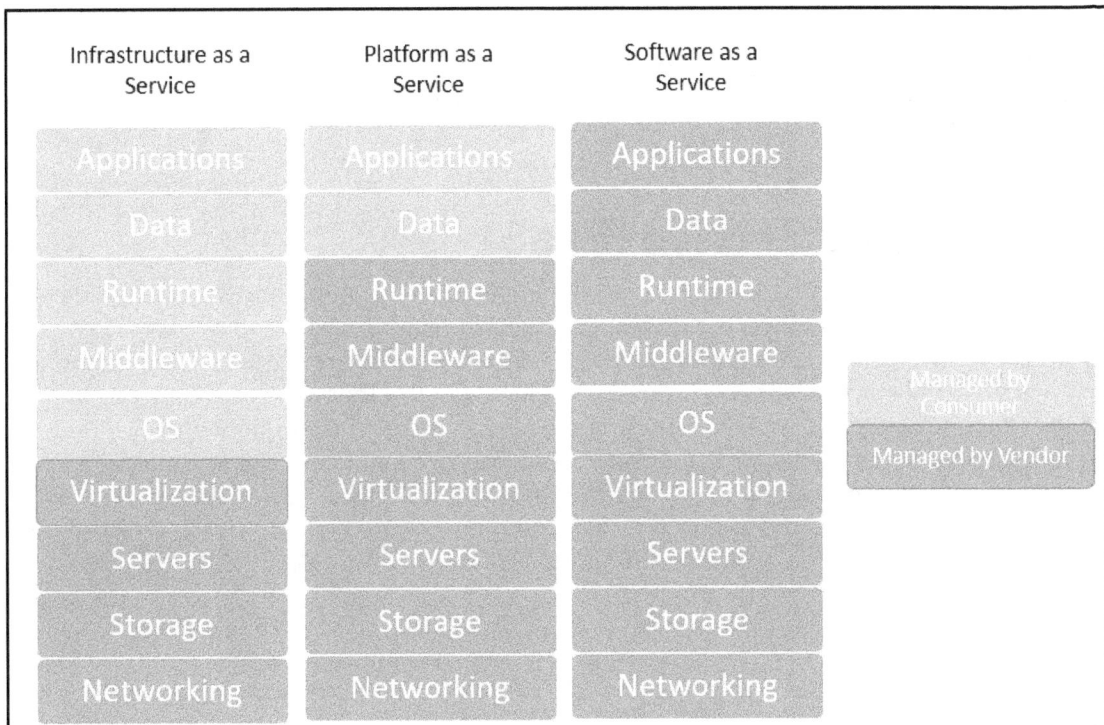

Infrastructure as a Service	Platform as a Service	Software as a Service	
Applications	Applications	Applications	
Data	Data	Data	
Runtime	Runtime	Runtime	
Middleware	Middleware	Middleware	
OS	OS	OS	Managed by Consumer
Virtualization	Virtualization	Virtualization	Managed by Vendor
Servers	Servers	Servers	
Storage	Storage	Storage	
Networking	Networking	Networking	

Figure 1: Cloud Services – IaaS, PaaS, and SaaS

Figure 1 shows the three categories of service available through cloud providers and the layers that are comprised in each service. These layers are stacked vertically on each other and each layer in the stack is colored differently depending on who manages it customer or provider. From *Figure 1*, it is clear that for IaaS, a cloud provider is responsible for providing, controlling, and managing layers from the network layer up to the virtualization layer. Similarly, for PaaS, a cloud provider controls and manages from the hardware layer up to the runtime layer, while the consumer controls only the application and data layers.

Infrastructure as a Service (IaaS)

As the name suggests, Infrastructure as a Service are infrastructure services provided by a cloud provider. This service includes the physical hardware and its configuration, network hardware and its configuration, storage hardware and its configuration, load balancers, compute, and virtualization. Any layer above virtualization is the responsibility of the consumer. The consumer can decide to use the provided underlying infrastructure in whatever way best suits their requirements. For example, consumers can consume the storage, network, and virtualization to provision virtual machines on top of it. It is then consumer's responsibility to manage and control the virtual machines and the software deployed within it.

Platform as a Service (PaaS)

Platform as a Service enables consumers to deploy their applications and services on the provided platform, consuming the underlying runtime, middleware, and services. The cloud provider provides the services from infrastructure to runtime. The consumers cannot provision virtual machines as they cannot access and control them. Instead, they can only control and manage their applications. This is a comparatively faster method of development and deployment because now the consumer can focus on application development and deployment. Examples of Platform as a Service include Azure Automation, Azure SQL, and Azure App Services.

Software as a Service (SaaS)

Software as a Service provides complete control of the service to the cloud provider. The cloud provider provisions, configures, and manages everything from infrastructure to the application. It includes the provisioning of infrastructure, deployment and configuration of applications, and provides application access to the consumer. The consumer does not control and manage the application, and can use and configure only parts of the application. They control only their data and configuration. Generally, multi-tenant applications used by multiple consumers, such as Office 365 and Visual Studio Team Services, are examples of SaaS.

Advantages of using cloud computing

There are multiple distinct advantages of using cloud computing. The major among them are as follows:

- **Cost effective**: Cloud computing helps organizations to reduce the cost of storage, networks, and physical infrastructure. It also prevents them from having to buy expensive software licenses. The operational cost of managing these infrastructures also reduces due to lesser effort and manpower requirements.
- **Unlimited capacity**: Cloud provides unlimited resources to the consumer. This ensures applications will never get throttled due to limited resource availability.
- **Elasticity**: Cloud computing provides the notion of unlimited capacity and applications deployed on it can scale up or down on an as-needed basis. When demand for the application increases, cloud can be configured to scale up the infrastructure and application by adding additional resources. At the same time, it can scale down unnecessary resources during periods of low demand.
- **Pay as you go**: Using cloud eliminates capital expenditure and organizations pay only for what they use, thereby providing maximum return on investment. Organizations do not need to build additional infrastructure to host their application for times of peak demand.
- **Faster and better**: Cloud provides ready-to-use applications and faster provisioning and deployment of environments. Moreover, organizations get better-managed services from their cloud provider with higher service-level agreements.

We will use **Azure** as our cloud computing provider for the purpose of demonstrating samples and examples. However, you can use any cloud provider that provides complete end-to-end services for DevOps.

We will use multiple features and services provided by Azure across IaaS and PaaS. We will consume **Operational Insights** and **Application Insights** to monitor our environment and application, which will help capture relevant telemetry for auditing and monitoring purposes. Azure virtual machines running Windows Containers will be provisioned and they will act as our hosting platform. We will use Windows Server 2016 as the target operating system for our applications. Azure Resource Manager (ARM) and templates, which we will look into in detail in the next chapter, as our choice of framework and deployment automation. We will also use Desired State Configuration and PowerShell for configuration management within virtual machines and containers.

We will use Visual Studio Team Services, a suite of PaaS services on cloud provided by Microsoft, to set up and implement our end-to-end DevOps practices. Microsoft also provides the same services as part of **Team Foundation Services** (**TFS**) as an on-premises solution.

Technologies like Pester, DSC, and PowerShell can be deployed and configured to run on any platform. These will help both in the validation of our environment and in the configuration of both application and environment, as part of our configuration management process.

We will introduce a sample application in Chapter 5, *Building a Sample Application*, and the entire application lifecycle management will be implemented through DevOps practices. Windows Server 2016 is our target platform for deploying the application. Windows Server 2016 is a breakthrough operating system from Microsoft also referred to as Cloud Operating System. We will look into Windows Server 2016 in the following section.

Windows Server 2016

Windows Server 2016 has come a long way. All the way from Windows NT to Windows 2000 and 2003, then Windows 2008 (R2) and 2012 (R2), and now Windows Server 2016. **Windows NT** was the first popular Windows server among enterprises. However, the true enterprise servers were Windows 2000 and Windows 2003. The popularity of Windows Server 2003 was unprecedented and it was widely adopted. With Windows Server 2008 and 2008 R2, the idea of the data center took priority and enterprises with their own data center adopted it. Even the Windows Server 2008 series was quite popular among enterprises. In 2010, the Microsoft Cloud, Azure, was launched.

The first steps towards a cloud operating system were Windows Server 2012 and 2012 R2. They had the blueprints and technology to be seamlessly provisioned on Azure. Now, when Azure and cloud are gaining enormous popularity, Windows Server 2016 is released as a true cloud operating system. The evolution of Windows Server is shown in *Figure 2*:

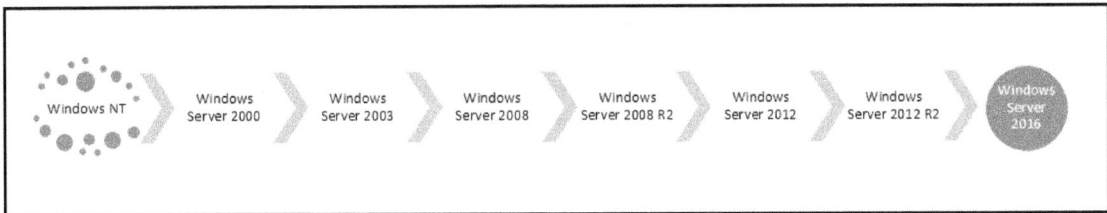

Figure 2: Windows Server evolution

Windows Server 2016 is referred to as a cloud operating system. It is built with cloud in mind. It is also referred to as the first operating system that enables DevOps seamlessly by providing relevant tools and technologies. It makes implementing DevOps simpler and easier through its productivity tools. Let us look briefly into these tools and technologies.

Application platform

Windows Server 2016 comes with multiple options for deploying and hosting applications. It provides the following:

- Windows Server 2016
- Nano Server
- Windows and Docker Containers
- Hyper-V Containers
- Nested virtual machines

Windows Server as a hosting platform

Windows Server 2016 can be used for hosting applications and consuming server functionalities. It provides the services necessary to make applications secure, scalable, and highly available. It also provides services like virtualization, directory services, certificate services, web server, databases that help in building enterprise scale applications and services.

Nano servers

Windows Server provides a new option to host applications and services called Nano servers. This is a new lightweight, scaled-down Windows Server containing only the kernel and drivers necessary to run as an operating system. They are also known as headless servers. They do not have any graphical user interface and the only way to interact and manage them is through remote PowerShell. Out-of-the-box, they do not contain any service or feature. The services need to be added to Nano servers explicitly before use. So far, they are the most secure servers from Microsoft. They are very lightweight and their resource requirements and consumption is less than 80% of a normal Windows server. The number of services running, the number of ports open, the number of active processes running and the amount of memory and storage required, are also less than 80% compared to normal Windows servers.

Even though Nano Server out of box just has the kernel and drivers, its capabilities can be enhanced by adding features and deploying any Windows application on it.

Windows Containers and Docker

Containers are one of the most revolutionary features added to Windows Server 2016 after Nano Server. With the popularity and adoption of Docker Containers on Linux, Microsoft has introduced container services in Windows Server 2016 and Windows 10.

Containers are operating system virtualization. This means that multiple containers can be deployed on the same operating system and each one of them will share the host operating system kernel. It is the next level of virtualization after server virtualization (virtual machines). Containers generate the notion of complete operating system isolation and independence, even though it uses the same host operating system underneath it. This is possible through the use of namespace isolation and image layering. Containers are created from images. Images are immutable and cannot be modified. Each image has a base operating system and a series of instructions that are executed against it. Each instruction creates a new image on top of the previous image and contains only the modification. Finally, a writable image is stacked on top of these images.

These images are combined into a single image, which can then be used for provisioning containers. A container made up of multiple image layers is shown in *Figure 3*:

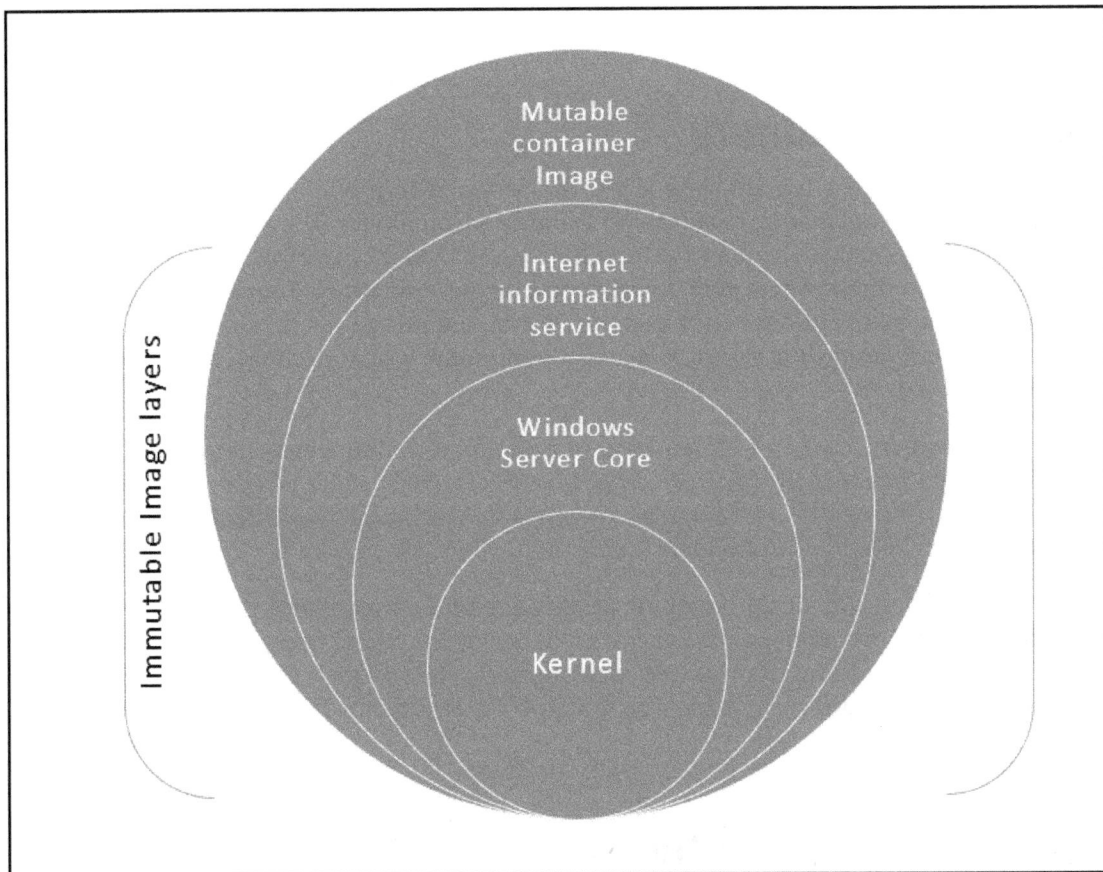

Figure 3: Containers made up of multiple image layers

Namespace isolation helps provide containers with pristine new environments. The containers cannot see the host resources and the host cannot view the container resources. For the application within the container, a complete new installation of the operating system is available. The containers share the host's memory, CPU, and storage.

Containers offer operating system virtualization, which means they can host only those operating systems supported by the host operating system. There cannot be a Windows Container running on a Linux host, and a Linux container cannot run on a Windows host operating system.

Hyper-V containers

Another type of container technology Windows Server 2016 provides is **Hyper-V** Containers. These containers are similar to Windows Containers. They are managed through the same Docker client and extend the same Docker APIs. However, these containers contain their own scaled down operating system kernel. They do not share the host operating system but have their own dedicated operating system, and their own dedicated memory and CPU assigned in exactly the same way virtual machines are assigned resources.

Hyper-V Containers bring in a higher level of isolation of containers from the host. While Windows Containers run in full trust on the host operating system, Hyper-V Containers do not have full trust from the host's perspective. It is this isolation that differentiates Hyper-V Containers from Windows Containers.

Hyper-V Containers are ideal for hosting applications that might harm the host server affecting every other container and service on it. Scenarios where users can bring in and execute their own code are examples of such applications. Hyper-V Containers provide adequate isolation and security to ensure that applications cannot access the host resources and change them.

Nested virtual machines

Another breakthrough innovation of Windows Server 2016 is that virtual machines can host virtual machines. Now, we can deploy multiple virtual machines containing all tiers of an application within a single virtual machine. This is made possible through software-defined networks and storage.

Enabling microservices

Nano servers and Containers help provide advanced lightweight deployment options through which we can now deconstruct the entire application into multiple smaller, independent services, each with their own scalability and high availability configuration, and deploy them independent of each other. **Microservices** help in making the entire DevOps lifecycle agile. With microservices, changes to services do not demand that every other microservice undergo entire test validation. Only the changed service needs to be tested rigorously, along with its integration with other services. Compare this to a monolithic application. Even a single small change will result in having to test the entire application. Microservices help in that it requires smaller teams for its development, testing of a service can happen independently of other services, and deployment can be done for each service in isolation.

Continuous integration, continuous deployment, and continuous delivery for each Micro service can be executed in isolation rather than compiling, testing, and deploying the whole application every time there is a change.

Reduced maintenance

Because of their intrinsic nature, Windows Nano servers and Containers are lightweight and quick to provision. They help in quick provision and configuration of environments and reduce overall time needed for continuous integration and deployment. Also, these resources can be provisioned on Azure on-demand within a few minutes. Because of their small footprint in terms of size, storage, memory, and features, they need less maintenance. These servers are patched less often, have fewer hot-fixes, they are secure by default, and have less chance of failing, which makes them ideal for development operations. The operations team needs to spend fewer hours maintaining these servers compared to normal servers. This reduces overall cost for the organization and help DevOps ensure a high-quality delivery.

Configuration management tools

Windows Server 2016 comes with Windows Management Framework 5.0 installed by default. **Desired State Configuration** (**DSC**) is the new configuration management platform available out-of-the-box in Windows Server 2016. It has a rich, mature set of features that enables configuration management for both operating system and applications. With DSC, the desired state and configuration of environments are authored as part of Infrastructure as Code and executed on every server on a scheduled basis. They help check the current state of servers with the documented desired state and bring them back to the desired state. DSC is available as part of PowerShell and it helps with authoring DSC configuration documents.

Windows Server 2016 provides a PowerShell unit testing framework known as **PESTER**. Historically, unit testing for infrastructure environments was always missing as a feature. PESTER enables the testing of infrastructure provisioned either manually or through Infrastructure as Code using DSC configuration or ARM templates. These help with the operational validation of the entire environment, bringing in a high level of cadence and confidence in continuous integration and deployment processes.

Deployment and packaging

Package management helps in deployment of utilities and tools through automation. It is a new concept in the Windows world. Package management has been ubiquitous in the Linux world for a long time. Packing management helps search, save, install, deploy, upgrade, and remove software packages from multiple sources and repositories on demand. There are public repositories such as **Chocolatey, NuGet**, and **PSGallery** available storing readily deployable packages. Tools such as NuGet can connect these repositories, download packages and help in overall package management. They also help with the versioning of packages. Applications that rely on a specific package version can download it on an as-needed basis. Package management helps with the building of environments and application deployment. Package deployment is much easier and faster with this out-of-the-box Windows feature.

Visual Studio Team Services

Now it's time to focus on another revolutionary online service – Visual Studio Team Services – that seamlessly enables continuous integration, continuous deployment, and continuous delivery. In fact, it would be more appropriate to call it a suite of services available under a single name. VSTS is a PaaS provided by Microsoft and hosted on cloud. The same service is available as (**Team Foundation Server (TFS)** on on-premises data centers. All examples used in this book use VSTS.

According to Microsoft, VSTS is a cloud-based collaboration platform that helps teams share code, track work, and shipping software. It was previously known as **Visual Studio Online (VSO)** and recently been renamed as VSTS. It is an enterprise software development tool and service that enables organizations to provide automation facilities to their end-to-end application lifecycle management process, from planning, to deployment, to getting real-time feedback from software systems users. This increases the maturity and capability of an organization to deliver high quality software systems to their customers again and again.

Successful software delivery involves bringing numerous processes and activities together efficiently. These include executing and implementing various agile processes, increasing collaboration among teams, seamless and automatic transition of artifacts from one phase of SDLC to another phase, and deployment to multiple environments. It is important to track and report on these activities, to measure and take action on these findings, and ultimately improve the delivery process. VSTS makes it simple and easy. It provides a whole suite of services that enable the following:

- Collaboration among every team member by providing a single interface for the entire application lifecycle management process
- Collaboration among development teams using source code management service
- Collaboration among test teams using test management service
- Automated validation of code and packaging through continuous integration using Build Management service
- Automated validation of application functionality and deployment, and configuration of multiple environments through continuous deployment and delivery using Release Management service
- Tracking and work item management using Work Management service

Figure 4 shows all the services available from the VSTS top navigation bar:

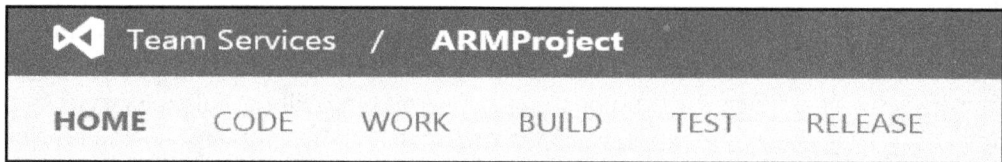

Figure 4: VSTS services

Source code management service

The source code management service, also known as **Version control system**, is one of the flagship services from VSTS. Source code version control helps store the code in a repository that can either be centralized or distributed. It also helps in versioning the code. Versioning helps maintain multiple copies of the same files, with a new copy created when the code gets updated. It helps with viewing the history of the code, comparing code between different versions, and retrieving previous versions.

We will need a VSTS account to be created before it can be used. We will look into the details of creating a VSTS account later in this chapter. Creating an account also creates a team project collection in which team projects can be created. The team project collection is a container that provides a security boundary and additional services such as agent pools. After an account is created, the next step is to create a team project. After a team project is created, the user is automatically redirected to the project dashboard. Each team project is based on a type of process. This process was previously known as **Process Templates** in VSO. The process determines how the requirements are broken down into features or user stories and tasks. It also provides a mechanism to manage them through work-item tracking. There are three types of processes available out-of-the-box in VSTS:

- **Scrum**: The Scrum process is for teams who follow the Scrum framework for their application development lifecycle.
- **Agile**: The Agile process is for teams using Agile methodology.
- **CMMI**: The **Capability Maturity Model Integration** (**CMMI**) process is a comparatively more formal process for executing projects. It mainly focuses on continuous improvement through telemetry.

Each of the processes, whether Scrum, Agile, or CMMI, involves different ways of executing projects and demands a complete book for itself. We will not go into detail in this book.

The code link on the top navigation bar will take us to the source code management control panel. This is shown in *Figure 5*:

Figure 5: Source code link

A team project in VSTS is a security boundary and logical container that provides all the services we mentioned in the previous section. VSTS allows for the creation of multiple projects within a single account. By default, a repository is created with the creation of a project. However, VSTS allows for the creation of additional repositories within a single project. The relationship between the VSTS account, projects, and repository is shown in *Figure 6*:

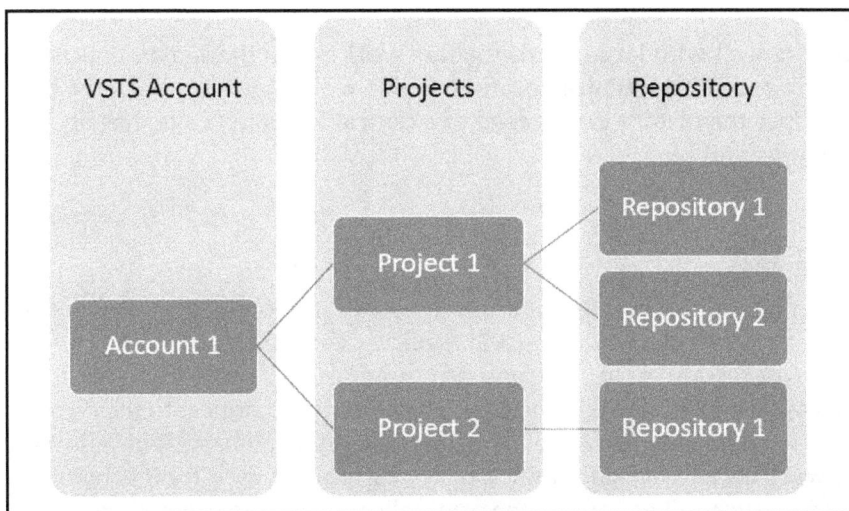

Figure 6: Relationship between VSTS account, team projects, and repositories

VSTS provides two types of repositories, as follows:

- Git
- **Team Foundation Version Control (TFVC)**

It also provides the flexibility to choose between Git or TFVC source control repositories. There can also be combination of **Team Foundation Server** (**TFS**) and TFVC repositories available within a single project.

Team Foundation Version Control

TFVC is the traditional and centralized way of implementing version control in which there is a central repository, which developers work on directly in connected mode to check-in their changes. If the central repository is offline or unavailable, developers cannot check-in their code and have to wait for it to go online and become available. Other developers can see only the checked-in code. Developers can group multiple changes into a single change set for checking-in code changes that are logically grouped to form a single change. TFVC locks the code files that are undergoing edits. Other developers can read the locked file but they cannot edit it. They have to wait for the prior edit to be complete and release the lock before they can make their own edits. A history of check-ins and changes is maintained on the central repository, while the developers have a working copy of the files but not the history.

TFVC works very well with large teams that are working on the same projects. This allows control over source code at a central location. It also works the best when the project is for a long duration since the history is managed at a central location. TFVC has no issues working with large and binary files.

Exploring Git

Git, on the other hand, is a modern distributed way of implementing version control where the developers can work on their own local copies of code and history in offline mode. Each developer has a local copy of the code and its entire history. They can make changes to the code and can commit to the local repository. They can then connect to the central repository in order to synchronize their local repository on an as-needed basis. This allows every developer to work on any file since they will be working on their local copy only. Branching in Git does not create another copy of the original code and is extremely quick to create.

Git works well with smaller teams. With larger teams, there is a substantial overhead to manage multiple pull requests to merge the code on a central repository. It also works best for smaller duration projects as the history will not get too large to be downloaded and manageable on every developer's local repository. Branching and merging is a breeze with advanced options.

Git is the recommended way of using source control because of the rich functionality it provides. We will use Git as repository for our sample application in this book.

Build Management service

Another very important service in VSTS is the **Build Management service**. The main task of the Build Management service is to provide continuous integration service to projects.

As we already know by now, continuous integration is the process of compiling, building, and validating code. It is about deploying code onto a test environment and validating the code quality, code coverage, and whether the code bits are in working condition. Build services help automate this entire process. Similar to source code management, the build service is scoped at the team project level. In each team project, VSTS allows the creation of multiple build definitions and templates. Each build definition is attached to a branch of a repository. This could be a Git or a TFVC repository. Templates act as the basic building blocks for definitions. They can be a starting place for the creation of custom build definitions, with activities already defined in the definition. A build definition can also be saved as a template and reused to create other build definitions. In this section, we will introduce the concepts first and then show how it is implemented or configured.

The build definition consists of multiple activities that run in sequence, one after another, like a pipeline. Each activity is responsible for executing a single task within the overall build pipeline. *Figure 7* shows an example of a build definition consisting of six tasks created using a Visual Studio build template:

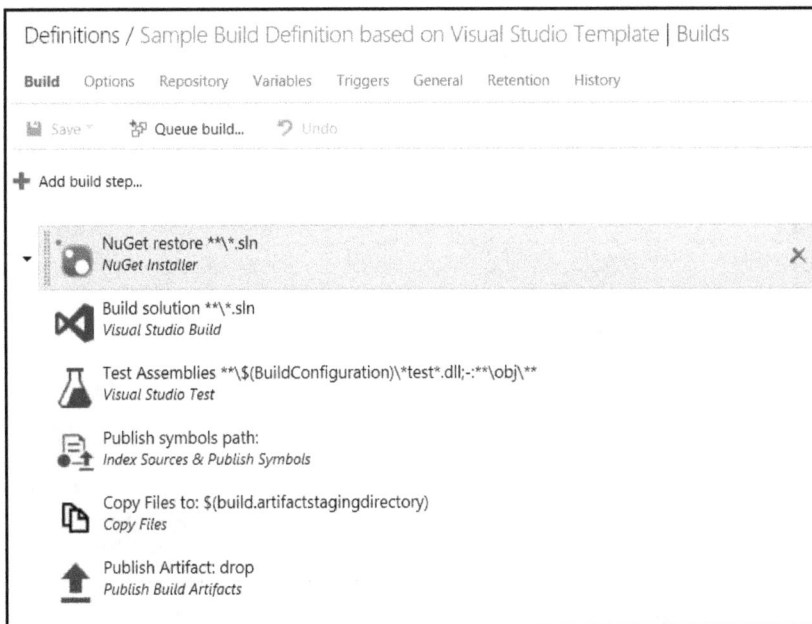

Figure 7: Sample build definition based on a Visual Studio template

These tasks are responsible for the following:

- Restoring the NuGet packages needed by the solution
- Building the entire solution, which in turn builds every project within it
- Executing unit tests on the compiled code
- Publishing a symbol path that helps in debugging
- Copying the generated and compiled assemblies to a destination folder
- Publishing the artifacts on the VSTS server

There are many more tasks available which can be used to augment the build definition further. *Figure 8* shows the tasks available for build definition. There is also a marketplace where more tasks can be made available to the build definition. It is important to note at this stage that the same tasks are available for both build and release definitions. There is no difference in their configuration and execution, whether they are executed as part of a build or release definition:

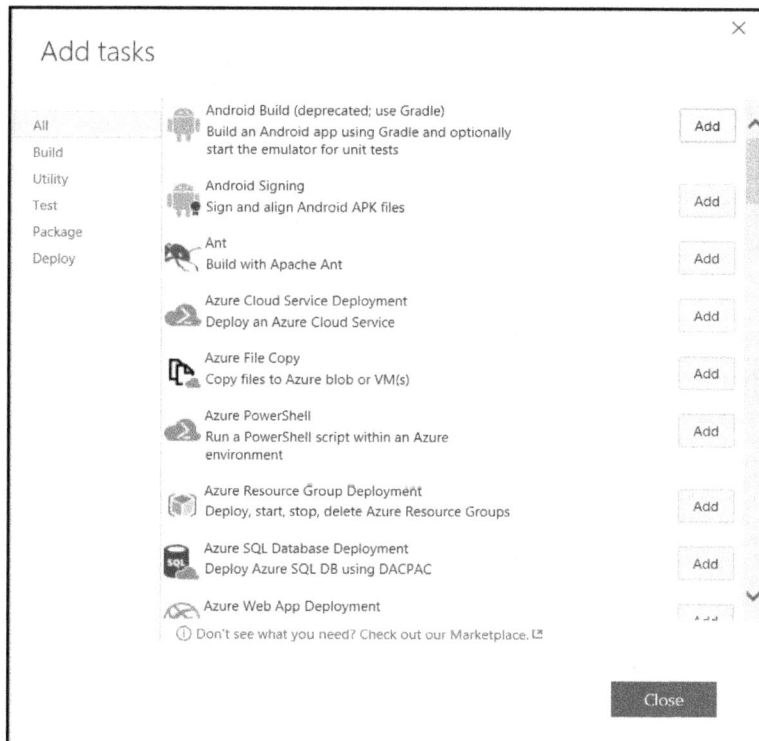

Figure 8: Build tasks

Executing Build Definitions

Build definitions need build environments in order to be executed. Tasks in a build definition have pre-requisites which should be available on build servers. VSTS provides built-in build servers out-of-the-box with prerequisites already installed on them. They are available to every account for the execution of build definitions. However, VSTS is flexible enough to accept our own custom-built servers for the execution of build definitions.

Build architecture

Figure 9 depicts the VSTS build architecture. Every build server should have build agents installed and running on it. Build agents are Windows services configured to interact and work with the VSTS build service. The agents are grouped together to form an agent pool. An agent pool is defined at the VSTS account level and there can be multiple agent pools defined. VSTS provides a default agent pool, named **Hosted**. All VSTS-provided servers are part of the hosted agent pool:

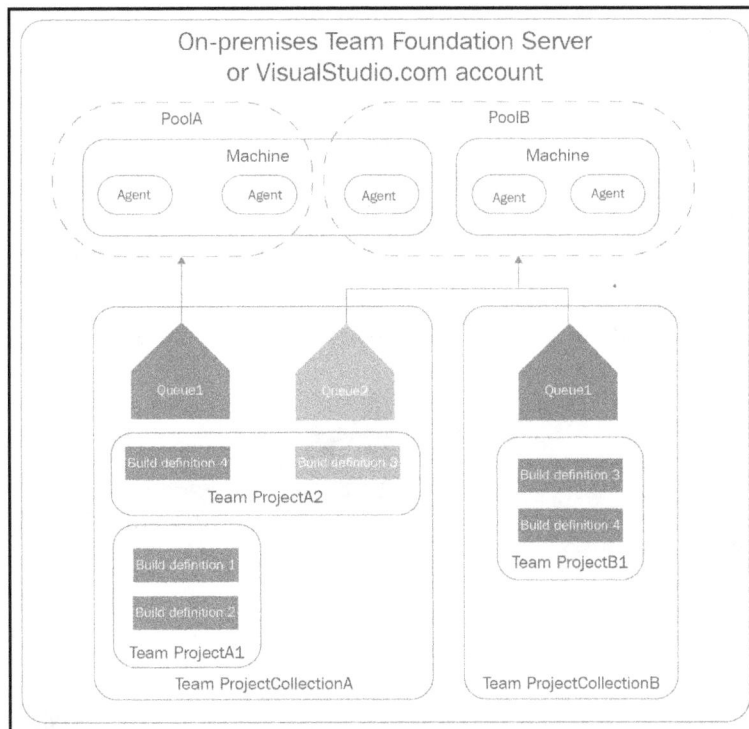

Figure 9: Relationship between agents, pools, and queues

Agents, agent pools, and agent queues

The relationship between build servers, agents, agent pools, and agent queues is shown in *Figure 9*.

Multiples can be installed on a build server.

Each of these agents belongs to a single agent pool. An agent cannot belong to multiple agent pools.

An agent queue is mapped to a single agent pool. A queue cannot be mapped to multiple agent pools however a single agent pool can be used by multiple agent queues.

Queuing Build Definitions

Build definitions are queued before they can be executed. When queuing a build definition, the name of the agent queue on which it should be queued should be provided. A queue is tied and mapped to an agent pool. Any available agent in the pool that meets the capabilities needed by the build definition eventually picks up the request and executes it.

Configuring a Build definition

The **Build Management** control panel can be reached via the **Builds** sub-menu in the **Build & Release** link on the top navigation bar. Clicking on the **+ New** button available at the top-right of the window will start a new build definition wizard. *Figure 10* shows the **Create new build definition** wizard:

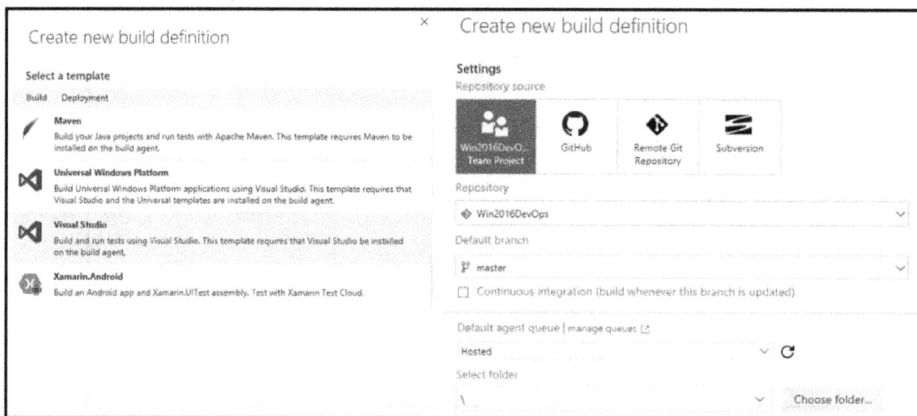

Figure 10: Creating a build definition

Selecting a **Build** template and providing an appropriate repository name, branch name, and agent queue information will create a build definition in draft mode with a few activities in it. The build definition control panel is shown in *Figure 11*:

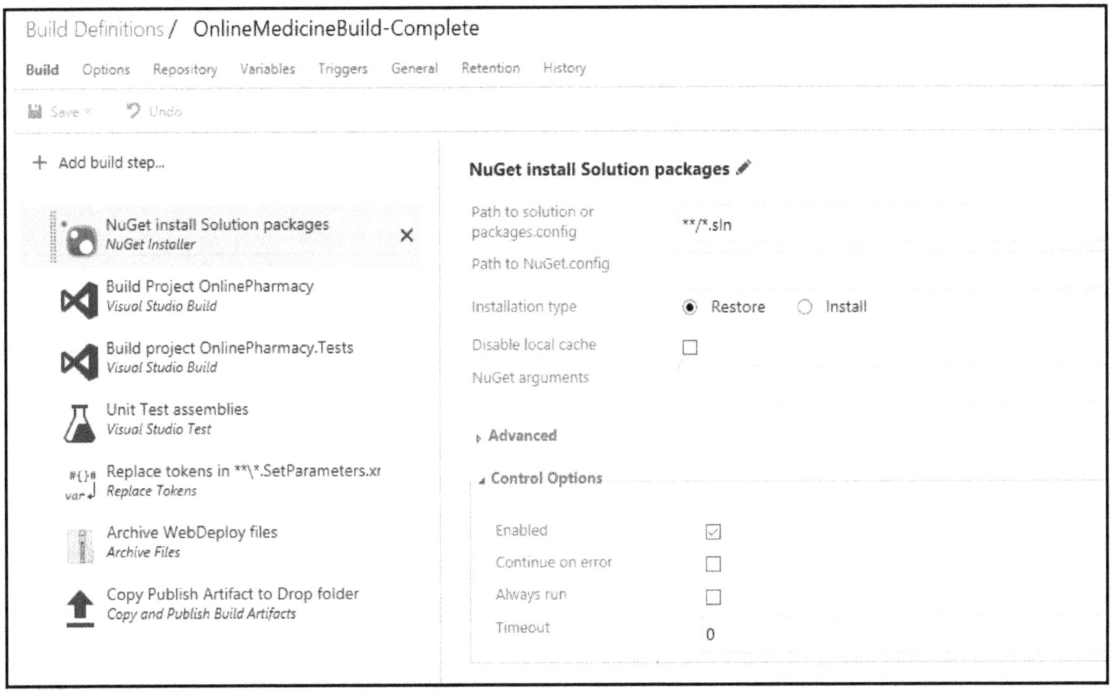

Figure 11: Build control Panel

There are two levels of configuration for each build definition – Build level and Task level configuration.

- **Build level configuration**: These configurations affect the entire build definition and execution process. It also provides the options to save and queue the build definition from any tab:
    - **Build**: This tab lists every task that comprises the build definition. Configuration for every task can be done from this tab. Refer to *Figure 11* for a visual example.

- **Options**: This tab is used to build multiple configurations such as debug, release, or any other configuration defined in the project. Selecting **Multi-Configuration** shows further options. We can provide comma-separated configuration names, select whether each of these configurations should run in parallel or in sequence, and select whether these configurations should stop if an error occurs. It also allows us to create a new work item (**Bug, Epic, Feature, Task, Test case, User story, Issue**) when the build fails by checking the **Create Work Item on Failure** checkbox. This is shown in *Figure 12*:

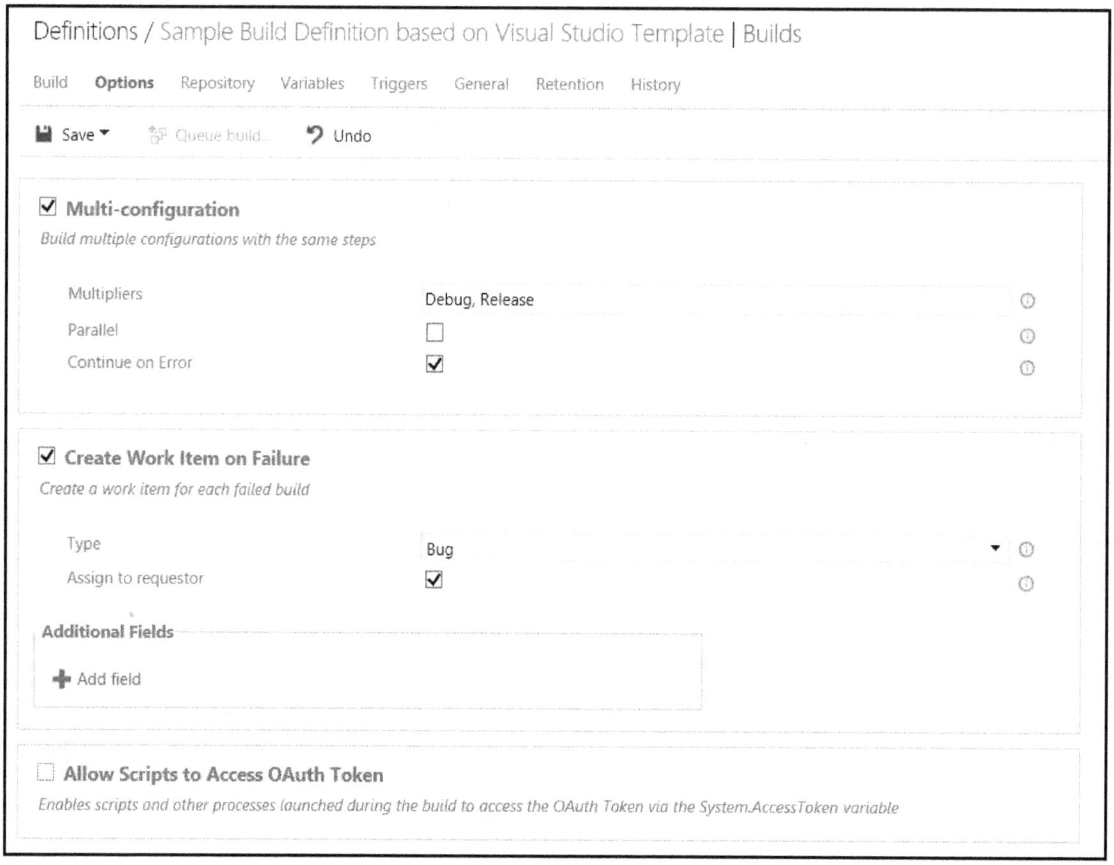

Definitions / Sample Build Definition based on Visual Studio Template | Builds

Build **Options** Repository Variables Triggers General Retention History

💾 Save ▼   Queue build...   ⤺ Undo

☑ **Multi-configuration**
Build multiple configurations with the same steps

Multipliers	Debug, Release
Parallel	☐
Continue on Error	☑

☑ **Create Work Item on Failure**
Create a work item for each failed build

Type	Bug ▼
Assign to requestor	☑

Additional Fields
➕ Add field

☐ **Allow Scripts to Access OAuth Token**
Enables scripts and other processes launched during the build to access the OAuth Token via the System.AccessToken variable

Figure 12: Options tab for build definition

- **Repository**: The options shown here are different based on the type of repository. For a Git-based repository type, information about the repository and its branch in the project should be provided. The **Clean** option removes untracked files and branches from the repository. **Label sources** helps provide labeling for the source code files and versions them for easy identification. To report on the build status the corresponding option should be checked. If code is reused from another repository, the sub module should also be checked out. This is shown in *Figure 13*:

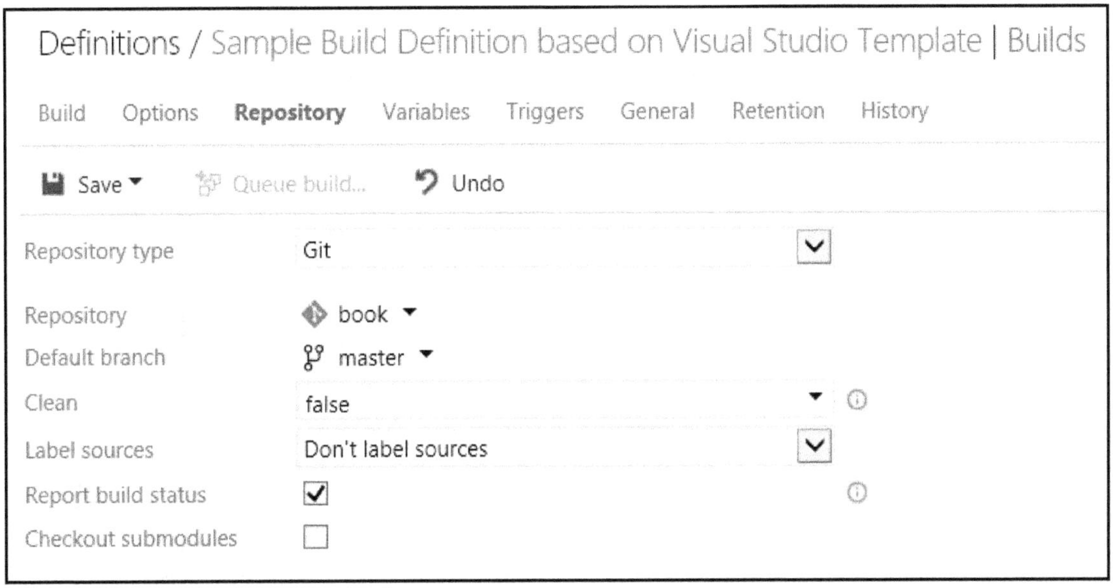

Definitions / Sample Build Definition based on Visual Studio Template | Builds

Build   Options   **Repository**   Variables   Triggers   General   Retention   History

Save ▾   Queue build...   Undo

Repository type	Git
Repository	book ▾
Default branch	master ▾
Clean	false
Label sources	Don't label sources
Report build status	✔
Checkout submodules	☐

Figure 13: Repository tab of build definition

- **Variables**: This tab helps make the build definition generic and reusable. It helps remove hard coding and changes the behavior of the build definition during execution. It also helps use the same value in multiple places within the same definition. There are a set of predefined variables available out of box. In addition, new variables can be defined by the user. Each variable has a name and a value. A variables can also be encrypted using the secret lock button. Moreover, **Allow at Queue Time** enables the availability of the same variable during manual queuing providing an opportunity to change its value before execution. *Figure 14* shows the **Variables** tab in a build definition:

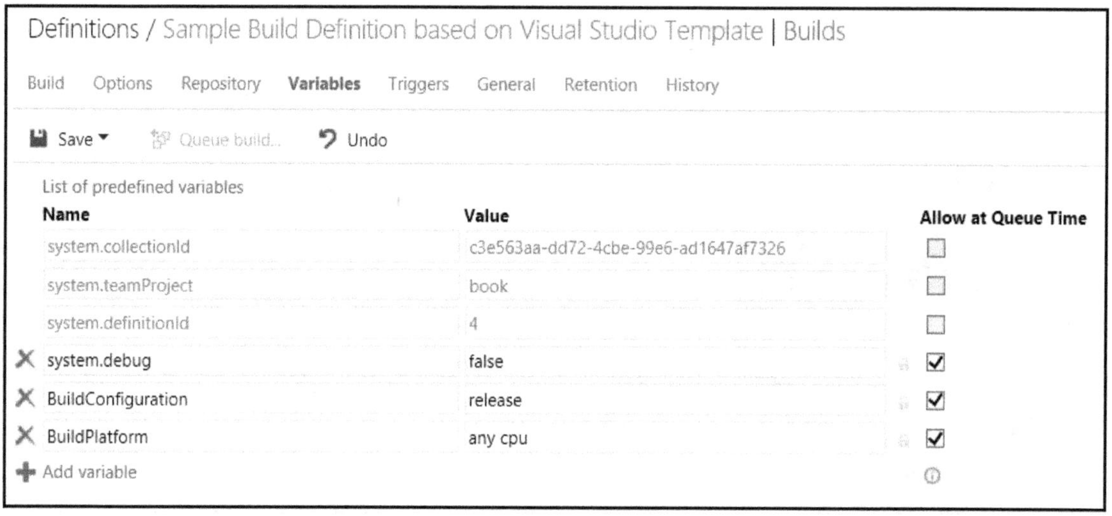

Definitions / Sample Build Definition based on Visual Studio Template | Builds

Build   Options   Repository   **Variables**   Triggers   General   Retention   History

💾 Save ▾   Queue build...   ↻ Undo

List of predefined variables

Name	Value	Allow at Queue Time
system.collectionId	c3e563aa-dd72-4cbe-99e6-ad1647af7326	☐
system.teamProject	book	☐
system.definitionId	4	☐
✕ system.debug	false	☑
✕ BuildConfiguration	release	☑
✕ BuildPlatform	any cpu	☑
➕ Add variable		ⓘ

Figure 14: Variables tab of a build definition

- **Triggers**: A build can be initiated manually as a scheduled activity and/or as a continuous integration. When **Continuous integration (CI)** is chosen, any commit or check-in of code will initiate the build process by queuing it to an agent queue. *Figure 15* shows the **Triggers** tab of the build definition:

Definitions / Sample Build Definition based on Visual Studio Template | Builds

Build   Options   Repository   Variables   **Triggers**   General   Retention   History

💾 Save ▾   Queue build...   ↩ Undo

☐ **Continuous integration (CI)**
Build each check-in.

☐ **Scheduled**
Build matching branches for each schedule.

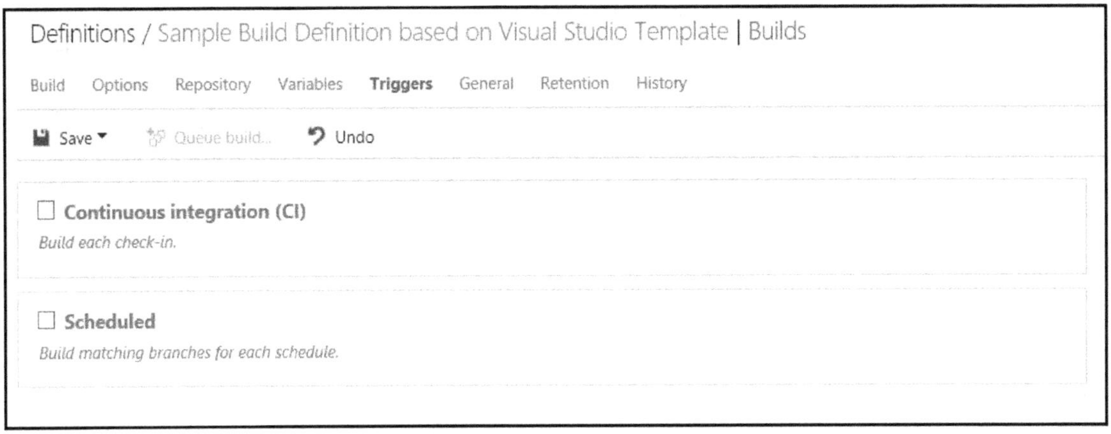

Figure 15: Triggers tab of the build definition

- **General**: This tab allows us to choose the queue for the submission of our build definition. If the build needs access across projects in the account, **Project Collection** should be chosen as the authorization scope. Otherwise, **Current Project** should be chosen. **Description** provides more information about the build definition. Each build is given a unique number and if we want more useful names for the build, **Build number format** can be used to define them. The **Demands** section lists the capabilities a build agent must possess for successful execution of the definition. A build will not execute if the demands are not satisfied. **Build job timeout in minutes** provides control to VSTS to cancel the build execution if it does not finish within the given time. *Figure 16* shows the **General** tab of a build definition:

Definitions / Sample Build Definition based on Visual Studio Template | Builds

Build   Options   Repository   Variables   Triggers   **General**   Retention   History

💾 Save ▾   Queue build...   ↺ Undo

Default agent queue	Hosted ☑	↻ Manage
Build job authorization scope	Project Collection ☑	ⓘ
Description		
Build number format	$(date:yyyyMMdd)$(rev:.r)	ⓘ
Build job timeout in minutes	60	ⓘ
Badge enabled	☐	ⓘ

Demands

Name	Type	Value
msbuild	exists	
visualstudio	exists	
vstest	exists	

➕ Add demand

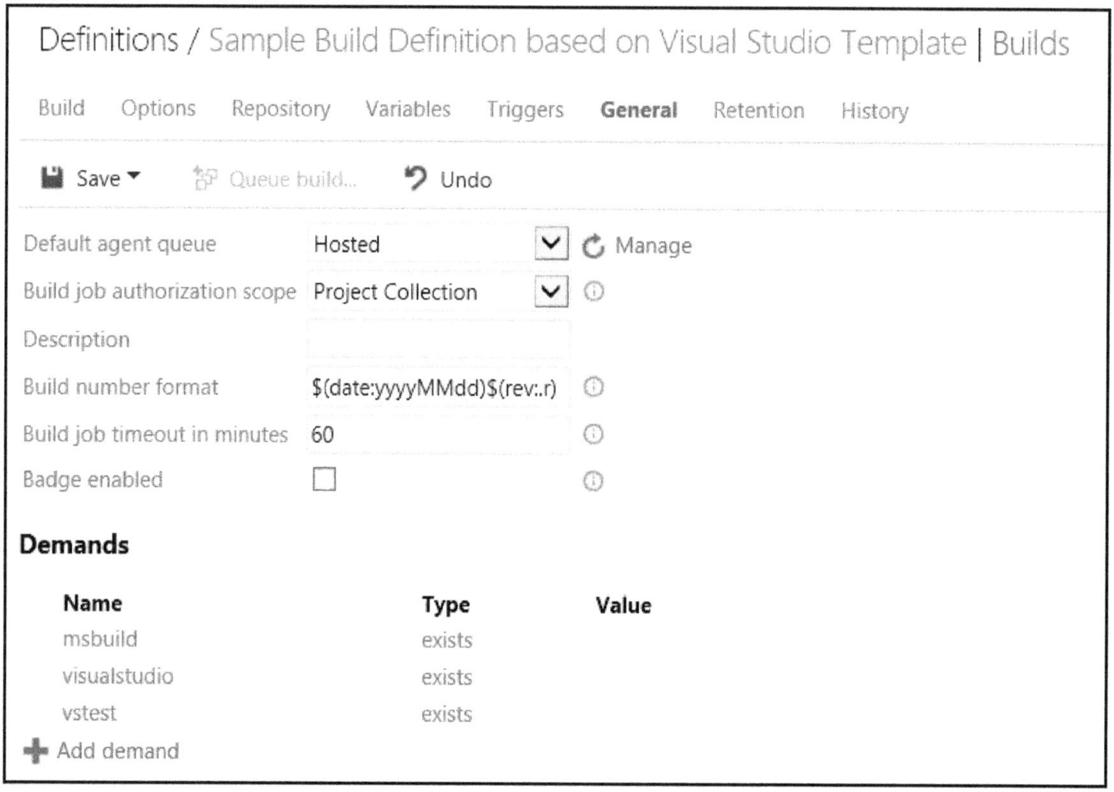

Figure 16: General tab of a build definition

- **Retention**: VSTS stores logs and other information for every build execution. This tab allows setting the number of days to retain various aspects of build output. *Figure 17* shows the **Retention** tab:

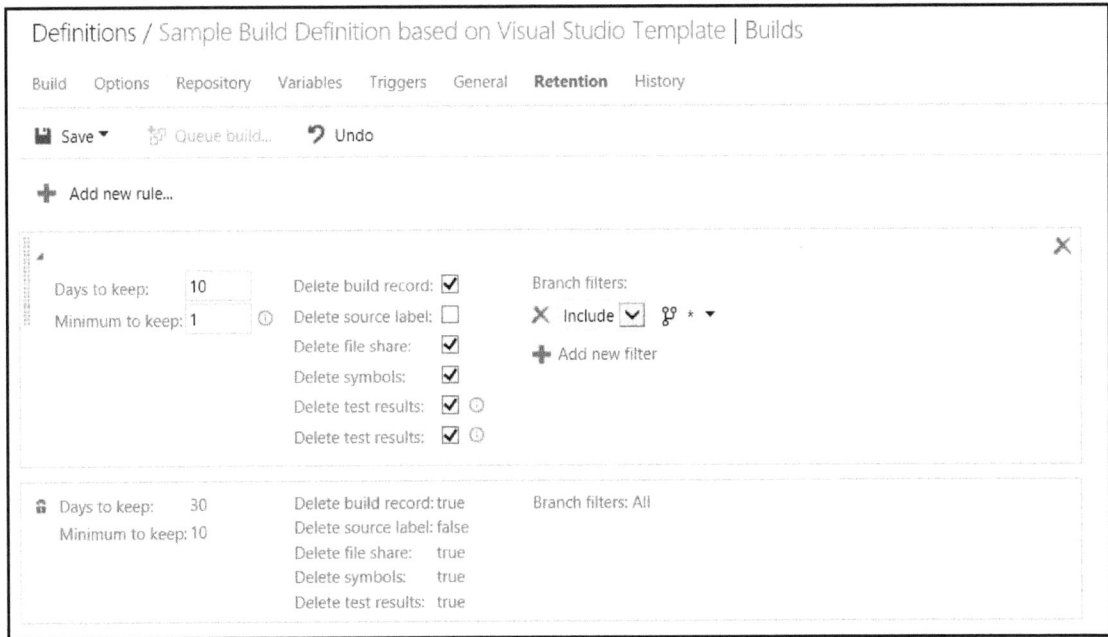

Definitions / Sample Build Definition based on Visual Studio Template | Builds

Build   Options   Repository   Variables   Triggers   General   **Retention**   History

Save ▾   Queue build...   Undo

➕ Add new rule...

Days to keep:	10	Delete build record: ✔	Branch filters:
Minimum to keep:	1	Delete source label: ☐	✕ Include ▾ 🔀 * ▾
		Delete file share: ✔	➕ Add new filter
		Delete symbols: ✔	
		Delete test results: ✔	
		Delete test results: ✔	

Days to keep: 30   Delete build record: true   Branch filters: All
Minimum to keep: 10   Delete source label: false
                      Delete file share: true
                      Delete symbols: true
                      Delete test results: true

Figure 17: Retention tab of the build definition

- **History**: VSTS maintains the history of changes made to the build definition. This was not possible in earlier versions of VSTS. It provides version control for the build definition itself and allows reversion back to a previous version and comparison between multiple versions of the same definition:

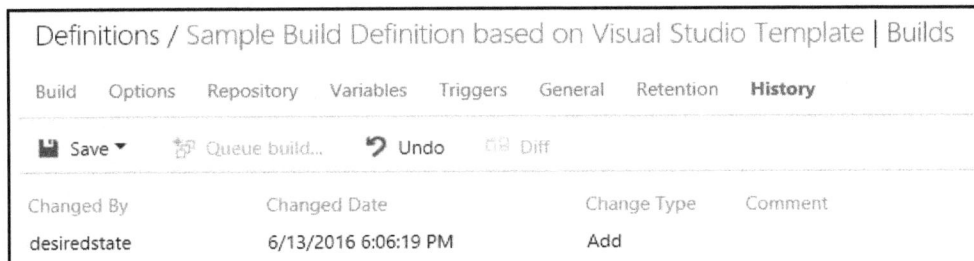

Definitions / Sample Build Definition based on Visual Studio Template | Builds

Build   Options   Repository   Variables   Triggers   General   Retention   **History**

Save ▾   Queue build...   Undo   Diff

Changed By	Changed Date	Change Type	Comment
desiredstate	6/13/2016 6:06:19 PM	Add	

Figure 18: History tab of the build definition

There are further configuration options available through the **Build Definition** context menu. Among the most important of them is the **Security** configuration. The **Security** configuration allows us to provide contributor, administrator, and authoring permissions to users and groups. This is shown in *Figure 19*:

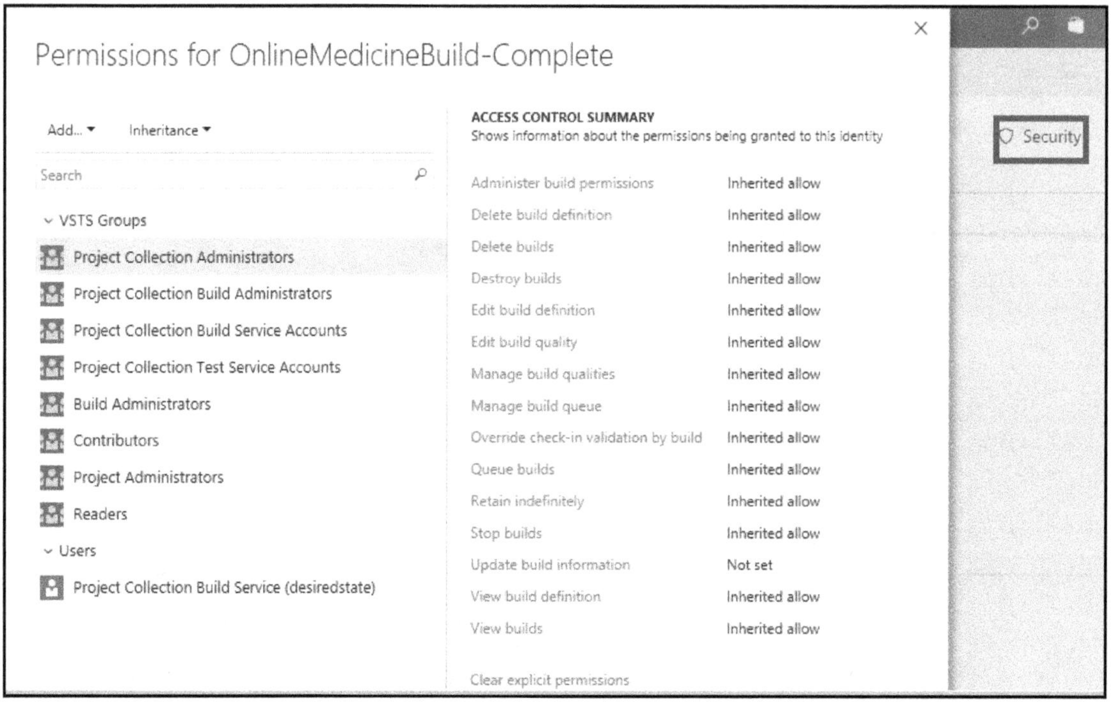

Figure 19: Build definition security configuration

The **Queue build** button lists a build definition to a queue and executes it.

- **Task level configuration**: Each task has its own set of configurations to work on. There are different requirements for different tasks. *Figure 20* shows the **Build solution** task. This is responsible for compiling every project within a solution. It accepts the solution file path and multiple configurations related to NuGet. These include path to `NuGet.config`, whether to restore or install `NuGet` packages, disabling the NuGet cache, and NuGet arguments. The advanced section accepts the path to `NuGet.exe`:

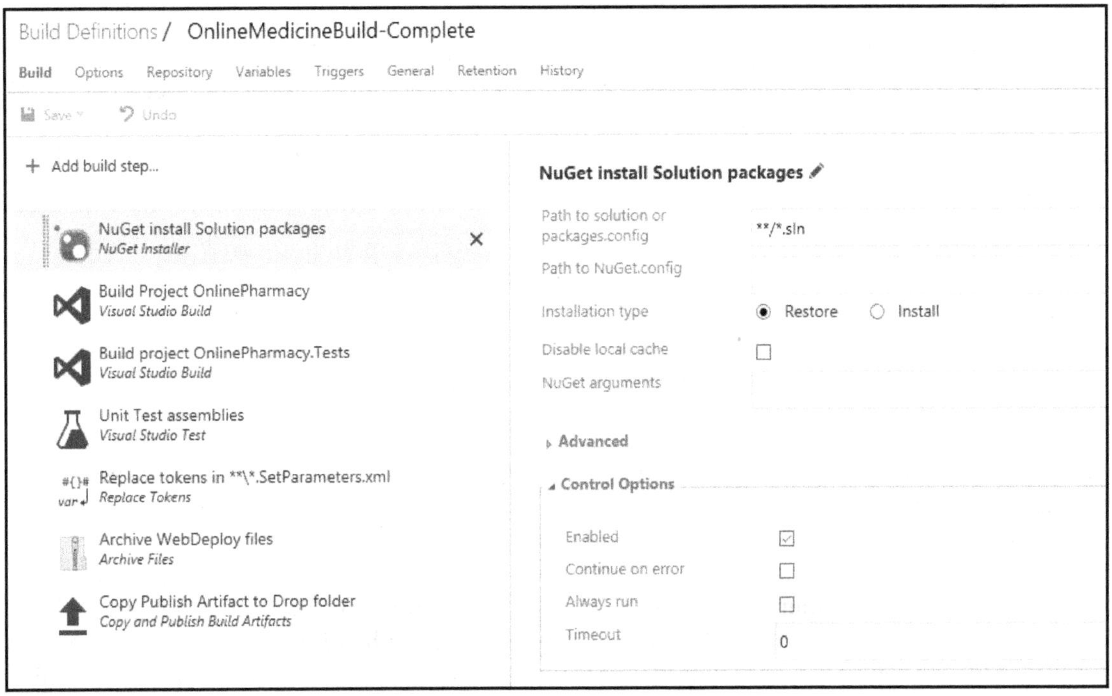

Build Definitions / OnlineMedicineBuild-Complete

Build Options Repository Variables Triggers General Retention History

Save Undo

+ Add build step...

NuGet install Solution packages
NuGet Installer   ✕

Build Project OnlinePharmacy
Visual Studio Build

Build project OnlinePharmacy.Tests
Visual Studio Build

Unit Test assemblies
Visual Studio Test

Replace tokens in ***.SetParameters.xml
Replace Tokens

Archive WebDeploy files
Archive Files

Copy Publish Artifact to Drop folder
Copy and Publish Build Artifacts

NuGet install Solution packages 🖉

Path to solution or packages.config	***.sln
Path to NuGet.config	
Installation type	◉ Restore ○ Install
Disable local cache	☐
NuGet arguments	

▸ **Advanced**

◢ **Control Options**

Enabled	☑
Continue on error	☐
Always run	☐
Timeout	0

Figure 20: Build solution task within the build definition

- The **Control Options** section has an additional configuration that controls the entire task. These configurations are common to all the tasks available in VSTS build and release definitions. **Control Options** is shown in *Figure 20*.
- The **Enabled** check refers to whether this task participates in build execution. It is not executed if the check is removed. By default, it is in the checked state.

- A build execution fails when any task within it fails. The **Continue on error** check helps change this setting and allows us to continue executing the build even if this tasks fails.
- **Always run** ensures that a given task always executes, even if there are build failures from other tasks.

Release Management service

Now it's time to look at how VSTS can help with continuous deployment and continuous delivery. We already know by now that continuous deployment refers to the deployment of application on multiple environments, including pre-production and production environments, through automation. This involves both the provisioning and configuration of environments and applications.

The Release Management service helps automate the deployment and configuration to multiple environments. It helps execute validation tests, such as functional tests, on these environments. The Release Management service help implement both continuous deployment and delivery. Similar to Source Code and Build mMnagement, the Release Management service is scoped at the project level. For each project, VSTS allows the creation of multiple release definitions.

Each release definition consists of multiple environment definitions, each environment representing a deployment target. Test, staging, and production are examples of environments. Release Management executes these environment definitions and each environment can be configured to run in parallel or in sequence after a prior environment execution. Each environment definition would typically consist of provisioning and configuring multiple servers, deploying and configuring application components on these servers, and validating the application. Although the configuration of environments within a release definition could be different, from a DevOps perspective, they should be similar.

Each environment definition consists of multiple activities that run in sequence, one after another, like a pipeline. Each activity is responsible for executing a single task within the overall environment pipeline. *Figure 21* shows a release definition example consisting of two environments, authoring and production, each with multiple activities in its pipeline. Each contains the same tasks. However, their configuration is different for each environment:

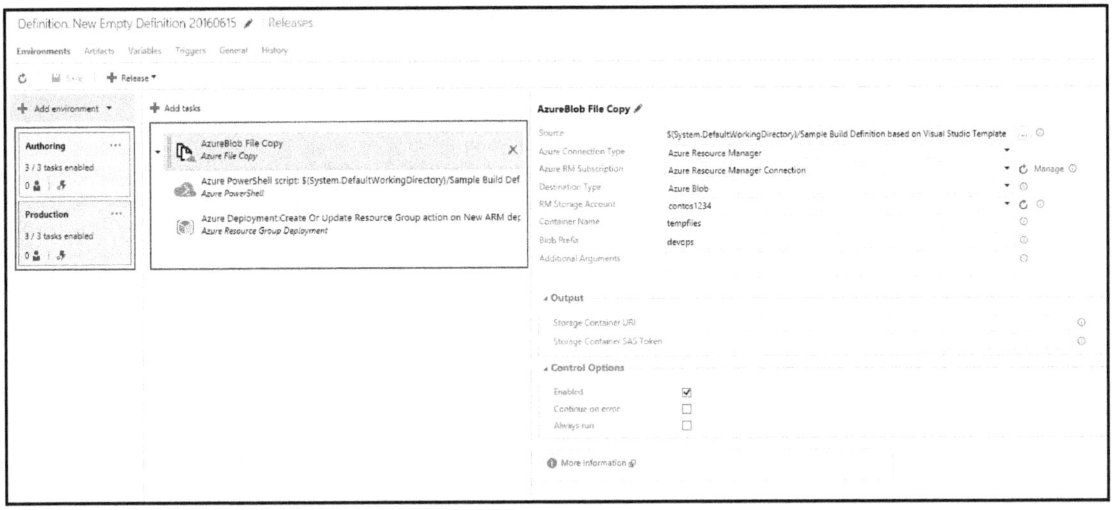

Figure 21: Release definition with two environments

It may be recollected that tasks are available to both build and release definitions are common in VSTS. *Figure 8* in this chapter shows the rich set of tasks available for build and release definitions.

The release pipeline gets its inputs in the form of artifacts. One of the final steps in continuous integration is to drop the generated package to a specified location. Release Management considers the output from a build execution as an artifact. It also considers files stored in Git and TFVC repositories as artifacts.

Executing release definitions

Release definitions need release environments in order to be executed. The tasks in a release and environment definition have pre-requisites, and those should be available on the release servers. VSTS provides built-in release servers out-of-the-box, with prerequisites installed on them. They are available to every account in VSTS for the purpose of executing release definitions. However, at the same time, VSTS is flexible enough to accept our own custom release servers for the execution of release definitions.

Release Management architecture

The Release Management architecture is the same as that of Build Management, which is depicted in *Figure 9*. Every release server should have a release agent installed and running on it. Release agents are Windows services that are configured to interact and work with the VSTS Release Management service.

Executing a release definition in turn executes the environment definitions. Each release environment is configured to use an agent queue. This agent queue selected during release definition creation becomes the agent queue configuration for the first environment. Each environment definition can be configured to use a particular agent queue and a request is queued on the agent queue for each environment. An agent queue is formed at the project-collection level and multiple queues can be created. When queuing an environment definition, VSTS expects the artifact that should be used within its pipeline.

Release definition configuration

The Release Management control panel can be reached through the **Release** sub-menu of the **Build & Release** link on the top navigation bar. Clicking on the **+ New** button available in the top-right of the browser window will initiate the creation of a new release definition:

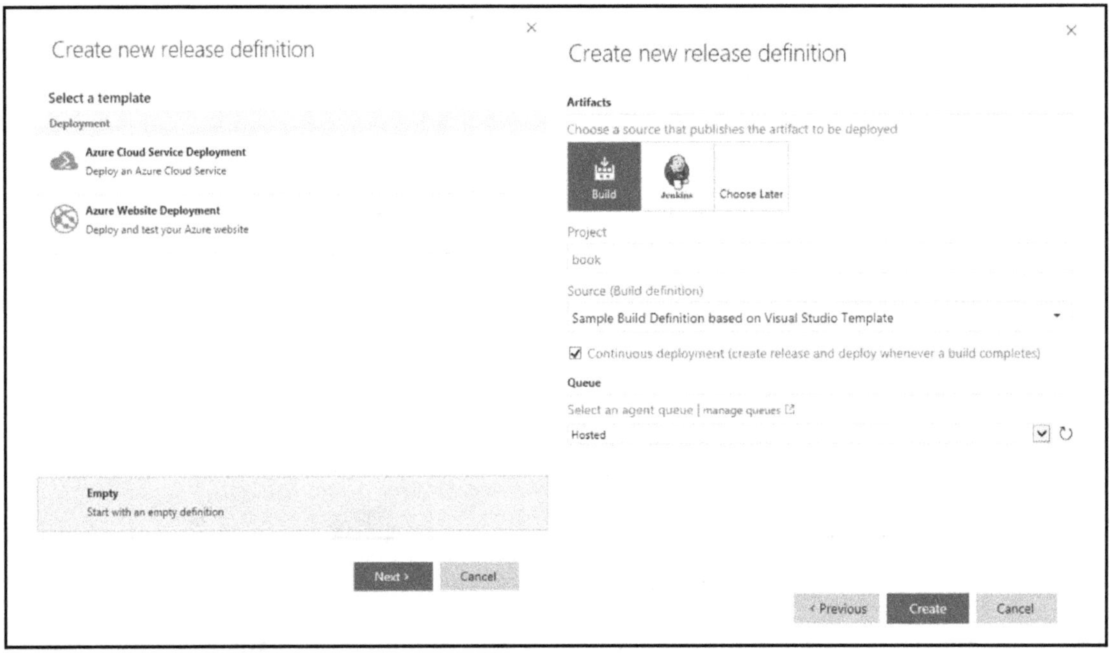

Figure 22: Creating a new release definition

Figure 22 shows the **Create new release definition** user interface. Selecting a release template and providing source artifacts and agent queue information will create a release definition in draft mode. The queue agent selected here will become the default queue agent for first environment within the release definition. If the **Empty** template is chosen, VSTS will create an environment named **Environment 1** with no tasks in it. The same release definition is shown in *Figure 23*:

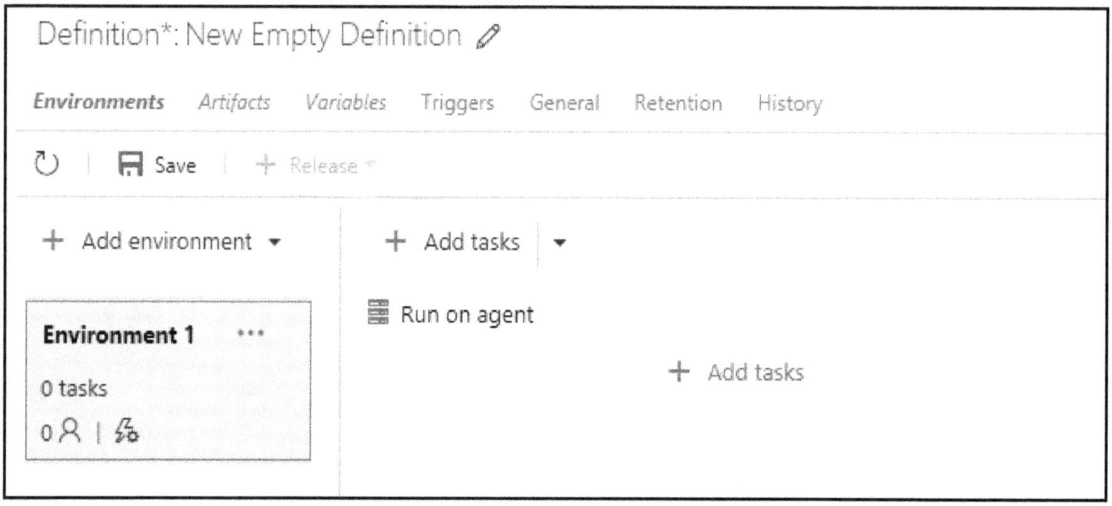

Figure 23: Empty release definition

There are three levels of configuration for each release definition–Release level, Environment level and Task level configuration.

- **Release level configuration**: This configuration affects the entire release definition and execution. It also provides the option to save the release definition from any tab.
    - **Environments**: This tab lists every environment available in the release definition. It also comprises all the tasks that are part of the environment definition. Individual task configuration can be done from this tab.

- **Artifacts**: This tab helps configure the link to the artifacts. The artifacts can come from a build execution or from a repository. Build artifacts can be chosen from any project in a Visual Studio account and repository artifacts can choose any repository and select project within the VSTS account. The artifacts type can be Jenkins, Git, TFVC, and GitHub apart from VSTS Build. The **Artifacts** user interface is shown in *Figure 24*:

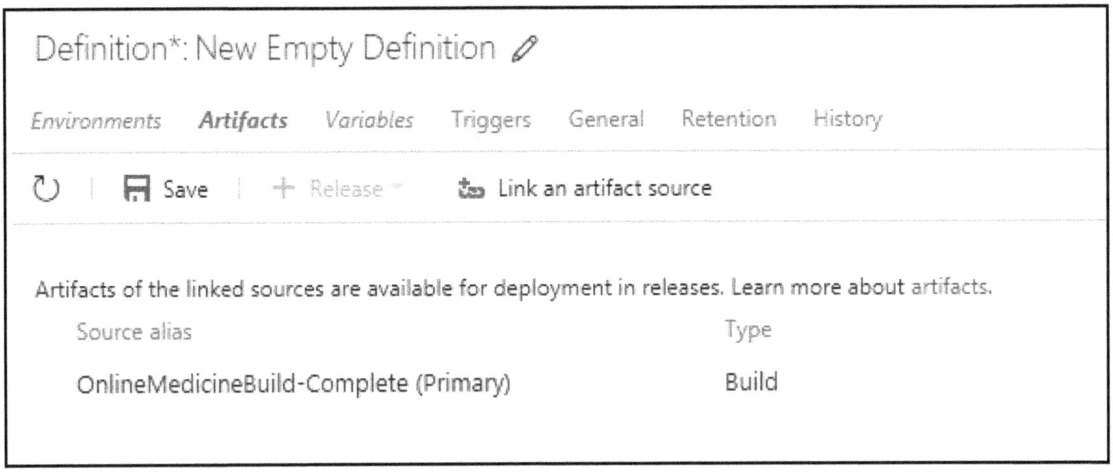

Definition*: New Empty Definition 🖉

Environments   ***Artifacts***   *Variables*   *Triggers*   *General*   *Retention*   *History*

↻ | 💾 Save | ＋ Release ▾   ⮑ Link an artifact source

Artifacts of the linked sources are available for deployment in releases. Learn more about artifacts.

Source alias	Type
OnlineMedicineBuild-Complete (Primary)	Build

Figure 24: Artifacts tab in release definition

- **Variables**: This tab helps make the release definition generic and reusable. They help remove hard coding and change the behavior of a release definition during execution. They also help use the same value in multiple places within the same definition. There is a set of predefined variables available. In addition, new variables can be defined by the user. Each variable has a name and value. Variables can also be encrypted using the secret lock button. These are release-level variables. This is shown in *Figure 25*. There is another set of variables, known as **Environment variables**, that are defined at the environment level. We will look at them when we talk about environment level configuration in the following section:

Definition: OnlineMedicineRelease-Complete ✎ | Releases

Environments   Artifacts   **Variables**   Triggers   General   Retention   History

↻ | 🖫 Save | + Release ▾

Variable Groups

Include variable groups to use the variables in this release definition. You can manage variable groups here.

No variable groups are linked.

Link variable group(s)

Variables

Define custom variables to use in this release definition. View list of pre-defined variables

Name	Value
🗑 StorageAccountName	win2016devops1
🗑 ContainerName	armt
🗑 resourceGroupName	win2016devops
🗑 StorageSAS	********
+ **Add variable**	

Figure 25: Variables tab in release definition

- **Triggers**: Release can be initiated manually or as a scheduled activity or as continuous deployment. If **Continuous Deployment** is chosen as an option, the availability of any new build version or any new commit/check-in of code (if the continuous integration is configured on the linked build) will start the release process by queuing it to the agent queue. The artifacts configuration determines whether to use the build output or new commits in the code repository to initiate the release. The build version must be chosen manually as an artifact if release is manually initiated. This is shown in *Figure 26*. Trigger configuration is also available at the environment level and we will look into it when we discuss environment-specific configuration in the following section:

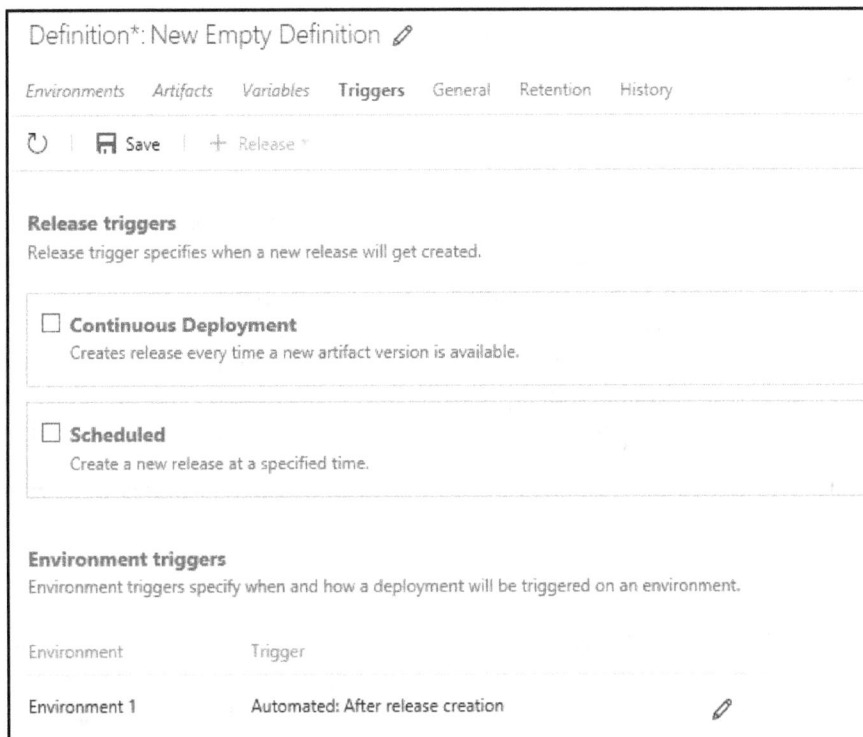

- **General**: This tab allows you to configure the release name. Every release is given a unique number, and **Release name format** helps provide more useful names for the releases. The **General** tab is shown in *Figure 27*:

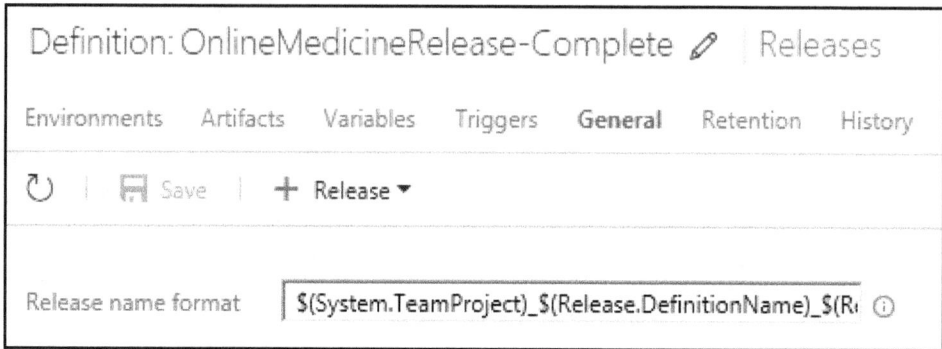

Figure 27: General tab in release definition

- **Retention**: VSTS stores logs and other information for every release execution. This tab allows to set the number of days for which to retain the release logs.
- **History**: VSTS maintains the history of changes made to the release definition, which was not possible in earlier versions of VSTS. This provides version control for the release definition itself and allows reversion back to a previous version and comparison between multiple versions of same definition. The **History** details are shown in *Figure 28*:

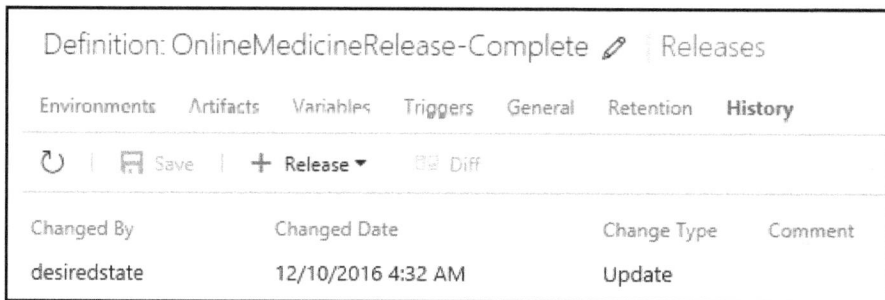

Figure 28: History tab in release definition

There is further configuration available through the release definition context menu. Among the more important of them is the **Security** configuration. **Security** configuration allows you to provide contributor, administrator, and authoring permissions to different team members. The steps to configure security for the release definition are the same as those for the build definition.

Clicking on the **Release** button and then on the **Create Release** item creates a new release, enlists the environments on agent queues, and starts executing them.

- **Environment level configuration**: This configuration affects an individual environment's definition and execution. Each environment has a button with the symbol: **....** Clicking on it and then on any one of the menu items – **Assign approvers...**, **Agent queues**, **Configure variables**, or **Deployment conditions**, will show the user interface for configuring that environment. Environment Context Menu is shown in *Figure 29*:

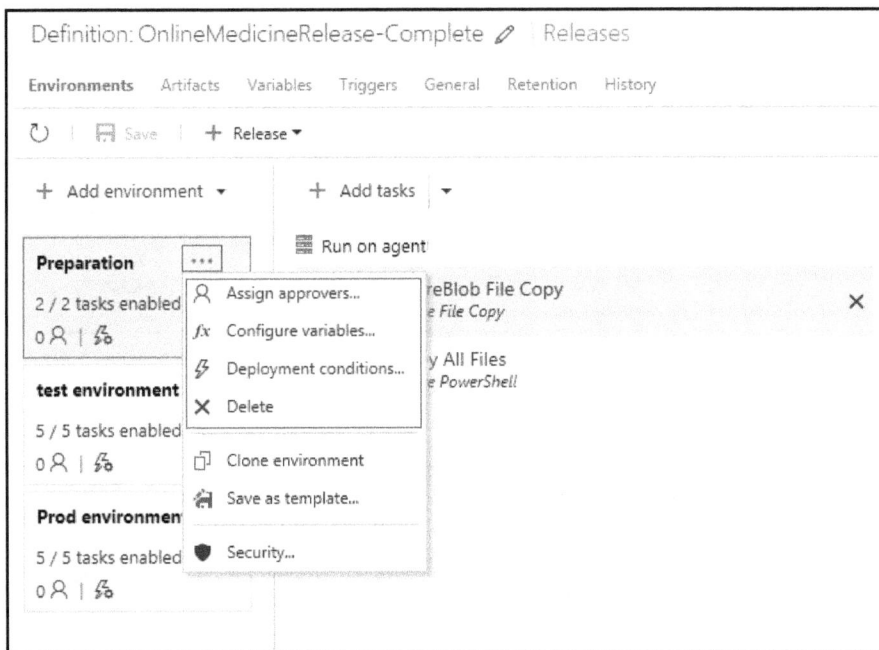

Figure 29: Environment contextual menu

You can delete an environment definition from its contextual menu, as shown in *Figure 30*:

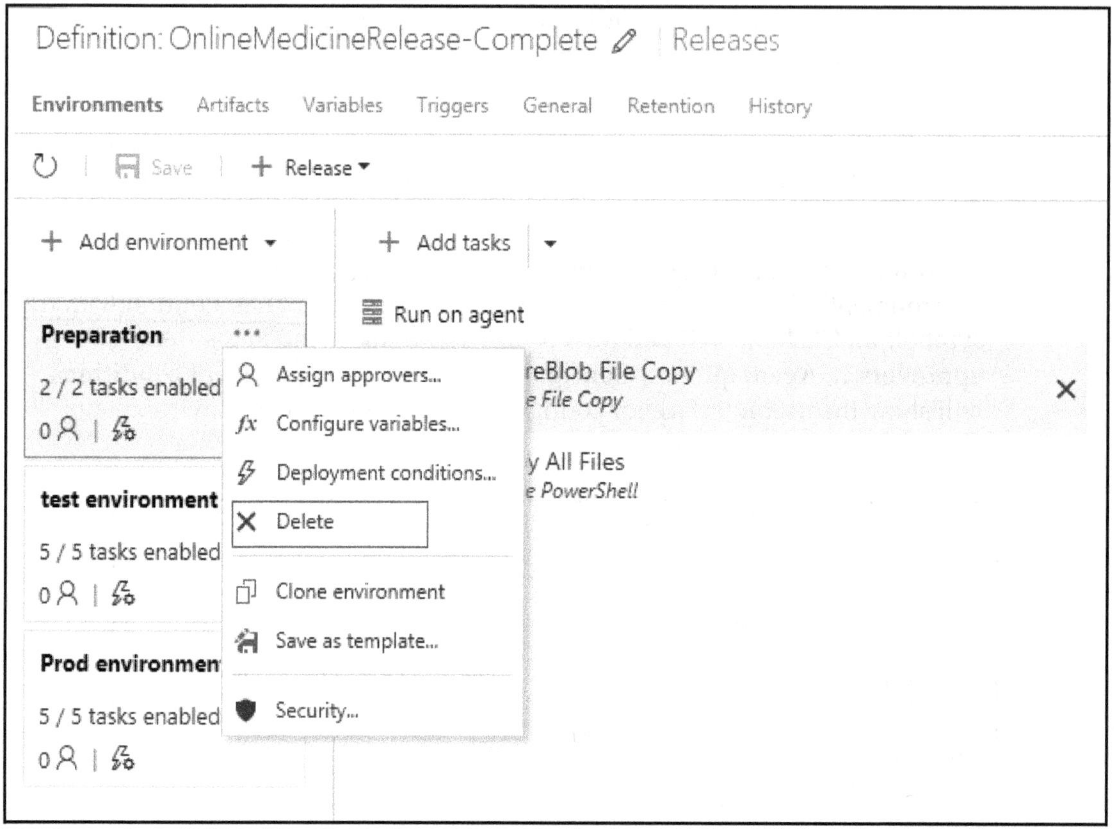

Figure 30: Deleting an environment definition

- **Approvals**: Approvals play a pivotal role in Release Management because they affect multiple environments that are strategic and important to applications and organizations. Approvals can be sought prior to the execution of an environment definition from a user/group, or they can be configured to be approved automatically. Similarly, we can configure both pre-deployment and post-deployment approvals for an environment. This is shown in *Figure 31*:

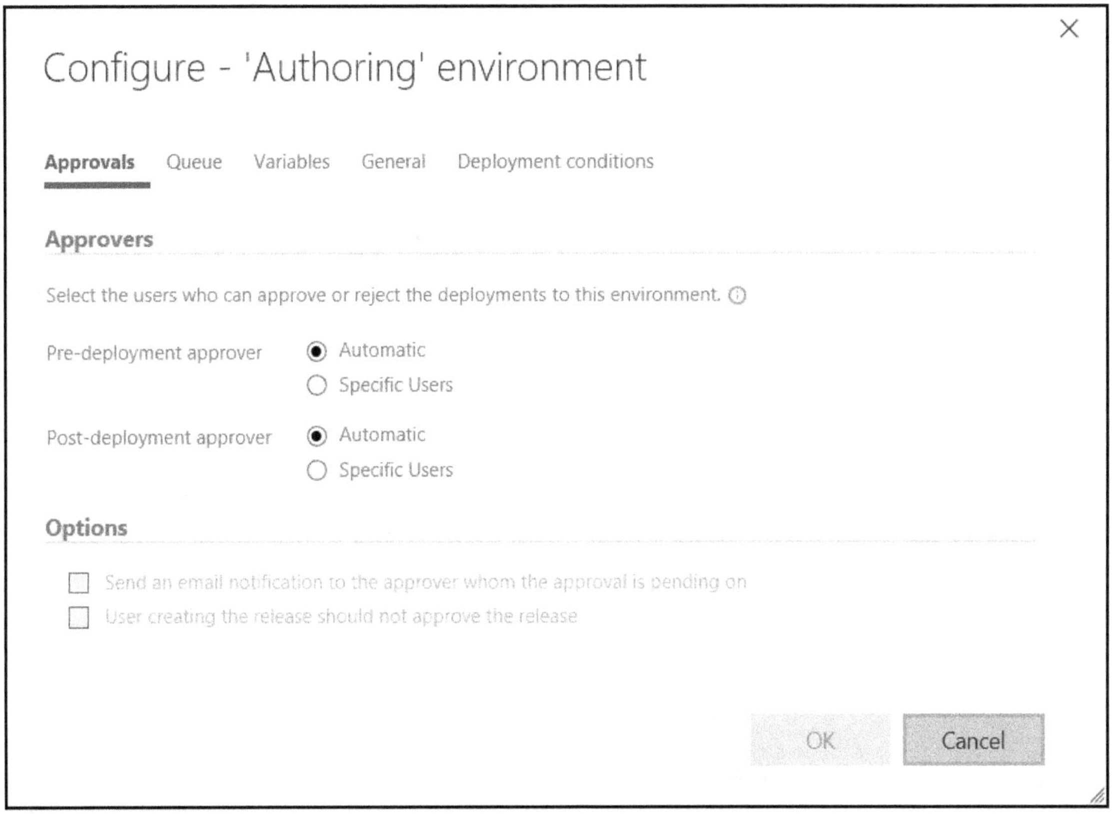

×

Configure - 'Authoring' environment

Approvals   Queue   Variables   General   Deployment conditions

Approvers

Select the users who can approve or reject the deployments to this environment. ⓘ

Pre-deployment approver   ● Automatic
                          ○ Specific Users

Post-deployment approver ● Automatic
                          ○ Specific Users

Options

☐ Send an email notification to the approver whom the approval is pending on
☐ User creating the release should not approve the release

OK   Cancel

Figure 31: Approvals tab in environment definition

- **Queue**: This tab can override the default agent queue. The **Demands** section lists the capabilities a release agent must have for successful execution of the definition. Release will not execute if the demands are not satisfied. The queue configuration is shown in *Figure 32*:

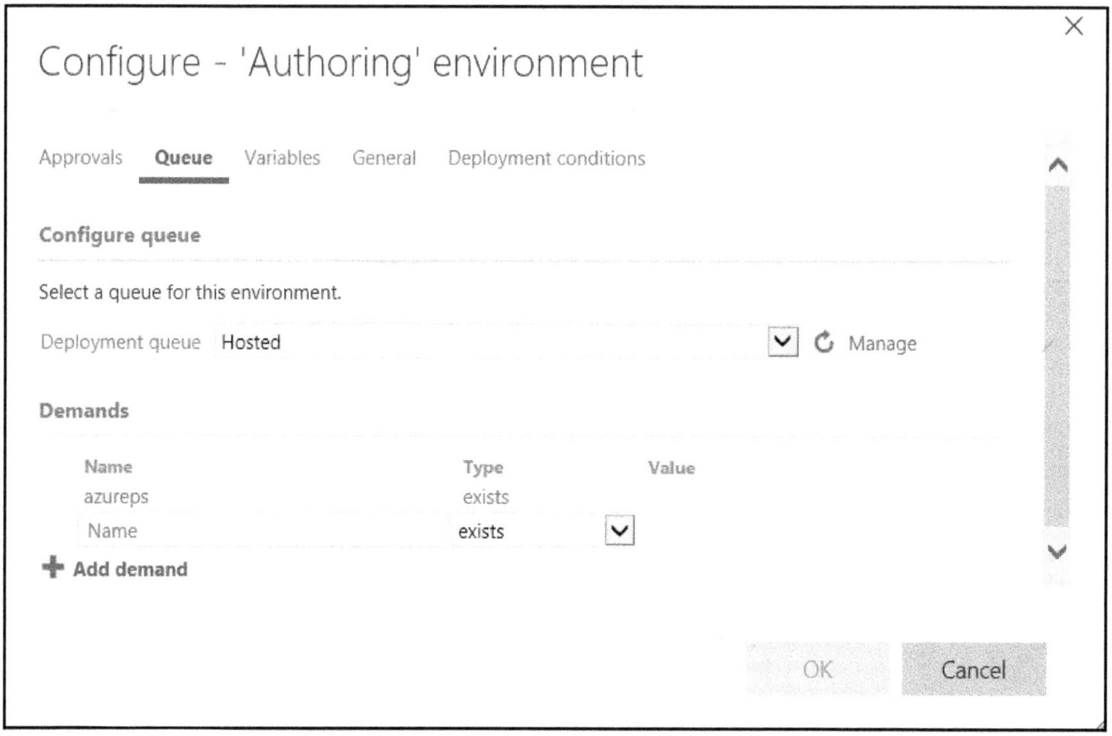

Figure 32: Queue configuration in environment definition

- **Variables**: The concept of variables is the same as that discussed in the release-level configuration section. Environment also provides the same set of predefined variables as provided at the release level. In addition, new variables can be defined by the user. The release-level variables are accessible at the environment level and can also be overridden here by declaring a variable with the same name. Environment level variables are visible only within the environment they are defined in. This is shown in *Figure 33*:

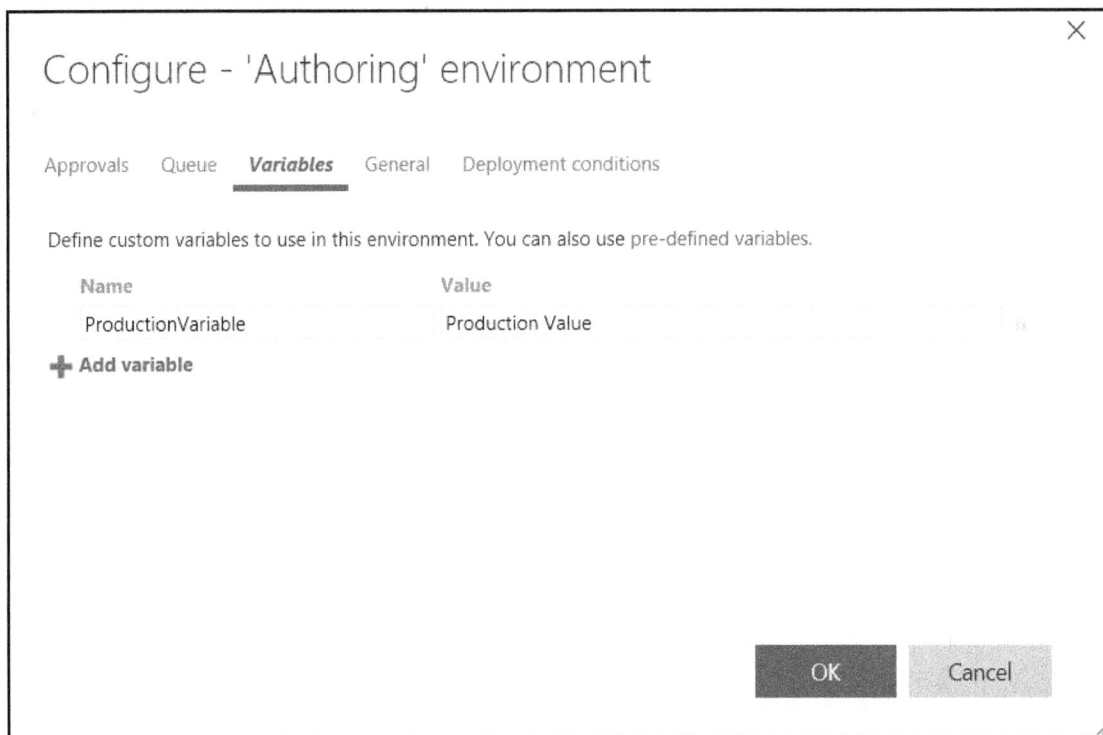

Figure 33: Variable configuration in environment definition

- **General**: This tab allows the configuration of e-mail notifications and you may also provide a name for the owner of the environment. **Skip artifacts download** ensures that the artifacts are not downloaded to the agent prior to starting the deployment. **Deployment timeout in minutes** provides control to VSTS to cancel the environment execution if it does not finish within the time provided. This is shown in *Figure 34*:

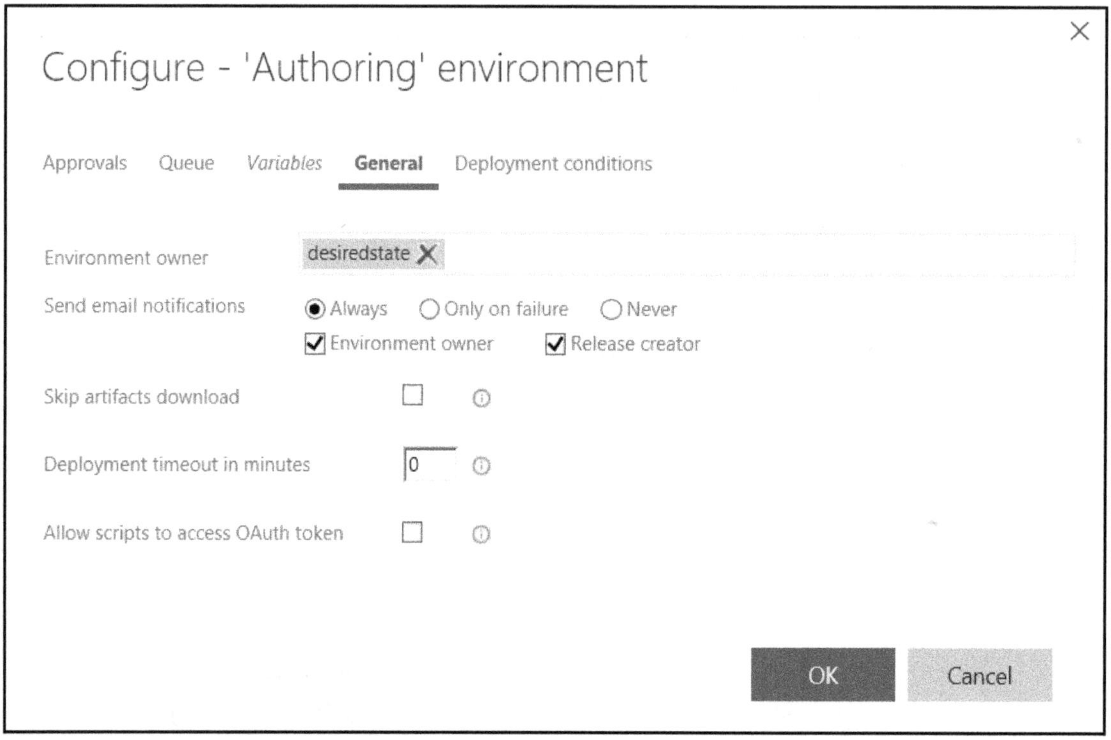

Figure 34: General configuration in environment definition

- **Deployment conditions**: Environment release can be initiated manually. It can be triggered automatically, after the creation of a release from the release definition, as a scheduled activity, or as part of continuous deployment. This is shown in *Figure 35*:

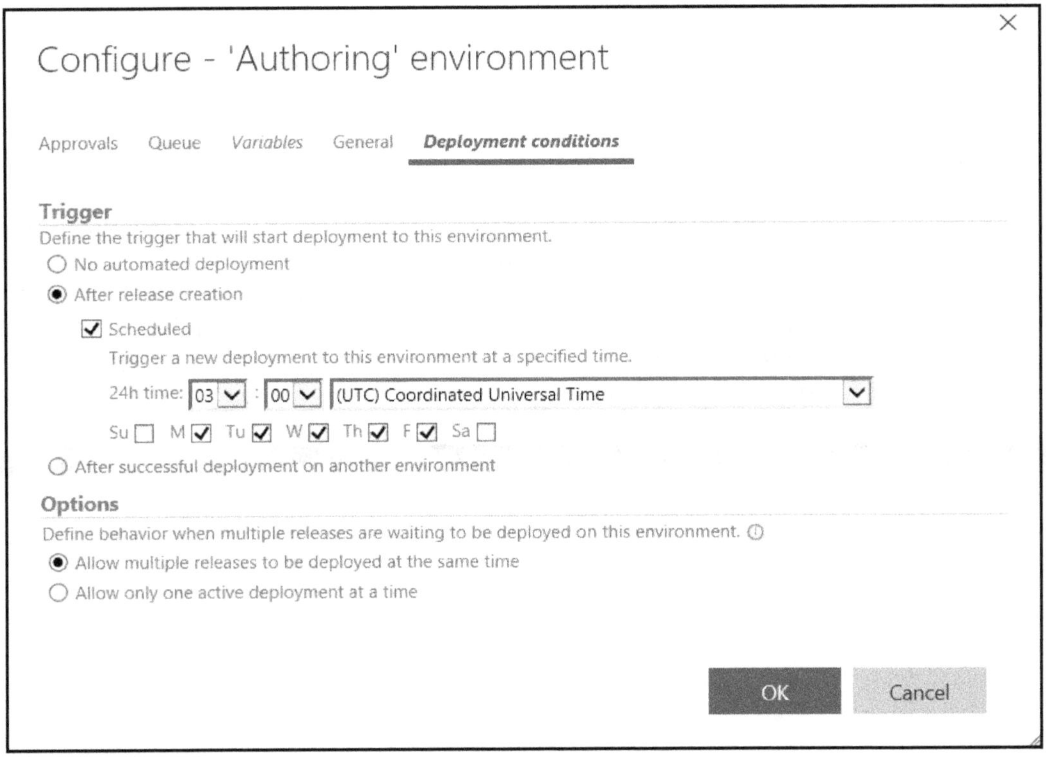

Figure 35: Deployment configuration in environment definition

- **Task-level configuration**: Release definitions have same tasks available for configuration as those available to build definitions. We have already covered this during our discussion about build task level configuration.

Setting up a cloud environment

Azure and VSTS accounts are crucial for implementing DevOps processes. In this chapter, we will look at the steps to create both VSTS and Azure accounts, and in Chapter 5, *Building a Sample Application*, we will set up the development environment for our application.

Visual Studio Team Services

The primary prerequisite for creating an account with VSTS is to have a Microsoft account. Microsoft accounts were previously known as **Live** accounts. This is a free account that can be set up through `https://signup.live.com/` to access Microsoft services such as Skype, OneDrive, Outlook, Hotmail, and more.

Another way to create a VSTS account is to have a **Work or School account**, which refers to an enterprise and its e-mail accounts.

One account, either a Microsoft account or a Work or School account, is necessary to create a VSTS account. After provisioning these accounts, browsing through `https://go.microsoft.com/fwlink/?LinkId=307137&clcid=0x409` will start a wizard to create a VSTS account. It will ask you to log in with your Microsoft or Work account. After login, pick a unique name through which your VSTS account is identified. This is shown in *Figure 36*. You can also select the type of repository – **Git** or **Team Foundation Version Control**. By clicking on the **Change details** link, select a preferred region and the process types (**CMMI**, **SCRUM**, and **Agile**) to manage the work. This is shown in *Figure 37*:

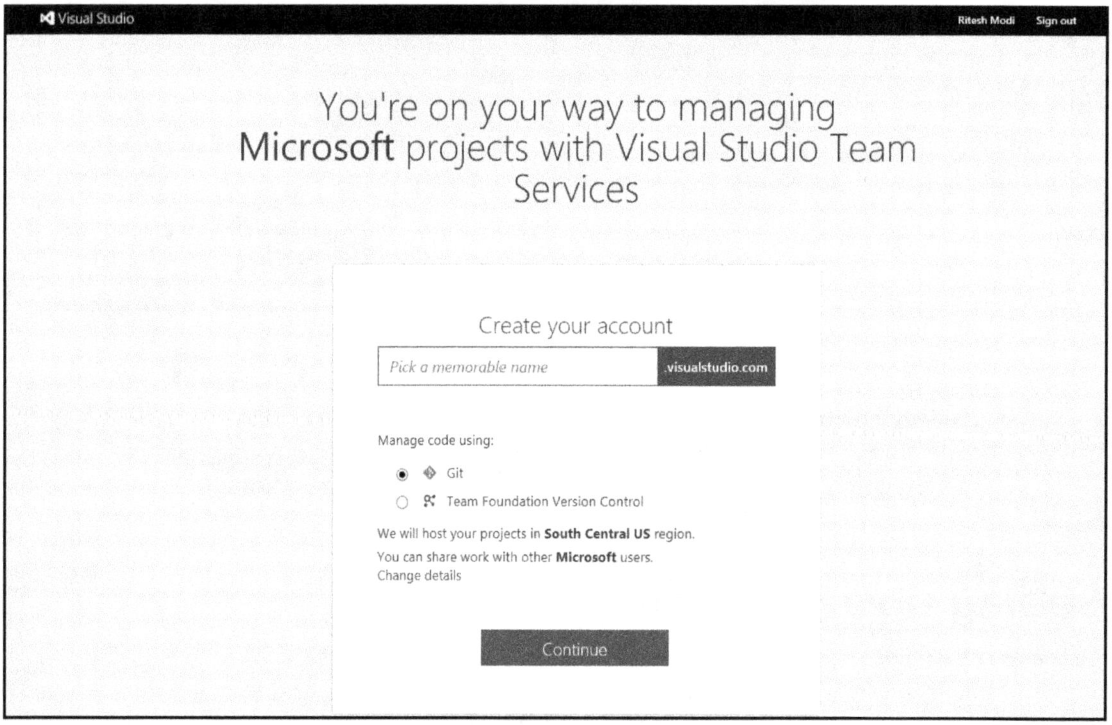

Figure 36: Creating a VSTS account

Click on the **Continue** button and in a few seconds, your account will be created as shown in *Figure 37*.

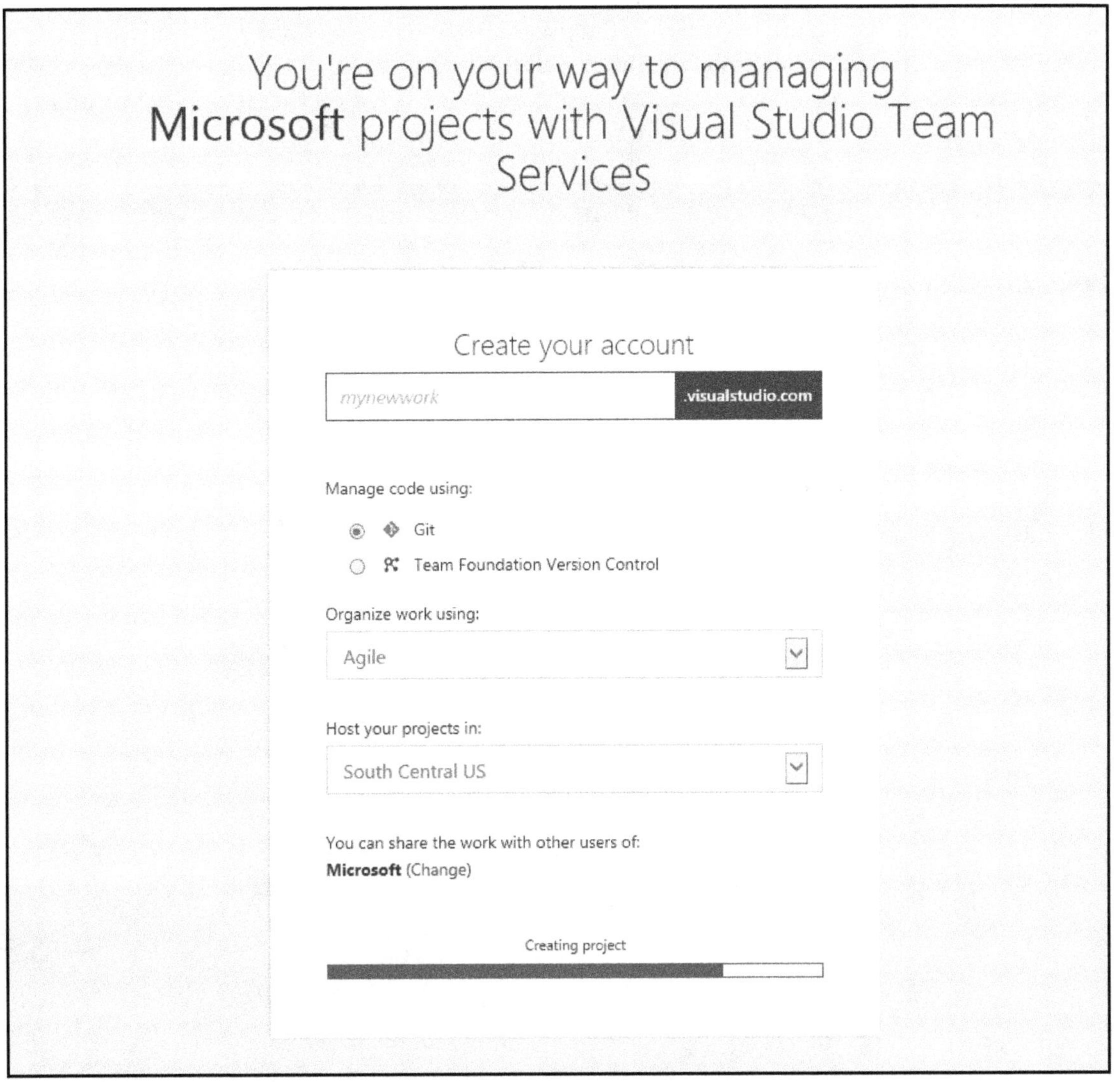

Figure 37: Creating a VSTS account

Azure account

The primary prerequisite for creating an account with Microsoft Azure is to either have a Microsoft or a Student/Work account. In the preceding section, we looked at how to create a Microsoft account. Once you have a valid account, navigate to `https://account.windowsazure.com` from your browser. Click on the **SIGN IN** button in the extreme top-right corner of the page. This is shown in *Figure 38*:

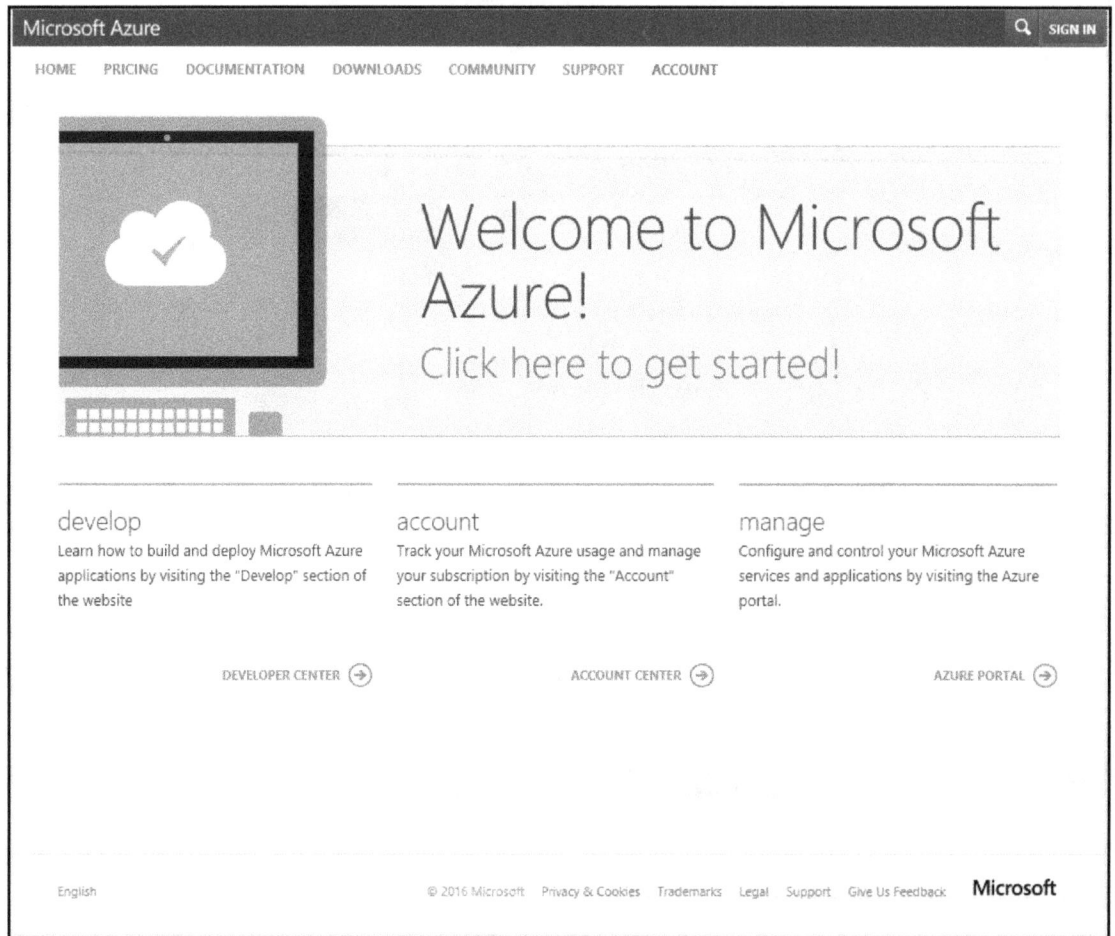

Figure 38: Azure start page for creating a subscription

This will navigate to the login page for your Microsoft or Work/School account. I used an Outlook account to obtain a subscription and tenant from Azure. This is shown in *Figure 39*:

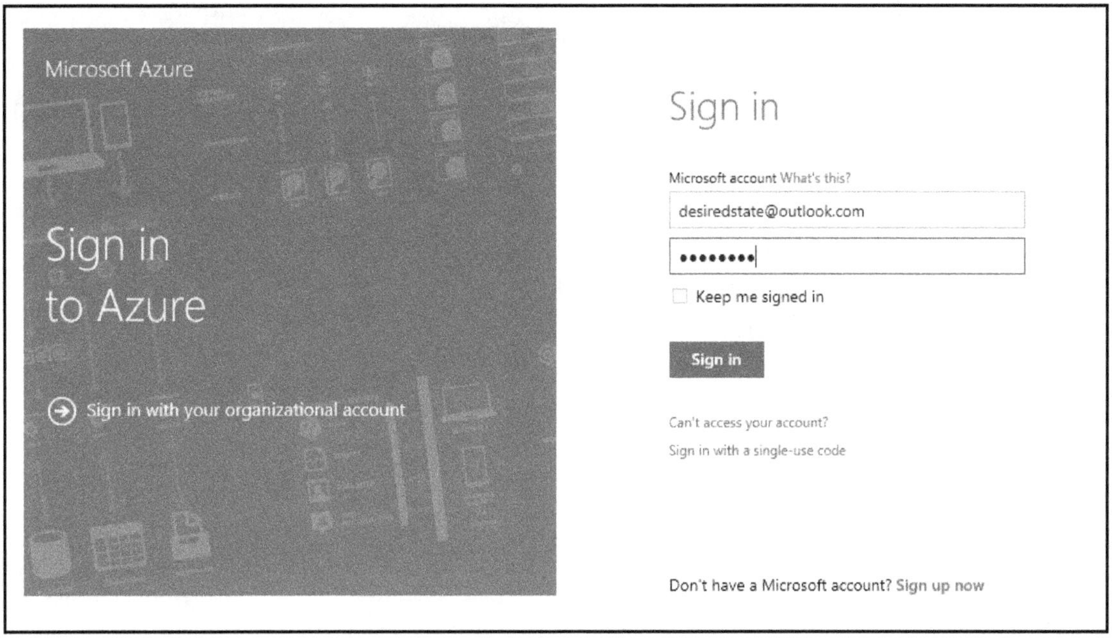

Figure 39: Azure login screen

Logging into Azure will take you to the screen shown in *Figure 40*. Click on the **Sign up** link:

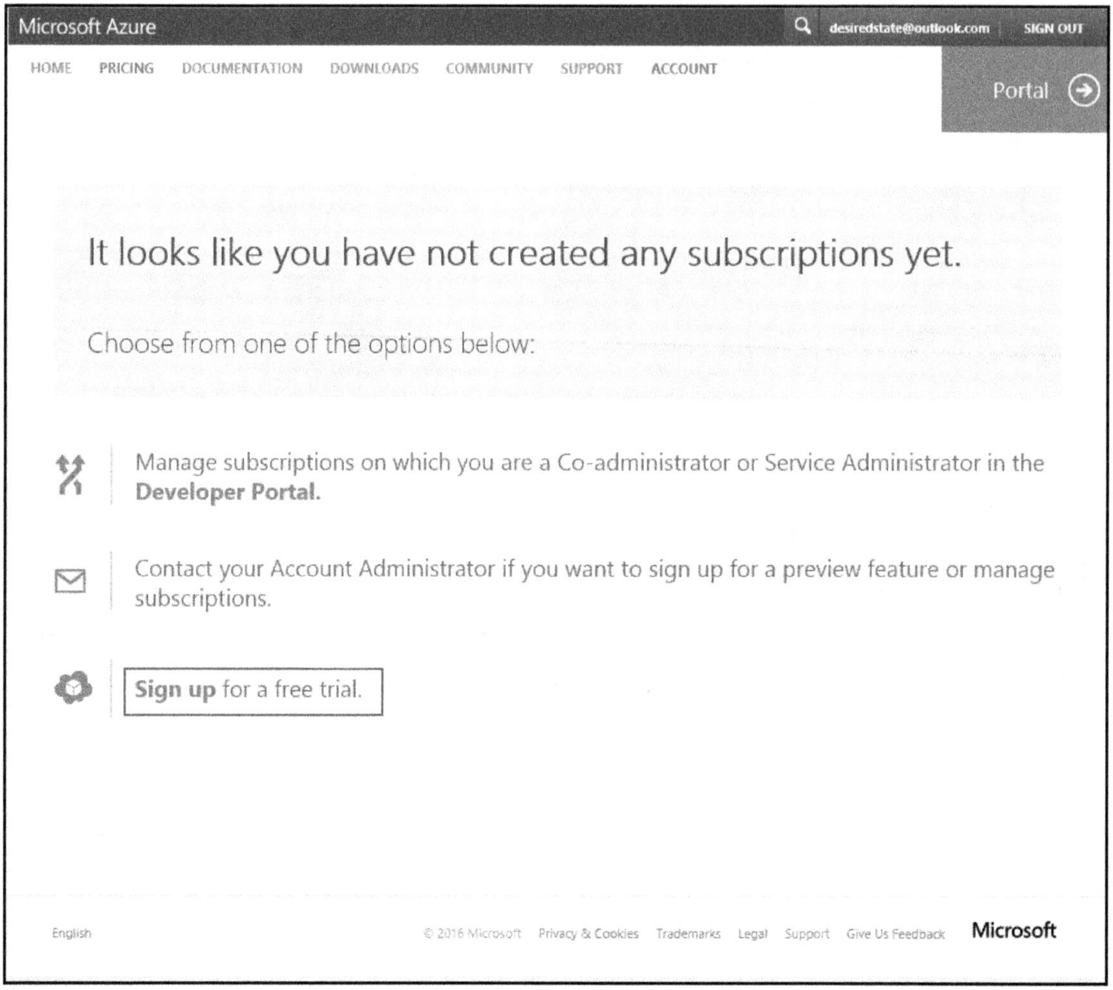

Figure 40: Sign up with Azure

This will show the details of your account. It will also ask you to verify your credit card and validate your account via your phone. This is shown in *Figure 41*. Once you have accepted the agreement terms, click on **Sign up** to create a tenant and subscription in Azure:

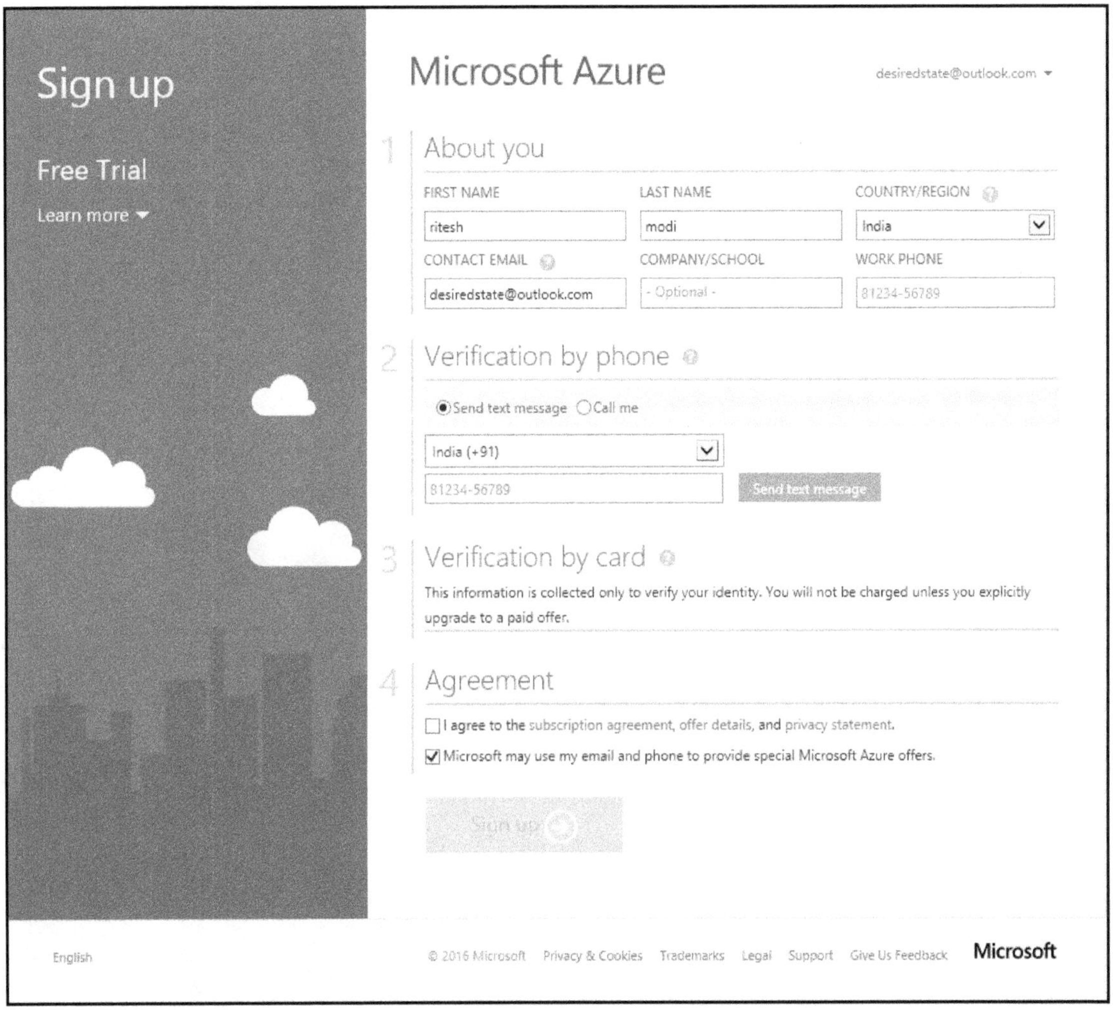

Figure 41: Azure subscription creation

Summary

We have covered a lot of ground in this chapter. The first chapter introduced DevOps concepts and this chapter discussed mapping technology to those concepts. In this chapter, we saw the impetus DevOps can get from technology. We looked at cloud computing and the different services provided by cloud providers. From there, we went on to look at the benefits Windows Server 2016 brings to DevOps practices and how Windows Server 2016 makes DevOps easier and faster with its native tools and features. Towards the end of the chapter, we explored VSTS, which forms the core for DevOps practices, by implementing continuous integration, continuous deployment, and delivery. You should now have a good grasp of the tools and technology used to implement DevOps. We created an account in VSTS for our DevOps process and created a subscription on Azure used for hosting our platform and application.

In the following chapter, we will get into the details of each of these technologies and use them in practice.

3
DevOps Automation Primer

Azure was launched in early 2010 with **Azure Service Management (ASM)** as its base technology platform for provisioning, organizing, and managing IaaS and PaaS services. During the Build 2014 event, Microsoft introduced a new Azure technology platform, **Azure Resource Manager (ARM)**. There are inherent issues with Azure Service Management in terms of performance, concurrency, extensibility, and scalability of services. It was becoming difficult for Microsoft to introduce newer, consistent, and scalable services because of the way ASM was designed and architected. Azure Resource Manager was introduced to overcome these challenges and provide an architecture that is extensible, scalable, and provide additional advance features not available with ASM.

Before 2014, **System Center Configuration Manager (SCCM)** was the prime configuration management software from Microsoft and with cloud gaining popularity, there was need of a lightweight configuration management platform that could easily scale and run everywhere including cloud and on-premises. **Desired State Configuration (DSC)** was launched in 2014 as part of **Windows Management Framework (WMF)** 4.0 and has become stable and robust with the release of WMF 5.0. Windows Server 2016 and Windows 10 come with WMF 5.0 installed out-of-the-box. DSC is a lightweight configuration management platform capable of running and configuring multiple operating systems, services, and environments. PowerShell has long been a part of Windows. It is the de-facto standard and used ubiquitously for administration and the management of infrastructure, environment, and services.

In this chapter, I will introduce Azure Resource Manager, describe its concepts, benefits and advantages, architecture, and show some of its features. The chapter will continue with Azure Resource Manager templates. Templates are a deployment feature of ARM and enables Infrastructure as Code and DevOps implementation. I will show how templates are defined and authored, its features and components like linking, dependencies, expressions, monitoring and auditing deployments, and tools for authoring them.

Next, PowerShell will be introduced. It is a scripting language and command-line shell used for automation, administration, and management of servers, services and environments. A PowerShell-based utility Pester will be another important topic in this chapter. Pester is a unit and integration testing tool for PowerShell scripts and environments. It helps in validating infrastructure and environments through assertion, comparing desired with actual output. The chapter ends with how all these technologies come together and help in enabling DevOps. DSC is based on PowerShell. Azure templates use both DSC and PowerShell for provisioning and management of Azure resources. I will try to cover these technologies as much as possible in this chapter. However, because this book is on DevOps, these topics will not be covered in complete detail as each of them demands their own book.

Subsequent sections will introduce DSC, describe its different architectures and concepts, show its configuration features, how it manages environments using dependencies, partial configuration, PowerShell cmdlets, and DSC resources.

Azure Resource Manager

ARM is the successor of ASM. Although both platforms are operational and available as of writing this chapter, Microsoft is moving toward using ARM as a platform for all future deployments.

ARM and ASM

ASM has inherent constraints and some of the major ones are discussed here:

- ASM deployments are slow and blocking. Operations are blocked if an earlier operation is already in progress.
- Parallelism is a challenge in ASM. It is not possible to execute multiple transactions successfully in parallel. The operations in ASM are linear and executed one after another. Either there are parallel operation errors or they will get blocked.
- Resources in ASM are provisioned and managed in isolation from each other. There is no relation between ASM resources. Grouping of services and resources, configuring them together is not possible.
- Cloud services are the unit of deployment in ASM. They are reliant on affinity groups and not scalable due to its design and architecture.

- Granular and discreet roles and permissions cannot be assigned to resources in ASM. Users are either service administrators or co-administrators in the subscription. They either get full control on resources or do not have access to them at all.
- ASM provides no deployment support. Deployments are either manual or you will need to resort to writing procedural scripts in PowerShell or .NET.
- ASM APIs were not consistent between resources.

ARM advantages

ARM provides distinct advantages and benefits over ASM. They are:

- **Grouping**: ARM allows grouping of resources together in a logical container. These resources can be managed together and undergo a common lifecycle as a group. This makes it easier to identify related and dependent resources.
- **Common lifecycle**: Resources in a group have the same lifecycle. These resources can evolve and be managed together as a unit.
- **Role-Based Access Control**: Granular roles and permissions can be assigned to resources providing discreet access to users. Users can have only those rights that are assigned to them.
- **Deployment support**: ARM provides deployment support in terms of templates enabling DevOps and Infrastructure as Code. The deployments are faster, consistent, and predictable.
- **Superior technology**: Cost and billing of resources can be managed as a unit. Each resource group can provide their usage and cost information.
- **Manageability**: ARM provides advance features such as security, monitoring, auditing, and tagging features for better manageability of resources. Resources can be queried based on tags. Tags also provide cost and billing information for resources tagged similarly.
- **Migration**: Easier migration and update of resources within, as well as across, resource groups.

ARM concepts

With ARM, everything in Azure is a resource. Examples of resources are virtual machine, network interfaces, public IP address, storage accounts, virtual networks, and more. ARM is based on concepts related to resource providers and resource consumers. Azure provides resources and services through multiple resource providers that are consumed and deployed in groups.

Resource providers

These are services responsible for providing resource types through Azure Resource Manager. The top level concept in ARM are resource providers. These providers are containers for resource types. Resource types are grouped into resource providers. They are responsible for deploying and managing the resources. For example, a virtual machine resource type is provided by a resource provider called **Microsoft.Compute Namespace**. The REST API operations are versioned in order to distinguish between them. The version naming is based on the dates on which they are released by Microsoft. It is necessary that a related resource provider is available to a subscription in order to deploy a resource. Not all resource providers are available to a subscription out of the box. If a resource is not available in the subscription, one has to check if the required resource provider is available in a given region. If that is available, the user can explicitly register in the subscription.

Resource types

These are an actual resource specification defining its public API interface and implementation. It implements the working and operations supported by the resource. Similar to resource providers, resource types also evolve over time with regard to their internal implementation and have multiple versions for its schema and public API interface. The version names are based on dates that they are released on by Microsoft as a preview or **General Availability (GA)**. The resource types become available to a subscription after a resource provider is registered to it. Also, not every resource type is available in every Azure region. The availability of a resource is dependent on the availability and registration of a resource provider in an Azure region and must support the API version needed for provisioning it.

Resource groups

Resource groups are a unit of deployment in ARM. They are containers grouping multiple resource instances in a security and management boundary. A resource group is uniquely named in a subscription. Resources can be provisioned on different Azure regions yet belong to the same resource group. It provides additional services to all resources within it. Resource groups provide metadata services like tagging which enables categorization of resources, policy-based management of resources, Role-Based Access Control, protection of resources from accidental deletion or updates, and more. As mentioned before, they have a security boundary and users not having access to a resource group cannot access resources contained within it. Every resource instance needs to be part of a resource group or else it cannot be deployed.

Resource and resource instances

Resources are created from resource types and should be unique within a resource group. The uniqueness is defined by the name of the resource and its type together. In OOPS parlance, resource instances can be referred to as objects while resource types can be referred to as a class. The services are consumed through the operations supported and implemented by resource instances. They define properties that should be configured before usage. Some are mandatory properties while others are optional. They inherit the security and access configuration from its parent resource group. These inherited permissions and role assignments can be overridden for each resource. A resource can be locked in such a way that some of its operations can be blocked and not made available to roles, users, and groups even though they have access to it. They can be tagged for easy discoverability and manageability.

Azure Resource Manager

Azure Resource Manager is the technology platform and orchestration service from Microsoft that ties up all components discussed earlier. It brings Azure resource providers, resources, and resource groups together to form a cohesive cloud platform. It helps in registration of resource providers to subscriptions and regions, it makes the resource types available to resource groups, makes the resource and resource APIs accessible to the portal and other clients, and authenticates access to resources. It also enables features like tagging, authentication, Role-Based Access Control, resource locking, and policy enforcement for subscriptions and its resource groups. It provides the same deployment and management experience whether through portal or client-based tools like PowerShell or a command-line interface.

Azure Resource Manager architecture

Figure 1 shows the architecture of Azure Resource Manager and its components. As shown in the figure, Azure Subscription comprises of multiple resource groups. Each resource group contains resource instances that are created from resource types available in the resource provider.

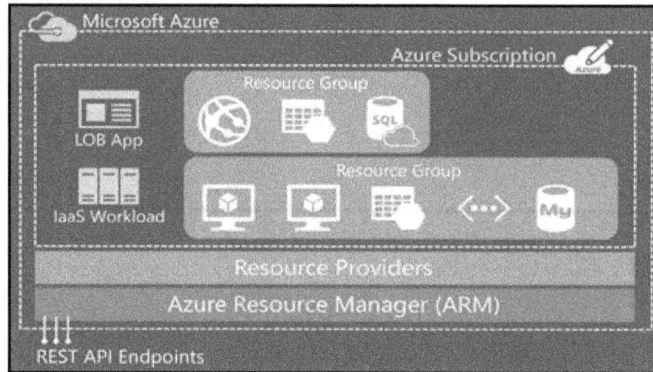

Figure 1: Azure Resource Manager architecture

Azure Resource Manager features

The following are some of the major features provided by Azure Resource Manager:

Role-Based Access Control

Azure Active Directory (**AAD**) authenticates users to provide access to subscriptions, resource groups, and resources. ARM implements OAuth and RBAC within the platform, enabling authorization and access control to resources, resource groups, and subscriptions based on roles assigned to a user or group. A permission defines access to operations on a resource. These permissions could allow or deny access to the resource. A role definition is a collection of these permissions. Roles map AAD users and groups to the permissions. Roles are subsequently assigned to a scope which can be an individual, collection of resources, resource group, or subscription. The AAD identities (users, groups and service principles) added to a role gain access to the resource according to permissions defined in the role. ARM provides multiple roles out-of-the-box. It provides system roles like Owner, Contributor, Reader, and more. It also provides resource-based roles like SQL DB contributor, virtual machine contributor, and more. ARM allows the creation of custom roles.

Tags

Tags are name value pairs that add additional information and metadata to resources. Both resources and resource groups can be tagged with multiple tags. Tags help in categorization of resources for better discoverability and manageability. Resources can be quickly searched and identified easily. Billing and cost information can be fetched for resources that have the same tags applied. While this feature is provided by ARM, an IT administrator defines its usage and taxonomy with regard to resources and resource groups. Taxonomy and tags for example, can be defined based on departments, resource usage, location, projects, or any other criteria deemed fit from a cost, usage, billing, and search perspective. These tags can then be applied to resources. Tags defined at the resource group level are not inherited by its resources.

Policies

Another security feature provided by ARM are policies. Custom policies can be created to control access to the resources. Policies are defined conventions and rules and must be adhered to while interacting with resources and resource groups. The policy definition contains explicit denial of actions on resources or access to resources. By default, every access is allowed if it is not mentioned in the policy definition. These policy definitions are assigned to resource, resource group, and subscriptions scope. It is important to note that these policies are not replacements or substitutes for RBAC. In fact, they complement and work together with RBAC. Policies are evaluated after a user is authenticated by AAD and authorized by the RBAC service. ARM provides JSON-based policy definition language for defining policies. Some of the examples of policy definition are that it must tag every provisioned resource or resources can only be provisioned to specific Azure regions.

Locks

Subscriptions, resource groups, and resources can be locked to prevent accidental deletion and updates by an authenticated user. Locks applied at higher levels flow downstream to child resources. Locks applied at subscription level, lock every resource group and resources within it.

Multi-region

Azure provides multiple regions for the provisioning and hosting of resources. ARM allows resources to be provisioned at different locations and yet reside within the same resource group. A resource group can contain resources from different regions.

Idempotent

This feature ensures predictability, standardization, and consistency in resource deployment by ensuring that every deployment will result in the same state of resources and their configuration no matter the number of times it is executed.

Extensible

ARM architecture provides extensible architecture to allow creation and plugging of newer resource providers and resource types into the platform.

Azure Resource Manager templates

In an earlier section, we witnessed deployment features such as multi-service, multi-region, extensible, and idempotent provided by ARM. ARM templates are primary means of provisioning resources in ARM. ARM templates provide implementation support for ARM deployment features.

ARM templates provide a declarative model through which resources, their configuration, scripts, and extensions are specified. ARM templates are based on **JavaScript Object Notation (JSON)** format. They use the JSON syntax and conventions to declare and configure resources. JSON files are text-based, human friendly, and easily readable files. They can be stored in a source code repository and have version control. They are also a means to represent Infrastructure as Code that can be used to provision resources in an Azure resource group again and again, predictably, consistently, and uniformly. A template needs a resource group for deployment. It can only be deployed to a resource group and the resource group should exist before executing template deployment. A template is not capable of creating a resource group.

Templates provide the flexibility to be generic and modular in their design and implementation. Templates provide the ability to accept parameters from users, declare internal variables, help in defining dependencies between resources, link resources within same or different resource groups, and also execute other templates. They also provide scripting language type expressions and functions that make them dynamic and customizable at runtime.

Template basics

A bare minimum template that actually does nothing is shown here:

```
{
    "$schema":
    "http://schema.management.azure.com/schemas/2015-01-01/
    deploymentTemplate.json#",
    "contentVersion": "1.0.0.0",
    "parameters": {
    },
    "variables": {
    },
    "resources": [
    ],
    "outputs": {
    }
}
```

A template has four important sections–parameters, variables, resources, and outputs. In the preceding template, there are no defined parameters, variables, resources, or outputs. Resources is the only mandatory JSON section while the rest are optional. The schema element defines the **Uniform Resource Identifier** (**URI**) that contains the model a template should be bound and adhered to. It contains the definition for all elements that can be defined in a template. The model itself contains references to all Azure resource schema that can be defined in a template. Schemas help at the design time validation of the template. Each template has a contentVersion element. This element defines the version of the template. Template version numbers are used when invoking and executing nested templates. The parameter, variable, and output sections are JSON objects while the resources section is a JSON object array that can contain multiple JSON objects each representing a resource.

Parameters

Parameters help to create generic and customizable templates. Parameters are defined in templates where the values are provided by the user as arguments as part of deployment. This encourages the use of the same template for multiple different environments such as development, test, production, and other types of environments. Multiple parameters can be defined in a template. Let's look at a sample parameter definition containing two parameters – firstParameter and secondParameter. The first parameter is of string type and can hold any one of two allowed values. The default value is FirstValue and has maxLength and minLength as validators. Metadata helps in adding additional context and information. Description is added as part of the firstParameter metadata. Similarly, secondParameter is of int type with validators on acceptable values, minimum values, and maximum values:

```
"parameters": {
    "firstParameter": {
        "type": "string",
        "allowedValues": [
            "FirstValue",
            "SecondValue"
        ],
        "defaultValue": "FirstValue",
        "maxLength": 20,
        "minLength": 10,
        "metadata": {
            "description": "My first parameter"
        }
    },
    "secondParameter": {
        "type": "int",
        "allowedValues": [
            10,
            20
        ],
        "defaultValue": 10,
        "maxValue": 20,
        "minValue": 10,
        "metadata": {
            "description": "My second parameter"
        }
    }
}
```

Templates provide attributes for defining parameters as shown in code. The explanation of these attributes are mentioned in the following table:

Attribute Name	Data type	Mandatory	Description
type	A valid value from a given list. See description for valid values	Required	Valid data types are string, secureString, int, bool, object, secureObject, and array.
defaultValue	Depends on data type	Optional	Default values are used if the value is not provided.
allowedValues	Array	Optional	Valid values can only be one of the provided values.
minValue	Integer	Optional	Minimum value for int type parameter.
maxValue	Integer	Optional	Maximum value for int type parameter.
minLength	Integer	Optional	Minimum length for string or array type parameter.
maxLength	Integer	Optional	Maximum length for string or array type parameter.
Metadata	Object	Optional	Can be any valid JSON object.

Variables

Variables are similar to parameters but the values are defined internally, within the template itself, and are not provided externally by a user. The value of a variable is part of the variable declaration itself. Variables are declared once and should be unique within a template. They can be placed anywhere within a template where a JSON string is expected. They make templates dynamic, manageable, and changes can be done to it easily. The value of a variable is substituted during deployment at all places it's used in the template. Variables are of JSON object data type. Let's look at a sample definition of a variable as shown here:

```
"firstVariable": {
        "networkName": "FirstNetwork",
        "subnets": [
            {
                "subnetName": "FrontEnd",
                "subnetIPRange": "10.0.0.0/24"
            },
            {
```

```
                        "subnetName": "BackEnd",
                        "subnetIPRange": "10.0.1.0/24"
                }
        ]
    }
```

Resources

Resources are array types that can hold multiple resource declarations. Arrays in JSON are represented by square brackets [] and objects by wriggly brackets {}. Each resource is an object declaring its desired configuration. Each resource has two types of properties – properties that provide information to ARM about the name, type, version, and location of the resource and properties that configure the resource itself. The mandatory properties of a resource are as follows:

- `name`: It represents the name of the resource instance
- `apiVersion`: It specifies the version of the REST API to be used for provisioning
- `location`: Azure region of the resource
- `type`: The resource provider namespace along with resource type name for creating a resource instance

Each resource has its specific configuration requirements and they will differ from one resource to another. These configurations configure the resource and its inner working. Let's look at how to define resources in a template. There are two resource declarations in the resources section of the template.

The first resource instance is named `storageaccount` provisioned at the `West Europe` Azure region based on the resource provider, `Microsoft.Storage` and resource type, `storageAccounts` and its version is `2015-06-15`.

```
"resources": [
        {
                "type": "Microsoft.Storage/storageAccounts",
                "name": "storageaccount",
                "apiVersion": "2015-06-15",
                "location": "West Europe",
                "properties": {
                    "accountType": "Standard_LRS"
                }
        },
        {
                "apiVersion": "2015-05-01-preview",
                "type": "Microsoft.Network/publicIPAddresses",
```

```
        "name": "myPublicIPAddress",
        "location": "West Europe",
        "properties": {
            "publicIPAllocationMethod": "Static",
            "dnsSettings": {
                "domainNameLabel": "mypublicipaddress"
            }
        }
    }
}
]
```

The first resource instance is named myPublicIPAddress provisioned at the West Europe Azure region based on the resource provider, Microsoft.Network and resource type, publicIPAddresses and its version is 2015-05-01-preview. Both the resources have a properties element which describes the resource-specific configurations. The StorageAccounts resource type has dependency on the accountType property which defines whether the storage account should be Locally redundant, Zone redundant, Geo redundant or Read-access Geo redundant. Similarly, PublicIpAddresses resource type has dependency on the allocation method which can be dynamic or static. dnsSettings provides a DNS name to the public IP address.

Outputs

Outputs represents the return values from templates as the result of executing or deploying them. The outputs section can be customized to contain multiple objects, each returning values. Each object in the outputs section has two properties – the type of return value and the value of return type. type refers to data types which we saw in the previous section and value refers to the actual data or object returned by the template. The output section is executed and returns a value only if the template was executed and deployed successfully. Let's look at how to define outputs in a template:

```
"outputs": {
    "myOutput": {
        "type": "string",
        "value": "Resource Group deployed successfully !!"
    }
}
```

In the code listing, a single output; `myOutput` is defined. It is of string type and will return the text on successful execution of the template.

Expressions and functions

ARM extends JSON by adding additional features in terms of expressions and functions. These are not available in JSON out-of-the-box and Microsoft added them to make templates dynamic and customizable. Expressions and functions are evaluated at deployment and they help in adding scripting language semantics to templates. Expressions are defined using square brackets and can appear anywhere a JSON string is expected in a template. The return value from an expression is always in JSON format.

There are numerous functions provided by ARM templates and can be categorized into string functions, numeric functions, array functions, deployment functions, and resource functions.

- Numeric functions help when working with integers such as adding, subtracting, and dividing numbers.
- String functions help when working with string literals like concatenation of strings, splitting of strings into arrays, replacing a part of a string, getting substrings from original strings, and more.
- Array functions help in working with array values in a template such as concatenating two arrays, splitting an array, retrieving sub-elements of an array, and more.
- Deployment functions help in getting values from variables, parameters, and more.
- Resource functions help in working with resources like getting their ID, current location and subscription, getting properties of resources, and more. Some of the important resource functions are **reference**, **resourceId**, **subscription**, and **resourceGroup**. For a complete list of functions available for templates visit the following URL:
  `https://azure.microsoft.com/en-in/documentation/articles/resource-group-template-functions/#resource-functions`

Nested resources

Resources can be nested within other resources. However, both the parent and the child resource should support nesting. Not all resources can be nested. Examples of nested resources are PowerShell extension resources within a virtual machine parent resource. Other examples of nested resource are Service Bus queues, relays and topics resource and they should reside within a Service Bus namespace resource. Nesting means that the child resource is part of a parent resource although the declaration of child resources in a template can be within the parent resource or outside of it. There is a special naming consideration to be taken care of while declaring a child resource outside of a parent resource. It is important to note that contained resources are dependent on the parent resource and cannot exist without it.

Some examples of expressions and functions are shown for better understanding:

- Concatenating two strings

    ```
    [ concat( 'String 1', 'string2' ) ]
    ```

- Adding two numbers

    ```
    [ Add ( 10, 20 ]
    ```

A minimal template

Let's look at a complete ARM template consisting of parameters, variables, resources, and output. This template also uses expressions and functions. The purpose of this template is to provision an Azure storage account. This template takes in one `storageAccountName` parameter of `string` type. Storage names must be a minimum of three characters and cannot be more than 24 characters in length. A couple of variables; `storageApiVersion` and `storageAccountType` are defined with valid values. The resources section declares a single resource. The value for the resource name is derived from the `storageAccountName` parameter. The resource provider is `Microsoft.Storage` and resource type is `storageAccounts`. The value for `apiVersion` is retrieved from the `storageApiVersion` variable and the value for storage account resource-specific `accountType` property is retrieved from the `storageAccountType` variable. The storage account is provisioned at the same location of resource group itself. ARM provides the `resourceGroup` function for retrieving the current resource group on which the deployment is in progress. Finally, the `outputs` section outputs the status of successful execution of deployment:

```
{
    "$schema":
```

```
         "http://schema.management.azure.com/schemas/2015-01-01/
         deploymentTemplate.json#",
         "contentVersion": "1.0.0.0",
         "parameters": {
             "storageAccountName": {
                 "type": "string",
                 "minLength": 3,
                 "maxLength": 24,
                 "metadata": {
                     "Description": "Storage account name"
                 }
             }
         },
         "variables": {
             "storageApiVersion": "2015-06-15",
             "storageAccountType": "Standard_LRS"
         },
         "resources": [
             {
                 "type": "Microsoft.Storage/storageAccounts",
                 "name": "[parameters('storageAccountName')]",
                 "apiVersion": "[variables('storageApiVersion')]",
                 "location": "[resourceGroup().location]",
                 "properties": {
                     "accountType": "[variables('storageAccountType')]"
                 }
             }
         ],
         "outputs": {
             "TemplateOutput": {
                 "type": "string",
                 "value": "[concat(parameters('storageAccountName'),' storage
     account was successfully created!!')]"
             }
         }
     }
```

We will use this template in subsequent section for deployment to the Azure resource group.

ARM template tools

Working with ARM templates requires tools for both authoring and deployment.

ARM templates are simple text-based JSON files. They can be authored using any text-based editor however, for faster and easy authoring, IntelliSense support for template and its resource configuration, Visual Studio Code, or Visual Studio 2013/2015 can be used. Visual Studio provides a rich interface, project template, IntelliSense, and deployment script for templates. This book uses Visual Studio 2015 for authoring of all ARM templates.

Although templates can be authored manually through the Azure portal, it is not recommended as it is error prone and time consuming to author templates from there.

Authoring tools

In this book, we will use Visual Studio 2015 for authoring ARM templates. See the following steps for creating a template:

1. The first step is to install Visual Studio 2015 community edition on the development box. The development environment contains Windows server 2016 technical preview operating system. This is because Windows 10 does not yet support Windows Containers and Docker. Eventually, when Windows 10 starts supporting Windows Container and Docker, it should be used as a development platform. Visual Studio community edition is available from `https://www.visua lstudio.com/en-us/downloads/download-visual-studio-vs.aspx`. Click on **Download Community Free** button to start downloading Visual Studio. This is shown here in *Figure 2*:

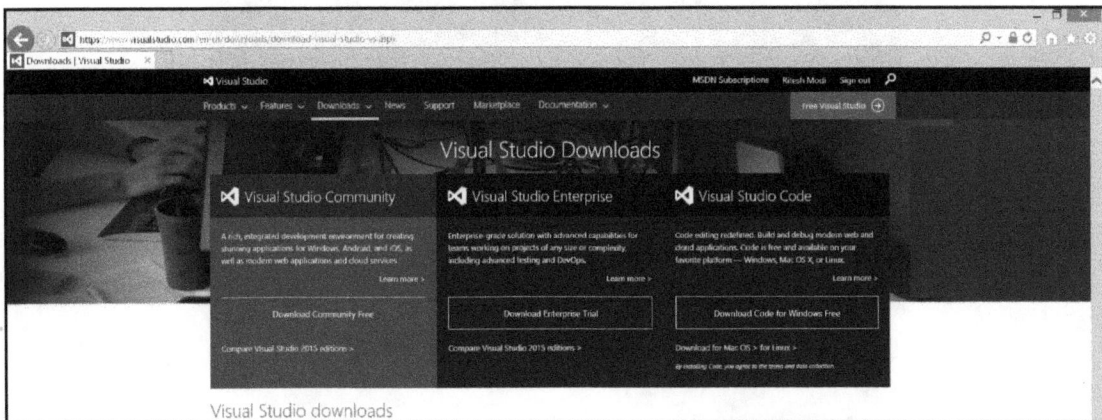

Figure 2: Visual Studio site for downloading the community edition

2. A setup file is downloaded and executed. It will prompt a window asking for installation location and type of installation. Accept **Default** and click on **Install**. This is shown in *Figure 3*:

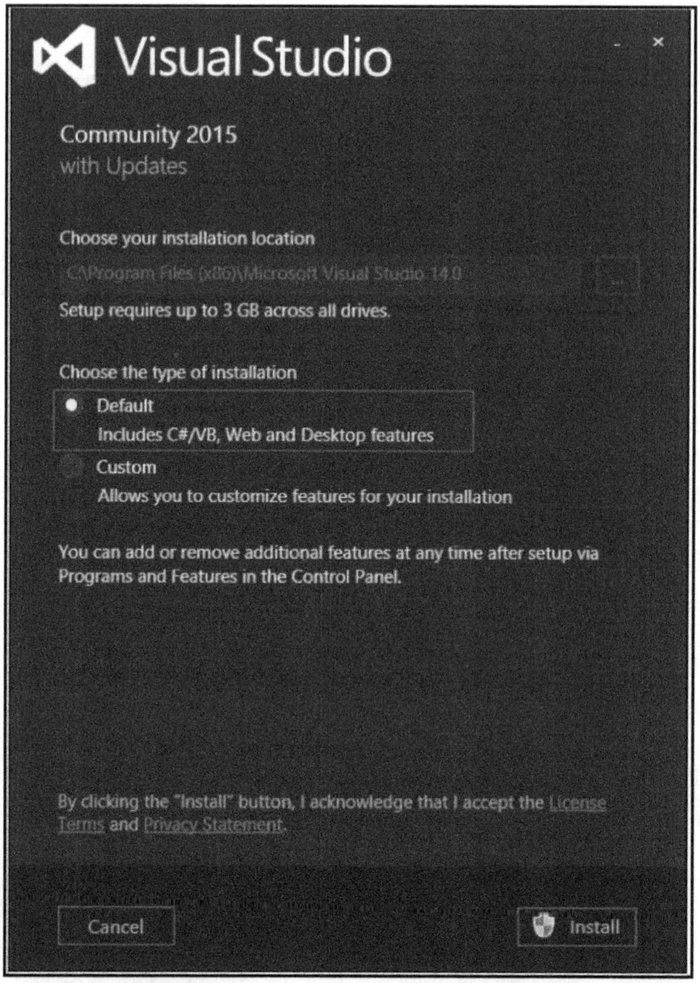

Figure 3: Installing Visual Studio 2015 community edition

3. After Visual Studio is installed, Azure tools for Visual Studio should be installed. The installer is available at `https://azure.microsoft.com/en-us/tools/` shown in *Figure 4*. Click on the button, **Download Azure Tools for Visual Studio**:

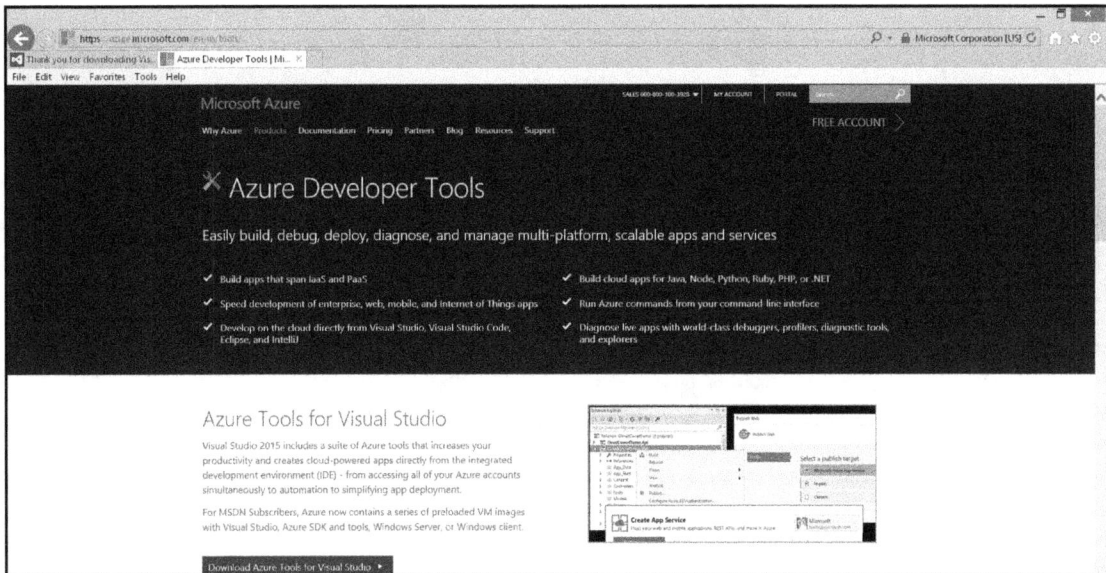

Figure 4: Site for Azure Tools for Visual Studio

4. This will invoke a **Web Platform Installer** for installing **Microsoft Azure SDK for .NET(VS 2015)** as shown in *Figure 5*. Click on the **Install** button to install Azure tools. Another prompt to accept the license agreement is shown. Click **Accept** to start the installation of tools. This will also install Visual ARM Visual Studio template for authoring ARM templates:

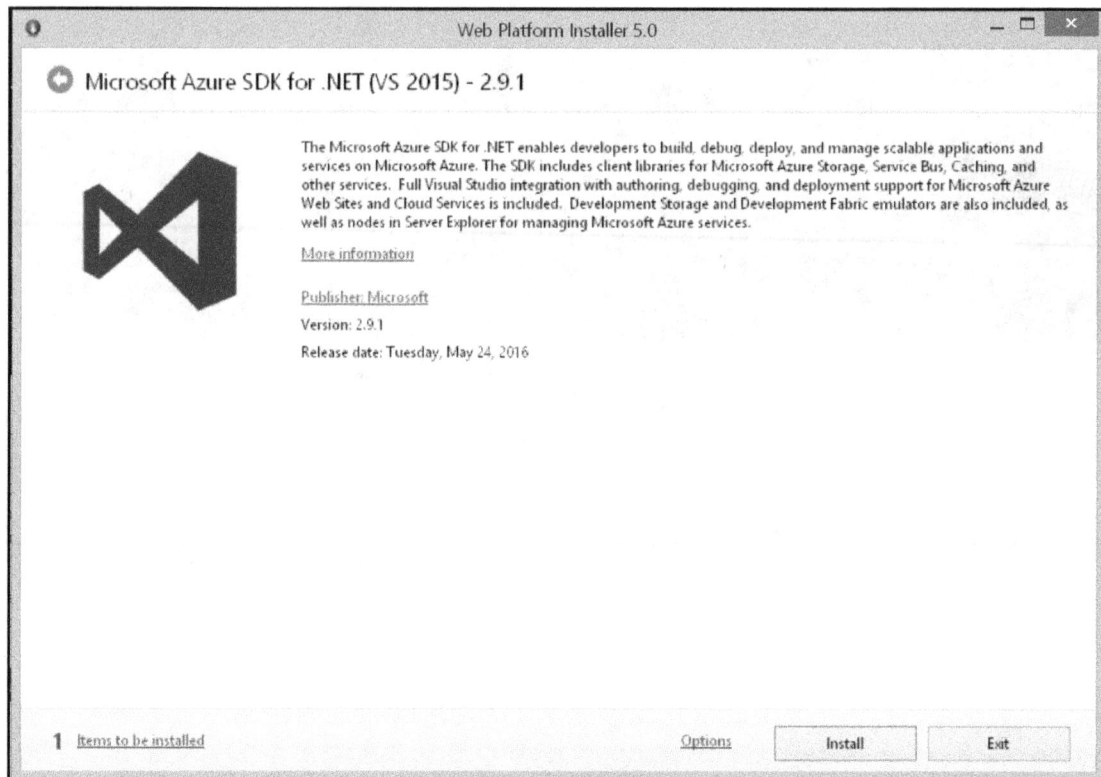

Figure 5: Web Platform Installer

5. Open Visual Studio and select **New Project** | **Azure Resource Group** from the **Cloud** category. Name the project **MinimalTemplate**, provide `C:\templates` as location, the **Solution name** defaults to the name of the project (you can change the solution name to a different name from the project name) and click **OK** as shown in *Figure 6*:

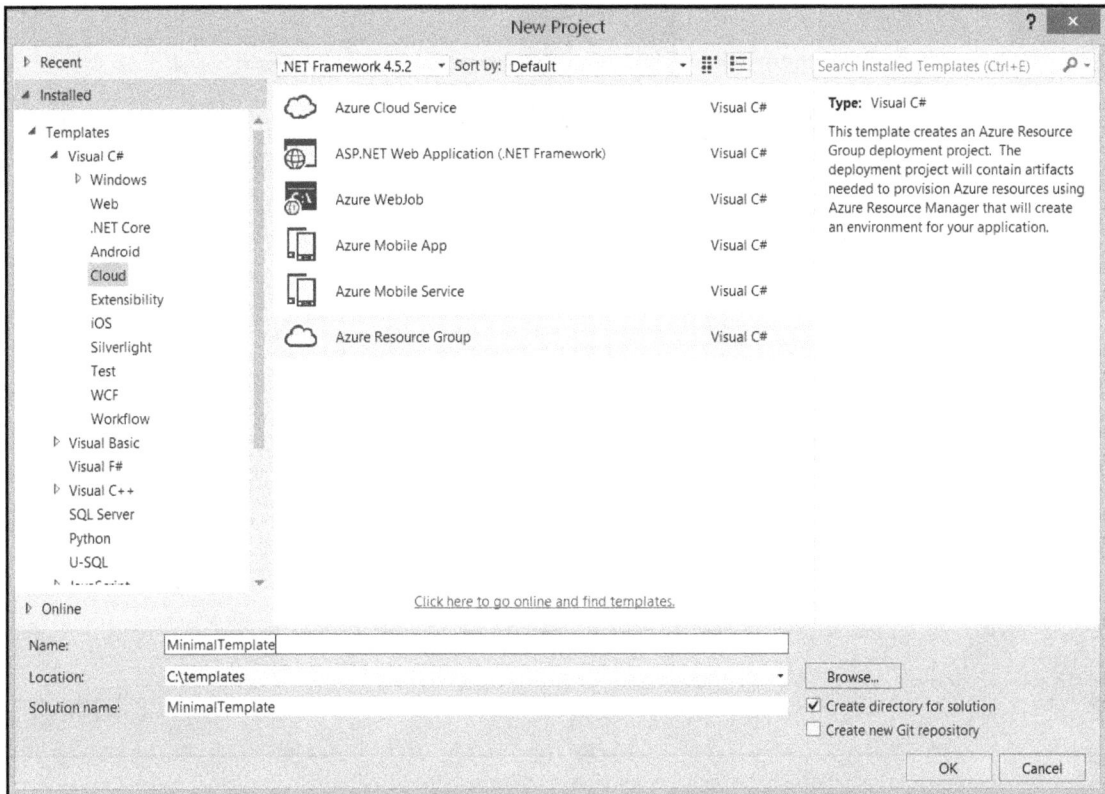

Figure 6: Visual Studio project creation for Azure Resource Group

6. Select **Blank Template** from the list of templates and click **OK** as shown in *Figure 7*. This will create a solution and Azure Resource group project within it:

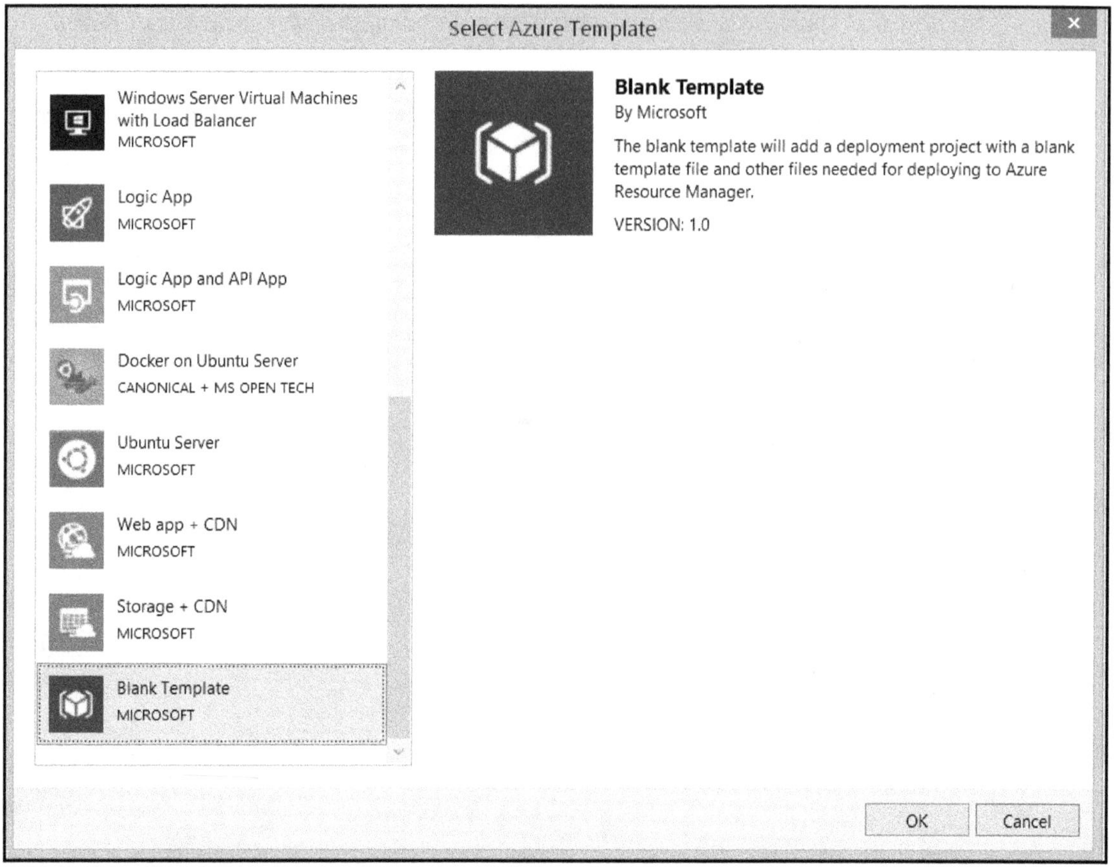

Figure 7: Selecting Blank Template for project

7. The resultant**Blank Template** is shown here in *Figure 8*:

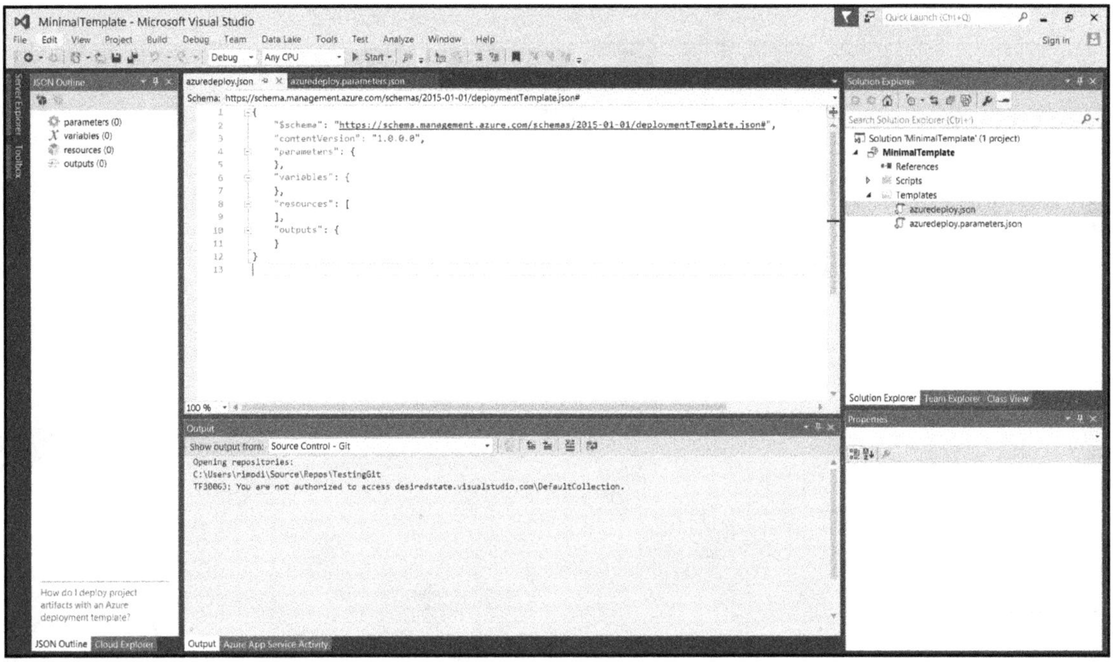

Figure 8: An empty blank Azure Resource Group Template

8. Modify the `azuredeploy.json` file to reflect the minimal template we created earlier in this chapter as shown in *Figure 9* and save the entire project:

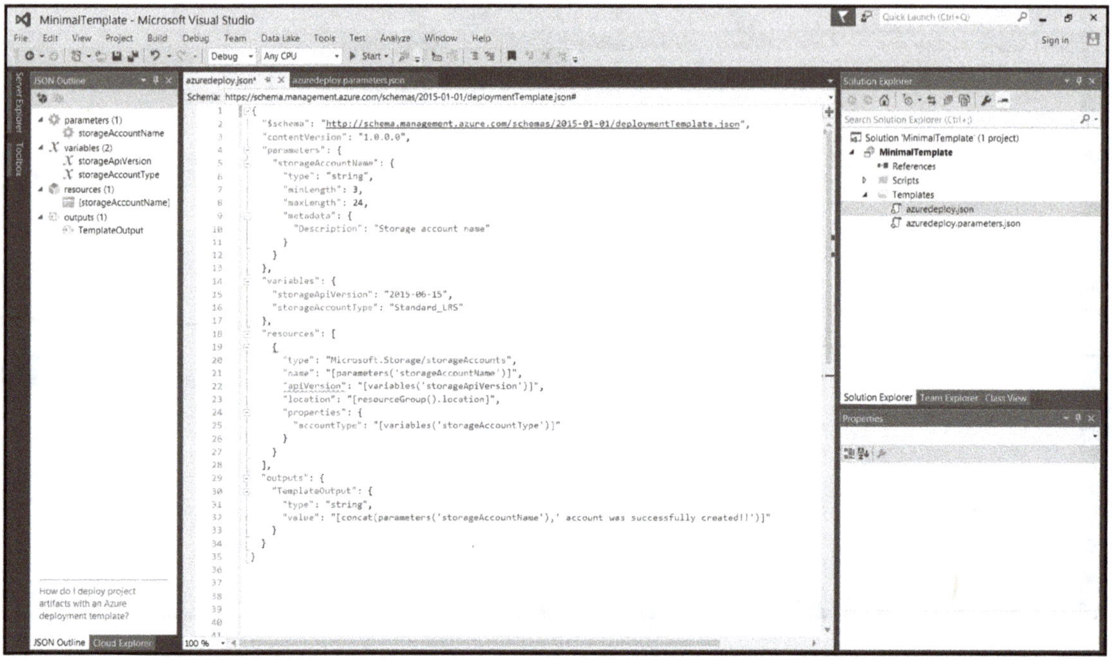

Figure 9: Minimal Template in Visual Studio

9. More resources can be added to template by using the **JSON Outline** pane. It has an **Add Resource** button that can be used for the same. Later, we will deploy this template using PowerShell in this chapter.

Deployment tools

Templates can be deployed to a resource group in multiple ways, prominent among them are:

- PowerShell
- Azure command-line interface
- REST APIs
- Azure portal

This book uses PowerShell and the Azure Resource Manager module for deploying ARM templates to resource groups. We will look into steps for using PowerShell for deployment of templates when we discuss PowerShell in detail in the next section.

Deployments

PowerShell allows two modes of deployment of templates. They are as follows:

- Incremental
- Complete

Incremental deployment adds resources declared in the template that don't exist in a resource group and leaves resources unchanged in a resource group that are not part of a template definition, leaves resources unchanged in a resource group that exist in both the template and resource group with the same configuration state.

Complete deployment on the other hand, adds resources declared in a template to the resource group, deletes resources that do not exist in the template from the resource group, and leaves resources unchanged that exist in both the resource group and template with the same configuration state.

PowerShell

PowerShell is an object-based, command-line shell and scripting language used for administration, configuration, and management of infrastructure and environments. It is built on top of .NET framework and provides automation capabilities. PowerShell was released in 2006 as version on Windows. PowerShell version 5 is the current version that is available in Windows Server 2016 and Windows 10 out-of-the-box. PowerShell 5 is also available as part of the WMF 5.0.

PowerShell has truly become a first class citizen among IT administrators and automation developers for managing and controlling the Windows environment. Today, almost every Windows environment and its components can be managed by PowerShell. Similarly, almost every aspect of Azure subscription can also be managed by PowerShell.

PowerShell can be divided into two components:

- **PowerShell** engine: This is the core engine responsible for executing the PowerShell commands executed through the command line, pipelines, scripts, and functions. The engine provides the execution environment and context in terms of security, concurrency, threading, base .NET framework, extended type system, modules, logging, and auditing. The PowerShell engine exposes runspace interfaces that are used by PowerShell hosts for interacting with it.
- **PowerShell host**: These are user-facing applications or command line interfaces responsible for interacting with the user, accepting inputs from them and passing them to the PowerShell engine for execution using the runspace interface provide by the engine. The return values from the engine are displayed to the user using the same host. Each PowerShell host has its own configuration that is accessible through a host provided system variable; $Host. There are two hosts provided out-of-the-box in Windows. They are:
    - `PowerShell.exe`
    - PowerShell **Integrated Scripting Environment** (ISE)

PowerShell ISE provided added functionality for authoring PowerShell scripts apart from being a command line interface.

PowerShell features

PowerShell provides lots of features and capabilities and demands a complete book by itself. In this book, we will look into some of the important aspects of PowerShell relevant to us for DevOps.

Cmdlets

PowerShell provides small executable commands called cmdlets which execute a single task or operation. There are hundreds and thousands of cmdlets available in PowerShell. My own machine running Windows 8.1 has more than 3000 cmdlets available. There is a cmdlet available for almost every administration and management activity in PowerShell. Cmdlet names follow verb-noun naming conventions. For example, the `Get-Process` cmdlet is responsible for retrieving all running processes in a system. `Get` refers to the verb or action being performed and `Process` refers to the subject or noun under consideration. PowerShell accepts object-oriented objects as arguments for their parameters and returns back well-defined objects as the return value.

Pipeline

PowerShell is an object-based language which helps in implementing the concepts of pipelines. Pipelines refer to a series of cmdlets defined in a single statement, executed one after another where the output of the previous cmdlet becomes the input of the next cmdlet. Pipelines are defined using the pipe character |.

An example of a pipeline is shown here:

```
Get-Process -Name Notepad | Stop-Process
```

The code shows two cmdlets `Get-Process` and `Stop-Process` in a pipeline. Execution of the statement executed the first cmdlet first. `Get-Process` outputs objects of type, `System.Diagnostics.Process`. If Notepad is running on the system, it will return an object containing details about its process. The same process object is sent to `Stop-Process` cmdlets as input arguments which stops the Notepad process from running.

Variables

PowerShell provides support for variables which are temporary storage locations in memory to store values that can be used and changed subsequently. They help in making script granular, flexible, and maintainable. PowerShell does not mandate to specify data types while defining variables. In such cases, PowerShell implicitly decides the data type based on values assigned to the variable. When a variable is defined with a data types qualifier, it can accept only those values that adhere to the rules of its data type. The native PowerShell variable data types are string, char, byte, int, long, bool, decimal, single, double, array, and hashtable. Variables in PowerShell are defined using the dollar symbol $.

Examples of variables are:

- The following code assigns a string value to the OSName variable:

```
$OSName = "Windows Server 2016"
```

Note the $ sign prefixed to OSName.

- The following code assigns the same `string` value to the `OSName` variable however this time, the data type is provided explicitly:

```
[string] $OSName = "Windows Server 2016"
```

> Variables can be referred to by their names prefixed with the dollar `$` symbol.
> `$OSName` would print the value stored in `OSName` variable.

Scripts and modules

PowerShell is also a scripting language. We can use cmdlets, functions, pipelines, and variables within scripts as well. Scripts are reusable code that can be executed multiple times. They encapsulate code, function, data, and logic in a script file with the ps1 extension. The scripts can be loaded and executed in the current execution environment using a technique called **Dot-sourcing**. Dot-sourcing refers to PowerShell syntax to load a file using dot notation as shown here. Please note the `.` preceding the script path:

```
. ./SampleScript.ps1
```

PowerShell modules are the means to share scripts, functions, and cmdlets with others. Modules are packaged in a specific format that can be readily deployed on any Windows system. There are well defined locations in the Windows operating system that house modules. System modules are available at:
`C:\Windows\System32\WindowsPowershell\v1.0\Modules` while modules from third-party sources are available at `C:\Program Files\WindowsPowershell\Modules`. The `C:\` drive refers to the system drive here which might be different for you.

The `Get-Module` cmdlet provides information about all currently loaded modules while `Get-Module -ListAvailable` provides information about all modules that are available on the system but not loaded in the workspace.

Azure PowerShell development environment

PowerShell will be used heavily in this book throughout all chapters. Since all our environments would be hosted on Azure, the Azure PowerShell module will be a core module for managing Azure through PowerShell. One of the ways to deploy ARM templates is through PowerShell. Before we can use PowerShell to deploy templates in resource groups, we need to install the Azure ARM PowerShell modules. These modules provide the cmdlets, functions, and code to connect and authenticate to Azure, create resource groups, and deploy templates in them. They also provide functionality to peek into the Azure resource group logs to check the status of deployment and also troubleshoot issues. The Azure PowerShell module is available through Web Platform Installer as well as through PowerShell gallery. Windows Server 2016 and Windows 10 provides package management and `PowerShellGet` modules for quick and easy downloading and installation of PowerShell modules from PowerShell gallery. The cmdlets from these modules are already configured with Powershell gallery source and repository information. The `PowerShellGet` module provides the `Install-Module` cmdlet for downloading and installing modules on system. Installation of modules is a simple activity. Simply, copy the module files at well-defined module locations.

Before moving ahead in this section, there should be a PowerShell host, either PowerShell or PowerShell ISE opened as an administrator. Downloading and installing modules requires administrative privileges.

AzureRM modules enable working with Azure ARM from a client machine using PowerShell. Let's download and install the AzureRM module using the Install-Module cmdlet. Before using any cmdlet, we should explicitly import the module into the current workspace as a good practice, although PowerShell will auto load the module if it's not already loaded. This is shown here:

```
Import-module PowershellGet
Install-Module -Name AzureRM -Verbose
```

The `Install-Module` cmdlet is dependent on the `NuGet` provider to interact with NuGet-based repository. The first time a package management cmdlet is used, it will ask to download the same. Click on **Yes** to any prompts related to downloading `NuGet` provider. This is shown in *Figure 10*:

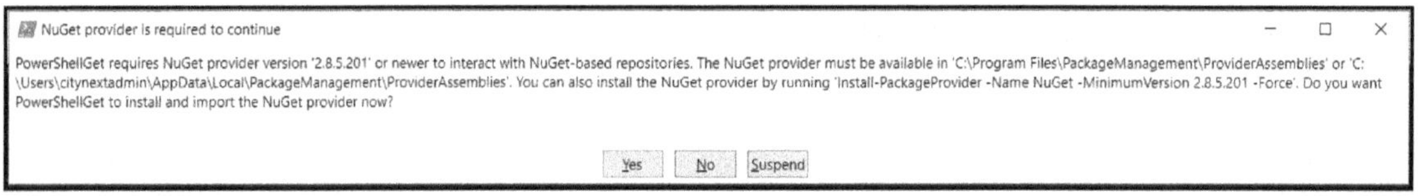

Figure 10: Permission to install NuGet package provider

There will be another prompt stating that the module is downloaded from an **Untrusted repository**. **PSGallery** repository is not trusted by default. Click **Yes** to download the provider. This is shown in *Figure 11*:

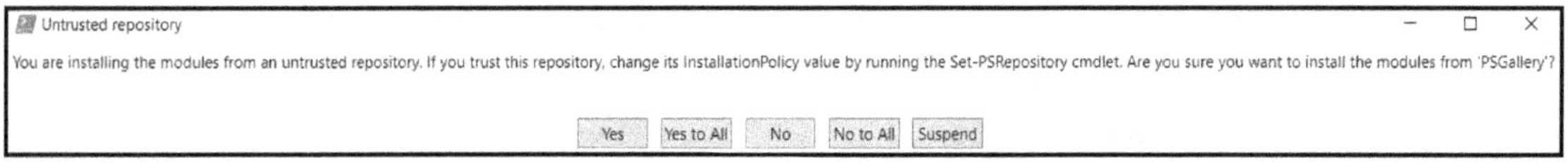

Figure 11: Permission to download from untrusted repository

These prompts can be disabled by using the `Force` switch as shown here:

```
Install-Module -Name AzureRM -Verbose -Force
```

The `AzureRM` module is a container module that references individual sub-modules each representing a resource provider namespace. `AzureRM` functionality is divided into multiple modules, each AzureRM sub-module representing an ARM resource provider and they contain provider-specific cmdlets and functionality. `AzureRM` modules can be used to install all sub-modules in one go and it can also be used to install individual sub-modules. In the preceding code, `AzureRM` module is downloaded and installed on the machine it is executed on. This will download all modules related to `AzureRM`. Similarly, to install only a individual or set of modules, the following code can be used. To install individual modules, the explicit names should be provided to this cmdlet. The first line installs a single `AzureRM.Compute` module and the second one installs two sub-modules: `AzureRM.Storage` and `AzureRM.Network`:

```
Install-Module -Name AzureRM.Compute -Verbose
Install-Module -Name AzureRM.Storage, AzureRM.Network -Verbose
```

Before we can do anything with resource groups and templates, we should authenticate with Azure. This is done through the `Login-AzureRMAccount` cmdlet as shown here:

```
Login-AzureRmAccount
```

It is to be noted that cookies must be allowed on the computer from where the authentication is initiated.

This cmdlet can be configured to use the username and password defined in code or it will open a login window. This is shown in *Figure 12*. Please enter a valid username and password to authenticate and login to Azure:

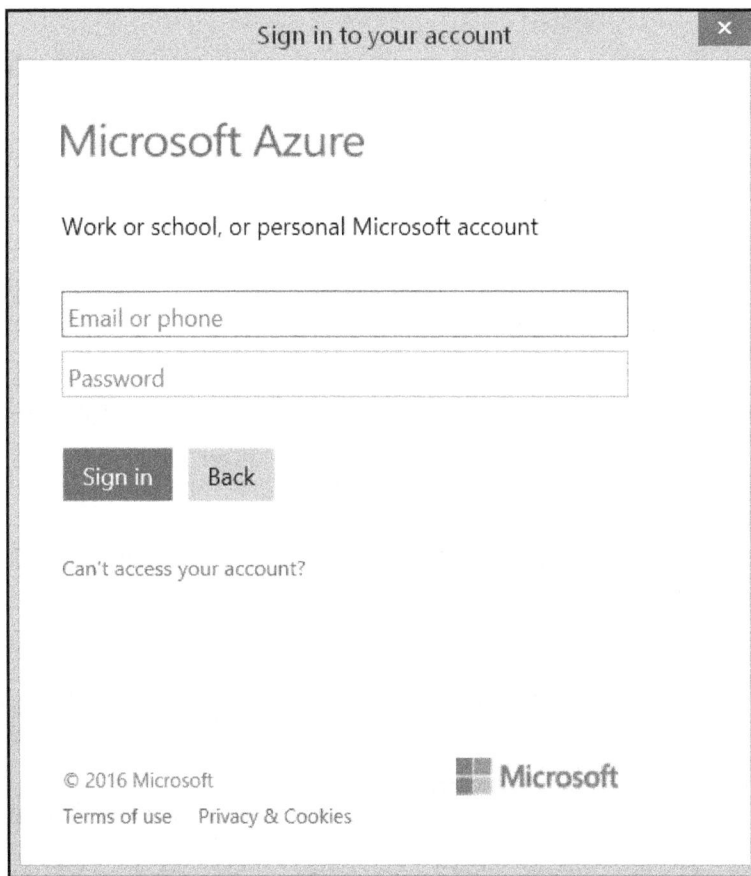

Figure 12: Azure login window using PowerShell

As seen before, templates are deployed within a Resource group. We should be able to create a resource group using PowerShell and then deploy a template within it after successful login to Azure. The code to create a resource group is shown here:

```
Import-module AzureRM.Resources
New-AzureRmResourceGroup -Name "myResourceGroup" -Location "West Europe" -
Verbose
```

Here, the Name refers to the name of a newly-created resource group and Location refers to a valid Azure region for the resource group to be created. Verbose provides additional information while executing the cmdlet.

After the resource group is created, templates can be deployed into it.

To deploy a template, cmdlet New-AzueRmResourceGroupDeployment can be used and this is shown here:

```
New-AzureRmResourceGroupDeployment -Name "FirstDeployment" -ResourceGroup
"myResourceGroup" -TemplateFile "C:\template\azureDeploy.json" -verbose
```

Here Name refers to the name of deployment which is any valid name that can be used to identify the deployment, resource group refers to the name of resource group where this deployment will provision resources and TemplateFile refers to the file location of the ARM template.

To deploy the minimal template that was created earlier, execute the following command from any PowerShell editor. It is to be noted that the storage name must be unique across Azure, and resource group must be unique within a subscription. The resource group is named azureRG provisioned at West Europe region. The Minimal Template takes storageAccountName as a parameter. This parameter must be supplied while deploying the template as shown here:

```
New-AzureRmResourceGroup -Name "azureRG" -Location "West Europe" -Force -
Verbose
New-AzureRmResourceGroupDeployment -Name "Deploy1" -ResourceGroupName
"azureRG"
-Mode Incremental -TemplateUri
"C:\templates\MinimalTemplate\MinimalTemplate
\Templates\azuredeploy.json" -Verbose -storageAccountName "auniquename"
```

Pester

Now, it's time to visit another PowerShell utility called Pester. Pester helps in defining and executing tests on PowerShell scripts, functions, and modules. These could be unit tests, integration tests, or operational validation tests. Pester is an open source utility freely downloadable from GitHub as a PowerShell module. It is also available out-of-the-box on Windows 10. We will use Pester to define unit tests and operational validation tests and also execute them in continuous integration build pipelines and continuous deployment release pipelines in this book. As of writing this book, Pester 3.0 is the latest stable version available for download and the same is used.

Pester helps in defining unit tests in a simple English style language using simple constructs like `Describe` and `It` and validates them through assertions. Pester can be downloaded as a ZIP file from `https://github.com/pester/pester/archive/master.zip`. After downloading, the ZIP file should be unblocked and its content should be extracted to a well-defined module location. We already know that modules live at both `$env:windir\system32\WindowsPowershell\v1.0\modules` and `$env:ProgramFiles\WindowsPowershell\modules` and Pester should be extracted to any one of these folder locations. We will use the modules folder from `$env:ProgramFiles` to store the Pester module.

Installing Pester

This step is not required to be performed on Windows Server 2016 or a Windows 10 machine since the Pester module is available on them by default.

On machines with WMF 5.0, package management module should be used to download and install Pester instead of the next steps.

The code shown next should be executed on servers on which Pester is not available by default. Pester is available by default only on Windows Server 2016 and Windows 10. The code shown next is also depended on WMF 4.0.

The steps mentioned in the previous section will be automated through PowerShell for installing Pester. The entire script `Install-Pester.ps1` is shown here:

```
Param(
  # folder location for storing the temp pester downloaded files
  [string]$tempDownloadPath
)
# create a temp folder for downloading pester.zip
New-Item -ItemType Directory -Path "$tempDownloadPath" -Force
```

```
# download pester.zip from GitHub
Invoke-WebRequest -Uri https://github.com/pester/pester/archive/master.zip
-OutFile "$tempDownloadPath\pester.zip"

# files from internet are generally blocked. unblocking the archive file
Unblock-File -Path "$tempDownloadPath\pester.zip"

# extracting files from archive file to Well-defined modules folders
Expand-Archive -Path "$tempDownloadPath\pester.zip" -DestinationPath
"$env:ProgramFiles\WindowsPowershell\Modules" -Force

# renaming the folder from pester-master to pester
Rename-Item -Path "$env:ProgramFiles\WindowsPowershell\Modules\Pester-
master" -NewName "$env:ProgramFiles\WindowsPowershell\Modules\Pester" -
ErrorAction Continue

# test to check if pester module is available
Get-Module -ListAvailable -name pester
```

Use the code shown here to execute the script and install Pester on a system. This code assumes that the `Install-Pester.ps1` script is available at `C:\temp`

```
C:\Install-Pester.ps1 -tempDownloadPath "C:\temp"
```

Let me explain each line within the script.

The script starts with accepting a single parameter `$tempDownloadPath` of `string` type. This path should be provided by the caller as argument to the script:

```
Param (
  # folder location for storing the temp pester downloaded files
  [string]$tempDownloadPath
)
```

The next statement creates a new folder at the location provided by the user. `Force` ensures that an error is not generated even if a folder with the same name exists:

```
New-Item -ItemType Directory -Path "$tempDownloadPath" -Force
```

Then, the `Invoke-WebRequest` cmdlet is used to download the Pester archive file from GitHub and store the downloaded file as `pester.zip` to the user's folder:

```
Invoke-WebRequest -Uri https://github.com/pester/pester/archive/master.zip
-OutFile "$tempDownloadPath\pester.zip"
```

By default, downloaded ZIP files are blocked and cannot be used without unblocking them. Code shown next unblocks the downloaded `pester.zip` file using `Unblock-File` cmdlet.

```
Unblock-File -Path "$tempDownloadPath\pester.zip"
```

Next, the archive file is expanded and all its files and folders are extracted to the modules folder which is a well-defined module location:

```
Expand-Archive -Path "$tempDownloadPath\pester.zip" -DestinationPath
"$env:ProgramFiles\WindowsPowershell\Modules" -Force
```

The extracted folder name is `Pester-master` however; the name should be `Pester`. The `Rename-Item` cmdlet is used to rename `pester-master` to `pester`. This cmdlet will throw an error if the folder named `Pester-master` does not exist. Normally, the script will terminate if an error occurs. With `ErrorAction` as `continue`, `Rename-item` will throw an error but script execution will not stop:

```
Rename-Item -Path "$env:ProgramFiles\WindowsPowershell\Modules\Pester-
master" -NewName "$env:ProgramFiles\WindowsPowershell\Modules\Pester" -
ErrorAction Continue
```

Finally, a small test is conducted to ensure the Pester module is available using the `Get-Module` cmdlet. If this cmdlet outputs the `name` and `version` of the `pester` module, it means that Pester is successfully installed on the machine:

```
Get-Module -ListAvailable -name pester
```

Writing tests with Pester

Pester provides an easy to use `New-Fixture` cmdlet. Executing this cmdlet creates two files. The first file is for authoring PowerShell scripts and functions and the second file is for authoring unit tests for code in the first file. This cmdlet also ties both the files together by generating scaffolding code in such a way that the entire script in first file is loaded into the workspace of the second file when the second file containing unit tests are executed using the concept of Dot-sourcing. The scaffolding code ensures that PowerShell scripts and functions are available to the test cases for invocation. Pester should be able to execute any code from the first file that are referred to in test cases. It is important to understand that `New-Fixture` cmdlet helps in importing a script into another workspace. This can be done manually by Dot-sourcing the script files into the Pester unit tests file. In fact, `New-fixture` cmdlet also dot-sources the script file into a unit tests file.

Understanding Pester is much easier by experiencing it rather than going through theory. Let's understand Pester through a scenario of writing a simple function for adding two numbers and corresponding tests for testing the same.

1. Let's create a folder at `C:\` that will store script as well as tests. Let's name it `Addition`.

2. From any PowerShell host execute the commands shown here to generate the scripting files. The `cd` command changes the directory to the `C:` drive. `Import-Module` cmdlet imports the Pester module into the current workspace and `New-Fixture` cmdlet from the Pester module creates the script files at the `Addition` folder location. It will generate two files: `Add-Numbers.ps1` and `Add-Numbers.Tests.ps1`:

```
cd C:\
Import-Module -Name Pester
New-Fixture -Path "C:\Addition" -Name "Add-Numbers"
```

The script generated in `Add-Numbers.ps1` will contain the logic that should be tested and an empty `Add-Numbers` function created is shown here:

```
function Add-Numbers {
}
```

The script generated in `Add-Numbers.Tests.ps1` is shown here.

```
$here = Split-Path -Parent $MyInvocation.MyCommand.Path
$sut = (Split-Path -Leaf $MyInvocation.MyCommand.Path)
-replace '\.Tests\.', '.'
. "$here\$sut"
Describe "Add-Numbers" {
    It "does something useful" {
        $true | Should Be $false
    }
}
```

The first three statements get the path of the `add-Numbers.ps1` script file and loads it in the current runspace using Dot-sourcing.

The variable, `$here` contains the parent folder of `Add-Numbers.Tests.ps1` in `C:\Addition`.

The second statement gets the file name of the tests script file as Add-Numbers.Tests.ps1 and replaces the \.Tests\. with a single . then assigns it to the variable, $sut. $sut contains the Add-Numbers.ps1 value which is actually our script file containing application logic.

The third statement simply combines both the folder path and script file name and loads it by Dot-sourcing it. This makes our Add-Numbers function available to the test cases defined in the tests script file.

The last three statements refer to a single test case generated by New-Fixture cmdlet.

Describe refers to a collection of tests cases. It is a container that can contain multiple tests. It is actually a function defined in the Pester module that accepts a script block. It should reflect the component getting tested.

It refers to a single test case and its naming should indicate the nature of test performed. It is also a function defined in the Pester module that accepts a script block. This script block contains the actual tests and assertions. The assertions determine whether the test is successful or not. A successful assertion is shown in green color while failures are shown in red color. Should be is an assertion command. There are multiple assertions provided by Pester such as Should be, Should BeExactly, Should match, Should Throw and more.

3. Modify the Add-Number.ps1 script file with real code. The Add-Number script looks like the following:

```
function Add-Numbers {
    param (
        [int] $Num1,
        [int] $Num2
    )
    return $Num1 + $Num2
}
```

The Add-Numbers function has been modified to accept two parameters, Num1 and Num2 both of integer data type. It adds both the numbers and returns back the same to the caller.

4. The `Add-Numbers.tests.ps1` script has been modified by removing the default test provide by Pester and adding two test cases within the same `Describe` section. The `Describe` section has been renamed to `test cases adding two numbers`

The first test named `checking when both the numbers are positive` declares two variables; `$FirstNumber` and `$Secondnumber` and assigns values to them. It invokes the `Add-Number` function passing both the variables as arguments to it. The return value from the function is piped and asserted (verified). Similarly, the second test named `checking when one number is positive and another negative` again declares two variables `$FirstNumber` and `$Secondnumber` and assign values to them. However, this time the value of one of the variables is negative. It invokes the `Add-Number` function passing both the variables as arguments to it. The return value from the function is piped and asserted:

```
$here = Split-Path -Parent $MyInvocation.MyCommand.Path
$sut = (Split-Path -Leaf $MyInvocation.MyCommand.Path)
-replace '\.Tests\.', '.'
. "$here\$sut"
Describe "test cases adding two numbers" {
    it "checking when both the numbers are positive" {
        $FirstNumber = 10
        $SecondNumber = 20
        Add-Numbers -Num1 $FirstNumber -Num2 $SecondNumber |
        should be 30
    }
    it "checking when one number is positive and another negative"
    {
        $FirstNumber = -10
        $SecondNumber = 20
        Add-Numbers -Num1 $FirstNumber -Num2 $SecondNumber |
        should be 10
    }
}
```

5. Its time now to run the tests. The test can be executed by using `Invoke-Pester` cmdlet provided by the Pester module. This cmdlet takes the path of the `Tests` scripts file. Execute the cmdlet as shown here to execute the tests written earlier:

```
Invoke-Pester -Script "C:\Addition\Add-Numbers.Tests.ps1"
```

This will invoke the scripts and execute all the test cases described in it. The same is shown in *Figure 13*. The green color denotes a successful test case and red one means a failed test case.

```
PS C:\> Invoke-Pester -Script "C:\Addition\Add-Numbers.Tests.ps1"
Describing test cases adding two numbers
 [+] checking when both the number are positive 405ms
 [+] checking when One number is positive and another negative 99ms
Tests completed in 504ms
Passed: 2 Failed: 0 Skipped: 0 Pending: 0

PS C:\>
```

Figure 13: Executing Pester unit tests

Pester real-time example

Let's work on another example on Pester. This time we will write tests for ensuring whether a website and its related applications are in a working condition on a web server. This time New-Fixture is not used for generating the script files. Instead, both the application code and test cases are written from scratch using a PowerShell ISE editor.

Both the code for provisioning of web server artifacts and related tests are within the same file although they can be in different files as seen before.

The entire code is shown here. The script is stored at C:\temp\Test-WebServer.ps1. A CreateWebSite function is defined taking four parameters. These parameters capture inputs for the application pool name ($appPoolName), website name ($websiteName), its port number ($port), and the path referred by the website ($websitePath). The function first creates an **Internet Information Server** (**IIS**) application pool first using New-WebAppPool cmdlet and $appPoolName parameter and then creates a IIS website using New-Website cmdlet using all the four parameters:

```
function CreateWebSite
{
    param(
    [string] $appPoolName,
    [string] $websiteName,
    [uint32] $port,
    [string] $websitePath

    )
```

```
            New-WebAppPool -Name $appPoolName
            New-Website -Name $websiteName -Port $port -PhysicalPath
            $websitePath -ApplicationPool $appPoolName -Force
    }

    Describe "Status of web server" {
        BeforeAll {
            CreateWebSite -appPoolName "TestAppPool"
            -websiteName "TestWebSite" -port 9999 -websitePath
            "C:\InetPub\Wwwroot"
        }
        AfterAll {
            Remove-Website -Name "TestWebSite"
            Remove-WebAppPool -Name TestAppPool
        }
        context "is Website already exists with valid values" {
         it "checking whether the website exists" {
            (Get-Website -name "TestWebSite").Name | should be "TestWebSite"
         }
         it "checking if website is in running condition" {
            (Get-Website -name "TestWebSite").State  | should be "Started"
         }
        }
    }
```

The test cases are written in the same file. A `Describe` named `Status of web server` is defined and represents a group of test cases. A special construct `BeforeAll` and `AfterAll` is used within the `Describe` block. `BeforeAll` runs the script within it just once for all test cases in a `Describe` block before the execution of the first `it` block. Similarly, the script within `AfterAll` is executed after all the test cases (`it` blocks) are executed. They are typically used for setting up and cleaning up the environment. Here, we invoke our `CreateWebSite` function within the `BeforeAll` block to provision our application pool and website. Both the application pool and website is removed in the `AfterAll` block. This ensures that the environment is in the same state as before the start of the tests.

`Context` is also a new container construct that can contain and group multiple test cases (`it` blocks). Context does not affect the execution of tests. They remain the same as before however it adds additional metadata and groups tests based on condition. For example, a context is a group of test cases with different valid values while another context is a group of test cases with invalid values.

There are two test cases implemented. The test case `checking whether the website exists` uses the `Get-Website` cmdlet to get the name of the website and asserts on it. The test case, `checking if website is in running condition` again uses the same cmdlet but checks its status property and compares with `Started` value for assertion.

Executing the above script with `Invoke-Pester` cmdlet shows the result as shown in *Figure 14*.

```
Invoke-Pester -Script "C:\temp\Test-WebServer.ps1"
```

```
PS C:\> Invoke-Pester -Script "C:\Addition\Add-Numbers.Tests.ps1"
Describing test cases adding two numbers
  [+] checking when both the number are positive 405ms
  [+] checking when One number is positive and another negative 99ms
Tests completed in 504ms
Passed: 2 Failed: 0 Skipped: 0 Pending: 0

PS C:\> Invoke-Pester -Script "C:\test-WebServer.ps1"
Describing Status of web server

Name                     State          Applications
----                     -----          ------------
TestAppPool              Started

Name          : TestWebSite
ID            : 3
State         : Started
PhysicalPath  : C:\InetPub\Wwwroot
Bindings      : Microsoft.IIs.PowerShell.Framework.ConfigurationElement

    Context is Website already exists with valid values
    [+] checking whether the website exists 557ms
    [+] checking if website is in running condition 15ms
Tests completed in 573ms
Passed: 2 Failed: 0 Skipped: 0 Pending: 0


PS C:\>
```

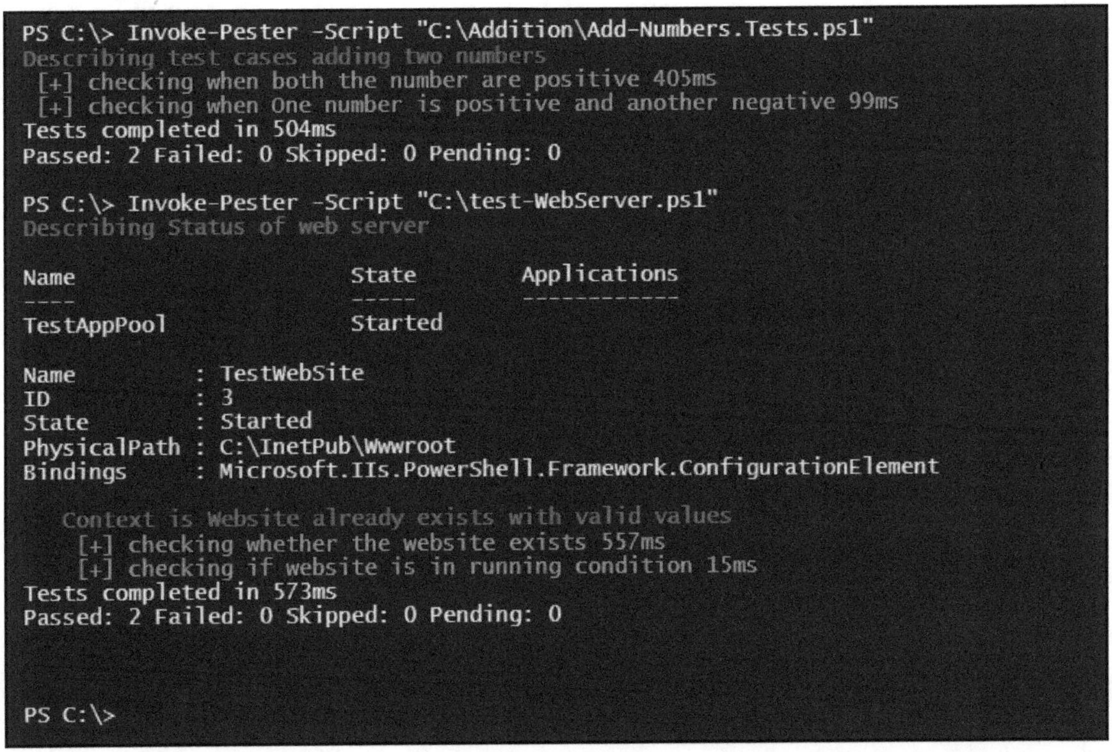

Figure 14: Executing Pester tests

It is important to note the naming pattern of `Describe`, `Context`, and `it` blocks. They have been named in such a way that the result of executing the unit tests can be read as simple English which is meaningful and provide enough context about the tests that are successful and ones that failed.

Desired State Configuration

Desired State Configuration is a new configuration management platform from Microsoft built as an extension to PowerShell. DSC was originally launched as part of WMF 4.0. It is available as part of WMF 4.0 and 5.0 for all Windows Server operating systems above Windows 2008 R2. WMF 5.0 is available out-of-the-box on Windows Server 2016 and Windows 10. It uses the core infrastructure of **Web Services for Management (WSMan)** and **Windows Remote Management (WinRM)** for its working. It is an extension to PowerShell and adds language constructs, features, and cmdlets for easy authoring and execution of configuration across heterogeneous environments.

DSC is a declarative language enabling Infrastructure as Code by representing and describing the entire infrastructure and its configuration through code. DSC configuration files are simple `.ps1` script files that can be stored in source control repositories for version control.

DSC represents the target state and configuration for environments through code. It represents what the environment state and configuration should look like. The how part is not required because it is taken care of by DSC internally.

DSC will be used in the release pipeline to configure multiple environments and application configuration.

DSC Push architecture

Figure 15 depicts a DSC Push architecture.

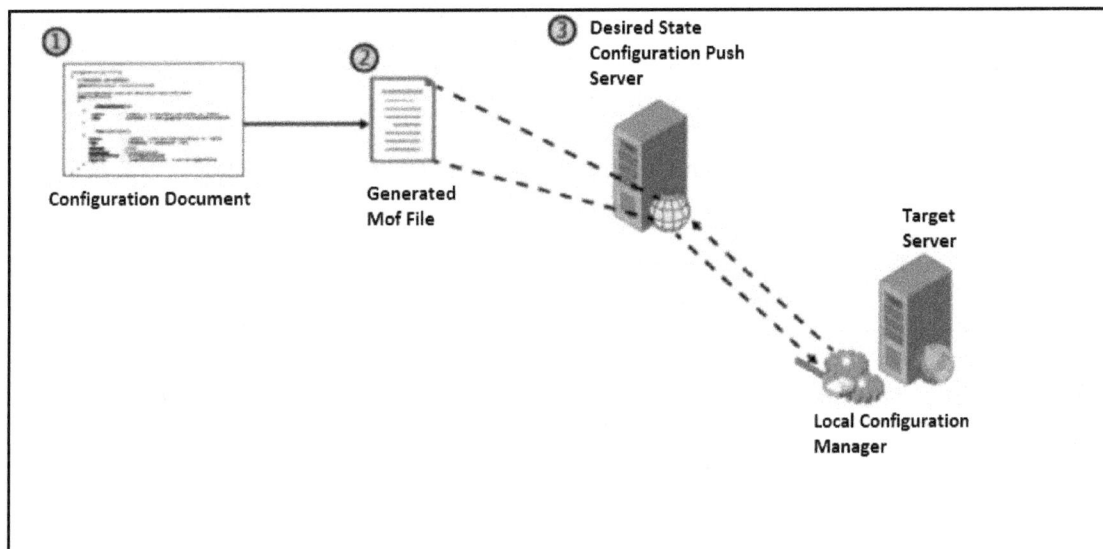

Figure 15: Desired State Configuration Push architecture

A simple DSC is shown here:

```
Configuration EnableWebServer
{
    Import-DscResource -ModuleName 'PSDesiredStateConfiguration'
    Node WebServer01
    {
        WindowsFeature IIS
        {
            Name = "Web-Server"
            Ensure = "Present"
        }
    }
}
EnableWebServer -OutputPath "C:\DSC-WebServer" -Verbose
Start-DscConfiguration -Path "C:\DSC-WebServer" -Wait -Force -Verbose
```

The code declares `EnableWebServer` configuration. This configuration is responsible for ensuring the presence of the `Web-Server` (IIS) Windows feature on a `WebServer01` computer. The node name should be changed reflecting an actual computer name in your network. Notice that the configuration does not use any scripting or programming to provision a web server. The configuration is merely providing the intent and its configuration values, the rest is taken care of by DSC resources internally. The node section comprises of names of computers that this configuration is applicable to. `WindowsFeature` mentioned in Configuration is a DSC resource that actually provides the logic for provisioning of Windows features on a target computer. The how part is taken care of by these DSC resources.

Executing the above configuration as shown in the code, generates the configuration **Management Object Format** (**MOF**) file for each node name in configuration at the folder location provided to the path parameter. If the path parameter is omitted, the MOF files will be generated in the current working folder. These MOF files are pushed to target nodes by DSC using the `Start-DscConfiguration` cmdlet. This cmdlet takes the path parameter as input representing the folder containing MOF files, loads all MOF files, and sends them to their respective computer nodes using the MOF file names.

Alternatively, you can also provide the `ComputerName` parameter to `Start-DSCConfiguration` cmdlet which will load a MOF file matching the `ComputerName` and push it to that node only. This is shown here:

```
Start-DscConfiguration -Path "C:\DSC-WebServer" -ComputerName WebServer01 -
Wait -Force -Verbose
```

Installing WMF 4.0 or 5.0 on client nodes ensures the installation of DSC **Local Configuration Manager** (**LCM**). It is the responsibility of LCM on these client nodes to accept the configuration sent to it and execute them on the local machine. LCM treats the received configuration as Golden configuration. LCM is configured to run periodically, checking the current state of configuration with a Golden desired state of configuration. If it finds any deviation, it brings back the configuration and environment back to a desired state. This ensures that target servers and their configuration can be auto-remediated in case there are changes applied to them.

DSC resources must be available at the client nodes for LCM to periodically check and auto-remediate the configuration. They help LCM in validating the current resource configuration with desired configuration, bringing back the current configuration to a desired configuration. Earlier we witnessed a single DSC resource in configuration. There are more than 300 DSC resources available to be used within configurations. While DSC comes with few out-of-the-box DSC resources, it is possible to author custom DSC resources. DSC provided resources are:

- WindowsProcess
- WindowsFeature
- Service
- Environment
- File
- Archive
- User
- Group
- Package
- Log
- Script

DSC Pull architecture

We've seen one of the DSC architecture implementations called the **Push mode**. DSC comes in two architectural implementation modes:

- DSC Push mode
- DSC Pull mode

In Pull mode, the configurations are not pushed to client nodes. Instead, LCM on client nodes are configured with appropriate endpoint information through which it is able to connect and download configuration from DSC Pull servers and execute them on a local server. It is needless to say that DSC Pull servers need to be created and available with appropriate published configuration files before they are fetched by LCM.

DSC Pull mode is a decentralized and a scalable way of enabling configuration management. Hundreds and thousands of client nodes can simultaneously pull configurations automatically without any manual intervention. DSC resources can also be downloaded along with configuration files eliminating the need to preinstall resources on client nodes before executing the configuration. It is much more manageable and flexible compared to DSC Push mode. We will be using DSC Pull server and configuration to create our base container images.

The DSC Pull architecture is shown in *Figure 16*:

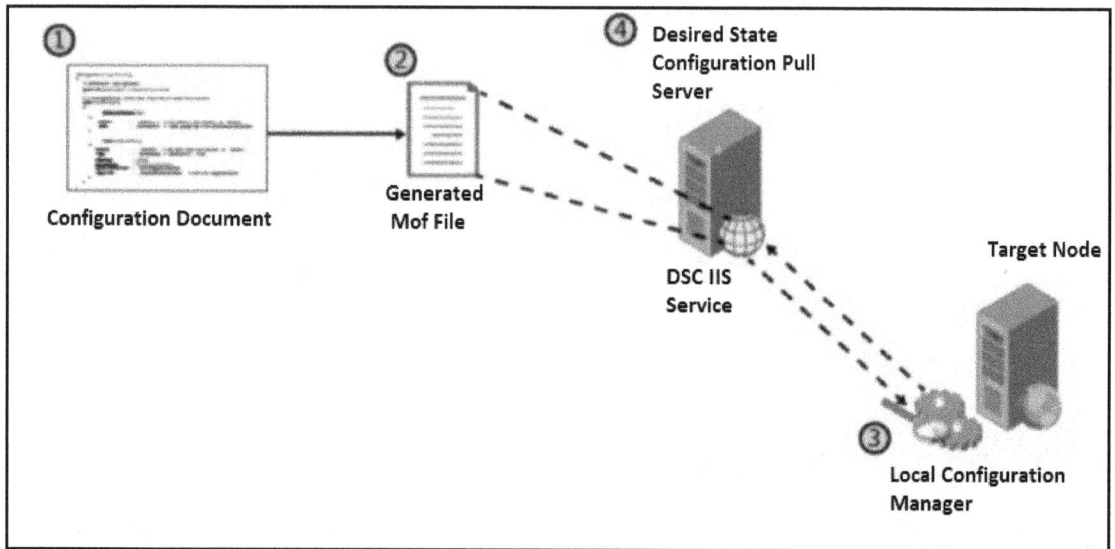

Figure 16: Desired State Configuration Pull architecture

Initially, DSC configuration is authored as PowerShell scripts. Then DSC MOF file is generated based on authored PowerShell scripts, and eventually the MOF files are published to a Pull server. The LCM of the client node then downloads the configuration and reconfigures the node according to the configuration.

Figure 17 shows the DSC Pull mode request flow between client node and Pull server.

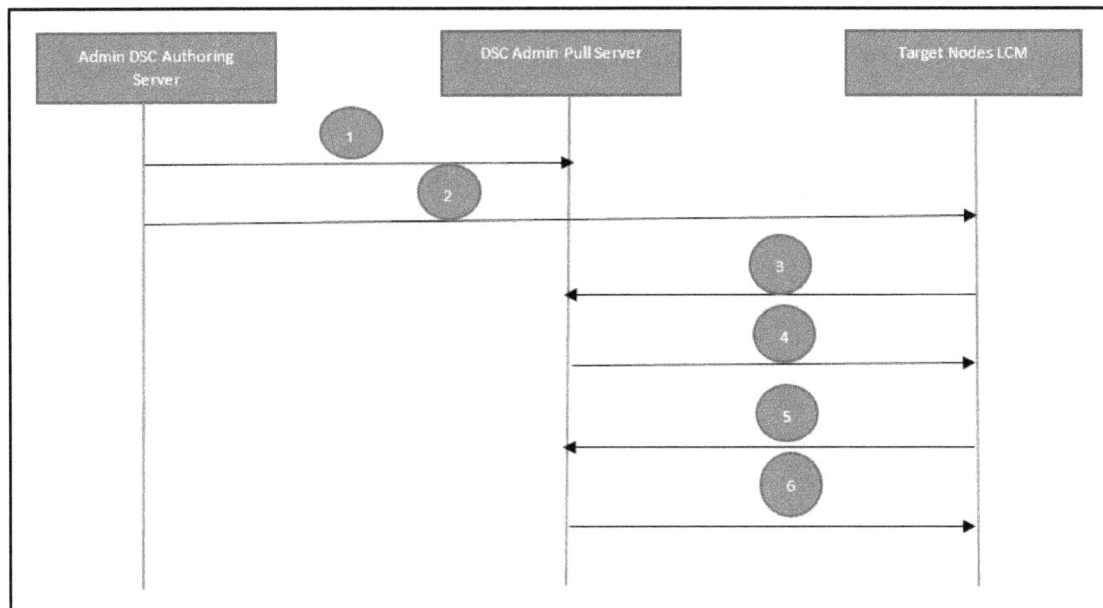

Figure 17: Desired State Configuration Pull flow sequence

The following sequence of operations happens during Pull mode

1. The configuration developer creates the configuration, generates MOF files and other artifacts, and copies them to a pre-defined folder location on the DSC Pull server. This is simply a copy-paste operation.
2. The DSC administrator configures the LCM of every client node with information about Pull server endpoint, configuration details, and frequency to pull configuration.
3. The client node sends requests to the Pull server for fetching configuration.
4. The Pull server on receiving the request, responds by sending configuration information.
5. Steps 2 to 4 are repeated based on configured frequency.
6. For every request received, a response is sent with configuration information to the client nodes.

Pull configuration example

This chapter assumes that you already have a working Pull server in your network. In case, you do not have a Pull server available, complete steps for creating a Pull server is provided in appendix 1 in this book which would create a Pull server with endpoint URL `https://10.4.0.4:9100/PSDSCPullServer.svc/` on port `9100`:

The following configuration will to explain how to set up DSC Pull configuration:

```
Configuration EnableWebServer
{
    Import-DscResource -ModuleName 'PSDesiredStateConfiguration'
    Node EnableWebServer
    {
        WindowsFeature IIS
        {
            Name = "Web-Server"
            Ensure = "Present"
        }
    }
}
```

You will notice that the name of Node is no longer a computer node name. This is because any node can pull this configuration from the Pull server. The node name is of high significance in DSC. The Node name decides the name of the generated MOF file. With pull architecture, even the name of configuration has impact on the way these configurations are downloaded by the target node. The name used reflects the intent of the configuration.

You will also notice that `start-DscConfiguration` cmdlet is not used for this configuration. `Start-DscConfiguration` is used to push configuration to target nodes. For Pull server configurations, there are two additional requirements:

- Instead of pushing, configurations are deployed to a well-known folder path known to Pull server. Pull server can be an IIS website or a **Server Message Block** (**SMB**) share. In this book, IIS websites will be configured as a Pull server. The Pull server is configured with this folder path in its `web.config` file. When a request for configuration arrives at the Pull server, the website accesses this folder path, loads and sends back the configuration. By default, this folder location is
  `$env:ProgramFiles\WindowsPowershell\DSCService\Configuration`.
  We generate MOF files as we did in the Push scenario by executing the configuration with output path as
  `$env:ProgramFiles\WindowsPowershell\DSCService\Configuration`.
  This would generate the MOF file within the output path folder. This is shown here:

  ```
  EnableWebServer -OutputPath "$env:ProgramFiles\
  WindowsPowershell\DSCService\
  Configuration" -Verbose
  ```

- A checksum/hash should be generated for each MOF file. This hash is saved in a `.mof.checksum` file along with the original MOF file. Each `.mof` file should have a corresponding `.mof.checksum` file with same name. This checksum is important for LCM to validate and decide if it needs to download the configuration from the Pull server. Every time a LCM on a node pulls a configuration, it sends the hash it already has to the Pull server. If the hash is different on the Pull server, the configuration is downloaded otherwise it would mean the configuration on the node is the same as that on Pull server. To generate the checksum and write it to a file, DSC provides a cmdlet `New-DscChecksum`. Its usage is shown here. It takes `configuratioPath` as the path to the configuration MOF file and `Outpath` as the folder location to generate the corresponding checksum file:

  ```
  New-DSCCheckSum -ConfigurationPath
  "$env:ProgramFiles\WindowsPowershell\DSCService\
  Configuration\
  EnableWebServer.mof"  -OutPath
  "$env:ProgramFiles\WindowsPowershell\DSCService\
  Configuration" -Force
  ```

- It is to be noted that if the `ConfiguationPath` parameter refers to a folder rather an MOF file, the checksum file will be generated for all MOF files at location referred to by the `ConfiguationPath` parameter. This is shown here:

```
New-DscCheckSum -ConfigurationPath "$env:ProgramFiles\
WindowsPowershell\DSCService\Configuration"
-OutPath "$env:ProgramFiles\WindowsPowershell\DSCService\
Configuration" -Force
```

The configuration can now be pulled by any authorized and configured computer node. After storing configurations on the Pull server, the LCM of computer nodes should be configured so that they can pull configurations from the Pull server.

To configure LCM on a target node, DSC configuration should be created containing resources specific to LCM. The MOF file should be generated, pushed to target nodes, and executed locally on target nodes. The approach to push LCM configuration to the target node is the same as that of any other configuration using `Start-DscConfiguration` cmdlet. However, there are differences in the way the configurations are authored. This is explained next.

DscLocalConfigurationManager() attribute

LCM configuration has the `DscLocalConfigurationManager()` attribute at a configuration level. This attribute ensures and enforces that only configuration related to LCM are allowed within the configuration. There are three resources used in this example:

- `Settings`
- `ConfigurationRepositoryWeb`
- `PartialConfiguration`

The Settings resource configures the LCM with multiple properties. If you want to view LCM properties, use `Get-DscLocalConfigurationManager` cmdlet to list all properties along with their values. The properties used in this example are explained here:

Property Name	Description
`ConfigurationModeFrequencyMins`	Represents the frequency (in minutes) at which the LCM attempts to execute and apply the current configuration on the target node. The default value is 15. It should be either set to an integer multiple of `RefreshFrequencyMins` or vice-versa.
`RefreshMode`	Possible values are `Push` (the default), `Disabled`, and `Pull`. In the Push configuration, the configuration must be pushed to each target node. In the Pull mode, a Pull server should be available in hosting configurations, for LCM to contact, access, download, and apply the configurations.
`RefreshFrequencyMins`	Represents the frequency (in minutes) at which the LCM contacts the Pull server to download the current configuration. This value can be set in conjunction with `ConfigurationModeFrequencyMins`. When `RefreshMode` is set to `PULL`, the target node contacts the Pull server at an interval set by `RefreshFrequencyMins` and downloads the current configuration. At the interval set by `ConfigurationModeFrequencyMins`, LCM applies the latest configuration that was downloaded onto the computer node. The default value is `30`.

ConfigurationMode	This property has three possible values. This property determines how LCM should behave in the event of configuration drifts or availability of newer configuration. It can take the following values: ApplyAndAutoCorrect: LCM keeps executing the configuration on a regular basis (specified by ConfigurationModeFrequencyMins) without checking whether the configuration is different or not. ApplyAndMonitor: In this mode, which is the default, LCM compares the configuration specified on the Pull server with the configuration file on the target node. If a difference is detected, the discrepancy is reported in logs, but does not apply the new configuration. ApplyOnly: In this mode, LCM does not automatically run in the background. If a Pull server is configured, it will check with the server periodically and only if a new configuration is present, it will apply that configuration to the target node.
RebootNodeIfNeeded	Certain configuration changes on a target node might require it to be restarted. Computer node will restart if value is $true. If value of this property if $false (the default value), the configuration will complete, but the node will not be restarted automatically. It should be restarted manually.

ConfigurationRepositoryWeb

ConfigurationRepositoryWeb defines details about web-based Pull server. The three properties of this resource used in this example provide enough information to connect to the Pull server. CertificateID and AllowUnsecureConnection are other available properties but not used in this example. CertificateID refers to the certificate thumbprint for authenticating to Pull server and AllowUnsecureConnection accepts a Boolean value determining whether unauthenticated access to Pull server is allowed.

Property Name	Description
ServerURL	The URL of the Web-based Pull server. A dummy URL is provided in code shown next and should be changed to a valid Pull server url.
RegistrationKey	This registers target node with the Pull server. It is a common key used by both pull server and target nodes. The key is defined on Pull server and only an IT administrator should have knowledge about it. The key has been masked in code shown next. The reader should provide their registration key. The RegistrationKey is used in conjunction with ConfigurationNames. It is ignored when using ConfigurationID
ConfigurationNames	The names of configuration files that are to be pulled by target node are available on Pull server at a well-defined folder accessible by the Pull server website. Here, the sample configuration available on Pull server is WebFeatures

Partial Configurations

The PartialConfiguration section defines the Configuration source that should be used to deploy the configuration on a computer node. PartialConfiguration help in downloading multiple configurations from different Pull servers and apply all of them together on a local node. In this example, we have used a single configuration in ConfigurationRepositoryWeb and a single PartialConfiguration section, but more configurations can be added to the ConfigurationNames property of ConfigurationRepositoryWeb and multiple partial configuration sections can be defined corresponding to those configurations. It is important to note that the name of partial configuration must available in ConfigurationNames property of ConfigurationRepositoryWeb. Moreover, the name must also match to the name of the original configuration based on which MOF file is generated. We mentioned at the beginning of this section that ConfigurationNames are quite important in Pull scenarios.

In short, the PartialConfiguration names should match the name of the original configuration, the name of MOF file, and the name should also be available as part of ConfigurationNames property of ConfigurationRepositoryWeb. If these names do not match, LCM on computer nodes will not be able to pull configuration information from Pull servers. The RefreshMode property defined in settings section can be overridden in this section with a different value.

Pushing LCM Configuration

Finally, the configuration is pushed to the localhost computer node (in this case the configuration is authored on local computer) and executed to effect changes to LCM configuration using `Set-DSCLocalConfigurationManager` cmdlet. This cmdlet is responsible for pushing and updating only Local Configuration Manager configuration. It cannot be used for pushing other types of configuration.

The configuration assumes that the LCM configuration is authored on the node that would act as a client to Pull server. This is the reason the node name is `localhost` in code shown next. However, if you want the following configuration to be authored on any other server, it is possible to do so. In that case, the node name in code should change to the actual name of the node and `start-DscConfiguration` should either, not use the computer name altogether, or should provide the actual node name to `ComputerName` parameter as argument.

Pull server information like `RegistrationKey`, endpoint URL, and `ConfigurationNames` should be gathered before the following script is executed. The `RegistrationKey` is available from the `RegistrationKeys.txt` file available in the `$env:ProgramFiles\WindowsPowerShell\DscService` folder on Pull server. The endpoint URL of Pull server can be obtained from IIS.

```
[DscLocalConfigurationManager()]
configuration PartialConfigurationDemo
{
    Node localhost
    {
        Settings
        {
            ConfigurationModeFrequencyMins = 30
            RefreshMode = 'Pull'
            RefreshFrequencyMins = 30
            ConfigurationMode = "ApplyandAutoCorrect"
            RebootNodeIfNeeded = $true
        }

        ConfigurationRepositoryWeb IISConfig
        {
            ServerURL = "https://10.4.0.4:9100/PSDSCPullServer.svc/"
            RegistrationKey = "xxxxxxxx-xxxx-xxxx-xxxx-xxxxxxxxxxxx"
            ConfigurationNames = @("EnableWebServer")
        }
        PartialConfiguration EnableWebServer
        {
            Description = 'Configuration for installing Web server'
            ConfigurationSource = '[ConfigurationRepositoryWeb]IISConfig'
```

```
            RefreshMode = 'Pull'
        }
    }
}
PartialConfigurationDemo -OutputPath "C:\LCMConfiguration" -Verbose
Set-DscLocalConfigurationManager -path "C:\LCMConfiguration" -force -
verbose
Update-DscConfiguration -Wait -Verbose
Start-DscConfiguration -UseExisting -Wait -Force -Verbose
```

After the LCM settings are configured, it's time to connect to Pull server, download, and execute the configuration on the target node. The configuration is pulled using `Update-DscConfiguration` cmdlet. It does not accept any parameters and runs as a job by default. To execute this cmdlet in synchronous mode, the `-wait` switch can be used as shown before. `Verbose` switch provides additional execution steps when this cmdlet is executed.

After pulling configuration the configuration is executed and applied using `Start-DscConfiguration` cmdlet. It is asked to use existing configuration through `UseExisting` switch, `wait` switch runs the cmdlet in synchronous mode, force switch pushes configuration to target nodes even when the LCM on target node is configured with pull configuration and verbose switch provides additional information about the execution.

If there are no errors while executing the code shown here, IIS will be installed, available and configured on target node. This can be verified by accessing `http://localhost/` using browser in your local machine. You should see *IISStart* screen.

Summary

This was a technology-heavy chapter and we covered different technologies that will help in automation of provisioning and managing environments. We started with Azure Resource Manager and its features and concepts. Then, we moved on to Azure Resource Manager templates, described various components of templates and how to author them, constructed a simple minimal template, used tools for authoring templates and then deployed them through PowerShell. Then, we discussed PowerShell as a command-line and scripting language that helps in automation and administration of infrastructure and environment. We also discussed some of its most important concepts like variables, pipelines, cmdlets, scripts, and modules. We covered the PowerShell script unit testing tool, Pester. We tried to understand Pester and its concepts using two examples. Finally, we discussed Desired State Configuration as a configuration platform with its Pull and Push architecture, their process flow, and ways to use configuration files to configure target computer nodes.

4

Nano, Containers, and Docker Primer

May you live in interesting times - translation from a Chinese proverb

We are in the midst of revolutionary changes in the technology world. Over the last few years, the pace of innovation has been so rapid that anything that is new today becomes old in a few days. Even though the change is fast, there are innovations that rewrite history and change the way we look at providing and consuming computing services. Container technology and Nano Servers are major among these innovations.

In this chapter, we will explore the basic concepts of **WindowsContainers** and **NanoServer**, provision them on Azure, look at their differences, and explore the building blocks related to them on the Windows platform. Windows Containers is a new technology introduced with Windows Server 2016. Containers are not a new technology in Linux world; they have been available on the Linux platform for more than a decade and are highly successful. Windows Containers are managed through Docker binaries. Docker tools are used to manage Windows Containers on the Windows platform similar to the way they manage Docker Containers on the Linux platform.

Virtualization

If we look back at the history of computing, the 1970s were dominated by mainframe computing. During the 80s and 90s, personal computing and client-server technology was the flavor. The first decade of this century was characterized by two major trends: virtualization and mobile computing. Today, we are again in midst of trend-changing phenomena with the concept of containerization of applications and services.

To understand Containers better, let's take a step back and understand virtualization. Virtualization was a breakthrough innovation that completely changed the way physical servers were looked at. It refers to the abstraction of a physical object into a logical object. Virtualization of physical servers enabled the creation of multiple virtual servers, better known as virtual machines. These virtual machines consumed and shared the same physical CPU, memory, storage, and other hardware with the physical server on which they were hosted. This enabled faster and easier provisioning of application environments on demand, providing high availability and scalability with reduced cost. One physical server was enough to host multiple virtual machines, each virtual machine containing its own operating system and hosting services on it. There was no longer any need to buy additional physical servers for deploying new applications and services. The existing physical servers were sufficient to host more virtual machines. Furthermore, as part of rationalization, many physical servers were consolidated into a few with the help of virtualization.

Each virtual machine contains the entire operating system and each virtual machine is completely isolated from other virtual machines, including the physical hosts. Although a virtual machine uses the hardware provided by the host physical server, it has full control over its assigned resources and its environment. These virtual machines can be hosted on a network similar to a physical server with its own identity.

One of the drawbacks of virtual machines is that each virtual machine contains the complete operating system. This means that running multiple virtual machines will run multiple operating systems on a physical host. Each operating system consumes a major portion of hardware resources, the same resources that could be utilized by applications and services if they were hosted on a physical server. Another issue with virtual machines is that it still consumes a lot of time to provision them. Although the time required to provision them is less than provisioning a physical server, it is still considerably high in this fast-paced world. Furthermore, the footprint of a virtual machine runs in gigabytes and has the potential to be reduced significantly.

Containers

Containers are also a virtualization technology; however, they do not virtualize a physical server. Instead, a Container is an operating-system-level virtualization. What this means is that Containers share the operating system kernel provided by the host among themselves along with the host. Multiple containers running on a host (physical or virtual) share the host operating system kernel. Containers ensures that they reuse the host kernel instead of each having a dedicated kernel to themselves.

Containers are also completely isolated from the host and other Containers, much like a virtual machine. Containers use Windows storage filter drivers and session isolation for providing isolation of operating system services such as the filesystem, registry, processes, and networks. Each Container gets its own copy of operating system resources. The Container has the perception that it has a complete new, untouched operating system and resources. This arrangement provides lots of benefits, as follows:

- Containers are faster to provision. They do not need to provision the operating system and its kernel services. They are available from the host operating system.
- Containers are lightweight and require fewer computing resources compared to virtual machines. The operating system resource overhead is no longer required in Containers.
- Containers are much smaller in size compared to virtual machines.
- Containers help in solving the problems related to managing multiple application dependencies in an intuitive, automated, and simple manner. Containers provide infrastructure to define all application dependencies in a single place.

Containers are an inherent part and feature of Windows Server 2016 and Windows 10; however, they are managed and accessed using a Docker client and Docker daemon. Windows provides PowerShell cmdlets for managing Containers but they are in alpha phase at the time of writing.

Each Container has a single main process that must be running for the Container to exist. A Container will stop when this process ends. Also, a Container can either run in interactive mode or in detached mode like a service.

Figure 1 shows all the technical layers that enable Containers. The bottommost layer provides the core infrastructure in terms of network, storage, load balancers, and network cards. At the top of the infrastructure is the compute layer, consisting of either a physical server or both physical as well as virtual servers on top of a physical server. This layer contains the operating system with the ability to host Containers. The operating system provides the execution driver that the layers above use to call kernel code and objects to execute Containers. Microsoft has created **Host Container System Shim** (**HCSShim**) for managing and creating Containers and uses Windows storage filter drivers for image and file management. The Container environment isolation ability is provided to Windows session. Windows Server 2016 and Nano Server provide the operating system and enable the Container features and also execute the user-level Docker client and Docker engine.

The Docker engine uses the services of HCSShim, storage filter drivers, and sessions to spawn multiple Containers on the server, each containing a service, application, or database:

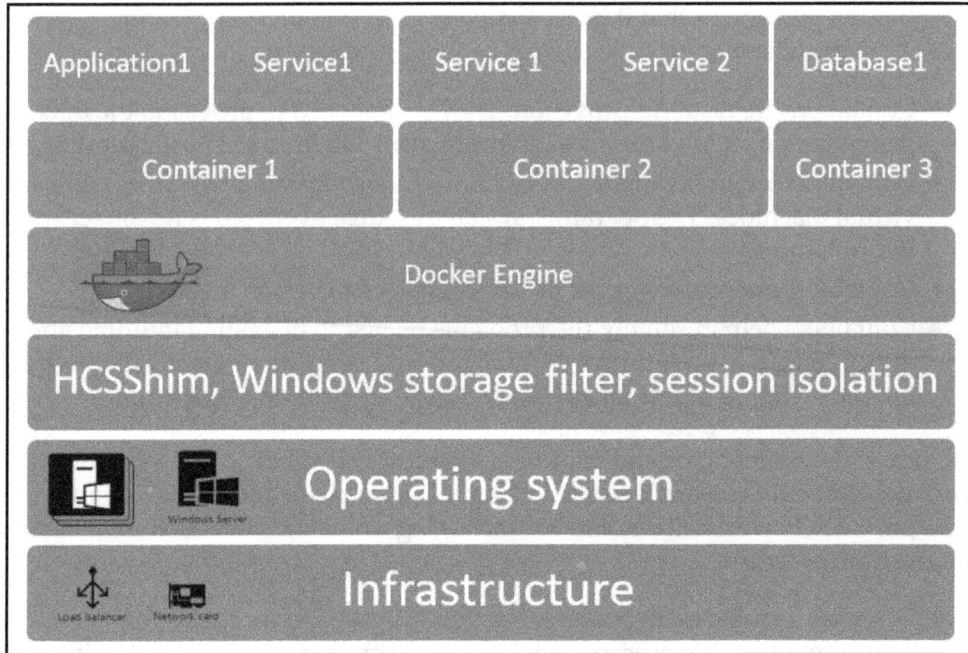

Figure 1: Container architecture

The next section will navigate through some of the important concepts related to Containers.

Docker

Docker provides management features to Windows Containers. It comprises two executables:

- Docker daemon
- Docker client

The Docker daemon is the workhorse for managing Containers. It is a Windows service responsible for managing all activities on the host related to Containers. The Docker client interacts with the Docker daemon and is responsible for capturing inputs and sending them across to the Docker daemon. The Docker daemon provides the runtime, libraries, graph drivers, and engine to create, manage, and monitor Containers and images on the host server. It also provides capabilities to create custom images that are used for building and shipping applications to multiple environments.

Container host

The **Container host** is the host operating system with the capability and features of Windows Containers turned on. It also hosts the Docker daemon and its client. The Docker daemon must be present on the Container host although the Docker client can be used from another server connecting remotely to the daemon. The Container host can be a physical or a virtual server running either on the cloud like Azure or deployed on-premises.

Container images

Images are one of the most important concepts to understand in Container technology. Every Container is based on an image. Images contains a base operating system, system libraries, drives for interacting with the hardware and operating system, system applications, services, and utilities. They also contain configured applications and services. An analogy to understand images better is to compare them with object-oriented classes. Images are similar to object-oriented classes implinting behavior and properties while Containers are similar to objects created from those classes. An image is a blueprint based on which Containers are created. Docker provides a centralized registry and repository for public images. Microsoft also provides its own repository and registry for Windows-based images. These base images can be used to create custom images. All custom images should be based on a base image. Windows Containers uses a Windows storage filter driver for managing images. Images are read-only files. Once created, they cannot be modified. An image from which Containers are created in turn consists of multiple sub images. Every image consists of a stack of these layers linked together. These sub layers are reusable and can be part of multiple images. A layer can comprise a new configuration, a modified configuration provided from the layer underneath it, deployment of an application or service, or a combination of any of these. Each layer of an image is stored as a file. Windows uses the storage filter driver technology to combine all the layer files to create the final image. When a Container is created, a read/write image layer is added on top of all the layers. It is this topmost layer that is used by the Container for all its write operations. Images are stored in a local repository referred to by a name.

They also have tag information associated to them that helps in assigning versions to them. This enables multiple images with different versions to be available on the same Container host. The image architecture is shown in *Figure 2*. In this architecture, a base image is used and a couple of instructions are executed on a base image one after another to create a final image through `Dockerfile`. Each instruction creates an image layer represented through an identifier on top of the previous layer. `Dockerfile` will be explained in considerable detail later in this chapter. The code for `Dockerfile` is also available in the same section:

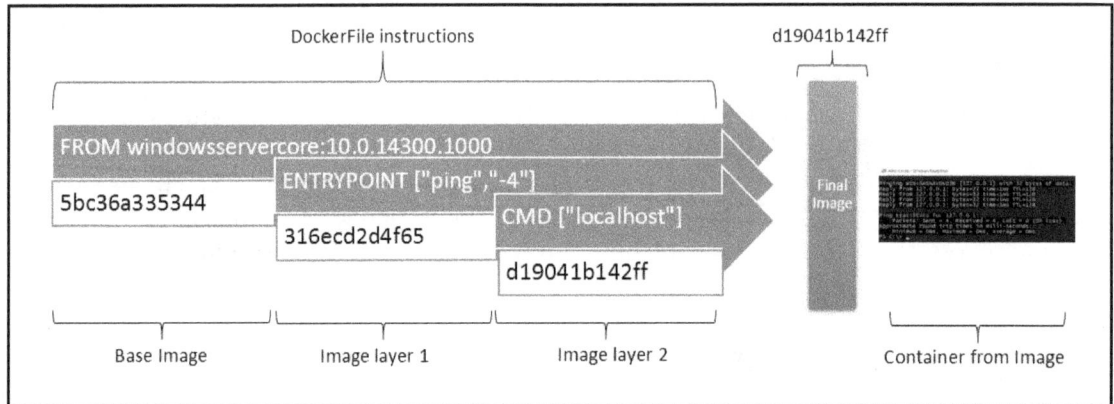

Figure 2: Image architecture

Microsoft provides two base images – **WindowsServerCore** and NanoServer. We will be creating our own custom images in `Chapter 7`, *Configuration Management*, discussing configuration management. There are two ways to create images. `Dockerfile` is a file containing instructions to create an image. `Dockerfile` approach should be used to define images from sctrach while existing running Containers can also be saved as an image. We will introduce `Dockerfile` and its instruction commands later in this chapter.

Docker Hub/Docker Registry

This is the centralized registry for hosting and sharing images. The registry is hosted at `https://hub.docker.com/` and anyone having access to it can search, find, and download images. It helps in sharing images with co-workers, customers, and others. A registry contains multiple repositories and they can be either public or private repositories.

Installing a Windows Server 2016 Container on Azure

There are multiple ways to install and create a Container environment on Windows Server 2016 on Azure. The environment can be provisioned through pure PowerShell scripting, .NET, Azure **Command Line Interface** (**CLI**) or through ARM templates. The ARM templates can be deployed through multiple technologies, including PowerShell. We will create development, testing, and pre-production environments coding, running, testing, and deploying our custom web-based application on Windows Containers. We will describe the step-by-step process to create a Container environment using Windows Server 2016. The steps for building a Container environment on Windows 10 are exactly the same as for Windows Server 2016. All our environment apart from the development environment will be based on Windows Server 2016. The development environment will be on Windows 10. Docker is also introducing a **Docker for Windows** installer for creating a Docker environment on the Windows platform; however, at the time of writing, Docker for Windows creates and deploys a Linux Moby virtual machine that hosts the Docker daemon and manages the Container environment. In this book, we will enable the Docker Container environment using Windows 10 as the development environment and deploy our application in Containers for development. All our environments will be provisioned on Azure cloud virtual machines, and so before creating a Container environment, we will provision the virtual machine.

Provisioning Azure virtual machines

Azure virtual machines will be provisioned through PowerShell. For creating virtual machines on Azure using PowerShell, follow these steps using the PowerShell **Integrated Scripting Environment** (**ISE**):

1. Log in to the Azure subscription as shown here. You should have a valid Azure subscription with credentials to log in. A login screen appears when using `Login-AzureRmAccount` without any parameters. There are ways to overcome the appearance of the login screen using the concept of **Service Principal** in Azure which will be explained in `Chapter 7`, *Configuration Management*:

```
Login-AzureRmAccount
```

2. This step is optional and should be executed only if the account used to log in to Azure has access to multiple subscriptions and you want to use a particular subscription for creating the virtual machine. You should provide the subscription name and send it as argument to the `set-AzureRmContext` cmdlet. This is shown here and <<xxxxxxxx>> should be replaced with your subscription name:

```
Set-AzureRmContext -SubscriptionName <<xxxxxxxx>>
```

3. Declare a few variables to hold names for the storage account, resource group, location of Azure resources, and virtual machine name, as shown here. The name of the resource group should be unique within the subscription, the name of virtual machine must be unique within a resource group, and the name of the storage account must be unique on the Internet. The majority of Azure cmdlets define both location and resource group name as parameters and `$locationRG` and `$rgName` variables should be used for them:

```
$storageAccountName = "myContainerstore"
$locationRG = "westus"
$rgName = "ContainerRG"
$vmName = "myContainerVM"
```

4. Create a new resource group using `New-AzureRmResourceGroup` cmdlet, passing the resource group and location names as arguments:

```
New-AzureRmResourceGroup -Name $rgName -Location $locationRG
```

5. Virtual machine files must reside on the storage account. Create a new storage account using `New-AzureRmStorageAccount` cmdlet, providing storage account name and location as values to its parameters. The return value from the cmdlet is stored in `$storageAccount` variable. This is shown here:

```
$storageAccount = New-AzureRmStorageAccount -ResourceGroupName
$rgName -Name
$storageAccountName -Type "Standard_GRS" -Location $locationRG
```

6. Virtual machines must also reside on a virtual network. The code shown next creates a virtual network and a subnet within it. After creation, the subnet object passed as argument to virtual network. The subnet object is created using `New-AzureRmVirtualNetworkSubnetConfig` cmdlet providing `10.0.0.0/24` as the value for `AddressPrefix` parameter. This subnet IP range must be part of the overall virtual machine IP addressing scheme. The virtual network is created using `New-AzureRmVirtualNetwork` with `10.0.0.0/16` value as `AddressPrefix` parameter . `AddressPrefix` is the IP range of the network and also subnets together must have IP ranges as subset of this range. This is shown here:

```
$singleSubnet = New-AzureRmVirtualNetworkSubnetConfig -Name
singleSubnet -AddressPrefix 10.0.0.0/24
$vnet = New-AzureRmVirtualNetwork -Name TestNet -ResourceGroupName
$rgName
-Location $locationRG -AddressPrefix 10.0.0.0/16 -Subnet
$singleSubnet
```

7. Create a public IP address and DNS name used to connect to the newly created virtual machine over the Internet. A public IP address is dynamically allocated to the virtual machine using `New-AzureRmPublicIpAddress` cmdlet. This is shown here:

```
$pip = New-AzureRmPublicIpAddress -Name TestPIP -ResourceGroupName
$rgName -Location $locationRG -
AllocationMethod Dynamic -DomainNameLabel $vmName
```

8. Create a network interface card for the virtual machine. This network card is attached to the virtual machine at one end and the virtual network subnet on the other end. `New-AzureRmNetworkInterface` accepts the name, resource group, location, and subnet ID as parameter. This is shown here:

```
$nic = New-AzureRmNetworkInterface -Name TestNIC -ResourceGroupName
$rgName -Location $locationRG
-SubnetId $vnet.Subnets[0].Id -PublicIpAddressId $pip.Id
```

9. Create a credential object using the `Get-Credential` cmdlet. This cmdlet will open a login window accepting the username and password. The provided username and password will be stored in the `$cred` variable. This variable will be used while provisioning the virtual machine. This credential object will be used to create an administrator user within new virtual machine. This is shown here:

```
$cred = Get-Credential -Message "Type the name and password
of the local administrator account."
```

10. Create a new virtual machine configuration object using the `New-AzureRmVMConfig` cmdlet. It accepts the **Virtual Machine** (**VM**) name, size of the VM, and availability set information. We are not using availability sets. `VMName` and the size of the VM are provided as values to the cmdlet and the config object is stored in the `$vm` variable. This is shown here:

```
$vm = New-AzureRmVMConfig -VMName $vmName -VMSize "Standard_A4"
```

11. The next step is to provide operating system configuration to the VM configuration created in the earlier step. The `Set-AzureRmVMOperatingSystem` cmdlet accepts operating system name, credentials for the operating system, and also accepts switches to determine whether it's a Windows or a Linux operating system, whether VM agents must be installed while creating the virtual machine and whether Windows updates should be configured. It is important to note that the previously created `$vm` config object is used as a parameter to this cmdlet. This enables this cmdlet to add operating system information to the config object as shown here:

```
$vm = Set-AzureRmVMOperatingSystem -VM $vm -Windows -ComputerName
$vmName -Credential $cred -ProvisionVMAgent -EnableAutoUpdate
```

12. In this step, Azure image information is provided to the previously created config object. Virtual machines are based on images maintained by Azure. Each virtual machine is based on an image. The `Set-AzureRmVMSourceImage` cmdlet accepts `PublisherName`, `Offer`, and `Sku` as parameters. It is here we provide the information that Windows Server 2016 should be used as our virtual machine operating system. The `Sku` value `2016-Datacenter-with-Containers` will provision a Windows Server 2016 at the time of writing this chapter. This is shown here:

    ```
    $vm = Set-AzureRmVMSourceImage -VM $vm -PublisherName
    MicrosoftWindowsServer
    -Offer WindowsServer -Skus 2016-Datacenter-with-Containers -Version
    "latest"
    ```

13. Add the previously created network interface card to the virtual machine using the `Add-AzureRmVMNetworkInterface` cmdlet that accepts the virtual machine config object and ID of network card. This is shown here:

    ```
    $vm = Add-AzureRmVMNetworkInterface -VM $vm -Id $nic.Id
    ```

14. Add operating system and data disk information to the virtual machine. We will only create the operating system disk in this guide. The first statement creates a complete URL for storing the virtual machine disk file. The location of this disk file is within the storage account we created earlier. Files stored in Azure storage accounts are referred using `https://<<storageaccountname>>.blob.core.windows.net/<<Containe rname>>/<<blobname>>` format.. The expression `$storageAccount.PrimaryEndpoints.Blob.ToString()` provides the domain name for the newly created storage account. The `vhd` is the Container used by default for storing virtual machine **Virtual Hard Disk** (VHD) files. The `Set-AzureRmVMOSDisk` cmdlet accepts the name of the virtual machine, the storage location where the virtual machine disk file should be created, and the source from where the base disk information should be copied. This is shown here:

    ```
    $osDiskUri = $storageAccount.PrimaryEndpoints.Blob.ToString() +
    "vhds/WindowsVMosDisk.vhd"
    $vm = Set-AzureRmVMOSDisk -VM $vm -Name $vmName -VhdUri $osDiskUri
    -CreateOption fromImage
    ```

15. Create the virtual machine using the $vm config object through the New-AzureRmVM cmdlet. This is shown here:

```
New-AzureRmVM -ResourceGroupName $rgName -Location $locationRG
-VM $vm
```

The newly created resource group should now contain all the resources we created, including the virtual machine. This is shown in *Figure 3:*

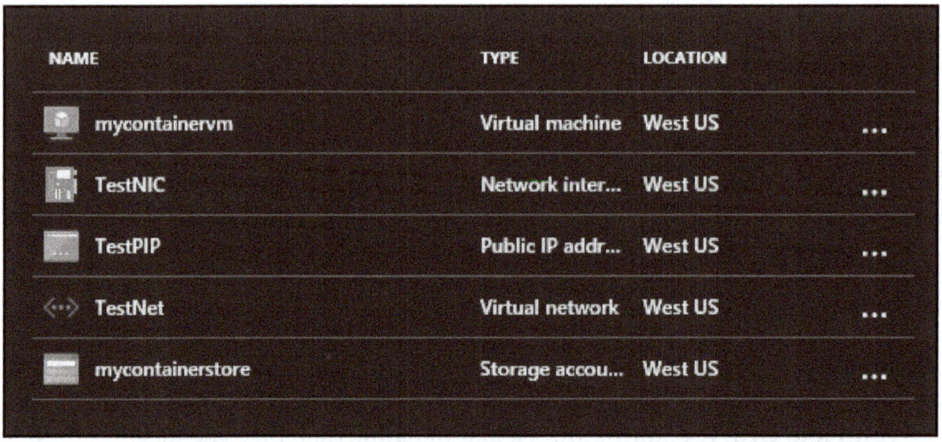

NAME	TYPE	LOCATION	
mycontainervm	Virtual machine	West US	...
TestNIC	Network inter...	West US	...
TestPIP	Public IP addr...	West US	...
TestNet	Virtual network	West US	...
mycontainerstore	Storage accou...	West US	...

Figure 3: Resources in resource group

Connect to the newly created virtual machine and log in to it. All the steps mentioned henceforth should be executed from within the virtual machine.

16. Containers infrastructure can be installed on Windows Server 2016 using the PackageManagement module. Microsoft recently developed a new package provider DockerMsftProvider that will be used for installing Docker and container infrastructure. However, to make DockerMsftProvider provider available on Windows Server 2016, NuGet provider must be available. To install NuGet provider, execute the following PowerShell statement on the server using the PowerShell console:

```
Install-PackageProvider -Name "NuGet" -MinimumVersion 2.8.5.201
-force -ForceBootstrap -Confirm:$false -Verbose
```

17. Now `DockerMsftProvider` can be installed by executing the following PowerShell statement:

```
Install-Module -Name DockerMsftProvider -RequiredVersion "1.0.0.1"
-Force -verbose
-Confirm:$false -SkipPublisherCheck
```

18. Next, using the newly downloaded `DockerMsftProvider` provider, a new package `docker` should be downloaded and installed. This will internally enable the `Container` Windows feature, download the Docker engine and Docker client binaries, install them in the `Program` files folder location, and enable them for usage. This is shown next:

```
Install-Package -Name docker -ProviderName DockerMsftProvider
-Force -ForceBootstrap
-confirm:$false -Verbose
```

Installing Container features requires a restart of the server, which can be done using the following command:

```
Restart-Computer
```

19. After the server reboot, again open the PowerShell ISE. At this moment, the container infrastructure is ready; however, there are no images available on the server using which Containers can be created. To download the `windowsservercore` image, execute the following statement. Please note the image name, it is case-sensitive:

```
docker pull microsoft/windowsservercore
```

20. To search all available images for the Windows environment provided by Microsoft, execute the following command:

    ```
    docker search microsoft
    ```

    The table following shows all images available on public repository having Microsoft within their names:

```
PS C:\> docker search microsoft
NAME                                        DESCRIPTION                                     STARS   OFFICIAL    AUTOMATED
microsoft/sample-django:windowsservercore   Django installed in a Windows Server Core ...   1                   [OK]
microsoft/dotnet35:windowsservercore        .NET 3.5 Runtime installed in a Windows Se...   1       [OK]        [OK]
microsoft/sample-golang:windowsservercore   Go Programming Language installed in a Win...   1                   [OK]
microsoft/sample-httpd:windowsservercore    Apache httpd installed in a Windows Server...   1                   [OK]
microsoft/iis:windowsservercore             Internet Information Services (IIS) instal...   1       [OK]        [OK]
microsoft/sample-mongodb:windowsservercore  MongoDB installed in a Windows Server Core...   1                   [OK]
microsoft/sample-mysql:windowsservercore    MySQL installed in a Windows Server Core b...   1                   [OK]
microsoft/sample-nginx:windowsservercore    Nginx installed in a Windows Server Core b...   1                   [OK]
microsoft/sample-python:windowsservercore   Python installed in a Windows Server Core ...   1                   [OK]
microsoft/sample-rails:windowsservercore    Ruby on Rails installed in a Windows Serve...   1                   [OK]
microsoft/sample-redis:windowsservercore    Redis installed in a Windows Server Core b...   1                   [OK]
microsoft/sample-ruby:windowsservercore     Ruby installed in a Windows Server Core ba...   1                   [OK]
microsoft/sample-sqlite:windowsservercore   SQLite installed in a Windows Server Core ...   1                   [OK]
microsoft/sample-golang:nanoserver          Go Programming Language installed in a Nan...   1                   [OK]
microsoft/sample-httpd:nanoserver           Apache httpd installed in a Nano Server ba...   1                   [OK]
microsoft/sample-mysql:nanoserver           MySQL installed in a Nano Server based con...   1                   [OK]
microsoft/sample-nginx:nanoserver           Nginx installed in a Nano Server based con...   1                   [OK]
microsoft/sample-node:nanoserver            Node installed in a Nano Server based cont...   1                   [OK]
microsoft/sample-python:nanoserver          Python installed in a Nano Server based co...   1
microsoft/sample-rails:nanoserver           Ruby on Rails installed in a Nano Server b...   1                   [OK]
microsoft/sample-redis:nanoserver           Redis installed in a Nano Server based con...   1                   [OK]
microsoft/sample-ruby:nanoserver            Ruby installed in a Nano Server based cont...   1                   [OK]
```

Figure 4: Search results from the Docker search command

21. To verify the Container environment, execute the `docker` command as shown here:

    ```
    docker --version
    ```

    This should show the current version and build of the Docker engine as shown here:

    ```
    PS C:> docker --version
    Docker version 1.12.2-cs2-ws-beta, build 050b611
    ```

    Execute the following command to check whether there are any Containers available. `ps` refers to the listing of Containers. The `-a` switch denotes all Containers in any state (stopped, running, paused):

    ```
    docker ps -a
    ```

Since we have not created any Containers, the results should show an empty list as shown here:

```
docker ps -a
CONTAINER ID    IMAGE    COMMAND    CREATED    STATUS    PORTS    NAMES
```

Finally, execute the command shown here to check whether there are any images available:

```
docker images
```

Since we have downloaded a single image, the result should show an empty image list as shown here:

```
REPOSITORY TAG IMAGE ID CREATED SIZE
microsoft/windowsservercore latest 7baaa272ad7d 3 weeks ago 9.42 GB
```

22. To create and start a container, execute the following command. It runs a container in daemon mode and also maps port `8080` on `docker` host with port `80` on the Container.

```
docker run -d -p 8080:80 microsoft/windowsservercore ping
-t localhost
```

23. We have already seen that Containers are created from images and every image has a base image on which it is based. Microsoft has provided two base images for Containers.

- **WindowsServerCore**: This image should be used for creating Windows Server Core based Containers. It does not have any GUI but still has full-blown Windows features for deploying any enterprise-scale application.
- **NanoServer**: This image should be used to create Containers on Nano Server virtual machines or Hyper-V Containers on any Windows server.

Installing Windows Nano Server on Azure

Similar to Windows Server 2016, there are multiple ways to install and create a Nano Server environment on Azure. Nano Server can be provisioned on Azure through pure PowerShell scripting or through ARM templates. The ARM templates can be deployed through PowerShell. The Windows Server Container environment was provisioned through PowerShell. We will use ARM templates to deploy Nano Server on Azure. The template will remain almost the same as the one used to create a Windows Server 2016 environment with small differences. I will point out these differences as we go along in this section. Nano Server is a new technology on the Windows platform and is introduced with Windows Server 2016. At the time of writing, there are not many features available on Nano Servers since it is an evolving technology with newer features getting introduced frequently. We will describe step by step the process to create a Nano Server and you will be able to create them using the same steps when Nano Server is released and feature-rich. Nano Server does not have a GUI and can be only managed remotely.

A valid asymmetric certificate should be deployed in Nano Server to securely access it from remote machines. Certificates are not created by default within an Azure virtual machine when provisioned through ARM. We will use **Azure Key Vault** for storing our certificate. The certificate will be generated on a local machine and uploaded to Key Vault, and the ARM template will have elements to connect, access, and deploy a certificate in Nano Server.

Provisioning Nano Server

Nano Servers are lightweight operating systems and their creation steps are similar to those of virtual machines. For creating a Nano Server on Azure using the Azure Resource Manager template, follow these steps:

1. Open any PowerShell ISE editor as an administrator and log in to the Azure subscription as shown here. This step of connecting to an Azure subscription is the same as when the Windows Server 2016 Container environment was created:

   ```
   Login-AzureRmAccount
   ```

2. Select an appropriate Azure subscription:

   ```
   Set-AzureRmContext -SubscriptionName <<xxxxxxxx>>
   ```

3. Declare variables to hold names for the resource group and Azure location. Create a new resource group using `New-AzureRmResourceGroup` and passing the resource group and location name as arguments:

```
$locationRG = "westeurope"
$rgName = "NaNoServerRG"
New-AzureRmResourceGroup -Name $rgName -Location $locationRG
```

4. Since this section shows the steps to create a Nano Server, a self-signed certificate is used. In an actual scenario and environment, a valid certificate should be purchased and deployed instead of using a self-signed certificate. Create a self-signed wildcard certificate using the `New-SelfSignedCertificate` cmdlet as shown here. A certificate has a subject name that represents the certificate. It must be same as that of our Nano Server or a wildcard name that can be used for multiple subjects. We will create `TestNanoServer` in the West Europe region and Azure will generate the DNS name as `TestNanoServer.westeurope.cloudapp.azure.com` for our Nano Server. The certificate is stored in the local machine certificate store of the machine running this command and can be used for any virtual machine in the West Europe region:

```
New-SelfSignedCertificate -DnsName *.westeurope.cloudapp.azure.com
-CertStoreLocation
Cert:LocalMachineMy
```

Export the certificate from the local store and save it on the local filesystem as a `.pfx` file. A `.pfx` file contains the certificate's private key and is secured using a password. This is shown in *Figure 5*:

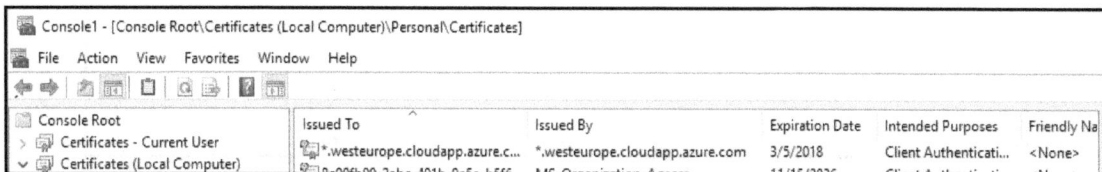

Figure 5: Certificate in local computer personal store

Right-click on ***.westeurope.cloudapp.azure.com | Certificate | All Tasks** and then**Export**. It will open a wizard to export the certificate as a `.pfx` file. This is shown in *Figure 6*:

Figure 6: Certificate Export Wizard start screen

Click the **Next** button as shown in *Figure 6*.

Select the **Yes, export the private key** option in the **Export Private Key** screen as shown in *Figure 7*:

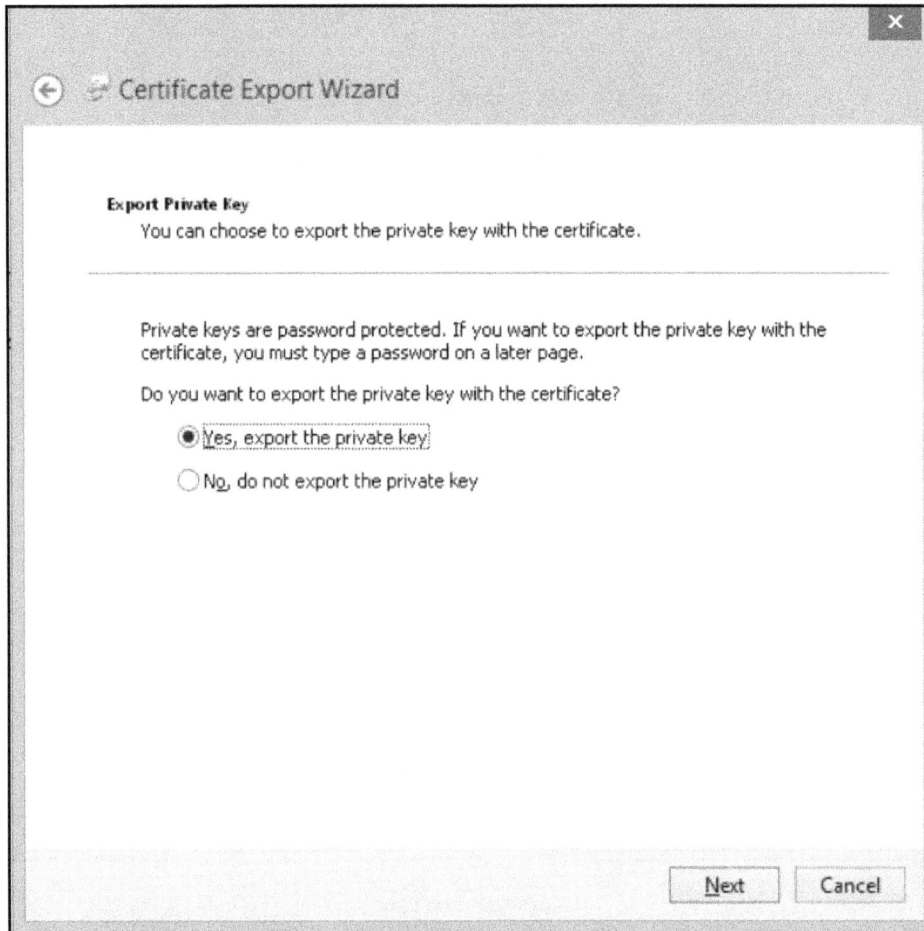

Figure 7: Export certificate with private key

Leave the default values in this screen as is and click **Next** as shown in *Figure 8:*

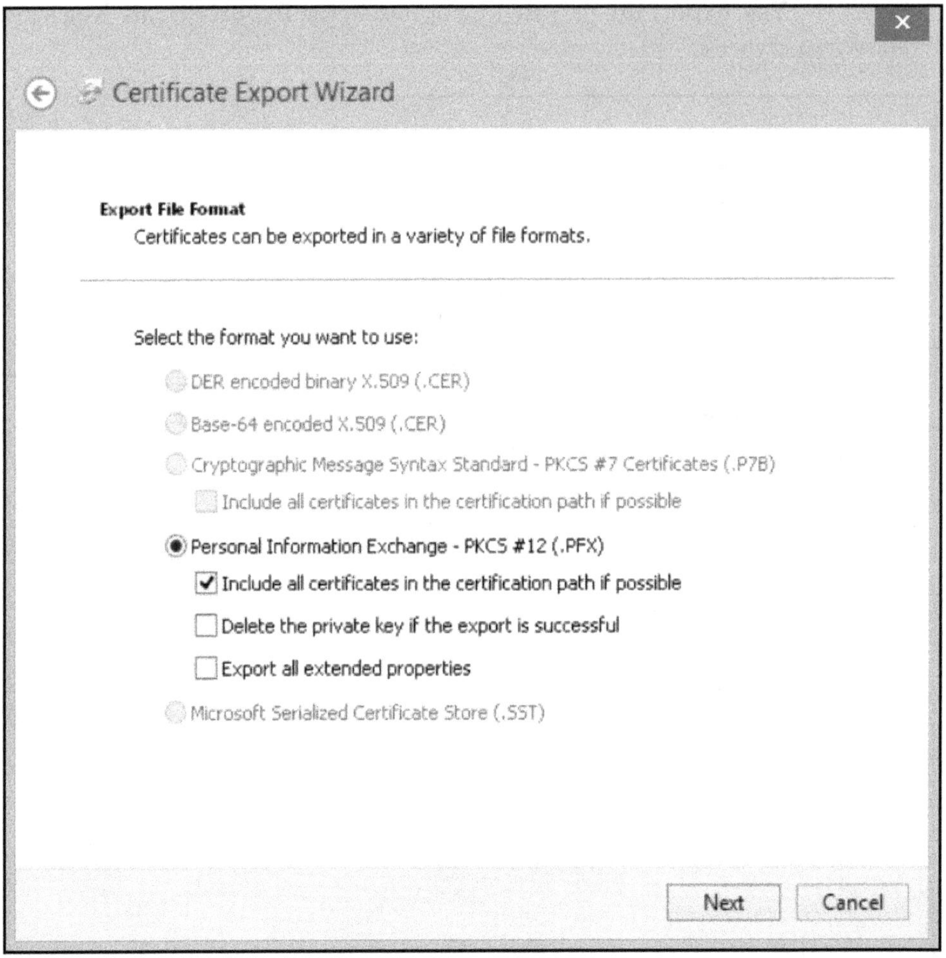

Figure 8: Certificate file format

Select the **Password** checkbox and provide both password and confirm password values as shown in *Figure 9*. This password will be needed when storing the certificate in Azure Key Vault. Click **Next** to move further:

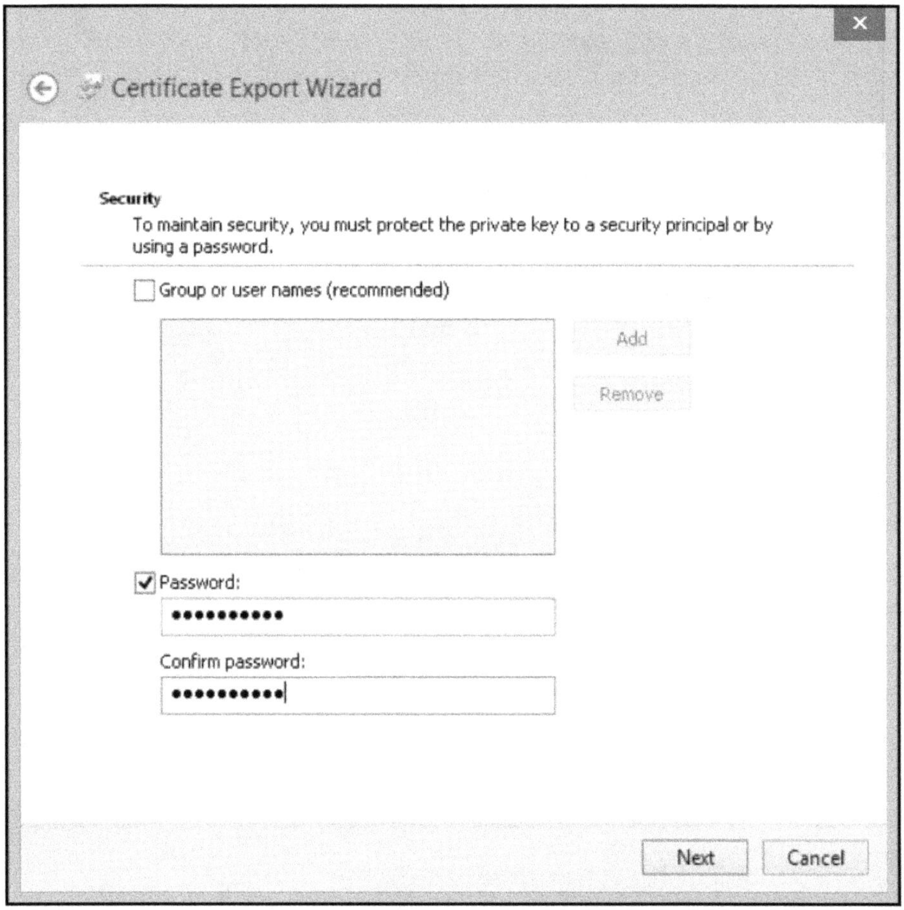

Figure 9: Certificate password

Provide the file location for storing the exported certificate as shown in *Figure 10*. Clicking **Next** should provide the message that the export was successful.

Figure 10: Export file path for certificate

5. Create a new Azure Key Vault in the selected subscription using the `New-AzureRmKeyVault` cmdlet as shown here. `NanoSecrets` is the name of the vault and this vault can be used within the template as well as PowerShell deployments. Vaults come in two flavors:
    - Standard
    - Premium

```
New-AzureRmKeyVault -VaultName NanoSecrets
                    -ResourceGroupName $rgName
                    -Location $locationRG
                    -EnabledForTemplateDeployment
                    -EnabledForDeployment
                    -Sku standard
```

6. Load the contents of `nanocert.pfx` and convert it into `base64` encoding as shown here:

```
$certFile = "C:nanocert.pfx"
$certContent = get-content $certFile -Encoding Byte
$encodedCertContent =
[System.Convert]::ToBase64String($certContent)
```

7. Create a JSON object containing the encoded certificate content, the type of content and password that was provided while exporting the certificate. Azure Key Vault expects these details in JSON format. This is shown here. `jsonObject` is assigned a multiline string containing name value pairs:

```
$jsonObject = @"
{
"data": "$encodedCertContent",
"dataType" :"pfx",
"password": "<<Your password>>"
}
"@
```

8. Convert the `jsonObject` to byte encoding and then convert the bytes into `Base64` encoding. This is shown here:

```
$jsonObjectBytes =
[System.Text.Encoding]::UTF8.GetBytes($jsonObject)
$jsonEncoded =
[System.Convert]::ToBase64String($jsonObjectBytes)
```

9. Convert the `Base64.JSON` object into a secure string using the `ConvertTo-SecureString` cmdlet. This secure string is stored in Azure Key Vault as a secret using the `Set-AzureRmKeyVaultSecret` cmdlet. Now this certificate can be used in ARM templates while provisioning a Nano Server in the West Europe region. A name is provided to the secret for identification. It has been named as `NanoCert`. This is shown here:

```
$secret = ConvertTo-SecureString -String $jsonEncoded -AsPlainText
-Force
Set-AzureKeyVaultSecret -VaultName "NanoSecrets" -Name "NanoCert"
-SecretValue $secret
```

This cmdlet will output the unique URL for accessing the certificate. Take note of this URL as it will be needed while authoring the ARM template.

10. Open Visual Studio 2015 and select **New Project**. From the resultant window, select the **AzureResourceGroup** template from the **Cloud** template. Provide a name and location for the project (`C:templates` in my computer) and select **Blank Template**. This will generate an empty template named `azuredeploy.json`, which is shown in *Figure 11*:

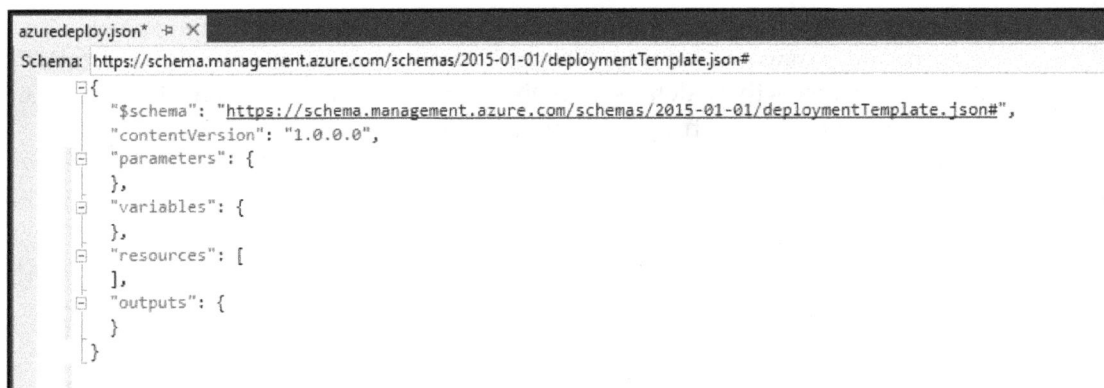

```
azuredeploy.json*
Schema: https://schema.management.azure.com/schemas/2015-01-01/deploymentTemplate.json#
{
    "$schema": "https://schema.management.azure.com/schemas/2015-01-01/deploymentTemplate.json#",
    "contentVersion": "1.0.0.0",
    "parameters": {
    },
    "variables": {
    },
    "resources": [
    ],
    "outputs": {
    }
}
```

Figure 11: Blank ARM template in visual studio 2015

11. We will modify this file and it will eventually be used to create a Nano Server on Azure.

12. The `parameters` section should look as shown here:

```
"parameters": {
        "adminUsername": {
            "type": "string",
```

```
                    "defaultValue": "<<your nano server username>>",
                    "minLength": 1,
                    "metadata": {
                        "description": "Username for the Nano Server."
                    }
                },
                "adminPassword": {
                    "type": "securestring",
                    "defaultValue": "<<your nano server password>>",
                    "metadata": {
                        "description": "Password for the Nano Server."
                    }
                },
                "dnsNameForPublicIP": {
                    "type": "string",
                    "minLength": 1,
                    "defaultValue": "nanoserver123",
                    "metadata": {
                        "description": "Globally unique DNS Name for the
                        Public IP used to access the Nano Server."
                    }
                },
                "windowsOSVersion": {
                    "type": "string",
                    "defaultValue": "2016-Nano-Server",
                    "allowedValues": [
                        "2016-Nano-Server"
                    ],
                    "metadata": {
                        "description": "The Windows version for the VM.
                        This will pick  Nano Server by default.
                        Allowed values: 2016-Nano-Server."
                    }
                }
        },
```

Four parameters are added to the parameters section of the template. The first parameter refers to the `username` for the Nano Server, the second one refers to the `password` for the Nano Server. The `password` cannot be more than 20 characters long, end with a period(.), or contain the following characters: / " [ ] : | < > + = ; , ? * @. The default values for both `username` and `password` must be changed before using the template. These two are used for authenticating and connecting to the Nano Server. This server will be available and accessed from the Internet. It is good practice to provide a DNS name through which this server can be addressed globally. It should be uniquely named in an Azure region. The OS version `2016-Nano-Server-Technical-Preview` is the `sku` that creates a Nano Server virtual machine on Azure. This name changes in future and so it must be checked before using it.

It is to be noted that by changing the value of this variable, it is possible to provision a Windows Server 2016 instead of a Nano Server. The `Windows-Server-Technical-Preview` should be used instead of the `2016-Nano-Server-Technical-Preview`. These names will undergo changes when they are generally available to everyone.

13. The `variables` section should look as shown here:

```
"variables": {
        "imagePublisher": "MicrosoftWindowsServer",
        "imageOffer": "WindowsServer",
        "OSDiskName": "osdiskforwindowssimple",
        "nicName": "myVMNic",
        "addressPrefix": "10.0.0.0/16",
        "subnetName": "Subnet",
        "subnetPrefix": "10.0.0.0/24",
        "vhdStorageType": "Standard_LRS",
        "publicIPAddressName": "myPublicIP",
        "publicIPAddressType": "Static",
        "vhdStorageContainerName": "vhds",
        "vmName": "MyNanoVM",
        "vmSize": "Standard_A4",
        "virtualNetworkName": "MyVNET",
        "vnetId": "[resourceId('Microsoft.Network/virtualNetworks',
        variables('virtualNetworkName'))]",
        "subnetRef": "[concat(variables('vnetId'), '/subnets/',
        variables('subnetName'))]",
        "vhdStorageName": "[concat('vhdstorage',
        uniqueString(resourceGroup().id))]"
    },
```

The following table provides description for each of these variables:

Variable name	Description
imagePublisher	The publisher of the Nano Server image.
imageOffer	The offer for the Nano Server image.
vhdStorageName	The name of the storage account for hosting Container and vhd files as blobs.
vhdStorageContainerName	Name of the Container in the storage account for storing the Nano Server vhd file.
vhdStorageType	Storage is of multiple types – Local redundant, Zone redundant, Geo redundant and Read-access Geo redundant.
virtualNetworkName	The name of the virtual network creating for hosting the Nano Server.
subnetName	The subnet name on which the Nano Server is created. Subnets are part of the virtual network.
addressPrefix	The address range for the virtual network divided into multiple subnets.
subnetPrefix	Address range that is a subset of the virtual network address range.
vnetId	The ID of the virtual network used for referencing it in the template. Declaring it as a variable makes cleaner templates and it can be used at multiple places.
subnetRef	The ID of the virtual network subnet for referencing it in the template. Declaring it as a variable makes cleaner templates and it can be used at multiple places.
publicIPAddressName	The name of the public IP resource declared in the resources section.
publicIPAddressType	Static or dynamic public IP address.
VMName	The name of the Nano Server.
VMSize	The size of the Nano Server.
nickname	The name of the network interface card attached to the Nano Server.
OSDiskName	The name of the Nano Server vhd file.

14. After defining parameters and variables, now let's focus on adding resources. Add the `StorageAccount` resource from `Microsoft.Storage` provider namespace as shown here:

```
{
    "type": "Microsoft.Storage/storageAccounts",
    "name": "[variables('vhdStorageName')]",
    "apiVersion": "2015-06-15",
    "location": "[resourceGroup().location]",
    "tags": {
        "displayName": "StorageAccount"
    },
    "properties": {
        "accountType": "[variables('vhdStorageType')]"
    }
},
```

The following table provides description for each of these properties:

Resource property name	Description
type	The resource `type` from the provider namespace based on which the resource instance is created. The resource provider is `Microsoft.Storage` and the resource type is `storageAccounts`.
name	The name of the resource instance.
apiVersion	The version of the provider REST API.
location	Location of the provisioned resource instance. The location is obtained through the `location` property returned by the `resourceGroup()` function that returns its current location.
tags	The `displayName` tag added. More tags can be added based on multiple criteria, as discussed in Chapter 3, *DevOps Automation Primer*.
properties: accountType:	This is a storage account specific property. The type of storage account type is defined in the variable section.

15. Add the `publicIPAddresses` resource from the `Microsoft.Network` provider namespace as shown here:

```
{
    "type": "Microsoft.Network/publicIPAddresses",
    "name": "[variables('publicIPAddressName')]",
    "apiVersion": "2015-06-15",
    "location": "[resourceGroup().location]",
    "tags": {
        "displayName": "PublicIPAddress"
    },
    "properties": {
        "publicIPAllocationMethod":
                "[variables('publicIPAddressType')]",
        "dnsSettings": {
            "domainNameLabel":
                "[parameters('dnsNameForPublicIP')]"
        }
    }
},
```

The following table provides description for each of these properties:

Resource property name	Description
type	The resource provider is `Microsoft.Network` and resource type is `publicIPAddresses`.
name	The name of the resource instance.
apiVersion	The version of the provider REST API.
location	Location of the provisioned resource instance. The location is obtained through the `location` property returned by the `resourceGroup()` function that returns its current location.
tags	The `displayName` tag added. More tags can be added based on multiple criteria, as discussed in `Chapter 3`, *DevOps Automation Primer*.
publicIPAllocationMethod	This is a public IP address specific property. The allocation of a public IP address is static as defined in the variables section.
domainNameLabel	This is a resource specific property, part of the `dnsSettings` property. Its value is derived from parameters provided by the user. If the user does not provide a value, a default value is used.

16. Add the `networkSecurityGroups` resource from the `Microsoft.Network` provider namespace as shown here. A **Network Security Group** (**NSG**) containing three inbound rules is added in the template. The NSG rules open the **Remote Desktop Protocol** (**RDP**) port (3389), **Remote PowerShell** port (5985), and **Secure Remote PowerShell** port (5986). This NGS will be applied to all virtual machines and Nano Servers hosted on the virtual network subnet created in this template later:

```
{
        "type": "Microsoft.Network/networkSecurityGroups",
        "name": "[concat(variables('vmName'),'_nsg1')]",
        "apiVersion": "2015-05-01-preview",
        "location": "[resourceGroup().location]",
        "properties": {
            "securityRules": [
                {
                    "name": "RDP",
                    "properties": {
                        "description": "RDP",
                        "protocol": "Tcp",
                        "sourcePortRange": "*",
                        "destinationPortRange": "3389",
                        "sourceAddressPrefix": "*",
                        "destinationAddressPrefix": "*",
                        "access": "Allow",
                        "priority": 200,
                        "direction": "Inbound"
                    }
                },
                {
                    "name": "WinRM",
                    "properties": {
                        "description": "WinRM",
                        "protocol": "Tcp",
                        "sourcePortRange": "*",
                        "destinationPortRange": "5985",
                        "sourceAddressPrefix": "*",
                        "destinationAddressPrefix": "*",
                        "access": "Allow",
                        "priority": 400,
                        "direction": "Inbound"
                    }
                },
                {
                    "name": "WinRMs",
                    "properties": {
                        "description": "WinRMs",
```

```
                          "protocol": "Tcp",
                          "sourcePortRange": "*",
                          "destinationPortRange": "5986",
                          "sourceAddressPrefix": "*",
                          "destinationAddressPrefix": "*",
                          "access": "Allow",
                          "priority": 500,
                          "direction": "Inbound"
                      }
                  }
              ]
          }
      },
```

The following table provides description for each of these properties:

Resource property name	Description
type	The resource provider is Microsoft.Network and resource type is networkSecurityGroups.
name	The name of the resource instance. The name is defined as a combination of vmname defined in variables and _nsg.
apiVersion	The version of the provider REST API.
location	Location of the provisioned resource instance. The location is obtained through the location property returned by the resourceGroup() function that returns its current location.
Properties -> securityRules	This is an array type resource specific property that defines multiple NSG rules objects. Three rules are defined in this example. Each rule has a name and rule specific properties.
Properties -> securityRules -> properties	Each NSG rule object contains its name, description, protocol(tcp), sourcePortRange (* denotes from any source port), desintationPortRange (3389, 5985, 5986), sourceAddressPrefix (* denotes from any source IP address), destinationAddressPrefix (* denotes to any destination IP address), access is allowed, each rule having a distinct priority and direction is Inbound.

17. Add the `virtualNetworks` resource from the `Microsoft.Network` provider namespace as shown here:

```
{
    "type": "Microsoft.Network/virtualNetworks",
    "name": "[variables('virtualNetworkName')]",
    "apiVersion": "2015-06-15",
    "location": "[resourceGroup().location]",
    "dependsOn": [
    "[concat('Microsoft.Network/
     networkSecurityGroups/',
concat(variables('vmName'),'_nsg1'))]"
    ],
    "tags": {
        "displayName": "VirtualNetwork"
    },
    "properties": {
        "addressSpace": {
            "addressPrefixes": [
                "[variables('addressPrefix')]"
            ]
        },
        "subnets": [
            {
                "name": "[variables('subnetName')]",
                "properties": {
                    "addressPrefix":
                    "[variables('subnetPrefix')]",
                    "networkSecurityGroup": {
                        "id":
                        "[resourceId('Microsoft.Network/
                        networkSecurityGroups',
concat(variables('vmName'),'_nsg1'))]"
                    }
                }
            }
        ]
    }
},
```

The following table provides description for each of these properties:

Resource property name	Description
type	The resource provider is Microsoft.Network and resource type is virtualNetworks.

name	The name of the resource instance.
apiVersion	The version of the provider REST API.
location	Location of the provisioned resource instance. The location is obtained through the location property returned by the resourceGroup() function that returns its current location.
dependsOn	It contains the name of the resource this resource is dependent on. The current resource will start provisioning only after the dependent resources are successfully provisioned. VirtualNetwork is dependent on the networkSecurityGroup resource defined earlier. Resources can be referred to other resources defined within the same template using their provider name combined with resource type and resource instance name.
tags	The displayName tag added. More tags can be added based on multiple criteria, as discussed in Chapter 3, *DevOps Automation Primer*.
Properties -> addressSpace -> addressPrefixes	This is a virtual network specific property. This is an array that can contain multiple address prefixes. In this example, a single addressPrefix is defined referred from the variables section.
Properties -> subnets	This is an array type resource specific property that defines multiple subnet objects for a virtual network. We have defined just one subnet. The subnet object contains its name, addressPrefix, that gets its value from the variables section and reference to the NSG created earlier. Resources can be referred to other resources defined within the same template using the resourceId function that accepts the target resource provider name, resource type, and resource instance name.

18. Add the networkInterface resource from the Microsoft.Network provider namespace as shown here:

```
{
    "type": "Microsoft.Network/networkInterfaces",
    "name": "[variables('nicName')]",
    "apiVersion": "2015-06-15",
    "location": "[resourceGroup().location]",
    "tags": {
        "displayName": "NetworkInterface"
    },
```

```
"dependsOn": [
    "[concat('Microsoft.Network/publicIPAddresses/',
    variables('publicIPAddressName'))]",
    "[concat('Microsoft.Network/virtualNetworks/',
    variables('virtualNetworkName'))]"
],
"properties": {
    "ipConfigurations": [
        {
            "name": "ipconfig1",
            "properties": {
                "privateIPAllocationMethod": "Static",
                "PrivateIpAddress": "10.0.0.4",
                "publicIPAddress": {
                    "id":
                    "[resourceId('Microsoft.Network/
                    publicIPAddresses',
                    variables('publicIPAddressName'))]"
                },
                "subnet": {
                    "id": "[variables('subnetRef')]"
                }
            }
        }
    ]
},
},
```

The following table provides description for each of these properties:

Resource property name	Description
type	The resource provider is `Microsoft.Network` and resource type is `networkInterfaces`.
name	The name of the resource instance. The name is defined in the variables (`nicName`).
apiVersion	The version of the provider REST API.
location	Location of the provisioned resource instance. The location is obtained through the `location` property returned by the `resourceGroup()` function that returns its current location.

dependsOn	It contains the name of the resource this resource is dependent on. The `NetworkInterface` resource is dependent on both public IP address and virtual network. The current resource will start provisioning only after the dependent resources are successfully provisioned.
tags	The `displayName` tag added. More tags can be added based on multiple criteria as discussed in `Chapter 3`, *DevOps Automation Primer*.
Properties -> ipConfigurations	This is an array type resource specific property that defines multiple IP configurations. Each network interface can have multiple IP configurations assigned. In this example, a single IP configuration is provisioned. Each IP configuration has a name property.
Properties -> ipConfigurations -> properties	Each IP configuration object contains its name, `privateIPAllocationMethod` (static internal IP is assigned to Nano Server), `PrivateIPAddress` (`10.0.0.4` is assigned to Nano Server), `PublicIPAddress` (refers to the `PublicIPAddress` resource created in earlier step) and `subnet` (refers to `subnet` in virtual network on which Nano Server will be hosted).

19. Add the `virtualMachines` resource from the `Microsoft.Compute` provider namespace as shown here:

```
{
    "type": "Microsoft.Compute/virtualMachines",
    "name": "[variables('vmName')]",
    "apiVersion": "2015-06-15",
    "location": "[resourceGroup().location]",
    "tags": {
        "displayName": "VirtualMachine"
    },
    "dependsOn": [
        "[concat('Microsoft.Storage/storageAccounts/',
        variables('vhdStorageName'))]",
        "[concat('Microsoft.Network/networkInterfaces/',
        variables('nicName'))]"
    ],
    "properties": {
        "hardwareProfile": {
            "vmSize": "[variables('vmSize')]"
        },
        "osProfile": {
```

```json
            "secrets": [
                {
                    "sourceVault": { "id": "/subscriptions/
                    xxxxxxxx-xxxx-xxxx-xxxx-xxxxxxxxxxxx/
                    resourceGroups/NaNoServerRG/
                    providers/Microsoft.KeyVault/
                    vaults/nanoSecrets" },
                    "vaultCertificates": [
                        {
                            "certificateUrl":
                            "https://nanoSecrets.vault.
                            azure.net:443/
                            secrets/NanoCert/
                            xxxxxxxxxxxxxxxx
                            xxxxxxxxxxxxxxxx",
                            "certificateStore": "My"
                        }
                    ]
                }
            ],
            "computerName": "[variables('vmName')]",
            "adminUsername":
                "[parameters('adminUsername')]",
            "adminPassword":
                "[parameters('adminPassword')]",
            "windowsConfiguration": {
                "provisionVMAgent": true,
                "enableAutomaticUpdates": true,
                "winRM": {
                    "listeners": [
                        {
                            "protocol": "Https",
                            "certificateUrl":
                            "https://nanoSecrets.vault.
                            azure.net:443/
                            secrets/NanoCert/
                            xxxxxxxxxxxxxxxxxx
                            xxxxxxxxxxxxxx"
                        }
                    ]
                }
            }
        },
        "storageProfile": {
            "imageReference": {
                "publisher":
                "[variables('imagePublisher')]",
                "offer": "[variables('imageOffer')]",
```

```
                    "sku": "[parameters('windowsOSVersion')]",
                    "version": "latest"
                },
                "osDisk": {
                    "name": "osdisk",
                    "vhd": {
                        "uri": "[concat('http://',
                        variables('vhdStorageName'),
                        '.blob.core.windows.net/',
                        variables('vhdStorageContainerName'),
                        '/', variables('OSDiskName'),
                        '.vhd')]"
                    },
                    "caching": "ReadWrite",
                    "createOption": "FromImage"
                }
            },
            "networkProfile": {
                "networkInterfaces": [
                    {
                        "id":
                        "[resourceId('Microsoft.Network/
                        networkInterfaces',
                        variables('nicName'))]"
                    }
                ]
            }
        }
    }
```

The following table provides description for each of these properties:

Resource property name	Description
type	The resource provider is Microsoft.Compute and resource type is virtualMachines.
name	The name of the resource instance. The name is defined in variables (vmName).
apiVersion	The version of the Microsoft.Compute provider REST API.
location	Location of provisioned resource instance. The location is obtained through the location property returned by the resourceGroup() function that returns its current location.

dependsOn	It contains the name of the resource this resource is dependent on. The virtual machine resource is dependent on both storage account and virtual network. The current resource will start provisioning only after the dependent resources are successfully provisioned.
tags	The displayName tag added. More tags can be added based on multiple criteria, as discussed in Chapter 3, *DevOps Automation Primer*.
hardwareProfile	It contains the vmSize property and determines the physical resource of the Nano Server in terms of number of CPUs and RAM. It gets its value from vmSize variable.
osProfile	There are five important properties in the osProfiles element. • Secrets: It contains the reference to secrets available in Azure Key Vault. It is necessary that we define secret references here for it to be used in subsequent sections in the template. It contains a reference to the Azure Key Vault created earlier using PowerShell and certificate URL uploaded to the same Key Vault. Values must be replaced for only subscription id in the template if all the steps are followed as shown in this section. The value for certificateURL is available from the output of *Step 9* after executing the Set-AzureKeyVaultSecret. • computerName: It refers to the name of the operating system in the Nano Server. It is this name the Nano Server will be referred by. It gets its value from the vmName variable. • Username for the Nano Server: The value is obtained from the adminUsername parameter. • Password for Nano Server: The value is obtained from the adminPassword parameter. • WindowsConfiguration: It configures the operating system with additional configuration. These include WinRM listener settings to use https and certificates. The certificate is downloaded from Azure Key Vault. It also provides configuration options to provision the virtual machine agent and options to enable Windows update after provisioning of the virtual machine. The Nano Server will have both the VM agent enabled and Windows update set as automatic. The value for the certificateURL is available from the output of step 9 after executing Set-AzureKeyVaultSecret.

Properties -> `storageProfile`	Storage profile deals with the source image used to create the virtual machine and storage location for storing the new operating system and data disks created for the virtual machine. The image reference includes the publisher name, offer name, and SKU details. There is no data disk for the Nano Server in this example. It has an operating system disk that is needed to host the operating system. The storage details are in the form `https://<<storage account name>>.blob.core.windows.net/<<Container name>>/<<blob name>>`. These values are obtained from variables.
Properties -> `networkProfile`	Network profile references the network interface card that should be attached to the virtual machine.

20. By this time, the Azure resource group, the ARM template, as well as the Key Vault have been constructed. The Key Vault also contains the certificate that will be deployed within the Nano Server and used for accessing it from a client. In this step, the ARM template will be deployed to provision all resources in the ARM template including the Nano Server. This first cmdlet `Test-AzureRmResourceGroupDeployment` validates the syntax and correctness of the template, and the second cmdlet `New- AzureRmResourceGroupDeployment` deploys the resource in the resource group. These concepts were covered in `Chapter 3`, *DevOps Automation Primer* and should be revisited as a reference:

```
Test-AzureRmResourceGroupDeployment -ResourceGroupName $rgName
-Mode Incremental
-TemplateFile "C:templatesazuredeploy.json" -Verbose
New-AzureRmResourceGroupDeployment -Name "Deployment1"
-ResourceGroupName $rgName -Mode
Incremental -TemplateFile "C:templatesazuredeploy.json" -Verbose
```

The path of the Azure resource manager template is `C:templates` in my development environment and it could be different in the reader's environment.

21. There is no user interface in a Nano Server and it should be administered remotely. PowerShell remoting should be used for accessing Nano Servers. The following code helps in connecting to the Nano Server from a remote machine.

The first two lines of code declare variables to store the public IP address of the Nano Server and secure PowerShell remoting port:

```
$hostName= "<<public ip address of nano server>>"
$winrmPort = "5986"
```

The next three lines of code declare the username for connecting to the Nano Server, converting it to a secure string, and constructing a `PSCredential` object using them. This credential object is used for authenticating with the Nano Server using PowerShell remoting:

```
$username = "<<provide your nano server username>>"
$pass = ConvertTo-SecureString -string "<<provide your nano server
password>>"
-AsPlainText -Force
$cred = New-Object -typename
System.Management.Automation.PSCredential
-argumentlist $username, $pass
```

Though optional when using a certificate from a known certificate authority, the next line of code is mandatory when using a self-signed certificate. It configures the PowerShell remoting session configuration for not checking certificate authority, common name, and revocation list:

```
$soptions = New-PSSessionOption -SkipCACheck -SkipCNCheck
-SkipRevocationCheck
```

The next line of code uses an interactive PowerShell remoting session to connect to the Nano Server using its public IP address on port 5986, credentials, and session configuration. It also uses the `UseSSL` switch to ensure that the certificate is used for the exchange of information. If this command executes successfully, you should be able to see a prompt that refers to a remote shell on the Nano Server:

```
Enter-PSSession -ComputerName $hostName -Credential $cred -port
$winrmPort -SessionOption $soptions -UseSSL
```

Using Docker client

Now that we have provisioned virtual machines and ensured that Docker infrastructure is available on them, it's time to focus on the `myContainervm` machine a Windows Server 2016 with Container on Azure that was provisioned using PowerShell. Docker client is used for interacting with Docker daemon by sending commands and arguments. Docker client is used for all Container, image, and network related operations.

Executing the `docker` command on the `cmd` command line or `PowerShell.exe` will show all Docker commands. This is shown here:

```
PS C:> docker
Usage: docker [OPTIONS] COMMAND [arg...]
       docker [ --help | -v | --version ]
A self-sufficient runtime for Containers.
Options:
  --config=%USERPROFILE%.docker              Location of client config
                                             file
 -D, --debug                                 Enable debug mode
 -H, --host=[]                               Daemon socket(s) to
                                             connect to
 -h, --help                                  Print usage
 -1, --log-level=info                        Set the logging level
 --tls                                       Use TLS; implied by
                                             --tlsverif
 --tlscacert=%USERPROFILE%.dockerca.pem      Trust certs signed only
                                             by thi
 --tlscert=%USERPROFILE%.dockercert.pem      Path to TLS certificate
                                             file
 --tlskey=%USERPROFILE%.dockerkey.pem        Path to TLS key file
 --tlsverify                                 Use TLS and verify the
                                             remote
 -v, --version                               Print version information
                                             and quit
Commands:
    attach    Attach to a running Container
    build     Build an image from a Dockerfile
    commit    Create a new image from a Container's changes
    cp        Copy files/folders between a Container and the local
              filesystem
    create    Create a new Container
    diff      Inspect changes on a Container's filesystem
    events    Get real time events from the server
    exec      Run a command in a running Container
    export    Export a Container's filesystem as a tar archive
    history   Show the history of an image
    images    List images
    import    Import the contents from a tarball to create a
              filesystem image
    info      Display system-wide information
    inspect   Return low-level information on a Container or image
    kill      Kill a running Container
    load      Load an image from a tar archive or STDIN
    login     Log in to a Docker registry
    logout    Log out from a Docker registry
    logs      Fetch the logs of a Container
```

```
        network   Manage Docker networks
        pause     Pause all processes within a Container
        port      List port mappings or a specific mapping for the
                  CONTAINER
        ps        List Containers
        pull      Pull an image or a repository from a registry
        push      Push an image or a repository to a registry
        rename    Rename a Container
        restart   Restart a Container
        rm        Remove one or more Containers
        rmi       Remove one or more images
        run       Run a command in a new Container
        save      Save one or more images to a tar archive
        search    Search the Docker Hub for images
        start     Start one or more stopped Containers
        stats     Display a live stream of Container(s) resource usage
                  statistics
        stop      Stop a running Container
        tag       Tag an image into a repository
        top       Display the running processes of a Container
        unpause   Unpause all processes within a Container
        update    Update configuration of one or more Containers
        version   Show the Docker version information
        volume    Manage Docker volumes
        wait      Block until a Container stops, then print its exit code
    Run 'docker COMMAND --help' for more information on a command.
    PS C:>
```

Docker commands can broadly be classified into the following categories:

- Container life cycle management
- Image management
- Monitoring commands
- Docker registry management

This chapter will delve into some of the important commands in each of these categories.

Container life cycle management

This category consists of commands that help in managing the Container life cycle. This includes starting, stopping, restarting, killing, pausing, and unpausing Containers.

Docker run

This is perhaps the most important command among all commands that start a Container based on an image. This command itself has a lot of options for configuring a Container while starting it. Before a Container can be created and made available from an image, Docker daemon performs a series of operations. These include:

- Loading the specified image from a global repository after downloading it, if it is not available in the local repository
- Creating a read/write image layer and adding it on top of all other image layers
- Attaching the Container to a network and assigning it an IP address
- Creating a Container and executing the default or RUN command provided application within it

The RUN command provides options to open and expose ports in the Container and map them to ports on the Container host. This allows the Container host to forward requests on its port to the Container port using port forwarding. The -p flag is used for mapping ports between Container and Container host. This is shown here:

```
docker run -i -t -p 8080:80 microsoft/windowsservercore powershell
```

In this example, port 8080 on the Container host is mapped to port 80 on a Container based on microsoft/windowsservercore image. Any request that comes on port 8080 on the Container host is forwarded to port 80 in the Container.

The RUN command also provides options to share files and folders between the Container host and Containers using volumes. The -v flag is used for mapping folders on a Container host with Containers. This is shown here:

```
docker run -i -t -p 8080:80 -v /c/users:/c/ microsoft/windowsservercore
powershell
```

In this example, the C:users folder on the Container host is mapped to c: on the Container.

The RUN command provides an option to name the Container using the -name option. When the Container name is not provided explicitly, Docker provides a dynamically generated name to it. This is shown here, with the Container name being testContainer:

```
Docker run -i -t --name testContainer -p 8080:80 -v /c/users:/c/  testimage
powershell
```

The RUN command also provides a provision to start a Container in an interactive manner by attaching a console to it. -i and -t are used to make a Container interactive and PowerShell at the end of the command attaches a PowerShell console to the Container.

Containers can also start in detached mode. In this mode, the Container runs in the background and there is no active interaction with the Container. Use -d instead of -i and -t for running a Container in detached mode.

There are many more options, such as linking Containers, assigning networks, and assigning values to environment variables, which are not covered in this chapter; you should refer to the online documentation on the docker run command at https://docs.docker.com/engine/reference/run/.

Docker ps

The ps lists all the running Containers on a Container host.

```
Docker ps
```

Using the same command with the -a flag lists all the Containers in running as well as stopped state:

```
Docker ps -a
```

Docker start

The start command starts a stopped Container:

```
Docker start <<name or id of Container>>
```

Docker stop

The stop command stops a running Container:

```
Docker stop <<name or id of Container>>
```

Docker rm

The `rm` command removes a stopped Container:

```
Docker rm <<name or id of Container>>
```

Docker restart

The `restart` command stops and starts a running Container:

```
Docker restart <<name or id of Container>>
```

Docker pause

The `pause` command freezes a running Container:

```
Docker pause <<name or id of Container>>
```

Docker unpause

The `unpause` command starts a paused Container:

```
Docker unpause <<name or id of Container>>
```

Image management

This category consists of commands that help in managing images. This includes building and removing images.

Docker build

This command helps in creating a new image from a `Dockerfile`. Its use is shown here:

```
Docker build -t <<name of image>> <<path of folder containing Dockerfile>>
```

This command sends the `Dockerfile` in a given folder along with other files in it to Docker daemon as build context. The instructions in the `Dockerfile` are executed to generate a new image. The `-t` flag provides a name for the image. There is a complete section on `Dockerfile` later in this chapter.

Docker commit

This command creates a new image by saving an existing Container. It is to be noted that the container should be in stopped state before it can be committed to an image. Its use is shown here:

```
Docker commit <<Container id>> <<Image name>>
```

Docker images

This command lists all the available images in the local repository. Its use is shown here:

```
Docker images
```

Docker rmi

This command removes an image from the local repository:

```
Docker rmi <<image id>>
```

Docker tag

This command tags an image into the local repository. The tag name helps in versioning images. Its use is shown here:

```
Docker tag <<image id or name>> <<tag name>>
docker tag [image-id] microsoft/windowsservercore:1.0.0.0
```

The image ID can be obtained by running the docker images command.

Monitoring commands

These commands help in getting information log and configuration information about Containers.

Docker logs

This command helps in getting the log information of a Container. Its use is shown here:

```
Docker logs <<Container id or name>>
Docker logs 51be6169e12a
```

Docker stats

This command helps in getting the resource usage of Containers. It includes information on CPU, memory, and network usage. This command does not produce results at the time of writing this book but eventually it should return values for resource usage. It is shown here:

```
Docker stats <<Container id or name>>
Docker stats 51be6169e12a
```

For getting resource usage for all Containers, run the same command without any Container information:

```
Docker stats
```

Docker inspect

This command helps in getting Container configuration details. It is shown here:

```
Docker inspect <<Container id or name>>
Docker inspect 51be6169e12a
```

Docker events

This command helps in getting real-time events and information from Docker Containers and images. To see it working, two consoles are needed. Within one of the shells, execute the command as shown here:

```
Docker events
```

This will capture all events from Containers, images, networks, and volumes. On another shell, work with Docker client to manage Containers, images, networks, and volumes. This will result in real-time updates to the previous shell with activities happening on this shell.

Docker registry management

Docker provides commands that make working with registries easier from the command line. There are many centralized registries available, such as Docker Hub and `https://quay.io/`. This book uses Docker Hub for all its registry purposes. Docker Hub is available at `https://hub.docker.com` and an account must be created before it can be used. Creating an account is simple and after its creation, log in to the account to create repositories.

These repositories store images and their metadata. For the purpose of this book, an account **windowsdevops** is created as shown in *Figure 12*:

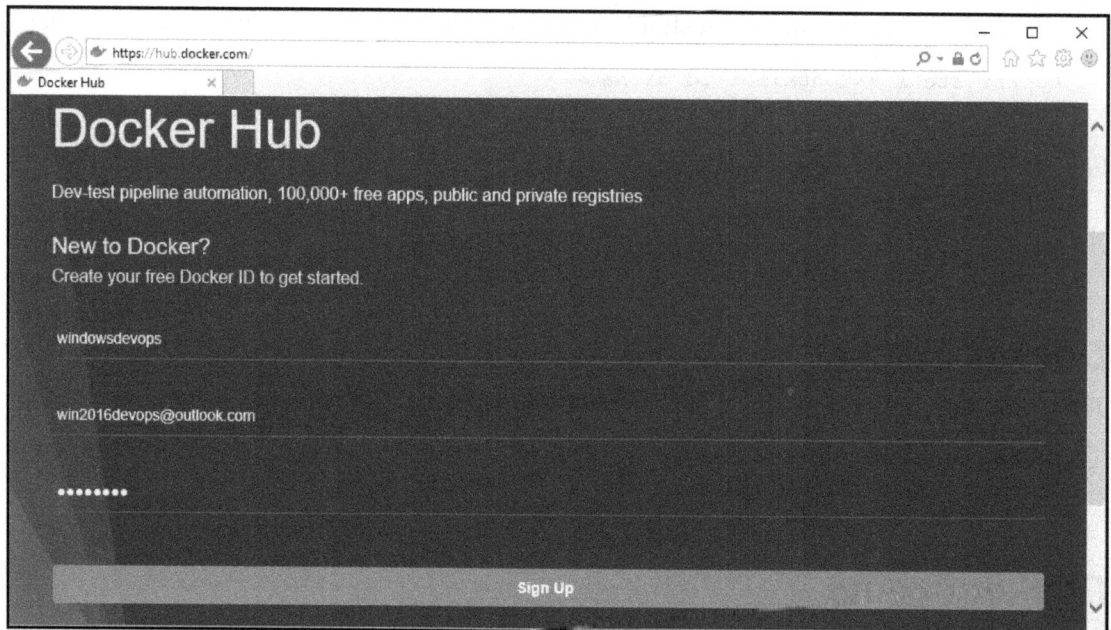

Figure 12: Signing up at hub.docker.com

After creating an account and logging in to it, repositories can be created as shown in *Figure 13* and *Figure 14:*

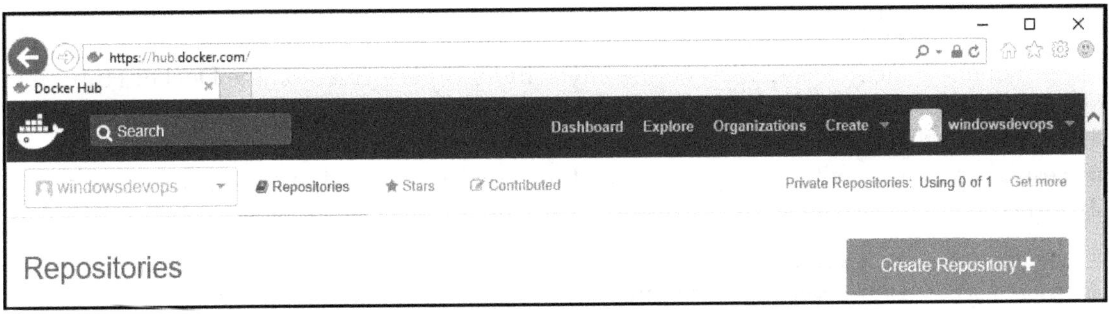

Figure 13: Dashboard after creating account

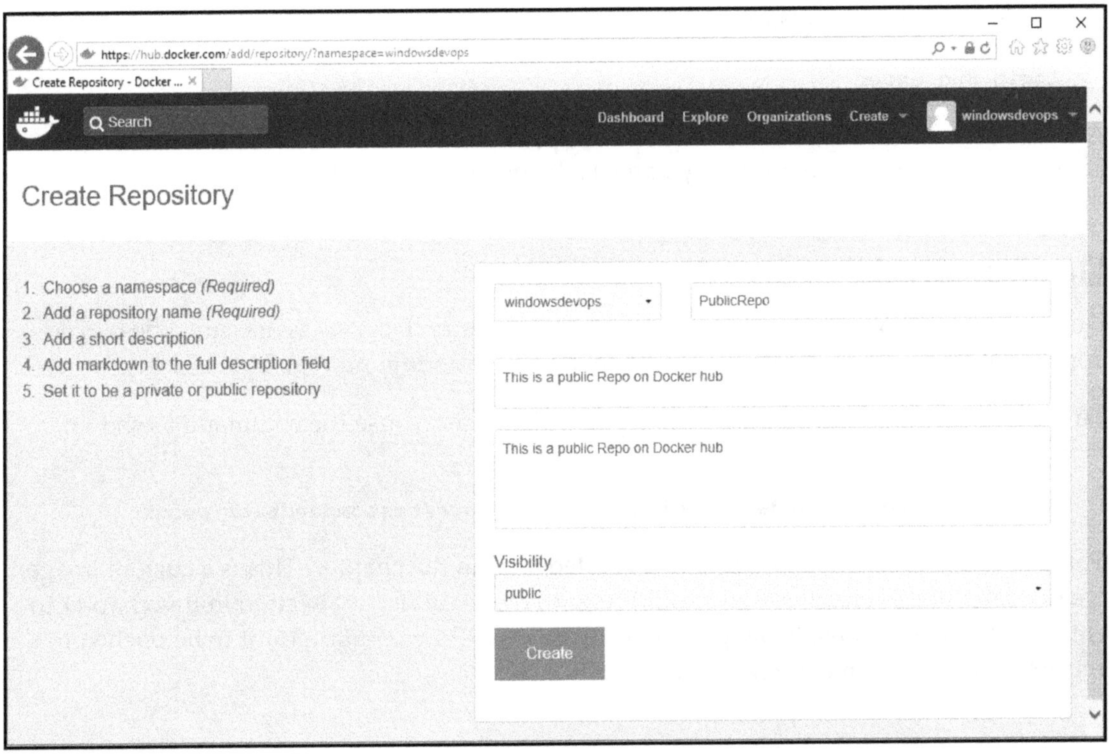

Figure 14: Create Docker Hub public repository

After a public repository is created, Docker client can be used to push, pull, and search it.

Docker login

User credentials must be supplied before any activity is performed on the Docker Hub registry. Docker client provides a `login` command for creating a session with the registry. After entering this command, it will prompt for username and password and after successful validation with the registry will allow you to push and pull images. Its use is shown here:

```
PS C:> docker login
Login with your Docker ID to push and pull images from Docker Hub. If you
don't have a Docker ID,
head over to https://h
ub.docker.com to create one.
Username: windowsdevops
Password:
Login Succeeded
```

A valid username and password should be supplied for successful login. In the example above, the `windowsdevops` registry name is the username used to log in.

Docker push

Docker `push` uploads local images to the Docker registry. Docker images must be tagged appropriately before they can be pushed to the `windowsdevops` registry.

To tag an image that can be pushed to a particular registry, use the command as shown here:

```
docker tag testcmdandentrypoint windowsdevops/testcmdandentrypoint
```

The `testcmdandentrypoint` image is created later in the chapter. This is a custom image created later in this chapter. You should refer to the `ENTRYPOINT` section in this chapter to create this image. It must be tagged as `registryname/imagename` for it to be pushed to the registry. Here, the name of registry is `windowsdevops`.

To push the newly tagged image, use the command as shown here:

```
PS C:> docker push windowsdevops/testcmdandentrypoint
The push refers to a repository
[docker.io/windowsdevops/testcmdandentrypoint]
316ecd2d4f65: Pushed
d19041b142ff: Pushed
latest: digest:
sha256:c2a845685b3883706e2fbb31addc7f3f36e13a19f63bfccf64401886a926c0a8
size: 733
```

Docker pull

Docker images can be pulled into local repository using this command. A valid login session must exist before images can be pulled from a registry.

To pull an image from repository, use the command as shown here:

```
PS C:> docker pull windowsdevops/testcmdandentrypoint
Using default tag: latest
latest: Pulling from windowsdevops/testcmdandentrypoint
Digest:
sha256:c2a845685b3883706e2fbb31addc7f3f36e13a19f63bfccf64401886a926c0a8
Status: Downloaded newer image for
windowsdevops/testcmdandentrypoint:latest
```

Here, the `Pull` command supplies the name of the registry and image for download.

Understanding Dockerfile

`Dockerfile` is the primary building block for creating Windows Container images. It is a simple text-based, human-readable file without any extension and is named `Dockerfile`. Although there is the mechanism to name it differently, generally it is named `Dockerfile`. We have already seen that every Container image is based on a base image; `Dockerfile` contains instructions to create a custom Container image from a base image. These instructions are executed sequentially from top to bottom by Docker daemon, the engine behind all activities related to Windows Containers. The instructions refer to the command and their parameters understood by Docker daemon. `Dockerfile` enables Infrastructure as Code practices by converting the application deployment and configuration into instructions that can be versioned and stored in a source code repository.

When building an image from `Dockerfile`, the file is sent to Docker daemon. For each instruction within `Dockerfile`, Docker daemon creates an intermediate transient short-lived Container, executes the instruction within it, and commits the Container as an image layer referable through a unique identifier. Finally, after the last instruction is executed, there will be a stack of image layers built from individual instruction, each added on top of the previous resultant layer. They are linked together to form an image from which a Windows Container can be created.

It is important to note that each image layer records and represents just the modification or changes induced as a result of executing a single instruction. This intermediate image layer is a reusable layer that can be referred by multiple Docker Images if those Docker images contains similar `Dockerfile` instruction.

Windows Containers implement an aggressive caching mechanism to provide improved user experience while building and generating images. Docker caches the intermediate image layer in memory while executing `Dockerfile`. Caching of layers is implemented for those instructions that are idempotent in nature. A layer is cached if the result of an instruction is deterministic and is the same every time it is executed. Repeated execution of the same `Dockerfile` can benefit from caching behavior as the instructions are not executed, instead it uses the cache layer. Caching helps in faster generation of images during iterative repeated execution of `Dockerfile`.

Docker build command

Docker provides a command to create an image from `Dockerfile` as shown here:

```
Docker build -t <<Name of image>> .
```

The `build` command takes a tag name referred by `-t` flag as input. This name is used to refer to the image. The period `.` specifies the current working directory in the shell prompt. As good practice, there should be a single `Dockerfile` in a directory. Other files needed to build a Container image can be stored within this directory and they will be sent to Docker daemon as part of the build context. These files are available and used by daemon if they are referred in `Dockerfile`.

Shell and Exec instruction forms

Instructions in `Dockerfile` can be authored in two forms.

- Shell form
- Exec form

Shell form

On Windows Server, PowerShell is used for executing shell commands. In Shell form, the arguments to instructions are provided similar to the way they are executed on a shell prompt as shown here:

```
RUN Powershell -Command Install-WindowsFeature web-server
```

In this example, `RUN` is the instruction provided by Docker, PowerShell is an executable that accepts the command parameter, and everything on the line after command parameter is argument to it. In this case, `Install-WindowsFeature Web-server` is the argument sent to the command for installing **Internet Information Service (IIS)** in the Container image.

When using this form, `cmd /s /c` is appended to every command by default.

Exec form

In the Exec form, the arguments to instructions are provided in JSON array format as shown here:

```
RUN ["Powershell", "Install-WindowsFeature", "web-server"]
```

In this form, the command is executed in the same way as it is executed in the shell prompt. There is no default command added to it. This form ensures the execution of instructions in their pure form without any modification. The Exec form is generally preferred and used as best practice. All `Dockerfile` instructions can be executed in shell as well as Exec form.

Dockerfile instructions

Docker provides a large number of instructions that can be used in `Dockerfile` for the generation of images. In this section, we will look at some of the important instructions at an introductory level. For complete information about all instructions in detail, refer to the Docker site at `https://docs.docker.com/engine/reference/builder/`. As a general rule, all Docker instructions are authored in capital letters to distinguish them easily from commands and their parameters.

COMMENT

`Dockerfile` provides support for comments. Comments are not executed by Docker daemon. They are meant for providing additional information about instructions to anyone reading the `Dockerfile`. Comments are represented through instructions starting with a hash symbol (#). Any text mentioned after the hash symbol is treated as a comment. A simple example of a comment in shown here in the first line:

```
# This image is based on microsoft/windowsservercore image
From microsoft/windowsservercore:latest
```

FROM

Every custom Docker must start with the `FROM` instruction. Every image must have a base image referenced on which it is based. Microsoft provides two base images for Windows Containers. They are:

- **WindowsServerCore**: It contains the complete Windows Server 2016 core
- **NanoServer**: It contains the Nano Server

Each image can have multiple tags in the local repository and this information should be provided in the `Dockerfile FROM` instruction for the daemon to pick up the correct image. If a tag is not provided, the daemon tries to load the *latest* image tag. The image must be tagged as `latest` before it can be used by the daemon.

The FROM instruction loads images from the local repository using name and version. If it cannot find an image matching this combination in the local repository, it tries to pull the image from a global registry. If it finds the image, it will download it along with any further dependent images it refers to. The two aforementioned Windows-based base images are not hosted on the default Docker public registry. They are hosted by Microsoft on Azure blob storage and they must be available in the local repository before the custom Dockerfile can use them. An example of using FROM instructions are shown here:

```
# This image is based on microsoft/windowsservercore image with latest
version
FROM microsoft/windowsservercore:latest
```

MAINTAINER

The MAINTAINER instruction helps in providing the author name for the generated image. Its use is shown here:

```
FROM microsoft/windowsservercore:latest
# This image is created and maintained by Ritesh Modi
MAINTAINER "Ritesh Modi"
```

It is to be noted that the first statement in a dockerfile should start from the FROM command.

COPY

The COPY instruction copies files and directories from the host (source) to the destination path in the Container environment. These files and directories must be available to the build context sent to Docker daemon while initiating the build. In other words, these files and folders must be placed in the same directory as that of Dockerfile to make them available to the build context.

It is to be noted that the destination path should use forward slashes instead of back slashes.

It takes the format shown here:

```
# Shell form
COPY <<source file or folder>> <<destination file or folder>>
# Exec form
COPY ["<<source file or folder>>", "<<destination file or folder>>"]
```

And its use is shown here. This example copies `samplefile.txt` to the `C:` drive in the Container:

```
# This image is created and maintained by Ritesh Modi
# It shows the usage of COPY instruction
FROM microsoft/windowsservercore
COPY samplefile.txt C:/
```

ADD

The `ADD` instruction is similar to the `COPY` instruction with additional capabilities. It not only allows copying files and folders from the build context but also from remote locations including the Internet.

The `ADD` instruction copies files and directories from the host (source) to the destination path in the Container environment. These files and directories must be available to the build context sent to Docker daemon while initiating the build. It can also download files from the Internet.

It is to be noted that the destination path should use forward slashes instead of back slashes.

It takes the format as shown here:

```
# Shell form
ADD <<source file or folder>> <<destination file or folder>>
# Exec form
ADD ["<<source file or folder>>", "<<destination file or folder>>"]
```

An Exec form should be used if there are spaces in either the source or destination path. Its use is shown here. This example copies `samplefile.txt` to the `C:` drive in the Container:

```
# This image is created and maintained by Ritesh Modi
# It shows the usage of ADD instruction
FROM microsoft/windowsservercore
ADD samplefile.txt C:/
```

The next example downloads a file from the Internet:

```
ADD https://www.python.org/ftp/python/3.5.1/python-3.5.1.exe
/C:/python-3.5.1.exe
```

WORKDIR

WORKDIR helps in setting the current working folder in the Container environment. All instructions after using this instruction will execute within the context of the current working folder unless it is changed again using the WORKDIR instruction. By default, the current working directory in the Windows Container is C:. In the example shown next, the current working directory is C:Windows.

It takes the format shown here:

```
WORKDIR <<Path to current working folder>>
And its usage is shown here
# This image is created and maintained by Ritesh Modi
# It shows the usage of WORKDIR instruction
WORKDIR "C:windows"
```

EXPOSE

This instruction informs Docker daemon that any Container created from this image would listen on the network port specified as part of its argument. The port would not be accessible during the building of an image but would be available at runtime while creating the Container. The port is accessible at Container creation time only when using the -p flag in Docker run command. The -p flag take the source port on the host machine and destination port in Container environment, and maps them such that any request arriving on the host machine with the source port is forwarded to the Container on the destination port.

It takes the format shown here:

```
EXPOSE <<Port number>>
```

And its use is shown here:

```
# It shows the usage of EXPOSE instruction
EXPOSE 1433
```

ENV

ENV refers to environment variables in Windows Containers. This instruction helps in setting up environment variables in Containers that are available during runtime. It also helps in passing values to Containers while starting them. They help in making Containers generic and configurable.

Docker `run` provides an `-ENV` option that can be used to override the value provided in `Dockerfile`.

It takes two different formats as shown here:

```
# In first statement, the entire string after Key and first blank is
treated as value
ENV <<Key>> <<Value>>
ENV <<Key>> = <<Value>>
```

And its sample usage is shown here:

```
# This image is created and maintained by Ritesh Modi
# It shows the usage of E instruction. A default value is provided that can
be overridden using -e option of docker run command
ENV "DomainName" "DefaultDomainName"
```

To override the value of an environment variable defined in a `Dockerfile`, use the `-e` option while executing the `docker run` command as shown here. The image name must be replaced with an actual image name before executing the following command:

```
docker run -it -e DomainName=WindowsServer <<ImageName>> powershell
```

VOLUME

VOLUME helps in sharing a directory on the host with the Container environment. Every write action to the filesystem and data stored in the Container is written on the topmost layer of the Container image. This image layer is volatile, and gets deleted when the Container is stopped and removed. Every time a Container starts, a new fresh environment is created and previous stored data is not available. To persist and make data available across the Container life cycle, volumes should be used. The shared folder available in the Container environment is actually stored on the host machine at the `C:ProgramDatadockervolumes` folder location. In a running Container, any data stored in this folder gets stored on the host and is available irrespective of the state of the Container.

It takes the format shown here:

```
VOLUME "<<path in Container>>"
VOLUME ["<<path in Container>>"]
```

And its use is shown here. Anything stored in the logs directory in a container will be available on the host machine:

```
# It shows the usage of VOLUME instruction
VOLUME C:logs
```

VOLUME can also be created using the Docker run command with a –v flag. The advantage of using volumes with the run command is that both the source on the host and the destination in the Container paths can be provided. With Dockerfile, only the Container mount point can be specified, which gets mapped to a folder determined by Docker on the host. This is shown here. The folder C:logs on the host is shared within the container as data directory at the C: drive. The image name must be replaced with an actual image name before executing the following command:

```
docker run –it –v c:logs:C:data <<image name>> powershell
```

RUN

RUN instruction specifies commands that are executed in intermediate Containers during the build process and the results of which are captured into the new Container image. These commands can include anything that is possible using PowerShell and a command-line utility tool, such as installing and configuring software, configuring operating systems, and building file and folder layouts.

It takes the format shown here:

```
# Shell form
RUN <<Executable and its arguments>>
# Exec form
RUN ["<<Executable>>", "<<param1>>", "<<param2>>"]
```

And its use is shown here. It installs IIS using a Shell form:

```
# It shows the usage of RUN instruction using shell form
# It shows the usage of RUN instruction using shell form
RUN Powershell Install-WindowsFeature Web-Server
```

PowerShell is the executable that would execute the Install-WindowsFeature cmdlet to install the Web-Server feature in the Container image. The next example shows the same activity using an Exec form:

```
# It shows the usage of RUN instruction using Exec form
RUN ["Powershell", "Install-WindowsFeature", "Web-Server"]
```

It is to be noted that when using any filesystem path with an Exec form, it must be escaped using double back slashes instead of a single back slash:

```
RUN ["Powershell", "New-Item", "C:NewFolder"]
```

CMD

CMD instruction specifies the default command to be executed when creating a Container . Multiple CMD instructions can be present in a Dockerfile; however, only the last CMD instruction is relevant and executed as part of the creation of a Container. The CMD instruction provides a default executable to run when no explicit executable is provided while starting a Container through the Docker run command. At the same time, Docker provides flexibility to be override the default CMD executable in Dockerfile and execute the executable provided through Docker run command.

It takes the format shown here:

```
# Shell form
CMD <<Executable and its arguments>>
# Exec form
CMD ["<<Executable>>", "<<param1>>", "<<param2>>"]
```

And its use is shown here. It installs IIS using a Shell form:

```
# It shows the usage of CMD instruction using shell form
CMD Powershell
```

PowerShell is the executable that would execute in the Container image. The next example shows the same activity using the Exec form:

```
# It shows the usage of CMD instruction using Exec form
CMD ["Powershell"]
```

The console parameter in run command becomes optional while creating a container in an interactive mode for an image containing this instruction as shown here. The image name must be replaced with an actual image name before executing the following command:

```
docker run -it <<Image name>>
```

ENTRYPOINT

ENTRYPOINT instruction is similar to the CMD instruction in that it provides a default executable with arguments when starting a Container. However, there is a slight difference. The ENTRYPOINT instruction does not allow overriding of the executable command through the Docker run command. This instruction makes the Container look like an executable and as if the executable is hardcoded in the Container image.

It takes the format shown here:

```
# Shell form
ENTRYPOINT <<Executable and its arguments>>
# Exec form
ENTRYPOINT ["<<Executable>>", "<<param1>>", "<<param2>>"]
```

And its use is shown here. It pings the local machine using the Shell form:

```
# It shows the usage of ENTRYPOINT instruction using shell form
ENTRYPOINT Powershell ping 127.0.0.1 -t
```

PowerShell is the executable that would execute the ping executable continuously. The next example shows the same activity using the Exec form:

```
# It shows the usage of ENTRYPOINT instruction using Exec form
ENTRYPOINT ["Powershell","ping", "127.0.0.1", "-t"]
```

ENTRYPOINT can work together with the CMD instruction to bring flexibility in providing arguments to ENTRYPOINT at runtime while creating a Container through the Docker run command. When CMD is used with the ENTRYPOINT instruction, CMD provides arguments to the executable mentioned in the ENTRYPOINT instruction. This is shown here:

```
# It shows the usage of ENTRYPOINT and CMD instruction working together
ENTRYPOINT ["ping","-4"]
CMD ["localhost"]
```

The image can be built for Dockerfile using the following command:

```
Docker Build -t testcmdandentrypoint "<<path to Dockerfile folder>>"
```

If the Dockerfile is available in the C:df folder, the command will look as shown here:

```
Docker Build -t testcmdandentrypoint "C:df"
```

And the result would look as shown here. The identifiers in this example would be different for readers:

```
PS C:> docker build -t testcmdandentrypoint "c:df"
Sending build context to Docker daemon 2.048 kB
Step 1 : FROM microsoft/windowsservercore
---> 5bc36a335344
Step 2 : ENTRYPOINT ping -4
---> Running in 4529614439e8
---> 0b66180d227a
Removing intermediate Container 4529614439e8
Step 3 : CMD localhost
---> Running in 6fbbfcf5f08a
---> a317a8345283
Removing intermediate Container 6fbbfcf5f08a
Successfully built a317a8345283
PS C:>
```

Creating a Container from an image built from this `Dockerfile` will output the ping result from the localhost. The value `localhost` is provided as argument by the CMD instruction to the `ENTRYPOINT` instruction. The command to start a Container from the test image is shown here:

```
Docker run -i -t testcmdandentrypoint
```

And the result is shown here:

```
Pinging WIN-SHSNAVDV03B [127.0.0.1] with 32 bytes of data:
Reply from 127.0.0.1: bytes=32 time<1ms TTL=128
Reply from 127.0.0.1: bytes=32 time<1ms TTL=128
Reply from 127.0.0.1: bytes=32 time<1ms TTL=128
Reply from 127.0.0.1: bytes=32 time<1ms TTL=128
Ping statistics for 127.0.0.1:
    Packets: Sent = 4, Received = 4, Lost = 0 (0% loss),
Approximate round trip times in milli-seconds:
    Minimum = 0ms, Maximum = 0ms, Average = 0ms
PS C:>
```

However, if a Container is starting with explicit values after the image name in the Docker run command, these values replace the default CMD instruction values and are used as argument to the ENTRYPOINT instruction. This is shown here with bing.com being used as value to use for ping:

```
Docker run -i -t testcmdandentrypoint bing.com
And the result is shown here.
Pinging bing.com [204.79.197.200] with 32 bytes of data:
Reply from 204.79.197.200: bytes=32 time<1ms TTL=120
Reply from 204.79.197.200: bytes=32 time=1ms TTL=120
Reply from 204.79.197.200: bytes=32 time=1ms TTL=120
Reply from 204.79.197.200: bytes=32 time=1ms TTL=120
Ping statistics for 204.79.197.200:
    Packets: Sent = 4, Received = 4, Lost = 0 (0% loss),
Approximate round trip times in milli-seconds:
    Minimum = 0ms, Maximum = 1ms, Average = 0ms
PS C:>
```

Summary

This chapter again covered a lot of ground from a technology perspective. It introduced some of the most important and latest technologies that make DevOps easier and relevant. The industry is adopting Containers as part of its deployment strategies and baking them into its DevOps practices. In this chapter, Containers, along with some of their important concepts, were introduced. Steps to create a Container-enabled virtual machine on Azure were illustrated using PowerShell. Next, steps to create a Nano Server virtual machine on Azure were provided using ARM templates. This took care of two different ways to deploy Container-enabled environments on Azure. After this, Docker clients and Docker engines were introduced. Some of the important commands were explained using the Docker client to manage the Container life cycle, images, monitoring, and registries. Finally, Dockerfile was discussed at length, along with its instructions. They help in creating custom images. This chapter will form the backbone to the rest of the chapters, as environments, Docker client, and Dockerfile are used extensively in this book.

5
Building a Sample Application

In previous chapters, we briefly delved into multiple technologies that enable and help implement DevOps. We discussed tools like Visual Studio Team Services providing continuous integration, deployment, and delivery services; Azure Infrastructure as a Service, providing infrastructure and platform services to provision and host environments needed during software development phases like development, testing, pre-production, and production; declarative and imperative scripting languages such as JSON, ARM Templates, PowerShell, Desired State Configuration, and Pester to automate provisioning, configuration and the testing of environments. We experienced newer platforms introduced with Windows Server 2016 including Nano Server and Windows Containers for hosting applications as well.

This chapter will provide an overview of a sample web-based application named **Online Pharmacy** built using ASP.NET MVC and Azure SQL. The goal of application is to enable readers to quickly deploy it with minimal changes on the development environment. It is not a full-fledged functional production-ready application implementing the best practices of web development. It is just good enough to help in decoding and implementing DevOps principles and practices.

This chapter is accompanied with complete source code for this sample application, and readers are encouraged to use it to experience it. They can also modify and extend it according to their need. This chapter is not step-by-step guide to create this application, but it explores major concepts and components used during building this application.

Now, it's time to get an overview of sample application that can be used as medium to implement and showcase DevOps principles and practices throughout this book in subsequent chapters.

Experiencing the application

Online Pharmacy is a simple data-based application built for fictional pharmacy shops with three user stories:

- Create, edit, delete, view history, and the details of drugs
- Add, edit, delete, and view history, and the details of drugs inventory
- Add, edit, delete, and view history, and the details of drug sales

The home page of sample application is shown in *Figure 1*.

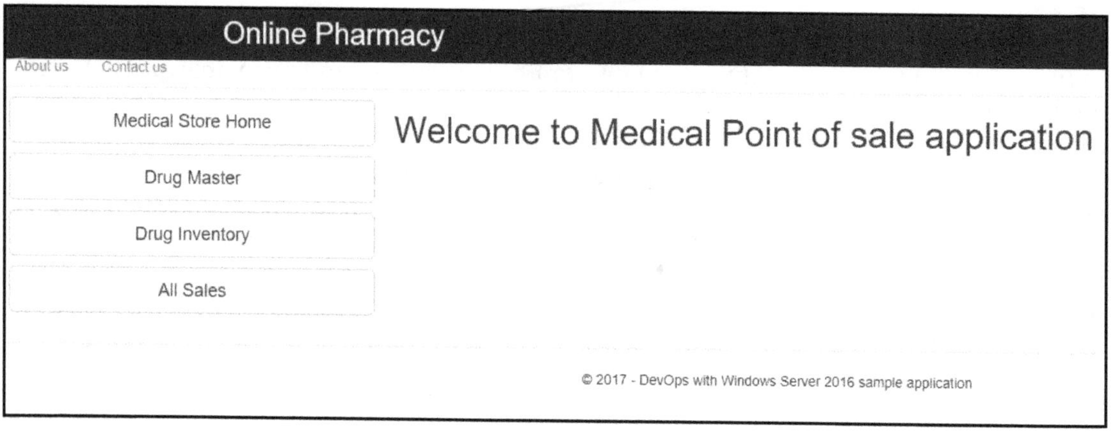

Figure 1: Online pharmacy home page

There are three important links at the left-hand side navigation pane. The **Drug Master** button leads to the drug management landing page, which by default lists all drugs. Specific drug information can be managed by editing, deleting, and creating new medicines from here. This is shown in *Figure 2*.

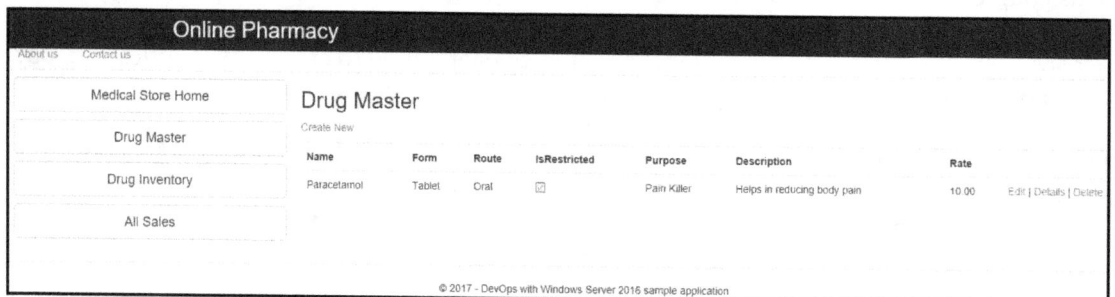

Figure 2: A sample application drug management page

After a drug is on boarded, its inventory can be added and managed using the **Drug Inventory** button on the left navigation pane. Each inventory item can be individually edited, deleted, and details can be viewed from here. This is shown in *Figure 3*.

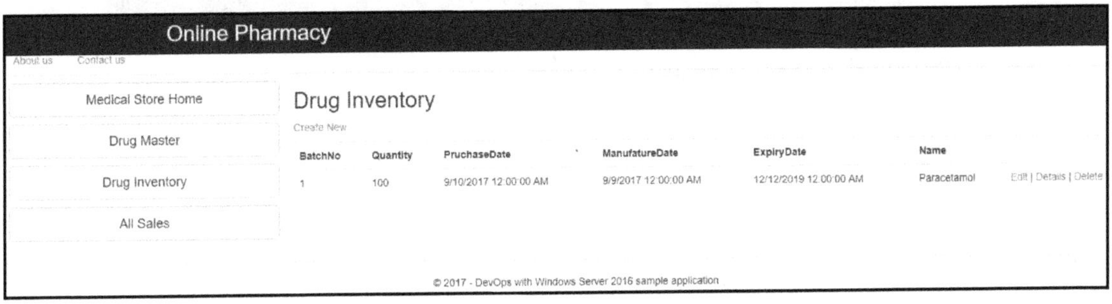

Figure 3: A sample application drug inventory master page

Once both drugs and their inventory are added, the application enables selling them to customers. The **All Sales** button in the left-hand side navigation pane is an entry point to sales functionality and helps in navigating to sales landing page, which by default lists all the sales done till date. This is shown in *Figure 4*.

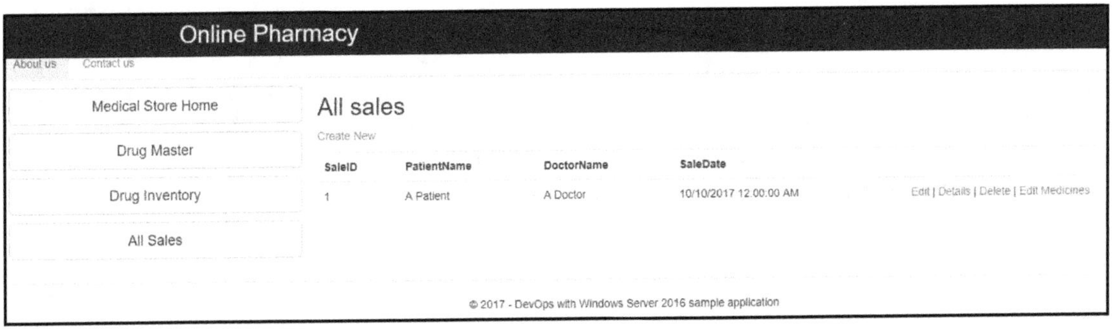

Figure 4: The sample application drug sale management page

There can be multiple drugs sold as part of every sale. Drug line items can be managed using the **Edit** link available to each sale. This is shown in *Figure 5*.

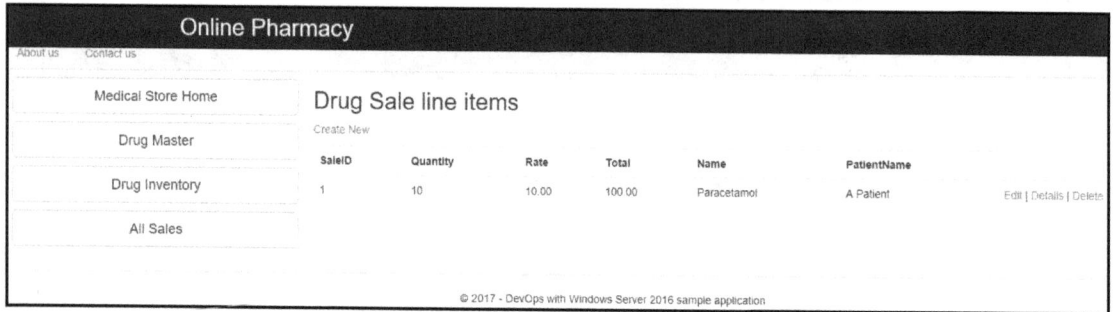

Figure 5: The sample application drug sale line items

Readers are free to add additional functional features, security features such as authentication, authorization, advance validation, and technology components such as caching.

Application architecture

It is a simple two-tier architecture with web application deployed in **Internet Information Service (IIS)** as a frontend database and Azure SQL Server as backend database. The application connects to the database using connection string defined in `web.config`. The connection string is generated and stored in `web.config` using the Entity Framework.

IIS web application is hosted on Windows Containers on multiple load balanced Azure Virtual Machines. This is shown in *Figure 6*.

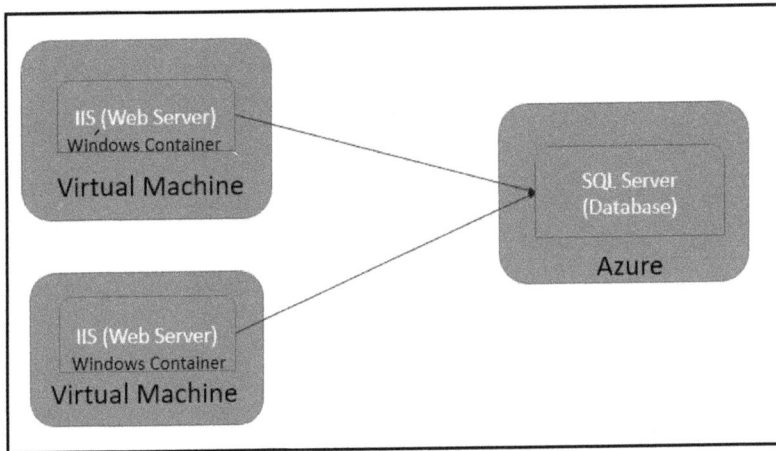

Figure 6: The sample application architecture

Preparing development environment

In Chapter 3, *DevOps Automation Primer,* we installed Visual Studio 2015 Community Edition on Windows Server 2016 machine. It is to be noted that the development environment can be Windows 10 machine as well. Windows Server 2016 environment will be used as development environment in this book. Next step in setting up the development environment is provision Azure SQL Server and Database. SQL Server 2014 Management Studio is needed to work with Azure SQL and it can be downloaded from https://www.microsoft.com/en-us/download/details.aspx?id=42299.

Select **MgmtStudio 64BITSQLManagementStudio_x64_ENU.exe** as shown in *Figure 7* here.

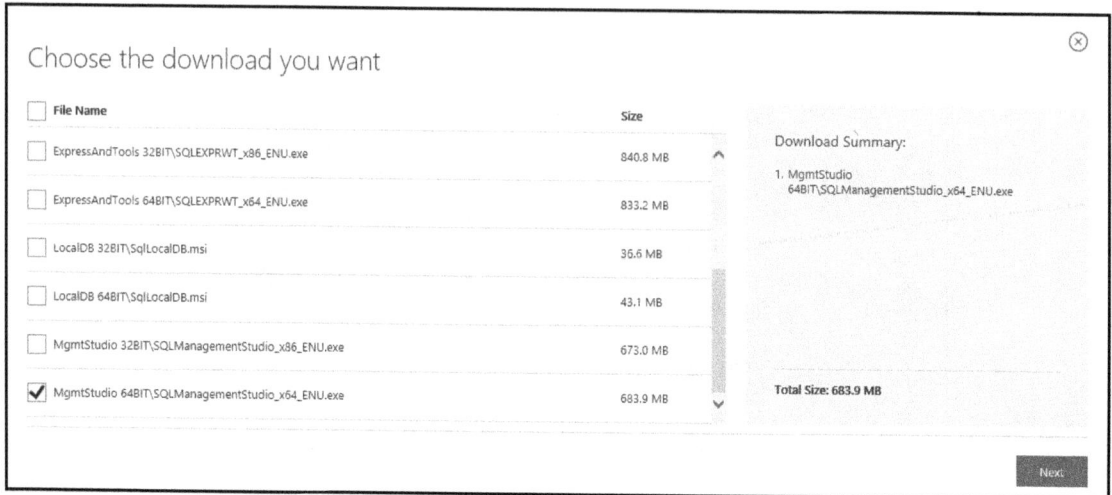

Figure 7: SQL Server Management Studio download

Save the executable and extract the setup files to an appropriate location.

One of the prerequisite of SQL Server 2014 Management Studio is the availability of .NET 3.5 runtime on development box. Since our development box is an Azure virtual machine, the Windows Server 2016 image files are not available to install additional features like .NET 3.5. There are multiple ways to install .NET 3.5. When installing .NET 3.5, it asks for the physical location of binaries. Windows server binaries are not available within the virtual machine by default on Azure. The binaries for .NET 3.5 should be downloaded or copied over to the virtual machine. In this case, we download a Windows Server 2016 image on to the local machine, mount it and extract the binaries related to .NET 3.5. To install .NET 3.5, a Windows Server 2016 server image must be downloaded from `https://www.mi crosoft.com/en-us/evalcenter/evaluate-windows-server-2016`, mounted on a drive, and `sxs` folder in `sources` folder containing **microsoft-windows-netfx3-ondemand-package.cab** should be copied to development environment. The `sxs` folder is copied to `C:` drive on development virtual machine. This is shown in *Figure 8*.

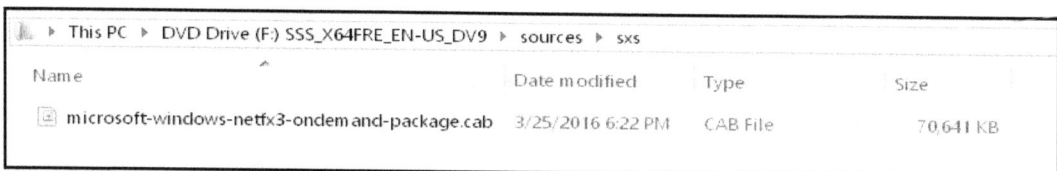

Figure 8: .NET 3.5 runtime source file in mounted ISO image

Now, .NET 3.5 can be installed using Server manager by providing the copied folder as alternate path. This is shown in *Figure 9*.

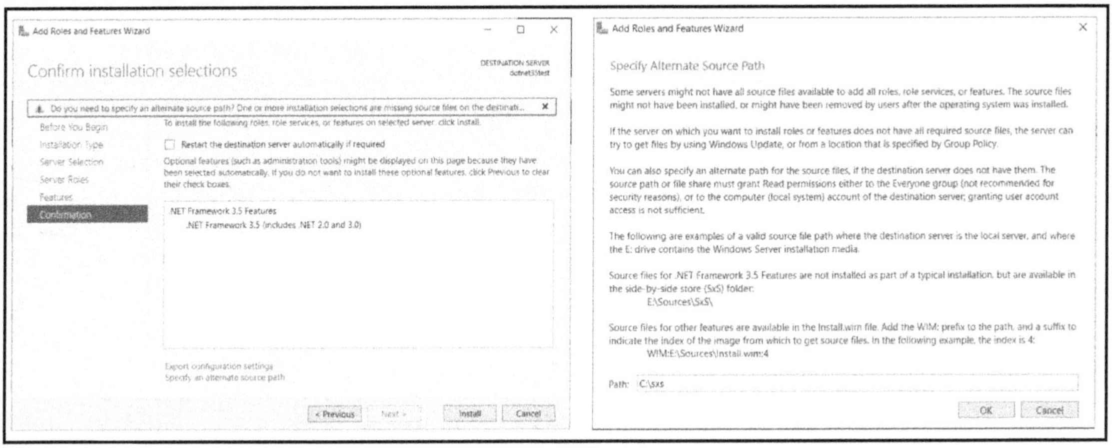

Figure 9: Installing .NET 3.5 feature using alternate source path

The step of installing .NET 3.5 runtime is needed only for the development environment. It is not needed in test, pre-production, production or any other environment because these environments would be hosted within windows containers and SQL Server Management Studio is not required on these environments.

After the .NET 3.5 pre-requisite is installed, start the SQL Server Management Studio installation process by executing the extracted `Setup.exe` file.

Installing SQL Server Management Studio

On development environment, developers will frequently work with databases. This requires installation of SQL Server Management Studio to connect to Azure SQL databases.

1. SQL Server Management Studio is only required on development box for connecting to Azure SQL and authoring of database tables. It is not required on test, authoring, pre-production or production environments. Start installation using `SQLManagementStudio_x64_ENU.exe`.

2. Select **SQL Server stand-alone installation** option and **Accept** the license terms as shown in *Figure 10*. The setup will install necessary files and run rules to check whether there are potential problems while installing SQL Server. It will show warnings and failures, and they should be rectified before proceeding.

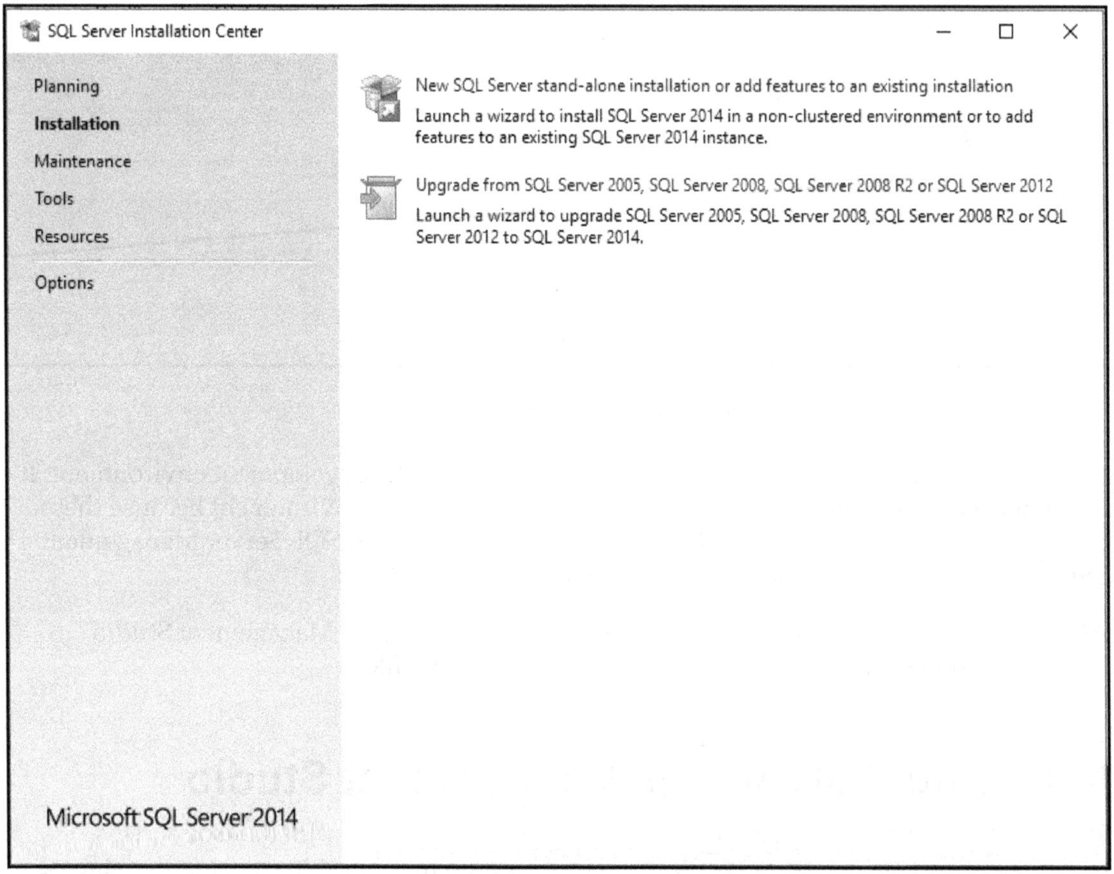

Figure 10: SQL Server Management Studio installation

3. Select the features as shown in *Figure 11* on the **Feature Selection** screen.

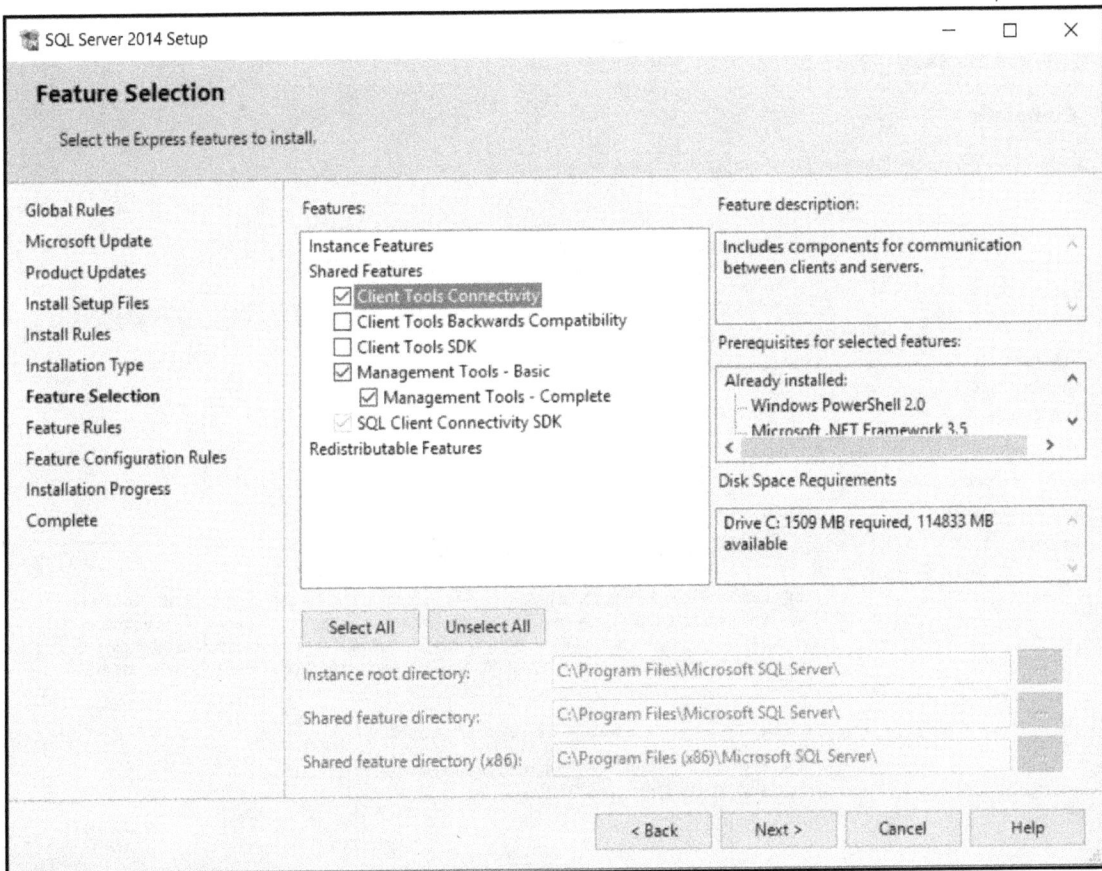

Figure 11: SQL Server Management tool feature selection

4. The installation process will take some time to complete and once complete should show the status as shown in *Figure 12*.

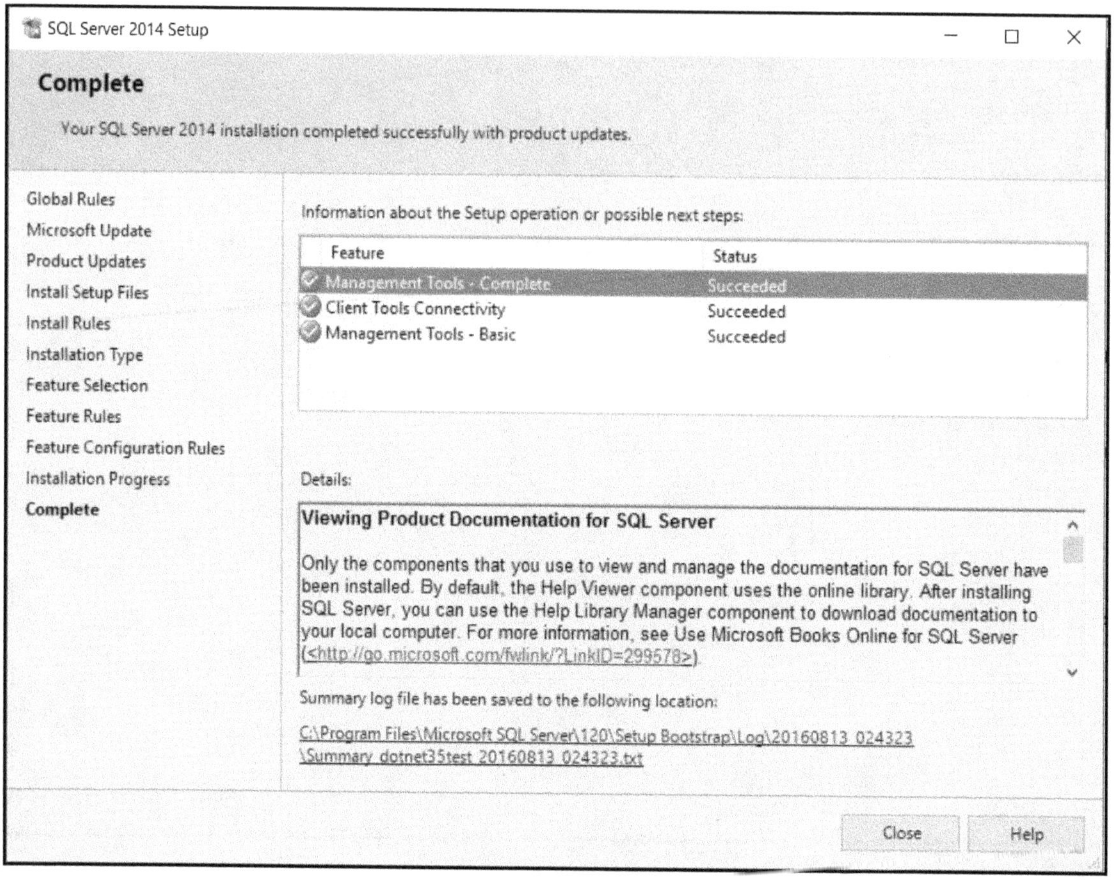

Figure 12: The successful installation of the SQL Server Management Studio

Creating Azure SQL Server and SQL database

After Installing SQL Server Management Studio, its time to provision Azure SQL Server and database. Following steps should be executed for the same:

1. Login into Azure subscription using appropriate credentials. Navigate to **SQL Database** and create a new SQL server and database as shown in *Figure 13*.

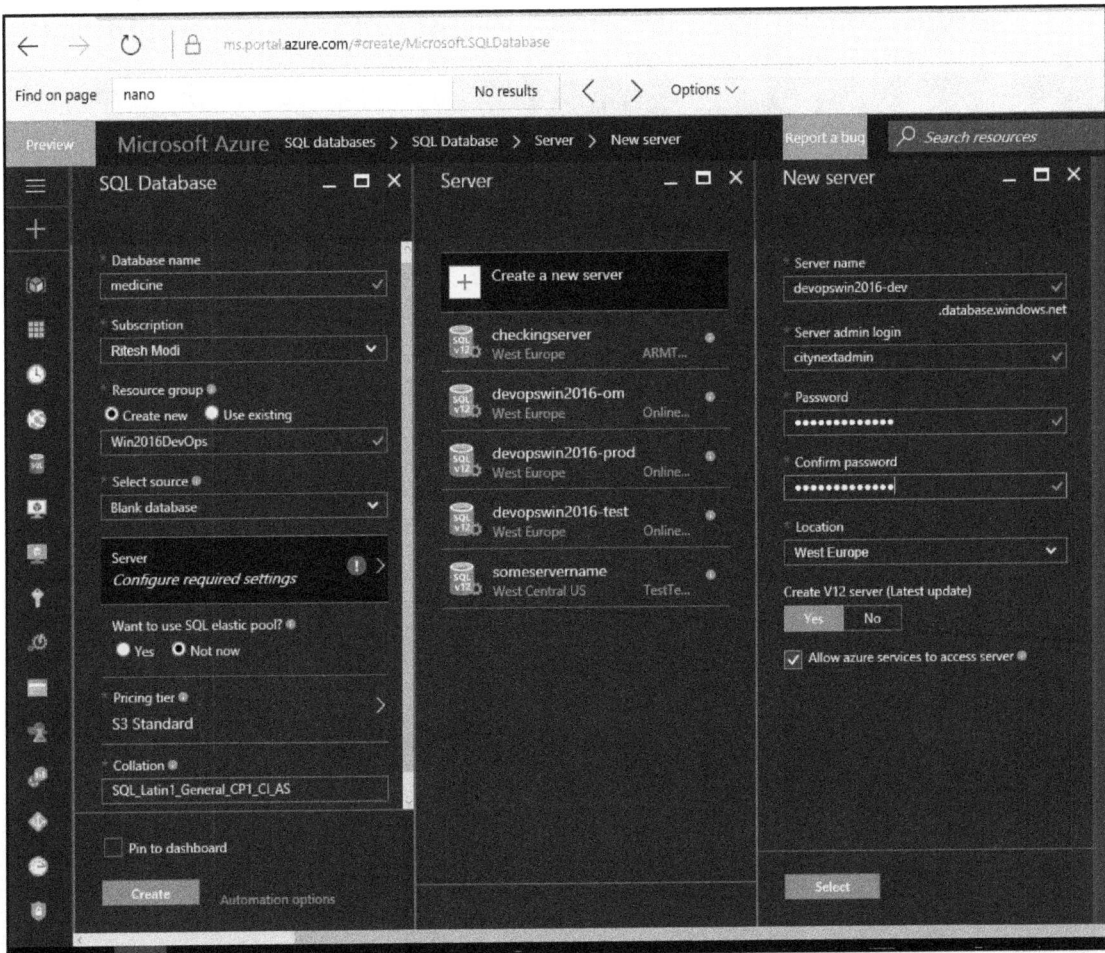

Figure 13: Provision Azure SQL server and database

2. Name the Database as **medicine**, select appropriate subscription, provide resource group name, **Blank database** as source, **devopswin2016-dev** as server name, provide credentials and location. Click the **Create** button on database blade to start creating both server and database.

3. After the server and database are provisioned, navigate to the server properties blade and click on **Firewall** menu item. The next *Figure 14* shows the Firewall configuration blade. Click on **Add client IP** to add the development machine IP address to the list of IP addresses allowed to connect to Azure SQL and database.

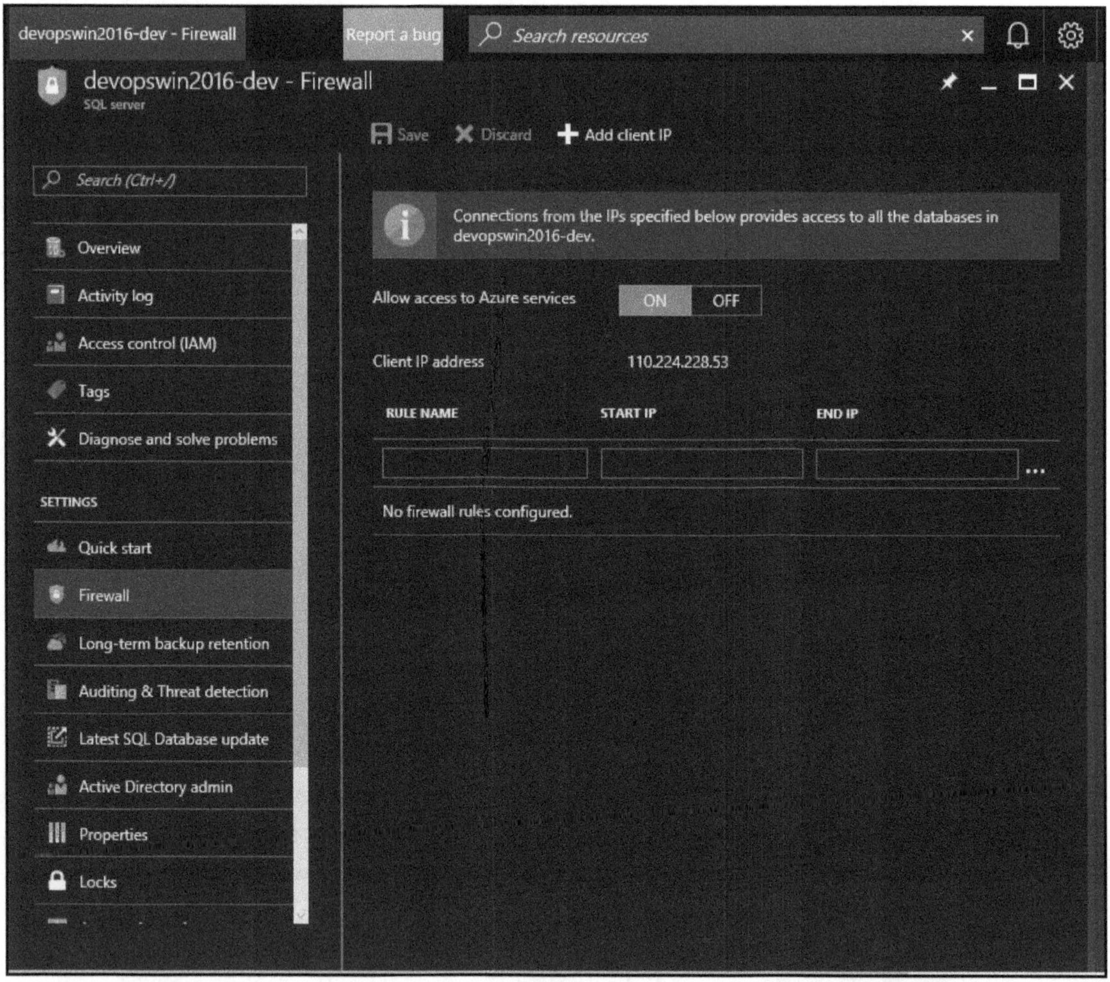

Figure 14: Adding client IP as to Azure SQL Server Firewall list

Creating database tables

Now that both Management Studio and SQL Database are provisioned, the provided `OnlineMedicine.sql` script can be executed within Management Studio to create the database structure on SQL Database.

Open Management Studio and connect to Azure SQL using its DNS name. The DNS information is available from Azure SQL server blade as shown here in *Figure 15*.

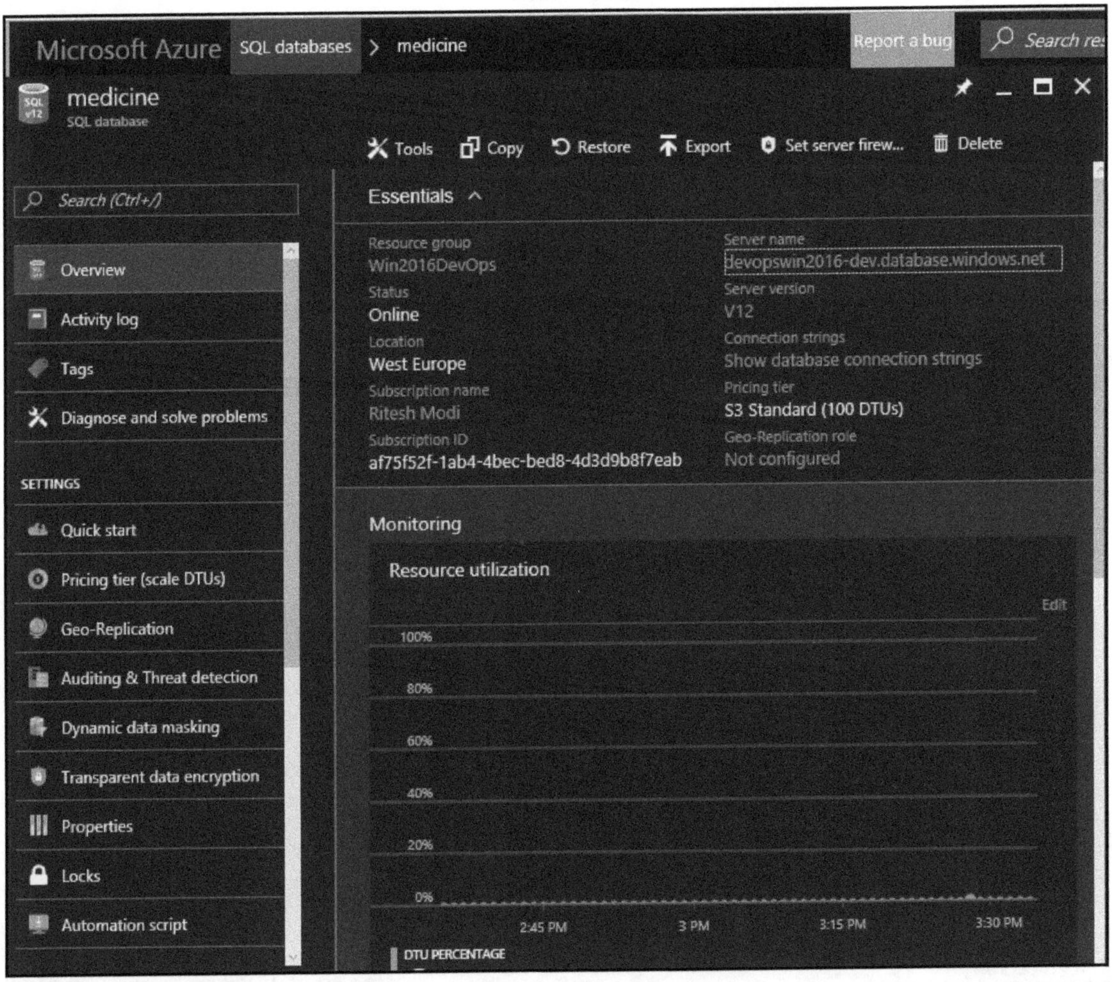

Figure 15: Finding the Azure SQL server DNS name and IP address

The `onlinePharmacy.sql` file contains the entire SQL script for the creation of table. It is important to note that this script does not contain script to create a database. Both Azure SQL server and database should be available before executing this script. On all environments apart from development environment, both the server and database are created using Azure Resource Manager Templates.

Also, if a developer changes any database object on development environment should add/remove/change the relevant script in this file to ensure that database schema in development and all other environments are same.

The steps for the same are shown here:

1. Open SQL Server Management Studio and open `OnlinePharmacy.sql` file from location storing this file.

2. Ensure that **medicine** is shown as current database. Run the entire script using *F5* key or **Run** command from toolbar. It will create the database and table structure with appropriate relationships as shown in *Figure 16*.

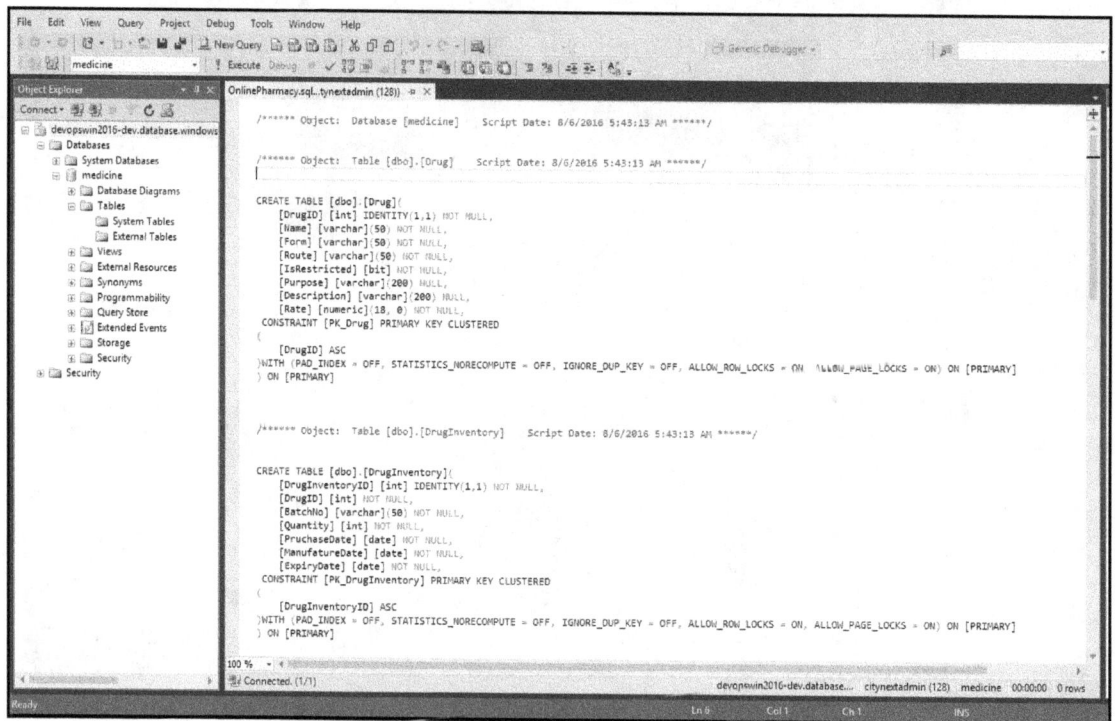

Figure 16: Executing sample SQL script on Azure SQL Server

Next, it's time to understand the database schema.

Understanding database schema

Defining and designing database schema requires a complete book by itself. They are full-blown topics, and we will make it simple for the purpose of our sample application and book. With this in perspective, a single database with four tables are defined. The important point here is to show how a database and its objects are deployed and configured in containers rather than the complexity of designing a database schema.

The database schema containing four tables and its columns are shown in *Figure 17*.

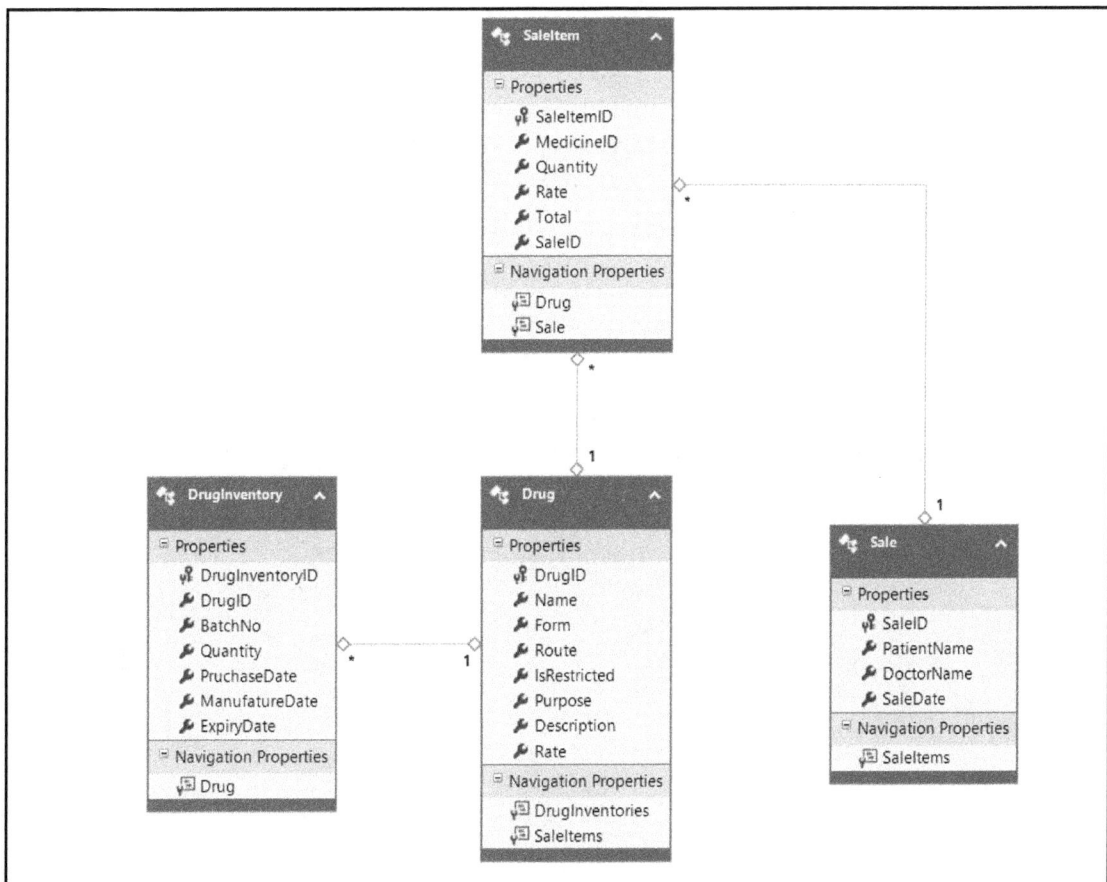

Figure 17: SQL database schema for Online Pharmacy sample application

The **Drug** table holds information about drugs/medicines and its attributes. The **DrugID** column is auto-generated identity column. The value for this column is not provided by frontend web application or any other source. It is auto generated when an entry is made into the table. The **DrugInventory** table holds the available stock of a drug. It is related to **DrugID** column of **Drug** table through referential integrity constraints (primary and foreign keys). The **Sale** table contains details about Patient, Doctor and is related to **SaleItems** table that contains details about all drugs sold as part of sale process. **SaleItem** is also linked to the **Sale** table through primary-foreign key referential integrity constraints. The **SaleItem** table also references **Drug** table to ensure that only drugs available in this table can be sold. The database schema `OnlinePharmacy.sql` is available as part of accompanied source code.

Setting up Visual Studio solution

After creating database structure, it's time to focus on visual studio solution. As mentioned before, the code accompanied with chapter should be used as application under DevOps practices.

A Visual Studio solution **OnlinePharmacy** with three projects is available for use.

The first project **OnlinePharmacy** is an ASP.NET MVC Web Application, the second project **OnlinePharmacy.Configuration** consists of templates and scripts related to configuration management and Infrastructure as code for the application and the last project **OnlinePharmacy.Tests** is unit testing project for the web application project.

The entire source code for all three projects is accompanied with this chapter. Next, let's explore the solution and its contained projects

Open Visual Studio 2015 Community edition, select and open **OnlinePharmacy** solution. The entire solution structure is shown in *Figure 18*.

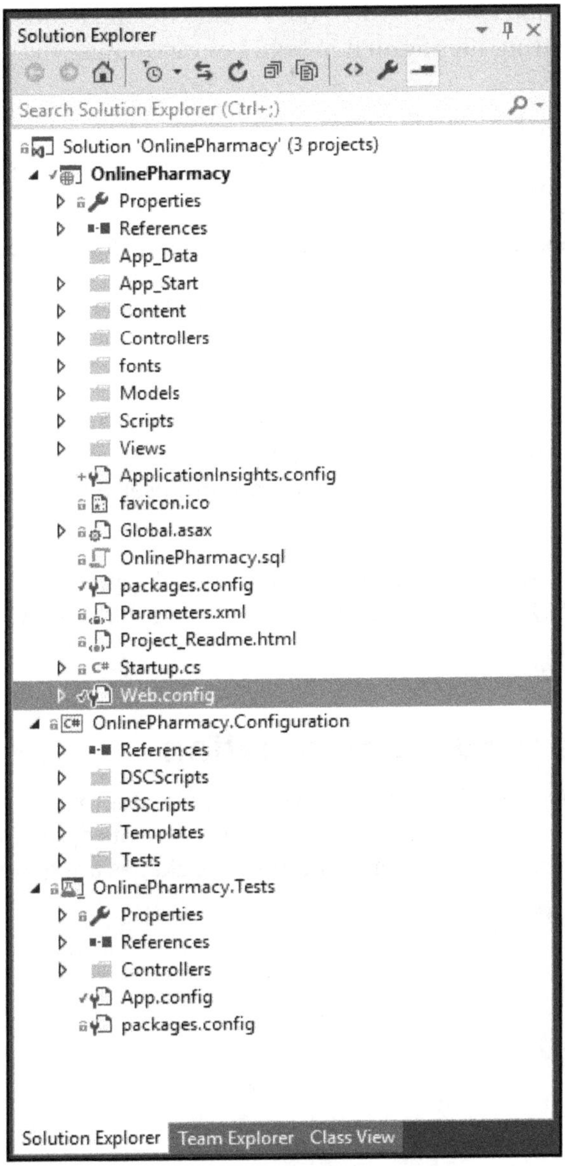

Figure 18: Visual Studio solution structure

Modify web.config connection string

Web application needs a connection string to connect to Azure SQL. This connection string is stored in web application's `web.config` file as shown here. Readers are advised to change the connection string highlighted in bold before running the application.

```
<connectionStrings>
<add name="medicineEntities"
connectionString="metadata=res://*/Models.PharmacyModel.csdl|res://*/Models
.PharmacyModel.ssdl|res://*/Models.PharmacyModel.msl;provider=System.Data.S
qlClient;provider connection string=&quot;data
source=tcp:devopswin2016.database.windows.net,1433;initial
catalog=medicine;Password=xxxxxxxxxx;User
ID=xxxxxxxxxx;MultipleActiveResultSets=True;App=EntityFramework&quot;"
providerName="System.Data.EntityClient" />
</connectionStrings>
```

The `web.config` connection string change is the only change needed to be performed within the solution to make it work on development environment. The changes in connection string should reflect appropriate password, user ID, data source and initial catalog.

I want to provide emphasis that IP address of your development environment must be registered with Azure SQL server Firewall rules. Missing this step will result in exceptions from the application.

Publish profile for web application

The **OnlinePharmacy** web application will eventually be deployed using web deploy packages generated in build pipeline for all the environments apart from development environment. For development environment, these packages are generated using a publish profile.

A publish profile named **Release** is already created within the project. You can view the profile by right clicking on the project and select **Publish** from context menu as shown in *Figure 19*.

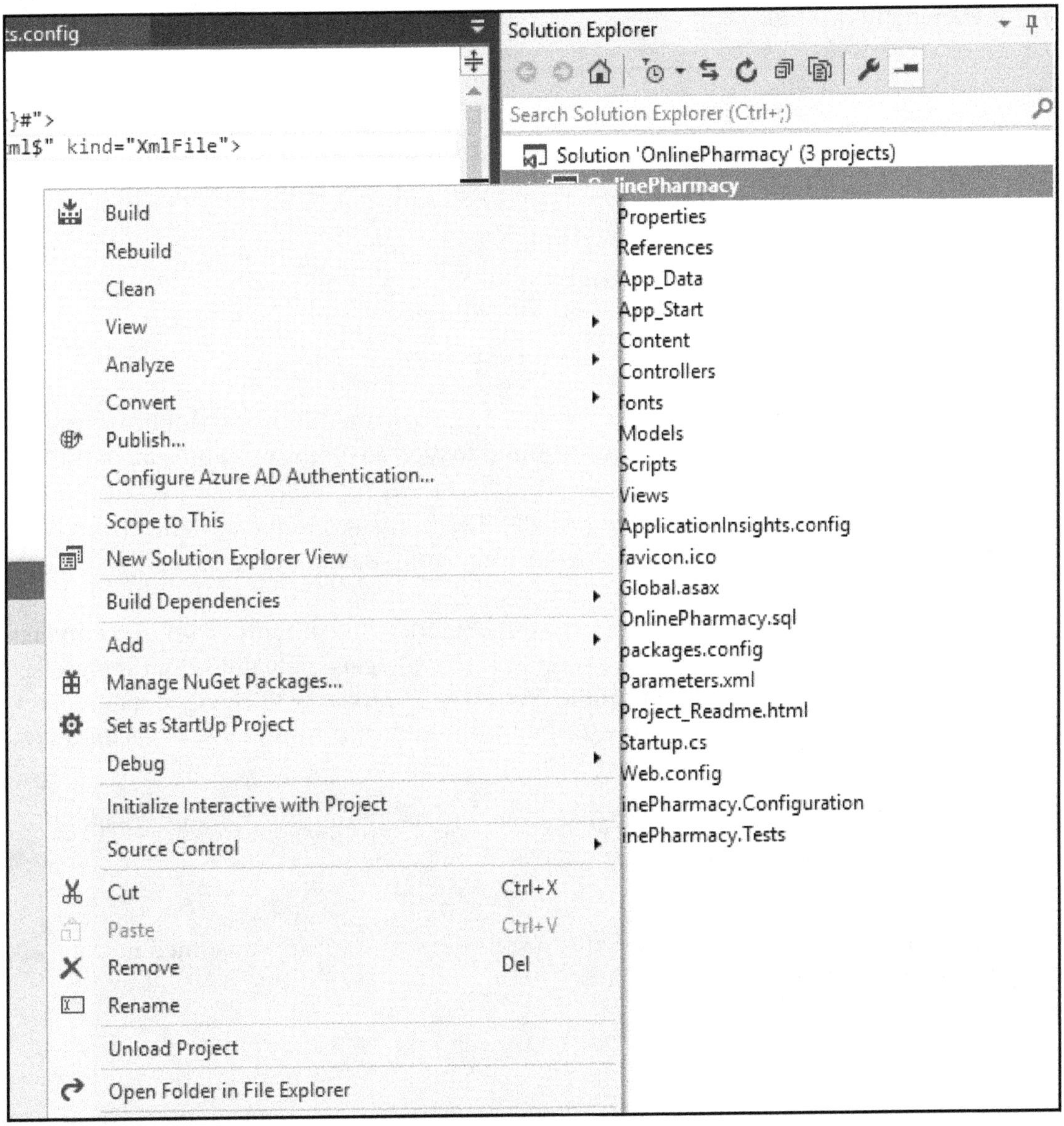

Figure 19: Viewing Publish profile

On the resultant wizard, you can change the location of web deploy packages currently at `C:Packages`.

The packages get generated while building the project. Web deploy packages generates five files as shown in *Figure 20*.

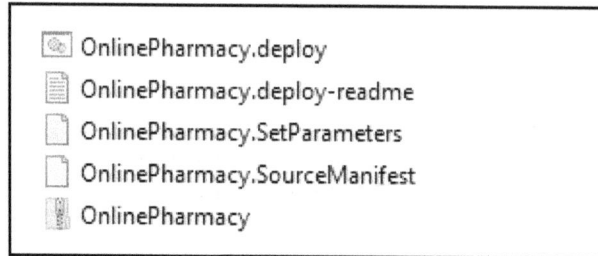

Figure 20: Generated web deploy files

- A `[project name].zip` file: This package contains all the assemblies, files, database scripts, and resources required to recreate your web application on a IIS web server.
- A `[project name].deploy.cmd` file: This contains a set of parameterized web deploy commands that publish your web deployment package to a IIS web server.
- A `[project name].SetParameters.xml` file: This provides a set of parameter values to the `MSDeploy.exe` command. This file gets the values from the project configuration and **Publish** profile. Values in this file can be changed manually or can use `Parameters.xml` file to change the values at runtime which is discussed next.

More details on this subject is available at `https://www.asp.net/web-forms/overview/deployment/web-deployment-in-the-enterprise/configuring-parameters-for-web-package-deployment`.

You should not change other settings in this profile because they are consumed in `Chapter 9`, *Continuous Integration*, in build pipeline.

Parameters.xml

As mentioned before, the web application will be deployed using web deploy packages using build pipeline on IIS. The Website name in IIS can be different for different environment. This file helps in parameterizing properties and settings that vary between destination environments. The build pipeline in `Chapter 9`, *Continuous Integration*, changes the website name dynamically. `Parameters.xml` file works along with web deploy packages and help pass website name values at runtime. Readers are recommended to view code for this file available at root of web application. For more understanding with regard to usage of `Parameters.xml` file refer to link `https://msdn.microsoft.com/en-us/library/ff398068(v=vs.110).aspx`.

Running the sample application

The **OnlinePharmacy** web application should already be set as startup project. If not set it as a startup project as shown here in *Figure 21* and start the application using *F5* key or **Start** command from toolbar.

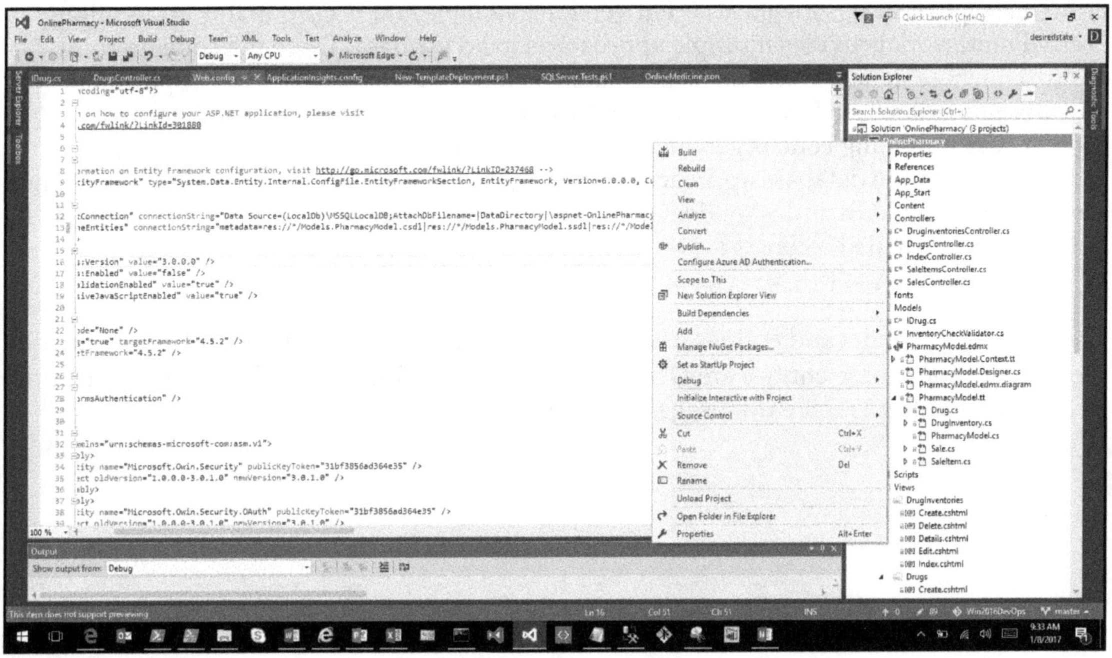

Figure 21: Setting up startup project in Visual Studio

Understanding Visual Studio Solution

The steps mentioned in the sections till the end of unit testing are provided with two purposes in mind.

- Explain the MVC and Entity Framework concepts.
- Discuss important aspects of how this sample application is created. This knowledge will be useful to create your own MVC application.

You may ignore to perform these steps in your development environment as *Setting up Development Environment to run Sample Web App* section has already explained steps to consume the accompanying code.

Entity Framework

Web application interacts and stores data in SQL Server database. Microsoft provides Entity Framework as object-relationship mapping tool to fast track data access development. Entity Framework 6.0 is the most recent version available and is used in this application. Entity Framework provides multiple approaches to access data. There is a code first approach where database schema is generated from models and code in an application. There is also a database first approach in which necessary models, entities, database context, and plumbing code is generated from database schema. The **OnlinePharmacy** application uses the database approach. However, readers are free to use any approach they are comfortable and their design demands. More details about steps used to create Entities and model is provided at `https://www.asp.net/mvc/overview/getting-started/databa se-first-development/creating-the-web-application`.

The application model and entities used in this application are available in `Models` folder of web application. These entities are **Drug, DrugInventory, Sale**, and **SaleItem** are generated as a result of Entity Framework usage. These entities are shown in *Figure 22*.

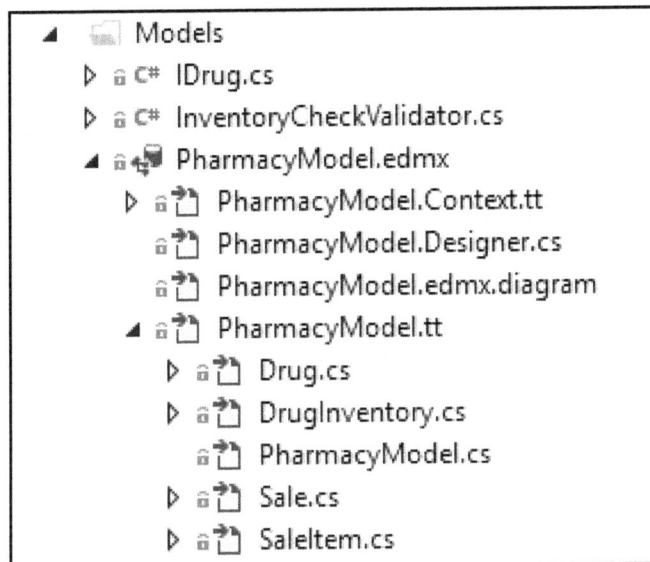

Figure 22: Entity models in sample web application

Both the connection string and entities are generated through Entity Framework wizard. If there are subsequent changes in database schema after generating the model, either the model needs to be updated using Visual Studio or the existing model should be deleted before regenerating the model.

There are no changes done to the generated entities apart from a single change. A custom validator **InventoryCheckValidator** is added as an attribute to quantity property of **SaleItem** class. This validator class checks the availability of a drug/medicine in inventory before it can be sold. The code for this class is available in accompanied source code. The class implements the `ValidateAttribute` abstract class and the `IsValid` method. This method queries and sums all inventories added for a medicine as well as sums up all quantities sold in past and compares the difference between them with current sale quantity. It returns an appropriate message with success or failure as result. Readers are encouraged to look into the code from available source code.

Controllers and Views

Now that database, model, and data connection has been set up, it's time to look into controllers and views. The web application uses the **ASP.NET Web Application** template from **Web** section as shown in *Figure 23*.

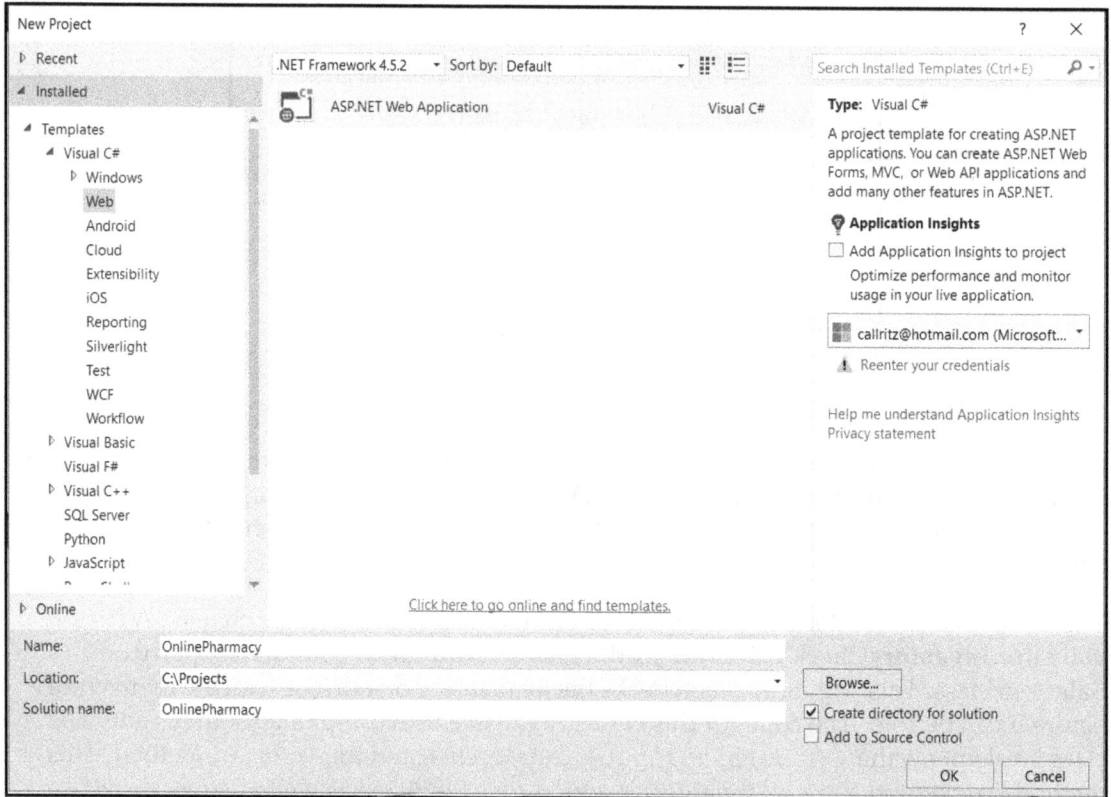

Figure 23: Selecting ASP.NET Web Application project template

.NET framework 4.5.2 is selected as framework selection. **Application Insights** checkbox is checked. The project name is **OnlinePharmacy**. The type of project as shown in *Figure 24* selected is **MVC** from **ASP.NET 4.5.2 Templates** with **Add unit tests** project added. By default, the name of the project would be the name of ASP.NET MVC project with *tests* appended as suffix and the default name is used for unit test project.

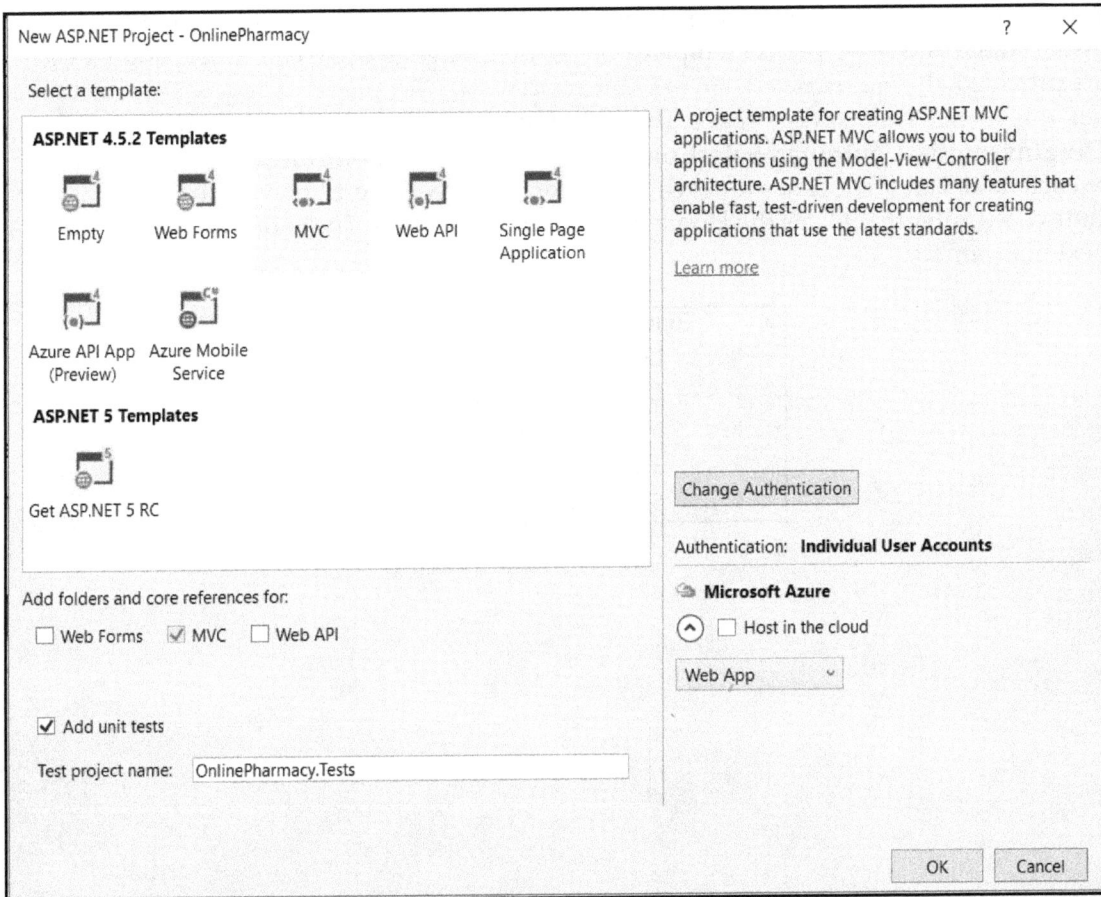

Figure 24: Selecting MVC as project template and adding unit tests project

Alternatively, these two projects could be created after starting from a blank template and adding new projects to it.

Controllers

Both the controllers sand views are generated using the scaffolding feature provided by visual studio and MVC project template. Steps used for generating controllers and views are provided at `https://www.asp.net/mvc/overview/getting-started/database-first -development/generating-views`. There are four controllers, **DrugsController**, **DrugInventoriesController**, **SalesController** and **SaleItemsController**, one corresponding to each model and five views for each controller. There is an additional controller **IndexController** that forms the Home page of the application. The controllers are shown next in *Figure 25*.

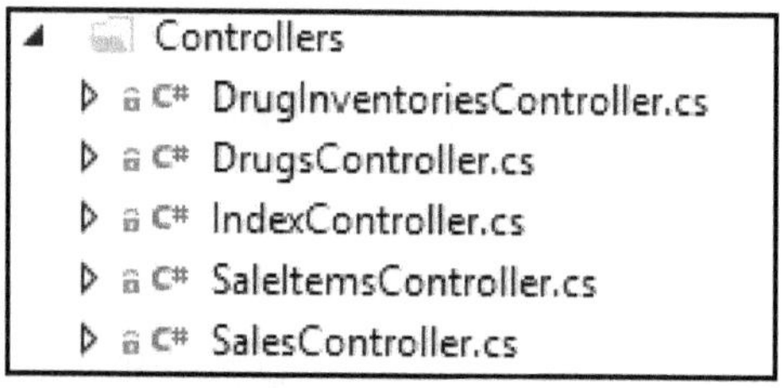

Figure 25: Controllers in visual studio sample web project

Views

As mentioned, there are five major views per controller. These views are used while creating, deleting, editing, listing and homepage for each controller and model. These are shown next in *Figure 26*.

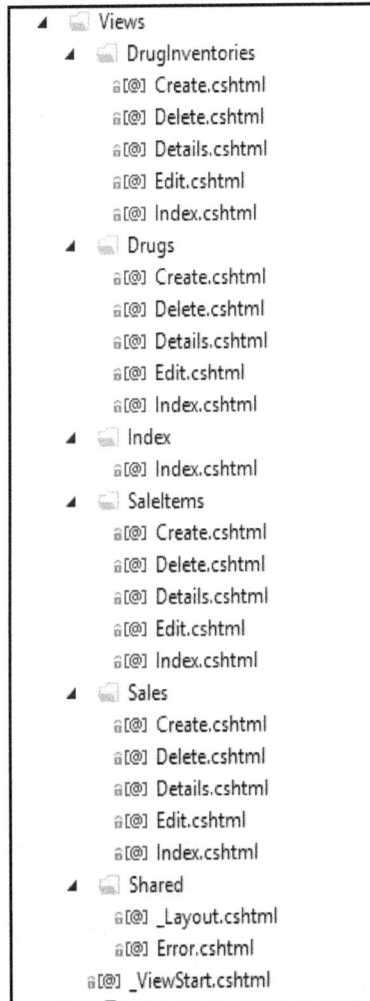

Figure 26: Views in visual studio sample web project

After the code is generated, appropriate changes in views and controllers are done to compose the application.

> Readers are advised to refer to accompanied source code to understand the code changes.

By default, the application shows the index view related to the **index** controller. This is achieved by modifying the **Start Action** project properties as shown in *Figure 27*.

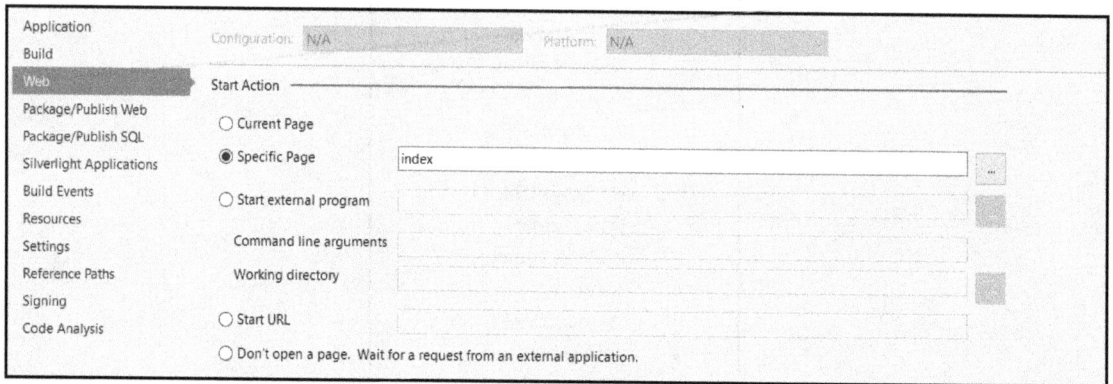

Figure 27: Setting start action to index controller

Configuration management

A new class library project is added to host all configuration management related scripts, templates and configuration. It has four folders

- DSCScripts: This folder contains all Desired State Configuration related scripts
- PSScript: This folder contains all PowerShell scripts
- Templates: This folder contains Azure Resource Manager Templates and DockerFile
- Tests: This folder contains Pester unit and Operational Validation tests

All these files in the project are discussed in details from Chapter 7, *Configuration Management*, to Chapter 10, *Continuous Delivery and Deployment*.

Unit testing

Controllers are the core for working of the **ASP.NET MVC** application. They are the first point of contact for request and coordinates both with models and views to send response back to user. Unit testing refers to the process of testing every code path in isolation to verify its actual working compared with an expected result. Unit test are written as part of unit testing process and includes multiple small and discrete tests.

Although a fully functional application consists of hundreds and thousands of unit tests, for the purpose of **OnlinePharmacy** sample application, few unit test are written and executed to demonstrate unit testing process as part of DevOps continuous integration practice and validate the correctness of code.

In general, controllers invoke data access operations either directly in its class or indirectly by delegating data access operations to some dedicated class. In both cases, the calls are time-consuming and resource intensive in nature. Having hundreds of tests each creating database connection, working on data, and eventually tearing them down takes considerable long time to execute them. As a general rule, it should not considerable long time to execute unit test in a continuous integration pipeline. Every commit or check-in of code will execute unit test, and they should execute without any time lag. To overcome and execute tests quickly, mock and fake objects should be used through dependency injection to simulate data access from controllers rather than invoking them directly.

Both the approaches of accessing data directly or working through mock and fake objects are correct in their own right and can be used depending on how many tests are to be executed, whether data is allowed to be accessed for unit testing and time consumed for data operations.

In this chapter, mock objects are used for unit testing along with controllers for a single Entity. Readers should complete unit test for other entities as an exercise after referring to source code for unit test. The sample application has five controllers, and **DrugController** is used for the purpose of showcasing the approach of mocking data access objects.

Also, readers should judge the best approach for themselves based on guidelines provided here.

The unit test project was already created while creating the **OnlinePharmacy** solution. The project structure is shown here in *Figure 28*.

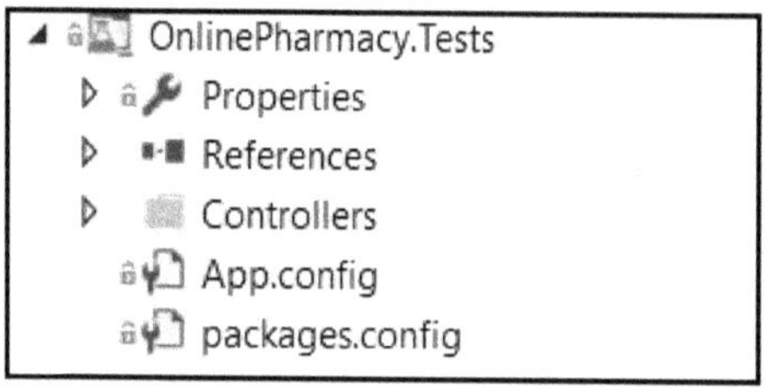

Figure 28: The unit test project structure

The unit testing project **OnlinePharmacy.Tests** by default creates a `Controllers` folder. The unit test code for controllers should be hosted in this folder.

Furthermore, the unit test will be testing controllers and instantiating objects from controller and model classes. To make these classes available to a unit testing project, a reference to **OnlinePharmacy** assembly must be taken. This is shown in *Figure 29*. Right-click on references item and select **Add Reference**. Select **Project** and ensure that the **OnlinePharmacy** project is selected.

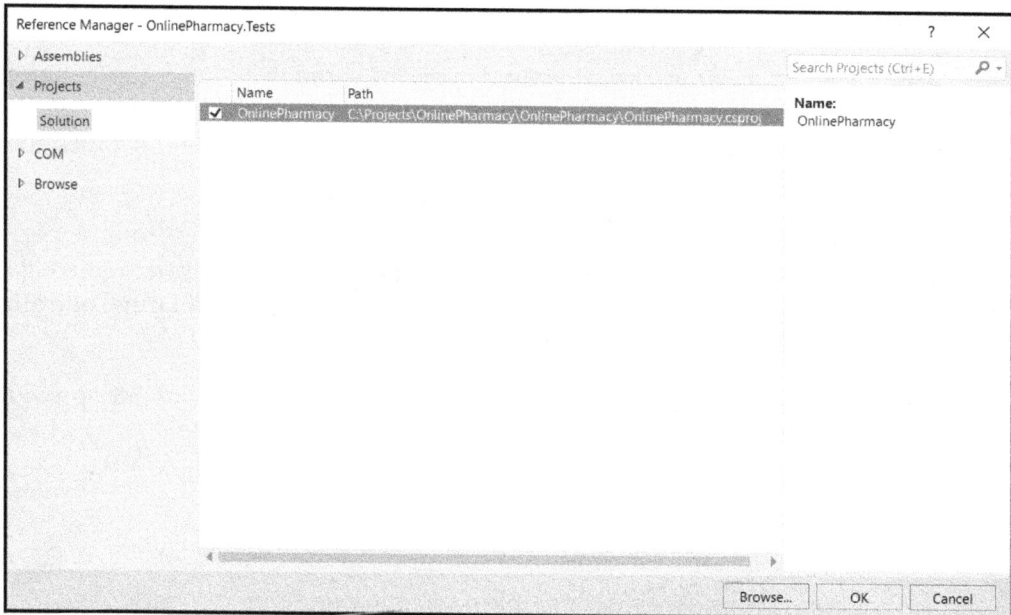

Figure 29: Setting up references to OnlinePharmacy project assembly

Right-click on the `Controllers` folder, click on **Add** and select the **unit test menu** item. This will create a new class `UnitTest1` in file `UnitTest1.cs`. Rename the file to `DrugUnitTests.cs`. Also rename the class to `DrugControllerTests` and remove all code within the class.

Unit testing DrugController

The code generated by Visual Studio for controllers accesses the data context directly by default. The implementation of `DrugController` is modified such that it no more accesses data context directly. Instead a new interface, `IDrug` is declared with methods that performs data access operations within the `Model` folder. The code for `IDrug` interface is shown here:

```
public interface IDrug
    {
        IEnumerable<Drug> GetAllDrugs();
        void CreateDrug(Drug newDrug);
        void EditDrug(Drug oldDrug);
        void DeleteDrug(Drug oldDrug);
        Drug GetDrugDetails(int? id);
    }
```

- The `GetAllDrugs` method returns all drugs available in `Drug` table
- The `CreateDrug` method should create a new Drug entry in `Drug` table
- The `EditDrug` method should update and modify existing Drug in `Drug` table
- The `DeleteDrug` method should delete a Drug from `Drugs` table
- The `GetDrugDetails` method should provide details about a particular drug represented by `DrugID`

A class `DrugRepository` is defined in the same class file implementing the `IDrug` interface. The code for `DrugRepository` is shown here:

```
public class DrugRepository : IDrug
    {
        private medicineEntities db = new medicineEntities();
        public void CreateDrug(Drug newDrug)
        {
            db.Drugs.Add(newDrug);
            db.SaveChanges();
        }
        public void DeleteDrug(Drug oldDrug)
        {
```

```
            db.Drugs.Remove(oldDrug);
            db.SaveChanges();
        }
        public void EditDrug(Drug oldDrug)
        {
            db.Entry(oldDrug).State = EntityState.Modified;
            db.SaveChanges();
        }
        public IEnumerable<Drug> GetAllDrugs()
        {
            return db.Drugs.ToList();
        }
        public Drug GetDrugDetails(int? id)
        {
            Drug drug = db.Drugs.Find(id);
            return drug;
        }
    }
```

The code for interacting with data context is the same as that witnessed in controller class. The data context code has been removed from controller and placed in five discreet methods in the DrugsController class. The DrugsController class instead of accessing data context will access DrugRepository class.

DrugsController is further modified by adding a new parameterized constructor. This constructor accepts any object derived from the IDrug interface and stores it in a private variable. All methods in the DrugsController class uses this object to perform its data-based operations. A new mock repository class will be created implementing the IDrug interface and passed to controller class using parameterized constructor. When the methods of the DrugsController class are invoked, they will invoke the mock repository methods instead of the DrugRepository class.

The code for the DrugsController class is shown here:

```
using System;
using System.Collections.Generic;
using System.Data;
using System.Data.Entity;
using System.Linq;
using System.Net;
using System.Web;
using System.Web.Mvc;
using OnlinePharmacy.Models;
using System.Web.Routing;
namespace OnlinePharmacy.Controllers
{
```

```
public class DrugsController : Controller
{
    private IDrug _drugObject;
    public DrugsController()
    {
        _drugObject = new DrugRepository();
    }
    public DrugsController(IDrug _drug)
    {
        _drugObject = _drug;
    }
    // GET: Drugs
    public ActionResult Index()
    {
        return View("Index",_drugObject.GetAllDrugs());
    }
    // GET: Drugs/Details/5
    public ActionResult Details(int? id)
    {
        if (id == null)
        {
            return new HttpStatusCodeResult(HttpStatusCode.BadRequest);
        }
        Drug drug = _drugObject.GetDrugDetails(id);
        if (drug == null)
        {
            return HttpNotFound();
        }
        return View("Details",drug);
    }
    // GET: Drugs/Create
    public ActionResult Create()
    {
        return View("Create");
    }
    // POST: Drugs/Create
    [HttpPost]
    [ValidateAntiForgeryToken]
    public ActionResult Create([Bind(Include =
    "DrugID,Name,Form,Route,IsRestricted,Purpose,
    Description,Rate")] Drug drug)
    {
        if (ModelState.IsValid)
        {
            _drugObject.CreateDrug(drug);
            return new RedirectToRouteResult(new
            RouteValueDictionary(new {
            action = "Index", controller = "Drugs" }));
```

```
        }
        return View("Create",drug);
    }
    // GET: Drugs/Edit/5
    public ActionResult Edit(int? id)
    {
        if (id == null)
        {
            return new HttpStatusCodeResult(HttpStatusCode.BadRequest);
        }
        Drug drug = _drugObject.GetDrugDetails(id);
        if (drug == null)
        {
            return HttpNotFound();
        }
        return View("Edit",drug);
    }
    // POST: Drugs/Edit/5
    [HttpPost]
    [ValidateAntiForgeryToken]
    public ActionResult Edit([Bind(Include =
    "DrugID,Name,Form,Route,IsRestricted,Purpose,
    Description,Rate")] Drug drug)
    {
        if (ModelState.IsValid)
        {
            _drugObject.EditDrug(drug);
            return new RedirectToRouteResult(new
            RouteValueDictionary(new {
            action = "Index", controller = "Drugs" }));
        }
        return View("Edit", drug);
    }
    // GET: Drugs/Delete/5
    public ActionResult Delete(int? id)
    {
        if (id == null)
        {
            return new HttpStatusCodeResult(HttpStatusCode.BadRequest);
        }
        /* Drug drug = db.Drugs.Find(id); */
        Drug drug = _drugObject.GetDrugDetails(id);
        if (drug == null)
        {
            return HttpNotFound();
        }
        return View("delete", drug);
    }
```

```
// POST: Drugs/Delete/5
[HttpPost, ActionName("Delete")]
[ValidateAntiForgeryToken]
public ActionResult DeleteConfirmed(int id)
{
    Drug drug = _drugObject.GetDrugDetails(id);
    _drugObject.DeleteDrug(drug);
    return new RedirectToRouteResult(new
    RouteValueDictionary(new {
    action = "Index", controller = "Drugs" }));
}
    }
}
```

It can be seen that by default `DrugsController` uses the data access `DrugRepository` class, but using the new constructor, the data access class can be overridden with a mock object that instead of accessing database would provide in-memory data to the controller.

Mocking Drug data access class

A new class file `MockDrugRepository.cs` is added to the `Controllers` folder in the unit test project, and a class `MockDrugRepository` is defined in this file. This class implements the `IDrug` interface and implements all the methods provided by it. However, instead of accessing database context, this class creates a list data structure in-memory and uses it as its database. The entire code for this class is shown here:

```
using System;
using System.Collections.Generic;
using System.Linq;
using System.Text;
using System.Threading.Tasks;
using OnlinePharmacy.Controllers;
using OnlinePharmacy.Models;
namespace OnlinePharmacy.Tests.Controllers
{
    public class MockDrugRepository : IDrug
    {
        private List<Drug> drugs = new List<Drug>();
        public MockDrugRepository()
        {
            drugs = new List<Drug>
            {
                new Drug {
                    DrugID  = 1,
                    Description = "Paracetamol drug",
```

```
                        Form = "tablet",
                        IsRestricted = false,
                        Name = "Paracetamol",
                        Purpose = "Body pain killer",
                        Rate = 10,
                        Route = "Oral"
                },
                new Drug {
                        DrugID  = 2,
                        Description = "Percocet drug",
                        Form = "tablet",
                        IsRestricted = true,
                        Name = "Percocet",
                        Purpose = "Body pain killer",
                        Rate = 20,
                        Route = "Oral"
                }
        };
}
public void CreateDrug(Drug newDrug)
{
    drugs.Add(newDrug);
}
public void DeleteDrug(Drug oldDrug)
{
    drugs.Remove(oldDrug);
}
public void EditDrug(Drug oldDrug)
{
    var drug = drugs.Where(d => d.DrugID ==
    oldDrug.DrugID).FirstOrDefault();
    drugs.Remove(drug);
    drugs.Add(oldDrug);
}
public IEnumerable<Drug> GetAllDrugs()
{
    return drugs;
}
public Drug GetDrugDetails(int? id)
{
    return drugs.SingleOrDefault(d => d.DrugID == id);
}
        }
    }
```

Objects created from this class will be injected into the controller using its parameterized constructor in all our unit test for DrugsController.

Drug controller unit tests

Any class decorated with the [TestClass] attribute is treated as a class containing a unit test and any method within a unit test class with the [TestMethod] attribute is treated as a single discreet unit test. For the purpose of testing the drug controller class with mock data access, 13 unit test are written. There can be more unit tests for this controller, but these unit tests are good representation.

A common pattern in all the tests is that each of them creates a new instance of mock data repository class MockDrugRepository and passes it as argument to the new DrugsController class. Methods of controller classes are invoked, which eventually invokes the methods within the mock object.

The unit test cases along with their code is shown here:

- IndexViewNameCheck: This unit test tests the name of the view returned by controller's Index action method:

```
[TestMethod]
        public void IndexViewNameCheck()
        {
            MockDrugRepository mock = new MockDrugRepository();
            DrugsController drug = new DrugsController(mock);
            ViewResult result = drug.Index() as ViewResult;
            Assert.AreEqual("Index", result.ViewName);
        }
```

- IndexObjectsCheck: This unit test tests that the collection returned by the controller's Index action method returns the expected objects:

```
[TestMethod]
public void IndexObjectsCheck()
{
    MockDrugRepository mock = new MockDrugRepository();
    DrugsController drug = new DrugsController(mock);
    ViewResult result = drug.Index() as ViewResult;
    IEnumerable<Drug> data = (IEnumerable<Drug>)result.Model;
    List<Drug> list = new List<Drug>(mock.GetAllDrugs());
    CollectionAssert.Contains(data.ToList(), list[0]);
    CollectionAssert.Contains(data.ToList(), list[1]);
}
```

- `IndexNotNullCheck`: This unit test checks that the return value from the controller's `Index` action method is not null:

```
[TestMethod]
    public void IndexNotNullCheck()
    {
        MockDrugRepository mock = new MockDrugRepository();
        DrugsController drug = new DrugsController(mock);
        ViewResult result = drug.Index() as ViewResult;
        Assert.IsNotNull(result);
    }
```

- `DetailsValidDrugIDCheck`: It checks that the `DrugID` returned by the `Details` action method is the same as expected:

```
[TestMethod]
public void DetailsValidDrugIDCheck()
{
    MockDrugRepository mock = new MockDrugRepository();
    DrugsController drug = new DrugsController(mock);
    ViewResult result = drug.Details(1) as ViewResult;
    Assert.AreEqual(1, ((Drug)result.Model).DrugID);
}
```

- `DetailsValidNameCheck`: It checks that the Name returned by the `Details` action method is the same as expected.

```
[TestMethod]
public void DetailsValidNameCheck()
{
    MockDrugRepository mock = new MockDrugRepository();
    DrugsController drug = new DrugsController(mock);
    ViewResult result = drug.Details(1) as ViewResult;
    Assert.AreEqual("Paracetamol", ((Drug)result.Model).Name);
}
```

- **DetailsNotNullCheck**: It checks that data returned by the controller's `Detail` action method is not null:

```
[TestMethod]
public void DetailsNotNullCheck()
{
    MockDrugRepository mock = new MockDrugRepository();
    DrugsController drug = new DrugsController(mock);
    ViewResult result = drug.Details(1) as ViewResult;
    Assert.IsNotNull(result);
}
```

- **DeleteViewNameCheck**: This unit test tests the name of the view returned by controller's `Index` action method. It first creates a new `Drug` object and then deletes the same:

```
[TestMethod]
public void DeleteViewNameCheck()
{
    MockDrugRepository mock = new MockDrugRepository();
    DrugsController drug = new DrugsController(mock);
    Drug newDrug = new Drug
    {
        DrugID = 10,
        Description = "A dummy medicine",
        Form = "Capsule",
        Route = "Oral",
        IsRestricted = false,
        Name = "Dummy",
        Purpose = "Does not do anything",
        Rate = 100
    };
    drug.Create(newDrug);
    RedirectToRouteResult result =
    (RedirectToRouteResult)drug.DeleteConfirmed(10);
    Assert.AreEqual("Index", result.RouteValues["action"]);
}
```

- `DeleteNullCheck`: This unit test tests that no `Drug` object is returned after deleting it using the controller's `DeleteConfirmed` action method:

```
[TestMethod]
public void DeleteNullCheck()
{
    MockDrugRepository mock = new MockDrugRepository();
    DrugsController drug = new DrugsController(mock);
    ViewResult deleteResult = drug.DeleteConfirmed(1) as
ViewResult;
    ViewResult result = drug.Details(1) as ViewResult;
    Assert.IsNull(result);
}
```

- `CreateNoNullCheck`: This unit test tests that controller's `Create` action method creates a new `Drug` object and that invoking `Details` method returns an object:

```
[TestMethod]
public void CreateNotNullCheck()
{
    MockDrugRepository mock = new MockDrugRepository();
    DrugsController drug = new DrugsController(mock);
    Drug newDrug = new Drug {
        DrugID = 3,
        Description = "Insulin injection",
        Form = "Inject",
        Route = "Injection",
        IsRestricted = false,
        Name = "Insulin",
        Purpose = "Sugar control",
        Rate = 100
    };
    ViewResult createResult = drug.Create(newDrug) as
ViewResult;
    ViewResult result = drug.Details(3) as ViewResult;
    Assert.IsNotNull(result);
}
```

- `CreateSuccessCheck`: This unit test tests that controller's `Create` action method creates a new `Drug` object and that invoking `Details` method returns the same object:

```
[TestMethod]
public void CreateSuccessCheck()
{
    MockDrugRepository mock = new MockDrugRepository();
    DrugsController drug = new DrugsController(mock);
```

```
        Drug newDrug = new Drug {
                DrugID = 5,
                Description = " Amoxicillin antibiotic",
                Form = "Liquid",
                Route = "Oral",
                IsRestricted = false,
                Name = "Amoxil",
                Purpose = "cold and cough",
                Rate = 50
            };
        ViewResult createResult = drug.Create(newDrug) as ViewResult;
        ViewResult result = drug.Details(5) as ViewResult;
        Assert.AreEqual(5, ((Drug)result.Model).DrugID);
    }
```

- **CreateViewNameCheck**: This unit test tests the name of the view returned by controller's `Create` action method. It creates a new `Drug` object:

```
    [TestMethod]
    public void CreateViewNameCheck()
    {
        MockDrugRepository mock = new MockDrugRepository();
        DrugsController drug = new DrugsController(mock);
        Drug newDrug = new Drug {
            DrugID = 4,
            Description = "Pencillin",
            Form = "Inject",
            Route = "Injection",
            IsRestricted = true,
            Name = "Pencillin",
            Purpose = "Antibiotic",
            Rate = 200
        };
        RedirectToRouteResult result =
(RedirectToRouteResult)drug.Create(newDrug);
        Assert.AreEqual("Index", result.RouteValues["action"]);
    }
```

- **EditViewNameCheck**: This unit test tests the name of the view returned by controller's `Edit` action method. It creates a new `Drug` object and then edits it:

```
    [TestMethod]
    public void EditViewNameCheck()
    {
        MockDrugRepository mock = new MockDrugRepository();
        DrugsController drug = new DrugsController(mock);
        Drug newDrug = new Drug {
```

```
            DrugID = 15,
            Description = "Galvus",
            Form = "tablet",
            Route = "Oral",
            IsRestricted = true,
            Name = "Galvus",
            Purpose = "Diabetes",
            Rate = 150
        };
        drug.Create(newDrug);
        newDrug.Purpose = "controls diabetes and sugar level";
        RedirectToRouteResult result =
(RedirectToRouteResult)drug.Edit(newDrug);
        Assert.AreEqual("Index", result.RouteValues["action"]);
    }
```

- EditValidCheck: This unit test tests that controller's Edit action method to return its updated object. It creates a new Drug object and then edits it:

```
[TestMethod]
public void EditValidCheck()
{
    MockDrugRepository mock = new MockDrugRepository();
    DrugsController drug = new DrugsController(mock);
    Drug newDrug = new Drug {
        DrugID = 16,
        Description = "Lucentis",
        Form = "tablet",
        Route = "Oral",
        IsRestricted = true,
        Name = "Lucentis",
        Purpose = "Eye Blindness",
        Rate = 150
    };
    drug.Create(newDrug);
    newDrug.Purpose = "Eye Blindness and color blindness";
    drug.Edit(newDrug);
    ViewResult result = drug.Details(16) as ViewResult;
    Assert.AreEqual("Eye Blindness and color blindness",
    ((Drug)result.Model).Purpose);
}
```

This unit test are executed in Visual Studio through the **Tests** menu as shown in *Figure 30*.

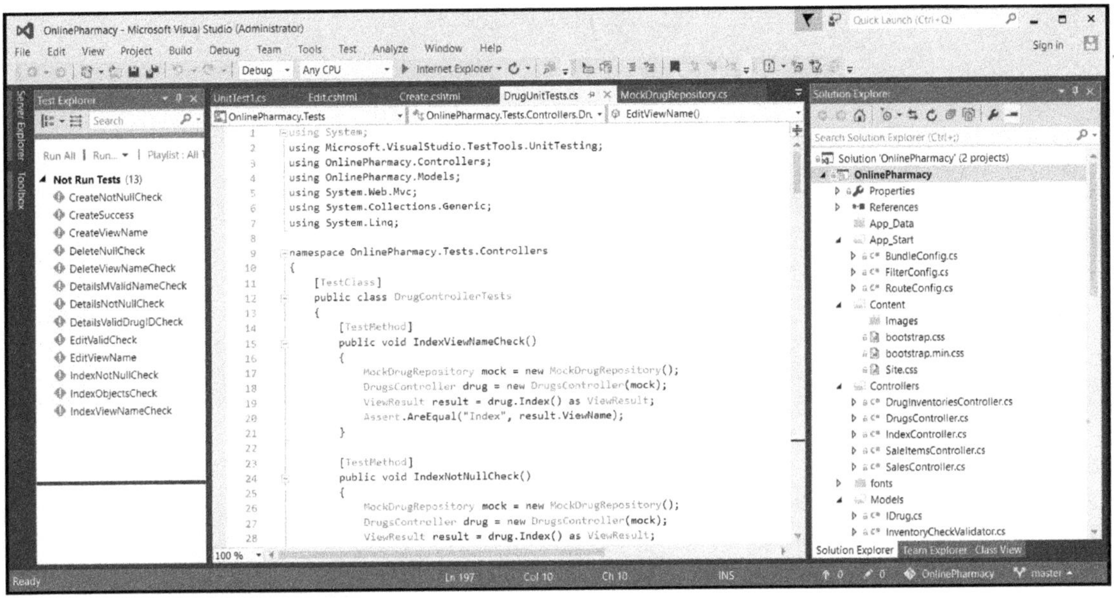

Figure 30: Visual Studio with drug controller unit test

Summary

This chapter introduced a sample web-based application, **OnlinePharmacy**. We need an application on which DevOps practices and principles can be applied and implemented. You as a reader will be working on a real application and need to understand the way DevOps can be applied to a sample application. This chapter talked about the concepts, components, and steps that were used to create an **ASP.NET MVC** web application that were also used to create the sample application. You are encouraged to refer to source code accompanying this chapter to understand the application and at the same time can create their own application in order to implement DevOps practices.

The next chapter will introduce a source code control mechanism for this sample application and show how it can be used to maintain source code for teams with multiple members across regions.

6
Source Code Control

In this chapter, we will learn one of the most important DevOps practices. Until now, we have explored the context around technology and a sample application was created to facilitate the implementation of DevOps practices. This and the next chapter collectively deal with Configuration Management. Although the next chapter deals with infrastructure and application Configuration Management, this chapter is about Source Code and Version Control Management, also known as **Source Configuration Management (SCM)**.

Configuration Management

Configuration Management is the process of applying code and configuration changes to services and applications while maintaining the history of those changes. Maintaining the history helps in reverting back to any previous valid version, helps in auditing and facilitates Release Management. Although Source Code and Configuration can be managed manually by developers by keeping multiple copies of code, it is a tedious and error-prone exercise. It is recommended to use and deploy automation tools for Configuration Management.

Configuration Management helps in three major aspects:

- **Change management**: Changes to application code and configuration should be managed and controlled. Code should be baselined, and any new development or changes should happen with reference to the baseline. Once the change is approved, developed, tested, and released, it becomes the new baseline and reference point. Developers working on these changes should have a replica of the baseline for their development environment. They should not work on the baseline version directly. These developments could be for bug fixes or new feature development. Adequate testing, validation, and verification are performed and, after management's approval, the changes should be pushed as a release to production.

- **Developing with multiple teams**: When multiple teams and developers are involved, it is recommended to have a common code repository and enabling collaboration. This common repository enables simultaneous and parallel changes and it should be capable of performing branching, merging, and conflict resolution for the source code. This directly improves productivity and collaboration among developers and teams. Such a repository also helps in auditing and security control.

- **Release management**: It is an absolute must for development and operations team to know the current configuration of applications and services on production and details about newer changes being developed as part of the next future release. Configuration management helps in recording these configuration changes as part of its history logs, and can help in rolling back releases to earlier valid working specific versions of configuration.

Source Configuration Management

Source Configuration Management and Version Control Management refer to the process of managing and controlling access and changes to Source Code. It involves storing source code and configurations within a repository with restrictive access, allowing authorized users to create, modify, update, and delete the source code and configurations in a controlled manner, and maintain the history of all such changes. It provides appropriate automation for code conflict resolution, parallel development paths, comparison of files, and reverting to previous specific versions. It records all changes to source code in its history logs over a period of time. Source Configuration Management and Version Control System helps in eliminating and maintaining multiple copies of the same files by developers and make them more productive by providing tools to identify their changes over a period of time and increase collaboration.

There are many SCM tools and products available today. Some are open source, whereas others are proprietary in nature. Some of the major tools are:

- Git
- VSTS
- TFS
- SVN
- CVS
- Perforce

There are two types of Source Configuration Management and version control:

- Centralized
- Distributed

Centralized

In a Centralized Source Configuration Management and Version Control System, a Centralized Server is designated as a version control server to which multiple developers can connect, interact, and collaborate. It helps in managing and controlling distributed teams dispersed across geographies. Centralized version control stores the source code files and manages all its version over a period of time in a centralized location. Developers normally are connected to this centralized repository on an continuous basis. They checkout files to modify them and check them in to commit changes within the repository. Developers only have a working copy of source code on their local system; however, they do not have the history of all changes made to the source code by every developer. The main advantage of this kind of Version Control System is full control lies with administrators and every developer is aware of the work done by other developers. It also helps collaboration among multi-location teams across geographies.

The main drawback of such a Version Control System is that they are a single point of failure. Any downtime can seriously affect productivity of and collaboration among developers. Also, it is suitable for smaller teams as they all are always connected to the central repository. A pictorial representation of Centralized Version Control System is shown in *Figure 1*.

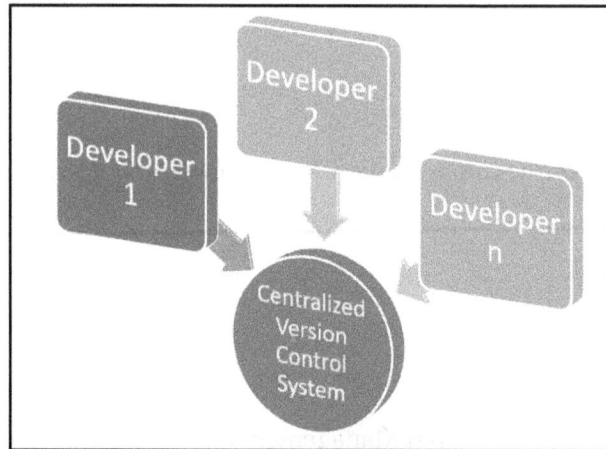

Figure 1: Centralized Version Control System

Some major Centralized Version Control Systems are TFVC, Perforce, and CVS.

Distributed

A Distributed Version Control System is an evolution from Centralized Version Control System. In a Distributed Version Control System, although a centralized repository is designated as a remote repository with which multiple developers can work, they are not continuously connected to it. In fact, developers have entire copy of the source code and version history on their local workstation. They work on this local copy and connect back to the central repository to synchronize their changes. In effect, every developer's machine is a mirror copy of the remote repository. A Distributed Version Control System has all the features of a Centralized Version Control System; however, there is no single point of repository failure and it provides a highly scalable ecosystem to developers. They connect to the remote repository when they need to synchronize their changes with it.

The Distributed Version Control Management system is shown in *Figure 2*:

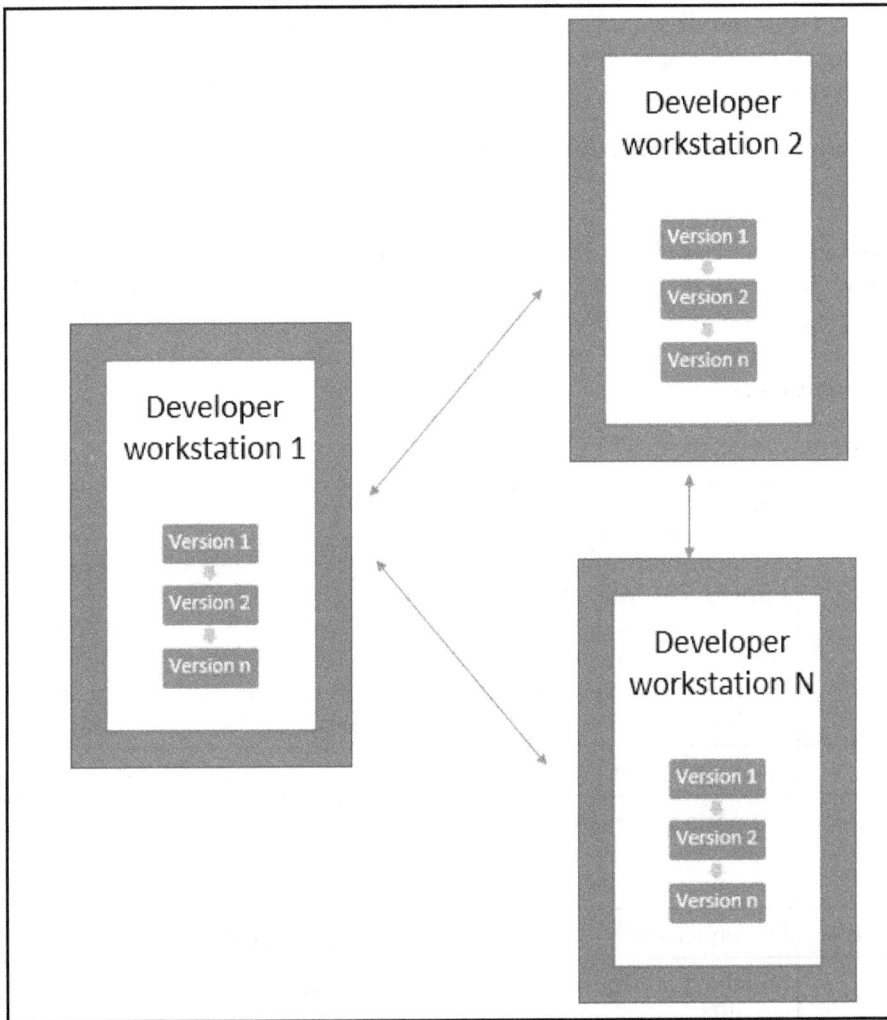

Figure 2: Distributed Version Control System

Git is one of the most used and famous Distributed Version Control System.

Visual Studio Team Services

Visual Studio Team Services (**VSTS**) provides Software Configuration Management and control services for source code. It has two types of repositories and teams can select them based on their needs:

- **Team Foundation Version Control** (**TFVC**)
- **Git**

TFVC is the traditional Centralized Source Code Management System, whereas Git is a relatively new distributed Source Code Management System. Git is the default repository in VSTS when creating a new repository. There was already an introduction to both Git and TFVC in `Chapter 2`, *DevOps Tools and Technologies*, and readers are advised to read it for a better understanding.

The main differences between TFVC and Git are shown in *Table 1*:

Type	Git	TFVC
Branching	Advance branching is possible through Git. Very fast to create branches. Does not copy files to create new branches. Supports branches on developer's local machine	Supports basic branching techniques. Copies files to create new branches. Creating branches is a time-consuming process, especially when the repository is large. Does not support local branching.
File size	Not suitable for large files	Supports large files
Merging	Supports advance merging strategies, such as fast forward, recursive, or resolve	Supports basic merging
Is Connected	Disconnected	Connected
Team size	Suitable for large teams. Highly scalable	Suitable for smaller teams
History availability	Repository history is available on every developer workstation	Repository history is not available on every developer workstation
Identifiers	Apply tags to commits	Apply labels to batch check-in

Table 1: Git versus TFVC

In this book, **Git repository** in VSTS is used for the sample application as a Source Code Management System.

Git 101

As mentioned before, Git is a Distributed Version Control Management System. Any folder on disk can be a Git repository. The only requirement to be a Git repository is that it should be Initialized or Cloned using the Git command-line. A Git repository contains files and folders along with a complete history of changes made to them. It also contains information about active, passive branches along with tags. All files and folders under the control of the Git repository are collectively called a **working tree**.

The Git repository can be either remote or local. Remote repositories are repositories hosted on the Internet and can be accessed from anywhere while local repositories are repositories hosted on the developer's workstation and accessible only to that developer. Remote repositories can be cloned as local repositories. When remote repositories are cloned, all files and folders (also known as the working tree) along with the entire repository history are copied to the developer's workstation. Developers work with this local repository actively and are not connected to the remote repository. When they have finished working on their code, the local repository can be synchronized with the remote repository. This synchronization updates the local repository with changes made in the remote repository from other developers but not available on the local repository and also update the remote repository with changes from the local repository. If there are conflicts, the developer can resolve them during this synchronization process.

It is to be noted that a Git remote repository is needed when multiple developers are working together and collaborating among themselves. It is also needed when the code needs to be highly available on a more stable hardware compared to the developer's workstation. A remote repository is not needed when the developer is working on a local repository and does not want those changes to be available on any other developer.

A remote Git repository can be created in VSTS within a Team Project. The local Git repository can be created using two different methods.

Git init

Git init initializes an empty Git repository with an empty history. The command can be executed using Git for Windows and is shown next:

```
Git init
```

It initializes a Git repository at the current folder location and adds a hidden .Git folder to it. This .Git folder is known as the Git repository and maintains the entire history of code changes over a period of time.

```
Git init <<folder location>>
```

It initializes a Git repository at given folder location and adds a hidden .Git folder to it.

Files or folders in a Git initialized repository can be either in a tracked or untracked state. The mere presence of a file or folder in the Git initialized directory does not mean that it is part of the Git repository. These files and folders are referred to as untracked files and folders. Git is not aware of any changes to untracked files.

Git follows a two-phase approach to ensure that files or folders can be tracked and are under the control of Git. The first phase is known as **staging**. When files and folders are staged, they are added and recorded in the Git repository but not yet committed to it. Blob (Binary large objects) objects are generated by Git for each added file and recorded in Git's index file within the .Git folder. The next phase is to commit the staged changes. Committing generates a commit object, which refers to the object graph of the working tree and stores the same in the Git repository. The Git commit object uniquely identifies a revision or version of all files and folders in a repository using an ID. The Git repository keeps track of all commit objects. The repository always points to the most recent Git commit object and when a new commit object is created, it moves the pointer to the new commit object. Each commit object also has a reference to its parent commit object. The commit graph is shown in *Figure 3*.

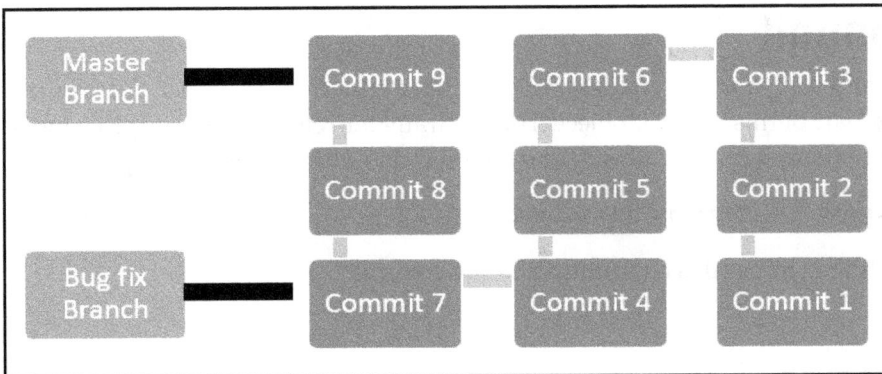

Figure 3: Git commit graph

The command `Git commit` creates and commits a new `commit` object.

Git clone

A Git repository can also be created by cloning an existing Git `local` or `remote` repository. The command for cloning a Git repository is shown here:

```
Git clone <<url of remote repository>>
```

or like this:

```
Git clone <<path to local Git repository>>
```

Git add

After a Git repository is created either using `Git init` or `Git clone`, to add a file or folder to the staging area, the `Git add` command is used. Using `.` with this command means that all tracked files with changes and untracked files are added to the staging area. The command is shown here:

```
Git add .
```

Git commit

The command `Git commit` creates and commits a new `commit` object. All files from staging are part of this `commit` object. The `m` parameter refers to a descriptive message associated with each `commit` object. The command is shown here:

```
Git commit -m "This is first commit"
```

The preceding command is committing a new commit.

Git branch

A branch in SCM is referred to as an independent path of development. A branch in Git is a pointer to a specific `commit` object. A separate copy is not created when creating a branch in Git. There can be multiple branches in a repository, each pointing to the same or different `commit` objects. Branching in Git does not copy, instead a pointer is created pointing to a particular version of files and folders by means of a `commit` object. Git branches are extremely lightweight and fast to create.

The command `Git branch` creates a new branch. This is shown here:

```
Git branch <<Branch name>>
```

Git merge

Branches are created for multiple purposes. Generally, the main branch is called the **master** branch. Multiple branches from the **master** branch are created for independent parallel development paths such as bug fixing, the development of new features, and releases. After these independent lines of development are complete, they are merged back to the main **master** branch. The process of synchronizing a branch into another branch is called **merging**. It not only merges file and folder content but also modifies the history of the repository. Merging can be as simple as copying or updating files and folders to the target branch without any conflicts. However, it can be complex when the same files and contents are changed in both the branches. In such cases, conflicts should be resolved by accepting the changes. Git provides multiple strategies for merging including fast-forward, resolve, rebasing, and recursive.

The command `Git merge` merges a branch referred by a branch name to a current branch. The command is shown here:

```
Git merge <<Branch name>>
```

Git remote

As mentioned earlier, a Git repository can be provisioned as a remote repository. The purpose of Git remote is to maintain up-to-date history from all developers with regard to content, hosted on the Internet. Developers will clone the remote repository to get the entire working tree and its history. Developers will periodically pull changes from the remote repository, which are committed and pushed by other developers, and push their own committed changes to the remote repository.

The command to pull changes from the remote repository is shown next:

```
Git pull origin master
```

Here, `origin` is an alias that refers to the URL of the remote repository and `master` refers to the branch name that needs to be pulled and merged into a local branch. It is to be noted that the `pull` command internally executes multiple commands. It first uses the `fetch` command to fetch the content and history into a local workstation and then executes the `merge` command to merge the remote changes to local changes:

The command to push changes to the remote repository is shown next:

```
Git push origin master
```

Here, `origin` is an alias that refers to the URL of the remote repository and `Master` refers to the branch name that needs to be pushed and merged into the `remote` branch:

Installing Git for Windows on the development environment

Visual Studio needs the Git toolkit to manage local repositories and interact with remote repositories. The Git for Windows tool available at `https://Git-scm.com/` is used in this book to work with the Git repository. This utility is not available on Windows operating systems and not installed along with Visual Studio. It can be downloaded and installed separately on the development environment from the provided URL. This is also shown in *Figure 4*.

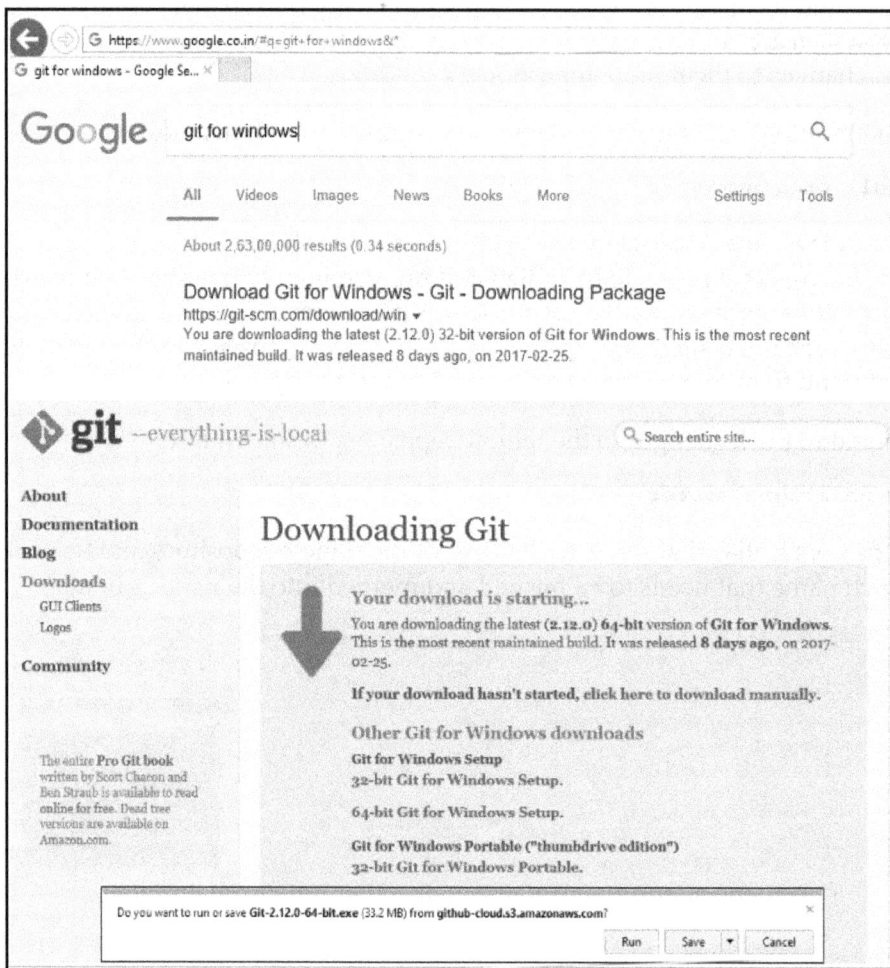

Figure 4: Git for Windows download URL

The setup can be executed after having been saved on a local disk or run directly. *Figure 5* shows the major steps for installing Git for Windows on a Windows 10 development workstation.

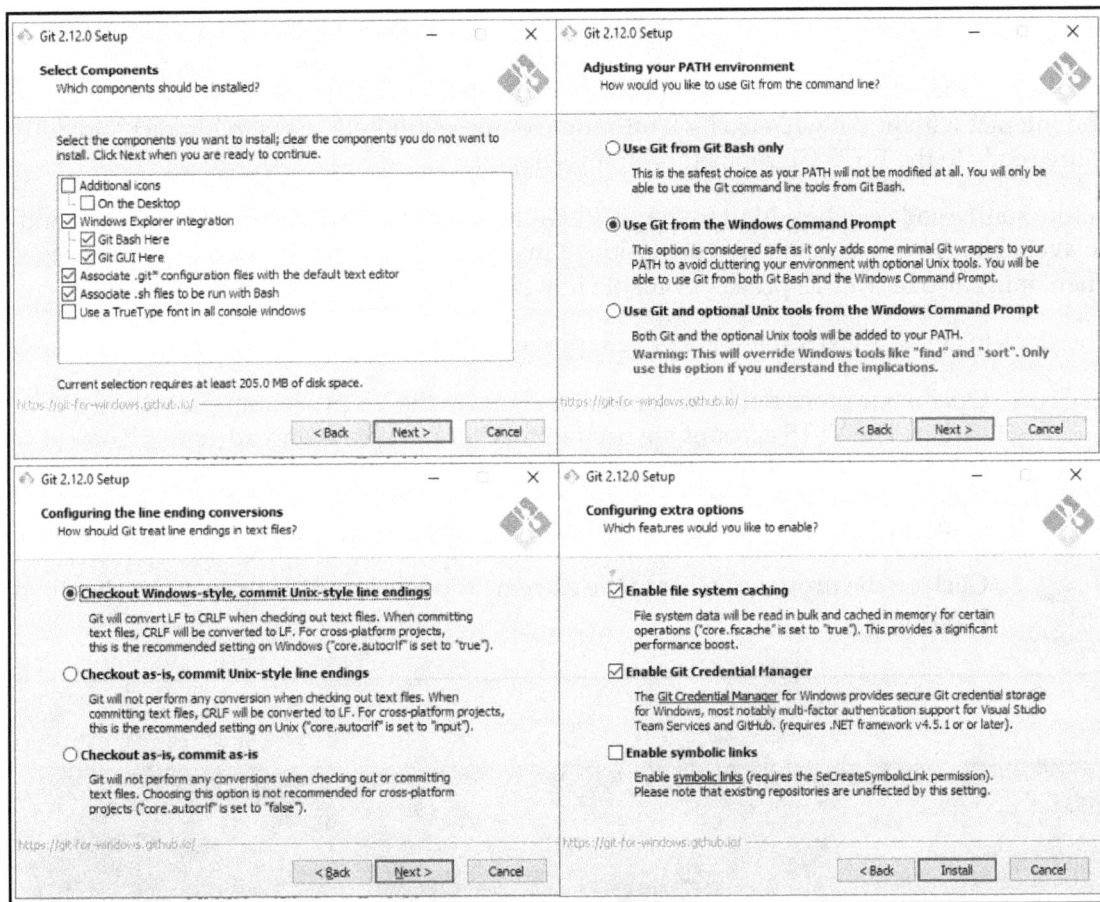

Figure 5: Git for Windows installation steps

Adding Online Pharmacy to the VSTS Git repository using Visual Studio 2015

In `Chapter 5`, *Building a Sample Application* a sample application *Online Pharmacy* was introduced. In this section, we will add the same to Visual Studio Team Service's Git repository. There are multiple different ways to add source code to the VSTS Git repository and interact with it. We will also look into some of these different ways to interact and add source code to the VSTS Git repository in this chapter.

Before source code can be added to the VSTS Git repository, a VSTS account must exist and be available. A VSTS account was provisioned in `Chapter 2`, *DevOps Tools and Technologies*. There must also be a VSTS project available in which a Git repository can be created.

The steps to create a VSTS Team Project are provided here:

1. Open your preferred browser and navigate to the VSTS account provisioned earlier. The VSTS account we used in this book can be found at: `https://desired state.visualstudio.com/`

   Readers are advised to create their own account.

2. Click on the drop-down list at the extreme top-left corner of the page as shown in *Figure 6*.

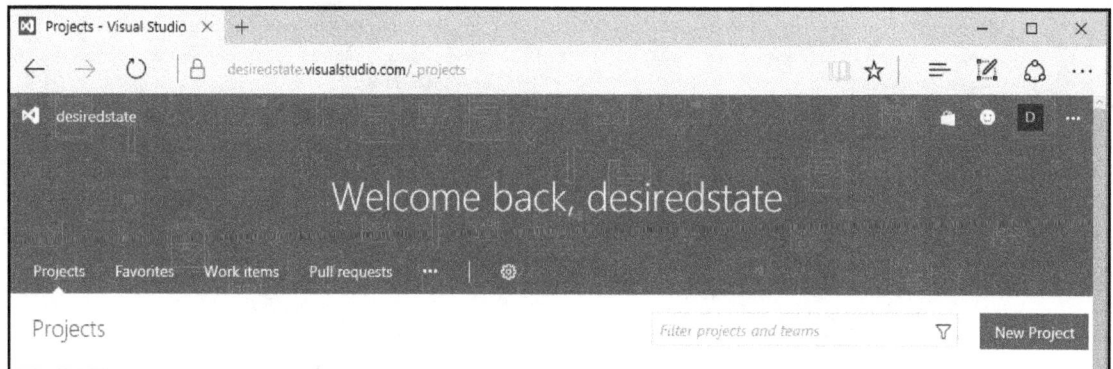

Figure 6: Selecting a new project in VSTS

3. The name of the Team Project used in this book is **Win2016DevOps**. Provide the
   project name, select **Agile** as the process template, and **Git** as the version control,
   and then click on the **Create project** button as shown in *Figure 7*.

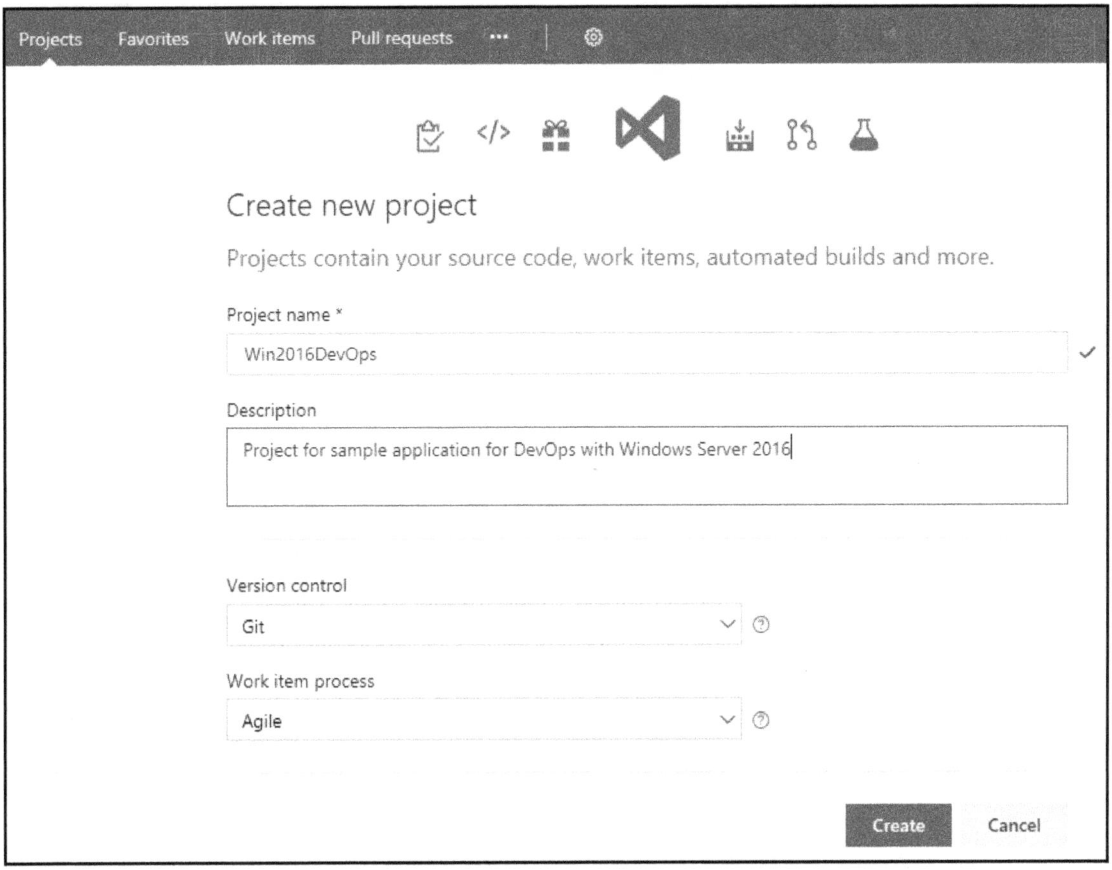

Figure 7: Creating a new VSTS project with a Git repository

From the resultant screen, note down the URL as shown in *Figure 8*. This URL will be needed in subsequent steps to configure Visual Studio Remotes in the development environment.

Win2016DevOps ☆

Briefly describe your project...

Get started with your new project!

ˇ   Clone to your computer

HTTPS | SSH   https://win2016devops.visualstudio.com/_git/Win2016DevOps   📋   **OR**   ⏻ Clone in Visual Studio   ˇ

Generate Git credentials

○ Having problems authenticating in Git? Be sure to get the latest version of Git for Windows or our plugins for IntelliJ, Eclipse, Android Studio or Windows command line.

Figure 8: A Git repository URL in VSTS

The first step is to configure Git on the local workstation with a user email ID and name. The 64-bit version of Git is by default installed in the `%Program files%` folder. Open `Git-bash.exe` and configure it with the user's e-mail and user name as shown here:

The prompt by default is made up of the currently logged-in user and machine name separated by @ symbol.

```
citynextadmin@DevVS MINGW64
$ Git config --global user.email "desiredstate@outlook.com"
citynextadmin@DevVS MINGW64
$ Git config --global user.name "DesiredState"
```

4. Once the e-mail and user configuration are done, Git can be used for managing repositories. Copy the `Win2016DevOps` folder from the `Chapter 5`, *Building a Sample Application* source code to your preferred file system location. This location will become your local Git repository. We have created this at `C:Projects`. This is shown as follows:

Navigate to the copied folder `Win2016DevOps`.

```
citynextadmin@DevVS MINGW64 ~
$ cd /c/projects/Win2016DevOps
```

The `init` command to initialize the Git repository.

```
citynextadmin@DevVS MINGW64 /c/projects/Win2016DevOps
$ Git init
```

This will initialize an empty Git repository.

Add all the copied files to the Git staging using the `Git add` command. Notice that `master` is appended to the path to show that it is a Git repository.

```
citynextadmin@DevVS MINGW64 /c/projects/Win2016DevOps (master)
$ Git add
```

5. Commit the newly add files to the local Git repository using the `Git commit` command as shown next.

```
citynextadmin@DevVS MINGW64 /c/projects/Win2016DevOps (master)
$ Git commit -m "adding DevOpsWin2016 artifacts to Git"
```

6. Now, we can start working with Visual Studio 2015. Open Visual Studio 2015 and click on **Team Explorer** as shown in *Figure 9*. There is no active connection to any project in VSTS.

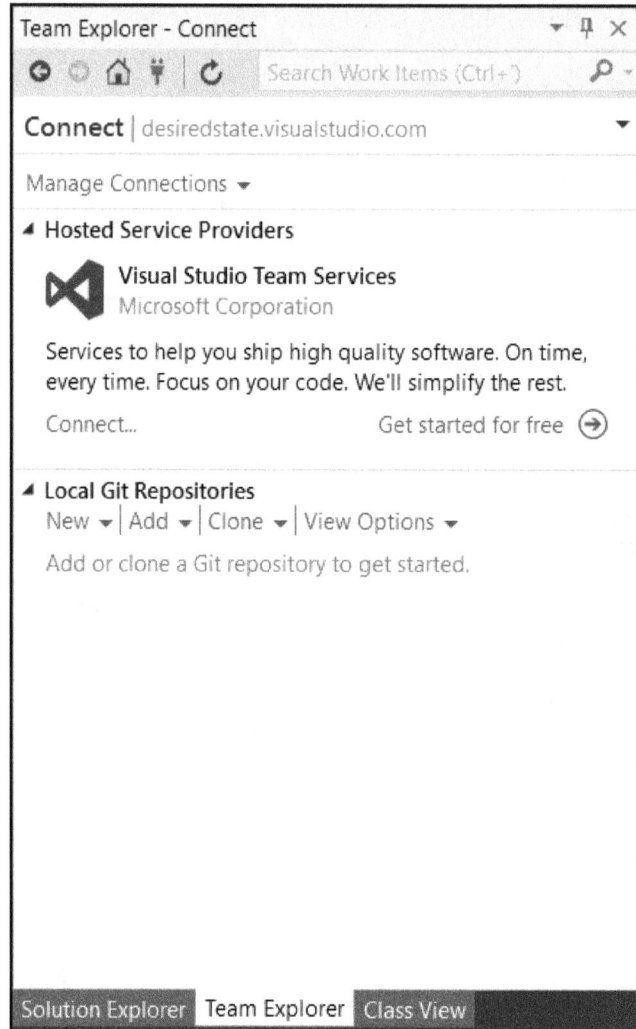

Figure 9: Team Explorer window in Visual Studio 2015

7. Within the **Local Git Repositories** section, click on **Add** to add the **OnlinePharmacy** solution to **Visual Studio**. The **Add** link allows us to add an existing local repository. Navigate to the folder `DevOpsWin2016` was copied to. In this case, it is `C:projectsWin2016DevOps`. Provide the location of the `project` folder and click on the **Add** button as shown on the left-hand of the screenshot in *Figure 11*. Right-click on the resulting repository and click on **Open** as shown on the right-hand screenshot in *Figure 10*.

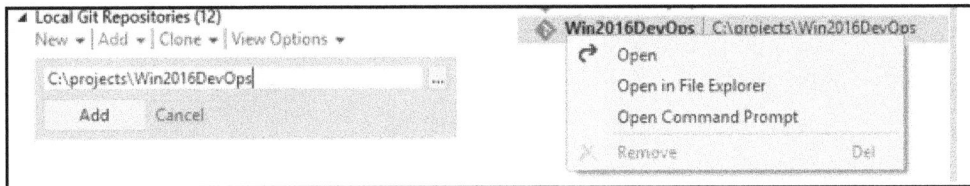

Figure 10: Adding existing Git Repository

8. The preceding step will open the **Home** dashboard for the repository. Click on the **Settings** button from the **Home** screen, to the **Settings** screen in **Team Explorer**. Click on **Repository Settings** on the **Settings** page to modify settings for the newly created local repository as shown in *Figure 11*. It is to be noted that no connection has yet been created to VSTS from a local repository.

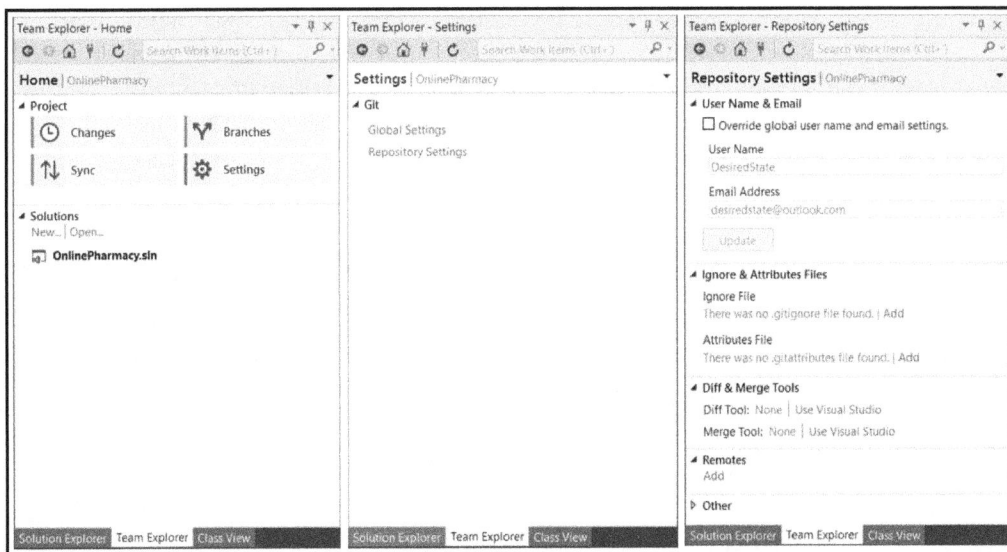

Figure 11: Setting a Repository Settings

9. Add a new remote to the **Repository Settings**. Provide **origin** as the name and the URL of the VSTS project that was copied earlier, as the **Fetch** and **Push** values. The **Fetch** and **Push** URL values should in general be the same. Click on the **Save** button as shown in *Figure 12*:

Figure 12: Adding remote information

10. Now that we have a local Git repository with a **master** branch and remotes configured with a remote VSTS account, it's time to push and publish the branch itself to the VSTS Git repository. Publishing the first branch will create the branch itself if it does not yet exist. In order to publish a branch, click on the Home button in **Team Explorer** and click on the Branch button as shown in *Figure 13*. Right-click on the **master** branch and select **Publish Branch** from the context menu. This will start the process of publishing the entire branch along with its source code to the VSTS account. Provide the appropriate credentials, if prompted.

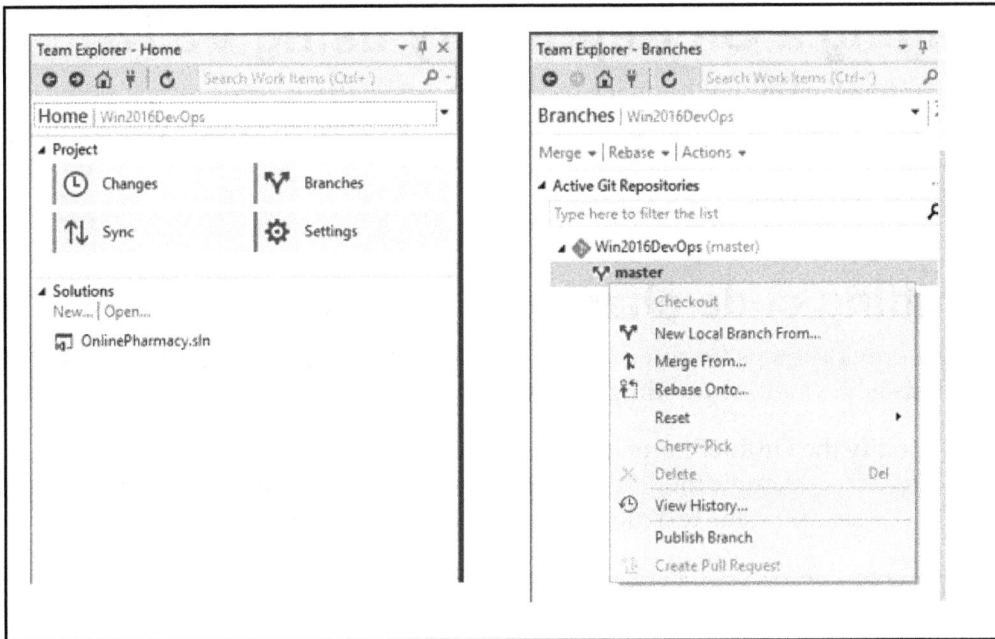

Figure 13: Publishing Branch to a remote Git repository

11. Publishing process takes a few minutes to push the local branch to the remote
    repository. Once it is complete, the **Team Explorer** screen should show that it has
    successfully published the source code in the **master** branch, and the VSTS **Code**
    hub shows that code has moved to the Git repository named **Win2016DevOps** as
    shown in *Figure 14*.

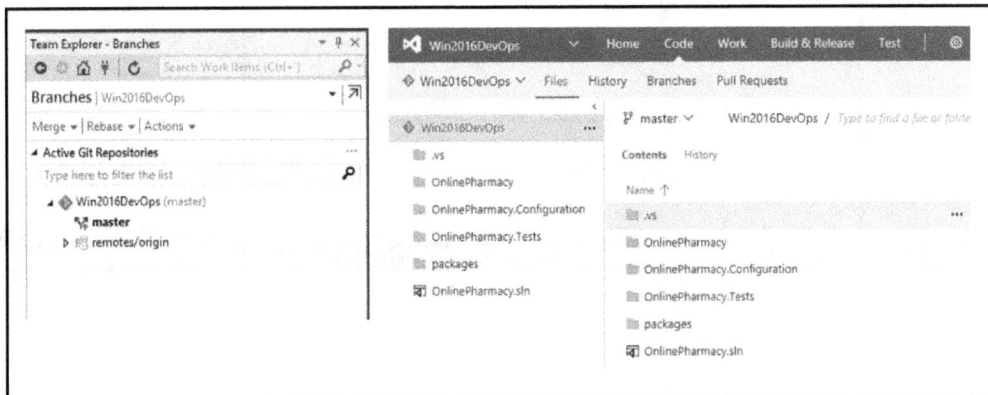

Figure 14: Source code in VSTS

Managing a Git Repository using VSTS

After onboarding the **OnlinePharmacy** solution on the VSTS Git repository, it's time to work on it as a developer. A developer typically will push his/her code to the repository and pull code submitted by others as well. This involves merging code and solving any arising conflict resolution.

Submitting code changes to a Git repository

This section provides steps for some of the common tasks performed by developers on an ongoing basis while they are building an application and changing code frequently.

1. Modify the **OnlinePharmacy** code in Visual Studio after opening the solution. In *Figure 15,* a sample modification is done to `Details.cshtml` file by adding a `<h2>` tag and some text along with it. Save the code changes.

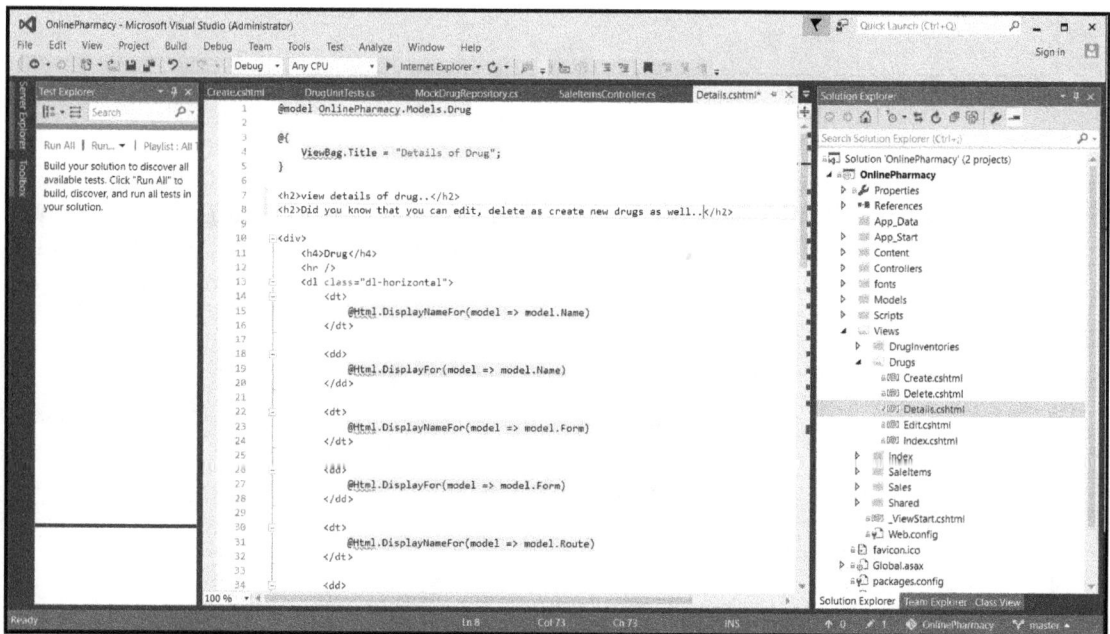

Figure 15: Modifying code

2. From the **Team Explorer** home screen, click on the **Changes** button. It will navigate to the **Changes** screen, listing modifications to all files in the local repository. Since there is a single change in our case, the `Details.cshtml` file is shown in **Changes** section of the screen. These represent files that are not tracked by Git. This is shown in *Figure 16*. Click on the + button corresponding to the **Changes** section.

Figure 16: Staging changes to local Git repository

3. Clicking on the + button will stage the changes in a local repository. Staging files is when Git starts tracking them. This is shown in *Figure 17*:

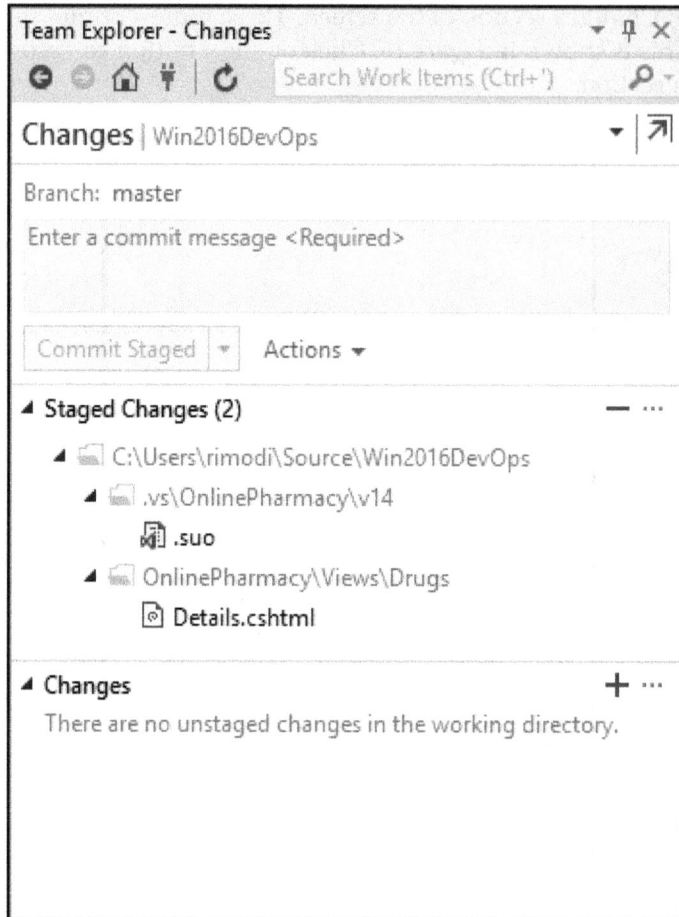

Figure 17: Committing staged changes to the local Git repository

4. Now the staged changes can be committed to the local Git repository. Provide a description/message and select the **Commit Staged and Push** command from the drop-down list. This action will connect to a remote Git repository and send the changes as a `commit` object to it. This `commit` object is then recorded in the remote repository. This is shown in *Figure 18*.

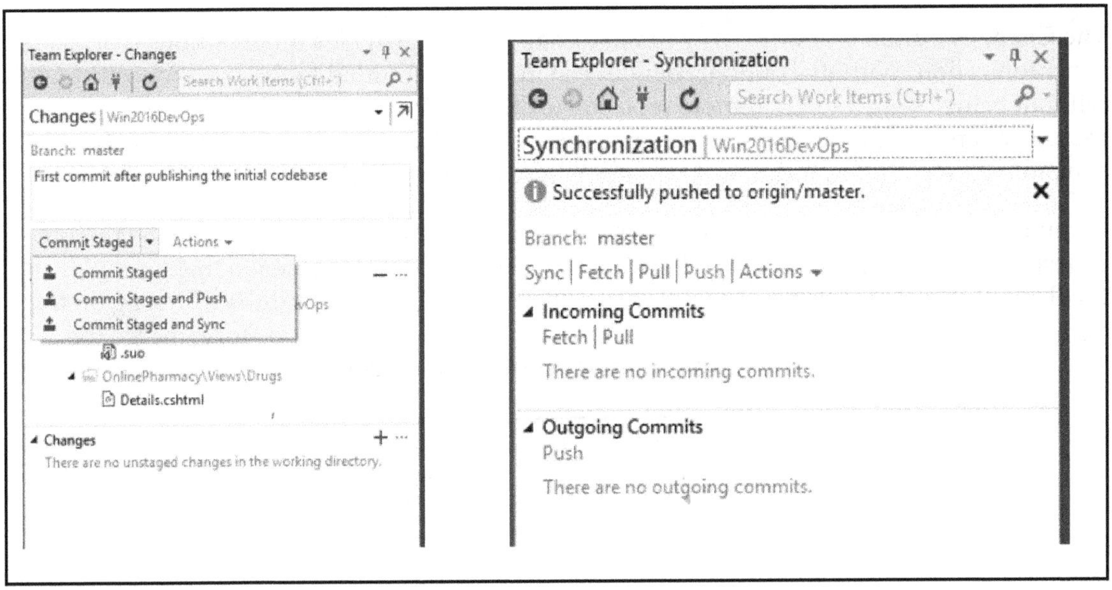

Figure 18: Synchronizing changes with a remote repository

Pulling code changes from a Git repository

Pulling refers to fetching the latest code from a remote repository and merging it with a local repository.

Pulling source code changes from a Git repository before publishing changes is always a good practice. This ensures that there are no difficult merge conflicts to be resolved later.

The two methods in VSTS for pushing changes to remote repository are

- Synchronization
- Pull

Team Explorer home screen provides the **Sync** button for synchronization. This is a more involved approach where a pull operation is first executed before pushing changes. Synchronization refers to fetching the latest code from a remote repository, merging it with the local repository and local changes and pushing the updated source code to the remote repository. Synchronization works with `commit` object. Synchronization not only pulls the source code but also pushes it to the remote repository.

The **Changes** button is another way to push changes and provides more options than synchronization. With this option, changes can just be committed to the local repository without being pushed to the remote repository; they can be committed to the local repository and pushed to the remote repository. It can also commit and perform a synchronization, that is, it can pull changes before pushing them to the remote repository.

If you choose the option of committing changes only without pushing them to the remote repository, the changes can be synchronized later using the option shown in *Figure 19* using the **Sync** button from the home window. It will show **Outgoing Commits**. Clicking on the **Sync** link will pull commits not available locally from the remote repository, merge the changes locally, and send the updated commits to a remote repository.

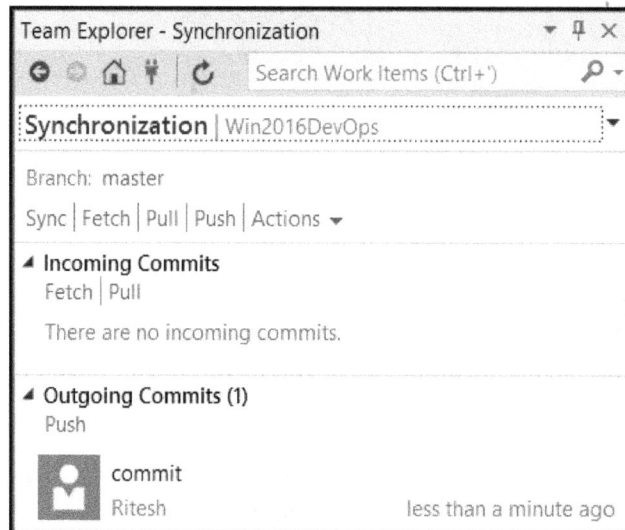

Figure 19: Visual Studio synchronization option

Alternatively, the **Pull** button can be used to pull changes that would internally **fetch** and **merge** remote changes with local changes. The `fetch` command in VSTS will simply fetch the changes but not merge them with the local code. The `merge` command should be used to merge the fetched code with the local repository. The `merge` command has been explained before in this chapter in the *Git 101* section.

Onboarding another developer for the same application

By this time, the **OnlinePharmacy** source code is on the VSTS Git repository and more developers are getting added to the project. To enable newer developers to be on boarded to the project so they can start working on the same code repository requires the following steps to be performed:

1. The developer should open Visual Studio 2015, navigate to **Team Explorer**, and click on the connection icon on its top navigation bar. Clicking on **Manage Connection** and selecting **Connect to Team project** will start the process of creating a connection to the remote VSTS Git project. Click on the **Servers** button, add the URL for the VSTS account created earlier, and finally close the connection dialog. This step might demand credentials to log in to VSTS, and they should be provided to successfully establish a connection. This is shown in *Figure 20*.

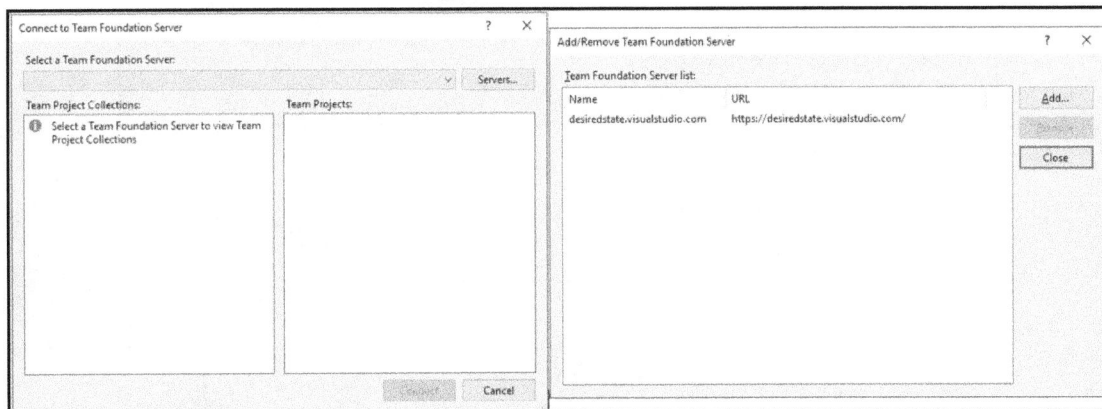

Figure 20: Creating new VSTS connection in Visual Studio

2. A new window with a list of all projects available in the provided account is shown in *Figure 21*. Select the **Win2016DevOps** project from the list.

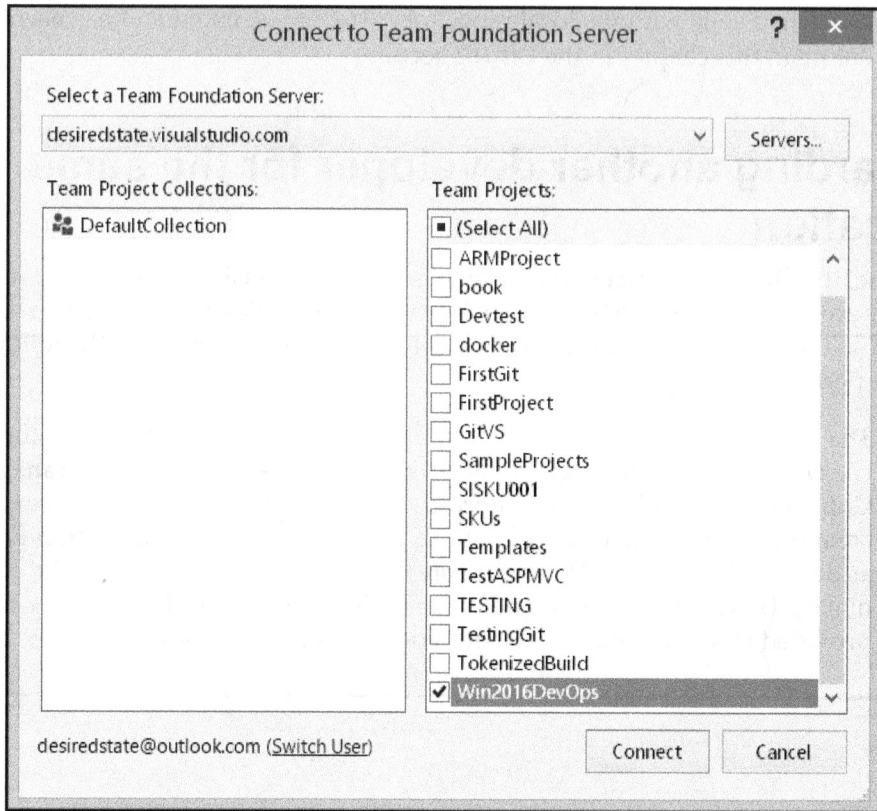

Figure 21: Selecting a VSTS project in Visual Studio

3. After successful connection, the project should be cloned into a local repository. This is shown in *Figure 22*. The first screenshot on left is suggesting that the remote repository should be cloned. Cloning refers to the process of copying the entire remote repository along with its history to a local repository. There are two links provided for cloning the remote repository. There is a prompt on the top of the **Team Explorer** window, and there is a **Clone Repository** link in the **Project** section. The result is the same no matter which option is used. Clicking on the link will prompt for the remote repository URL and local repository folder location as shown in the central screenshot. Clicking on the **Clone** button here will start the process of cloning the remote repository. The screenshot on the right shows the successful cloning:

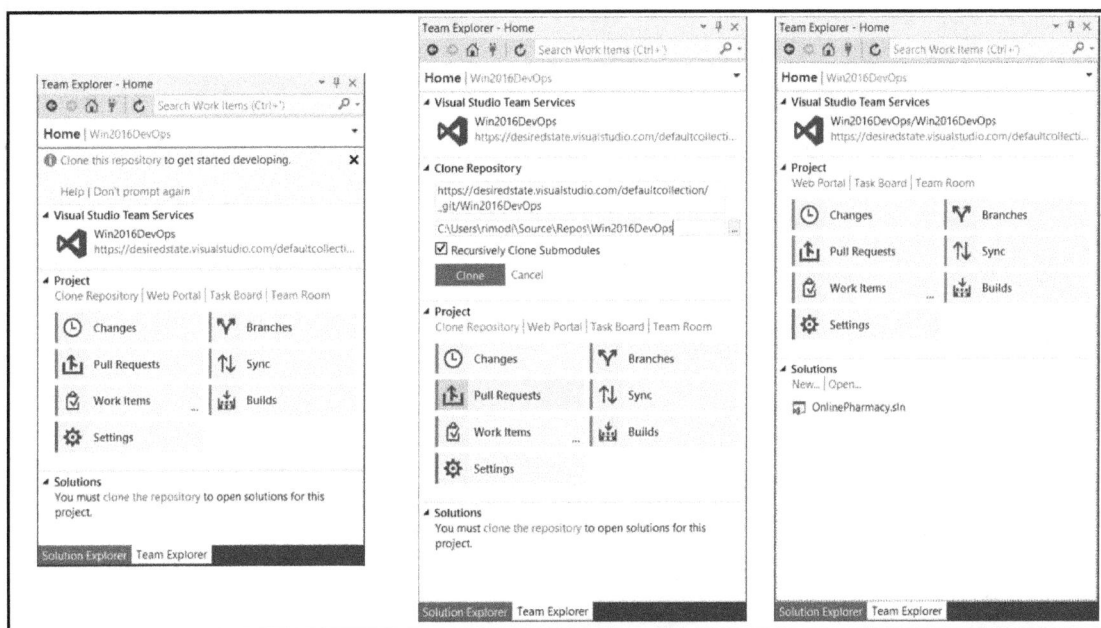

Figure 22: Cloning VSTS Git repository

4. After cloning, a developer should open the **Solutions** windows from **Team Explorer**. Right-click on the project and select the **Open** menu item from the **Team Explorer – Home** window. This will open the solution in Visual Studio. This is shown in *Figure 23*.

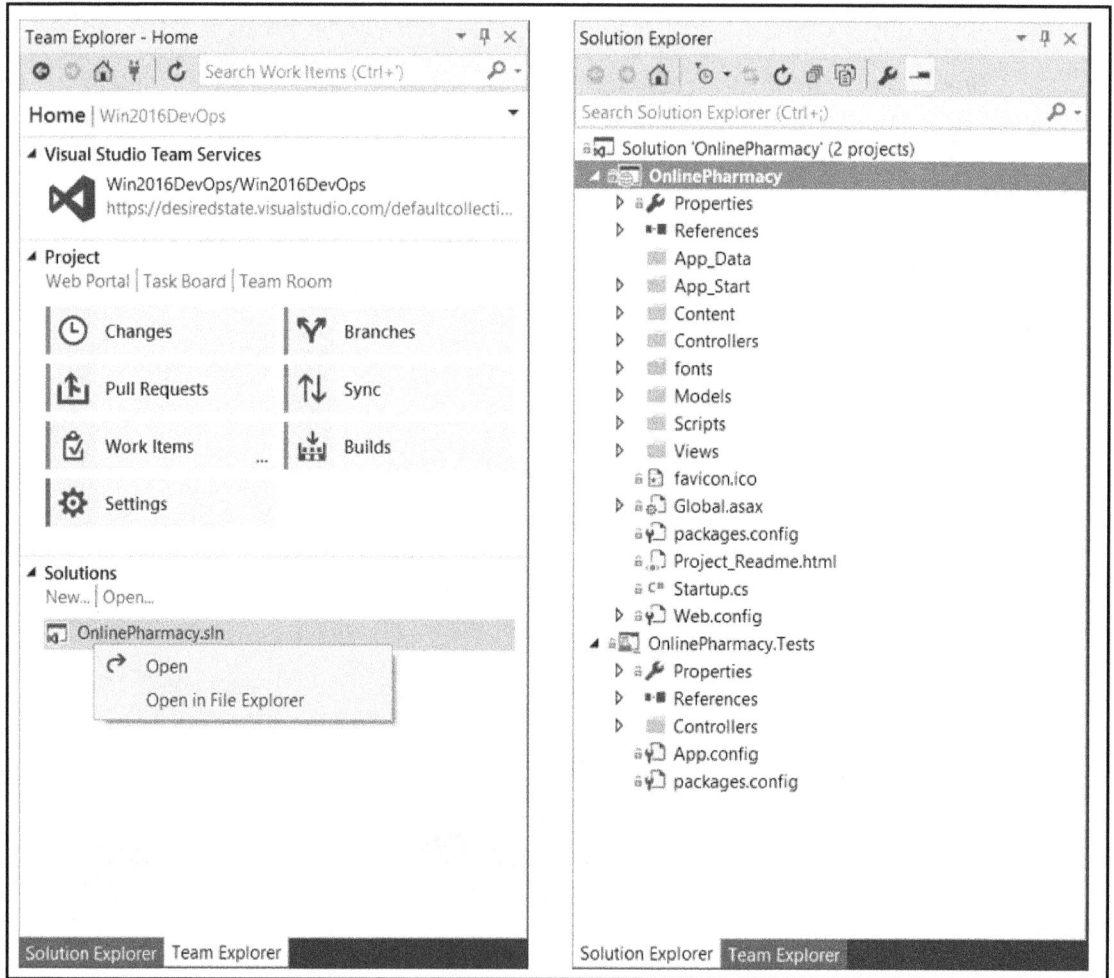

Figure 23: Opening the cloned project

Now the developer can start working on the code and pull, push, and synchronize changes to a remote repository.

Cloning and adding a solution to the VSTS Git repository

Previous sections in this chapters provided the steps to onboard an existing project by means of publishing to a remote repository from a local workstation. In this section, we will look into another way of onboarding a Visual Studio solution to the VSTS Git repository. In this example, a VSTS project is created, a clone of this empty repository is made on a local machine, and a new or existing project is added and pushed to a remote repository. The steps for the same are provided here:

1. Navigate to your already created VSTS account, log in, and create a new project by clicking on the **New team project** menu item. This is shown in *Figure 24*.

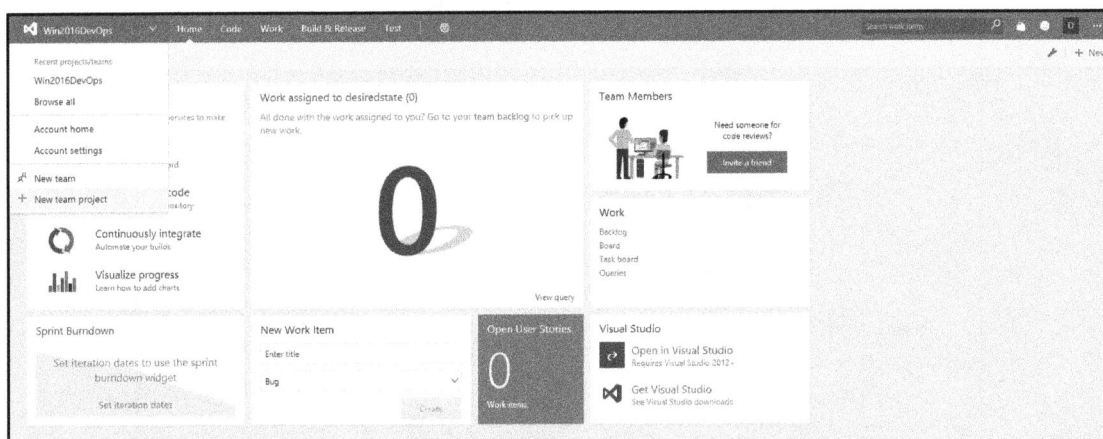

Figure 24: Creating a new VSTS project

2. Provide **ProjectCloneExample** as the **Project name**, an appropriate **Description**, **Agile** as the **Process template** value and Git as the **Version control** value. Click on the **Create project** button as shown in *Figure 25*.

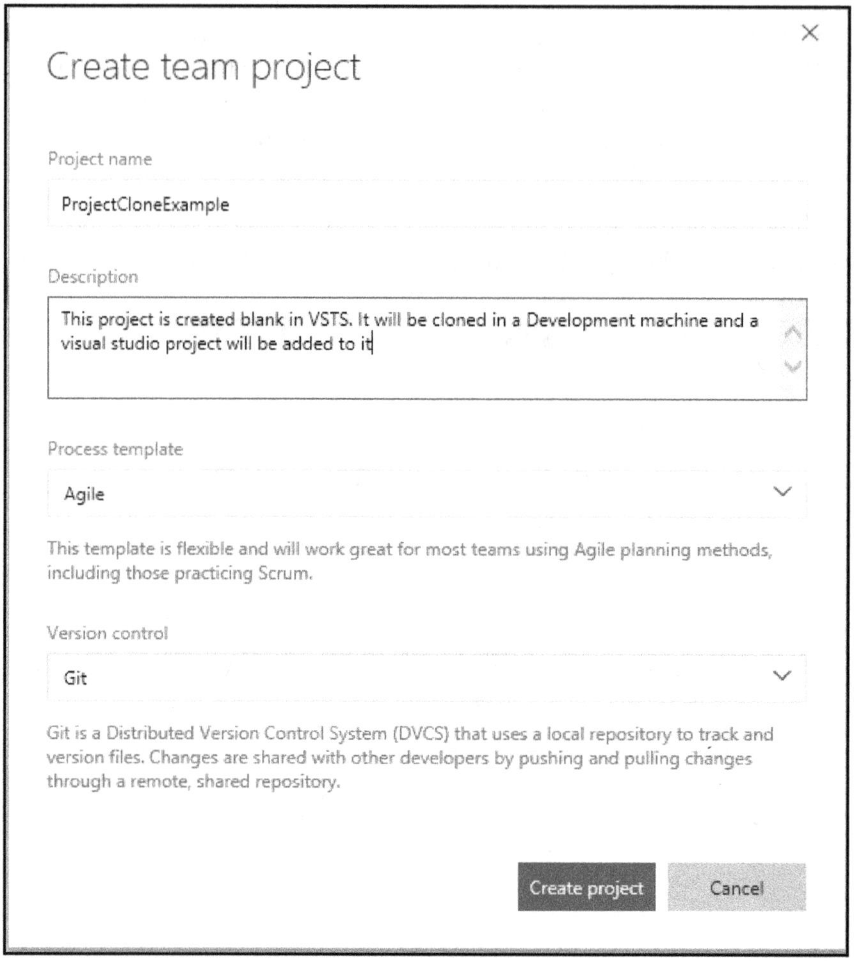

Figure 25: A project with a Git repository

3. On a local machine, start Visual Studio 2015, connect to your Team Service's account through **Team Explorer**, and select the newly created**ProjectCloneExample** project from the list of projects available in the account. This is shown in *Figure 26*.

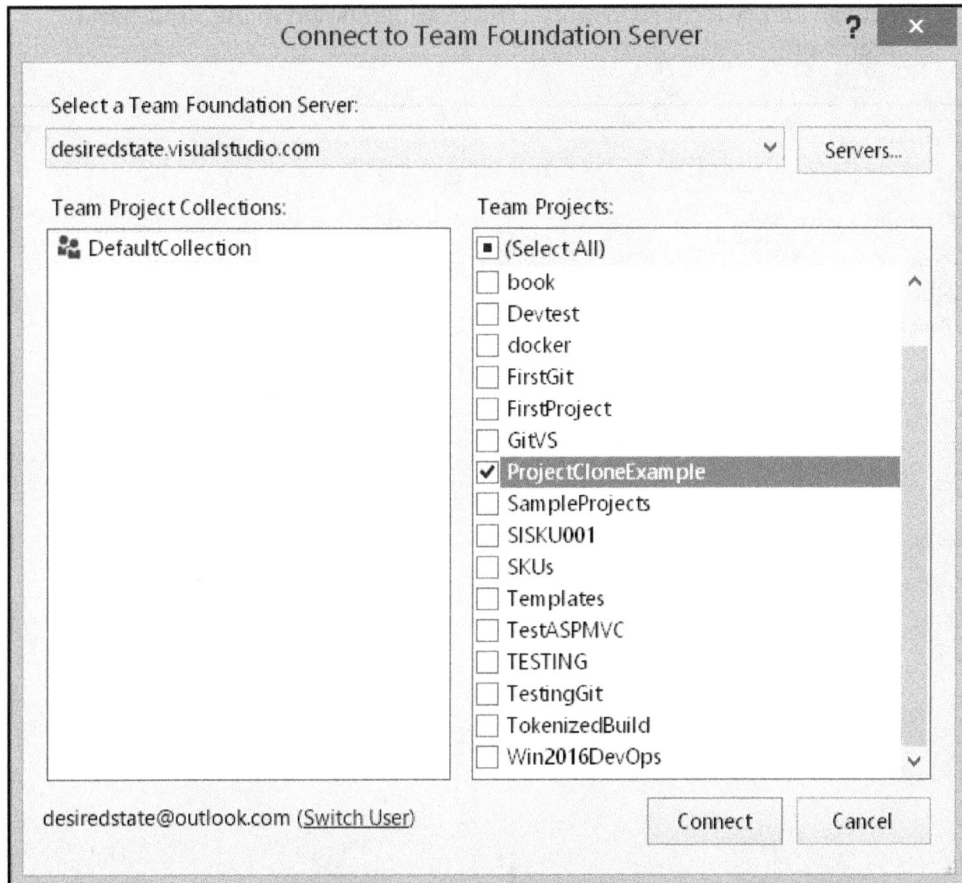

Figure 26: Selecting a VSTS project in Visual Studio

4. From the **Connect** screen in **Team Explorer**, click on the **Clone** link available at the **Local Git Repositories** section. In a previous section, we used the **Add** link instead of the **Clone** link. Values for the remote URL and local path should be provided as shown in *Figure 27*. Readers should provide their own environment-related values for both remote and local repositories. Click on the **Clone** button to create an empty local repository. The result is shown in the right-hand screenshot:

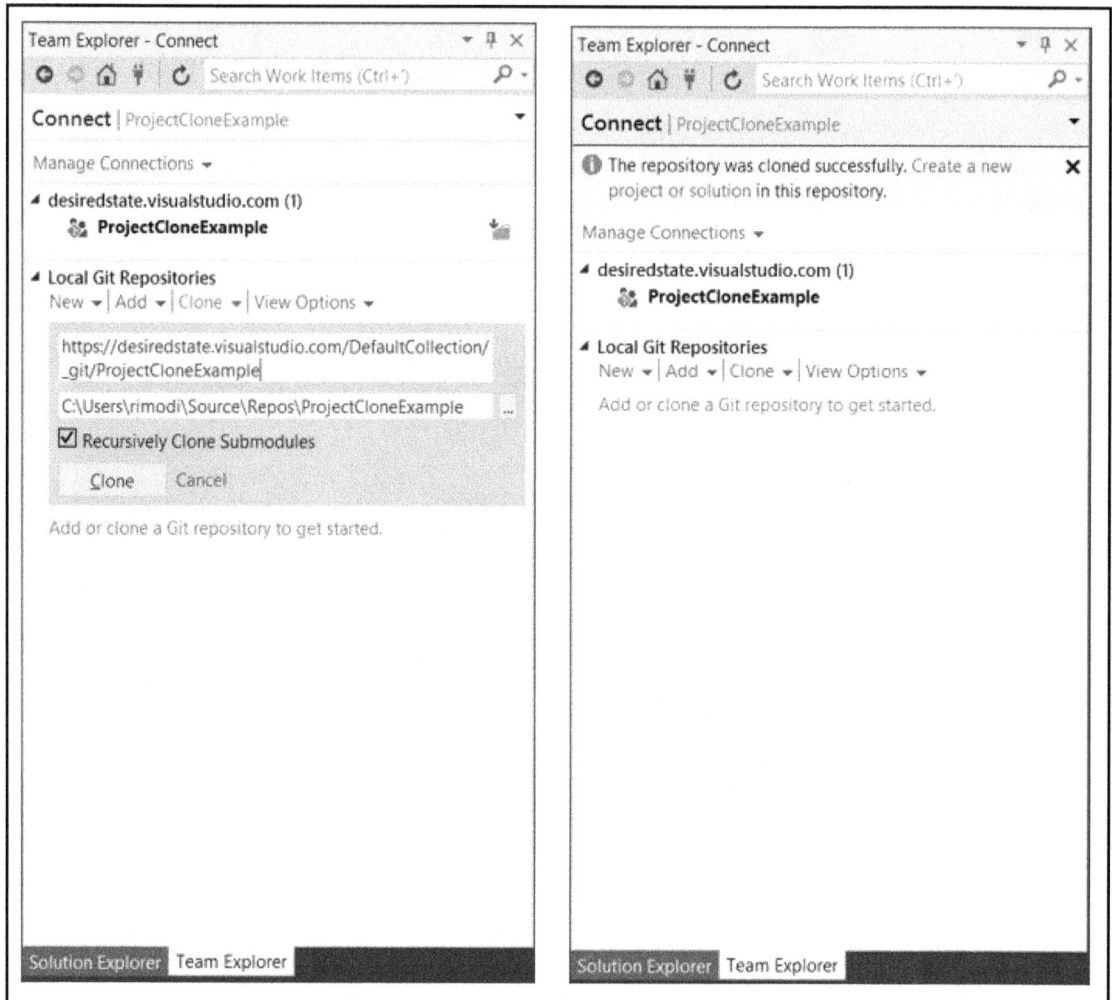

Figure 27: Cloning a Git repository

5. The URL for a remote repository is available from VSTS as shown in *Figure 28*.

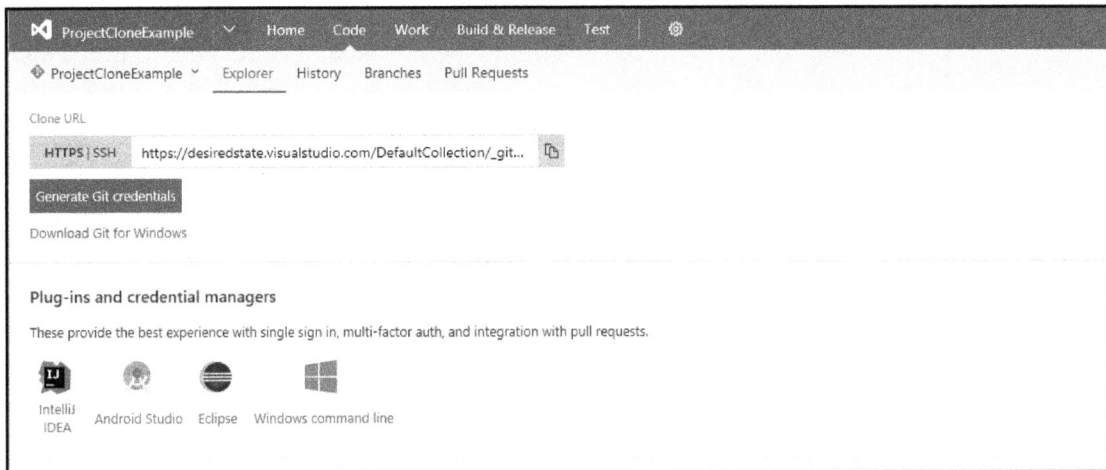

Figure 28: Git repository URL in VSTS

6. Open Visual Studio 2015 and create a new **ASP.NET Web Application** as shown in *Figure 29*. The location of the solution is the same path that was used for the local repository in step 4 while cloning a remote repository. Select a **Project** template (in this case, **MVC** template is selected) to create a new project. Instead of creating a new project, another option is to copy existing solution, projects, and code files to this folder.

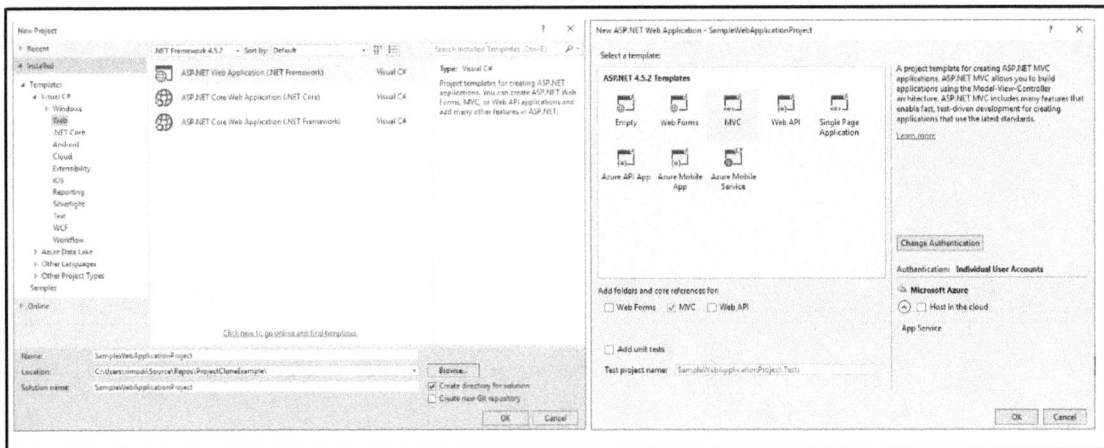

Figure 29: Creating a new ASP.NET MVC web application project in Visual Studio

7. After a new project is created, navigate to **Team Explorer** and click on the Home icon from its top navigation bar. From the **Home** window, click on the button. This will show all the files added to the working folder. This is shown in *Figure 30* **Changes** button. This will show all the files added to the working folder. This is shown in *Figure 30*.

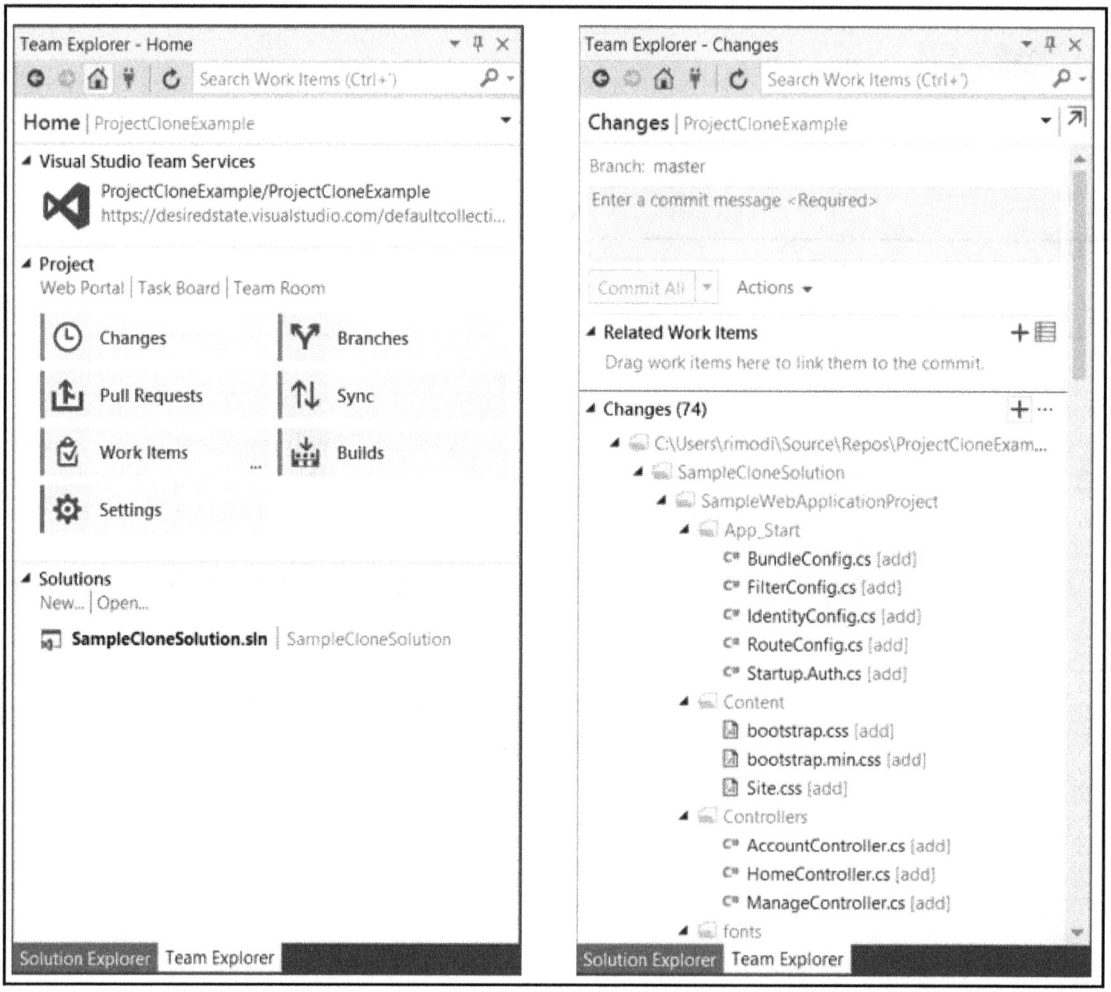

Figure 30: Untracked project files

8. Click on the + button corresponding to the **Staged Changes** section to add them to the staging area and commit the changes in the staging are into a local Git repository as shown in *Figure 31*. Provide an appropriate commit message and select the **Commit Staged and Push** menu item to push the changes to the remote repository after committing to a local repository.

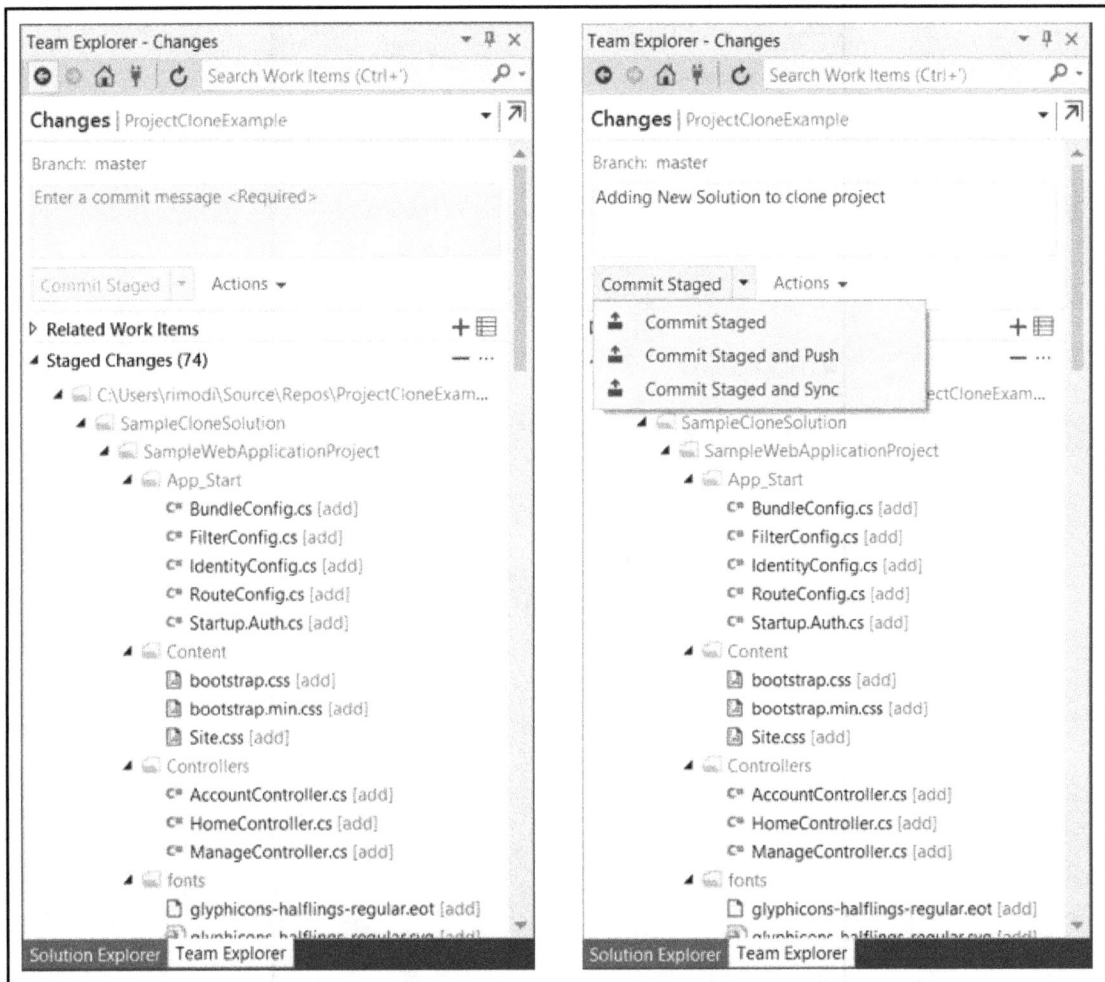

Figure 31: Staging, committing, and pushing changes

9. The screen after successfully committing and pushing code to a remote repository is shown in the left-hand screenshot of *Figure 32* and the right-hand screenshot shows the VSTS **Code** | **Explorer** with files recently published from a local repository.

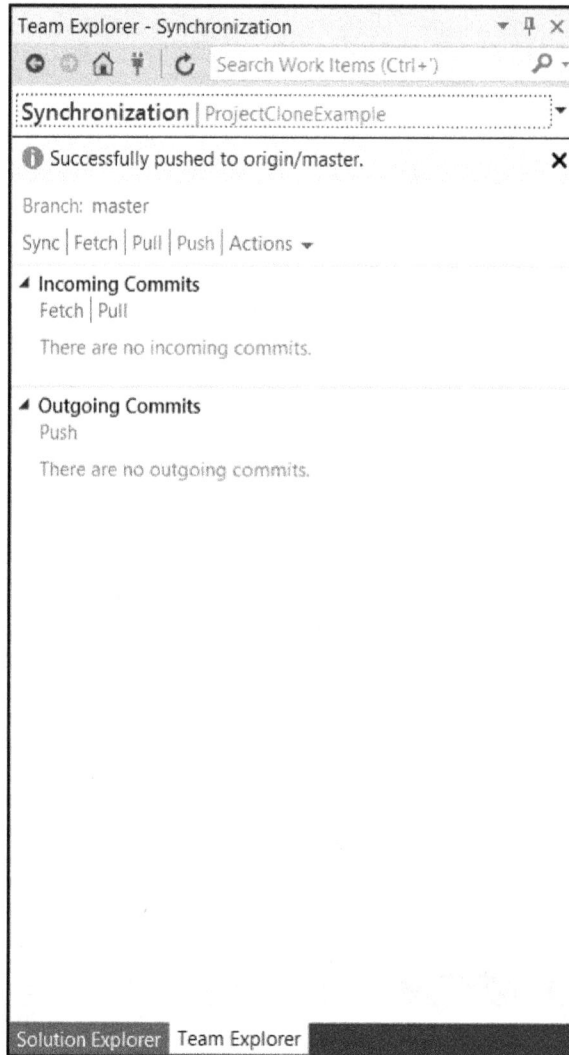

Figure 32: Updated code in the VSTS Git repository

Adding a project to the VSTS Git repository using the command-line tool

Since we already have the base code developed, this section will provide the steps to add existing source code to a GIT repository in VSTS.

Cloning and adding a solution to VSTS Git repository using the Git command-line tool

This example is similar to the previous example as explained in the *Adding Online Pharmacy to the VSTS Git repository using Visual Studio 2015* section of this chapter; the difference between these two examples is that the previous example used the Visual Studio user interface while this example uses the Git for Windows tool to work with the VSTS Git repository. The steps are shown here:

1. Navigate to your VSTS account, log in, and create a new project by clicking on the **New team project** menu item. This is shown in *Figure 33*.

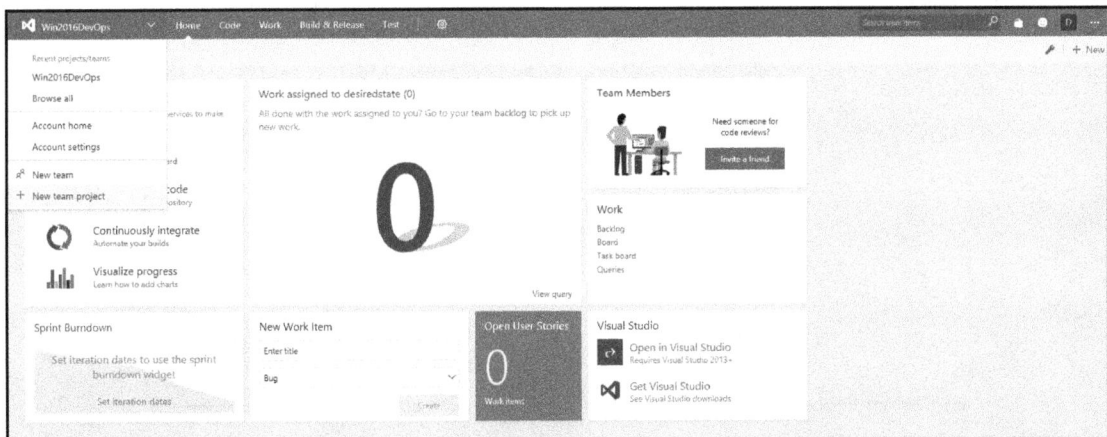

Figure 33: Creating a new VSTS project

2. Provide **ProjectCloneExampleGIT** as the **Project name**, an appropriate **Description**, **Agile** as the **Process template** value, and **Git** as **Version control** value. Click on the **Create project** button as shown in *Figure 34*.

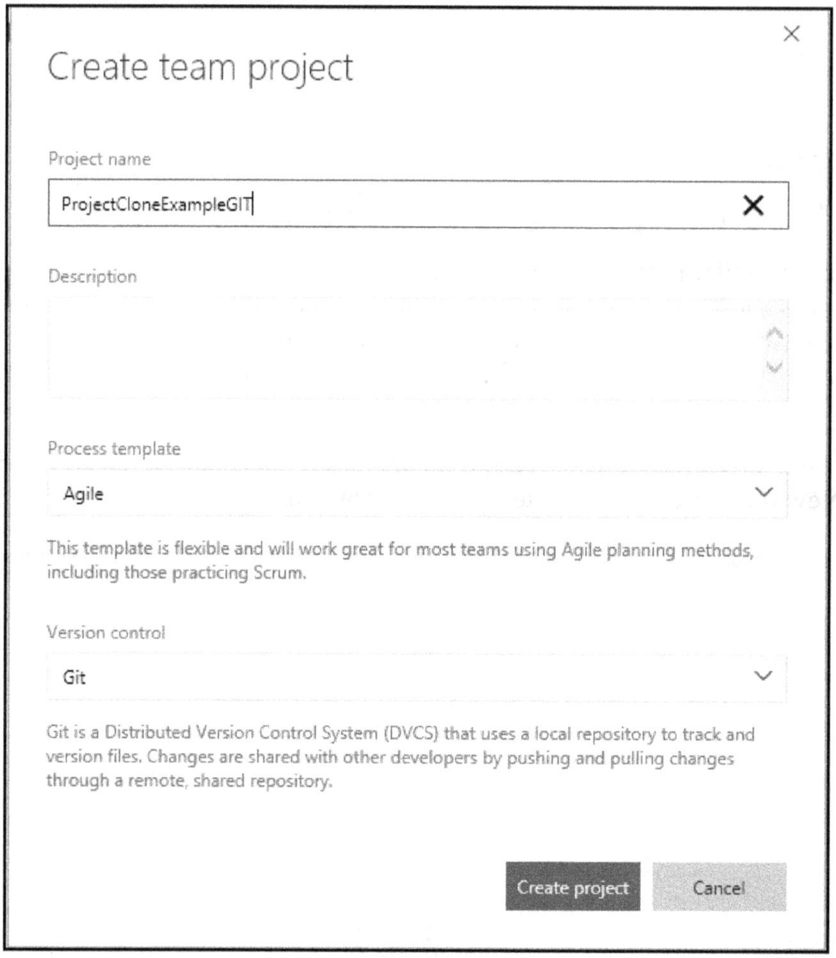

Figure 34: Creating a project with a Git repository

3. Open the Git utility and navigate to the `c:projects` folder as shown next:

```
citynextadmin@DevVS MINGW64 ~
$ cd /c/projects/
```

4. Clone the remote repository into a local folder as follows:

```
citynextadmin@DevVS MINGW64 /c/projects
$ Git clone
https://desiredstate.visualstudio.com/
DefaultCollection/_Git/ProjectCloneExampleGIT
The output from executing this command is shown next.
Cloning into 'ProjectCloneExampleGIT'...
warning: You appear to have cloned an empty repository.
Checking connectivity... done.
```

5. The `clone` command creates a folder at the `C:projects` location named `ProjectCloneExampleGIT`. This is shown in *Figure 35*.

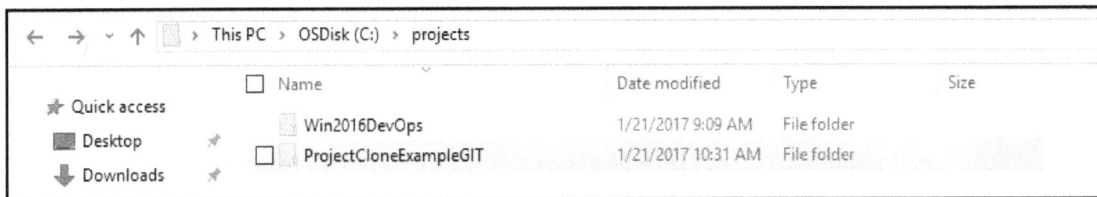

Figure 35: Project working tree files and folder

6. Create a new Visual Studio project as shown in *Figure 36* and *Figure 37*. An **MVCASP.NET Web application** with associated unit test projects is created for this example. Alternatively, readers can copy existing projects to this newly created folder instead of creating a new project.

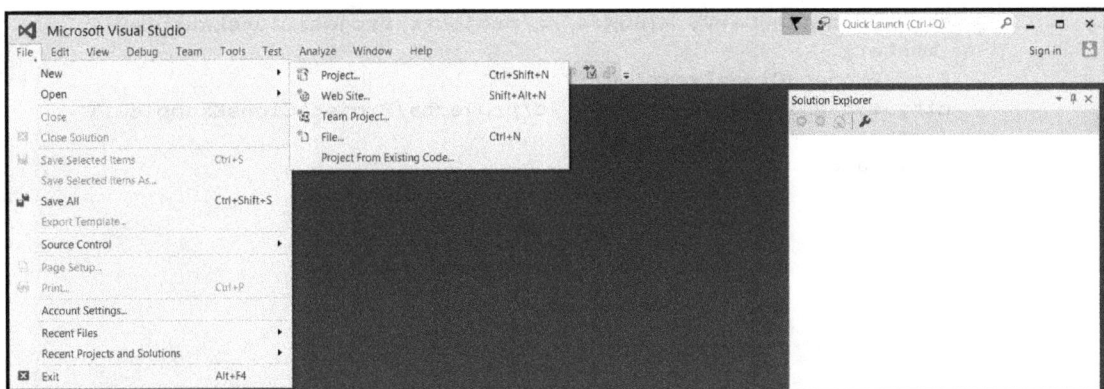

Figure 36: Creating new project in Visual Studio

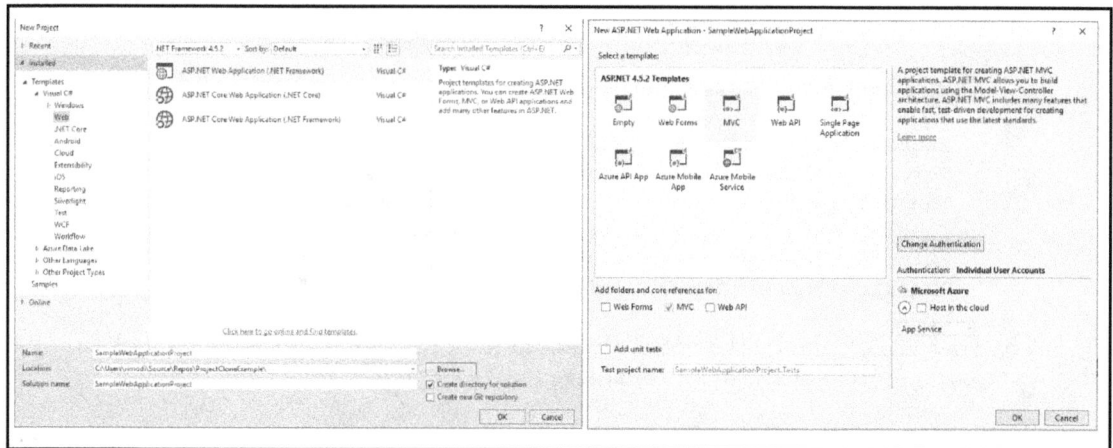

Figure 37: Selecting an ASP.NET MVC Web Application template

Note the project location. It is the same folder we created in step 3. This will generate project files at a given folder location. These files are still not a part of the Git repository.

The solution and project files should now be staged similar to the way Visual Studio was used to stage changed files. This is shown in here. The first command navigates to the newly created folder using the `cd` command. The `add` command adds the changes to the staging area, and `.` refers to all changes in the current folder:

```
citynextadmin@DevVS MINGW64 /c/projects/ProjectCloneExampleGIT
(master)
$ cd ProjectCloneExampleGIT/
citynextadmin@DevVS MINGW64 /c/projects/ProjectCloneExampleGIT
(master)
$ Git add .
```

7. Commit the staged changes to a local Git repository. This is done using the `commit` command. It accepts a message parameter to provide a description for the `commit` object. This is shown next. Multiple lines will be output with a few warning-related line feeds converted to carriage returns and line feeds but eventually the `commit` should succeed. The warning arises due to the differences in the way line feeds are interpreted in the Windows and Linux operating system.:

```
citynextadmin@DevVS MINGW64  /c/projects/ProjectCloneExampleGIT
(master)
$ Git commit -m "commit of sample project using GIT"
The output from executing this command is shown next.
[master (root-commit) 7ed1a40] commit of sample project using GIT
```

8. Finally, the local repository should push its changes to the remote repository. This is performed using the `push` command as shown next. The `origin` refers to the remote repository, and `master` refers to the **master** branch:

```
citynextadmin@DevVS  MINGW64 /c/projects/ProjectCloneExampleGIT
(master)
$ Git push origin master
The output from executing this command is shown next.
Counting objects: 294, done.
Delta compression using up to 8 threads.
Compressing objects: 100% (250/250), done.
Writing objects: 100% (294/294), 12.77 MiB | 233.00 KiB/s, done.
Total 294 (delta 37), reused 0 (delta 0)
remote: Analyzing objects... (294/294) (56086 ms)
remote: Storing packfile... done (944 ms)
remote: Storing index... done (199 ms)
To https://desiredstate.visualstudio.com/
DefaultCollection/_Git/ProjectCloneExampleGIT
* [new branch]      master -> master
```

9. At this point, navigating to the **ProjectCloneExampleGIT** project in VSTS will show the code published in step 9. This is shown in *Figure 39*.

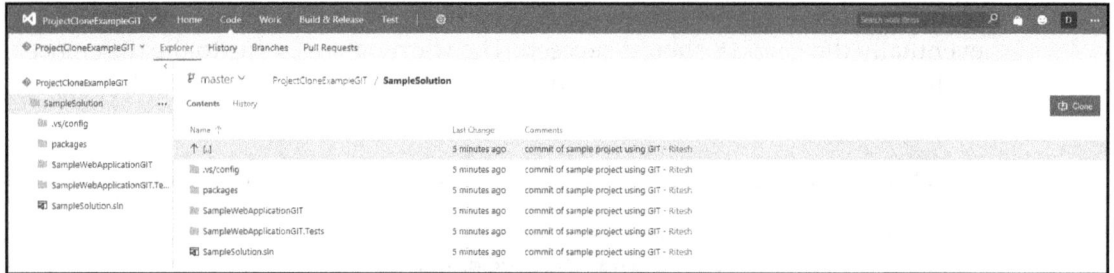

Figure 38: Code in a VSTS project

Summary

This chapter introduced Configuration Management from the SCCM perspective, which is one of the important DevOps practices. It discussed various aspects of Version Control System including the types of version control and capabilities provided by VSTS for both Centralized and Distributed Version Control System. Git is the focus of this book from the Version Control System point of view. Differences between Git and TFVC were discussed. We also gave a short introduction to Git, followed by adding our sample application **OnlinePharmacy** to the VSTS Git repository. We explored the steps to work with the VSTS Git repository, such as adding, committing, pushing, and synchronizing changes using Visual Studio and the Git command-line. We described how to onboard a new developer for the project published earlier and different ways to use Visual Studio to interact with the VSTS Git repository. In the next chapter, we will focus on Software Configuration Management related to Infrastructure as Code and application configuration.

7
Configuration Management

The previous chapter introduced **Source Code Configuration Management (SCCM)**. This chapter is a continuation of the earlier chapter, and it introduces infrastructure and application configuration management. An emerging concept in infrastructure configuration management is **Infrastructure as Code (IaC)**. It helps in bringing a high degree of consistency, predictability, and standardization not only in designing, developing, provisioning, and deployment of infrastructure but also in easing maintenance and upgrades on an ongoing basis. One of the major DevOps principles is configuration management related to infrastructure and application. `Chapter 5`, *Building a Sample Application* introduced *Online Medicine* as a sample application. The same application will be provisioned, deployed, and configured end to end as part of this chapter.

Infrastructure as Code

I am sure most of the readers would have come across situations where suddenly applications stop working. Servers containing application crash due to hardware failure, environment changes on servers which make applications unusable, and when IT administrators are trying to fix the problem using a trial and error strategy. There have been situations where a new environment needs to be built for applications and services but there is no automated way to provision them. The entire environments are built manually. The Operations teams have sleepless nights because they might have missed steps while building the environment manually. There is even the possibility of a wrong configuration being applied. It might be that documentation and automation scripts exist but still there is no way to have a high level of confidence, predictability, and consistency in deployment.

If you and your team have experienced such situations, DevOps with its configuration management principles implementing Infrastructure as Code can help overcome them.

Infrastructure as Code is a method, approach, and process to provision, deploy, and configure infrastructure and applications. It brings in high level of confidence and a faster understanding of overall steps and process. It suggests and recommends that provisioning, deployment, and configuration of infrastructure and applications should be done through automation. Scripts, templates, and code for automating should be treated as software code undergoing the same application life cycle management just like any other software, application, or service. They should be designed, built, tested, and deployed as general software, and all practices related to application development and testing should be applied to them. They should be version controlled and subjected to change management.

Infrastructure as Code converts the manual deployment and configuration steps in discreet reusable automation processes and scripts. It helps in maintaining the scripts as source code and develops them over a period of time through version control. They are tested for their functional accuracy and unit tested before they can be used for the purposes of provisioning, deployment, and configuration of any environment. After deployment, operational validation is conducted to ensure that the environments will function and behave as intended.

The success of Infrastructure as Code to a large extent depends on the level of automation implemented for provisioning, deployment, and configuration of infrastructure and applications. Without automation, it is difficult to achieve the purpose and principles of Infrastructure as Code.

Unit, integration and operational validation tests are integral to Infrastructure as Code. The scripts and templates should be tested for their behaviors usually through unit tests, in desired configuration states through integration and they should also be tested to check that they are working as expected functionally through operational validation. It should be part of continuous delivery and deployment process ensuring that these scripts and templates are always in a ready state to be used for deployment and configuration.

Objectives of Infrastructure as Code

Some of the major objectives of Infrastructure as Code are:

- **Predictability**: Components and resources provisioned, deployed, and configured as part of Infrastructure as Code should be in a good state and behave according to their intended configuration as stated in templates and scripts. There should not be any element of surprise in their intended state and behavior.
- **Deterministic**: Environments provisioned, deployed, and configured should be the same or similar across all environments, provided similar inputs are provided to resources and components. There should be one successful outcome which can be tested and measured appropriately whether they are executed on the same environment or on different environments
- **Consistency**: Infrastructure as Code should bring in a high level of consistency in components no matter how many times they are used to provision, deploy, and configure environments.
- **Idempotent/repeatability**: Infrastructure as Code should provision, deploy, and configure environments in the same manner and steps, and should leave them in the same state every time they executed.
- **Security**: Infrastructure as Code converts the manual steps into code and during this process there is a possibility that secrets and credentials may creep in within code, templates, and scripts. It is of the utmost importance that there should be no mention or hard-coding of any secrets and credentials in any scripts, templates, and code in any form.

Revisiting sample application architecture

Our sample application *Online Medicine* is a web based application with Azure SQL as its backend database. The frontend part of the web application is deployed within Windows Containers on Azure virtual machines. This is shown in *Figure 1*:

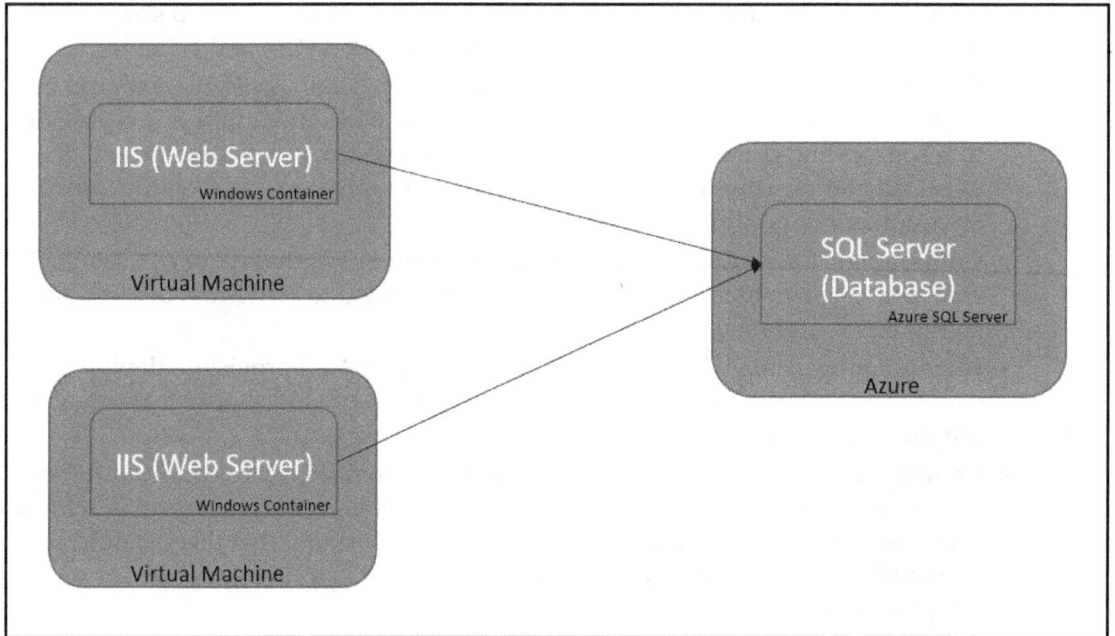

Figure 1: Sample application architecture

The component and deployment design of the sample application is depicted in *Figure 2*:

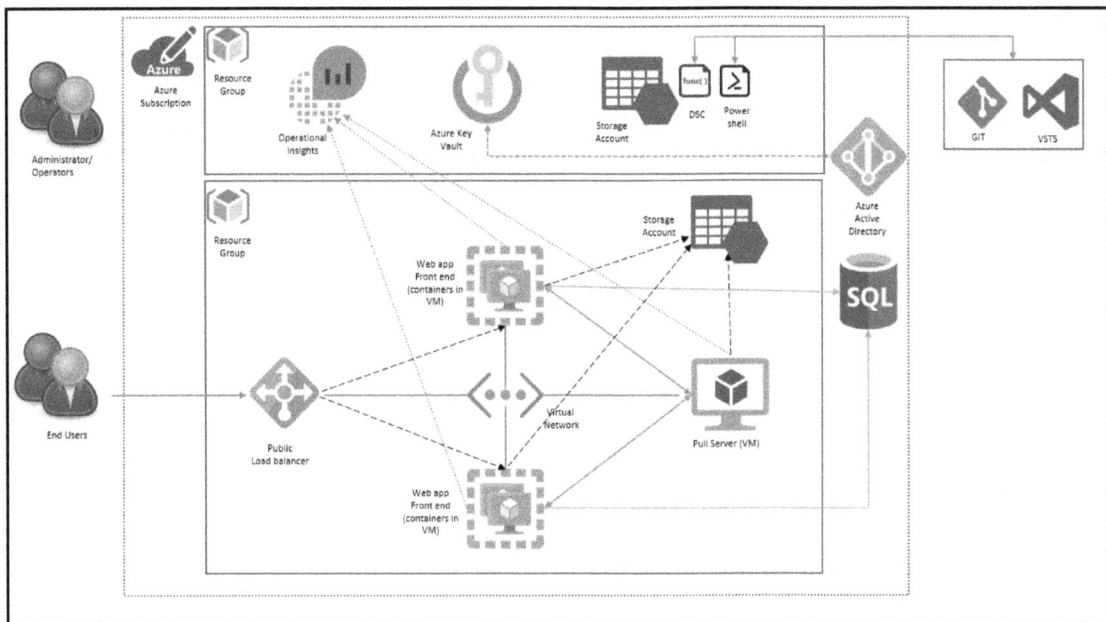

Figure 2: High level component architecture

The chapter is accompanied with source code that demonstrates the end-to-end Infrastructure as Code for our *Online Medicine* sample web application. The code is completely parameterized and almost all aspects of deployment and configuration can be customized. These parameterizations will be discussed along with code descriptions as we move along this chapter.

There are two resource groups created as part of the configuration management of the sample application. The first resource group contains a storage account storing scripts and code for enabling Infrastructure as Code, **Azure Key Vault**, and **Operational Insights**. All these three resources provide services to the application deployed in another resource group. The second resource group contains all application specific resources such as virtual machines, a storage account for storing vhd files for virtual machines, virtual networks, and more. It is technically possible to put all resources in a single resource group but it is a good practice to group resources in a single resource group having the same development life cycle. The major components in deployment architecture are explained next.

Azure Key Vault

Azure Key Vault is a secure service provided by Azure to store and manage secrets, keys, credentials, and any other information that should be treated as confidential. It stores all these confidential data in an encrypted format and is available to those users, groups, and service applications that have been provided explicit permissions to view or use them. For the purpose of the sample application, we will store information related to the following:

- Azure directory tenant ID
- Service application ID
- Azure SQL username
- Azure SQL password
- Azure SQL server name
- Azure SQL database name
- Operational Insights workspace ID
- Operational Insights workspace key
- Storage account keys
- Storage account secure access token
- VSTS username
- VSTS password
- Virtual machine username
- Virtual machine password

Operational Insights

Operational Insights is an audit and monitoring service provided by Azure to get real-time information about all changes, drifts, and events occurring within virtual machines. It provides a centralized workspace and dashboard for IT administrators for viewing, filtering and conducting drill-down searches on all changes, drifts, and events occurring on these virtual machines. It deploys agents on target virtual machines. Once deployed, these agents start sending all changes, events, and drifts information to the centralized workspace. All our web front virtual machines along with Pull Server virtual machines will be attached to Operational Insights as part of the configuration management.

Desired State Configuration Pull Server

This is a service that holds configuration documents (MOF files) for the sample application. It also maintains the database of all containers that are configured, registered with Pull Server, and pull configuration documents from it. The local configuration manager on these target containers periodically checks the availability of new configurations as well as drifts in the current configuration and reports back to Pull Server. It also has inbuilt reporting capabilities that provide information about nodes that are compliant as well as those which are non-compliant. A Pull Server is a IIS web application hosting Desired State Configuration Pull Server endpoint in our case. For the purpose of our sample application, a PowerShell script is executed to open relevant firewall ports, download appropriate packages, and install local certificates. It also downloads the SQL Server script for creating tables in Azure SQL for the purpose of the sample application. This virtual machine is based on Windows Server 2016 image. Pull Server is configured to run on port 9100 on these virtual machines for the purpose of demonstration using the sample application. The port number for Pull Server is dynamically assigned and can be changed while executing the accompanying source code.

For the purpose of this book, a single virtual machine designated to Pull Server is created. However, for the enterprise scenario, multiple virtual machines attached to a load balancer in a high availability configuration should be created for Pull Server. Pull Server is created from scratch, showing the details behind creating a Pull server. Azure provides a Desired State Configuration pull service through its Azure automation service and can be utilized as well as an alternative. In both the cases, the end result remains the same; however, the management of pull service is responsibility of Azure team. A Pull Server typically should have a certificate deployed and this is left as an exercise for the readers.

Azure storage account

Azure storage is a service provided by Azure to store files as **Blobs**. All scripts and code for automating the provisioning, deployment, and configuration of infrastructure and the sample application are stored in a VSTS Git repository and are packaged and deployed in the Azure storage account. Azure provides PowerShell script extension resources that can automatically download DSC and PowerShell scripts and execute them on virtual machines while executing Azure resource manager templates. This will be shown in detail in subsequent pages of this chapter. There are two Azure storage accounts provisioned for the purpose of the sample application. One is for storing the reusable scripts and templates and the other for storing virtual machine vhd files. They are defined in separate resource groups. This is to ensure that even when deprovisioning the resource group containing the sample application the scripts remain intact in their own storage account.

Azure virtual machines and containers

Two Azure virtual machines hosting containers for our sample *Online Medicine* web application are provisioned. Each virtual machine has a network card with a public IP assigned to it. They are attached to a virtual network with a private IP address assigned on the same network. The public IP for virtual machines is optional since they are attached to a public load balancer; however, for the purpose of demonstration and easier debugging, they are assigned to both the virtual machines. They should be removed in enterprise or production deployments. These virtual machines are based on a Windows Server 2016 image with a containers feature. The virtual machines host windows containers and Docker binaries to manage containers and images. Operational Insights agents are installed on virtual machines for monitoring the virtual machines. These agents could have been added to containers as well but that has been left as an exercise for the readers. To add an OMS agent to containers, `dockerfile` should be edited to download the agent and executed with the appropriate OMS workspace key and ID. PowerShell scripts are also executed on these virtual machines downloaded from the storage account to open relevant firewall ports, create container images, download appropriate packages, and install local certificates. The web application is configured to run on port `8080` on these virtual machines and containers for the purpose of demonstration using the sample application. The port number for the web application is dynamically assigned and can be changed while executing the accompanying source code.

Azure public load balancer

A public load balancer is attached to all web application virtual machines for sending requests to them in a round robin fashion. A public IP address and DNS name is assigned to a load balancer for accepting Internet requests. Although it can accept requests on any viable port, for the purpose of the sample application, it accepts HTTP web requests on port `8080` and routes the same to the virtual machines. It also probes on port `8080` on HTTP protocol with `/newapp/Index` as its path. The sample *Online Medicine* application can be browsed using the `http://<<public ip address of load balancer>>/newapp/Index` URL. Couple of **Network Address Translation (NAT)** rules are also opened so that they can be used to log in to the virtual machines using a remote desktop.

An alternative resource to the Azure public load balancer is the Azure application gateway, and depending on the scenario, this can be used and deployed. Again, it should be noted that port `8080` is configurable and used for demonstration purpose; however, any port can be used with the accompanied source code.

Azure SQL

Azure SQL is SQL **Platform as a Service** (**PaaS**) provided by Azure to host databases. Azure provides a secure platform to host databases and takes complete ownership to manage the availability, reliability, and scalability of the service. With Azure SQL, there is no need to provision custom virtual machines, or deploy SQL server, configure, and patch it. Instead, the Azure team does these activities behind the scene and also manages them on our behalf. It also provides firewall services enabling security and only IP addresses allowed by the firewall are allowed to connect and access it. The two virtual machines that will be provisioned to the host sample application in containers have distinct public IP addresses assigned to them and they are added to the Azure SQL firewall rules dynamically so that the web application can access its database seamlessly. The Azure SQL server and its database are created while executing the Azure resource manager template; however, tables in the database are created during the provisioning of Pull Server. It is to be noted that generally management virtual machines should execute such tasks but, for the sake of simplicity, the Pull Server virtual machine is used. In a real life scenario, it is recommended to use a separate virtual machine.

Security considerations

One of the most important consideration for Infrastructure as Code and configuration management is security. When representing infrastructure and applications for the provisioning, deployment, and configuration as code, it is quite possible to hardcode secrets and credentials within the scripts and templates, and they become part of the codebase. Even if not hardcoded within scripts and configuration documents, they might be supplied as parameters during the runtime execution by the Operations team. Either they would know the secrets beforehand or would get them from an IT administrator. In both cases, there is a possibility of security compromise.

Security is an inherent component of Infrastructure as Code for our sample application. To ensure that there are no security leaks, enough consideration and best practices are deployed while designing the artifacts. These are enterprise-scale security considerations and should be used in almost all cases. This chapter will also point out areas where security is not implemented for readers to implement them as an exercise.

Storing secrets and credentials

All secrets, credentials, and sensitive data are stored in an Azure Key Vault by an IT or security administrator. These secrets and confidential data are not known to anyone apart from the IT or security administrator creating them. This confidential information is fetched and pulled from the Azure Key Vault at runtime while provisioning and configuring infrastructure and is passed on to relevant resources and components. All secrets and credentials related to virtual machine, VSTS, Azure SQL, Azure active directory, storage accounts, and Operational Insights information are stored in the Azure Key Vault.

Secure login to Azure subscription

In `Chapter 3`, *DevOps Automation Primer*, we looked at using PowerShell cmdlet `Login-AzureRmAccount` to log in to the Azure subscription. Most of the provisioning, deployment, and configuration of environments happens through unattended execution using the VSTS release pipeline. It is imperative that the credentials parameter is used along with `Login-AzureRmAccount`. This parameter can only be used along with the Azure work subscription and is not allowed for Microsoft accounts. Even when using it along with a work subscription, it would fail if **Multi-Factor Authentication** (**MFA**) is enabled on the subscription. In short, the credentials parameter with `Login-AzureRMAccount` will work when MFA is not enabled and is working with the Azure work subscription. In the rest of the cases, credentials parameter will not work. To overcome all these limitations, **Active Directory** (**AD**) credential authentication along with service principals can be used to log in into Azure subscription. This solution works with any Azure subscription, whether it is a work or Microsoft account and it also does not matter if MFA is enabled or not. This is also a secure way to login to the Azure subscription without comprising any security. This book uses this approach for the purpose of configuration management and Infrastructure as Code.

The steps to use an AD password along with service principals to log in to the Azure subscription is shown later in this chapter. The service application will have owner rights on the subscription, and adequate permissions should also be provided to it in order to access and retrieve credentials and secrets from the Azure Key Vault. These concepts will become clearer once the readers go through the step-by-step guidance later in order to enable AD password authentication with service principals.

Storage account keys and shared access signature tokens

All code and scripts are treated as first-class citizens from a source code control perspective and stored in a Git VSTS repository. During the build stage, the build pipeline publishes these configuration scripts and code into an Azure storage account container as blobs. Storage account containers can be opened for access to the public on the Internet or can be kept private so that only privileged users can access them. To ensure that no-one has access to these configuration scripts and code, access to storage containers is kept private. Azure storage accounts help generate a **Shared Access Signature (SAS)** token that can be used to access private containers by anyone holding that token. Appropriate SAS tokens are generated and stored in the Azure Key Vault. This ensures that only the service application used to provision, deploy, and configure both the infrastructure and application can access the token and download scripts and code on virtual machines using the same.

Network Security Groups and firewalls

(**NSGs**Network Security Groups (NSGs) allow or disallow access to virtual machines on Azure at the network level. By way of whitelisting or blacklisting IP addresses and associated ports with them, NSGs help increase the security footprint of the servers. Firewalls allow access or remove access to ports at an operating system level. Both NSG and firewall configuration are used in the sample application to ensure that only authorized access is allowed to the server.

These security measures ensure that only privileged users can access the virtual machines, containers, storage accounts, and Azure SQL database, while, they can be accessed during installation by a service application. There is no hardcoding of any secret or credential in any form in code, templates, and scripts. No secrets or credentials are supplied as parameters to the scripts and templates not visible to the Operations team and release management team.

The IT administrator and deployment role

The IT administrator is responsible for provisioning infrastructure and services that are reused and consumed by multiple applications within the enterprise. The services provisioned by the IT administrator include centralized monitoring and log management, provisioning of Key Vaults, storage accounts, and service accounts that are consumed by individual application and release management to perform their deployment and management operations in their environments. Access to these services are constrained and limited to authorized administrators only.

An IT administrator will log in to the Azure subscription with his credentials and create a new Azure AD application, an Azure AD service application, and provide the owner's permissions to the service application on the subscription. Individual application owners and release management will use this Azure AD service application to log in to Azure and perform management actions to deploy, update, and configure their infrastructure and applications. They should not be using their individual account IDs to perform any action related to application and infrastructure management.

The IT administrator is responsible for storing secrets and credentials in the Azure Key Vault. A specific ARM template has been designed and build specifically for this purpose. The IT administrator will execute the template to store the secrets and confidential information in the Azure Key Vault. An IT administrator will pass on these credentials and secrets as a parameter to the ARM template. These secrets and credentials are neither available nor visible to the application and release teams. They would consume these credentials and secrets by consuming directly from the Key Vault. They do not have permissions to view these secrets and credentials.

The IT administrator is also responsible for provisioning a storage account for storing scripts, templates, and code.

The Operational Insights workspace is also provisioned so that application owners can use this service for centralized monitoring and application logging. The administrator can get intelligent information from this workspace about the availability, performance, scalability, and security aspects of every application using this service.

An release or deployment role is another important role responsible for provisioning, deploying, and configuring the infrastructure and application. They are also responsible for maintaining, managing, and monitoring both the infrastructure and application. Deployment is typically executed as part of the VSTS release pipeline by a VSTS release management user or manually by these operators. They do not have access to an Azure storage account, Azure Key Vault, Azure SQL, VSTS repositories, and virtual machines. They can log in to the Azure subscription using a service principal created by the IT administrator and perform management operations on their workloads.

Steps for deployment for an IT administrator

Before an IT administrator can provision centralized resources, he should be aware of the Azure tenant and subscription ID. He must also have owner privileges on the subscription. All common and centralized services are provisioned within an Azure resource group. These services are provisioned by executing PowerShell scripts and Azure resource manager templates. The `GeneralServices.json` template is deployed by an IT administrator to provision the Key Vault and Operational Insights workspace. The following steps should be executed for successful end-to-end provisioning, deployment, and configuration of common services. The administrator starts with the `PreCreate.ps1` PowerShell script and executes the ARM template for provisioning of resources. `PreCreate.ps1` is the starting script for an administrator to start the provisioning process. Before executing any of the steps mentioned next in this and the next chapter, please ensure that the latest Azure SDK and modules are installed on the machine used to configure the environment. Refer to `Chapter 3`, *DevOps Automation Primer*, for the steps to install Azure PowerShell modules. Azure SDK 2.9.6 can be installed from `https ://go.microsoft.com/fwlink/?LinkId=518003&clcid=0x409`.

PreCreate.ps1

`PreCreate.ps1` script is responsible for provisioning common and shared resources in a dedicated resource group. Resources in other resources group consume these resources.

1. Open any PowerShell console and execute the `PreCreate.ps1` script. It is available within the `OnlinePharmacy.ConfigurationPSScripts` folder in the accompanied code for `Chapter 5`, *Building a Sample Application*. The command to execute the script is shown here. The path must be replaced with actual path to the file. The script is executed using the concept of **dot-sourcing** which brings the entire script in to current scope.

```
C:UsersrimodiSourceWin2016DevOpsOnlinePharmacy.
ConfigurationPSScripts
Precreate.ps1
-location "West Europe"
-resourceGroupName "dimdum"
-subscriptionID "xxxxxxxxx"
-tenentID "xxxxxxxxxxx"
-storageAccountName "dimdadumnns"
-containerName "armt"
-workspaceName "dimdadumOMS"
-sqlServerName "dimdadumsqlsd"
-principalName "verify2101"
-passwordforServicePrincipal "xxxxxxxxx"
-templatePath "
C:SourceWin2016DevOpsOnlinePharmacy.
ConfigurationTemplatesGeneralServices.json"
-keyVaultName "dimdadumvault"
-resourceUsername "xxxxxxxxxxxx"
-resourcepassword "xxxxxxx"
```

It is important to note is that the values provided for `resourceGroupName`, `storageAccountName`, `containerName`, and `StorageSAS` should be used to update release pipeline variables. Furthermore, `OMSWorkspaceName`, `containerName`, and `wsResourceGroup` values should be updated in the environment level variables within a release pipeline. Any mismatch in the values of these variables will result in errors while executing the release pipeline. The details for release and environment variables are provided in `Chapter 10`, *Continuous Delivery and Deployment*. The value of `StorageSAS` variable is displayed on the console while executing the script. You should make a note of it and use it in the release pipeline in `Chapter 10`, *Continuous Delivery and Deployment*. If you forget to note down the SAS token, you can re-run the script to get the SAS token.

2. `PreCreate.ps1` accepts a few parameters. Parameters are declared for the deploy location, resource group name, subscription ID, tenant ID, storage account name, storage container name, OMS workspace name, and SQL server name. The values for these parameters are filled by the values in the previous step. These parameters are used across this script file and also sent as parameters to Azure resource manager templates. It logs in to the Azure subscription as an account administrator using `Login-AzureRmAccount` in interactive mode.

```
param
(
[string] $location,
[string] $resourceGroupName,
```

```
[string] $subscriptionID,
[string] $tenantID,
[string] $storageAccountName ,
[string] $containerName ,
[string] $workspaceName ,
[string] $sqlServerName,
[string] $principalName,
[string] $passwordforServicePrincipal ,
[string] $templatePath ,
[string] $keyVaultName ,
[string] $resourceUsername ,
[string] $resourcepassword
)
Login-AzureRmAccount
```

After logging in, selecting a subscription is a good practice using the Set-AzureRmContext cmdlet, especially if there are multiple subscriptions available for a given login:

```
Set-AzureRmContext -SubscriptionId $subscriptionID
```

3. Create a new Azure resource group using the New-AzureRmResourcegroup cmdlet and resourceGroupName variable. The next line creates a new storage account using the New-AzureRmStorageAccount cmdlet and storageAccountName variable This storage account is the storage for all automation scripts and code that are used by the Azure resource manager template to automatically download them on virtual machines during their provisioning. The storage account is created using PowerShell instead of the ARM template to demonstrate multiple approaches for the provisioning of resources.

```
New-AzureRmResourceGroup -Name $resourceGroupName -Location
$location -Force
if((Get-AzureRmStorageAccount -ResourceGroupName $resourceGroupName
-Name
$storageAccountName -ErrorAction SilentlyContinue) -eq $null)
{
        New-AzureRmStorageAccount -ResourceGroupName
        $resourceGroupName -Name
        "$storageAccountName" -Location $Location -Type
        Standard_LRS -Verbose
}
```

4. Retrieve the storage account and its primary key for subsequent usage in the script. This storage key will be passed on to the Azure resource manager template to be stored in the Azure Key Vault. Scripts and templates stored in the storage account are accessible to only those who possess this key.

```
$storage = Get-AzureRmStorageAccount -ResourceGroupName
$resourceGroupName -Name
"$storageAccountName"
$storageKey = Get-AzureRmStorageAccountKey -ResourceGroupName
$resourceGroupName -Name
"$storageAccountName"
```

5. A new container should be created within the newly created storage account with no public access. This container is like a folder storing script files and templates needed for infrastructure and application deployment using configuration management. Access to this container is constrained using the **Access Control List (ACL)**. This ensures that only privileged users holding either the account key or SAS token can access it. A new SAS token is generated with a 2-year expiry date. This token is stored in the Azure Key Vault. Any application deployment dependent on these scripts should use this token along with the blob URL to access the files during the provisioning of virtual machines. The token is also shown on the console and should be copied over to release management, as shown in Chapter 10, *Continuous Delivery and Deployment*.

```
if((Get-AzureStorageContainer -Name $containerName -Context
$storage.Context -ErrorAction SilentlyContinue) -eq $null)
{
    New-AzureStorageContainer -Name "$containerName"
                              -Permission Container
                              -Context $storage.Context
                              -Verbose
}
Set-AzureStorageContainerAcl -Permission Off -Name "$containerName"
-Context $storage.Context -Verbose
$sas = New-AzureStorageContainerSASToken -Name $containerName
-Permission rwdl
-ExpiryTime (Get-Date).AddYears(2) -Context $storage.Context
"********important********"
"*** Note down the SAStoken that should be updated in release
management ***"
$sas
"********important********"
```

6. The next step is to create an Azure service principal and service application. However, if both the application and principal preexist then instead of trying to create them, their configuration values are retrieved. The release and operations team uses this service principal to authenticate to the Azure subscription. It helps in logging in to Azure in a non-interactive manner which is a requirement to conduct a deployment in a release pipeline. There are multiple ways to authenticate to the Azure subscription using a service principle. These includes mechanism to use certificates, username-password combination, key credentials, and AD credentials. We have used the AD credentials approach for authenticating but readers can use a different approach if they so wish. A variable to hold the service principal name is declared and its placeholder value should be replaced with actual value. A .NET object of type `PSADPasswordCredential` is created and configured. The password value should be replaced with the actual password. It represents the credential object for the service application. `PSADPasswordCredential` type is defined in `Microsoft.Azure.Commands.Resource.dll` assembly as shown in the following code. This assembly should be loaded using the `Add-Type` cmdlet

The code queries Azure to find if a service principal with the given name exists already. If the service principal exists, it obtains its configuration and stores it in `sp` and `app` variables; otherwise, it creates them and stores them in these variables. These variables are used to store values in the Azure Key Vault.

The `sp` variable is of special interest because it contains the ID of the service principal. This IP is the username to be used in conjunction with the password provided to authenticate with the Azure subscription.

```
# path to assembly containing PSADPasswordCredential type
Add-Type -LiteralPath "${env:ProgramFiles(x86)}Microsoft
SDKsAzurePowerShellResourceManagerAzureResourceManager
AzureRM.ResourcesMicrosoft.Azure.Commands.Resources.dll
$psadCredential = New-Object
Microsoft.Azure.Commands.Resources.Models.ActiveDirectory.
PSADPasswordCredential
$startDate = Get-Date
$psadCredential.StartDate = $startDate
$psadCredential.EndDate = $startDate.AddYears(1)
$psadCredential.KeyId = [guid]::NewGuid()
$psadCredential.Password = $passwordforServicePrincipal
$homePage = "https://www." + $principalName + ".org"
$identifierUri = $homePage + "/example"
if((Get-AzureRmADServicePrincipal
        -ServicePrincipalName $identifierUri)
        -eq $null)
```

```
{
    $app = New-AzureRmADApplication -DisplayName
    $principalName -HomePage $homePage -IdentifierUris
    $identifierUri -PasswordCredentials $psadCredential
    $sp = New-AzureRmADServicePrincipal -ApplicationId
    $app.ApplicationId.Guid
    Start-Sleep -Seconds 30
    New-AzureRmRoleAssignment -RoleDefinitionName Owner
    -ServicePrincipalName $app.ApplicationId.Guid
}
else
{
    $sp = Get-AzureRmADServicePrincipal
    -ServicePrincipalName $identifierUri
    $app = Get-AzureRmADApplication -ApplicationId
    $sp[0].ApplicationId.Guid
}
```

7. Deploy the `GeneralServices.json` ARM template after testing for its validity. For the sake of simplicity, the same username and password are used for Azure SQL, VSTS accounts, and virtual machines. Readers should declare different usernames and passwords for each of them and also provide their specific details for placeholder values. Username and password for SQL server, VSTS, and virtual machines are stored in the Azure `keyVault`. They are stored as secure strings. The first two lines converts the username and password into their secure string equivalent. The `GeneralServices.json` file accepts parameters and the same are supplied to it using `Test-AzureRmResourceGroupDeployment` and `New-AzureRmResourceGroupdeployment` cmdlets. The `Test-AzureRmResourceGroupDeployment` cmdlet helps in validating the ARM template for its correctness and validity while `New-AzureRmResourceGroupdeployment` does the actual deployment of the resources in a resource group. The `GeneralServices.json` file is available within the `OnlinePharmacy.ConfigurationTemplates` folder of the accompanying code and its path must be replaced in the next lines of code.

```
$username = ConvertTo-SecureString -String $resourceUsername
-Force -AsPlainText
$password = ConvertTo-SecureString -String $resourcepassword
-Force -AsPlainText
Test-AzureRmResourceGroupDeployment
            -ResourceGroupName $resourceGroupName
            -TemplateFile $templatePath
            -keyVaultName $keyVaultName
            -tenantId "$tenentID"
            -sqlUserName $username
```

```
        -sqlPasswordName $password
        -VSTSUserName $username
        -VSTSPasswordName $password
        -VMUserName $username
        -VMPasswordName $password
        -deployLocation $location
        -workspaceName "$workspaceName"
        -objectId $sp.Id
        -storageKey $storageKey[0].Value
        -sasToken $sas
        -storageName "$storageAccountName"
        -sqlServerName "$sqlServerName"
        -Verbose
        New-AzureRmResourceGroupDeployment
        -Name Deploy1
        -ResourceGroupName $resourceGroupName
        -TemplateFile $templatePath
        -keyVaultName $keyVaultName
        -tenantId "$tenentID"
        -sqlUserName $username
        -sqlPasswordName $password
        -VSTSUserName $username
        -VSTSPasswordName $password
        -VMUserName $username
        -VMPasswordName $password
        -deployLocation $location
        -workspaceName "$workspaceName"
        -objectId $sp.Id
        -storageKey $storageKey[0].Value
        -sasToken $sas
        -storageName "$storageAccountName"
        -sqlServerName "$sqlServerName"
        -mode Incremental -Verbose
```

GeneralServices.json

Now it's time to look into the details of the `GeneralServices.json` ARM template.

`GeneralServices.json` provisions the Operational Insights workspace and Azure Key Vault along with the secrets and credentials needed by the *Online Medicine* sample application. The PowerShell script, `PreCreate.ps1`, sends parameters to the template and the definitions of those parameters are shown here.

Parameters

`GeneralServices.json` is a generic template defining multiple parameters as shown here:

```
"parameters": {
   "keyVaultName": {
      "type": "string",
      "metadata": {
         "description": "Name of the key vault"
      }
   },
   "tenantId": {
      "type": "string",
      "metadata": {
         "description": "Tenant ID for the subscription for access
         to the vault"
      }
   },
   "sqlServerName": {
      "type": "string",
      "metadata": {
         "description": "Name of Azure SQL server"
      }
   },
   "objectId": {
      "type": "string",
      "metadata": {
         "description": "Guid id of service principal"
      }
   },
   "keysPermissions": {
      "type": "array",
      "defaultValue": [ "all" ],
      "metadata": {
         "description": "Permissions to grant user to keys in
         the vault."
      }
   },
   "secretsPermissions": {
      "type": "array",
      "defaultValue": [ "all" ],
      "metadata": {
         "description": "Permissions to grant user to secrets in
         the vault."
      }
   },
   "vaultSku": {
```

```
      "type": "string",
      "defaultValue": "Standard",
      "allowedValues": [
        "Standard",
        "Premium"
      ],
      "metadata": {
        "description": "SKU for the vault"
      }
    },
    "enabledForDeployment": {
      "type": "bool",
      "defaultValue": true,
      "metadata": {
        "description": "Specifies if the vault is enabled for VM
        or Service Fabric deployment"
      }
    },
    "enabledForTemplateDeployment": {
      "type": "bool",
      "defaultValue": true,
      "metadata": {
        "description": "Specifies if the vault is enabled for
        ARM template deployment"
      }
    },
    "enableVaultForVolumeEncryption": {
      "type": "bool",
      "defaultValue": true,
      "metadata": {
        "description": "Specifies if the vault is enabled for volume
         encryption"
      }
    },
    "sqlUserName": {
      "type": "securestring",
      "metadata": {
        "description": "SQL username secret to store in the vault"
      }
    },
    "sqlPasswordName": {
      "type": "securestring",
      "metadata": {
        "description": "SQL password secret to store in the vault"
      }
    },
    "VMUserName": {
      "type": "securestring",
```

```
      "metadata": {
        "description": "VM username secret to store in the vault"
      }
    },
    "VMPasswordName": {
      "type": "securestring",
      "metadata": {
        "description": "VM password secret to store in the vault"
      }
    },
    "VSTSUserName": {
      "type": "securestring",
      "metadata": {
        "description": "VSTS username secret to store in the vault"
      }
    },
    "VSTSPasswordName": {
      "type": "securestring",
      "metadata": {
        "description": "VSTS password secret to store in the vault"
      }
    },
    "workspaceName": {
      "type": "string",
      "metadata": {
        "description": "OMS workspace name"
      }
    },
    "sasToken": {
      "type": "string",
      "metadata": {
        "description": "storage account SAS token"
      }
    },
    "storageKey": {
      "type": "string",
      "metadata": {
        "description": "storage account Key"
      }
    },
    "storageName": {
      "type": "string",
      "metadata": {
        "description": "storage account Name"
      }
    },
    "deployLocation": {
      "type": "string",
```

```
      "metadata": {
        "description": "Azure region for deployment"
      }
    },
    "serviceTier": {
      "type": "string",
      "defaultValue": "Free",
      "allowedValues": [
        "Free",
        "Standard",
        "Premium"
      ],
      "metadata": {
        "description": "Service Tier: Free, Standard, or Premium"
      }
    }
  }
},
```

Variables

There are no variables defined in the template.

The *Resources* section is the main section of the template where all resources are defined along with their properties.

Resources

The resources provisioned in this template are mentioned next.

Microsoft.OperationalInsights/workspaces

This resource gets the values for its `name`, `location`, and `sku` properties from parameters passed to the template by `PreCreate.ps1`.

```
{
    "apiVersion": "2015-11-01-preview",
    "type": "Microsoft.OperationalInsights/workspaces",
    "name": "[parameters('workspaceName')]",
    "location": "[parameters('deployLocation')]",
    "properties": {
      "sku": {
        "Name": "[parameters('serviceTier')]"
      }
    }
}
```

```
      }
```

Microsoft.KeyVault/vaults

The vault gets its `name` and `location` from parameters. By default, it is enabled for deployment for virtual machines and ARM template deployment. The access policy defines access and permissions to the Key Vault. In the code shown next, all permissions to `keys` and `secrets` are provided to the service principal defined earlier. The value of all comes from the `keysPermissions` and `secretsPermissions` parameters defined earlier. Valid permission values for the keys are all, create, import, update, get, list, delete, backup, restore, encrypt, decrypt, wrapkey, unwrapkey, sign, and verify. Valid permission values for secrets are all, get, set, list, and delete.

```
{
    "type": "Microsoft.KeyVault/vaults",
    "name": "[parameters('keyVaultName')]",
    "apiVersion": "2015-06-01",
    "location": "[resourceGroup().location]",
    "tags": {
      "displayName": "KeyVault"
    },
    "properties": {
      "enabledForDeployment": "[parameters('enabledForDeployment')]",
      "enabledForTemplateDeployment":
      "[parameters('enabledForTemplateDeployment')]",
      "enabledForVolumeEncryption":
      "[parameters('enableVaultForVolumeEncryption')]",
      "tenantId": "[parameters('tenantId')]",
      "accessPolicies": [
          {
            "tenantId": "[parameters('tenantId')]",
            "objectId": "[parameters('objectId')]",
            "permissions": {
             "keys": "[parameters('keysPermissions')]",
             "secrets": "[parameters('secretsPermissions')]"
            }
          }
      ],
      "sku": {
          "name": "[parameters('vaultSku')]",
          "family": "A"
      }
    }
}
```

Microsoft.KeyVault/vaults secrets

Secrets are nested resources within the `Microsoft.KeyVault/Vaults` resource. These resources are dependent on the parent resource for its provisioning.

The SQL server username nested resource is declared as shown here. The `dependson` property states that this resource should be provisioned only after the given parent resource is completely provisioned:

```
{
  "type": "secrets",
  "name": "sqlusername",
  "apiVersion": "2015-06-01",
  "properties": {
    "value": "[parameters('sqlUserName')]"
  },
  "dependsOn": [
    "[concat('Microsoft.KeyVault/vaults/',
    parameters('keyVaultName'))]"
  ]
}
```

The SQL server password nested resource is declared as shown here:

```
{
  "type": "secrets",
  "name": "sqlpassword",
  "apiVersion": "2015-06-01",
  "properties": {
    "value": "[parameters('sqlPasswordName')]"
  },
  "dependsOn": [
    "[concat('Microsoft.KeyVault/vaults/',
    parameters('keyVaultName'))]"
  ]
}
```

The virtual machine username resource is declared as shown here:

```
{
  "type": "secrets",
  "name": "vmusername",
  "apiVersion": "2015-06-01",
  "properties": {
    "value": "[parameters('VMUserName')]"
  },
  "dependsOn": [
    "[concat('Microsoft.KeyVault/vaults/',
    parameters('keyVaultName'))]"
  ]
}
```

The virtual machine password resource is declared as shown here:

```
{
  "type": "secrets",
  "name": "vmpassword",
  "apiVersion": "2015-06-01",
  "properties": {
    "value": "[parameters('VMPasswordName')]"
  },
  "dependsOn": [
    "[concat('Microsoft.KeyVault/vaults/',
    parameters('keyVaultName'))]"
  ]
}
```

The VSTS username resource is declared as shown here:

```
{
  "type": "secrets",
  "name": "vstsusername",
  "apiVersion": "2015-06-01",
  "properties": {
    "value": "[parameters('VSTSUserName')]"
  },
  "dependsOn": [
    "[concat('Microsoft.KeyVault/vaults/',
    parameters('keyVaultName'))]"
  ]
}
```

The VSTS password resource is declared as shown here:

```
{
  "type": "secrets",
  "name": "vstspassword",
  "apiVersion": "2015-06-01",
  "properties": {
    "value": "[parameters('VSTSPasswordName')]"
  },
  "dependsOn": [
    "[concat('Microsoft.KeyVault/vaults/',
    parameters('keyVaultName'))]"
  ]
}
```

The OMS workspace ID resource is declared as shown here. The `reference` function is an ARM template built-in function and helps in retrieving resource values. Here, it gets the value of the `customerId` value of the OMS workspace resource.

```
{
  "type": "secrets",
  "name": "WorkspaceID",
  "apiVersion": "2015-06-01",
  "properties": {
    "value": "[reference(parameters('workspaceName')).customerId]"
  },
  "dependsOn": [
    "[concat('Microsoft.KeyVault/vaults/',
    parameters('keyVaultName'))]"
  ]
}
```

The storage account SAS token resource is declared as shown here:

```
{
  "type": "secrets",
  "name": "sasToken",
  "apiVersion": "2015-06-01",
  "properties": {
    "value": "[parameters('sasToken')]"
  },
  "dependsOn": [
    "[concat('Microsoft.KeyVault/vaults/',
    parameters('keyVaultName'))]"
  ]
}
```

The storage account key resource is declared as shown here:

```
{
  "type": "secrets",
  "name": "storageKey",
  "apiVersion": "2015-06-01",
  "properties": {
    "value": "[parameters('storageKey')]"
  },
  "dependsOn": [
    "[concat('Microsoft.KeyVault/vaults/',
    parameters('keyVaultName'))]"
  ]
}
```

The storage name resource is declared as shown here:

```
{
  "type": "secrets",
  "name": "storageName",
  "apiVersion": "2015-06-01",
  "properties": {
    "value": "[parameters('storageName')]"
  },
  "dependsOn": [
    "[concat('Microsoft.KeyVault/vaults/',
    parameters('keyVaultName'))]"
  ]
}
```

The SQL server name resource is declared as shown here:

```
{
  "type": "secrets",
  "name": "sqlServerName",
  "apiVersion": "2015-06-01",
  "properties": {
    "value": "[parameters('sqlServerName')]"
  },
  "dependsOn": [
    "[concat('Microsoft.KeyVault/vaults/',
    parameters('keyVaultName'))]"
  ]
}
```

Outputs

There are no outputs defined for this template.

Steps for deployment of the operator or release pipeline

After the IT administrator has provisioned the common services on which the sample application is dependent on, an operator or release team can execute the step to provision, deploy, and configure the infrastructure and sample application.

The scripts described next are intended to run in the VSTS release pipeline. However, they can also be run manually using a PowerShell editor such as ISE. The script has code commented for authenticating to the Azure subscription using the service principal created earlier. They should remain commented while using them in the release pipeline and can be uncommented while executing the script manually. The release pipeline uses the concept of service endpoint which will be discussed in `Chapter 10`, *Continuous Delivery and Deployment*.

UploadScriptFiles.ps1

The first step in provisioning the sample application is to upload the PowerShell scripts, templates, and configuration files to the Azure storage provisioned by the IT administrator. These files are available as part of the sample application code files in the `OnlinePharmacy.Configuration` project folder. The purpose of this script is to upload the relevant files to the Azure storage so that they are available to Azure virtual machines while provisioning them.

This PowerShell script will be executed as part of continuous deployment through the VSTS release pipeline. It is to be noted that placeholder values should be provided before executing the scripts.

1. If you are executing the script interactively then log in to the Azure subscription using the service principal created earlier. The login needs the service principal ID and password along with the `TenantId` and `Subscription` ID. This step is not needed in the release management process and the code should remain commented.

   ```
   #$(username) = "[xxxxxxxxxxxxxxx]"
   ```

```
#$(passsword) = "[xxxxxxxxxxxxxxxxxxxxx]"
#$pass = ConvertTo-SecureString -String $passsword
-AsPlainText -Force
#$cred = New-Object System.Management.Automation.PSCredential
$username, $pass
#Login-AzureRmAccount -Credential $cred -TenantId $(TenantID)
-SubscriptionId $(SubscriptionID) -ServicePrincipal
#Set-AzureRmContext -SubscriptionId "[xxxxxxxxxxxxxxxxxxxxx]"
```

Retrieve the storage account and its primary key for uploading files to the storage account. The rest of the commands upload scripts to the storage account. These scripts are available in the Git repository while running in the release pipeline.

```
$storage = Get-AzureRmStorageAccount
-ResourceGroupName
$resourceGroupName -Name "$storageAccountName"
$storageKey = Get-AzureRmStorageAccountKey
-ResourceGroupName
$resourceGroupName -Name "$storageAccountName"

#This cmdlet publishes a dsc configuration to
Azure storage account after zipping it along with
all its dependent resources.

Publish-AzureRMVMDscConfiguration -ConfigurationPath
"$scriptsFilePathDSCScriptsInstallContainer.ps1"
-ContainerName "$containerName" -ResourceGroupName
$resourceGroupName -StorageAccountName $storageAccountName
-Force -Verbose

#This PowerShell script converts a virtual machine into
Pull Server. It also generates the DSC MOF configuration
documents by executing IISInstall.ps1 and # also the
OnlineMedicine.sql sql script for generating the database tables.

Set-AzureStorageBlobContent -File "$scriptsFilePath
PSScriptspullserver.ps1" -Container "$containerName"
-Blob "pullserver.ps1" -BlobType Block -Force -Context
$storage.Context

#This PowerShell script is executed on Pull Server and
responsible for generating DSC MOF document. These MOF
files are downloaded by containers to configure themselves.

Set-AzureStorageBlobContent -File "$scriptsFilePath
DSCScriptsIISInstall.ps1" -Container "$containerName"
-Blob "IISInstall.ps1" -BlobType Block -Force -Context
```

```
$storage.Context

#This PowerShell script is executed on all web application
related virtual machines to provision custom windows container
images based on dockerfile and generate containers from them.
These containers host the web application

Set-AzureStorageBlobContent -File "$scriptsFilePathPSScripts
ContainerConfig.ps1" -Container "$containerName"
-Blob "ContainerConfig.ps1" -BlobType Block -Force -Context
$storage.Context

# This command uploads the OnlinePharmacy.sql sql script file
to azure storage container and executed by Pull Server virtual
machine for provisioning table # structure

Set-AzureStorageBlobContent -File "$sqlFilePath"
-Container "$containerName" -Blob "OnlinePharmacy.sql"
-BlobType Block -Force -Context $storage.Context

# This command uploads the dockerfile to azure storage
container. This file is responsible for creating a custom
image for our sample web application.

Set-AzureStorageBlobContent -File "$scriptsFilePathTemplates
dockerfile" -Container "$containerName" -Blob "dockerfile"
-BlobType Block -Force -Context $storage.Context

# This PowerShell script is run within a windows container
and responsible for updating the sql connection string in
web.config file of web application based on data supplied
to it from Azure Key Vault.

Set-AzureStorageBlobContent -File "$scriptsFilePathPSScripts
ChangeConnectionString.ps1" -Container "$containerName"
-Blob "ChangeConnectionString.ps1" -BlobType Block -Force
-Context $storage.Context

# This zip file contains all the artifacts related to the
frontend aspect of ASP.NET MVC web application. It will
be used in conjunction with webdeploy utility for deploying in
IIS within windows container.

Set-AzureStorageBlobContent -File "$scriptsFilePathPSScripts
lcm.ps1" -Container "$containerName" -Blob "lcm.ps1" -BlobType
Block -Force -Context $storage.Context
```

2. Create a new Azure resource group named `OnlineMedicine`. Deploy the `OnlineMedicine.json` ARM template after testing for its validity. Parameters to this template are passed using another `json` file named `OnlineMedicine.parameters.json`. We will look into the details of both `OnlineMedicine.json` and `OnlineMedicine.parameters.json` in the next section:

```
New-AzureRmResourceGroup -Name OnlineMedicine
                         -Location "West Europe"
Test-AzureRmResourceGroupDeployment -ResourceGroupName testingDev6
                                    -TemplateFile "C:Templates
                                     OnlineMedicine.json"
                                    -TemplateParameterFile
                                    "C:Templates
                                    OnlineMedicine.parameters.json"
                                    -verbose
New-AzureRmResourceGroupDeployment -Name test1
                                   -ResourceGroupName testingDev6
                                   -TemplateFile "C:Templates
                                    OnlineMedicine.json"
                                   -TemplateParameterFile
                                   "C:Templates
                                   OnlineMedicine.parameters.json"
                                   -Verbose
```

Test-ARMTemplate.ps1

After preparing the common services and uploading the relevant scripts and templates to the Azure storage, it's time to start the process of deployment of the sample application. The entire infrastructure and application deployment is done through ARM template. The ARM template is responsible for provisioning resources on Azure and running scripts on virtual machines to configure them with the DSC Pull Server, Docker container, deploying the application and connecting it to the Azure SQL Server. However, before the ARM template is executed, it should be tested for its validity. The purpose of `Test-ARMTemplate` is to create a new resource group for the sample application and validate the `OnlineMedicine.json` ARM template. This script is executed from the release pipeline. The code for the entire script is shown next.

```
param(
    [string] $ARMTemplatePath,
    [string] $ARMTemplateParametersPath,
    [string] $resourceGroupName,
    [string] $OMSWorkspaceName,
```

```
        [string] $skuName,
        [string] $deploymentName,
        [string] $pullserverRegKey,
        [string] $pullserverPort,
        [string] $webAppPort,
        [string] $deployLocation,
        [string] $wsResourceGroup,
        [string] $containerName
)
New-AzureRmResourceGroup -Name $resourceGroupName -Location
$deployLocation -Force -Confirm:$false -Verbose
Test-AzureRmResourceGroupDeployment -ResourceGroupName
$resourceGroupName -TemplateFile "$ARMTemplatePath"
-TemplateParameterFile "$ARMTemplateParametersPath"
-workspaceName "$OMSWorkspaceName" -skuName $skuName
-pullserverRegKey $pullserverRegKey -pullserverPort
$pullserverPort -webAppPort $webAppPort -wsResourceGroup
$wsResourceGroup -deployLocation "$deployLocation"
-containerName "$containerName" -Verbose
```

The script action has multiple parameters and passes them to the `Test-AzureRmResourceGroupDeployment` cmdlet for verifying the validity of the template.

New-TemplateDeployment.ps1

After ensuring that the ARM template has no errors, it's time to execute the template and provision environment along with the application deployment. This script is very similar to `Test-ARMTemplate.ps1`. It takes the same parameters but instead of testing the template, this script starts the actual deployment process using the `New-AzureRmResourceGroupDeployment` cmdlet. This script is executed from the release pipeline. The entire script is shown here.

```
param(
    [string] $ARMTemplatePath,
    [string] $ARMTemplateParametersPath,
    [string] $resourceGroupName,
    [string] $OMSWorkspaceName,
    [string] $skuName ,
    [string] $deploymentName,
    [string] $pullserverRegKey,
    [string] $pullserverPort,
    [string] $webAppPort,
    [string] $deployLocation,
    [string] $wsResourceGroup,
    [string] $containerName
```

```
)
New-AzureRmResourceGroupDeployment -ResourceGroupName
$resourceGroupName -Name $deploymentName -TemplateFile
"$ARMTemplatePath" -TemplateParameterFile "$ARMTemplateParametersPath"
-workspaceName "$OMSWorkspaceName" -skuName $skuName
-pullserverRegKey $pullserverRegKey -pullserverPort
$pullserverPort -webAppPort $webAppPort -wsResourceGroup
$wsResourceGroup -deployLocation "$deployLocation"
-containerName "$containerName" -Mode Incremental -verbose
```

OnlineMedicine.parameters.json

There are multiple ways to send parameters to ARM templates. One of the ways we saw earlier was by sending parameters using PowerShell. Another option is to send parameters to the ARM template is by way of the `json` file. In this `json` file, the parameters section contains all the parameters with their corresponding values. While deploying the template, `New-AzureRMResourceGroupDeployment`. `TemplateParameterFile` argument can be used to specify the parameters file. All parameters defined in the parameters file will be passed as parameters to the ARM template. Also, this is an ideal approach to send Azure Key Vault-related parameters and their values to the template.

The `OnlineMedicine.parameters.json` file contains only parameters related to values that are stored in the Azure Key Vault. The vault is referred using its unique identifier, and there is a special capability provided by templates to refer to the Azure Key Vault using reference keywords.

It is to be noted that placeholder values should be replaced before executing the scripts and templates. The xx values should be replaced with an appropriate subscription ID, the ?? values should be replaced with the resource group name created by the IT administrator containing the Azure Key Vault, and the ** value should be replaced with the actual name of the Key Vault.

The parameters defined in the parameters file are as follows:

- SQL server username:

```
"sqlUserName": {
  "reference": {
    "keyVault": {
      "id": "/subscriptions/xxxxxxxx-xxxx-xxxx-xxxx-xxxxxxxxxxxx
      /resourceGroups/???????/providers/
      Microsoft.KeyVault/vaults/*****"
    },
    "secretName": "sqlUserName"
```

```
      }
    }
```

- SQL server password:

```
"sqlPassword": {
  "reference": {
    "keyVault": {
      "id": "/subscriptions/xxxxxxxx-xxxx-xxxx-xxxx-
      xxxxxxxxxxxx/resourceGroups/???????/providers/
      Microsoft.KeyVault/vaults/*****"
    },
    "secretName": "sqlPassword"
  }
}
VSTS username:
  "vstsUserName": {
    "reference": {
      "keyVault": {
        "id": "/subscriptions/xxxxxxxx-xxxx-xxxx-xxxx-
        xxxxxxxxxxxx/resourceGroups/???????/providers/
        Microsoft.KeyVault/vaults/*****"
      },
      "secretName": "vstsUserName"
    }
  }
```

- VSTS password:

```
"vstsPassword": {
  "reference": {
    "keyVault": {
      "id": "/subscriptions/xxxxxxxx-xxxx-xxxx-xxxx-
      xxxxxxxxxxxx/resourceGroups/???????/providers/
      Microsoft.KeyVault/vaults/*****"
    },
    "secretName": "vstsPassword"
  }
}
```

- Virtual machine user name:

```json
"vmUserName": {
  "reference": {
    "keyVault": {
      "id": "/subscriptions/xxxxxxxx-xxxx-xxxx-xxxx-
      xxxxxxxxxxxx/resourceGroups/???????/providers/
      Microsoft.KeyVault/vaults/*****"
    },
    "secretName": "vmUserName"
  }
}
```

- Virtual machine password:

```json
"vmPassword": {
  "reference": {
    "keyVault": {
      "id": "/subscriptions/xxxxxxxx-xxxx-xxxx-xxxx-
      xxxxxxxxxxxx/resourceGroups/???????/providers/
      Microsoft.KeyVault/vaults/*****"
    },
    "secretName": "vmPassword"
  }
}
```

- OMS workspace ID:

```json
"WorkspaceID": {
  "reference": {
    "keyVault": {
      "id": "/subscriptions/xxxxxxxx-xxxx-xxxx-xxxx-
      xxxxxxxxxxxx/resourceGroups/???????/providers/
      Microsoft.KeyVault/vaults/*****"
    },
    "secretName": "WorkspaceID"
  }
}
```

- Storage account SAS token:

```
"sasToken": {
  "reference": {
  "keyVault": {
    "id": "/subscriptions/xxxxxxxx-xxxx-xxxx-xxxx-
    xxxxxxxxxxxx/resourceGroups/???????/providers/
    Microsoft.KeyVault/vaults/*****"
  },
    "secretName": "sasToken"
  }
}
```

- Storage account key:

```
"storageKey": {
  "reference": {
    "keyVault": {
      "id": "/subscriptions/xxxxxxxx-xxxx-xxxx-xxxx-
      xxxxxxxxxxxx/resourceGroups/???????/providers/
      Microsoft.KeyVault/vaults/*****"
    },
      "secretName": "storageKey"
  }
}
```

- Storage account name:

```
"storageName": {
  "reference": {
    "keyVault": {
      "id": "/subscriptions/xxxxxxxx-xxxx-xxxx-xxxx-
      xxxxxxxxxxxx/resourceGroups/???????/providers/
      Microsoft.KeyVault/vaults/*****"
    },
      "secretName": "storageName"
  }
}
```

- Azure SQL server name:

```
"sqlServerName": {
  "reference": {
    "keyVault": {
      "id": "/subscriptions/xxxxxxxx-xxxx-xxxx-xxxx-
      xxxxxxxxxxxx/resourceGroups/???????/providers/
      Microsoft.KeyVault/vaults/*****"
    },
    "secretName": "sqlServerName"
  }
}
```

OnlineMedicine.json

The ARM template, `OnlineMedicine.json`, is the main template for deploying both the infrastructure and application for the sample application. It reuses the storage account, OMS workspace, and Azure Key Vault provisioned by an IT administrator . The PowerShell script, `New-TemplateDeployment.ps1`, executes the template in combination with the `parameters` file.

Parameters

`OnlineMedicine.json` is a generic template defining multiple parameters as shown following:

```
"workspaceName": {
    "type": "string",
    "defaultValue": "OnlineMedicineOMS",
    "metadata": {
      "description": "OMS workspace Name"
    }
},
"pullserverPort": {
  "type": "string",
  "defaultValue": "9100"
},
"webAppPort": {
  "type": "string",
  "defaultValue": "8080",
  "metadata": {
    "description": "Port number for web application"
  }
```

```
    },
    "skuName": {
      "type": "string",
      "defaultValue": "om",
      "metadata": {
         "description": "om - shot form for Online Medicine.
         used to uniquify names"
      }
    },
    "deployLocation": {
      "type": "string",
      "defaultValue": "West Europe",
      "metadata": {
        "description": "Location for provisioning of resources"}
    },
    "countVMs": {
      "type": "int",
      "defaultValue": 2,
      "metadata": {
         "description": "The name of the new Web application
         virtual machines."
      }
    },
    "vmSize": {
      "type": "string",
      "defaultValue": "Standard_D3",
      "metadata": {
         "description": "The size of virtual machines."
      }
    },
    "osSKU": {
      "type": "string",
      "defaultValue": "2016-Datacenter-with-Containers",
      "metadata": {
         "description": "Image SKU of virtual machines"
      }
    },
    "databaseName": {
      "type": "string",
      "defaultValue": "medicine",
      "metadata": {
        "description": "Name of SQL server database"
      }
    },
    "sqlUserName": {
      "type": "securestring",
      "metadata": {
        "description": "SQL server username passed from Azure key vault"
```

```
        }
      },
      "sqlPassword": {
        "type": "securestring",
        "metadata": {
          "description": "SQL server password passed from Azure key vault"
        }
      },
      "vstsUserName": {
        "type": "securestring",
        "metadata": {
          "description": "VSTS username passed from Azure key vault"
        }
      },
      "vstsPassword": {
        "type": "securestring",
        "metadata": {
          "description": "VSTS password passed from Azure key vault"
        }
      },
      "vmUserName": {
        "type": "securestring",
        "metadata": {
          "description": "Virtual Machine username passed from Azure key
vault"
        }
      },
      "vmPassword": {
        "type": "securestring",
        "metadata": {
          "description": "Virtual Machine password passed from Azure key
vault"
        }
      },
      "WorkspaceID": {
        "type": "securestring",
        "metadata": {
          "description": "OMS workspace ID passed from Azure key vault"
        }
      },
      "sasToken": {
        "type": "securestring",
        "metadata": {
          "description": "Storage account SAS token passed from Azure key
vault"
        }
      },
      "storageKey": {
```

```
      "type": "securestring",
      "metadata": {
        "description": "Storage Account key passed from Azure key vault"
      }
    },
    "storageName": {
      "type": "securestring",
      "metadata": {
        "description": "Storage account name passed from Azure key vault"
      }
    },
    "containerName": {
      "type": "string",
      "metadata": {
        "description": "Storage container name passed from Azure key vault"
      }
    },
    "sqlServerName": {
      "type": "securestring",
      "metadata": {
        "description": "SQL Server name passed from Azure key vault"
      }
    },
    "wsResourceGroup": {
      "type": "string",
      "defaultValue": "win2016devops",
      "metadata": {
        "description": "Name of resource group hosting key vault,
        storage account and OMS workspace"
      }
    },
    "collation": {
      "type": "string",
      "defaultValue": "SQL_Latin1_General_CP1_CI_AS",
      "metadata": {
        "description": "The database collation for governing
        the proper use of characters."
      }
    },
    "edition": {
      "type": "string",
      "defaultValue": "Basic",
      "allowedValues": [
        "Basic",
        "Standard",
        "Premium"
      ],
      "metadata": {
```

```
        "description": "The type of database to create."
    }
},
"maxSizeBytes": {
  "type": "string",
  "defaultValue": "1073741824",
  "metadata": {
    "description": "The maximum size, in bytes, for the database"
  }
},
"pullserverRegKey": {
  "type": "string",
  "defaultValue": "11111111-1111-1111-1111-111111111111",
  "metadata": {
    "description": "GU"
  }
},
"requestedServiceObjectiveName": {
  "type": "string",
  "defaultValue": "Basic",
  "allowedValues": [
    "Basic",
    "S0",
    "S1",
    "S2",
    "P1",
    "P2",
    "P3"
  ],
  "metadata": {
    "description": "Describes the performance level for Edition"
  }
}
}
```

Variables

Multiple variables are defined for internal working of the template. The following code shows all the declared variables in the template:

```
"storageAccountName": "[concat(parameters('skuName'),
uniqueString(resourceGroup().id))]",
"storageApiVersion": "2015-05-01-preview",
"storageType": "Standard_LRS",
"networkName": "[concat(parameters('skuName'), '-network')]",
"networkApiVersion": "2015-05-01-preview",
"networkAddressSpace": "10.0.0.0/16",
"publicIpName": "[concat(parameters('skuName'), '-publicIP')]",
```

```
"publicIPApiVersion": "2015-05-01-preview",
"PublicIpType": "Static",
"nicName": "[concat(parameters('skuName'), '-nic')]",
"nicApiVersion": "2015-05-01-preview",
"nicIpType": "Dynamic",
"vmName": "vm",
"vmApiVersion": "2015-05-01-preview",
"NSGName": "[concat(parameters('skuName'),'-NSG')]",
"NSGApiVersion": "2015-05-01-preview",
"accountid": "[concat('/subscriptions/',
subscription().subscriptionId,'/resourceGroups/',
parameters('wsResourceGroup'),'/providers/',
'Microsoft.OperationalInsights/workspaces/',
parameters('workspaceName'))]",
"sqlServerName": "[concat(parameters('sqlServerName'),
'-', parameters('skuName'))]"
```

Resources

The Azure resources provisioned through the template are shown here.

Microsoft.Compute/availabilitySets

Availability sets are required for multiple virtual machines to be attached to a load balancer. It provides high availability for applications associated with them. Azure will patch one server at a time, ensuring that an instance is always available to serve the requests.

```
{
    "type": "Microsoft.Compute/availabilitySets",
    "name": "webappAVSet",
    "apiVersion": "2015-05-01-preview",
    "location": "[parameters('deployLocation')]"
}
```

Microsoft.Storage/storageAccounts

This storage account is needed to store the vhd files of Pull Server and virtual machines. The code is self-explanatory. All of its properties get values from either variables or parameters.

```
{
    "type": "Microsoft.Storage/storageAccounts",
    "name": "[variables('storageAccountName')]",
    "apiVersion": "[variables('storageApiVersion')]",
    "location": "[parameters('deployLocation')]",
```

```
    "properties": {
      "accountType": "[variables('storageType')]"
    }
  }
```

Microsoft.Network/virtualNetworks

All virtual machines and load balancers are attached to a virtual network in the Azure resource manager. The network has two subnets with distinct address spaces. It is possible to create more subnets and readers are free to create them based on their preference.

```
{
  "name": "[variables('networkName')]",
  "type": "Microsoft.Network/virtualNetworks",
  "location": "[parameters('deployLocation')]",
  "tags": {
    "skuName": "[parameters('skuName')]"
  },
  "dependsOn": [
    "[concat('Microsoft.Network/networkSecurityGroups/',
    variables('NSGName'))]"
  ],
  "apiVersion": "[variables('networkApiVersion')]",
  "properties": {
    "addressSpace": {
      "addressPrefixes": [
        "[variables('networkAddressSpace')]"
      ]
    },
    "subnets": [
      {
        "name": "subnetad",
        "properties": {
          "addressPrefix": "10.0.0.0/24"
        }
      },
      {
        "name": "frontend",
        "properties": {
          "addressPrefix": "10.0.1.0/24",
          "networkSecurityGroup": {
            "id": "[resourceId('Microsoft.Network/
            networkSecurityGroups', variables('NSGName'))]"
          }
        }
      }
    ]
```

```
    }
  }
```

Microsoft.Network/networkSecurityGroups

Network security groups help in filtering the requests and allow only those that match the rules in the allowed list based on a combination of both IP address and ports. The ports opened through NSG are 80,443, 1433, 5985, 5986, 3389, 2375, and 2376, for Pull Server and the web application.

```
{
  "apiVersion": "[variables('NSGApiVersion')]",
  "type": "Microsoft.Network/networkSecurityGroups",
  "name": "[variables('NSGName')]",
  "location": "[resourceGroup().location]",
  "tags": {
    "skuName": "[parameters('skuName')]"
  },
  "properties": {
    "securityRules": [
      {
        "name": "rule80",
        "properties": {
          "protocol": "Tcp",
          "sourcePortRange": "*",
          "destinationPortRange": "80",
          "sourceAddressPrefix": "*",
          "destinationAddressPrefix": "*",
          "access": "Allow",
          "priority": 101,
          "direction": "Inbound"
        }
      },
      {
        "name": "rule443",
        "properties": {
          "protocol": "Tcp",
          "sourcePortRange": "*",
          "destinationPortRange": "443",
          "sourceAddressPrefix": "*",
          "destinationAddressPrefix": "*",
          "access": "Allow",
          "priority": 102,
          "direction": "Inbound"
        }
      },
      {
```

```
          "name": "rule1433",
          "properties": {
            "protocol": "Tcp",
            "sourcePortRange": "*",
            "destinationPortRange": "1433",
            "sourceAddressPrefix": "*",
            "destinationAddressPrefix": "*",
            "access": "Allow",
            "priority": 103,
            "direction": "Inbound"
          }
        },
        {
          "name": "rulePSUnsecured",
          "properties": {
            "protocol": "Tcp",
            "sourcePortRange": "*",
            "destinationPortRange": "5985",
            "sourceAddressPrefix": "*",
            "destinationAddressPrefix": "*",
            "access": "Allow",
            "priority": 104,
            "direction": "Inbound"
          }
        },
        {
          "name": "rulePSsecured",
          "properties": {
            "protocol": "Tcp",
            "sourcePortRange": "*",
            "destinationPortRange": "5986",
            "sourceAddressPrefix": "*",
            "destinationAddressPrefix": "*",
            "access": "Allow",
            "priority": 105,
            "direction": "Inbound"
          }
        },
        {
          "name": "RDP",
          "properties": {
            "protocol": "Tcp",
            "sourcePortRange": "*",
            "destinationPortRange": "3389",
            "sourceAddressPrefix": "*",
            "destinationAddressPrefix": "*",
            "access": "Allow",
            "priority": 106,
```

```
          "direction": "Inbound"
        }
    },
    {
      "name": "docker",
      "properties": {
        "protocol": "Tcp",
        "sourcePortRange": "*",
        "destinationPortRange": "2375",
        "sourceAddressPrefix": "*",
        "destinationAddressPrefix": "*",
        "access": "Allow",
        "priority": 107,
        "direction": "Inbound"
      }
    },
    {
      "name": "dockers",
      "properties": {
        "protocol": "Tcp",
        "sourcePortRange": "*",
        "destinationPortRange": "2376",
        "sourceAddressPrefix": "*",
        "destinationAddressPrefix": "*",
        "access": "Allow",
        "priority": 108,
        "direction": "Inbound"
      }
    },
    {
      "name": "pullserver",
      "properties": {
        "protocol": "Tcp",
        "sourcePortRange": "*",
        "destinationPortRange": "[parameters('pullserverPort')]",
        "sourceAddressPrefix": "*",
        "destinationAddressPrefix": "*",
        "access": "Allow",
        "priority": 109,
        "direction": "Inbound"
      }
    },
    {
      "name": "webserver",
      "properties": {
        "protocol": "Tcp",
        "sourcePortRange": "*",
        "destinationPortRange": "[parameters('webAppPort')]",
```

```
                    "sourceAddressPrefix": "*",
                    "destinationAddressPrefix": "*",
                    "access": "Allow",
                    "priority": 110,
                    "direction": "Inbound"
                }
            }
        ]
    }
}
```

Microsoft.Network/publicIPAddresses

The public IP address resource makes a virtual machine accessible on the Internet. This IP address will also be passed to SQL server database firewall rules to allow access from virtual machines.

```
{
    "apiVersion": "[variables('publicIPApiVersion')]",
    "type": "Microsoft.Network/publicIPAddresses",
    "name": "[concat('pipPS',variables('publicIpName'))]",
    "location": "[parameters('deployLocation')]",
    "tags": {
        "skuName": "[parameters('skuName')]"
    },
    "properties": {
        "publicIPAllocationMethod": "Static",
        "dnsSettings": {
            "domainNameLabel": "[concat(parameters('skuName'),
            'pullserver01')]"
        }
    }
}
```

Microsoft.Network/networkInterfaces

Every virtual machine needs a **Network Interface Card** (NIC) for communication with a virtual network and other resources. This NIC is provisioned for the Pull Server virtual machine. A public IP address and a dynamic internal IP address from a frontend subnet and are assigned to NIC.

```
{
    "name": "[concat('nicPS',variables('nicName'))]",
    "type": "Microsoft.Network/networkInterfaces",
    "location": "[parameters('deployLocation')]",
    "tags": {
```

```
            "skuName": "[parameters('skuName')]"
          },
          "dependsOn": [
            "[concat('Microsoft.Network/virtualNetworks/',
            variables('networkName'))]",
            "[concat('Microsoft.Network/publicIPAddresses/','pipPS',
            variables('publicIpName'))]"
          ],
          "apiVersion": "[variables('nicApiVersion')]",
          "properties": {
            "ipConfigurations": [
              {
                "name": "ipconfigps",
                "properties": {
                  "privateIPAllocationMethod": "Dynamic",
                  "subnet": {
                    "id":
  "[resourceId('Microsoft.Network/virtualNetworks/subnets/',
                    variables('networkName'), 'frontend')]"
                  },
                  "publicIPAddress": {
                    "id":
                    [resourceId('Microsoft.Network/publicIPAddresses',
                    concat('pipPS',variables('publicIpName')))]"
                  }
                }
              }
            ]
          }
        }
```

Microsoft.Compute/virtualMachines

This resource provisions a virtual machine based on a Windows Server 2016 image. This `sku` of Windows has a containers feature enabled by default. It is dependent on the Azure storage account on which its `vhd` will be stored , the virtual network, and SQL server. It is dependent on the SQL server because the Pull Server is also responsible for provisioning the table structure within the Azure SQL database. The NIC provisioned earlier is also assigned to it.

```
      {
        "apiVersion": "[variables('vmApiVersion')]",
        "type": "Microsoft.Compute/virtualMachines",
        "name": "[concat(variables('vmName'),'-pulls')]",
        "tags": {
          "skuName": "[parameters('skuName')]"
        },
```

```
"location": "[parameters('deployLocation')]",
"dependsOn": [
"[resourceId('Microsoft.Storage/storageAccounts',
variables('storageAccountName'))]",
"[resourceId('Microsoft.Network/networkInterfaces',
concat('nicPS',variables('nicName')))]",
"[resourceId('Microsoft.Sql/servers',
variables('sqlServerName'))]",
"[resourceId('Microsoft.Sql/servers/databases',
variables('sqlServerName'), parameters('databaseName'))]"
],
"properties": {
  "hardwareProfile": {
    "vmSize": "[parameters('vmSize')]"
  },
  "osProfile": {
    "computerName": "[concat(variables('vmName'),'-pulls')]",
    "adminUsername": "[parameters('vmUserName')]",
    "adminPassword": "[parameters('vmPassword')]"
  },
  "storageProfile": {
    "imageReference": {
      "publisher": "MicrosoftWindowsServer",
      "offer": "WindowsServer",
      "sku": "[parameters('osSKU')]",
      "version": "latest"
    },
    "osDisk": {
      "name": "osdisk",
      "vhd": {
        "uri": "[concat('http://',variables('storageAccountName')
        ,'.blob.core.windows.net/vhds0/','psvmdisk.vhd')]"
      },
      "caching": "ReadWrite",
      "createOption": "FromImage"
    },
    "dataDisks": [
      {
        "vhd": {
          "uri": "[concat('http://',variables('storageAccountName')
          ,'.blob.core.windows.net/vhds0/', 'pullserver-data-
          disk1.vhd')]"
        },
        "name": "pullserver-data-disk1",
        "caching": "None",
        "diskSizeGB": "1023",
        "lun": 0,
        "createOption": "empty"
```

```
          }
        ]
      },
      "networkProfile": {
        "networkInterfaces": [
          {
            "id": "[resourceId('Microsoft.Network/networkInterfaces',
            concat('nicPS',variables('nicName')))]"
          }
        ]
      }
    }
  }
}
```

Microsoft.Compute/virtualMachines/extensions – CustomScriptExtension

This is a nested resource of the `virtualMachines` resource. `CustomScriptExtension` helps in executing PowerShell scripts during the provisioning of virtual machines and provides an opportunity to deploy, provision, and configure additional services and utilities within the virtual machine. This resource has the capability of downloading scripts from Azure storage accounts on to virtual machines using Azure storage keys. This extension downloads two PowerShell scripts – `PullServer.ps1` and `IISInstall.ps1` on the Pull Server virtual machine.

Scripts running using this extension is responsible for provisioning Pull Server and deploying configurations.

- `PullServer.ps1` is responsible for provisioning of the DSC Pull Server on the virtual machine. It is also responsible for executing the SQL script for the application to generate table structures in Azure SQL as well as generating appropriate virtual machine certificates for accessing its security through PowerShell. This script will be discussed in depth in the next chapter.
- `IISInstall.ps1` is responsible for generating DSC configured documents and deploying them in Pull Server so that they can be accessed and downloaded by the local configuration manager of the target containers and configure themselves. This script will be discussed in the depth in next chapter.

Since it is a nested resource, it is dependent on its parent virtual machine resource. This extension is dependent on the successful provisioning of the virtual machine.

```
{
    "type": "Microsoft.Compute/virtualMachines/extensions",
    "name": "[concat(variables('vmName'),'-pulls','/powershellscript')]",
    "apiVersion": "2015-05-01-preview",
```

```
    "tags": {
       "skuName": "[parameters('skuName')]"
    },
    "location": "[parameters('deployLocation')]",
    "dependsOn": [
    "[concat('Microsoft.Compute/virtualMachines/',
    variables('vmName'),'-pulls')]"
    ],
    "properties": {
      "publisher": "Microsoft.Compute",
      "type": "CustomScriptExtension",
      "typeHandlerVersion": "1.4",
      "autoUpgradeMinorVersion": true,
      "settings": {
        "fileUris": [
          "[concat('https://', parameters('storageName'),
          '.blob.core.windows.net/', parameters('containerName'),
          '/pullserver.ps1')]",
          "[concat('https://', parameters('storageName'),
          '.blob.core.windows.net/', parameters('containerName'),
          '/IISInstall.ps1')]",
          "[concat('https://', parameters('storageName'),
          '.blob.core.windows.net/', parameters('containerName'),
          '/OnlinePharmacy.sql')]"
        ],
        "timestamp": "11",
        "commandToExecute": "[concat('powershell.exe -ExecutionPolicy
        Unrestricted -File pullserver.ps1', ' -port ',
        parameters('pullserverPort') , ' -sqlUsername ',
        parameters('sqlUserName') , ' -sqlPassword ',
        parameters('sqlPassword') , ' -sqlDatabaseName ',
        parameters('databaseName') , ' -servername ',
        variables('sqlServerName'), ' -webport ' ,
        parameters('webAppPort') , ' -regKey ' ,
        parameters('pullserverRegKey') )]"
      },
      "protectedSettings": {
      // "storageAccountName": "[parameters('storageName')]",
        "storageAccountKey": "[parameters('storageKey')]"
      }
    }
  }
}
```

Microsoft.Compute/virtualMachines/extensions – MicrosoftMonitoringAgent

This is again a nested resource of the `virtualMachines` resource. `MicrosoftMonitoringAgent` helps in installing OMS agents on the virtual machine and also in configuring it to connect to the OMS workspace defined in another resource group.

Since it is a nested resource, it is dependent on its parent virtual machine resource:

```
{
  "apiVersion": "2015-06-15",
  "type": "Microsoft.Compute/virtualMachines/extensions",
  "name": "[concat(variables('vmName'),'-pulls','/omsscript')]",
  "location": "[resourceGroup().location]",
  "dependsOn": [
  "[concat('Microsoft.Compute/virtualMachines/',
  variables('vmName'),'-pulls')]",
  "[resourceId('Microsoft.Compute/virtualMachines/extensions',
  concat(variables('vmName'),'-pulls') ,'powershellscript')]"
  ],
  "properties": {
    "publisher": "Microsoft.EnterpriseCloud.Monitoring",
    "type": "MicrosoftMonitoringAgent",
    "typeHandlerVersion": "1.0",
    "settings": {
      "workspaceId": "[parameters('WorkspaceID')]"
    },
    "protectedSettings": {
      "workspaceKey": "[listKeys(variables('accountid'),
      '2015-11-01-preview').primarySharedKey]"
    }
  }
}
```

Microsoft.Network/publicIPAddresses – for load balancer

The public IP address resource makes a virtual machine accessible on the Internet. This IP address is statically provisioned for the load balancer. A unique name should be provided and replaced for `domainNameLabel`.

```
{
  "apiVersion": "2015-05-01-preview",
  "type": "Microsoft.Network/publicIPAddresses",
  "name": "lbPublicIP",
  "location": "[resourceGroup().location]",
  "properties": {
    "publicIPAllocationMethod": "Static",
```

```
      "dnsSettings": {
        "domainNameLabel": "[concat(parameters('skuName'), '[xxxxx]')]"
      }
    }
  }
```

Microsoft.Network/loadBalancers

This resource provisions a public load balancer with a public IP address so that it can be accessed from the Internet. Two virtual machines would be connected to it, and it opens a load balancing rule to access the web application deployed within the containers on both the virtual machines. It also declares a couple of NAT rules so that both virtual machines can be reached using a remote desktop. There is also a probe element declared to continuously check whether the web application is alive on a provided port on both the virtual machines:

```
{
  "apiVersion": "2015-05-01-preview",
  "name": "containerLB",
  "type": "Microsoft.Network/loadBalancers",
  "location": "[resourceGroup().location]",
  "dependsOn": [
    "[resourceId('Microsoft.Network/publicIPAddresses','lbPublicIP')]"
  ],
  "properties": {
    "frontendIPConfigurations": [
      {
        "name": "ContainerLBFE",
        "properties": {
          "publicIPAddress": {
            "id": "[resourceId('Microsoft.Network/publicIPAddresses',
            'lbPublicIP')]"
          }
        }
      }
    ],
    "backendAddressPools": [
      {
        "name": "ContainerLBBE"
      }
    ],
    "loadBalancingRules": [
      {
        "name": "WebAppList",
        "properties": {
          "frontendIPConfiguration": {
            "id": "
```

```
                [resourceid('Microsoft.Network/loadBalancers/
                frontendIPConfigurations','containerLB','ContainerLBFE')]"
            },
            "backendAddressPool": {
              "id": "[resourceid('Microsoft.Network/loadBalancers/
              backendAddressPools', 'containerLB','ContainerLBBE')]"
            },
            "probe": {
              "id":
              "[resourceid('Microsoft.Network/
              loadBalancers/probes',
              'containerLB','WebLBPROBE')]"
            },
            "protocol": "tcp",
            "frontendPort": "[parameters('webAppPort')]",
            "backendPort": "[parameters('webAppPort')]",
            "enableFloatingIP": true
          }
        }
      ],
      "probes": [
        {
          "name": "WebLBPROBE",
          "properties": {
            "protocol": "http",
            "port": "[parameters('webAppPort')]",
            "requestPath": "/newapp/Index",
            "intervalInSeconds": "100",
            "numberOfProbes": "100"
          }
        }
      ],
      "inboundNatRules": [
        {
          "name": "NAT0",
          "properties": {
            "frontendIPConfiguration": {
            "id": "[resourceid('Microsoft.Network/loadBalancers/
            frontendIPConfigurations','containerLB','ContainerLBFE')]"
            },
            "protocol": "tcp",
            "frontendPort": "3389",
            "backendPort": 3389,
            "enableFloatingIP": false
          }
        },
        {
          "name": "NAT1",
```

```
                 "properties": {
                   "frontendIPConfiguration": {
                     "id": "[resourceid('Microsoft.Network/loadBalancers/
                     frontendIPConfigurations','containerLB','ContainerLBFE')]"
                 },
                 "protocol": "tcp",
                 "frontendPort": "13389",
                 "backendPort": 3389,
                 "enableFloatingIP": false
                 }
             }
         ]
     }
}
```

Microsoft.Network/publicIPAddresses – web application public IP addresses

The public IP address resource makes a virtual machine accessible on the Internet. An IP addresses are provisioned for each virtual machine.

```
{
  "apiVersion": "[variables('publicIPApiVersion')]",
  "type": "Microsoft.Network/publicIPAddresses",
  "name": "[concat('pip',copyIndex(1),variables('publicIpName'))]",
  "tags": {
    "skuName": "[parameters('skuName')]"
  },
  "location": "[parameters('deployLocation')]",
  "copy": {
    "count": "[parameters('countVMs')]",
    "name": "piploop"
  },
  "properties": {
    "publicIPAllocationMethod": "[variables('PublicIpType')]",
    "dnsSettings": {
      "domainNameLabel": "[concat('webapponlmed',
      parameters('skuName'), copyIndex(1))]"
    }
  }
}
```

Microsoft.Network/networkInterfaces – web application NICs

Multiple NICs are provisioned based on the number of virtual machines created for the web application. Each NIC has a public IP address as well and an internal IP assigned by its hosted network. The successful provisioning of the NIC is dependent on the successful provisioning of public IP addresses, load balancers, and availability sets. Both the NICs are bound to the load balancer so that requests from the load balancer can be routed to them.

```
{
  "name": "[concat('nic',copyIndex(1),variables('nicName'))]",
  "type": "Microsoft.Network/networkInterfaces",
  "location": "[parameters('deployLocation')]",
  "tags": {
    "skuName": "[parameters('skuName')]"
  },
  "copy": {
    "count": "[parameters('countVMs')]",
    "name": "nicloop"
  },
  "dependsOn": [
  "[concat('Microsoft.Network/publicIPAddresses/','pip'
  ,copyIndex(1),variables('publicIpName'))]",
  "[concat('Microsoft.Network/virtualNetworks/',
  variables('networkName'))]",
  "[concat('Microsoft.Network/loadBalancers/',
  'containerLB')]",
  "[resourceId('Microsoft.Compute/availabilitySets',
  'webappAVSet')]"
  ],
  "apiVersion": "[variables('nicApiVersion')]",
  "properties": {
    "ipConfigurations": [
      {
        "name": "ipconfig",
        "properties": {
          "privateIPAllocationMethod": "[variables('nicIpType')]",
          "subnet": {
            "id": "[resourceId('Microsoft.Network/virtualNetworks/
            subnets/', variables('networkName'), 'frontend')]"
          },
          "publicIPAddress": {
            "id": "  [resourceId('Microsoft.Network/publicIPAddresses',
            concat('pip',copyIndex(1),variables('publicIpName')))]"
          },
          "loadBalancerBackendAddressPools": [
            {
              "id": "[resourceid('Microsoft.Network/loadBalancers/
              backendAddressPools', 'containerLB','ContainerLBBE')]"
```

```
                    }
                ],
                "loadBalancerInboundNatRules": [
                  {
                     "id":
                     "[resourceId('Microsoft.Network/
                     loadBalancers/inboundNatRules',
                     'containerLB',concat('NAT', copyindex()))]"
                   }
                ]
              }
            }
          }
        ]
      }
    }
```

Microsoft.Compute/virtualMachines – web application virtual machines

This resource provisions multiple virtual machines based on the value of the NumVMs parameter. Virtual machines have the Windows Server 2016 operating system installed with the size determined by the vmSize template parameter. This Sku of Windows has a containers feature enabled by default. It is dependent on the Azure storage account, the virtual network, SQL server, NICs, and the availability set.

```
{
  "apiVersion": "[variables('vmApiVersion')]",
  "type": "Microsoft.Compute/virtualMachines",
  "name": "[concat(variables('vmName'),copyIndex(1))]",
  "location": "[parameters('deployLocation')]",
  "tags": {
    "skuName": "[parameters('skuName')]"
  },
  "copy": {
    "count": "[parameters('countVMs')]",
    "name": "vmloop"
  },
  "dependsOn": [
"[resourceId('Microsoft.Storage/storageAccounts',variables('storageAccountN
ame'))]",
    "[resourceId('Microsoft.Network/networkInterfaces',
    concat('nic',copyIndex(1),variables('nicName')))]",
    "[resourceId('Microsoft.Compute/availabilitySets', 'webappAVSet')]"
  ],
  "properties": {
    "hardwareProfile": {
      "vmSize": "[parameters('vmSize')]"
    },
```

```
          "availabilitySet": {
            "id": "[resourceId('Microsoft.Compute/availabilitySets',
            'webappAVSet')]"
          },
          "osProfile": {
            "computerName": "[concat('vm',copyIndex(1))]",
            "adminUsername": "[parameters('vmUserName')]",
            "adminPassword": "[parameters('vmPassword')]"
          },
          "storageProfile": {
            "imageReference": {
              "publisher": "MicrosoftWindowsServer",
              "offer": "WindowsServer",
              "sku": "[parameters('osSKU')]",
              "version": "latest"
            },
            "osDisk": {
              "name": "osdisk",
              "vhd": {
                "uri": "[concat('http://',variables('storageAccountName')
,'.blob.core.windows.net/vhds0/','vm',copyindex(1),'osdisk.vhd')]"
              },
              "caching": "ReadWrite",
              "createOption": "FromImage"
            }
          },
          "networkProfile": {
            "networkInterfaces": [
              {
                "id":
"[resourceId('Microsoft.Network/networkInterfaces',concat('nic',
                copyIndex(1),variables('nicName')))]"
              }
            ]
          }
        }
      }
    }
  }
```

Microsoft.Compute/virtualMachines/extensions – CustomScriptExtension

This extension downloads three PowerShell scripts–lcm.ps1, ChangeConnectionString.ps1, and ContainerConfig.ps1, a dockerfile and a ZIP file named deployment.zip. The ZIP file contains the webdeploy package of our sample application.

The virtual machine is configured to execute `ContainerConfig.ps1` first and is responsible for provisioning a new container image using the downloaded `dockerfile`. The `dockerfile` loads both `lcm.ps1` and `changeConnectionString.ps1` during its execution and executes both the PowerShell files to configure the containers local configuration manager configuration and update the connection string of the web application at `web.config`. The data for the connection string, such as a SQL username, a SQL password, a database, and a server name is passed to the container image.

`ContainerConfig.ps1` also generates appropriate virtual machine certificates to access its security through PowerShell. This extension runs on every virtual machine provisioned for container and web application deployment. All these files are discussed in depth in the next section.

Since it is a nested resource, it is dependent on its parent virtual machine resource. This extension is also dependent on the successful provisioning of the Pull Server PowerShell extension. It is because the configurations should be available on Pull Server before the local configuration manager can pull them.

```
{
    "name":
"[concat(variables('vmName'),copyIndex(1),'/powershellscript')]",
        "type": "Microsoft.Compute/virtualMachines/extensions",
        "location": "[parameters('deployLocation')]",
        "tags": {
          "skuName": "[parameters('skuName')]"
        },
        "copy": {
          "count": "[parameters('countVMs')]",
          "name": "scriptloop"
        },
        "apiVersion": "2015-06-15",
        "dependsOn": [
          "[concat('Microsoft.Compute/virtualMachines/',
          variables('vmName'),copyIndex(1))]",
          "[resourceId('Microsoft.Compute/virtualMachines/extensions',
          concat(variables('vmName'),'-pulls') ,'powershellscript')]"
        ],
          "properties": {
            "publisher": "Microsoft.Compute",
            "type": "CustomScriptExtension",
            "typeHandlerVersion": "1.4",
            "autoUpgradeMinorVersion": true,
            "settings": {
              "fileUris": [
                "[concat('https://', parameters('storageName'),
                '.blob.core.windows.net/', parameters('containerName'),
```

```
                   '/ContainerConfig.ps1')]",
                "[concat('https://', parameters('storageName'),
                '.blob.core.windows.net/', parameters('containerName'),
                '/dockerfile')]",
                "[concat('https://', parameters('storageName'),
                '.blob.core.windows.net/', parameters('containerName'),
                '/lcm.ps1')]",
                "[concat('https://', parameters('storageName'),
                '.blob.core.windows.net/', parameters('containerName'),
                '/Deployment.zip')]",
                "[concat('https://', parameters('storageName'),
                '.blob.core.windows.net/', parameters('containerName'),
                '/ChangeConnectionString.ps1')]"
            ],
            "timestamp": "11",
            "commandToExecute": "[concat('powershell.exe -ExecutionPolicy
            Unrestricted -File ContainerConfig.ps1 ', '-username ',
            parameters('vmUserName'),' -password ',
            parameters('vmPassword'),
            ' -pullip ',
            reference(concat('pipPS',
            variables('publicIpName')))
            .ipAddress, ' -regKey ', parameters('pullserverRegKey'),
            ' -port ',
            parameters('pullserverPort'), ' -sqlUsername ',
            parameters('sqlUserName'),' -sqlPassword ',
            parameters('sqlPassword') ,' -webport ',
            parameters('webAppPort'), ' -sqlServer ',
            variables('sqlServerName'), ' -databaseName ',
            parameters('databaseName') )]"
        },
        "protectedSettings": {
            // "storageAccountName": "[parameters('storageName')]",
            "storageAccountKey": "[parameters('storageKey')]"
        }
    }
}
```

Microsoft.Compute/virtualMachines/extensions – MicrosoftMonitoringAgent

This is again a nested resource of the `virtualMachines` resource.
`MicrosoftMonitoringAgent` helps in installing OMS agent on all virtual machines related to the web application and also to configure them to connect to the OMS workspace.

```
{
    "apiVersion": "2015-06-15",
```

```
"type": "Microsoft.Compute/virtualMachines/extensions",
"name": "[concat(variables('vmName'),copyIndex(1),'/omsscript')]",
"location": "[resourceGroup().location]",
"dependsOn": [
  "[concat('Microsoft.Compute/virtualMachines/'
  ,variables('vmName'),copyIndex(1))]",
  "[resourceId('Microsoft.Compute/virtualMachines/extensions',
  concat(variables('vmName'),copyIndex(1)),'powershellscript')]"
],
"copy": {
  "count": "[parameters('countVMs')]",
  "name": "omsloop"
},
"properties": {
  "publisher": "Microsoft.EnterpriseCloud.Monitoring",
  "type": "MicrosoftMonitoringAgent",
  "typeHandlerVersion": "1.0",
  "settings": {
    "workspaceId": "[parameters('WorkspaceID')]"
  },
  "protectedSettings": {
    "workspaceKey": "[listKeys(variables('accountid'),
    '2015-11-01-preview').primarySharedKey]"
  }
 }
}
}
```

Microsoft.Sql/servers, databases, firewallRules

This resource provisions the Azure SQL server, databases, and `firewallrules`. Since the IP addresses belonging to Pull Server and web application virtual machines should be allowed to access the SQL server and database, they are dynamically added to the `firewallrules` using `reference` function provided by ARM templates. Accordingly, this resource is also dependent on all three IP addresses belonging to Pull Server and the web application. The firewall rule named `AllowAllWindowsAzureIps` allows all Azure services to connect to the Azure SQL server and database.

Since it is a nested resource, it is dependent on its parent virtual machine resource:

```
{
"name": "[variables('sqlServerName')]",
"type": "Microsoft.Sql/servers",
"location": "[resourceGroup().location]",
"tags": {
  "displayName": "SqlServer"
},
```

```
"apiVersion": "2014-04-01-preview",
"dependsOn": [
  "[resourceId('Microsoft.Network/publicIPAddresses',concat('pip1',
  variables('publicIpName')))]",
  "[resourceId('Microsoft.Network/publicIPAddresses',concat('pip2',
  variables('publicIpName')))]",
  "[resourceId('Microsoft.Network/publicIPAddresses',concat('pipPS',
  variables('publicIpName')))]"
],
"properties": {
  "administratorLogin": "[parameters('sqlUserName')]",
  "administratorLoginPassword": "[parameters('sqlPassword')]",
  "version": "12.0"
},
"resources": [
  {
    "name": "[parameters('databaseName')]",
    "type": "databases",
    "location": "[resourceGroup().location]",
    "tags": {
      "displayName": "Database"
    },
    "apiVersion": "2014-04-01-preview",
    "dependsOn": [
      "[variables('sqlserverName')]"
    ],
    "properties": {
      "edition": "[parameters('edition')]",
      "collation": "[parameters('collation')]",
      "maxSizeBytes": "[parameters('maxSizeBytes')]",
      "requestedServiceObjectiveName":
      "[parameters('requestedServiceObjectiveName')]"
    }
  },
  {
    "type": "firewallrules",
    "apiVersion": "2014-04-01-preview",
    "dependsOn": [
      "[variables('sqlServerName')]"
    ],
    "location": "[resourceGroup().location]",
    "name": "AllowAllWindowsAzureIps",
    "properties": {
      "endIpAddress": "0.0.0.0",
      "startIpAddress": "0.0.0.0"
    }
  },
  {
```

```
        "type": "firewallrules",
        "apiVersion": "2014-04-01-preview",
        "dependsOn": [
          "[variables('sqlServerName')]"
        ],
        "location": "[resourceGroup().location]",
        "name": "webapp1",
        "properties": {
          "endIpAddress": "[reference(concat('pip1',
          variables('publicIpName'))).ipAddress]",
          "startIpAddress": "[reference(concat('pip1',
          variables('publicIpName'))).ipAddress]"
        }
      },
      {
        "type": "firewallrules",
        "apiVersion": "2014-04-01-preview",
        "dependsOn": [
          "[variables('sqlServerName')]"
        ],
        "location": "[resourceGroup().location]",
        "name": "webapp2",
        "properties": {
          "endIpAddress": "[reference(concat('pip2',
           variables('publicIpName'))).ipAddress]",
          "startIpAddress": "[reference(concat('pip2',
          variables('publicIpName'))).ipAddress]"
        }
      },
      {
        "type": "firewallrules",
        "apiVersion": "2014-04-01-preview",
        "dependsOn": [
          "[variables('sqlServerName')]"
        ],
        "location": "[resourceGroup().location]",
        "name": "pullserver",
        "properties": {
          "endIpAddress": "[reference(concat('pipPS',
          variables('publicIpName'))).ipAddress]",
          "startIpAddress": "[reference(concat('pipPS',
          variables('publicIpName'))).ipAddress]"
        }
      }
    ]
  }
```

Outputs

The outputs are helpful to retrieve values of provisioned resources and execute Pester test cases using them.

```
"webappPort": {
    "type": "string",
    "value": "[parameters('webAppPort')]"
},
"pullserverPort": {
  "type": "string",
  "value": "[parameters('pullserverPort')]"
},
"numberofvms": {
  "type": "int",
  "value": "[parameters('countVMs')]"
},
"vmsize": {
  "type": "string",
  "value": "[parameters('vmSize')]"
},
"ossku": {
  "type": "string",
  "value": "[parameters('osSKU')]"
},
"databaseName": {
  "type": "string",
  "value": "[parameters('databaseName')]"
},
"sqlServer": {
  "type": "string",
  "value": "[variables('sqlServerName')]"
},
"resourceGroupName": {
  "type": "string",
  "value": "[resourceGroup().name]"
},
"deployLocation": {
  "type": "string",
  "value": "[resourceGroup().location]"
},
"skuName": {
  "type": "string",
  "value": "[parameters('skuName')]"
},
"pullServerPublicIPAddress": {
  "type": "string",
  "value":
```

```
      "[reference(concat('pipPS',variables
      ('publicIpName'))).ipAddress]"
    },
    "VM01PublicIPAddress": {
      "type": "string",
      "value":
      "[reference(concat('pip1',variables
      ('publicIpName'))).ipAddress]"
    },
    "VM02PublicIPAddress": {
      "type": "string",
      "value":
      "[reference(concat('pip2',variables
      ('publicIpName'))).ipAddress]"
    },
    "loadBalancerPublicIPAddress": {
      "type": "string",
      "value": "[reference('lbPublicIP').ipAddress]"
    },
    "storageName": {
      "type": "string",
      "value": "[variables('storageAccountName')]"
    },
    "nicNameforVM1": {
      "type": "string",
      "value": "[concat('nic1',variables('nicName'))]"
    },
    "nicNameforVM2": {
      "type": "string",
      "value": "[concat('nic2',variables('nicName'))]"
    },
    "lbfrontendIPConfiguration": {
      "type": "string",
      "value":
      "[reference('containerLB').
      frontendIPConfigurations[0].name]"
    },
    "lbbackendAddressPool": {
      "type": "string",
      "value":
      "[reference('containerLB').
      backendAddressPools[0].name]"
    },
    "lbloadBalancingRules": {
      "type": "string",
      "value":
      "[reference('containerLB').
      loadBalancingRules[0].name]"
```

```
    },
    "lbinboundNatRule1": {
      "type": "string",
      "value":
      "[reference('containerLB').
      inboundNatRules[0].name]"
    },
    "lbinboundNatRule2": {
      "type": "string",
      "value":
      "[reference('containerLB').
      inboundNatRules[1].name]"
    },
    "networkSecurityGroupName": {
      "type": "string",
      "value": "[variables('NSGName')]"
    },
    "vmUserName": {
      "type": "string",
      "value": "[parameters('vmUserName')]"
    },
    "vmPassword": {
      "type": "string",
      "value": "[parameters('vmPassword')]"
    }
}
```

Summary

This was a big chapter, and a lot of miles and technology were covered here. This chapter started with explaining the concepts related to Infrastructure as Code and its principles. Our sample web application architecture was revisited along with details of its deployment architecture. Configuration management for both the infrastructure and application is designed from the ground-up with special emphasis on security and modularity. The chapter then provided a step-by-step guidance to be executed by an IT administrator and deployment operators. All the code shown in this chapter is accompanied with source code and can be used, changed, and extended. This chapter was primarily about building the configuration management and artifacts related to Infrastructure as Code.

The next chapter will continue on the same topic. It will focus on testing the configuration management artifacts related to Infrastructure as Code and also explain the scripts used for provisioning the environment. It will perform operational validation for environments under consideration and ensure that the sample application works as intended after provisioning it.

8
Configuration Management and Operational Validation

The previous chapter started with configuration management, and this chapter continues and concludes the same. In this chapter, apart from configuration management, unit testing and operational validation of environments will be introduced. One of the principles of Infrastructure as Code is that the scripts and environments are unit tested. The operational validation of environments is performed to ensure that the application and environment are not only in desired state but are also ready operationally. Pester was introduced in `Chapter 3`, *DevOps Automation Primer*, and it is a primary tool used for the unit testing environment using PowerShell. The operational validation module is used in order to perform the operational validation.

This chapter will continue with the explanation of the scripts needed in order to deploy and configure the environment and application. Toward the end, it will discuss unit testing and the operational validation of environments in detail.

Steps for deployment through the release pipeline

The VSTS release pipeline executes tasks, and some of these tasks internally executes custom scripts. The scripts executed by the release pipeline are described next.

PullServer.ps1

The **Desired State Configuration** (**DSC**) Pull Server is essentially an IIS web application with endpoints that accepts requests from target nodes, records their current status, sends configuration documents, and enables management-related functionality. `PullServer.ps1` script is responsible for provisioning a Pull Server from scratch on a virtual machine. Detailed instructions and commands used for the creation of Pull Server are part of this script. This script is also responsible for creating database tables in Azure SQL. The portion of script that runs SQL scripts on Azure SQL should be moved as an exercise to an Azure function or executed through a management-related virtual machine. Pull Server listens on a dedicated port either on a HTTP or HTTPS protocol. The Pull Server under consideration is using HTTP protocol; however, readers are encouraged to use the HTTPS protocol as a good practice. There are a lot of activities happening in this script. Apart from creating Pull Server, it also downloads DSC and executes it to store at a well-known defined location-DSC Pull Server. The registration key (GUID) is an important concept of Pull Server. It registers a target node with the Pull Server. It is a shared key used by both Pull Server and target nodes. The key is defined on Pull Server, and only an IT administrator uses it while configuring individual nodes. The registration key is used in conjunction with `ConfigurationNames` when pulling a configuration from Pull Server. It is ignored when `ConfigurationID` is used to pull the configuration. This registration key is needed to configure the local configuration manager of containers so that they can connect to Pull Server and download and execute configurations. Later in this chapter, readers will come across the `IISInstall` DSC configuration. This configuration is responsible for creating a web server environment. It accepts a port number on which the IIS website will be configured using DSC.

The script accepts the Pull Server port number, Azure SQL username, password, server name, database name, web application port number, and DSC registration key as parameters. This script will be executed on the Pull Server virtual machine, and all parameters will be passed to it during template execution through the **Custom Script Extension** resource:

```
param (
[string] $port = 9100,
[string] $sqlUsername,
[string] $sqlPassword,
[string] $sqlDatabaseName,
[string] $servername,
[string] $webport,
[string] $regKey
)
```

A new certificate is generated to be used as the SSL certificate for the Pull Server web application. It is provided so that readers can configure their Pull Server running on the HTTPS protocol as an exercise:

```
# certificate for DSC Pull Server
if ((Get-ChildItem -Path Cert:\LocalMachine\My -DnsName $env:COMPUTERNAME)
-eq $null)
{
$cert = New-SelfSignedCertificate -CertstoreLocation Cert:\LocalMachine\My
`-DnsName $env:COMPUTERNAME
}
```

A few variables are declared for internal working of the script.

```
# variables declared and used in script
$ComputerName = "Localhost"
$IISWindowsFeature = "Web-Server"
$NET45WindowsFeature = "NET-Framework-45-Features"
$ODataWindowsFeature = "ManagementOData"
$DSCWindowsFeatureName = "DSC-Service"
$PULLServerWebDirectory = "C:\PSDSCPullServer"
$PULLServerSubDirectory = "bin"
$iisAppPoolName = "DSCPullServer"
$iisAppPoolDotNetVersion = "v4.0"
$iisAppName = "PSDSCPullServer"
$certificateThumbPrint = $cert.Thumbprint
```

Next, Windows server features, Internet Information Server, .NET 4.5, oData service, and DSC-services are installed on Pull Server:

```
# installing IIS windows feature
Install-WindowsFeature -Name $IISWindowsFeature -IncludeManagementTools -
ComputerName $ComputerName
# installing .NET 4.5 windows feature
Install-WindowsFeature -Name $NET45WindowsFeature -IncludeManagementTools -
ComputerName $ComputerName
# installing OData windows feature
Install-WindowsFeature -Name $ODataWindowsFeature -IncludeManagementTools -
ComputerName $ComputerName
# installing DSC windows feature
Install-WindowsFeature -Name $DSCWindowsFeatureName -IncludeManagementTools
-ComputerName $ComputerName
```

A new directory is created to act as a home for Pull Server files and folders. This folder represents the physical path of the Pull Server website:

```
# creating folder for hosting DSC Pull Server web files
New-item -Path $PULLServerWebDirectory -ItemType Directory -Force -
Confirm:$false
```

A new subdirectory named `bin` is created within the website root directory:

```
# creating bin folder within DSC Pull Server root directory
New-item -Path $($PULLServerWebDirectory + "" + $PULLServerSubDirectory) -
ItemType Directory -Force -Confirm:$false
```

The DSC-service Windows feature installs DSC-related files on the server. These files should be copied over to the Pull Server website root directory created in the previous step. The following files are generated and copied:

- `Global.asax`
- `PSDSCPullServer.mof`
- `PSDSCPullServer.svc`
- `PSDSCPullServer.xml`
- `PSDSCPullServer.config,`
- `IISSelfSignedCertModule.dll`
- `Microsoft.Powershell.DesiredStateConfiguration.Service.dll`
- `Devices.mdb`

Code listed next provides steps to copy and provision these files to appropriate folders on filesystem:

```
# copying relevant items to DSC Pull Server root directory
# global.asax
Copy-Item -Path
"$pshome\modules\psdesiredstateconfiguration\pullserver\Global.asax" -
Destination "$PULLServerWebDirectory\Global.asax" -Force -Confirm:$false
# copying relevant items to DSC Pull Server root directory
# PSDSCPullServer.mof
Copy-Item -Path
"$pshome\modules\psdesiredstateconfiguration\pullserver\PSDSCPullServer.mof
" -Destination "$PULLServerWebDirectory\PSDSCPullServer.mof" -Force -
Confirm:$false
# copying relevant items to DSC Pull Server root directory
# PSDSCPullServer.svc
Copy-Item -Path
"$pshome\modules\psdesiredstateconfiguration\pullserver\PSDSCPullServer.svc
```

```
" -Destination "$PULLServerWebDirectory\PSDSCPullServer.svc" -Force -
Confirm:$false
# copying relevant items to DSC Pull Server root directory
# PSDSCPullServer.xml
Copy-Item -Path
"$pshome\modules\psdesiredstateconfiguration\pullserver\PSDSCPullServer.xml
" -Destination "$PULLServerWebDirectory\PSDSCPullServer.xml" -Force -
Confirm:$false
# copying relevant items to DSC Pull Server root directory
# PSDSCPullServer.config
Copy-Item -Path
"$pshome\modules\psdesiredstateconfiguration\pullserver\PSDSCPullServer.con
fig" -Destination "$PULLServerWebDirectory\web.config" -Force -
Confirm:$false
# copying relevant items to DSC Pull Server root directory
# IISSelfSignedCertModule.dll
Copy-Item -Path
"$pshome\modules\psdesiredstateconfiguration\pullserver\IISSelfSignedCertMo
dule.dll" -Destination "$($PULLServerWebDirectory + "" +
$PULLServerSubDirectory + "\IISSelfSignedCertModule.dll")" -Force -
Confirm:$false
# copying relevant items to DSC Pull Server root directory
# Microsoft.Powershell.DesiredStateConfiguration.Service.dll
Copy-Item -Path
"$pshome\modules\psdesiredstateconfiguration\pullserver\Microsoft.Powershel
l.DesiredStateConfiguration.Service.dll" -Destination
"$($PULLServerWebDirectory + "" + $PULLServerSubDirectory +
"\Microsoft.Powershell.DesiredStateConfiguration.Service.dll")" -Force -
Confirm:$false
# copying relevant items to DSC Pull Server root directory
# Devices.mdb
Copy-Item -Path
"$pshome\modules\psdesiredstateconfiguration\pullserver\Devices.mdb" -
Destination "$env:programfiles\WindowsPowerShell\DscService\Devices.mdb"
```

Every website in IIS has an internal ID assigned to it. Next, a new ID is generated for to be created a website:

```
# get next website id
$siteID = ((Get-Website | % { $_.Id } | Measure-Object -Maximum).Maximum +
1)
```

A check is made for the availability of the IIS application pool related to Pull Server. If this pool exists, it is reused; otherwise, a new application pool is created:

```
# check if app pool with given name already exists
# create if it does not exist
if ( (Get-Item IIS:\AppPools\$iisAppPoolName -ErrorAction SilentlyContinue)
```

```
-eq $null)
{
    $null = New-WebAppPool -Name $iisAppPoolName
    $appPoolItem = Get-Item IIS:\AppPools\$iisAppPoolName
    $appPoolItem.managedRuntimeVersion = "v4.0"
    $appPoolItem.enable32BitAppOnWin64 = $true
    $appPoolItem.processModel.identityType = 0
    $appPoolItem | Set-Item
}
```

Similar to an application pool, a check is made for the pre-existence of the IIS website related to Pull Server. If it exists, it is reused; otherwise, a new website is created. The `port` parameter is used to configure the website. After it is created and configured, the website is started. Note that line configuring website with the certificate is commented. It can be uncommented to use the HTTPS protocol.

```
# check if website with given name already exists
# create if it does not exist
if ( (Get-Website -Name $iisAppName) -eq $null)
{
    $webSite = New-WebSite -Name $iisAppName `
                            -Id $siteID `
                            -Port $port `
                            -IPAddress "*" `
                            -PhysicalPath $PULLServerWebDirectory `
                            -ApplicationPool $iisAppPoolName #`
                            #-Ssl
# Remove existing binding for $port
Remove-Item IIS:\SSLBindings\0.0.0.0!$port -ErrorAction Ignore
# Create a new binding using the supplied certificate
# $null = Get-Item CERT:\LocalMachine\MY\$certificateThumbPrint | New-Item
IIS:\SSLBindings\0.0.0.0!$port
}
# start web site
Start-Website -Name $iisAppName
```

Next, the `web.config` elements are unlocked:

```
# modify web.config for website
$appcmd = "$env:windir\system32\inetsrv\appcmd.exe"
& $appCmd set AppPool $appPoolItem.name
/processModel.identityType:LocalSystem
& $appCmd unlock config -section:access
& $appCmd unlock config -section:anonymousAuthentication
& $appCmd unlock config -section:basicAuthentication
& $appCmd unlock config -section:windowsAuthentication
```

The incoming GUID value that represents the registration key is assigned to a temporary variable. There can be an alternate strategy to generate a registration key every time a Pull Server is created or modified; however, this discretion is left to the reader's judgement. It is recommended to use a pre-determined registration key to avoid a broken DSC setup:

```
# generate new guid for registration key
$guid = $regKey
```

A new file `RegistrationKeys.txt` is generated containing the incoming registration key GUID value. Any node that wants to connect to this Pull Server and download a configuration based on `ConfigurationNames` must send this registration key along with a request to Pull Server:

```
# store registration key in RegistrationKeys.txt
# at C:\Program Files\WindowsPowerShell\DscService
New-Item -ItemType File -Value $guid -Path "C:\Program
Files\WindowsPowerShell\DscService" -Name "RegistrationKeys.txt" -Force -
confirm:$false
```

The next set of instructions load the Pull Server `web.config` and add entries to its `AppSettings` section. These configuration settings let the Pull Server know the location of registration keys, the configuration document store, modules store, database location, database provider, and connection string to use for connecting to the database:

```
# load web.config content
$xml = [XML](Get-Content "$PULLServerWebDirectory\web.config")
$RootDoc = $xml.get_DocumentElement()
# add dbprovider appsetting element if it does not exists to web.config.
if (($xml.configuration.appSettings.add.Where({$PSItem.key -eq
'dbprovider'})).key `
-eq $null)
{
   $subnode = $xml.CreateElement("add")
   $subnode.SetAttribute("key", "dbprovider")
   $subnode.SetAttribute("value", "System.Data.OleDb")
   $RootDoc.appSettings.AppendChild($subnode)
}
# add dbconnectionstr appsetting element if it does not exists to
web.config.
if (($xml.configuration.appSettings.add.Where({$PSItem.key -eq
'dbconnectionstr'})).key
`
-eq $null)
{
   $subnode = $xml.CreateElement("add")
   $subnode.SetAttribute("key", "dbconnectionstr")
   $subnode.SetAttribute("value", `
```

```
  "Provider=Microsoft.Jet.OLEDB.4.0;Data Source=C:\Program
  Files\WindowsPowerShell\DscService\Devices.mdb;")
  $RootDoc.appSettings.AppendChild($subnode)
}
# add ConfigurationPath appsetting element if it does not exists to
web.config.
if (($xml.configuration.appSettings.add.Where({$PSItem.key -eq
'ConfigurationPath'})).key -eq $null)
{
    $subnode = $xml.CreateElement("add")
    $subnode.SetAttribute("key", "ConfigurationPath")
    $subnode.SetAttribute("value", "C:\Program
    Files\WindowsPowerShell\DscService\Configuration")
    $RootDoc.appSettings.AppendChild($subnode)
}
# add ModulePath appsetting element if it does not exists to web.config.
if (($xml.configuration.appSettings.add.Where({$PSItem.key -eq
'ModulePath'})).key -eq $null)
{
    $subnode = $xml.CreateElement("add")
    $subnode.SetAttribute("key", "ModulePath")
    $subnode.SetAttribute("value", "C:\Program
    Files\WindowsPowerShell\DscService\Modules")
    $RootDoc.appSettings.AppendChild($subnode)
}
# add RegistrationKeyPath appsetting element if it does not exists to
web.config.
if (($xml.configuration.appSettings.add.Where({$PSItem.key -eq
'RegistrationKeyPath'})).key -eq $null)
{
    $subnode = $xml.CreateElement("add")
    $subnode.SetAttribute("key", "RegistrationKeyPath")
    $subnode.SetAttribute("value", "C:\Program
Files\WindowsPowerShell\DscService")
    $RootDoc.appSettings.AppendChild($subnode)
}
# save web.config with changes
$xml.Save("$PULLServerWebDirectory\web.config")
```

A Firewall rule is enabled to allow access to the port on which the Pull Server web application is running:

```
# open firewall rule for Pull Server web application port defined by
incoming parameter
if (!(Get-NetFirewallRule | where {$_.Name -eq "PullServerRule"})) {
New-NetFirewallRule -Name "PullServerRule" -DisplayName "pullport" -
Protocol tcp -LocalPort $port -Action Allow -Enabled True
}
```

Now, it's time to deploy the real configurations on Pull Server that are downloaded by nodes. These configurations are dependent on DSC resources not available out-of-the-box on the Windows platform. Package management is used to download and install these resources on the server. The DSC configuration to be deployed on Pull Server is dependent on xWebAdministration and xWebDeploy packages and its DSC resources. The next set of script lines first configures the package management and then installs these two packages.

It is a good practice to provide the exact version details while installing packages. If version information is not provided, the latest packages are downloaded, which might contain breaking changes compared with packages against which the configurations are built:

```
# Create a new folder for executing DSC configuration
New-Item -Path $PSScriptRoot\IISInstall -ItemType Directory -Force -
Confirm:$false
# Registering Nuget as Package source
Register-PackageSource -Name Nuget -Location https://www.nuget.org/api/v2/
-ProviderName Nuget -Trusted -Force -ForceBootstrap
# Registering Chocolatey as Package source
Register-PackageSource -Name chocolatey -Location
http://chocolatey.org/api/v2/
ProviderName chocolatey -Trusted -Force -ForceBootstrap
# installing xWebAdministration DSC resources
install-module -Name xWebAdministration -RequiredVersion 1.14.0.0 -Force
Confirm:$false
# installing xWebDeploy DSC resources
install-module -Name xwebdeploy -RequiredVersion 1.2.0.0 -Force -
Confirm:$false
```

By now, the Pull Server is created and is fully functional; however, it still does not contain any configurations that target servers might be interested in them for downloading and consuming them. IISInstall.ps1 is downloaded along with the dependent packages. It defines the configuration that will be explained later in this chapter while covering IISInstall.ps1 script. It is deployed at a Pull Server well-known configuration folder location. This script is executed to ensure that there is a valid DSC configuration available on Pull Server that sample web application containers can download and configure themselves:

```
# Executing IIsInstall.ps1 to generate and deploy DSC configuration
# files on Pull Server used by containers to configure their
# IIS settings
if((Get-Item 'C:\Program
Files\WindowsPowerShell\DscService\Configuration\IISInstall.mof' `
-ErrorAction SilentlyContinue) -eq $null)
{
    . $PSScriptRoot\IISInstall.ps1 -webport $webport
}
```

The next set of lines execute SQL script on Azure SQL. The script connects to Azure SQL using incoming parameters and executes the OnlinePharmacy.sql downloaded from the Azure storage account along with other script files. This SQL script creates the table structure within the Azure SQL database:

```
# connect to Azure SQL database and create table structure for
# sample onlone medicine web application
try
{
    $ConnectionString = "Password=$sqlPassword;Persist Security
    Info=False;User
    ID=$sqlUsername; `
    Initial Catalog=$sqlDatabaseName;Data
Source=$servername.database.windows.net"
    $cmdtext = Get-Content -Path "$PSScriptRoot\OnlinePharmacy.sql"
    $con = New-Object "System.Data.SqlClient.SQLConnection"
    $sqlcmd = New-Object "System.Data.SqlClient.SqlCommand"
    $con.ConnectionString = $ConnectionString
    $con.Open()
    $sqlcmd.connection = $con
    $sqlcmd.CommandText = "Select count(*) from dbo.Drug"
    $output = $sqlcmd.ExecuteScalar()
    if($output -lt 0 -or $output -eq $null )
    {
        $sqlcmd.CommandText = $cmdtext
        $sqlcmd.CommandType = [System.Data.CommandType]::Text
        $result = $sqlcmd.ExecuteNonQuery()
```

```
    }
}
catch
{
    $sqlcmd.CommandText = $cmdtext
    $sqlcmd.CommandType = [System.Data.CommandType]::Text
    $result = $sqlcmd.ExecuteNonQuery()
}
```

One of the last steps is to configure the virtual machine with a certificate and **Windows Remote Management** (**WinRM**) settings so that it can be connected remotely from the Internet using the HTTPS protocol. This step will eventually help Pester test cases to connect to virtual machines in order to execute them:

```
$HostName = $env:computername
$cert = Get-ChildItem -Path cert:\LocalMachine\My\* -DnsName $HostName -
ErrorAction SilentlyContinue
if ($cert -eq $null)
{
    $cert = New-SelfSignedCertificate -CertstoreLocation
Cert:\LocalMachine\My -DnsName
    $HostName
}
get-childitem -Path WSMan:\localhost\Listener\ | where {$_.keys[0] -
contains 'Transport=HTTPS'} | Remove-Item -Force -Confirm:$false -Recurse
New-Item -Path WSMan:\LocalHost\Listener -Transport HTTPS -Address * -
CertificateThumbPrint $cert.Thumbprint -Force | out-null
Restart-Service winrm | out-null
New-NetFirewallRule -DisplayName 'Windows Remote Management (HTTPS-In)' -
Name 'Windows Remote Management (HTTPS-In)' -Profile Any -LocalPort 5986 -
Protocol TCP -Enabled True -Confirm:$false -ErrorAction Continue
```

The registration key is sent to the output stream so that it can be consumed by dependent components:

```
# registrationkey is set for output
# used for setting the LCM configuration of containers
# to connect to this Pull Server
Write-Output $guid.Guid
```

IISInstall.ps1

This is a DSC configuration deployed on a Pull Server used by containers in other virtual machines to configure their IIS environment. This configuration is responsible for ensuring that IIS and other ASP.NET MVC-related Windows features are installed and available and a new web application pool and a website are created in IIS. This script accepts a single parameter to configure the port of the sample web application in IIS. The website runs on the HTTP protocol on the port number provided as an incoming parameter. This DSC configuration is dependent on DSC resource modules `xWebAdministration`. This script is executed by `PullServer.ps1`, and it ensures that `xWebAdministration` is downloaded and installed before executing the script.

The configuration is executed to generate the MOF file. A corresponding checksum file is generated for the configuration, which is a mandatory step for configurations to be deployed in Pull Server. Both the configuration MOF and DSC checksum file are copied over to the well-known Pull Server configuration folder located at **Program Files** | **WindowsPowerShell** | **DscService** | **Configuration**. The entire script is shown here.

This script creates an application pool named `MedicinePool` and IIS website named `MVCWebSite`:

```
param(
    [string] $webport
)
Configuration IISInstall
{
# module containing basic DSC resources
Import-DscResource -ModuleName 'PSDesiredStateConfiguration'
# module containing IIS related DSC resources
Import-DscResource -ModuleName 'xWebAdministration'
Node localhost
  {
      # installs IIS windows feature
      WindowsFeature IIS
      {
          Name = "Web-Server"
          Ensure = "Present"
      }
      # installs .NET 4.5 windows feature
      WindowsFeature DotNet
      {
          Name = "net-framework-45-Core"
          Ensure = "Present"
          DependsOn = "[WindowsFeature]IIS"
      }
```

```
    # installs ASP.NET 4.5 windows feature
    WindowsFeature AspNet45
    {
        Ensure = "Present"
        Name = "Web-Asp-Net45"
        DependsOn = "[WindowsFeature]DotNet"
    }
    # creates a new IIS application pool
    xWebAppPool WebsiteApplicationPool
    {
        Name = "MedicinePool"
        Ensure = "Present"
        State = "Started"
        DependsOn = "[WindowsFeature]AspNet45"
    }
    # creates a new directory for IIS website
    file CreateDirectory
    {
        DestinationPath = "C:\Inetpub\MVCWebsite"
        Ensure = "Present"
        Type = "Directory"
        DependsOn = "[xWebAppPool]WebsiteApplicationPool"
    }
    # creates a new Website in IIS
    xWebsite CreateWebsite
    {
        Name = "MVCWebSite"
        PhysicalPath = "C:\Inetpub\MVCWebsite"
        Ensure = "Present"
        State = "Started"
        ApplicationPool = "MedicinePool"
        BindingInfo = MSFT_xWebBindingInformation{
        port ="$webport"; protocol ="http"
    }
    DependsOn = "[file]CreateDirectory"
  }
 }
}
# generate the MOF file at same location of this script
IISInstall -OutputPath "$PSScriptRoot\IISInstall"
# generate checksum for DSC configuration
New-DSCCheckSum -ConfigurationPath "$PSScriptRoot\IISInstall" -OutPath
"$PSScriptRoot\IISInstall" -Force
# copy the MOF configuration to Pull Server well known configuration folder
Copy-Item -LiteralPath "$PSScriptRoot\IISInstall\localhost.mof" -
Destination
"$env:ProgramFiles\WindowsPowerShell\DscService\Configuration\IISInstall.mo
f" -Force
```

```
# copy the DSC Checksum to Pull Server well known configuration folder
Copy-Item -LiteralPath "$PSScriptRoot\IISInstall\localhost.mof.checksum"-
Destination
"$env:ProgramFiles\WindowsPowerShell\DscService\Configuration\IISInstall.mo
f.checksum"-Force
```

ContainerConfig.ps1

This is the starting and master script for all the virtual machines-related web application frontend. After the virtual machines related to the sample web application are provisioned, this script is executed on each one of them. The script is responsible for managing all the scripts and web application files provided by the Custom Script Extension on the virtual machines. It unzips the web application `deployment.zip` file and opens Firewall rules for multiple ports including the web application port. Because the image used to create the virtual machines already has containers installed, it does not download and install Docker binaries, Docker clients, and Docker daemons on the virtual machine. The virtual machine has two Docker images: `microsoft/windowsservercore` and `microsoft/nanoserver` available by default in its local repository. A custom Docker image is used in order to provision the sample `OnlinePharmacy` web application. This image is named IIS for the purpose of this book. The script checks whether there is already a container image named IIS on the virtual machines. If this image is not available, it invokes and executes the `dockerfile` to build a new container image. The `dockerfile` ensures that it creates a new image based on `microsoft/windowsservercore` and completes all its instructions to install IIS, run DSC configuration downloaded from Pull Server, install utilities such as `webdeploy` using package management, deploy the web application files, and change the web application web.config connection string.

The explanation of the script is provided here.

The script accepts the virtual machine username and password, the Pull Server IP address, its port number, registration key, Azure SQL username, password, server, and database name, and web application port number as parameters:

```
param
(
    [string] $username,
    [string] $password,
    [string] $port,
    [string] $regKey,
    [string] $pullip,
    [string] $sqlUsername,
    [string] $sqlPassword,
    [string] $webport,
```

```
    [string] $sqlServer,
    [string] $databaseName
)
```

The script copies the original files to a subdirectory and removes the original files:

```
$HostName = $env:computername
"Downloading all files"
# creates a new folder at root directory
New-Item -Path $PSScriptRoot\downloads -ItemType Directory -Force -
Confirm:$false
# next four instructions copies the files to newly created folder
Copy-Item -LiteralPath $PSScriptRoot\ChangeConnectionString.ps1 -
Destination $PSScriptRoot\downloads\ChangeConnectionString.ps1 -Force
Copy-Item -LiteralPath $PSScriptRoot\Deployment.zip -Destination
$PSScriptRoot\downloads\Deployment.zip -Force
Copy-Item -LiteralPath $PSScriptRoot\lcm.ps1 -Destination
$PSScriptRoot\downloads\lcm.ps1 -Force
Copy-Item -LiteralPath $PSScriptRoot\dockerfile -Destination
$PSScriptRoot\downloads\dockerfile -Force
# next four statements deletes the original files
Remove-Item "$PSScriptRoot\Deployment.zip" -Force -Confirm:$false
Remove-Item "$PSScriptRoot\ChangeConnectionString.ps1" -Force -
Confirm:$false
Remove-Item "$PSScriptRoot\lcm.ps1" -Force -Confirm:$false
Remove-Item "$PSScriptRoot\dockerfile" -Force -Confirm:$false
```

The script unzips the downloaded `deployment.zip` file containing ASP.NET MVC web application files in the subdirectory and deletes the original ZIP file:

```
"$PSScriptRoot\downloads\Deployment.zip"
# this script section unzips the deployment.zip containing web application
file
if( (get-item -Path $PSScriptRoot\downloads\Deployment -force -ErrorAction
SilentlyContinue) -eq $null )
{
    Add-Type -AssemblyName System.IO.Compression.FileSystem
    function Unzip
    {
        param([string]$zipfile, [string]$outpath)
        [System.IO.Compression.ZipFile]::ExtractToDirectory($zipfile,
$outpath)
    }
    Unzip "$PSScriptRoot\downloads\Deployment.zip"
"$PSScriptRoot\downloads"
}
# deletes the original deployment.zip file
Remove-Item "$PSScriptRoot\downloads\Deployment.zip" -Force -Confirm:$false
```

It opens a couple of Firewall ports for Docker and the web application. The web application port is determined dynamically as a parameter to the script:

```
# open firewall rule for port 2375 used by Docker client and Daemon
if (!(Get-NetFirewallRule | where {$_.Name -eq "Docker"})) {
    New-NetFirewallRule -Name "Docker" -DisplayName "Docker" -Protocol tcp
-LocalPort 2375 -Action Allow -
    Enabled True
}
# open firewall rule for dynamic port used by web application
if (!(Get-NetFirewallRule | where {$_.Name -eq "webapp"})) {
    New-NetFirewallRule -Name "webapp" -DisplayName "webapp" -Protocol tcp
-LocalPort $webport -Action
    Allow -Enabled True
}
```

The Windows container feature should already be installed by default because of the chosen Azure OS image; however, the next lines of code ensures that Windows Container feature is already installed on virtual machine. It will install this feature if not already installed.

```
# install containers windows feature if not already installed
if( (Get-WindowsFeature -Name containers) -eq $null )
{
    Install-WindowsFeature containers
}
```

A new PowerShell `session` object is created. New containers will be created within the newly created `session` object. To create a new session, and remote into it, PowerShell remoting is used.

```
# preparing to remote on local machine
# this is needed because the newly downloaded
# docker binaries are not picked by existing
# powershell session
$username1 = "$HostName\$username"
$username1
$pass = ConvertTo-SecureString $password -AsPlainText -Force
$cred = New-Object System.Management.Automation.PSCredential $username1,
$pass
$soptions = New-PSSessionOption -SkipCACheck -SkipCNCheck -
SkipRevocationCheck
# creating a new PSSession
$s = New-PSSession -ComputerName $env:computername -Credential $cred -
SessionOption $soptions
```

The custom image is named `iis`, and a check is made to ensure that it already exists on the virtual machine. If not, a new container image is created using the `dockerfile` downloaded on the virtual machine. The `dockerfile` internally uses `lcm.ps1` and `ChangeConnectionString.ps1` to configure the web application environment. The script passes the necessary arguments to `dockerfile` to dynamically generate the image:

```
# Remoting on local machine to check and create
# custom windows container image for
# web application
Invoke-Command -Session $s -ScriptBlock { param($pathfiles, $pullip, $port,
$regKey, $sqlUsername,$sqlPassword, $sqlServer, $databaseName)
   Set-Location $pathfiles
   $aa = Docker images
   $toCreateImage = $false
    for($i = 0; $i -lt $aa.Length; $i++){
      if($aa[$i].StartsWith("iis")){
           $toCreateImage = $false
           break;
      }
      else
      {
           $toCreateImage = $true
      }
   }
if ($toCreateImage -eq $true )
{
    docker build --build-arg ipaddress=$pullip --build-arg port=$port --
build-arg regkey=$regKey --build-
    arg sqlUsername=$sqlUsername --build-arg sqlPassword=$sqlPassword --
build-arg sqlServer=$sqlServer --
    build-arg databaseName=$databaseName -t iis .
        Restart-Service Docker | out-null
}
} -ArgumentList $PSScriptRoot\downloads, $pullip, $port, $regKey,
$sqlUsername,$sqlPassword, $sqlServer, $databaseName | Out-Null
```

A container is created on all web frontend related virtual machines using the newly created the custom image using the `docker run` command. It is important to note that the port number on host virtual machine is mapped to the same port number internal to the container. Readers are free to map other ports other than the one shown here:

```
# Remoting on local machine to create container
# based on custom container image
Invoke-Command -Session $s -ScriptBlock { param($webport)
    $portStr = $webport + ":" + $webport
  docker run -d -p $portStr iis
} -ArgumentList $webport| Out-Null
```

Finally, a virtual machine certificate is generated in order to securely connect through PowerShell:

```
# checking if certificate for virtual machine exists already
# if not create a new certificate for secure remote powershell access to
virtual machine
$cert = Get-ChildItem -Path cert:\LocalMachine\My\* -DnsName $HostName -
ErrorAction SilentlyContinue
if ($cert -eq $null)
{
    $cert = New-SelfSignedCertificate -CertstoreLocation
Cert:\LocalMachine\My -DnsName $HostName
}
get-childitem -Path WSMan:\localhost\Listener\ | where {$_.keys[0] -
contains 'Transport=HTTPS'} | Remove-Item -Force -Confirm:$false -Recurse
New-Item -Path WSMan:\LocalHost\Listener -Transport HTTPS -Address * -
CertificateThumbPrint $cert.Thumbprint -Force | out-null
Restart-Service winrm | out-null
New-NetFirewallRule -DisplayName 'Windows Remote Management (HTTPS-In)' -
Name 'Windows Remote Management (HTTPS-In)' -Profile Any -LocalPort 5986 -
Protocol TCP -Enabled True -Confirm:$false -ErrorAction Continue
```

dockerfile

The `dockerfile` helps in building custom container images. Chapter 4, *Nano, Containers, and Docker Primer* provides a good introduction to the `dockerfile`, and it should be referred to while going through this section. The comments before each instruction provide details about the action performed. This `dockerfile` is building a new container image for the sample web application.

This template performs the following steps to generate an image `iis` for our sample application:

1. This image is built on top of the `microsoft/windowsservercore` image provided by Microsoft. At the time of writing, there are only two base images available: `windowsservercore` and `nanoserver`.

2. The next set of instructions in `dockerfile` declares arguments that are passed as parameters by `ContainerConfig.ps1` during the build phase of the image. These are used for connecting and downloading DSC configurations from Pull Server as well as changing the SQL connection strings in `web.config`.

3. The next command installs **Internet Information Services** (**IIS**) and other ASP.NET MVC Windows features including .NET 4.5.

4. A DSC configuration downloaded from Pull Server has dependency on the `xWebApplication` and `xWebdeploy` packages. They are downloaded from the PowerShell gallery using the package management module after registering `Nuget` and `Chocolatey` sources. While registering these two sources, if their corresponding package providers are missing, they are also installed.

5. The default files from the `wwwroot` folder are removed. The default web application and application pool are removed.

6. `Lcm.ps1` is added to the context, stored within the image in a folder, and executed. This configures the local configuration manager of the container image and downloads the DSC configuration from Pull Server. The configuration from Pull Server is executed, which is responsible for creating a sample application-specific website and application pool in IIS.

7. The `Chocolatey` utility is downloaded and installed. `webdeploy` package is also downloaded and installed using `Chocolatey`.

8. The deployment package containing the entire ASP.NET MVC sample application is executed.

9. The SQL connection string is modified in `web.config` by executing the `ChangeConnectionString.ps1`.

10. Finally, a loop is created to ensure that the containers do not exit when running in detached mode using this image.

After this image is created, containers from this image can be provisioned in order to serve requests for a web application. This image is created on both the web application virtual machines by `ContainerConfig.ps1` script that runs automatically as the Custom Script Extension after the virtual machines are provisioned. The entire code for `dockerfile` is listed here:

```
# escape=`
# base image on which custom image is based on
FROM microsoft/windowsservercore
# argument ipaddress used during building of image
# refers to Pull Server ip address
ARG ipaddress="0.0.0.0"
# argument port used during building of image
# refers to Pull Server port
# used for accesing Pull Server
ARG port="9100"
# argument regkey used during building of image
# refers to Pull Server registration key
ARG regkey="xxxxxxxx-xxxx-xxxx-xxxx-xxxxxxxxxxxx"
# argument sqlUsername used during building of image
# used in changing connection string in web.config
ARG sqlUsername="xxxxxxxxx"
# argument sqlPassword used during building of image
# used in changing connection string in web.config
ARG sqlPassword="xxxxxxxxx"
# argument sqlPassword used during building of image
# used in changing connection string in web.config
ARG sqlServer="xxxxxxxxx"
# argument sqlPassword used during building of image
# used in changing connection string in web.config
ARG databaseName="xxxxxxxxx"
# installing IIS and its related windows feature
RUN powershell -Command Install-WindowsFeature web-server, Web-Default-Doc, `
    Web-Dir-Browsing, Web-Http-Errors, Web-Static-Content, Web-Http-Logging, `
    Web-Request-Monitor, Web-Stat-Compression, Web-Filtering, Web-Windows-Auth, `
    Web-Net-Ext45, Web-Asp-Net45, Web-ISAPI-Ext, Web-ISAPI-Filter, Web-Metabase
# installing .NET 4.5
RUN ["Powershell", "install-windowsfeature","NET-Framework-45-Core" ]
# creating a new Docker folder
RUN powershell -Command New-Item -Path c:\docker -ItemType Directory -Force
# Registering Nuget as Package source
RUN powershell -Command Register-PackageSource -Name Nuget `
    -Location https://api.nuget.org/v3/index.json `
```

```
        -ProviderName Nuget -Trusted -Force -ForceBootstrap
# Registering Chocolatey as Package source
RUN powershell -Command Register-PackageSource -Name chocolatey `
        -Location http://chocolatey.org/api/v2/ `
        -ProviderName chocolatey -Trusted -Force -ForceBootstrap
# installing xWebAdministration DSC resources
RUN powershell -Command install-module -Name xWebAdministration `
        -RequiredVersion 1.14.0.0 `
        -Force -Confirm:$false -Verbose
# installing xWebDeploy DSC resources
RUN powershell -Command install-module -Name xwebdeploy `
        -RequiredVersion 1.2.0.0 `
        -Force -Confirm:$false -Verbose
# removing default iisstart.htm file
RUN powershell -Command Remove-Item C:\inetpub\wwwroot\iisstart.htm
# removing default iisstart.png file
RUN powershell -Command Remove-Item C:\inetpub\wwwroot\iisstart.png
# removing default web site website from IIS
RUN powershell -Command Remove-Website -Name 'Default Web Site'
# removing default application pool from IIS
RUN powershell -Command Remove-WebAppPool -Name 'DefaultAppPool'
# adding lcm.ps1 to docker folder created previously
ADD lcm.ps1 c:\docker
# adding ChangeConnectionString.ps1 to docker folder created previously
ADD ChangeConnectionString.ps1 c:\docker
# executing lcm.ps1 for changing the LCM configuration of image
# the LCM should pull configuration from Pull Server
# specified in parameters
RUN powerShell -Command c:\docker\lcm.ps1 -port %port% -regKey %regkey% -
ipaddress %ipaddress%
# Download Chocolatey installar and install the same
RUN powershell -Command install-package -name webdeploy -ProviderName
chocolatey -RequiredVersion 3.5.2 -Force -ForceBootstrap -Verbose
# adding the web application file from deployment folder
ADD \Deployment C:\Deployment
# changing the current working directory to deployment folder
WORKDIR C:\\Deployment
# execute the webdeploy package commandline from deployment folder
RUN C:\Deployment\OnlinePharmacy.deploy.cmd /Y
# execute ChangeConnectionString.ps1 and change connectionstring in
web.config
RUN powerShell -Command c:\docker\ChangeConnectionString.ps1 -sqlUsername
%sqlUsername% -sqlPassword %sqlPassword% -sqlServer %sqlServer% -
databaseName %databaseName%
CMD powershell -command while ($true) { Start-Sleep -Seconds 3600 }
```

It is to be noted that dockerfile used in this book purposefully uses each command to generate a new image layer. It is possible to group some of these commands and execute as a single command. This has been done to explain concepts in a verbose manner for the readers.

Readers should optimize dockerfiles by grouping related commands into single command. This would generate lesser image layers.

An example of grouping commands together is shown following:

```
FROM microsoft/windowsservercore
RUN powershell -Command new-item -ItemType Directory -Name "test-1" ; \
new-item -ItemType Directory -Name "test-2"; \
new-item -ItemType Directory -Name "test-3"; \
new-item -ItemType Directory -Name "test-4";
```

The template shown here will create four folders in C:\ in container but will generate a single image layer compared to four layer when executed as individual commands.

lcm.ps1

This script is loaded by dockerfile while creating a custom Windows container image for the web application. The purpose of this script is to change the configuration of the DSC local configuration manager settings of the container image. By default, DSC LCM is configured with the push mode. The LCM is modified to pull partial configurations from Pull Server.

The script accepts Pull Server IP address, its port number, and registration key as parameters:

```
param
(
    [string] $port,
    [string] $regKey,
    [string] $ipaddress
)
```

Both the IP address and port are concatenated together to form a Pull Server URL.

```
# ipaddress and port number are concatenated
$str = "$ipaddress" + ":" + "$port"
```

All configurations for modifying local configuration manager settings are decorated with the `DSCLocalConfigurationManager` attribute. Because this configuration will modify the LCM configuration of the container image whose name cannot be ascertained beforehand, the node name is set as `localhost`. The settings section helps in modifying the general properties of LCM, and they are modified to ensure that the node can pull configurations.

LCM uses `ConfigurationRepositoryWeb` properties in order to connect to a Pull Server. Every Pull Server has a unique registration key that LCM should use in conjunction with `ConfigurationNames` to download configurations.

Previously, a configuration document, `IISInstall` was deployed on Pull Server. The LCM of the container image downloads and applies the `IISInstall` configuration on the local Windows container image. LCM can have multiple `ConfigurationRepositoryWeb` defined, each representing a different Pull Server. Partial configuration helps in downloading and applying multiple configurations simultaneously on a target node by LCM. In this script, a single partial configuration is defined that pulls the `IISInstall` configuration from the defined Pull Server:

```
[DSCLocalConfigurationManager()]
configuration PartialConfigurationDemo
{
    Node localhost
    {
        Settings
        {
            ConfigurationModeFrequencyMins = 30
            RefreshMode = 'Pull'
            RefreshFrequencyMins = 30
            ConfigurationMode = "ApplyandAutoCorrect"
            RebootNodeIfNeeded = $true
        }
        ConfigurationRepositoryWeb IISConfig
        {
            ServerURL = "http://$($str)/psdscpullserver.svc"
            RegistrationKey = "$regkey"
            ConfigurationNames = @("IISInstall")
            AllowUnsecureConnection = $true
        }
        PartialConfiguration IISInstall
        {
            Description = 'Configuration for the IIS'
            ConfigurationSource = '[ConfigurationRepositoryWeb]IISConfig'
            RefreshMode = 'Pull'
        }
```

```
        }
    }
```

After the configuration is defined, it should be executed to generate the appropriate MOF file from it. The LCM changes are applied using `Set-DscLocalConfigurationManager` and `Update-DscConfiguration` pulls the partial configurations from Pull Server. The configurations are stored locally with a pending status. Finally, the configuration is applied to the Windows container image with the help of `Start-DscConfiguration`:

```
# generate the configuration MOF file
PartialConfigurationDemo -OutputPath "$PSScriptRoot\Output" -Verbose
# send and apply the configuration to DSC LCM
Set-DscLocalConfigurationManager -Path "$PSScriptRoot\Output" -Verbose
# download the partial configuration from Pull Server
Update-DscConfiguration -Wait -Verbose
# apply the partial configuration on local container image
Start-DscConfiguration -UseExisting -Wait -Force -Verbose
```

ChangeConnectionString.ps1

This script is loaded by `dockerfile` while creating the custom Windows container image for the web application. The web application, `web.config`, contains a connection string order to connect to Azure SQL. After the web application is deployed using the `webdeploy` utility within the container image, this script is invoked to update the connection string to reflect actual SQL username, password, Server and Database name.

The script accepts the SQL username, password, Server and Database name as parameters:

```
param
(
[string] $sqlUsername,
[string] $sqlPassword,
[string] $sqlServer,
[string] $databaseName
)
```

The web application internally uses entity framework to interact with Azure SQL database. The script is responsible for updating username, password, Server and Database name of a connection string. The connection string is defined using three parts for easier changes:

```
# connection string prefix used by entity framework
$constrPrefix = "metadata=res://*/Models.PharmacyModel.csdl|`
                res://*/Models.PharmacyModel.ssdl|`
                res://*/Models.PharmacyModel.msl;`
```

```
                    provider=System.Data.SqlClient;`
                    provider connection string='"
# connection string suffix
$constrSuffix = "MultipleActiveResultSets=True;App=EntityFramework';"
# connection string with username and password
# from Azure Key vault
$connectionString = "Password=$sqlPassword;`
                    Persist Security Info=False;`
                    User ID=$sqlUsername;`
                    Initial Catalog=$databaseName;`
                    Data Source=$sqlServer.database.windows.net;"
# complete connection string
$connectionString = $constrPrefix + $connectionString + $constrSuffix
```

The content of the web.config file is loaded, and using the xPath query, all the connection strings available in web.config are queried:

```
# loading web.config content
$xml = [XML](Get-Content "C:\inetpub\MVCWebsite\newapp\web.config")
# loading all connection strings from web.config using xPath
$nodes = $xml.SelectNodes("/configuration/connectionStrings/add")
```

Finally, all the connection strings are looped through, and when an appropriate connection string is found, it is replaced with a new connection string and saved into the web.config file:

```
# looping through connection strings
foreach($node in $nodes) {
    if($node.name -eq 'medicineEntities')
    {
        # match found for specific connectionstring
        # update the connection string
        $node.SetAttribute("connectionString", $connectionString);
    }
}
# save the updated content to web.config
$xml.Save("C:\inetpub\MVCWebsite\newapp\web.config")
```

PreparePesterEnvironment.ps1

This script is executed from the release pipeline. A new release server is assigned by VSTS while executing a release and to ensure that the Pester module is available on the resultant release server, this script uses package management module to download Pester and related modules. Both OperationValidation and the Pester module are made available on the release server before executing Pester test cases. The code for this script is shown next.

Both `Nuget` and `Chocolatey` are installed and configured. Using them, `Pester` and the `OperationValidation` module are made available to the release server:

```
Register-PackageSource -Name Nuget -Location https://www.nuget.org/api/v2/
-ProviderName Nuget -Trusted -Force -ForceBootstrap
# Registering Chocolatey as Package source
Register-PackageSource -Name chocolatey -Location
http://chocolatey.org/api/v2/ -ProviderName chocolatey -Trusted -Force -
ForceBootstrap
# installing xWebAdministration DSC resources
install-module -Name Pester -RequiredVersion "3.4.3" -Scope CurrentUser -
Force -Confirm:$false
# installing xWebDeploy DSC resources
install-module -Name OperationValidation -RequiredVersion 1.0.1 -Scope
CurrentUser -Force -Confirm:$false
Get-command -Module Pester | select name
Get-command -Module Microsoft.PowerShell.Operation.Validation | select name
```

Execute-Pester.ps1

Once Pester binaries are available on a release server, Pester test cases can be executed on it. The `Execute-Pester.ps1` script is responsible for executing both `Pester` and `OperationValidation` tests. The script is quite simple. It accepts four parameters and uses them with `Invoke-Pester` cmdlet.

The scripts are executed as a group using the `Invoke-Pester` cmdlet. This cmdlet takes in a folder path, and every test script from the folder is executed one after another.

Every test script, whether unit or operational, takes in two parameters:

- Release name
- Resource group name

These two parameters are passed on to the `Invoke-Pester` cmdlet, which in turn passes them to the test scripts:

```
param (
    [string] $releaseName,
    [string] $resourceGroupName,
    [string] $testScriptPath,
    [string] $operationTestsPath
)
Invoke-Pester -Script @{Path = "$testScriptPath"; Parameters = @{
deploymentName = "$releaseName" ; resourceGroupName = "$resourceGroupName"
```

```
}}
Invoke-Pester -Script @{Path = "$operationTestsPath"; Parameters = @{
deploymentName = "$releaseName" ; resourceGroupName = "$resourceGroupName"
}}
```

Environment unit tests

After provisioning the resources, it is important to test them. Tests should be executed on these resources to verify that they are provisioned successfully, configured according to given values, and are in the expected desired state.

Chapter 5, *Building a Sample Application*, introduced the OnlinePharmacy.Configuration project within the overall sample solution. This project contains the Tests folder containing both unit and operational validation tests.

Pester was introduced in Chapter 3, *DevOps Automation Primer*. It is used to execute the test cases defined in this section. The UnitTests folder contains all the Pester tests. The test cases are defined in PowerShell script files, one for each resource that should be tested.

These tests can be executed manually by executing the scripts directly using a PowerShell console. It can also be executed using the VSTS release pipelines. The preferred mechanism to execute these tests is through the VSTS release pipeline. After provisioning an environment, these unit tests should be executed against it. Chapter 10, *Continuous Delivery and Deployment*, will introduce release pipelines and way to execute these scripts from it. When executing these tests from the release pipeline, the connection to the Azure subscription is configured using VSTS service endpoints. These concepts will become clear in Chapter 10, *Continuous Delivery and Deployment*; however, if readers want to execute these tests manually, they should already be logged in to the subscription using the service application created in the previous chapter through the PreCreate.ps1 script file.

Each test script takes in two parameters—the name of the deployment and the resource group name. The deployment name is the unique release name autogenerated by VSTS while executing a release pipeline. A release pipeline has access to this value using the $(Release.ReleaseName) variable. Each script also has a BeforeAll section that executes Get-AzureRmResourceGroupDeployment with the provided parameters to retrieve the output values defined in the template in Chapter 7, *Configuration Management*. These output values are filled with values after the successful execution completion of the template.

Some of the scripts also query the resource directly using these output values.

Unit testing availability set

The availability set provides high availability when multiple virtual machines containing the same service are deployed in it. In this case, there should be two virtual machines associated with the availability set, and it should be provisioned in the same location as that of the virtual machines. It should also have a reference to both the virtual machines. The code for unit testing availability sets is shown next. The availability set tests are defined in `Availabilityset.Tests.ps1`:

```
<#
  Purpose:
       Verify that Azure availabilitySet resource is provisioned and
configured appropriately.
  Action:
       Run Get-AzureRmAvailabilitySet available in given resource group.
  Expected Result:
       The name of availabiltyset matches.
       AvailabilitySet is provisioned successfully.
       The location is appropriatly set
       It contains two virtual machines
       It has reference to vmvm1 virtual machine
       It has reference to vmvm2 virtual machine
#>
param(
    [string] $deploymentName,
    [string] $resourceGroupName
)
Describe "Availability Sets" {
 BeforeAll {
     $deployment = (Get-AzureRmResourceGroupDeployment -ResourceGroupName
$resourceGroupName -Name
     $deploymentName)
     $webappPort = $deployment.Outputs.webappPort.Value
     $pullserverPort = $deployment.Outputs.pullserverPort.Value
     $numberofvms = $deployment.Outputs.numberofvms.Value
     $location = $deployment.Outputs.deployLocation.Value
     $vmsize = $deployment.Outputs.vmsize.Value
     $ossku = $deployment.Outputs.ossku.Value
     $databaseName = $deployment.Outputs.databaseName.Value
     $resourceGroupName = $deployment.Outputs.resourceGroupName.Value
     $skuName= $deployment.Outputs.skuName.Value
   }
 $avset = Get-AzureRmAvailabilitySet -ResourceGroupName $resourceGroupName
     It "Availability set exists with given name" {
         $avset.Name | should be "webappAVSet"
     }
     It "Availability set state is good.." {
```

```
            $avset.StatusCode | should be "OK"
    }
    It "Availability set exists within given Azure location" {
            $avset.Location | should be $location
    }
    It "Availability set has references to two VMs" {
            $ref = $avset.VirtualMachinesReferences
            $ref.Count | should be $numberofvms
    }
    It "Availability set has references to first VMs" {
            $ref = $avset.VirtualMachinesReferences
            $ref[0].Id.Contains("VM1") | should be $true
    }
    It "Availability set has references to second VMs" {
            $ref = $avset.VirtualMachinesReferences
            $ref[1].Id.Contains("VM2") | should be $true
    }
}
```

Unit testing virtual networks

Virtual networks are necessary for the creation of virtual machines. They provide a network for virtual machines to communicate among themselves and also to the outside world. They provides internal IP addresses to virtual machines and provide the ability to define multiple subnets. Each virtual network has its own address prefix, and the subnets have a subset of the address prefix defined by the virtual network. A single virtual network with two subnets is defined in order to deploy the sample solution. Both the Pull Server and web application virtual machines are deployed in the same frontend subnet, although they could have been defined in separate subnets. The code for unit testing virtual networks and their subnets are shown later. A NSG is also applied to the frontend subnet. The virtual network tests are defined in `VirtualNetworks.Tests.ps1`:

```
<#
  Purpose:
        Verify that Azure virtual network resource is provisioned and
configured appropriately.
  Action:
        Run Get-AzureRmVirtualNetwork available in given resource group with
a given name.
  Expected Result:
        The count of subnets in virtual network is two
        The name of the two subnets are subnetad and frontend.
        The address prefix of virtual network matches.
        The address prefix of both virtual network subnets matches.
        virtual network is provisioned successfully.
```

```
        Its two subnets are provisioned successfully.
        The location is set appropriately
        The frontend subnet has applied Network security group represented
by Om-NSG
#>
param(
    [string] $deploymentName,
    [string] $resourceGroupName
)
Describe "Virtual network" {
 BeforeAll {
     $deployment = (Get-AzureRmResourceGroupDeployment -ResourceGroupName
$resourceGroupName -Name
     $deploymentName)
     $webappPort = $deployment.Outputs.webappPort.Value
     $pullserverPort = $deployment.Outputs.pullserverPort.Value
     $numberofvms = $deployment.Outputs.numberofvms.Value
     $location = $deployment.Outputs.deployLocation.Value
     $vmsize = $deployment.Outputs.vmsize.Value
     $ossku = $deployment.Outputs.ossku.Value
     $databaseName = $deployment.Outputs.databaseName.Value
     $resourceGroupName = $deployment.Outputs.resourceGroupName.Value
     $skuName= $deployment.Outputs.skuName.Value
   }
   $network = (Get-AzureRmVirtualNetwork -ResourceGroupName
   $resourceGroupName -Name $($skuName + "-
   network"))
       It "virtual network address space is {10.0.0.0/16}.." {
          $network.AddressSpace.AddressPrefixes | should be "10.0.0.0/16"
       }
       It "virtual network location is $location .." {
          $network.Location | should be "$location"
       }
       It "virtual network count of subnets is 2 .." {
          $network.Subnets.Count | should be 2
       }
       It "virtual network subnet name is subnetad .." {
          $network.Subnets[0].Name | should be "subnetad"
       }
       It "virtual network subnet name is frontend .." {
          $network.Subnets[1].Name | should be "frontend"
       }
       It "virtual network subnetad subnet address prefix is
       10.0.0.0/24.." {
          $network.Subnets[0].AddressPrefix | should be "10.0.0.0/24"
       }
       It "virtual network subnetad subnet address prefix is
       10.1.0.0/24.." {
```

```
        $network.Subnets[1].AddressPrefix | should be "10.0.1.0/24"
    }
    It "virtual network subnetad subnet has om-NSG applied to it.." {
        ($network.Subnets[1].NetworkSecurityGroup).Id.Contains(
        $($skuName + "-NSG")) | should be $true
    }
    It "virtual network was provisioned successfully" {
        $network.ProvisioningState | should be "Succeeded"
    }
    It "virtual network subnetad was provisioned successfully.." {
        $network.Subnets[0].ProvisioningState | should be "Succeeded"
    }
    It "virtual network frontend subnet was provisioned successfully.."
{
        $network.Subnets[1].ProvisioningState | should be "Succeeded"
    }
}
```

Unit testing Network Security Groups

Network Security Groups (**NSGs**) are one of the security mechanisms to limit access to Azure virtual machines. NSGs are applied at a virtual network subnet or a network interface level. A sample solution applies NSG at the subnet level. Applying NSG at the subnet level ensures that all virtual machines on the subnet get the same security filters. The same NSG filters are applied to both Pull Server and web application virtual machines. However, separate security groups could have been applied if they were deployed on separate subnets. As a best practice, virtual machines of a similar nature and hosting similar applications should be in a subnet with a unique NSG assigned to it. The exercise to have separate subnets and NSGs is left for readers to implement. NSGs provide an option to allow or disallow access to a port in combination with the source and destination IP addresses. Port 80, 443, 1433, 5985, 5986, 3389, 2375, 2376, the Pull Server port, and the web application port should be opened on the NSG for the application to work as intended. The code for unit testing NSG is shown later. The NSG tests are defined in NetworkSecurityGroups.Tests.ps1:

```
<#
  Purpose:
    Verify that Azure network security group resource is provisioned and
configured appropriately.
  Action:
    Run Get-AzureRmNetworkSecurityGroup available in given resource group
with a given name.
  Expected Result:
    NSG resource is provisioned successfully.
```

```
        NSG for port 443 is allowed for incoming requests
        NSG for port 80 is allowed for incoming requests
        NSG is applied to frontend subnet of virtual network
        NSG for port 1433 is allowed for incoming requests
        NSG for port 5985 is allowed for incoming requests
        NSG for port 5986 is allowed for incoming requests
        NSG for port 3389 is allowed for incoming requests
        NSG for port 2375 is allowed for incoming requests
        NSG for port 2376 is allowed for incoming requests
        NSG for port web application port is allowed for incoming requests
        NSG for port Pull Server port is allowed for incoming requests
#>
param(
    [string] $deploymentName,
    [string] $resourceGroupName
)
Describe "Network Security group" {
  BeforeAll {
    $deployment = (Get-AzureRmResourceGroupDeployment -ResourceGroupName
$resourceGroupName -Name
    $deploymentName)
    $webappPort = $deployment.Outputs.webappPort.Value
    $pullserverPort = $deployment.Outputs.pullserverPort.Value
    $numberofvms = $deployment.Outputs.numberofvms.Value
    $location = $deployment.Outputs.deployLocation.Value
    $vmsize = $deployment.Outputs.vmsize.Value
    $ossku = $deployment.Outputs.ossku.Value
    $databaseName = $deployment.Outputs.databaseName.Value
    $resourceGroupName = $deployment.Outputs.resourceGroupName.Value
    $skuName= $deployment.Outputs.skuName.Value
    $NSGName= $deployment.Outputs.networkSecurityGroupName.Value
}
It "NSG resource was provisioned successfully.." {
    $rule = ((Get-AzureRmNetworkSecurityGroup -Name $NSGName -
ResourceGroupName $resourceGroupName))
    $rule.ProvisioningState | should be "Succeeded"
}
It "NSG is applied to frontend subnet of virtual network" {
    $rule = ((Get-AzureRmNetworkSecurityGroup -Name $NSGName -
ResourceGroupName
    $resourceGroupName).Subnets[0].Id)
    $rule.Contains('frontend') | should be $true
}
It "NSG for port 80 is allowed for incoming requests" {
    $rule = ((Get-AzureRmNetworkSecurityGroup -Name $NSGName -
ResourceGroupName
    $resourceGroupName).SecurityRules.Where{$_.name -eq
"rule80"}).DestinationPortRange
```

```
    $rule | should be 80
}
It "NSG for port 443 is allowed for incoming requests" {
    $rule = ((Get-AzureRmNetworkSecurityGroup -Name $NSGName -
ResourceGroupName
    $resourceGroupName).SecurityRules.Where{$_.name -eq
"rule443"}).DestinationPortRange
    $rule | should be 443
}
It "NSG for port 1433 is allowed for incoming requests" {
    $rule = ((Get-AzureRmNetworkSecurityGroup -Name $NSGName -
ResourceGroupName
    $resourceGroupName).SecurityRules.Where{$_.name -eq
"rule1433"}).DestinationPortRange
    $rule | should be 1433
}
It "NSG for port 5985 is allowed for incoming requests" {
    $rule = ((Get-AzureRmNetworkSecurityGroup -Name $NSGName -
ResourceGroupName
    $resourceGroupName).SecurityRules.Where{$_.name -eq
"rulePSUnsecured"}).DestinationPortRange
    $rule | should be 5985
}
It "NSG for port 5986 is allowed for incoming requests" {
    $rule = ((Get-AzureRmNetworkSecurityGroup -Name $NSGName -
ResourceGroupName
    $resourceGroupName).SecurityRules.Where{$_.name -eq
"rulePSsecured"}).DestinationPortRange
    $rule | should be 5986
}
It "NSG for port 3389 is allowed for incoming requests" {
    $rule = ((Get-AzureRmNetworkSecurityGroup -Name $NSGName -
ResourceGroupName
    $resourceGroupName).SecurityRules.Where{$_.name -eq
"RDP"}).DestinationPortRange
    $rule | should be 3389
}
It "NSG for port 2375 is allowed for incoming requests" {
    $rule = ((Get-AzureRmNetworkSecurityGroup -Name $NSGName -
ResourceGroupName
    $resourceGroupName).SecurityRules.Where{$_.name -eq
"docker"}).DestinationPortRange
    $rule | should be 2375
}
It "NSG for port 2376 is allowed for incoming requests" {
    $rule = ((Get-AzureRmNetworkSecurityGroup -Name $NSGName -
ResourceGroupName
    $resourceGroupName).SecurityRules.Where{$_.name -eq
```

```
"dockers"}).DestinationPortRange
    $rule | should be 2376
}
It "NSG for port $webappPort is allowed for incoming requests" {
    $rule = ((Get-AzureRmNetworkSecurityGroup -Name $NSGName -
ResourceGroupName
    $resourceGroupName).SecurityRules.Where{$_.name -eq
"webserver"}).DestinationPortRange
    $rule | should be $webappPort
}
It "NSG for port $pullserverPort is allowed for incoming requests" {
    $rule = ((Get-AzureRmNetworkSecurityGroup -Name $NSGName -
ResourceGroupName
    $resourceGroupName).SecurityRules.Where{$_.name -eq
"pullserver"}).DestinationPortRange
    $rule | should be $pullserverPort
}
}
```

Unit testing load balancer

The Azure load balancer provides the ability to distribute requests to multiple virtual machines. External load balancers have both a public IP and internal IP assigned to them while internal load balancers only have a internal IP assigned. Load balancers have load balancing rules assigned to them, and based on these rules, the requests are distributed among virtual machines. Load balancers also have a probe configuration that continually probes the virtual machines on the provided port. The sample solution uses HTTP with port 8080 using the /newapp/Index path continually with an interval of 100 seconds. It also probes 100 times. Load balancers also have frontend configuration with NAT rules and a public IP address assigned to it. It has a backend pool with references to virtual machine network interfaces.The load balancer tests are defined in LoadBalancer.Tests.ps1:

```
<#
  Purpose:
    Verify that Azure Load balancer resource is provisioned and configured
appropriately.
  Action:
    Run Get-AzureRmLoadBalancer available in given resource group with a
    given name.
    Run Get-AzureRmLoadBalancerRuleConfig available in given resource group
    with a given name.
    Run Get-AzureRmLoadBalancerProbeConfig available in given resource
    group with a given name.
    Run Get-AzureRmLoadBalancerInboundNatRuleConfig available in
    given resource group with a given name.
```

Run Get-AzureRmLoadBalancerBackendAddressPoolConfig available in given resource group with a given name.
Run Get-AzureRmLoadBalancerFrontendIpConfig available in given resource group with a given name.
Expected Result:
Load balancer rule for frontend web application port is configured
Load balancer rule for backend web application port is configured
Load balancer rules is associated with backend address pool
Load balancer rule is associated with frontend IP configuration
Load balancer rule is associated with Tcp protocol
Load balancer rule uses the Default load distibution algorithm
Load balancer rule is provisioned successfully
Load balancer rule is associated with probe object
Load balancer probe is configured to be executed 100 times
Load balancer probe is configured to be executed in 100 seconds interval
Load balancer probe is associated with load balancer rules
Load balancer probe is configured for web application port
Load balancer probe is configured on http protocol
Load balancer probe is configured successfully
Load balancer probe is configured to probe /newapp/index path
Load balancer Nat config with frontend port 3389 for first virtual machine
Load balancer Nat config with backend port 3389 for first virtual machine
Load balancer Nat config with backend port 3389 for first virtual machine
Load balancer Nat config with frontend port 13389 for second virtual machine
Load balancer Nat config is on Tcp protocol for both virtual machines
Load balancer Nat config is configured successfully for both virtual machine
Load balancer backend address pool is connected to nic on first virtual machine
Load balancer backend address pool is connected to nic on second virtual machine
Load balancer frontend ip configuration is associated with load balancer public ip
Load balancer frontend ip configuration is associated with NAT to first virtual machine
Load balancer frontend ip configuration is associated with NAT to second virtual machine
Load balancer frontend ip configuration is associated with load balancing rules
Load balancer frontend ip configuration private internal ip is assigned dynamically
Load balancer backend address pool is provisioned successfully

```
        Load balancer backend address pool is connected to Nic of
        first virtual machine
        Load balancer backend address pool is connected to Nic of
        second virtual machine
#>
param(
    [string] $deploymentName,
    [string] $resourceGroupName
)
Describe "Load balancer" {
 BeforeAll {
    $deployment = (Get-AzureRmResourceGroupDeployment -ResourceGroupName
$resourceGroupName -Name
    $deploymentName)
    $webappPort = $deployment.Outputs.webappPort.Value
    $pullserverPort = $deployment.Outputs.pullserverPort.Value
    $numberofvms = $deployment.Outputs.numberofvms.Value
    $location = $deployment.Outputs.deployLocation.Value
    $vmsize = $deployment.Outputs.vmsize.Value
    $ossku = $deployment.Outputs.ossku.Value
    $databaseName = $deployment.Outputs.databaseName.Value
    $resourceGroupName = $deployment.Outputs.resourceGroupName.Value
    $skuName= $deployment.Outputs.skuName.Value
    $lbfrontendIPConfiguration=
$deployment.Outputs.lbfrontendIPConfiguration.Value
    $lbbackendAddressPool= $deployment.Outputs.lbbackendAddressPool.Value
    $lbloadBalancingRules= $deployment.Outputs.lbloadBalancingRules.Value
    $lbinboundNatRule1= $deployment.Outputs.lbinboundNatRule1.Value
    $lbinboundNatRule2= $deployment.Outputs.lbinboundNatRule2.Value
    $nicNameforVM1= $deployment.Outputs.nicNameforVM1.Value
    $nicNameforVM2= $deployment.Outputs.nicNameforVM2.Value
}

    $lb = Get-AzureRmLoadBalancer -Name containerLB -ResourceGroupName
$resourceGroupName
It "Load balancer rule for frontend port $webappPort is configured.." {
    (Get-AzureRmLoadBalancerRuleConfig -LoadBalancer $lb).FrontendPort |
should be $webappPort
}
It "Load balancer rule for backend port $webappPort is configured.." {
    (Get-AzureRmLoadBalancerRuleConfig -LoadBalancer $lb).BackendPort |
should be $webappPort
}
It "Load balancer rules is associated with backend address pool.." {
    (Get-AzureRmLoadBalancerRuleConfig -LoadBalancer
    $lb).BackendAddressPool.Id.Contains($lbbackendAddressPool) | should be
$true
}
It "Load balancer rule is associated with frontend IP configuration.." {
```

```
    (Get-AzureRmLoadBalancerRuleConfig -LoadBalancer
    $lb).FrontendIPConfiguration.id.Contains($lbfrontendIPConfiguration) |
should be $true
}
It "Load balancer rule is associated with Tcp protocol" {
    (Get-AzureRmLoadBalancerRuleConfig -LoadBalancer $lb).Protocol | should
be "Tcp"
}
It "Load balancer rule uses the Default load distibution algorithm.." {
    (Get-AzureRmLoadBalancerRuleConfig -LoadBalancer $lb).LoadDistribution
| should be "Default"
}
It "Load balancer rule is provisioned successfully.." {
    (Get-AzureRmLoadBalancerRuleConfig -LoadBalancer $lb).ProvisioningState
| should be "Succeeded"
}
It "Load balancer rule is associated with probe object.." {
    (Get-AzureRmLoadBalancerRuleConfig -LoadBalancer
$lb).Probe.Id.Contains('WebLBPROBE') | should be
    $true
}
It "Load balancer probe is configured to be executed 100 times.." {
    (Get-AzureRmLoadBalancerProbeConfig -LoadBalancer $lb).NumberOfProbes |
should be 100
}
It "Load balancer probe is configured to be executed in 100 seconds
interval.." {
    (Get-AzureRmLoadBalancerProbeConfig -LoadBalancer
$lb).IntervalInSeconds | should be 100
}
It "Load balancer probe is associated with load balancer rules.." {
    (Get-AzureRmLoadBalancerProbeConfig -LoadBalancer
    $lb).LoadBalancingRules[0].Id.Contains($lbloadBalancingRules) | should
be $true
}
It "Load balancer probe is configured on port $webappPort .." {
    (Get-AzureRmLoadBalancerProbeConfig -LoadBalancer $lb).Port | should be
$webappPort
}
It "Load balancer probe is configured on http protocol.." {
    (Get-AzureRmLoadBalancerProbeConfig -LoadBalancer $lb).Protocol |
should be "http"
}
It "Load balancer probe is configured successfully.." {
    (Get-AzureRmLoadBalancerProbeConfig -LoadBalancer
$lb).ProvisioningState | should be "Succeeded"
}
It "Load balancer probe is configured to probe /newapp/index path .." {
```

```
        (Get-AzureRmLoadBalancerProbeConfig -LoadBalancer $lb).RequestPath |
should be "/newapp/Index"
}
It "Load balancer Nat config with frontend port 3389 for first virtual
machine.." {
        (Get-AzureRmLoadBalancerInboundNatRuleConfig -LoadBalancer
$lb)[0].FrontendPort | should be "3389"
}
It "Load balancer Nat config with backend port 3389 for first virtual
machine.." {
        (Get-AzureRmLoadBalancerInboundNatRuleConfig -LoadBalancer
$lb)[0].BackendPort | should be "3389"
}
It "Load balancer Nat config with backend port 3389 for first virtual
machine.." {
        (Get-AzureRmLoadBalancerInboundNatRuleConfig -LoadBalancer
$lb)[1].BackendPort | should be "3389"
}
It "Load balancer Nat config with frontend port 13389 for second virtual
machine.." {
        (Get-AzureRmLoadBalancerInboundNatRuleConfig -LoadBalancer
$lb)[1].FrontendPort | should be "13389"
}
It "Load balancer Nat config is on Tcp protocol for both virtual
machines.." {
        (Get-AzureRmLoadBalancerInboundNatRuleConfig -LoadBalancer
$lb).Protocol | should be @('Tcp','Tcp')
}
It "Load balancer Nat config is configured successfully for both virtual
machine.." {
        (Get-AzureRmLoadBalancerInboundNatRuleConfig -LoadBalancer
$lb).ProvisioningState | should be
        @('Succeeded','Succeeded')
}
It "Load balancer frontend ip configuration is associated with load
balancer public ip .." {
        (Get-AzureRmLoadBalancerFrontendIpConfig -LoadBalancer
$lb).PublicIpAddress.Id.Contains('lbPublicIP')
        | should be $true
}
It "Load balancer frontend ip configuration is associated with NAT to first
virtual machine .." {
        (Get-AzureRmLoadBalancerFrontendIpConfig -LoadBalancer
        $lb).InboundNatRules[0].Id.Contains($lbinboundNatRule1) | should be
$true
}
It "Load balancer frontend ip configuration is associated with NAT to
second virtual machine.." {
```

```
    (Get-AzureRmLoadBalancerFrontendIpConfig -LoadBalancer
    $lb).InboundNatRules[1].Id.Contains($lbinboundNatRule2) | should be
$true
}
It "Load balancer frontend ip configuration is associated with load
balancing rules resource.." {
    (Get-AzureRmLoadBalancerFrontendIpConfig -LoadBalancer
    $lb).LoadBalancingRules[0].Id.Contains($lbloadBalancingRules) | should
be $true
}
It "Load balancer frontend ip configuration private internal ip is assigned
dynamically.." {
    (Get-AzureRmLoadBalancerFrontendIpConfig -LoadBalancer
$lb).PrivateIpAllocationMethod | should be
    "Dynamic"
}
It "Load balancer backend address pool is provisioned successfully.." {
    (Get-AzureRmLoadBalancerBackendAddressPoolConfig -LoadBalancer
$lb).ProvisioningState | should be
    "Succeeded"
}
}
```

Unit testing Azure SQL

Azure SQL provides SQL as a service. Azure SQL hosts an SQL database and has Firewall rules that allow requests from only whitelisted IP addresses. Both the web applications and Pull Server virtual machine public IP addresses are added to the list of allowed Firewall rules. The code for unit testing Azure SQL is shown next. The Azure SQL tests are defined in SQLServer.Tests.ps1:

```
<#
  Purpose:
    Verify that Azure SQL resource is provisioned and configured
appropriately.
  Action:
    Run Get-AzureRmSqlServer available in given resource group with a given
name.
    Run Get-AzureRmSqlDatabase available in given resource group with a
given name.
    Run Get-AzureRmSqlServerFirewallRule available in given resource group
with a given name.
  Expected Result:
    Get SQL server with given name
    Get SQL server location
    Get SQL Server database with given name
```

```
     Get SQL Server database with firewall rules related to first virtual
machine
     Get SQL Server database with firewall rules related to second virtual
machine
     Get SQL Server database with firewall rules related to pullserver
virtual machine
     Get SQL Server database with firewall rules related to all azure
services
#>
param(
    [string] $deploymentName,
    [string] $resourceGroupName
)
Describe "SQL SERVER" {
 BeforeAll {
    $deployment = (Get-AzureRmResourceGroupDeployment -ResourceGroupName
$resourceGroupName -Name
    $deploymentName)
    $webappPort = $deployment.Outputs.webappPort.Value
    $pullserverPort = $deployment.Outputs.pullserverPort.Value
    $numberofvms = $deployment.Outputs.numberofvms.Value
    $location = $deployment.Outputs.deployLocation.Value
    $vmsize = $deployment.Outputs.vmsize.Value
    $ossku = $deployment.Outputs.ossku.Value
    $databaseName = $deployment.Outputs.databaseName.Value
    $resourceGroupName = $deployment.Outputs.resourceGroupName.Value
    $skuName= $deployment.Outputs.skuName.Value
    $sqlServer= $deployment.Outputs.sqlServer.Value
}
    $server = Get-AzureRmSqlServer -ResourceGroupName $resourceGroupName
    $database = Get-AzureRmSqlDatabase -ServerName $sqlServer -
ResourceGroupName $resourceGroupName
    DatabaseName $databaseName
    $firewall = Get-AzureRmSqlServerFirewallRule -ResourceGroupName
$resourceGroupName -ServerName
    $sqlServer
It "Get SQL server with given name" {
    $server.ServerName | should be $("devopswin2016-" + $skuName)
}
It "Get SQL Server database with given name" {
    $database.Databasename | should be $databaseName
}
It "Get SQL Server database with Webapp1 firewall rules" {
    $webapp1Ipaddress = $firewall.Where{$_.FirewallRuleName -eq 'webapp1'}
| select startipaddress
    ExpandProperty startipaddress
    $firewall.Where{$_.FirewallRuleName -eq 'webapp1'} | select
FirewallRuleName -ExpandProperty
```

```
    FirewallRuleName | should be "webapp1"
}
It "Get SQL Server database with Webapp2 firewall rules" {
    $firewall.Where{$_.FirewallRuleName -eq 'webapp2'} | select
FirewallRuleName -ExpandProperty
    FirewallRuleName | should be "webapp2"
    $webapp2Ipaddress = $firewall.Where{$_.FirewallRuleName -eq 'webapp2'}
| select startipaddress -
    ExpandProperty startipaddress
}
It "Get SQL Server database with Pull Server firewall rules" {
    $firewall.Where{$_.FirewallRuleName -eq 'pullserver'} | select
FirewallRuleName -ExpandProperty
    FirewallRuleName | should be "pullserver"
    $pullserverIpaddress = $firewall.Where{$_.FirewallRuleName -eq
'pullserver'} | select startipaddress -
    ExpandProperty startipaddress
}
It "Get SQL Server database with AllowAllWindowsAzureIps firewall rules" {
    $firewall.Where{$_.FirewallRuleName -eq 'AllowAllWindowsAzureIps'} |
select FirewallRuleName -
    ExpandProperty FirewallRuleName | should be "AllowAllWindowsAzureIps"
    $AllowAllWindowsAzureIps = $firewall.Where{$_.FirewallRuleName -eq
'AllowAllWindowsAzureIps'} | select
    startipaddress -ExpandProperty startipaddress
}
}
```

Unit testing Azure SQL Firewall

The IP addresses in Azure SQL Firewall rules should match the public IP address of the web application and Pull Server virtual machines. They should also allow traffic from any Azure service. The code for unit testing Azure SQL Firewall rules is shown here. The Azure SQL Firewall tests are defined in SQLFirewallIPAddresses.Tests.ps1:

```
<#
  Purpose:
    Verify that Azure SQL firewalls have valid Ip address belonging to two
virtual machine hosting web
    application.
  Action:
    Run Get-AzureRmSqlServer available in given resource group with a given
name.
    Run Get-AzureRmSqlDatabase available in given resource group with a
given name.
    Run Get-AzureRmSqlServerFirewallRule available in given resource group
```

```
    with a given name.
        Run Get-AzureRmPublicIpAddress available in given resource group with a
    given name.
      Expected Result:
        Public Ip address of VM vmvm1 matches to the Azure SQL firewall
        Public Ip address of VM vmvm2 matches to the Azure SQL firewall
    #>
    param(
        [string] $deploymentName,
        [string] $resourceGroupName
    )
    Describe "SQL Firewall IP Addresses"{
     BeforeAll {
        $deployment = (Get-AzureRmResourceGroupDeployment -ResourceGroupName
    $resourceGroupName -Name
        $deploymentName)
        $webappPort = $deployment.Outputs.webappPort.Value
        $pullserverPort = $deployment.Outputs.pullserverPort.Value
        $numberofvms = $deployment.Outputs.numberofvms.Value
        $location = $deployment.Outputs.deployLocation.Value
        $vmsize = $deployment.Outputs.vmsize.Value
        $ossku = $deployment.Outputs.ossku.Value
        $databaseName = $deployment.Outputs.databaseName.Value
        $resourceGroupName = $deployment.Outputs.resourceGroupName.Value
        $skuName= $deployment.Outputs.skuName.Value
        $sqlServer= $deployment.Outputs.sqlServer.Value
     }
        $server = Get-AzureRmSqlServer -ResourceGroupName $resourceGroupName
        $database = Get-AzureRmSqlDatabase -ServerName $sqlServer -
    ResourceGroupName $resourceGroupName -
        DatabaseName $databaseName
        $firewall = Get-AzureRmSqlServerFirewallRule -ResourceGroupName
    $resourceGroupName -ServerName
        $sqlServer
    It "Public Ip address of VM vm1 matches to the Azure SQL firewall " {
        $ipaddress = (Get-AzureRmPublicIpAddress -Name $("pip1" + $skuName + "-
    publicIP") -ResourceGroupName
        $resourceGroupName).IpAddress
        $webapp1Ipaddress = $firewall.Where{$_.FirewallRuleName -eq 'webapp1'}
    | select startipaddress -
        ExpandProperty startipaddress
        $webapp1Ipaddress | should be $ipaddress
    }
    It "Public Ip address of VM vm2 matches to the Azure SQL firewall " {
        $ipaddress = (Get-AzureRmPublicIpAddress -Name $("pip2" + $skuName + "-
    publicIP") -ResourceGroupName
        $resourceGroupName).IpAddress
        $webapp2Ipaddress = $firewall.Where{$_.FirewallRuleName -eq 'webapp2'}
```

```
| select startipaddress -
    ExpandProperty startipaddress
    $webapp2Ipaddress | should be $ipaddress
}
}
```

Unit testing the count of virtual machines

The solution comprises of three virtual machines–one virtual machine for DSC Pull Server and two virtual machines for hosting web application. It should be noted that the number of virtual machines for the web application is configurable. The code for unit testing the count of virtual machines is shown here. The virtual machine count tests are defined in VirtualMachineCount.Tests.ps1:

```
<#
  Purpose:
    Verify the count of virtual machines in resource group .
  Action:
    Run Get-AzureRmVM available in given resource group with a given name.
  Expected Result:
    count of virtual machine in resource group
#>
param(
    [string] $deploymentName,
    [string] $resourceGroupName
)
Describe "Check the existance of Web front end and Pull Server virtual
machine" {
 BeforeAll {
    $deployment = (Get-AzureRmResourceGroupDeployment -ResourceGroupName
$resourceGroupName -Name
    $deploymentName)
    $webappPort = $deployment.Outputs.webappPort.Value
    $pullserverPort = $deployment.Outputs.pullserverPort.Value
    $numberofvms = $deployment.Outputs.numberofvms.Value
    $location = $deployment.Outputs.deployLocation.Value
    $vmsize = $deployment.Outputs.vmsize.Value
    $ossku = $deployment.Outputs.ossku.Value
    $databaseName = $deployment.Outputs.databaseName.Value
    $resourceGroupName = $deployment.Outputs.resourceGroupName.Value
    $skuName= $deployment.Outputs.skuName.Value
 }
    $vms = Get-AzureRmVM -ResourceGroupName $resourceGroupName
It "count of virtual machine in resource group" {
    $vms.Count | should be ($numberofvms +1)
}
```

```
}
```

Unit testing virtual machine 01

Virtual machines contain Docker containers that host a web application. Virtual machines are created using an image, **Windows 2016 with Containers** from Microsoft. The virtual machine needs a storage account to store its vhd file, a virtual network for communicating with other machines, a network interface card to talk to the network, and extensions to execute scripts. Azure provides multiple sizes for virtual machines. It is important to choose an appropriate size of virtual machine as it has a cost associated with it. The code for unit testing the first virtual machine is shown here. The virtual machine 01 tests are defined in VM01.Tests.ps1:

```
<#
  Purpose:
    Verify that virtual machine VM01 is provisioned and configured
appropriately.
  Action:
    Run Get-AzureRmVM available in given resource group with a given name.
  Expected Result:
    Virtual machine location is as intended
    Virtual machine is part of availability set
    Virtual machine size is Standard_D3
    Virtual machine is attached to NIC
    Virtual machine image is from appropriate Offer
    Virtual machine image is from appropriate publisher
    Virtual machine image is from appropriate sku
#>
param(
    [string] $deploymentName,
    [string] $resourceGroupName
)
Describe "web front end Virtual Machines vm01" {
 BeforeAll {
    $deployment = (Get-AzureRmResourceGroupDeployment -ResourceGroupName
$resourceGroupName -Name
    $deploymentName)
    $webappPort = $deployment.Outputs.webappPort.Value
    $pullserverPort = $deployment.Outputs.pullserverPort.Value
    $numberofvms = $deployment.Outputs.numberofvms.Value
    $location = $deployment.Outputs.deployLocation.Value
    $vmsize = $deployment.Outputs.vmsize.Value
    $ossku = $deployment.Outputs.ossku.Value
    $databaseName = $deployment.Outputs.databaseName.Value
    $resourceGroupName = $deployment.Outputs.resourceGroupName.Value
```

```
        $skuName= $deployment.Outputs.skuName.Value
        $nicNameforVM1= $deployment.Outputs.nicNameforVM1.Value
}
    $vm = Get-AzureRmVM -ResourceGroupName $resourceGroupName -Name vm1
It "virtual machine location is as intended" {
    $vm.Location | should be $location
}
It "Virtual machine is part of availability set" {
    $vm.AvailabilitySetReference.Id.Contains('WEBAPPAVSET') | should be
$true
}
It "Virtual machine size is $vmsize" {
    $vm.HardwareProfile.VmSize| should be "Standard_D3"
}
It "Virtual machine is attached to NIC " {
    $vm.NetworkInterfaceIDs[0].Contains("$nicNameforVM1")| should be $true
}
It "Virtual machine image is from appropriate Offer" {
    $vm.StorageProfile.ImageReference.Offer| should be 'WindowsServer'
}
It "Virtual machine image is from appropriate publisher" {
    $vm.StorageProfile.ImageReference.Publisher| should be
'MicrosoftWindowsServer'
}
It "Virtual machine image is from appropriate sku" {
    $vm.StorageProfile.ImageReference.Sku| should be $ossku
}
}
```

Unit testing virtual machine 02

This is similar to the first virtual machine. The code for both the virtual machines could have been written in a loop; however, for demonstration purposes, a separate script is written for both the virtual machines. There is another example later in this chapter that uses looping for both the virtual machines as well. The code for unit testing the second virtual machine is shown here. The virtual machine 02 tests are defined in VM02.Tests.ps1:

```
<#
  Purpose:
    Verify that virtual machine VM02 is provisioned and configured
appropriately.
  Action:
    Run Get-AzureRmVM available in given resource group with a given name.
  Expected Result:
    virtual machine location is as intended
```

```
        Virtual machine is part of availability set
        Virtual machine size is Standard_D3
        Virtual machine is attached to NIC
        Virtual machine image is from appropriate Offer
        Virtual machine image is from appropriate publisher
        Virtual machine image is from appropriate sku
#>
param(
    [string] $deploymentName,
[string] $resourceGroupName
)
Describe "web front end Virtual Machines VM02" {
 BeforeAll {
    $deployment = (Get-AzureRmResourceGroupDeployment -ResourceGroupName
$resourceGroupName -Name
    $deploymentName)
    $webappPort = $deployment.Outputs.webappPort.Value
    $pullserverPort = $deployment.Outputs.pullserverPort.Value
    $numberofvms = $deployment.Outputs.numberofvms.Value
    $location = $deployment.Outputs.deployLocation.Value
    $vmsize = $deployment.Outputs.vmsize.Value
    $ossku = $deployment.Outputs.ossku.Value
    $databaseName = $deployment.Outputs.databaseName.Value
    $resourceGroupName = $deployment.Outputs.resourceGroupName.Value
    $skuName= $deployment.Outputs.skuName.Value
    $nicNameforVM2= $deployment.Outputs.nicNameforVM2.Value
}
    $vm = Get-AzureRmVM -ResourceGroupName $resourceGroupName -Name vm2
It "virtual machine location" {
    $vm.Location | should be $location
}
It "Virtual machine is part of availability set" {
    $vm.AvailabilitySetReference.Id.Contains('WEBAPPAVSET') | should be
$true
}
It "Virtual machine size is $vmsize.." {
    $vm.HardwareProfile.VmSize| should be "Standard_D3"
}
It "Virtual machine is attached to NIC " {
    $vm.NetworkInterfaceIDs[0].Contains("$nicNameforVM2")| should be $true
}
It "Virtual machine image is from appropriate Offer" {
    $vm.StorageProfile.ImageReference.Offer| should be 'WindowsServer'
}
It "Virtual machine image is from appropriate publisher" {
    $vm.StorageProfile.ImageReference.Publisher| should be
'MicrosoftWindowsServer'
}
```

```
It "Virtual machine image is from appropriate sku" {
    $vm.StorageProfile.ImageReference.Sku| should be $ossku
}
}
```

Unit testing the DSC Pull Server virtual machine

This is again similar to the previous two virtual machines. The code for unit testing the Pull Server virtual machine is shown here. The Pull Server virtual machine tests are defined in `PullServer.Tests.ps1`:

```
<#
  Purpose:
    Verify that DSC Pull Server virtual machine is provisioned and
configured appropriately.
  Action:
    Run Get-AzureRmVM available in given resource group with a given name.
  Expected Result:
    virtual machine location is as intended
    Virtual machine is part of availability set
    Virtual machine size is Standard_D1
    Virtual machine is attached to NIC
    Virtual machine image is from appropriate Offer
    Virtual machine image is from appropriate publisher
    Virtual machine image is from appropriate sku
#>
param(
    [string] $deploymentName,
    [string] $resourceGroupName
)
Describe "Virtual Machines pullserver" {
 BeforeAll {
    $deployment = (Get-AzureRmResourceGroupDeployment -ResourceGroupName
$resourceGroupName -Name
    $deploymentName)
    $webappPort = $deployment.Outputs.webappPort.Value
    $pullserverPort = $deployment.Outputs.pullserverPort.Value
    $numberofvms = $deployment.Outputs.numberofvms.Value
    $location = $deployment.Outputs.deployLocation.Value
    $vmsize = $deployment.Outputs.vmsize.Value
    $ossku = $deployment.Outputs.ossku.Value
    $databaseName = $deployment.Outputs.databaseName.Value
    $resourceGroupName = $deployment.Outputs.resourceGroupName.Value
    $skuName= $deployment.Outputs.skuName.Value
}
    $vm = Get-AzureRmVM -ResourceGroupName $resourceGroupName -Name vm-
```

```
pulls
It "virtual machine location is as intended" {
    $vm.Location | should be $location
}
It "Virtual machine size is Standard_D1" {
    $vm.HardwareProfile.VmSize| should be $vmsize
}
It "Virtual machine is attached to NIC " {
    $vm.NetworkInterfaceIDs[0].Contains("nicPS" + $skuName + "-nic")|
should be $true
}
It "Virtual machine image is from appropriate Offer" {
    $vm.StorageProfile.ImageReference.Offer| should be 'WindowsServer'
}
It "Virtual machine image is from appropriate publisher" {
    $vm.StorageProfile.ImageReference.Publisher| should be
'MicrosoftWindowsServer'
}
It "Virtual machine image is from appropriate sku" {
    $vm.StorageProfile.ImageReference.Sku| should be '2016-Datacenter-with-
Containers'
}
}
```

Unit testing the DSC Pull Server operating system

It's time to test the configuration of the operating system and the DSC Pull Server. The DSC Pull Server is an IIS website with a web application pool. It has a defined port number. It is dependent on the web server and DSC service Windows feature; an appropriate Firewall port for Pull Server to work should be enabled and allowed access to. The code for unit testing the DSC Pull Server and operating system is shown here. The Pull Server operating system tests are defined in InsidePullServer.Tests.ps1:

```
<#
  Purpose:
    Verify that DSC Pull Server virtual machine is configured to accept
pull requests from DSC nodes.
  Action:
    Login into Pull Server hosted on Azure virtual machine using New-
PSSession.
  Expected Result:
    Web-server feature is installed
    SC-Service feature is installed
    DSC Pull Server web site exists
    DSC Pull Server web site is up and running
    DSC Pull Server web site is attached to appropriate application pool
```

```
    DSC Pull Server web site is running on https protocol
    DSC Pull Server web site is running on appropriate port
    DSC Pull Server web site is running on given physical path
    DSC Pull Server application pool exists
    DSC Pull Server application pool is up and running
    DSC Pull Server winrm service is available
    DSC Pull Server winrm service is up and running
    DSC Pull Server winrm service startup type is automatic
    Pull Server web application port is open on Pull Server.
    Pull Server winrm port 5985 is open on Pull Server
    Pull Server winrm port 5986 is open on Pull Server
    Pull Server Remote desktop port 3389 is open on Pull Server
#>
param(
    [string] $deploymentName,
    [string] $resourceGroupName
)
Describe "Inside Virtual Machines pullserver" {
 BeforeAll {
    $deployment = (Get-AzureRmResourceGroupDeployment -ResourceGroupName
$resourceGroupName -Name
    $deploymentName)
    $webappPort = $deployment.Outputs.webappPort.Value
    $pullserverPort = $deployment.Outputs.pullserverPort.Value
    $numberofvms = $deployment.Outputs.numberofvms.Value
    $location = $deployment.Outputs.deployLocation.Value
    $vmsize = $deployment.Outputs.vmsize.Value
    $ossku = $deployment.Outputs.ossku.Value
    $databaseName = $deployment.Outputs.databaseName.Value
    $resourceGroupName = $deployment.Outputs.resourceGroupName.Value
    $skuName= $deployment.Outputs.skuName.Value
    $vmUserName = $deployment.Outputs.vmUserName.Value
    $vmPassword = $deployment.Outputs.vmPassword.Value
    $pullServerPublicIPAddress =
$deployment.Outputs.pullServerPublicIPAddress.Value
  }
 beforeeach {
    $hostName= "$pullServerPublicIPAddress"
    $winrmPort = '5986'
    $username = $vmUserName
    $pass = ConvertTo-SecureString -string $vmPassword -AsPlainText -Force
    $cred = New-Object -typename System.Management.Automation.PSCredential
-argumentlist $username, $pass
    $soptions = New-PSSessionOption -SkipCACheck -SkipCNCheck -
SkipRevocationCheck
    $s = new-PSSession -ComputerName $hostName -Port $winrmPort -Credential
$cred -SessionOption $soptions
    -UseSSL
```

```
    }
    It "Web-server feature is installed" {
        $r = Invoke-Command -Session $s -ScriptBlock {(Get-WindowsFeature -name
web-server).Name}
        $r | should be "Web-Server"
    }
    It "DSC-Service feature is installed" {
        $r = Invoke-Command -Session $s -ScriptBlock {(Get-WindowsFeature -name
DSC-Service).Name}
        $r | should be "DSC-Service"
    }
    It "DSC Pull Server web site exists" {
        $r = Invoke-Command -Session $s -ScriptBlock {(Get-Website -Name
PSDSCPullServer).Name}
        $r | should be "PSDSCPullServer"
    }
    It "DSC Pull Server web site is up and running" {
        $r = Invoke-Command -Session $s -ScriptBlock {(Get-Website -Name
PSDSCPullServer).state}
        $r | should be "Started"
    }
    It "DSC Pull Server web site is attached to appropriate application pool" {
        $r = Invoke-Command -Session $s -ScriptBlock {(Get-Website -Name
PSDSCPullServer).applicationPool}
        $r | should be "DSCPullServer"
    }
    It "DSC Pull Server web site is running on https protocol" {
        $r = Invoke-Command -Session $s -ScriptBlock {(Get-Website -Name
        PSDSCPullServer).bindings.Collection.protocol}
        $r | should be "http"
    }
    It "DSC Pull Server web site is running on appropriate port" {
        $r = Invoke-Command -Session $s -ScriptBlock {(Get-Website -Name
        PSDSCPullServer).bindings.Collection.bindinginformation}
        $r | should be $("*:" + $pullserverPort + ":")
    }
    It "DSC Pull Server web site is running on given physical path" {
        $r = Invoke-Command -Session $s -ScriptBlock {(Get-Website -Name
PSDSCPullServer).PhysicalPath}
        $r | should be "C:\PSDSCPullServer"
    }
    It "DSC Pull Server application pool exists" {
        $r = Invoke-Command -Session $s -ScriptBlock {(Get-IISAppPool -Name
DscPullServer).Name}
        $r | should be "DSCPullServer"
    }
    It "DSC Pull Server application pool is up and running" {
        $r = Invoke-Command -Session $s -ScriptBlock {(Get-WebAppPoolState -
```

```
Name DscPullServer).Value}
    $r | should be "Started"
}
It "DSC Pull Server winrm service is available" {
    $r = Invoke-Command -Session $s -ScriptBlock {(Get-Service -Name
winrm).Name}
    $r | should be "winrm"
}
It "DSC Pull Server winrm service is up and running" {
    $r = Invoke-Command -Session $s -ScriptBlock {(Get-Service -Name
winrm).Status}
    $r | should be "4"
}
It "DSC Pull Server winrm service startup type is automatic" {
    $r = Invoke-Command -Session $s -ScriptBlock {(Get-Service -Name
winrm).StartType}
    $r | should be "2"
}
It "Pull Server web application port $pullserverPort is open on Pull
Server." {
    $r = Invoke-Command -Session $s -ScriptBlock { param($pullserverPort)
Test-NetConnection -Port
    $pullserverPort -ComputerName $env:COMPUTERNAME} -ArgumentList
$pullserverPort
    $r | should not be $null
}
It "Pull Server winrm port 5985 is open on Pull Server" {
    $r = Invoke-Command -Session $s -ScriptBlock {Test-NetConnection -Port
"5985" -ComputerName
    $env:COMPUTERNAME}
    $r | should not be $null
}
It "Pull Server winrm port 5986 is open on Pull Server" {
    $r = Invoke-Command -Session $s -ScriptBlock {Test-NetConnection -Port
"5986" -ComputerName
    $env:COMPUTERNAME}
    $r | should not be $null
}
It "Pull Server Remote desktop port 3389 is open on Pull Server" {
    $r = Invoke-Command -Session $s -ScriptBlock {Test-NetConnection -Port
"3389" -ComputerName
    $env:COMPUTERNAME}
    $r | should not be $null
}
 aftereach{
    Remove-PSSession -Session $s
 }
}
```

Unit testing the web application operating system

It's time to test the configuration of the operating system and web application operating system. `OnlinePharmacy` is an IIS website associated with its own web application pool. It is configured with a defined port number. It is dependent on the web server and Docker Windows feature. The appropriate Firewall port for it to work should be enabled and allowed access to. The web application is hosted within Windows containers. A custom image `IIS` should exist along with a container provisioned using it. The web application operating system tests are defined in `InsideFrontEndVirtualMachines.Tests.ps1`, as shown here:

```
<#
  Purpose:
    Verify that web application hosted on Azure virtual machine is
configured with container and images
    and hosting web application within containers.
  Action:
    Login into both virtual machines hosted on Azure using New-PSSession.
  Expected Result:
    Docker windows service is available on both virtual Machine
    Docker windows service is up and running on both virtual Machine
    Docker windows service is setup for automatic startup on both virtual
Machine
    Web-Server windows feature is available on both virtual Machine
    Containers windows feature is available on both virtual Machine
    Docker windows service is setup for automatic startup on both virtual
Machine
    Windows container image IIS exists on both virtual machines
    Windows container exists created using IIS image on both virtual
machine
    winrm service is available on both virtual Machine
    winrm service is up and running on both virtual Machine
    winrm service is setup for automatic startup on both virtual Machine
    OnlinePharmacy web application port is open on Pull Server.
    Pull Server winrm port 5985 is open on Pull Server
    Pull Server winrm port 5986 is open on Pull Server
    Pull Server Remote desktop port 3389 is open on Pull Server
#>
param(
    [string] $deploymentName,
    [string] $resourceGroupName
)
Describe "Inside Virtual Machines hosting web application container" {
 BeforeAll {
    $deployment = (Get-AzureRmResourceGroupDeployment -ResourceGroupName
$resourceGroupName -Name
```

```
    $deploymentName)
    $webappPort = $deployment.Outputs.webappPort.Value
    $pullserverPort = $deployment.Outputs.pullserverPort.Value
    $numberofvms = $deployment.Outputs.numberofvms.Value
    $location = $deployment.Outputs.deployLocation.Value
    $vmsize = $deployment.Outputs.vmsize.Value
    $ossku = $deployment.Outputs.ossku.Value
    $databaseName = $deployment.Outputs.databaseName.Value
    $resourceGroupName = $deployment.Outputs.resourceGroupName.Value
    $skuName= $deployment.Outputs.skuName.Value
    $vmUserName = $deployment.Outputs.vmUserName.Value
    $vmPassword= $deployment.Outputs.vmPassword.Value
}
for ($i=1; $i -le $numberofvms; $i++) {
    $hostName= "webapponlmed" + $skuName + $i +
".westeurope.cloudapp.azure.com"
    $winrmPort = '5986'
    $username = $vmUserName
    $pass = ConvertTo-SecureString -string $vmPassword -AsPlainText -Force
    $cred = New-Object -typename System.Management.Automation.PSCredential
-argumentlist $username, $pass
    $soptions = New-PSSessionOption -SkipCACheck -SkipCNCheck -
SkipRevocationCheck
    $s = new-PSSession -ComputerName $hostName -Port $winrmPort -Credential
$cred -SessionOption $soptions
    UseSSL
It "winrm service is available on webapp$($i)" {
    $r = Invoke-Command -Session $s -ScriptBlock {(Get-Service -Name
winrm).Name}
    $r | should be "winrm"
}
It "winrm service is up and running on webapp$($i)" {
    $r = Invoke-Command -Session $s -ScriptBlock {(Get-Service -Name
winrm).Status}
    $r | should be "4"
}
It "winrm service startup type is automatic on webapp$($i)" {
    $r = Invoke-Command -Session $s -ScriptBlock {(Get-Service -Name
winrm).StartType}
    $r | should be "2"
}
It "Docker service is available on webapp$($i)" {
    $r = Invoke-Command -Session $s -ScriptBlock {(Get-Service -Name
docker).Name}
    $r | should be "docker"
}
It "docker service is up and running on webapp$($i)" {
    $r = Invoke-Command -Session $s -ScriptBlock {(Get-Service -Name
```

```
docker).Status}
    $r | should be "4"
}
It "docker service startup type is automatic on webapp$($i)" {
    $r = Invoke-Command -Session $s -ScriptBlock {(Get-Service -Name
docker).StartType}
    $r | should be "2"
}
It "Web-server feature is installed on webapp$($i)" {
    $r = Invoke-Command -Session $s -ScriptBlock {(Get-WindowsFeature -name
web-server).Name}
    $r | should be "Web-Server"
}
It "Containers feature is installed on webapp$($i)" {
    $r = Invoke-Command -Session $s -ScriptBlock {(Get-WindowsFeature -name
containers).Name}
    $r | should be "containers"
}
It "Windows container image IIS exists on webapp$($i)" {
    $r = Invoke-Command -Session $s -ScriptBlock {$images = docker images;
    $images.where{$_.Contains('iis')}}
    $r | should not be $null
}
It "Windows container exists created using IIS image on webapp$($i)." {
    $r = Invoke-Command -Session $s -ScriptBlock {$container = docker ps -
a;
    $Container.where{$_.Contains('iis')}}
    $r | should not be $null
}
It "web application port $webappPort is open on webapp$($i)." {
    $r = Invoke-Command -Session $s -ScriptBlock {param($webappPort) Test-
NetConnection -Port $webappPort
    -ComputerName $env:COMPUTERNAME} -ArgumentList $webappPort
    $r | should not be $null
}
It "winrm port 5985 is open on webapp$($i)." {
    $r = Invoke-Command -Session $s -ScriptBlock {Test-NetConnection -Port
"5985" -ComputerName
    $env:COMPUTERNAME}
    $r | should not be $null
}
It "winrm port 5986 is open on webapp$($i)." {
    $r = Invoke-Command -Session $s -ScriptBlock {Test-NetConnection -Port
"5986" -ComputerName
    $env:COMPUTERNAME}
    $r | should not be $null
}
It "Remote desktop port 3389 is open on webapp$($i)." {
```

```
    $r = Invoke-Command -Session $s -ScriptBlock {Test-NetConnection -Port
"3389" -ComputerName
    $env:COMPUTERNAME}
    $r | should not be $null
}

    Remove-PSSession -Session $s
  }
}
```

Environment operational validation

Operational validation refers to the process of validating and verifying that the environments are not only provisioned and configured in the desired state but also are operational and running as intended. Although unit tests are performed on environments such as development, testing, and preproduction, operational validation can be executed against the production environment. However, this does not mean that operational validation cannot be executed against development, test, or any other environment. It can be executed against any environment.

Another important point to remember about operational validation is that it should not modify the environment while executing the tests. If it needs to perform any action that would eventually modify the environment, the tests should proactively create additional resources and use them. After completion of the tests, these temporary resources should be teared down.

Operational validation is a must have tool that should be employed for effective continuous delivery and deployment. Operational validation provides immediate feedback about a release to decide if it is suitable for going live on production. It can also execute tests such as A/B tests that can provide additional feedback about the deployment.

Operational validation can be executed through two different ways, as follows:

- Pester
- Operational validation module

Operational validation tests are Pester test cases authored and executed exactly in the same as way unit tests were shown earlier. The difference is in the scope of the tests. Although unit tests focus on an individual component and its working, operational validation checks for end-to-end working and operational effectiveness of the environment and application. Microsoft provides the operational validation module in order to execute operational tests for an environment. The operational validation module internally executes Pester test cases.

The tests should be converted into a PowerShell module for the operational validation module to be able to search and execute these test cases. The advantage operational validation module brings in is that it mandates that the tests are available as PowerShell modules. They can be easily searched and discovered easily on a computer. There is no need to use a file path in order to execute the tests. Moreover, these modules are easily shareable with communities, and other developers within and outside the team. These test modules are searchable, discoverable, identifiable, and they can be deployed using package management as well. Chapter 10, *Continuous Delivery and Deployment* will show the way to execute operational validation tests using Pester.

There are specific steps that are undertaken to use the operational validation module for operation validation test cases:

1. Create a folder structure expected by the operational validation module.
2. Write operational validation test cases.
3. Convert the tests into the PowerShell module.

The operational validation folder structure

The operational validation module expects test cases within specific folders and has a predefined folder structure. This helps the operational module to deterministically load and execute the operational validation tests.

An OnlineMedicine folder is created within the OperationalValidation folder. OnlineMedicine contains the OnlineMedicine.psd1 PowerShell data file and Diagnostics folder. The Diagnostics folder further contains two subfolders: Simple and Comprehensive. The Simple folder should contain simple test cases focusing on single resources, whereas the Comprehensive folder should contain integration and operational validation tests that involve more than one resource and are usually more time consuming than executing a simple test case.

To generate the `psd1` file in the `OnlineMedicine` folder, the `new-ModuleManifest` cmdlet can be used as shown here:

```
New-ModuleManifest -Path "..\
OnlinePharmacy.Configuration\tests\Operational
Validation\OnlineMedicine\OnlineMedicine.psd1"
```

Although the authoring and saving of script files happens within the overall `Project` folder, eventually, the `OnlineMedicine` module should be copied over to **Program Files | WindowsPowershell | Modules** directory of the machine on which the validation operations tests are executed.

The operational validation of the web application on the first virtual machine

As part of the operation validation, it is important to test whether the web application is reachable, whether it can send response to requests, and that the entire request-response mechanism is successful. The web application comprises multiple pages, and tests should be conducted in order to retrieve multiple pages successfully. The requests will only get a successful response if provisioning and configuration of every resource is in the desired state, and there are no deviations in them. The public IP address to the virtual machine is assigned at deployment time, and the web application port number is provided as a parameter by the administrator. The values for the public IP address and web application port number are available as part of the output from the template deployment. The code for operation validation tests is shown here. The operational validation tests for the first instance of the web application are defined in `WebAppVirtualMachine-01.Tests.ps1`:

```
<#
  Purpose:
    Verify the web application is operational on first virtual machine.
  Action:
    Run Invoke-WebRequest on multiple pages of web application.
  Expected Result:
    invoking the request for index page of web application and comparing
the returned status, text and
    description
    invoking the request for Drug's create page of web application and
comparing the returned status, text
    and description
    invoking the request for Drugs page of web application and comparing
the returned status, text and
    description
    invoking the request for Drug Inventory page of web application and
```

```
comparing the returned status,
    text and description
    invoking the request for sales page of web application and comparing
the returned status, text and
    description
#>
param(
    [string] $deploymentName,
    [string] $resourceGroupName
)
Describe "Web application requests to first virtual machine and container"
{
 BeforeAll {
    $deployment = (Get-AzureRmResourceGroupDeployment -ResourceGroupName
$resourceGroupName -Name
    $deploymentName)
    $vm01IP = $deployment.Outputs.vM01PublicIPAddress.value
    $webappPort= $deployment.Outputs.webappPort.value
}
It "invoking the request for index page of web application and comparing
the returned status, text and description.." {
    $parturl = $($($vm01IP) + ":" + $($webappPort))
    $indexPage = Invoke-WebRequest -UseBasicParsing -Uri
"http://$parturl/newapp/index"
    $indexPage.Content.Contains("Welcome to Medical Point of sale
application") | should be $true
    $indexPage.StatusCode | should be 200
    $indexPage.StatusDescription | should be "OK"
}
It "invoking the request for Drug's create page of web application and
comparing the returned status, text and description.." {
    $parturl = $($($vm01IP) + ":" + $($webappPort))
    $createDrug = Invoke-WebRequest -UseBasicParsing -Uri
"http://$parturl/newapp/Drugs/Create" -Method
    Get
    $createDrug.Content.Contains("Create new Drug Master - DevOps with
Windows Server 2016 sample
    application") | should be $true
    $createDrug.StatusCode | should be 200
    $createDrug.StatusDescription | should be "OK"
}
It "invoking the request for Drugs page of web application and comparing
the returned status, text and description.." {
    $parturl = $($($vm01IP) + ":" + $($webappPort))
    $drugs = Invoke-WebRequest -UseBasicParsing -Uri
"http://$parturl/newapp/Drugs"
    $drugs.Content.Contains("List of Drugs - DevOps with Windows Server
2016 sample application") | should
```

```
    be $true
    $drugs.StatusCode | should be 200
    $drugs.StatusDescription | should be "OK"
}
It "invoking the request for Drug Inventory page of web application and
comparing the returned status, text and description.." {
    $parturl = $($($vm01IP) + ":" + $($webappPort))
    $drugInventory = Invoke-WebRequest -UseBasicParsing -Uri
"http://$parturl/newapp/DrugInventories"
    $drugInventory.Content.Contains("List of inventory - DevOps with
Windows Server 2016 sample
    application") | should be $true
    $drugInventory.StatusCode | should be 200
    $drugInventory.StatusDescription | should be "OK"
}
It "invoking the request for sales page of web application and comparing
the returned status, text and description.." {
    $parturl = $($($vm01IP) + ":" + $($webappPort))
    $sales = Invoke-WebRequest -UseBasicParsing -Uri
"http://$parturl/newapp/Sales"
    $sales.Content.Contains("All sales.. - DevOps with Windows Server 2016
sample application") | should
    be $true
    $sales.StatusCode | should be 200
    $sales.StatusDescription | should be "OK"
  }
}
```

The operational validation of the web application on the second virtual machine

The operational validation tests for the second virtual machine are similar to the first one. The code for operation validation tests is shown here. The operational validation tests for the second instance of the web application are defined in WebAppVirtualMachine-02.Tests.ps1:

```
<#
  Purpose:
    Verify the web application is operational on second virtual machine.
  Action:
    Run Invoke-WebRequest on multiple pages of web application.
  Expected Result:
    invoking the request for index page of web application and comparing
the returned status, text and
    description
```

```
        invoking the request for Drug's create page of web application and
    comparing the returned status, text
        and description
        invoking the request for Drugs page of web application and comparing
    the returned status, text and
        description
        invoking the request for Drug Inventory page of web application and
    comparing the returned status,
        text and description
        invoking the request for sales page of web application and comparing
    the returned status, text and
        description
    #>
    param(
        [string] $deploymentName,
        [string] $resourceGroupName
    )
    Describe "Web application requests to first virtual machine and container"
    {
     BeforeAll {
        $deployment = (Get-AzureRmResourceGroupDeployment -ResourceGroupName
    $resourceGroupName -Name
        $deploymentName)
        $vm02IP = $deployment.Outputs.vM02PublicIPAddress.value
        $webappPort= $deployment.Outputs.webappPort.value
    }
    It "invoking the request for index page of web application and comparing
    the returned status, text and
    description.." {
        $parturl = $($($vm02IP) + ":" + $($webappPort))
        $indexPage = Invoke-WebRequest -UseBasicParsing -Uri
    "http://$parturl/newapp/index"
        $indexPage.Content.Contains("Welcome to Medical Point of sale
    application") | should be $true
        $indexPage.StatusCode | should be 200
        $indexPage.StatusDescription | should be "OK"
    }
    It "invoking the request for Drug's create page of web application and
    comparing the returned status, text
    and description.." {
        $parturl = $($($vm02IP) + ":" + $($webappPort))
        $createDrug = Invoke-WebRequest -UseBasicParsing -Uri
    "http://$parturl/newapp/Drugs/Create" -Method
        Get
        $createDrug.Content.Contains("Create new Drug Master - DevOps with
    Windows Server 2016 sample
        application") | should be $true
        $createDrug.StatusCode | should be 200
```

```
        $createDrug.StatusDescription | should be "OK"
}
It "invoking the request for Drugs page of web application and comparing
the returned status, text and
description.." {
    $parturl = $($($vm02IP) + ":" + $($webappPort))
    $drugs = Invoke-WebRequest -UseBasicParsing -Uri
"http://$parturl/newapp/Drugs"
    $drugs.Content.Contains("List of Drugs - DevOps with Windows Server
2016 sample application") | should
    be $true
    $drugs.StatusCode | should be 200
    $drugs.StatusDescription | should be "OK"
}
It "invoking the request for Drug Inventory page of web application and
comparing the returned status, text and description.." {
    $parturl = $($($vm02IP) + ":" + $($webappPort))
    $drugInventory = Invoke-WebRequest -UseBasicParsing -Uri
"http://$parturl/newapp/DrugInventories"
    $drugInventory.Content.Contains("List of inventory - DevOps with
Windows Server 2016 sample
    application") | should be $true
    $drugInventory.StatusCode | should be 200
    $drugInventory.StatusDescription | should be "OK"
}
It "invoking the request for sales page of web application and comparing
the returned status, text and description..." {
    $parturl = $($($vm02IP) + ":" + $($webappPort))
    $sales = Invoke-WebRequest -UseBasicParsing -Uri
"http://$parturl/newapp/Sales"
    $sales.Content.Contains("All sales.. - DevOps with Windows Server 2016
sample application") | should
    be $true
    $sales.StatusCode | should be 200
    $sales.StatusDescription | should be "OK"
  }
}
```

The operational validation of the web application using an Azure load balancer

The operational validation tests using a load balancer is the same as that of virtual machines; however, instead of using the public IP address of the virtual machines, the public IP address of load balancer is used. The code for operational tests using load balancer is shown next. The operational validation tests for the web application load balancer are defined in `WebAppLoadBalancer.Tests.ps1`:

```
<#
  Purpose:
    Verify the web application is operational using Azure Load balancer.
  Action:
    Run Invoke-WebRequest on multiple pages of web application.
  Expected Result:
    invoking the request for index page of web application and comparing
the returned status, text and
    description
    invoking the request for Drug's create page of web application and
comparing the returned status, text
    and description
    invoking the request for Drugs page of web application and comparing
the returned status, text and
    description
    invoking the request for Drug Inventory page of web application and
comparing the returned status,
    text and description
    invoking the request for sales page of web application and comparing
the returned status, text and
    description
#>
param(
    [string] $deploymentName,
    [string] $resourceGroupName
)
Describe "Web application requests to virtual machine and container using
load balancer" {
 BeforeAll {
    $deployment = (Get-AzureRmResourceGroupDeployment -ResourceGroupName
$resourceGroupName -Name
    $deploymentName)
    $lbip = $deployment.Outputs.loadBalancerPublicIPAddress.value
    $webappPort= $deployment.Outputs.webappPort.value
}
it "invoking the request for index page of web application and comparing
the returned status, text and
```

```
description.." {
    $parturl = $($($lbip) + ":" + $($webappPort))
    $fullurl = "http://$parturl/newapp/index"
    $indexPage = Invoke-WebRequest -UseBasicParsing -Uri (New-Object
System.Uri -ArgumentList "$fullurl")
    $indexPage.Content.Contains("Welcome to Medical Point of sale
application") | should be $true
    $indexPage.StatusCode | should be 200
    $indexPage.StatusDescription | should be "OK"
}
it "invoking the request for index page of web application and comparing
the returned status, text and description.." {
    $parturl = $($($lbip) + ":" + $($webappPort))
    $fullurl = "http://$parturl/newapp/index"
    $indexPage = Invoke-WebRequest -UseBasicParsing -Uri "$fullurl"
    $indexPage.Content.Contains("Welcome to Medical Point of sale
application") | should be $true
    $indexPage.StatusCode | should be 200
    $indexPage.StatusDescription | should be "OK"
}
it "invoking the request for Drug's create page of web application and
comparing the returned status, text and description.." {
    $parturl = $($($lbip) + ":" + $($webappPort))
    $fullurl = "http://$parturl/newapp/Drugs/Create"
    $createDrug = Invoke-WebRequest -UseBasicParsing -Uri "$fullurl" -
Method Get
    $createDrug.Content.Contains("Create new Drug Master - DevOps with
Windows Server 2016 sample
    application") | should be $true
    $createDrug.StatusCode | should be 200
    $createDrug.StatusDescription | should be "OK"
}
it "invoking the request for Drugs page of web application and comparing
the returned status, text and description.." {
    $parturl = $($($lbip) + ":" + $($webappPort))
    $fullurl = "http://$parturl/newapp/Drugs"
    $drugs = Invoke-WebRequest -UseBasicParsing -Uri "$fullurl"
    $drugs.Content.Contains("List of Drugs - DevOps with Windows Server
2016 sample application") | should
    be $true
    $drugs.StatusCode | should be 200
    $drugs.StatusDescription | should be "OK"
}
it "invoking the request for Drug Inventory page of web application and
comparing the returned status, text and description.." {
    $parturl = $($($lbip) + ":" + $($webappPort))
    $fullurl = "http://$parturl/newapp/DrugInventories"
    $drugInventory = Invoke-WebRequest -UseBasicParsing -Uri "$fullurl"
```

```
    $drugInventory.Content.Contains("List of inventory - DevOps with
Windows Server 2016 sample
    application") | should be $true
    $drugInventory.StatusCode | should be 200
    $drugInventory.StatusDescription | should be "OK"
}
it "invoking the request for sales page of web application and comparing
the returned status, text and description.." {
    $parturl = $($($lbip) + ":" + $($webappPort))
    $fullurl = "http://$parturl/newapp/Sales"
    $sales = Invoke-WebRequest -UseBasicParsing -Uri "$fullurl"
    $sales.Content.Contains("All sales.. - DevOps with Windows Server 2016
sample application") | should
    be $true
    $sales.StatusCode | should be 200
    $sales.StatusDescription | should be "OK"
  }
}
```

Unit and operational validation tests

Pester provides the `Invoke-Pester` PowerShell function in order to execute Pester test cases. It accepts a single script file as well as a path to the folder containing multiple test script files through the `Script` parameter:

```
Invoke-Pester -Script "$env:ProgramFiles\WindowsPowershell\Modules\Unit
Tests"
```

The preceding command executes all the test scripts while the following command executes test cases only in a single script file:

```
Invoke-Pester -Script "$env:ProgramFiles\WindowsPowershell\Modules\Unit
Tests\ Availabilityset.Tests.ps1"
```

Operational validation tests can be executed similar to the way unit tests are executed using `Invoke-Pester`. The operational validation module also provides a function `Invoke-OperationValidation` to execute operational validation test cases. `Invoke-OperationValidation` internally invokes the `Invoke-Pester` function in order to execute the test cases. If no parameters are specified for this function, it searches all the modules on the machine that adheres to the folder structure prescribed by the operational validation module and executes the tests within them. It has an option to choose if only simple or comprehensive tests are to be executed. By default, it executes both types of test cases. Even the `ModuleName` parameter can be specified containing the test cases. When the `ModuleName` parameter is provided, this function will search only for this module to execute the test cases.

The execution report of the operational validation module is different in format as compared with the Pester report although it internally uses the Pester module. However the Pester output can be included with the operational validation report.

The operational validation tests are executed directly using `Invoke-Pester` instead of `Invoke-OperationValidation` in `Chapter 10`, *Continuous Delivery and Deployment*.

Summary

This is the concluding chapter on configuration management, and again a lot of miles were covered in this chapter. This chapter covers the creation of a Pull Server, the configuration deployed on the DSC Pull Server, the configuration of web application virtual machines with a custom Docker image and container, `dockerfile` for defining a custom Docker image, local configuration manager updates to pull DSC configuration from the Pull Server, and modification of the connection string in web.config. After provisioning and configuring the environment, the chapter explained unit and operational validation tests for them. It provided information about various ways these tests can be executed using Pester and the operational validation module. All the code shown in this chapter is accompanied with the source code and can be used, changed, and extended. This chapter was primarily about building the configuration management and artifacts related to Infrastructure as Code and testing them in a continuous deployment and delivery process. The next chapter will be about continuous integration, explaining concepts and building build pipelines. Stay tuned!

9
Continuous Integration

Chapter 6, *Source Code Control*, provided detailed insight into the working of source code configuration management. Chapter 7, *Configuration Management* and Chapter 8, *Configuration Management and Operational Validation*, dealt with practices, principles, and implementation of application and infrastructure configuration management with the help of the **Online Medicine** sample application. The focus of this chapter is on another important practice of DevOps, that is, continuous integration.

Continuous integration is one of the main pillars of DevOps, directly effecting the application life cycle management of a project. This chapter will discuss continuous integration in depth. It will focus on the necessity of continuous integration, some of its important principles and implementation, and the configuration of **Visual Studio Team Services** (**VSTS**) to automate continuous integration.

Continuous integration

Continuous integration refers to the process of generating final deployable code packages because of changes in the source code. The goal of continuous integration is to keep the source code in a state that is always ready for deployment. The process can run at scheduled intervals, on demand, and whenever there is a change in the source code. The process consists of multiple tasks, and each task is responsible for executing a functionality. These functionalities include activities such as compiling code, unit testing, code coverage, code quality, and so on. Code changes can induce bugs and break the functionality of the application. Continuous integration ensures that code changes are compiled and tested immediately. It also ensures that immediate feedback is provided to the team in the case of failure. This can help teams take pro-active actions on fixing the issue. Continuous integration is executed by means of a build pipeline.

Why continuous integration?

Continuous integration brings in multiple advantages to the project implementing it. Every project has a finite budget, resources, and time. Projects are executed within these constraints. One of the goals of every enterprise is to optimize within these constraints, and bring out quality software products and services while reducing risks. Continuous integration helps in optimizing these constraints and streamlining the build and test process using automation.

Continuous integration automates the build and test process through build pipelines.

There are many advantages of implementing continuous integration. Some of the major advantages of continuous integration are mentioned here.

Fail fast and often

When a developer checks-in their code, the code is merged and integrated, and an automated build pipeline is executed to validate the correctness of the code and its outputs. If there is any bug, error, or issue, it is communicated to the developer in detail. The developer can identify the issue, and fix and test it, ensuring that the build process is not broken and the code meets the functional correctness of the solution at any given point of time.

High confidence and cadence

Continuous integration ensures that the code in the repository branch can always be compiled, tested, and ready for deployment to environments (including production). This entire process is automated to bring standardization and consistency in its execution. Stakeholders and the project management team will have a high level of confidence using the code for deployment to production and other environments. Now, compare it with a scenario where there is no continuous integration. Developers are free to check-in their code at their own will, which can run into weeks. Infrequent integration of code often leads to more code conflicts and regressions in other developers' code, which would be painful to resolve.

Better collaboration

Continuous integration provides immediate feedback to the developers when they push their code to the shared repository. The feedback is made available to all developers in the team. The issue could be directly related to the code and feature belonging to the developer, or it could induce issues in other developers' code and features. Developers interact and communicate in real time to solve issues arising out of pushing the code change.

Reduction of technical debt

"Technical debt is a concept in programming that reflects the extra development work that arises when code that is easy to implement in the short run is used instead of applying the best overall solution. As a change is started on a codebase, there is often the need to make other coordinated changes at the same time in other parts of the codebase or documentation. The other required, but uncompleted changes are considered debt that must be paid at some point in the future. Just like financial debt, these uncompleted changes keep incurring interest, making it cumbersome to build a project." -Wikipedia

When an automated build pipeline executes, it checks for issues arising out of compiling the solution, executing units, integration, and other tests. This ensures that if there are issues arising within the overall solution, it can be caught early and fixed rather than finding it sometime in future. It would be more difficult to fix the issue in the future compared to fixing it immediately.

Principles of Continuous Integration

Continuous integration is a mindset and guidance. It is based on certain principles, which make it highly effective. It does not prescribe ways to implement itself. Continuous integration does not talk of any individual tool, technology, or utility. It also does not mention the tasks that should be part of any continuous integration. However, it mentions that basic activities should be performed for effective continuous integration.

Automation

It is difficult to achieve continuous integration goals when implemented and executed manually. Automation should be used for implementing continuous integration. There should be a source code repository for developers to collaborate on code, an automated build pipeline that has the capability of executing both on demand as well as on triggers. It should also have the capability to execute build pipelines on schedule. Furthermore, the activities in build pipelines should have capabilities to compile the code, perform validation by executing different multiple types of tests, such as unit and integration tests, generate code drops, and provide a dynamic build name to uniquely identify it.

VSTS is a robust, feature-rich automation service for both build and release pipeline management. It provides automation capabilities to define and author build pipelines as well as execute, manage, report, and monitor build executions. VSTS was introduced in `Chapter 2`, *DevOps Tools and Technologies*, of this book, where its capabilities and features were demonstrated. Here are some of the capabilities of VSTS; it can:

- Define multiple build pipelines:
    - Variables to store commonly used data
    - Build activities or steps to define the pipeline
    - Build pipeline to move context and data across build activities and steps
- Manage build pipeline definitions:
    - Cloning
    - Saving into template
    - Editing definitions
    - Managing security for build definitions
    - Executing definitions
- Be link to the source code repository branch
- Trigger a build pipeline:
    - Manually
    - On schedule
    - Changes in repository branch
- Generate unique build label and identifiers
- Link with work items in the case of failure
- Provide version control for build definitions

- Execute build definitions on self-hosted servers as well as servers provided by VSTS
- Link with release management
- Integrate with open source tools

These capacities provided by VSTS will be discussed later in this chapter in detail. There are many more capabilities, and newer ones are getting added continuously on a regular basis. There is also a market place hosting third-party extensions, easily consumable within build pipelines. In fact, this chapter is accompanied with a sample build pipeline source code. The code for the build definition was exported from VSTS using a third-party extension called **Export/Import Build Definition**.

Single repository

Continuous integration yields better results with a single shared repository. If there are multiple repositories, each would have its own build pipeline. There would not be any out-of-the-box native sharing and collaboration between these build pipelines. However, if there is a single repository with build pipelines, there would be a single source to work with and all builds can happen from here. It is possible to have multiple branches, each having its own unique build pipeline or sharing a common pipeline. With a single repository, reporting can be done easily without combining data from multiple repositories.

Fast execution

Continuous integration will be more effective if the build pipeline executed in response to the code check can complete its execution faster. There should be immediate feedback to the developers about the quality of the code checked-in and they should be informed about any issues in the code. If the build pipeline takes hours or days to complete its activity, then the entire purpose of continuous integration gets defeated. The activities within a build pipeline should complete as soon as possible. If any activity within the build pipeline is consuming considerable time, analysis and refactoring should be done to check whether a subset can be moved to another pipeline. This differs from one project to another and should be evaluated on a case-to-case basis.

Reporting

Continuous integration should provide reports to its stakeholders. Centralized reporting and feedback should be enabled and provided to developers and management regarding the quality of code, execution of build pipelines, number of build failures and successes, root cause of build failures, logs from build the execution, compilation reports, unit tests, code coverage reports, and so on.

Security

Security plays a paramount role in continuous integration. The build pipeline accesses the source code repository, executes its activities, and steps on a build server. The build server should not be accessible to anyone apart from the build service account. The build definition should encrypt its variables both at definition and during runtime. Permissions in the build follow a hierarchical model. Defaults for all the permissions can be set at the team project level and can be overridden on an individual build definition. You are advised to visit `https://www.visualstudio.com/en-us/docs/build/concepts/policies/permissions#build-permissions` to understand permissions in details.

Continuous integration process

Continuous integration is a practice based on principles. It provides guidance regarding best practices and activities that should be performed and executed. However, it does not mandate any tool, utility, product, or service. It also does not prescribe processes that should be part of the build pipeline. It just says that there should be continuous integration that starts a build pipeline automatically to verify the build aspects of the solution, the quality of the solution by executing tests, and labels the execution with a unique name for identification.

However, as a practice, there are certain aspects that are common across software development and should be used across projects. In this chapter, we used those to implement continuous integration for the sample application, `OnlineMedicine`. The process of continuous integration is shown in the following image:

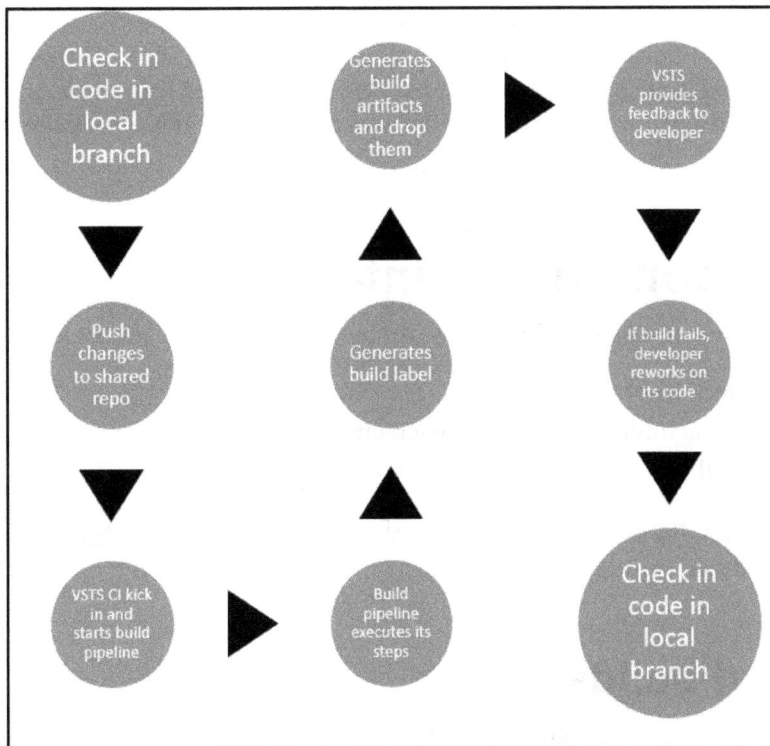

Figure 1: Sample continuous integration process

The continuous integration process can be broken down into nine high-level steps.

A developer checks-in or commits code into his local repository. A developer typically works on his local repository. Once he commits his changes into the local repository, he pushes his changes with the common shared repository used by all the developers. Continuous integration is associated with the common shared repository. VSTS is the platform used to implement continuous integration.

It monitors the repository for any new check-ins or commits. Once it sees that there is a new commit, it starts a new execution of the build pipeline. The build pipeline itself is composed of multiple steps, which we will discuss in detail later in this chapter. A new build label to identify the build execution uniquely is generated.

If the build execution is successful, a new build drop comprising build artifacts is created. However, if the build fails, the developer is informed about the error. The developer can rework on fixing the issue and restart the process of checking in into the local and then into the central shared repository. This is a continuous process that happens every time there is a change in code.

Types of continuous integration

There are three ways in which VSTS builds can be triggered. They are as follows:

- Scheduled
- Continuous integration (builds each check-in)
- Gated builds

So far, we have been discussing the second way, which is continuous integration. Now, we will discuss scheduled builds.

Scheduled builds

Scheduled builds refer to automatic build pipeline execution at a predetermined day and time. Multiple schedules can be configured for the same build pipeline and can include multiple branches from the same repository. Build pipelines are not dependent on the developer's check-in. These types of build pipelines are generally used as nightly and weekly builds during off-hours when no one is actively working on the shared common repository. The configuration of the same in VSTS is shown here.

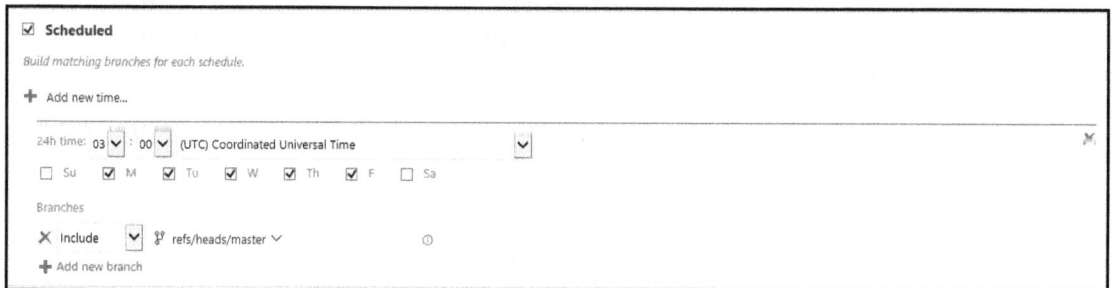

Figure 2: Scheduled build pipeline

In the preceding screenshot, a build has been scheduled to run at 3 a.m. on Monday, Tuesday, Wednesday, Thursday, and Friday, and it includes the source code from the **master** branch from the repository.

Continuous build

This executes a build pipeline whenever any developer checks in or commits code to the repository branch. Here is a screenshot:

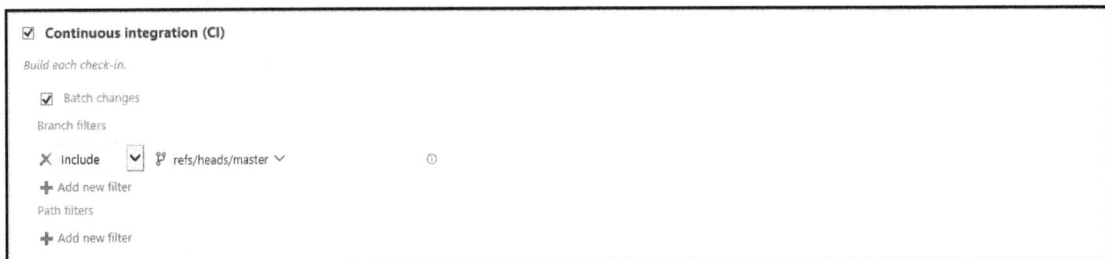

Figure 3: Sample continuous integration build pipeline

Batch changes in the preceding screenshot show an option used to sequence the execution of build definitions. This option batches all changes from developers into a single trigger and executes the build pipeline as soon as the previous build execution finishes. If this option is not checked, a build will be triggered for each check-in made by the developers.

Gated builds

Gated builds take a pessimist view of the check-in done by the developer. They allow the developer to check-in the code change into a repository only after the build is successful. If the build fails, the check-in is rejected. Gated builds can be configured through branch policies of a repository branch. This is not configured for the sample project.

Integration with source code configuration management

Build pipelines are generally integrated with source code repositories. In fact, integration between the source code repository and the build pipelines is an important automation aspect necessary for continuous integration to work seamlessly. The linking of a build definition with a repository is shown in the following screenshot. In our sample implementation, Git is chosen as the repository type. The user interface and options are different, depending on the repository type chosen. **Team Foundation Version Control (TFVC)** has different options compared to the ones shown in the screenshot. Other repository types include GitHub, subversion, and external GitHub. After choosing a repository type, a valid repository must be chosen. It is to be noted that multiple repositories can coexist within a VSTS project. A repository can host multiple branches, and an appropriate branch should be chosen to work along with build execution.

Label sources help in providing a unique label to the source code for identifying them after the build is complete. On selection of either **On successful build** or **On every build**, the label format text box appears. The label decides the naming convention for the source code identifier. Modules, LFS, sync, and shallow fetch are Git-specific concepts that are beyond the scope of this book. The **Clean options** removes untracked files and branches from the repository.

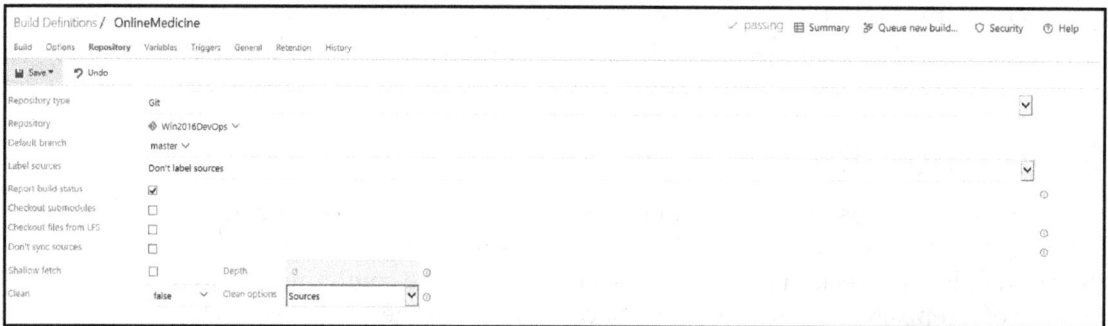

Figure 4: Integration with source code repository branch

Integration with work item management

Build pipeline can be integrated with VSTS work item management. This helps in opening a new bug or a work item when the build execution fails and assigning it to the requestor or developer who initiated the build by pushing his code to the repository. This is shown in the following screenshot. In this example, a **Bug** work item **Type** is created and assigned to the requestor. There are additional fields holding name value pairs that can also be filled while creating the work item:

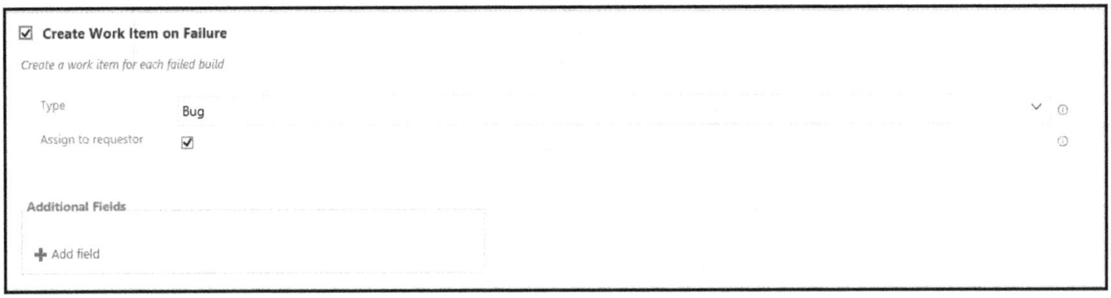

Figure 5: Integration with project work items

Build definition

VSTS provides an intuitive user interface for defining and building build definitions. A build definition comprises discrete individual steps and activities, and they together form the build process. Each project and solution has its unique requirements of the build process. Continuous integration does not provide any specification regarding what goes into a build pipeline. Continuous integration states that for it to be effective, it should have steps to ensure that the code can be compiled and its features and functionality can be tested. A build process for our Online Medicine sample application is shown here. This build pipeline comprises getting the latest version of code immediately after a developer checks-in the code, compiling code and generating binaries, executing unit tests and code coverage on the generated assembles, naming and versioning the build execution, and finally dropping the build artifacts to a location from where the release pipeline can pick and use them for provisioning the infrastructure and deploying the application. It is to be noted that there is a general tendency of provisioning and configuring a test environment and performing integration tests on it before finishing the execution of the build pipeline. Even the sample build pipeline in context could have been implemented the same way.

However, they are purposefully moved to the release pipeline (discussed in the next chapter) so that the build pipeline can be executed faster and provide feedback to the developer faster. It is at your discretion to implement the provisioning of the test environment and deploy the application in the build pipeline based on your project needs.

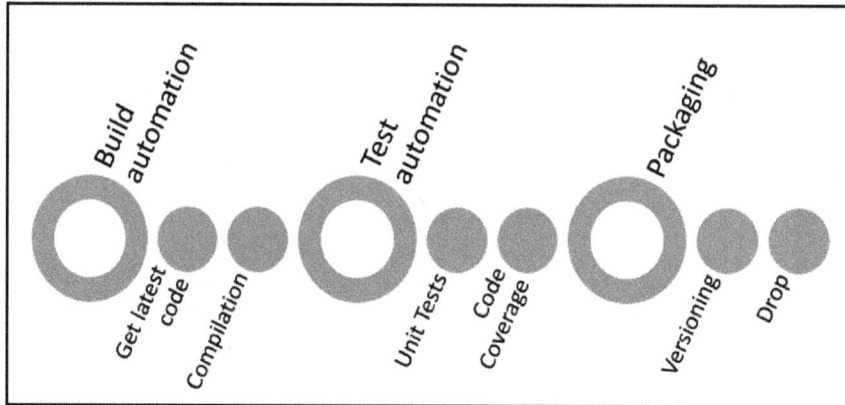

Figure 6: Build pipeline for Online Medicine sample application

Next, we will delve deeper in the configuration of the sample build pipeline for our Online Medicine sample application.

Defining variables

Variables help define common data elements reused at multiple places within the build definition. Also, changing its value can help update all the places it is used. Two variables, **Buildplatform** and **BuildConfiguration**, are defined for the Online Medicine build definition, and they are shown in the following screenshot. These variables are used while configuring build activities. Variables are defined by providing a name and value to it. The variable is referred by its name and has a default value. The default value can be overridden when starting a new execution of the build definition. There is also a lock icon against each variable. Selecting the lock icon will mask the value, and the value will not be visible on the user interface:

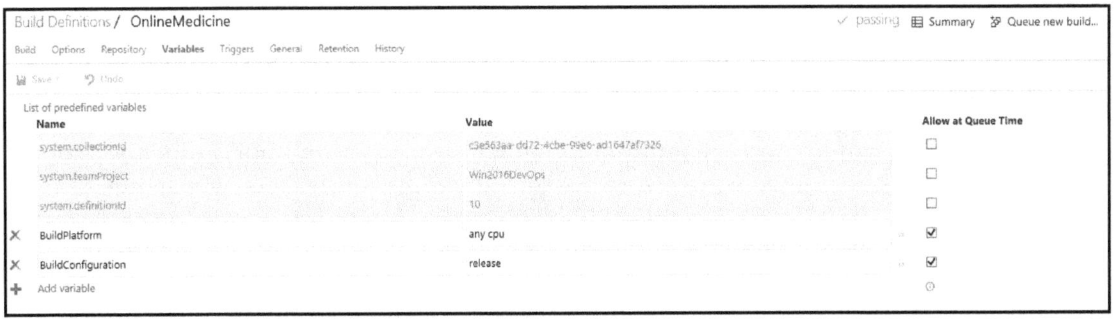

Figure 7: Online Medicine build definition variables

Build activities

This is a core and major part of the build definition where all the activities are defined and configured. The build activities are available from the **Build** tab of the build definition. It is these activities that are executed when a build pipeline is executed. These activities are executed in sequence and are responsible for performing a single functionality. Every build activity has four common properties as shown here:

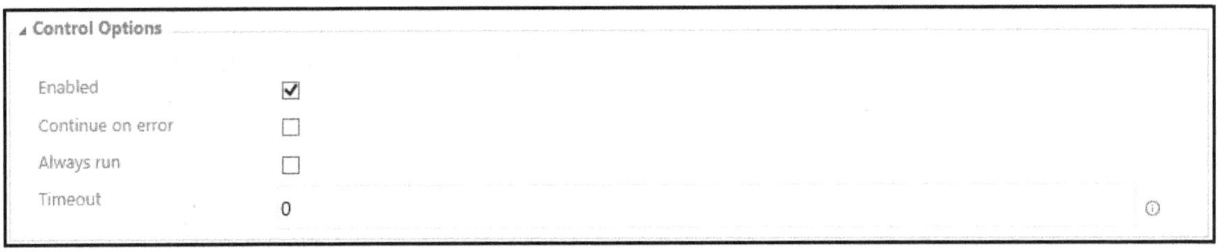

Figure 8: Common properties of activities

The **Enabled** property determines whether the activity will participate when the build definition is executed. This property becomes quite useful while building and testing the build definition.

The **Continue on error** property determines whether the activity and build pipeline should continue executing even if there are errors in executing this activity. The next activity will execute even when the activity in context fails. This property should remain unchecked as a best practice. If it is checked, it might provide unpredictable results during execution.

The **Always run** property ensures that the activity in context is executed even if the build fails.

The **Timeout** property determines the time lapse after which the activity will time out and throw an error. The default value of **0** means there is no timeout, and the activity will wait indefinitely for its completion.

The screenshot that follows shows the build activities for the Online Medicine build definition. It comprises of seven discrete steps, which are explained here:

1. The **NuGet installer** activity is for downloading and installing dependent binaries and executables.
2. The **Visual Studio Build** activity is for building and compiling the Online Medicine sample application project.
3. The **Visual Studio Build** activity is for building and compiling the Online Medicine unit tests project.
4. The **Visual Studio Test** activity is for executing unit tests on binaries generated on step 2. This step also performs the code coverage aspect of the application life cycle.
5. The **Replace Tokens** activity replaces the website name from `SetParameters.xml` used during the release pipeline. Here, the tokens are replaced and stored in the `SetParameters.xml` file.

6. The **Archive Files** activity is for generating the `deployment.zip` file needed during the release management.

7. The **Copy and Publish Build Artifacts** the source code and build artifacts, including the `deployment.zip` file, so that the release pipelines can pick them for provisioning and configuration of both the environment and the application.

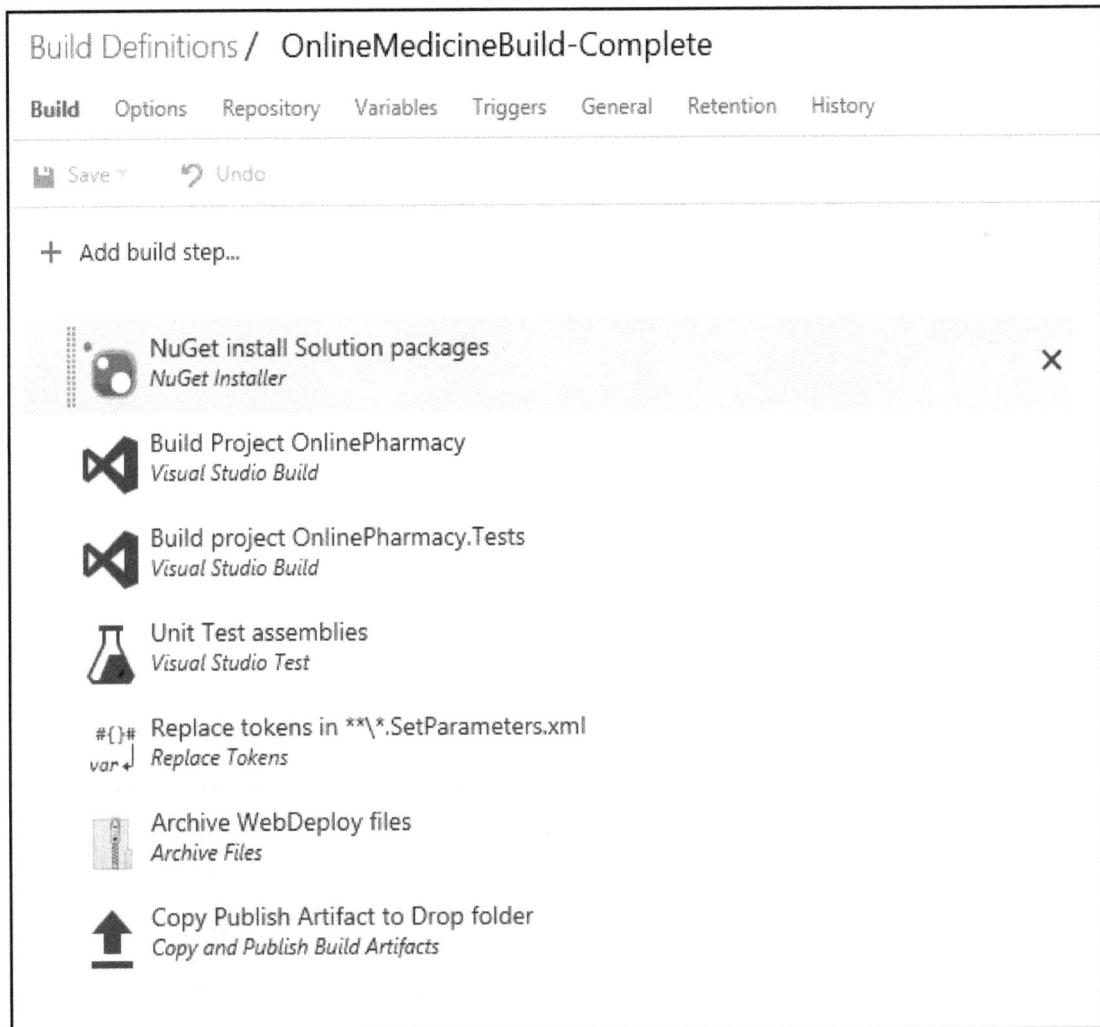

Build Definitions / OnlineMedicineBuild-Complete

Build   Options   Repository   Variables   Triggers   General   Retention   History

Save ▾   ⟲ Undo

+ Add build step...

NuGet install Solution packages
NuGet Installer   ✕

Build Project OnlinePharmacy
Visual Studio Build

Build project OnlinePharmacy.Tests
Visual Studio Build

Unit Test assemblies
Visual Studio Test

Replace tokens in ***.SetParameters.xml
Replace Tokens

Archive WebDeploy files
Archive Files

Copy Publish Artifact to Drop folder
Copy and Publish Build Artifacts

Figure 9: Online Medicine build definition

NuGet installer activity

The Online Medicine project is dependent on assemblies that are available through NuGet packages. These packages might not be available on the build server, so it is a good practise to add this activity before any build and test activity for installing dependencies.

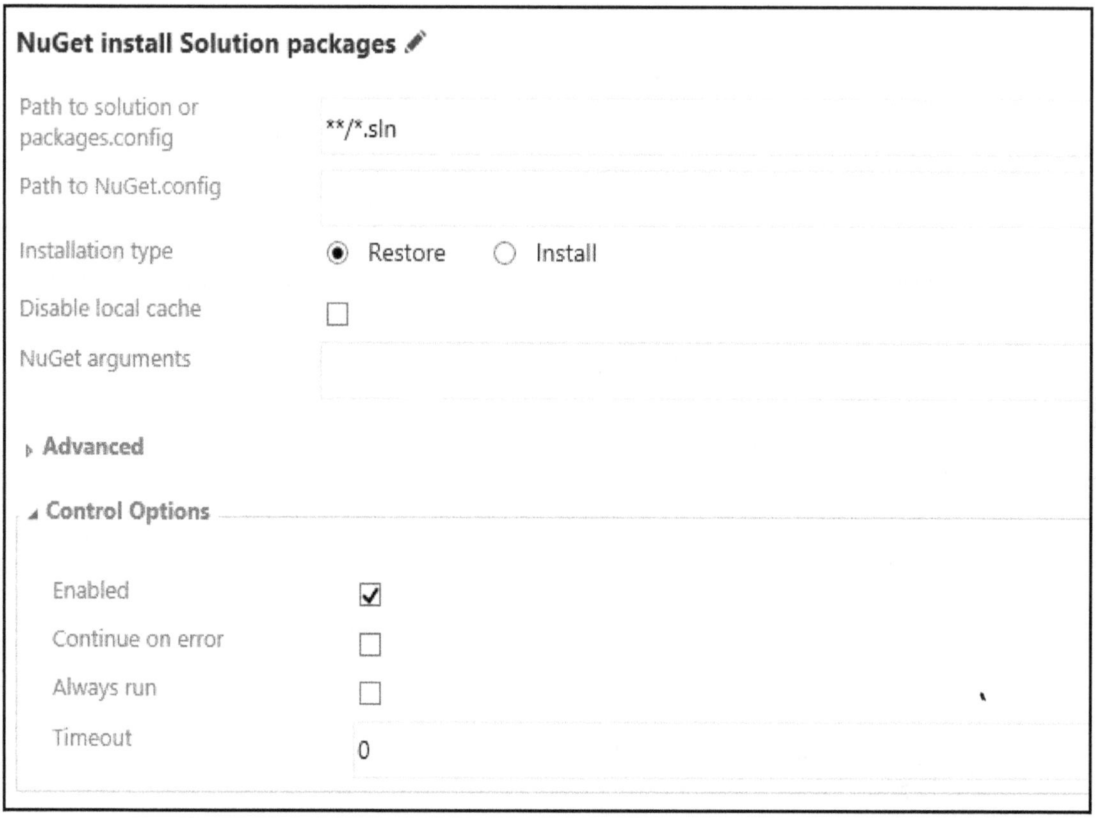

NuGet install Solution packages ✎

Path to solution or packages.config	**/*.sln
Path to NuGet.config	
Installation type	⦿ Restore ◯ Install
Disable local cache	☐
NuGet arguments	

▸ **Advanced**

◢ **Control Options**

Enabled	☑
Continue on error	☐
Always run	☐
Timeout	0

Figure 10: NuGet package install activity

In the preceding screenshot, the path to the solution file is provided in the **Path to solution or packages.config** text box using wildcard characters. The ****/*/.sln** characters here mean all solution files available in the current branch of the current repository. The **Installation type** is **Restore**, and the rest of the configuration options are left with their default settings.

Visual Studio Build activity for the OnlinePharmacy project

The Visual Studio Build activity helps in compiling the solution and its constituent projects. The solution property can take the path to the solution file or project file. The path can use wildcard characters to refer to multiple or exact matches. Since there are three projects in the OnlinePharmacy solution and the OnlinePharmacy.Configuration project should not be compiled, individual projects are used for compiling and building them. The solution path refers to the OnlinePharmacy project file containing the ASP.NET MVC web application.

Just to recall from the Chapter 7, *Configuration Management*, the web application binaries were archived in a ZIP file. This ZIP file contains web application binaries in the form of webdeploy packages. The command used to generate webdeploy packages within the Deployment folder is shown here, and they are the arguments provided to the **MSBuild** arguments. The webdeploy packages are generated and stored in the Deployment folder as denoted by the PackageLocation parameter:

```
/p:Configuration=Release /p:DeployOnBuild=true /p:DeployTarget=Package
/p:PackageLocation="./Deployment";PublishProfile=Release
```

Setting up **Clean** to true is like rebuilding the entire source code, while setting it up to false means an incremental build. It is set to be true, which will rebuild the entire project every time the build pipeline executes. The build configuration for the `OnlinePharmacy` project is shown here:

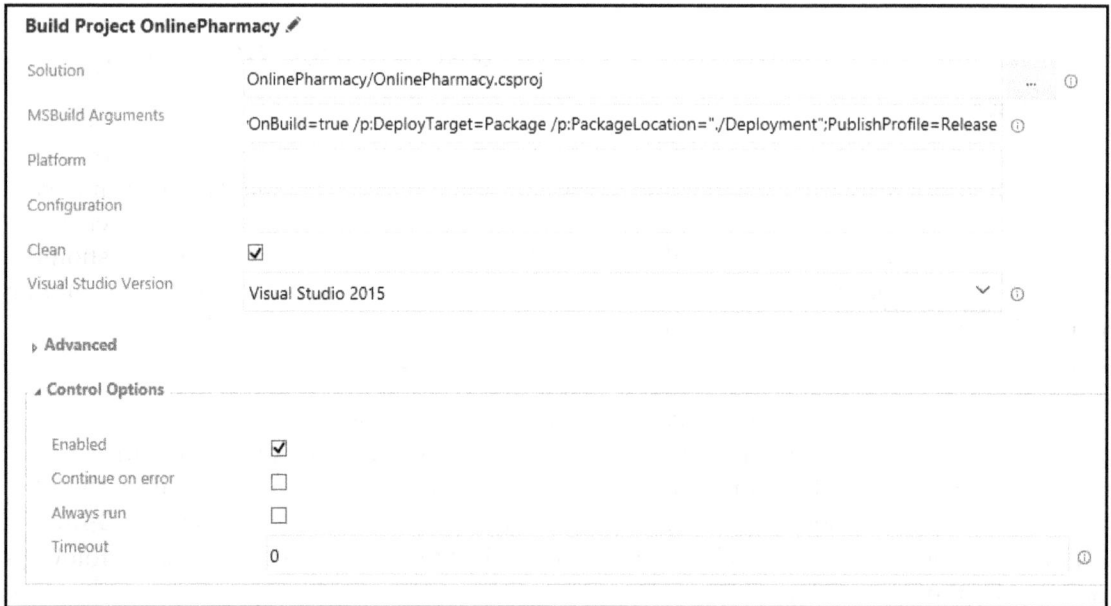

Build Project OnlinePharmacy 🖉

Solution	OnlinePharmacy/OnlinePharmacy.csproj
MSBuild Arguments	`OnBuild=true /p:DeployTarget=Package /p:PackageLocation="./Deployment";PublishProfile=Release`
Platform	
Configuration	
Clean	☑
Visual Studio Version	Visual Studio 2015

▸ **Advanced**

▴ **Control Options**

Enabled	☑
Continue on error	☐
Always run	☐
Timeout	0

Figure 11: Visual Studio Build activity to build Online Medicine web application

Visual Studio Build activity for the OnlinePharmacy test project

This activity is similar to the previous Visual Studio Build activity for the `OnlinePharmacy` project activity. However, in this step, instead of compiling the `OnlinePharmacy` project, the `OnlinePharmacy.Tests` project file is compiled. This project is related to uniting testing of the web application. The path of the project is provided to the solution property. There are no MSBuild arguments, and the rest of the property is blank or has default values. This is shown here:

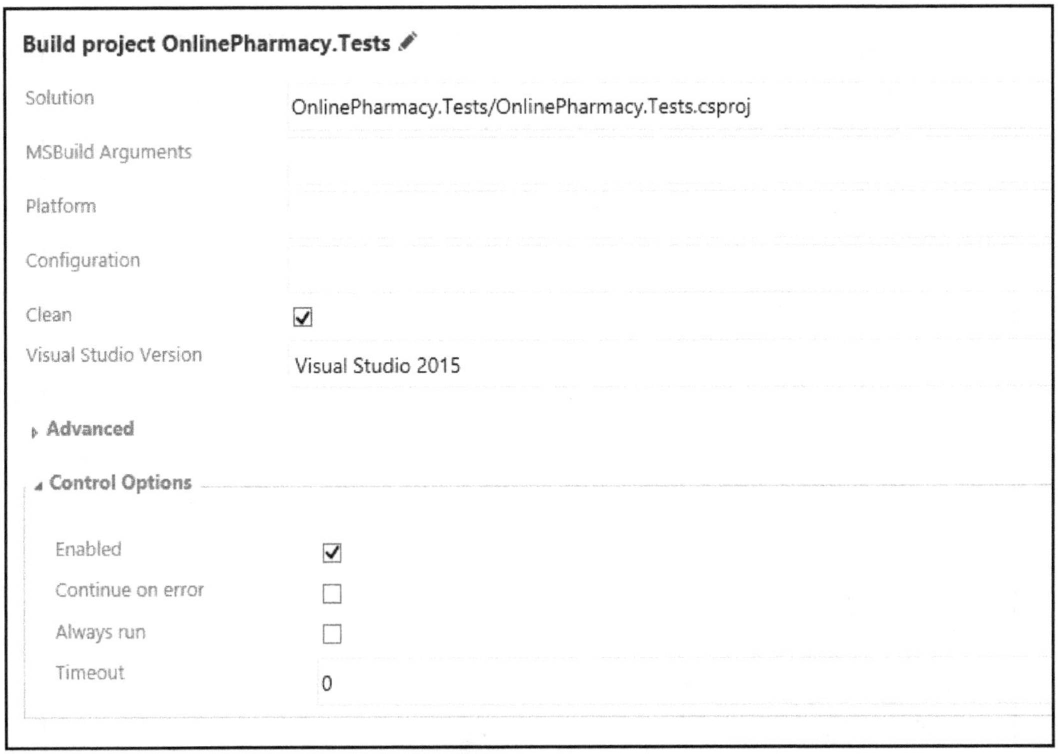

Build project OnlinePharmacy.Tests ✎	
Solution	OnlinePharmacy.Tests/OnlinePharmacy.Tests.csproj
MSBuild Arguments	
Platform	
Configuration	
Clean	☑
Visual Studio Version	Visual Studio 2015
▸ **Advanced**	
◢ **Control Options**	
Enabled	☑
Continue on error	☐
Always run	☐
Timeout	0

Figure 12: Visual Studio Build activity to build Online Medicine unit tests project

The Visual Studio Test activity for OnlinePharmacy project binaries

The Visual Studio Test activity, as shown in the following screenshot, is used to execute test cases available by compiling the unit tests project. These tests are executed on assemblies generated from compiling the `OnlinePharmacy` project. The **Code Coverage Enabled** checkbox is enabled, denoting that code coverage will also be performed along with unit tests. All other properties are either blank or with their default values. It is important to note that **Continue on error** is not checked for this activity. It means that the build execution will fail even when a single unit test fails:

Unit Test assemblies ✏

▲ **Execution Options**

Test Assembly	`**\*tests*.dll;-:**\obj\**`
Test Filter criteria	
Run Settings File	
Override TestRun Parameters	
Code Coverage Enabled	☑
Run In Parallel	☐

▸ **Advanced Execution Options**

▸ **Reporting Options**

▲ **Control Options**

Enabled	☑
Continue on error	☐
Always run	☐
Timeout	0

Figure 13: Visual Studio Test activity for executing unit tests and code coverage

Replace Tokens activity for updating the web application's name

The Online Medicine web application is packaged as a webdeploy package. The default value of the website in the webdeploy package's Setparameter.xml file is default web application. However, the sample application is deployed in a web application named **MVCWebApp**. MVCWebApp represents a web application with an **Internet Information Server (IIS)**. The idea behind Replace Tokens is to make the IIS website name dynamic, which can be determined at runtime. In this case, it happens to be MVCWebApp and could be anything depending on the name of the web application hosting the sample application. The Replace Tokens activity helps in replacing the name of the web application from the SetParameters.xml web deploy file to reflect the actual website that exists within the sample application environment IIS installation. The following screenshot shows that the SetParameters.xml file is represented as **Target files** within the deployment **Root directory**. The SetParameters.xml file has tokenized data represented with the #{ prefix and }# suffix. The rest of the configuration is either blank or default:

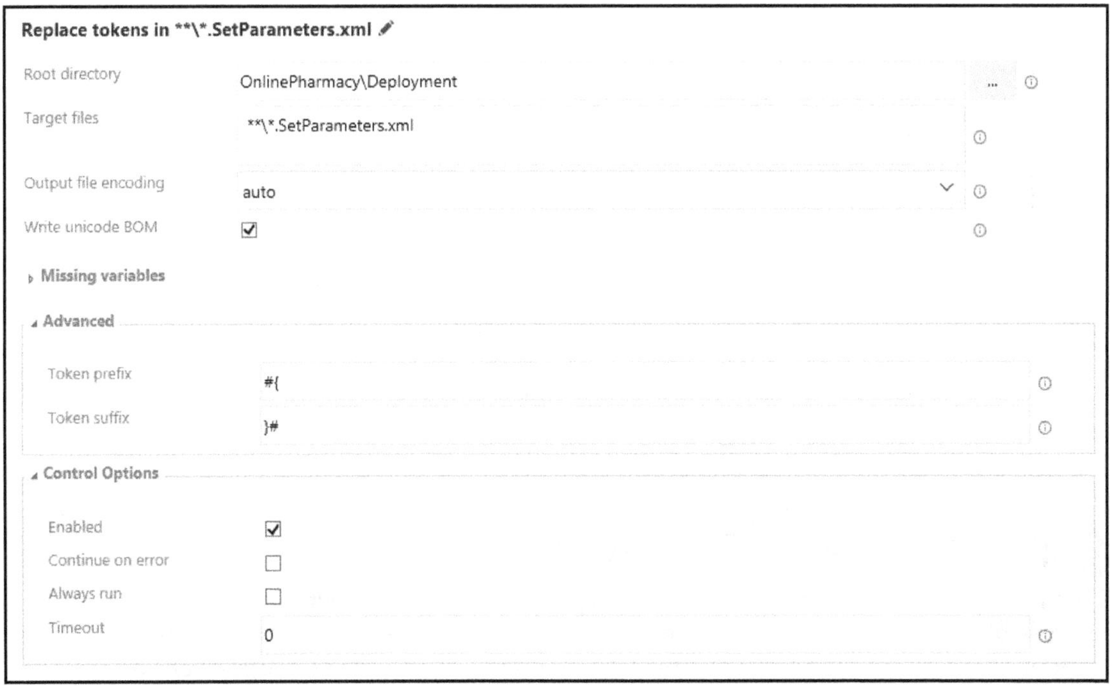

Replace tokens in ***.SetParameters.xml	
Root directory	OnlinePharmacy\Deployment
Target files	***.SetParameters.xml
Output file encoding	auto
Write unicode BOM	☑
▸ Missing variables	
⊿ Advanced	
Token prefix	#{
Token suffix	}#
⊿ Control Options	
Enabled	☑
Continue on error	☐
Always run	☐
Timeout	0

Figure 14: Replace token activity for replacing website name in webdeploy package

Archive Files activity for deployment.zip

The Archive Files activity helps in generating archive files. These files can have .zip, .7z, .tar, and .wim as extensions. As shown in the following screenshot, the newly generated `Deployment` folder by the Visual Studio build activity for the `OnlinePharmacy` project activity containing the `webdeploy` package is used as the `root` folder to archive. The archive type is the ZIP file. The output ZIP file is named as `deployment.zip` and would replace the file, if it already exists:

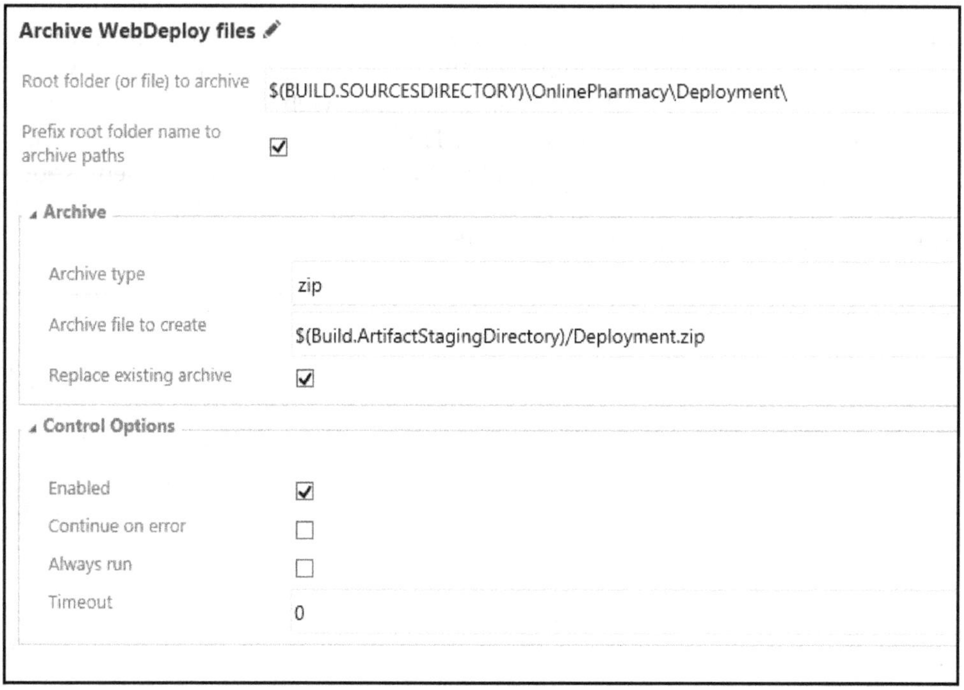

Figure 15: Archive activity to zip web deploy package

Copy and Publish Build Artifacts activity

Finally, once the main web application project and unit test project are compiled and built successfully, the unit tests and code coverage are executed on generated assemblies and `webdeploy` packages are packaged into the archive file. It's time to drop the entire code base along with the generated artifacts to a drop location. This is achieved using the Copy and Publish Artifacts activity.

This activity accepts a source `root` folder; in this case, it is empty, as shown in the following screenshot. An empty copy root means copy everything from the root folder recursively. The **Contents** property is configured with wildcard characters. The name of the folder is `Drop`, which could be any string value in this case. All files within this `Drop` folder are available and accessible to the release pipeline:

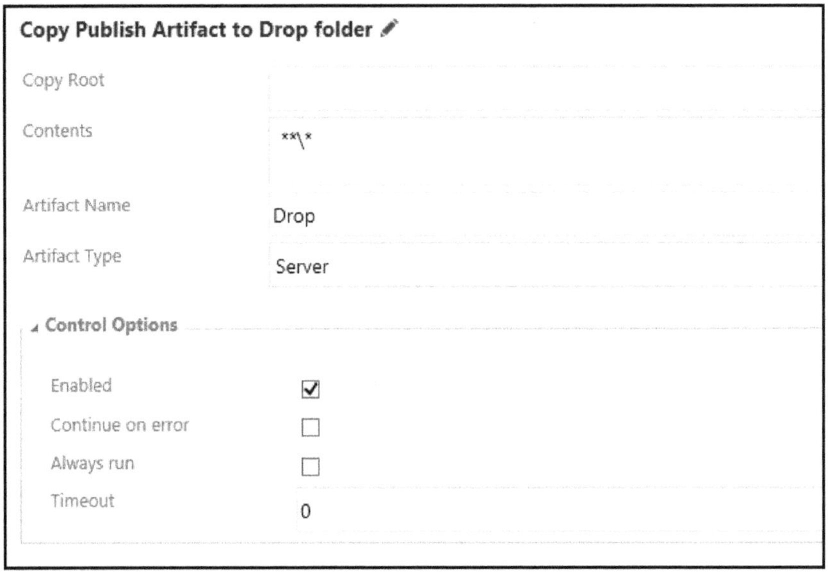

Copy Publish Artifact to Drop folder ✏

Copy Root	
Contents	***
Artifact Name	Drop
Artifact Type	Server

▴ **Control Options**

Enabled	☑
Continue on error	☐
Always run	☐
Timeout	0

Figure 16: Copy and Publish activity for code drop

Build options

The **Options** tab provides the ability to configure different aspects of execution of the build definition.

Generally, there is more than one project build configuration, that is, debug and release. Also, there is more than a single target platform, that is, x86 and x64. The build pipeline can be executed in various combinations of build configuration and target platforms. When selected, it accepts comma-separated values. Since we are building for any CPU type with only release build configuration, **BuildPlatform** and **Buildconfiguration** variables are reused here to refer to any CPU and release configuration. These build definitions for such combinations can run in parallel, depending on whether the parallel box is checked.

We have already discussed the configuration related to creating a work item when the build execution fails, as shown in the following screenshot.

The sample build definition does not utilize the **Allow Scripts to Access OAuth Token** configuration. This configuration should be selected if your scripts needs to access the VSTS API using the build process OAuth token:

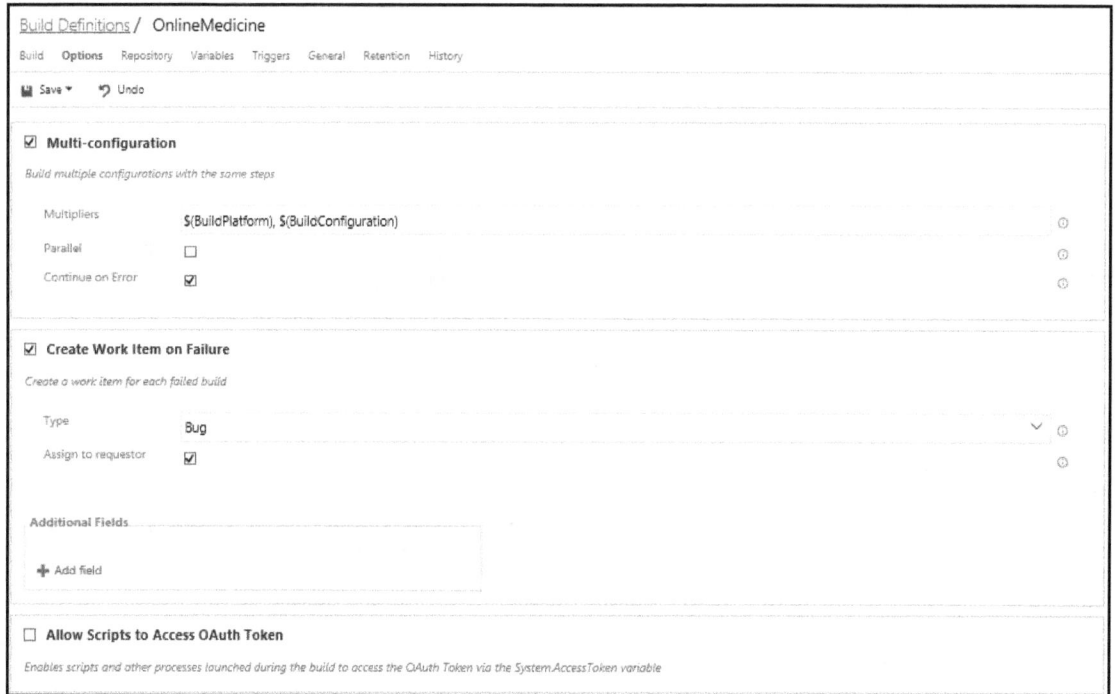

Figure 17: Options tab of build definition

Repository

The repository configuration for the sample build configuration is shown here. The details of the repository were explained in the previous section of this chapter.

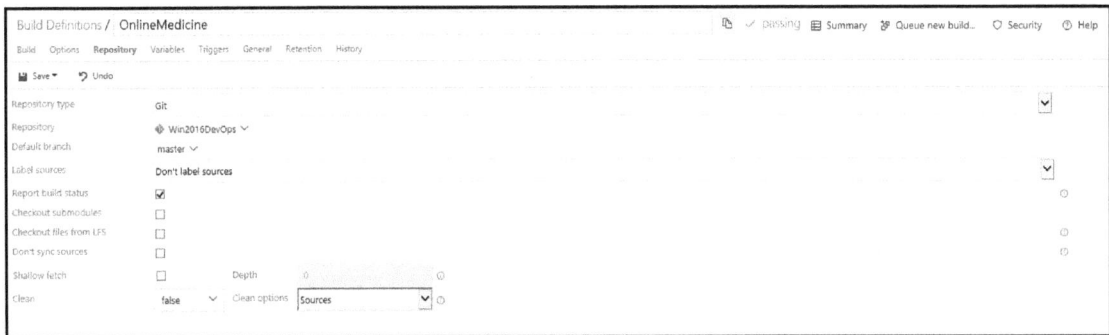

Figure 18: Repository tab of build definition

Triggers

Triggers were discussed earlier in the previous section of this chapter. The configuration of the Online Medicine build definition trigger for the Online Medicine sample application is shown next. For our build definition, both continuous and scheduled builds have been selected with the Master branch of our repository. Also, the scheduled build is supposed to run every day at 3.00 a.m. UST apart from weekends.

The time represents project-specific attributes where none of the developers would be working on the shared repository.

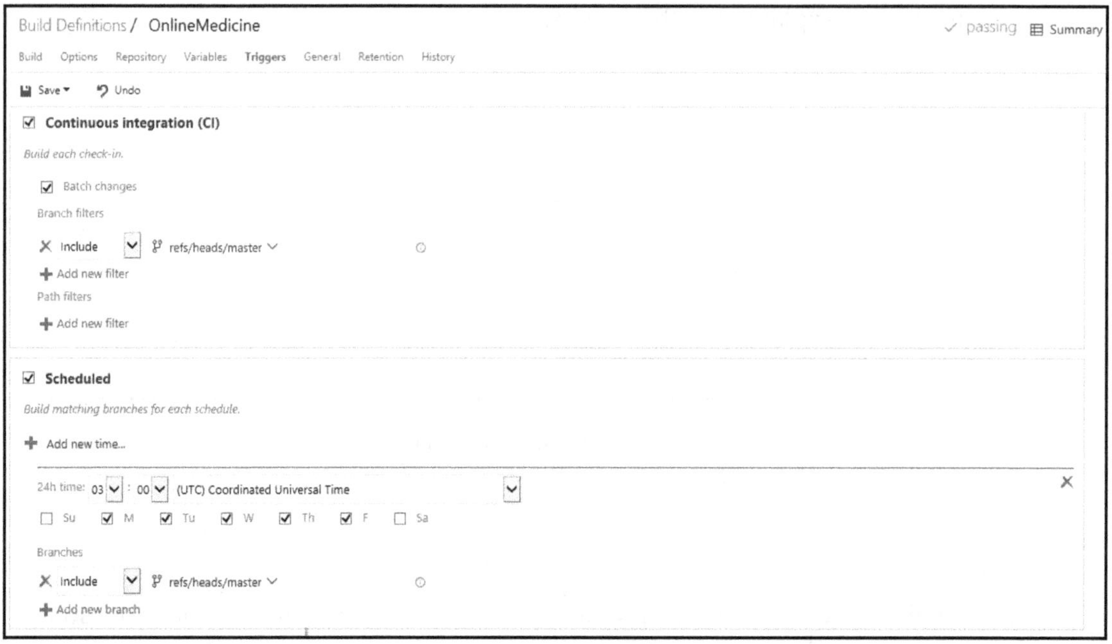

Figure 19: Triggers tab of build definition

General, retention, and history

The **General** tab in the following screenshot helps in configuring general build pipeline execution settings.

As we saw in `Chapter 2`, *DevOps Tools and Technologies*, the build pipelines can be executed on VSTS-provided servers as well as on project-provided servers. There can be multiple queues, each attached to different types of build servers. The **Default agent queue** helps in configuring the default queue to use when executing the build pipeline. This setting can be overridden when executing the build pipeline manually. In this case, we are using the **Hosted** option, which executes the build pipeline on VSTS-provided servers.

Description allows is to enter a description for the build definition and it is visible in the build status.

Build job authorization scope helps in defining and restricting access to a current project or **Project Collection**.

Every build pipeline execution gets a build label. The format for this is determined by VSTS when the **Build number format** is empty. The **Build number format** for the sample build definition is defined using variables having the project name, build definition name, branch name, the data of executing the pipeline, and the number of times the build has executed on the current date.

The **Build job timeout in minutes** setting determines the time lapse in minutes before the build fails.

If the status of build executions is required to be shown in external websites, the **Badge enabled** option can be selected, which will provide a URL that can be consumed. The format of the URL is like this:

https://desiredstate.visualstudio.com/_apis/public/build/definitions/576aa4ac-900c-417a-ae45-89abf7 cc26b4/10/badge

Figure 20: General tab of build definition

VSTS generates and stores a lot of data and information with every build. This includes build labels, reports, symbols, and logs. Retention refers to policies containing rules. Each rule defines the type of artifacts to be stored based on the number of days and number of builds. Proper retention policy will ensure that there is no unnecessary storage requirement. Rules are evaluated in order, from top to bottom. Rules are composed of a combination of days to keep and a minimum number of builds to keep. More restrictive rules should be placed above the more general purpose rules. For the sample build definition and project, the defaults have been used for retention configuration, as shown here:

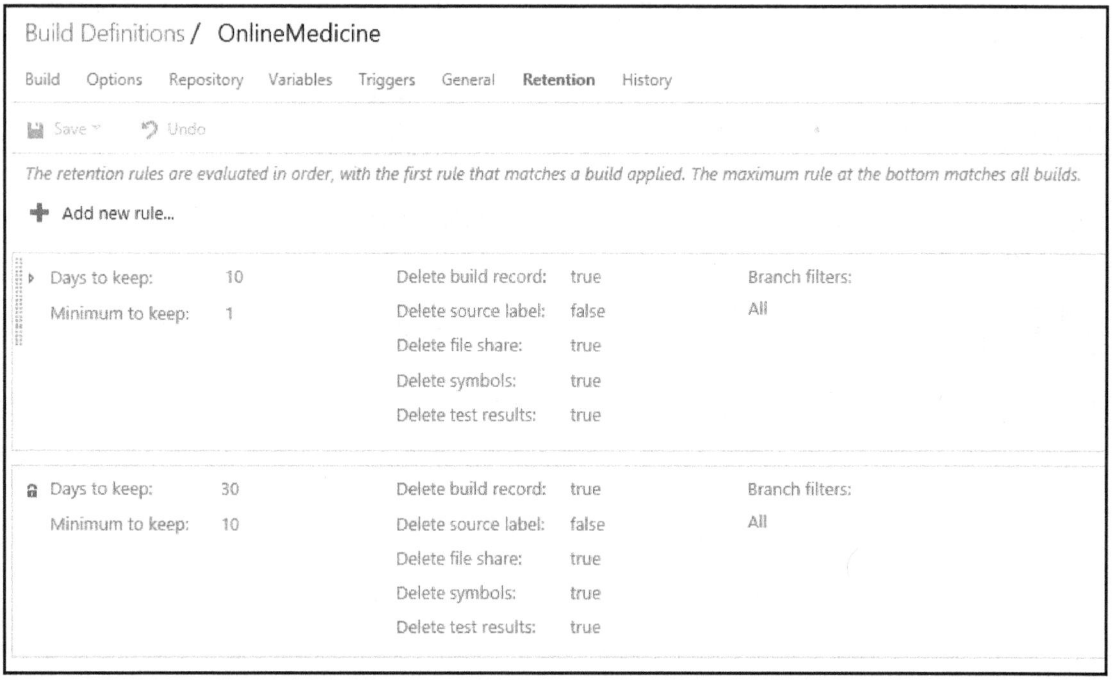

Build Definitions / OnlineMedicine			
Build Options Repository Variables Triggers General **Retention** History			

Save ▾   Undo

The retention rules are evaluated in order, with the first rule that matches a build applied. The maximum rule at the bottom matches all builds.

➕ Add new rule...

▸ Days to keep:	10	Delete build record:	true	Branch filters:
Minimum to keep:	1	Delete source label:	false	All
		Delete file share:	true	
		Delete symbols:	true	
		Delete test results:	true	

🔒 Days to keep:	30	Delete build record:	true	Branch filters:
Minimum to keep:	10	Delete source label:	false	All
		Delete file share:	true	
		Delete symbols:	true	
		Delete test results:	true	

* Figure 21: Retention tab of build definition

VSTS provides version control for build definitions as well. It means any changes, modification, and updates to the build definition itself are recorded in VSTS, providing a completely different history since the build definition was initially created. This is a very useful feature as it allows for comparison of build definitions between multiple changes and allows to reconcile the changes. The **Diff** button on the top menu helps in comparing two versions of the same build definition after selecting them from the list. This is shown here:

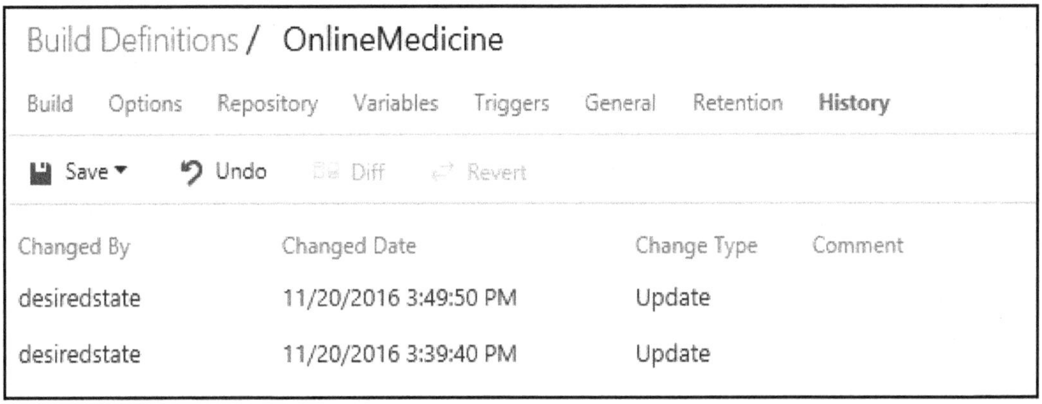

Build Definitions / OnlineMedicine								
Build	Options	Repository	Variables	Triggers	General	Retention	**History**	

💾 Save ▾	🔁 Undo	Diff	⤾ Revert	

Changed By	Changed Date	Change Type	Comment
desiredstate	11/20/2016 3:49:50 PM	Update	
desiredstate	11/20/2016 3:39:40 PM	Update	

Figure 22: History tab of build definition

Build pipeline execution

There are multiple places from where build definitions can be executed manually in VSTS. In this section, a couple of different ways are explained for executing a build definition.

Build definitions can be executed using the context menu available against each build definition, as show here:

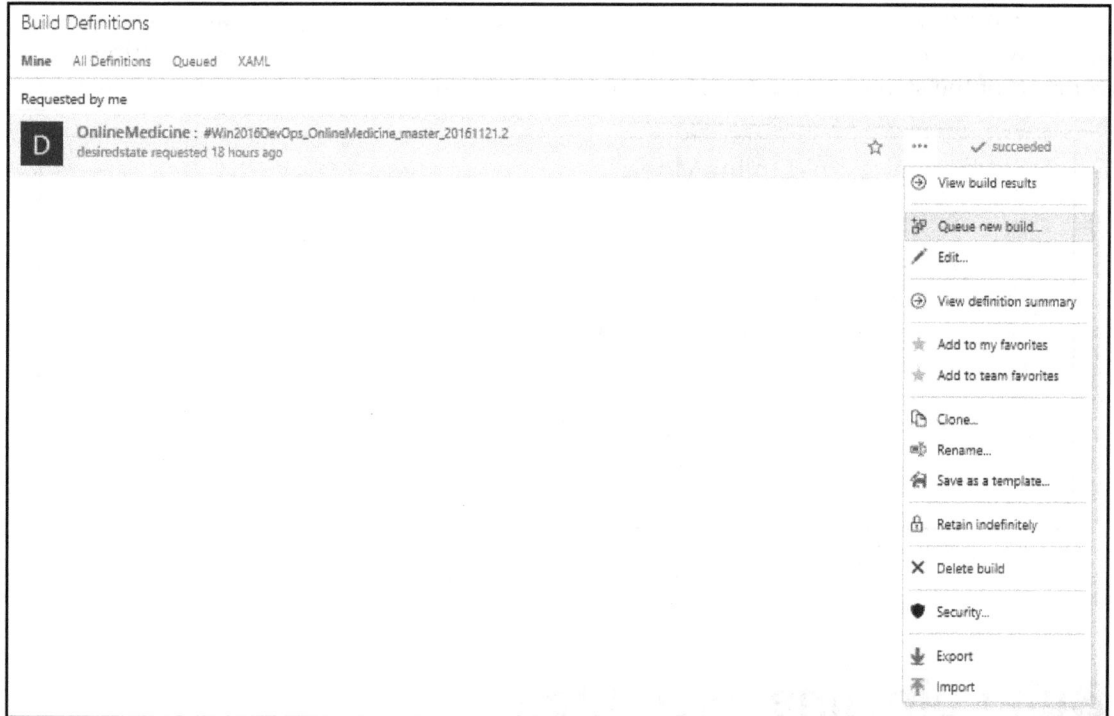

Figure 23: Queuing a build definition

If the build definition is in the edit mode, it can be executed by clicking on the **Queue new build** button in the top-right corner of the screen, as shown here:

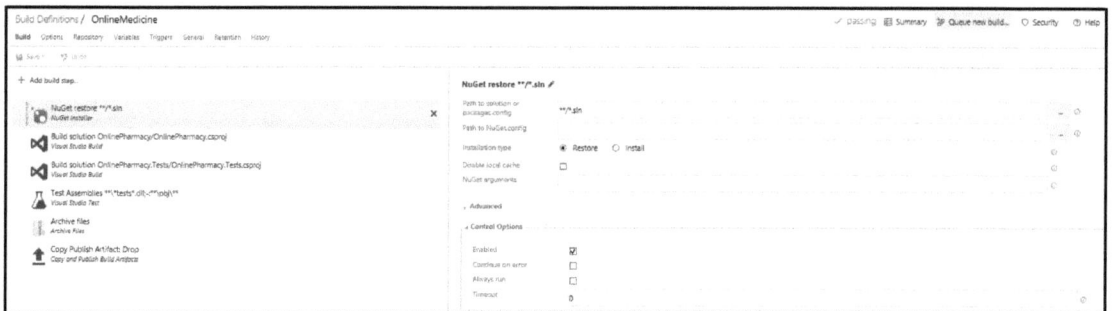

Figure 24: Another way to queue build definition

The build progress can be viewed in the console window. This is shown in the following screenshot. Here, the left pane shows the execution of all activities available in the build definition that are in the enabled state. The right pane shows the log messages from activities about their progress and status. Any message in red color denotes failure, while green color means success:

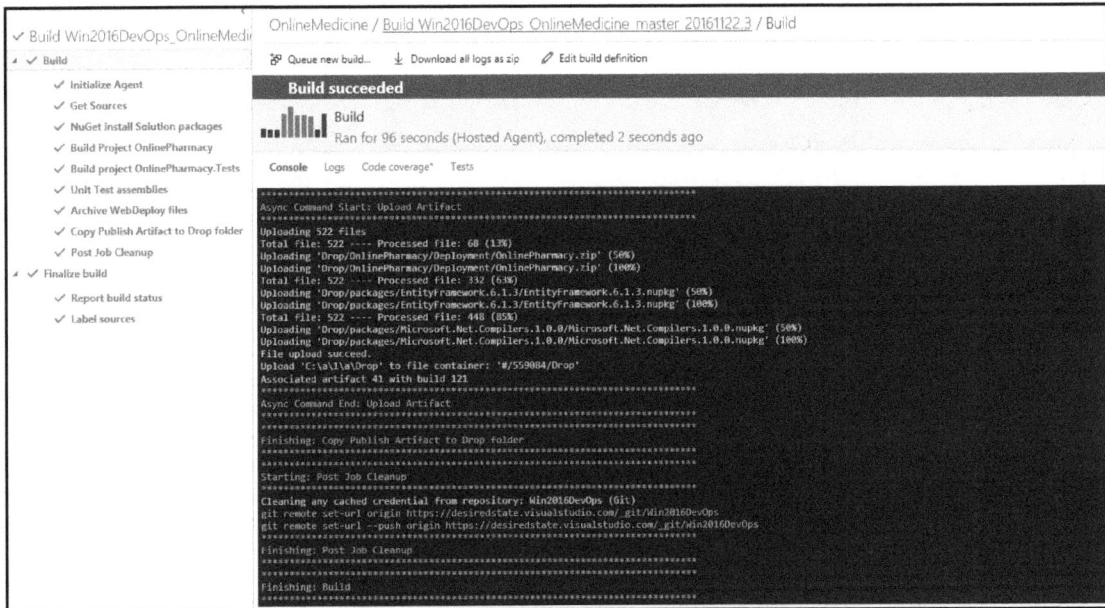

Figure 25: Build execution progress and logs

Summary

This chapter introduced continuous integration, its importance, and benefits, and also discussed in detail some of its important principles. Continuous integration is an evolution from manual processes for building and testing to automated delivery of code and artifacts to environments. It's a mechanism to tell developers about issues arising out of their code and helps in detecting failures earlier than later. A discussion on continuous integration cannot be complete without a discussion about build definitions and pipelines. Build pipelines are automation in application life cycle management. VSTS is the platform used for implementing continuous integration and build pipelines. Different types of build definitions, such as continuous and scheduled builds, were discussed, along with their integration to project work items and the source code repository.

Finally, the chapter explained the sample build definitions created for the Online Medicine sample application, along with their configuration and individual steps. These build activities are the main workhorse for getting the job of continuous integration done. Subsequently, continuous integration should be followed by continuous deployment and delivery. The next chapter will focus on continuous delivery and deployment, which uses the concepts of release pipelines and configuration management shown in the previous chapter.

10
Continuous Delivery and Deployment

The previous chapters have discussed in detail the major practices related to DevOps. The practices covered were configuration management and continuous integration. This chapter will discuss at length the concepts, principles, importance, strategies, and implementation related to continuous delivery and deployment. By the end of this chapter, we will have discussed in detail all the major DevOps practices with examples of their implementation.

Both continuous delivery and deployment DevOps practices are quite often used interchangeably, and the difference is not well understood by DevOps practitioners. However, there is a subtle difference between them. Readers should understand their differences and use them appropriately based on the context. The differences will become clear as we progress in this chapter.

However, before getting into the details about continuous delivery and deployment, it is important to understand the concept of release management and releases.

Understanding releases

In its simplest meaning, a release in software parlance means making software available to the end users. When a release is made, software features and functionality are made available to the end users for consumption. Releases are generally periodic in nature, and they can be done at any time–daily, weekly, monthly, yearly, or any combination of these depending on the nature of software, users, and value added into each release. A release consists of newer and updated functionality, completely tested and deployed on a production environment. Each release has a unique identifier through which it can be referred. A release is generally done on a production environment, but it can also involve deployment on multiple other environments such as test and staging. It depends on an organization as to how it would like to define a release along with the approval requirements. A release on any environment including a production environment involves getting approvals from stakeholders. Because every release involves multiple changes and bears the inherent risk of nonavailability and nonreliability of the application, every release demands approval from appropriate stakeholders and owners of the environments. Based on approvals, it is decided to release on environments. A release might consist of newer features or updates to existing features, bug fixes, or general improvements. With the majority of software getting developed using an agile application development life cycle, with each consisting of a small subset of features and functionality, there is a need for smaller, faster, and more frequent releases.

Release management

Release management refers to the process of managing releases. It involves planning, scheduling, controlling, and monitoring the complete application life cycle of software and ensuring that appropriate feedback is provided to stakeholders for effective decision making on pushing the release to production. It also involves deployment and configuration of both environments and applications. Multiple software changes are grouped together and referred collectively as a release. Stakeholders plan and decide which changes will be part of a release. They prioritize, schedule the release, and ensure that changes go through the quality gates before they are used on production. An agile application life cycle demands frequent releases, and release management ensures that release can be planned and executed frequently without risk. The adoption of agile practices without effective release management and frequent releases defeats the entire purpose of being agile. Release management helps in realizing the benefits of agile methodology. Release management is an integral component of both continuous delivery and deployment.

Continuous delivery

Continuous delivery is a DevOps practice. It refers to adopting the practice of generating quality application artifacts that are readily deployable in new or existing environments by executing quality checks on both the code and functionality by ensuring that the application meets both technical and functional specifications. Continuous delivery also ensures that the code in the main branch is always in a state that is readily deployable to any environment including a production environment. It helps in achieving a state that makes sure that the build and quality of software meets the specification and there are no surprises or risks in it being used for deployment to a production environment. It can also be referred as a state of readiness for the application code and configuration.

Application developers continually change code and to ensure that changes are acceptable only when they meet the functional and technical specification, they are deployed to an environment and successfully validated. If there are issues in build, deployment, and configuration of the environment and software, immediate feedback is provided to developers so that those issues can be fixed immediately.

Continuous deployment

Continuous deployment is a DevOps practice, and it refers to the practice of deployment of software artifacts to a new or existing production environment after ensuring that the application meets all the functional and technical requirements/specifications, deployed on multiple environments with no major issues or bugs. The definition is very similar to continuous delivery; however, an astute reader should have figured out that continuous deployment refers to the deployment and configuration of the environment and software on the production environment. Although continuous delivery is about being ready with regard to the application and environment by deploying the application on multiple environments, continuous deployment is about ensuring that the same artifacts are used for the production environment. The beauty of continuous deployment can be appreciated when a single change in the code is reflected on production after the changes undergo all the quality checks, are deployed and configured multiple times on different new as well as existing environments, executing automated code UI as well as performance tests, and finally executing operational validation on the production environment to verify that the application will act and behave as expected and end users are not surprised due to nonavailability, non-reliability, and reduced performance of the application. Deployment to production is dependent on approvals, and based on these approvals, releases are performed on production.

Some companies do not want to deploy on a production environment using automatic approvals. The stakeholders want to verify the release manually and ensure that deployment to production will not break the application, whereas others might want completely automated continuous deployment through automatic approvals. The decision to use manual approval viz-a-viz automatic approval depends on the maturity of the company, its people who are adopting DevOps practices, collaboration, technology adoption and implementation, robustness, and the completeness of the application life cycle. The stakeholders should have confidence that the application will continue to be operational even after the release and that the release can be rolled back to a previous stable release in case of an issue with the current release.

Why continuous delivery and deployment?

Software development is inherently a difficult exercise because it involves multiple processes, practices, and people. Some of the prominent reasons to adopt continuous delivery and deployment are mentioned next.

Detecting deployment issues early

As mentioned before, continuous delivery and deployment conduct frequent deployments to multiple environments. When a developer checks in their code, an automated build pipeline is executed, and after the build pipeline completes, deployment is conducted on a test environment where functional and technical verification and validation is performed. If there is any bug, error, or issue in deploying and configuring the environment and application, immediate feedback is provided to the developer informing about the failure. The developer can find the issue and fix it, thus ensuring that the release process does not fail and, at the same time, meets the functional correctness of the solution.

Eliminating surprises and risks

Continuous delivery and deployment ensure that the code in the repository branch can always be compiled, tested, and be ready for deployment to environments (including production). This entire process is automated, which brings standardization and consistency in the execution of the release pipeline. With such practices, surprises related to application and environment deployment and configuration on production can be reduced, and the entire deployment process can be made risk-free.

Reducing cost of change

Cost of change refers to time and effort invested to see a change on production. It also includes the time to resolve the issues arising due to releasing a change and bringing the production environment to a valid stable state. Automated continuous delivery and deployment eliminates or reduces manual tasks from the release process. This reduces both time and effort for moving changes to production. It also reduces bugs and issues in changes as both the code and its deployment process are verified on multiple environments before getting used on the production environment.

Pushing frequent changes to production

Continuous delivery and deployment deploys code on the environment whenever new packages are available from the continuous integration process. This ensures that code is verified against the deployment process and configuration whenever there is change in code. The resultant code is in a deployable state and can be pushed to production environments. This in turn helps in frequent releases on production while reducing the overall risks involved in a release.

Removing risky manual deployments

Manual environment provisioning and application deployment is a time-consuming, unpredictable, inconsistent and risky activity. It is highly error-prone when executed manually. The entire team is dependent on a couple of individuals being aware of conducting manual deployments. The steps are generally missed when performed manually, and the team gets into troubleshooting exercises. Sometimes, even the deployment documentation is also missing or not sufficient. Continuous deployment and delivery helps in complete automation of deployments on all environments.

Moving away from human dependency

It is better to write scripts and use them for deployment and configuration rather than doing it manually. However, the documentation to use the scripts are equally important, but they are generally missing. The scripts use different values for each environment and most often they are known to only a few members of the team. If there are multiple scripts, the complexity increases and the knowledge of ordering and sequencing becomes important for anyone conducting deployment. Continuous deployment and delivery help eliminate these issues using input values from configuration management tools and release pipeline variables. They also use automated processes rather than sequencing scripts manually. The entire release becomes process-dependent rather than human-dependent.

The principles of continuous deployment

Like continuous integration, continuous delivery and deployment is a culture, mindset, and guidance. It is based on adopting principles, which makes releasing applications and their life cycle efficient and effective. Some of the important principles are discussed next.

Automation as an enabler

It is difficult to achieve the benefits of continuous deployment and delivery when executed manually. It is important that automation is used to achieve their intent. Efforts should be made to automate every step and at the minimum should retrieve the artifacts generated by the build pipeline, execute deployment activities on multiple environments, and allow for the approval workflow before moving and deploying from one environment to another. There should be an automated release pipeline that has the capability of execution both on demand as well as based on triggers. It should also have the capability to execute release pipelines on the schedule. Furthermore, the activities in the release pipeline should have capabilities to deploy and configure both environments and the application. It should be able to perform the validation of environments and the application by executing operational validation tests. It should also provide feedback and deployment progress logs.

VSTS provides automation capabilities to define and author release pipelines/definitions as well as execute, manage, report, and monitor release executions. VSTS has very rich capabilities related to release management, including:

- Defining multiple release definitions/pipeline:
    - Variables for storing commonly used data
    - Release and deployment activities or steps for defining the pipeline
    - Releasing the pipeline to move context and data across release activities and steps
    - Defining multiple environments within each release definition
    - Each environment can have its own variables which not shared with other environments
    - Each environment has its own approval and deployment workflow
- Managing release pipeline definitions:
    - Cloning
    - Exporting a template
    - Editing definitions
    - Managing security for build definitions
    - Executing definitions
- Linking to the artifacts repository
- Executing the release pipeline
    - Manually
    - On schedule
    - Continuously because of changes in the code
- Generating a unique release label and identifiers
- The version control for release definitions
- Ability to execute release definitions on self-hosted servers as well as servers provided by VSTS

These are some of the rich capabilities provided by VSTS, and we will discuss them in detail later in this chapter. VSTS has many more automation capabilities, and they are getting continuously added on a regular basis. There is also a market place providing third-party activities that can be used within release pipelines.

Infrastructure as Code

While automation helps in bringing consistency and predictability, Infrastructure as Code helps in authoring declarative testable infrastructure scripts that are version controlled and these scripts are under the same application life cycle management process as the one that the application deploys. The scripts should execute unit and operational validation tests on the environment after the provisioning. This principle mandates that scripts and infrastructure configuration should be built and tested just like regular applications. It helps in increasing repeatability and testability of the environment.

Shortened execution time

Continuous deployment and delivery will be more highly effective if the release pipeline can complete its execution faster. This would decrease the deployment and provision time and provide immediate feedback to the developers about the quality of deployments. If the release pipeline takes hours or days to complete its process, then the entire purpose of continuous deployment and delivery gets defeated.

Reporting

Centralized reporting and feedback should be enabled and provided to both developers and management regarding the quality of the code, the execution of release pipelines, the number of release failures and successes, the root cause of release failures, and the logs from the release execution.

Secure deployments

Security plays an important role in continuous deployment and delivery. The release pipeline accesses the repository and executes its activities on a release server. The release server should not be accessible to anyone apart from the release service account. Every piece of data, credentials, and secrets should be encrypted. They should not be visible during both the design as well as runtime. The secrets should not even be visible in release logs. Appropriate policies, locks, and the compliance process should be enabled for secure deployments.

Continuous deployment process

Continuous deployment and delivery provides guidance about best practices and activities that should be executed in a typical release pipeline. However, it does not mandate any tool, utility, product, or service. It also does not provide any definite process that should be part of the release pipeline. It just says that there should be continuous deployment that should execute release pipeline because of the availability of newer packages.

However, as a practice, there are certain processes that are common across software development and should be used in almost every project. In this chapter, we used those to implement continuous deployment for the *Online Medicine* sample application. The process of continuous deployment is shown in *Figure 1*:

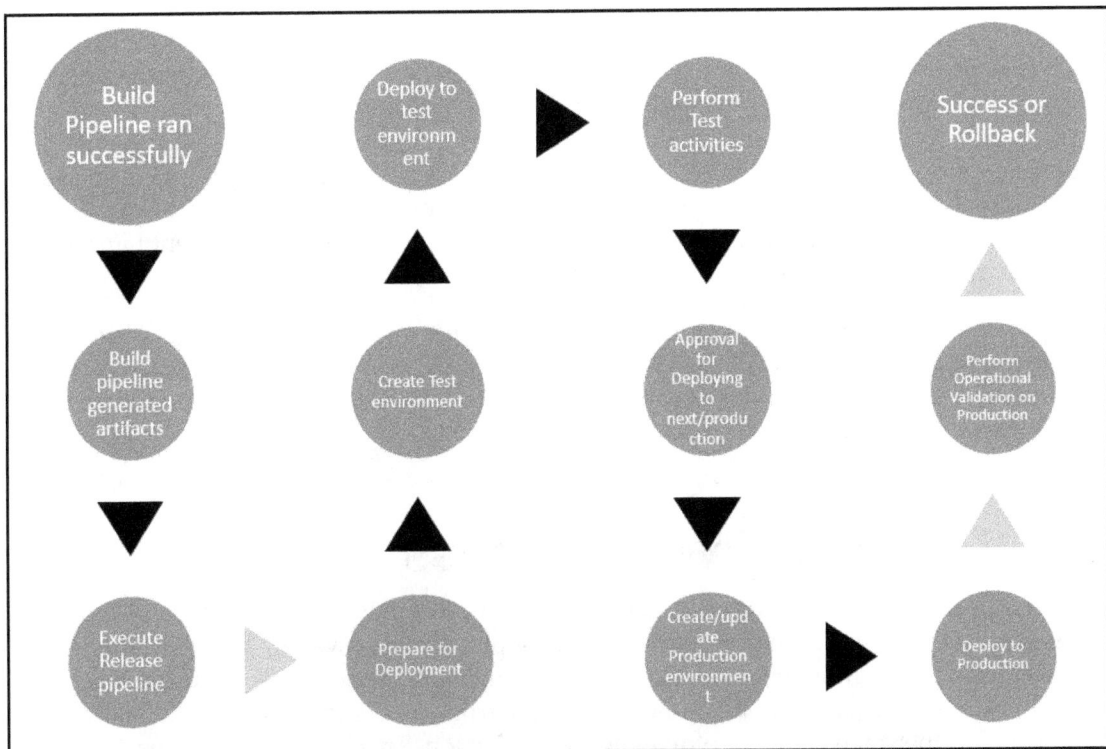

Figure 1: Sample continuous deployment process

The continuous deployment process in *Figure 1* is broken down in to 12 high-level steps. The sample continuous deployment process uses Azure as its target deployment platform.

A developer checks in or commits code into the repository. VSTS is the platform used for continuous deployment. It monitors the repository for any changes, executes the build pipeline, and generates build packages.

The release pipeline monitors the availability of new packages and starts executing the release pipeline associated with it. The release pipeline creates multiple environments for deployment. This includes executing scripts for uploading scripts and templates to Azure storage. Uploading scripts and template to storage helps with an easy distribution of scripts to virtual machines.

As part of the test environment, a test environment is provisioned and configured, an application is deployed and configured, and test activities are performed on application features and functionality. At the end, tests are executed on test environment to ensure that it is working as expected.

After ensuring that the deployment was satisfactory on the test environment, approvals are sought either automatically or manually to deploy into the next environment. The next environment could be any environment such as the staging environment, or it could be the production environment. No matter what environment it is, the steps remain the same as those executed for the test environment. Once they pass on this environment, the next environment is used for deployment. This process continues till the deployment happens on the production environment.

After deployment to production, operational validation tests are executed on production to ensure that application is working as desired and as expected. Based on the results of the operational validation, management and stakeholders can decide if they would like to accept the release or would roll back the same.

Continuous delivery process

Continuous delivery and continuous deployment go hand in hand together. Continuous delivery process is similar to that of continuous deployment; however, with the difference that it stops at deploying on an environment on which validation can be performed for both environment and application. It is conducted more from code and environment validation perspective rather than actual deployment on production. This is shown in *Figure 2*.

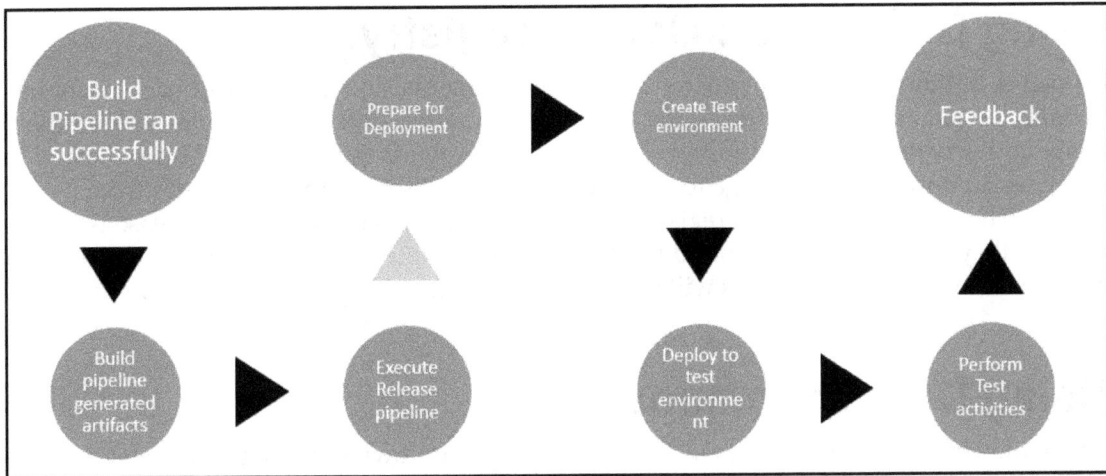

Figure 2: Sample continuous delivery process

Alternate strategies

In this book, the samples looked at an approach with a custom Pull Server deployed on a virtual machine, building a Docker image on all the environments with a `dockerfile` containing many instructions. This is one of the approaches for configuration management and continuous deployment. However, there are other approaches, and they should be evaluated before finalizing the strategy for configuration management and continuous deployment. In this section, we will discuss other alternate strategies that can be employed.

Using Azure automation for DSC Pull Server

Instead of creating a IaaS-based custom Pull Server on virtual machines, another strategy could be to use the Azure automation-provided PaaS DSC Pull Server. Although using the IaaS approach will provide more control over the Pull Server environment, the PaaS approach involves less maintenance and overheads. Some of the features might not be available as of the time of writing; however, they will be released in due course.

Using Docker hub/Docker registry

Instead of building Docker images for all the environments, an alternate approach could be to build the image once, execute all the tests on it, and after satisfactory results, upload the image to a private or public repository. All the environments that are part of the release pipeline can download the image to create containers instead of creating images from scratch. The advantage of using registries is that they can quicken the entire release process because they no longer need to build Docker images at runtime, while creating images at runtime for all the environments will ensure that all edge cases are well taken care off.

Using Docker compose

At the time of writing this book, Docker compose on Windows was at a nascent stage. Docker compose is a great tool for creating Docker images and containers as a solution through a single configuration file. An alternate approach to build images and containers is to use Docker compose instead of creating them directly on all the virtual machines.

Using Docker management tools such as Swarm or Kubernetes

At the time of writing this book, Swarm and Kubernetes on Windows were also at a nascent stage. These are great management tools providing features such as orchestration, scalability, deployment, and general management for Docker containers. These tools can be used to manage containers in different environments.

Types of releases

There are two ways in which VSTS can be configured to execute releases:

- Scheduled release
- Continuous deployment

We have been discussing continuous deployment in this chapter, and the next section talks about scheduled releases.

Scheduled releases

A scheduled release refers to automatic release pipeline execution at a predetermined schedule. Multiple schedules can be configured for each release pipeline and can include multiple source repositories. The release pipeline will execute at a given schedule and is not dependent on changes done to the code in the repository. These types of release pipelines are generally used on weekends during off-hours when generally there is no activity on the repository. The scheduling of a release is shown in *Figure 3*.

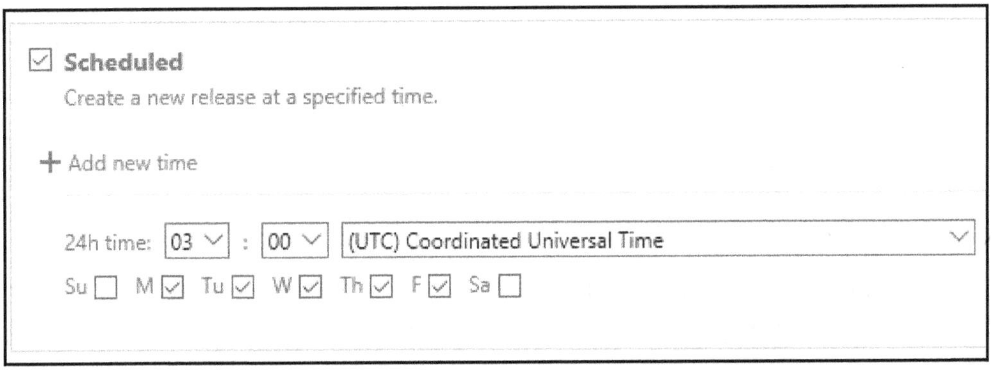

☑ **Scheduled**
   Create a new release at a specified time.

➕ Add new time

24h time: `03 ⌄` : `00 ⌄`   `(UTC) Coordinated Universal Time                    ⌄`
Su ☐   M ☑   Tu ☑   W ☑   Th ☑   F ☑   Sa ☐

Figure 3: Scheduled release pipeline

In *Figure 3*, a release has been scheduled to run at 3 a.m. on Monday, Tuesday, Wednesday, Thursday, and Friday.

Continuous deployment

Continuous deployment refers to the execution of release pipeline as and when a new version of the packages is available from a build pipeline. This is shown in *Figure 4*.

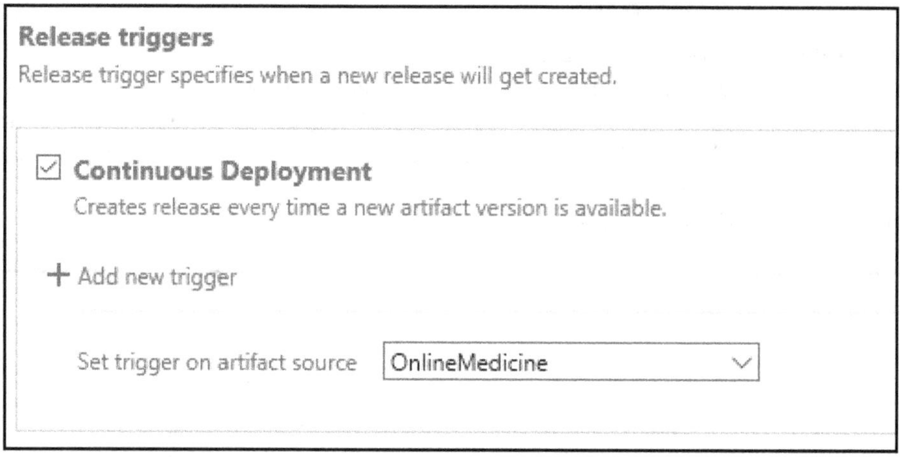

Figure 4: Sample continuous deployment release pipeline

Continuous deployment can also be triggered on the availability of different packages available from different sources arising out of multiple build pipelines.

Azure Resource Manager service endpoint

Before we get into discussing the release pipeline and definitions, it is important to understand VSTS service endpoints. Release and build pipelines by themselves are just repeatable workflows that execute one activity after another in sequence. They at times connect to external system and environments to perform their activities. In fact, most of the deploy tasks in VSTS are dependent on external environments. It could be related to conducting deployments on Azure Cloud, on-premise environments, or a combination of both. VSTS provides the facility of defining service endpoints centrally for a project, which can then be reused across all tasks in every build and release definition.

Since the *Online Medicine* sample application is completely deployed on Azure, VSTS release agents need to connect to Azure to provision, configure, and deploy environments and applications on it. VSTS provides the ability to connect to multiple types of external systems and environments. This is shown in *Figure 5*.

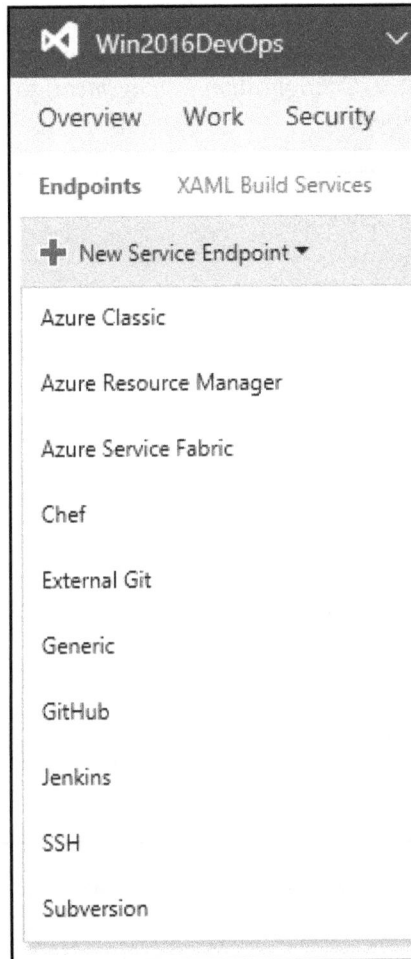

Figure 5: VSTS service endpoint types

This book uses **Azure Resource Manager** (**ARM**) for its cloud deployments. Clicking on the **Azure Resource Manager** menu item provides options to configure the ARM connection and endpoint. *Figure 6* shows a new ARM endpoint used within the sample release definition. **ARM Connection** is the name of the endpoint and is referred to in the release and build definition with this name. Information needed to connect to the Azure tenant is provided including the **Subscription ID**, **Subscription Name**, **Tenant ID**, application/client ID, and application key. The keys have been masked for security reasons; however, the reader should refer to Chapter 7, *Configuration Management,* to get details about how to get this information using PowerShell.

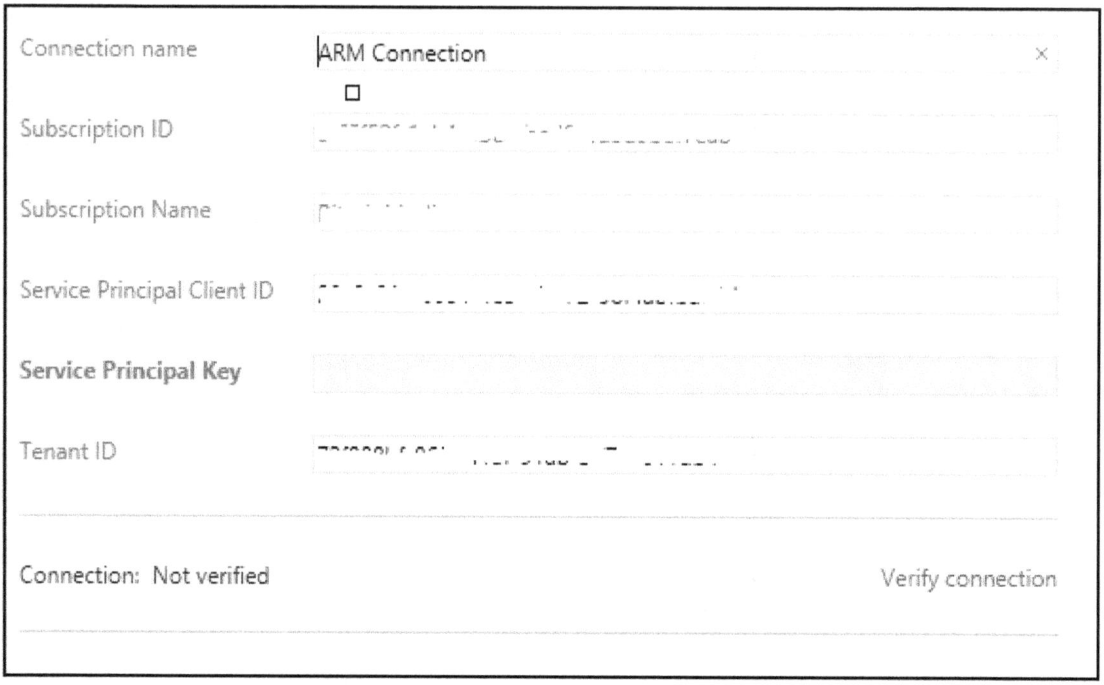

Connection name	ARM Connection
Subscription ID	
Subscription Name	
Service Principal Client ID	
Service Principal Key	
Tenant ID	
Connection: Not verified	Verify connection

Figure 6: Azure Resource Manager service endpoint

Release pipeline definition

VSTS provides a very intuitive user interface to define and build the release pipeline definition. The release definition comprises multiple discrete environments. Each environment block generally represents deployment to an environment. Examples of environments include test environments, staging environments, production environments, or any other environment. Each environment consists of multiple tasks that execute one after another as part of the overall deployment process. The transition from one environment to another is based on the approval workflow. Every project and solution has its unique requirements about its release process. Continuous deployment does not provide any specification regarding elements that should go into a release pipeline. Continuous deployment states that for it to be effective, it should have tasks that ensure that deployments are conducted and tested in an automated fashion.

A sample release process for our sample *Online Medicine* application is shown in *Figure 7*. This release pipeline comprises two environments representing the actual test and production environment. There is an additional environment preparation that does not conduct deployment but prepares the overall availability of scripts and templates at the Azure storage account. There could be many more environments in a release pipeline.

Each release definition is at least connected to an artifacts source. Every environment within the release definition starts by downloading the artifacts on the release server. This happens because each environment in effect can be executed on a separate release server. The preparation environment starts with getting the latest artifacts from a repository and uploads them to the Azure Blob storage. The artifacts consist of deployment scripts, templates, and DSC configurations. It also contains the `webdeploy` package built during the build pipeline. These artifacts are uploaded to the Azure storage so that any environment can download and use for its deployment. The preparation environment is configured to execute automatically whenever new artifacts are available. After the execution of the preparation environment, there is autoapproval to move to the execution of the next environment. This approval could potentially be configured to be manually approved.

After the preparation environment, the execution of the test environment is initiated. This environment is responsible for deployment to test the environment consisting of the provisioning and configuring environment on Azure, deploying the application within the Azure virtual machine Docker containers, and executing unit and operational tests to verify that the solution is behaving as expected.

There could have been more activities such as functional tests and coded UI tests within the test environment. These are not covered in this book because a few tasks are enough to understand release pipelines; however, readers should configure their pipelines with such tasks. After the successful execution of the test environment, there is autoapproval to move to the execution of the next environment, which happens to be the production environment in our case.

The production environment is exactly like the test environment. It has the same set of activities and executes the same scripts and templates. The only difference is that different parameters are used for the production environment compared to the test environment. Once the operational validation tests are positive, the stakeholders can decide to go live with the changes on production.

It is to be noted that there could have been many more environments in between the test and production environments; however, that depends on the project needs.

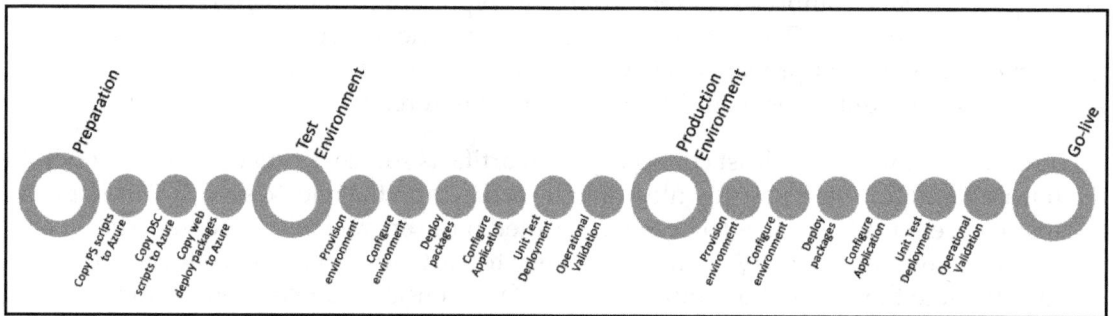

Figure 7: Release pipeline for Online Medicine sample application

Next, we will delve deeper into the configuration of the sample release pipeline for our *Online Medicine* sample application.

Variables configuration

Variables help define common data elements reused at multiple places within the release definition. Also, changing their values at one place can help update at all other places they are used. Four variables, **StorageAccountName**, **ContainerName**, **resourceGroupName**, and **StorageSAS**, are defined in *Online Medicine* release definition, and these are shown in *Figure 8*. **StorageAccountName** and **ContainerName** holds the name of the storage account and container storing the scripts and templates. **resourceGroupName** refers to the resource group holding common resources such as **Operational Management Workspace**, **Azure Key Vault**, and the storage account. Access to the storage account container is limited to users holding the **Secure Access Signature (SAS)** token. The storage SAS variable holds the value of the SAS token used to connect to the Azure storage account. These are global variables and can be used in any release task in any environment. Variables are defined by providing a name and a value. They are referred by their name and have a default value. There is also a lock icon against each variable. Selecting the lock icon will mask the value, and the value will not be visible on the user interface.

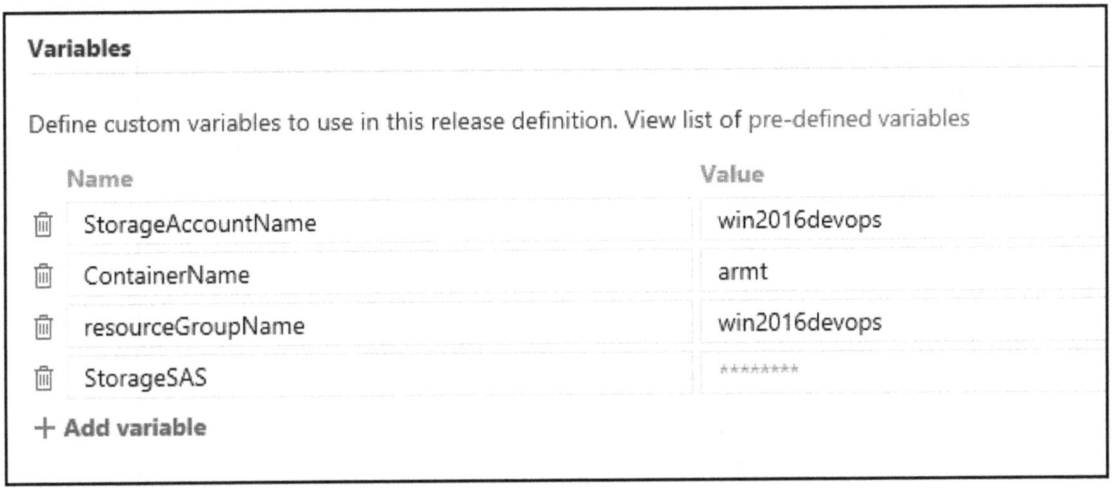

Variables

Define custom variables to use in this release definition. View list of pre-defined variables

Name	Value
StorageAccountName	win2016devops
ContainerName	armt
resourceGroupName	win2016devops
StorageSAS	********

+ **Add variable**

Figure 8: Online Medicine release definition global variables

Artifacts configuration

The artifacts configuration for a release definition allows it to be associated with multiple build pipelines. The artifacts configuration for the sample release definition is shown in *Figure 9*.

Release definitions and, in turn, environment definitions need artifacts that they can use to deploy on environments. Release definitions do not have access to the source code repository as build definitions do. Release definitions rely on the build definitions ability to generate packages based on the current snapshot of the source code repository. These artifacts are the source of truth for release definitions. As mentioned before, the artifacts are downloaded for every environment definition because of the simple fact that each environment definition can potentially run in a different release server.

The release definition should link itself to an appropriate build definition.

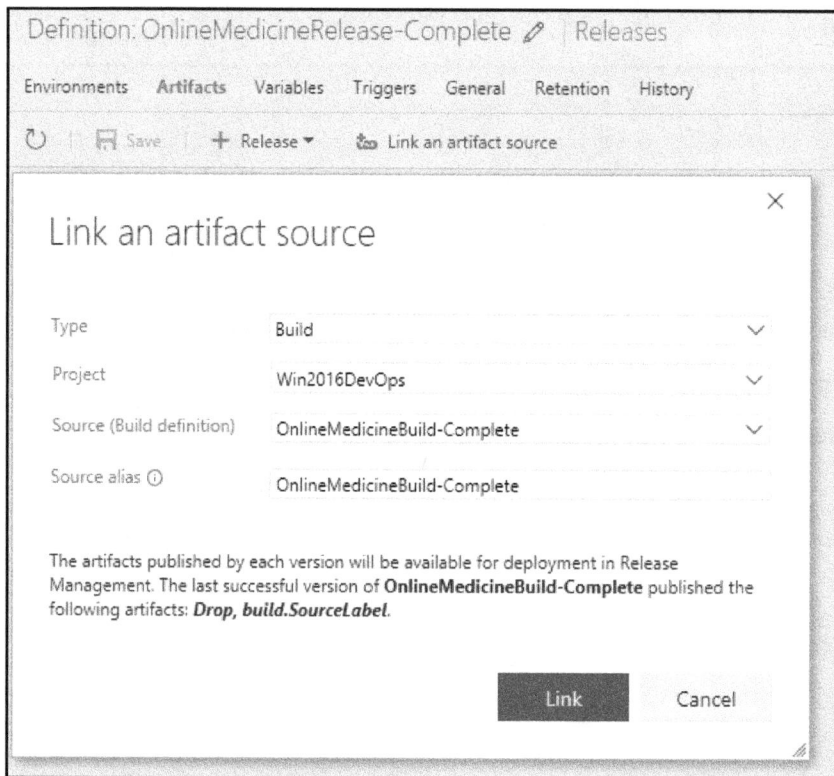

Figure 9: Artifacts tab of build definition

The artifacts can be sourced from multiple places. They can be sourced from packages generated during the VSTS build execution, directly from the VSTS Git or TFVC repository, packages generated by the Jenkins build execution, or from GitHub as code repository.

The **Type** field accepts build, GitHub, Git, TFVC, and Jenkins as artifact source.

The **Project** field denotes the VSTS project, and the **Source (Build definition)** field refers to the build definition name. **Source alias** is just another name to refer to an artifacts source.

Triggers configuration

Release triggers were discussed earlier in this chapter. There is another section, **Environment triggers**, within the **Triggers** section that was not discussed earlier. After a release is triggered, VSTS needs to identify a way to invoke the environment definition. Each environment can decide its own policy of getting triggered. *Figure 10* shows the configuration of **Environment triggers** for a sample release definition.

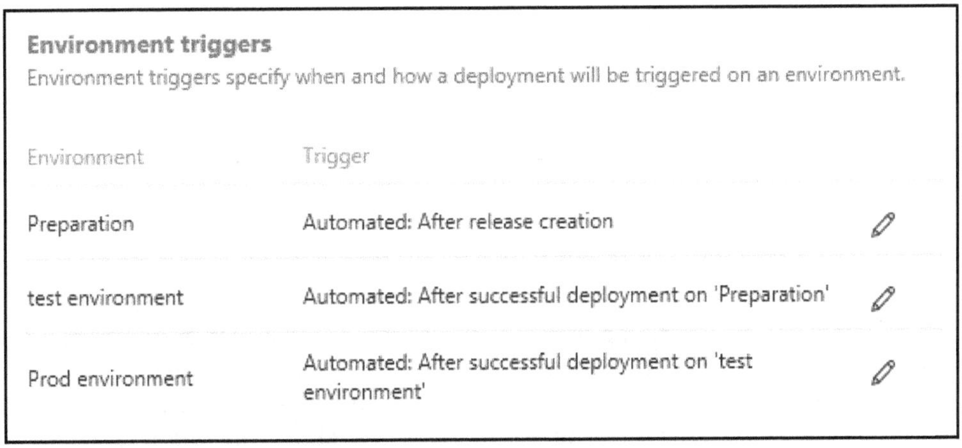

Figure 10: Triggers tab of build definition

The preparation environment is configured to start automatically after a release is created. The test environment is configured to be executed automatically after the successful deployment of the previous preparation environment, and the production environment is configured to be executed automatically after the successful deployment to the test environment. These are also called deployment conditions and further explained in the environment section of this chapter.

General, retention, and history

The **General** tab in *Figure 11* helps to configure the pattern for release names. Every release execution gets a release name, the format of which is determined by VSTS using the **Release name format** field. The **Release name format** for a sample release definition is defined using VSTS provided out-of-the-box release variables, such as the project name, release definition name, release ID, date of execution, and number of times the build has executed on any day. The build name format is shown here for reference:

$(System.TeamProject)_$(Release.DefinitionName)_$(Release.ReleaseId)_$(Date:yyyyMMdd)$(Rev:.r)

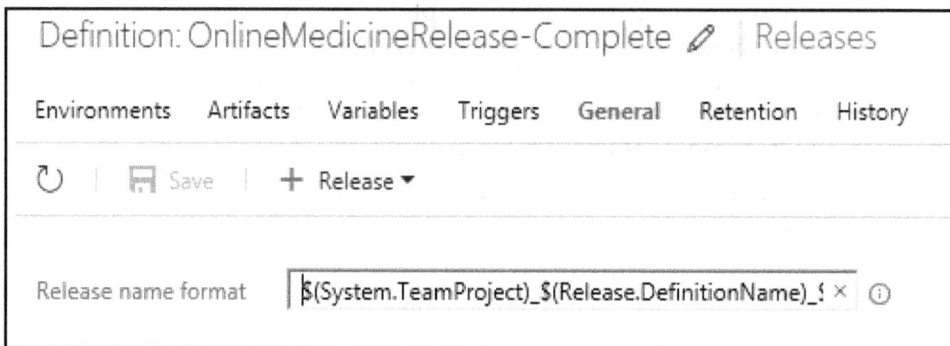

Figure 11: The General tab of build definition

VSTS generates and stores a lot of data and information with every release and environment execution. These includes release labels, reports, symbols, and more. Each environment has its own retention policy and can decide the number of days and number of release executions to store. Proper retention policy will ensure that there is no unnecessary usage of storage space on the project account. For the sample release definition and project, the defaults have been used for retention configuration as shown in *Figure 12*.

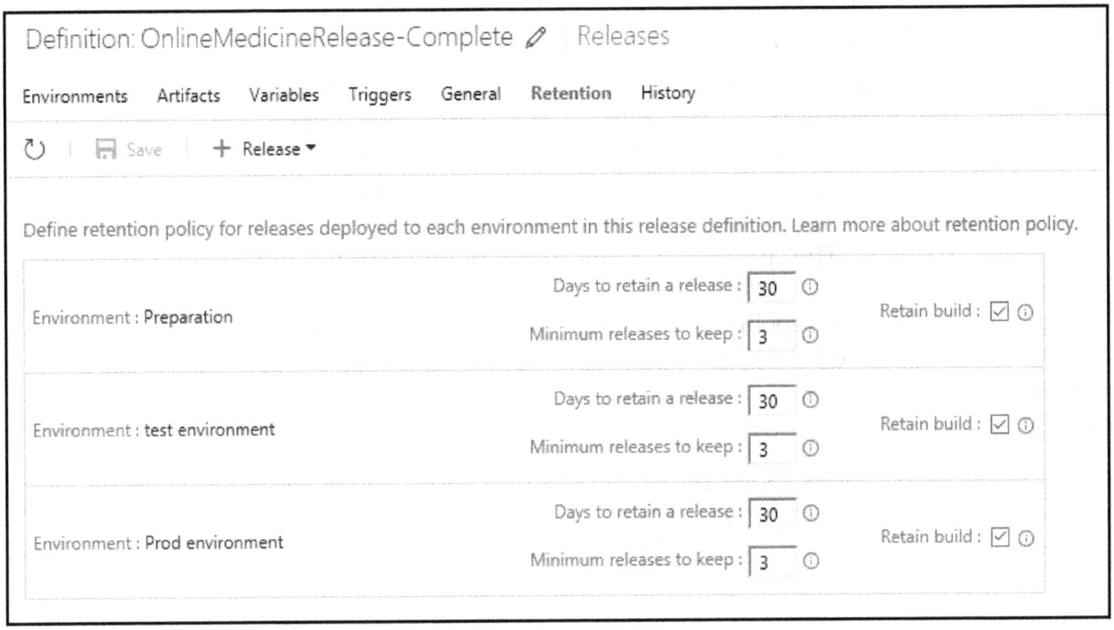

Figure 12: Retention tab of build definition

VSTS provides version control for release definitions as well. It means any changes, modification, and updates to the release definition will be recorded in VSTS, providing a complete history of all changes since the release definition is created. This is a very useful feature as it allows the comparison of release definitions between multiple changes over time and allows for reconciliation of the changes. The **Diff** button on the top menu helps in comparing two versions of the same release definition after selecting them in the list. This is shown in *Figure 13*.

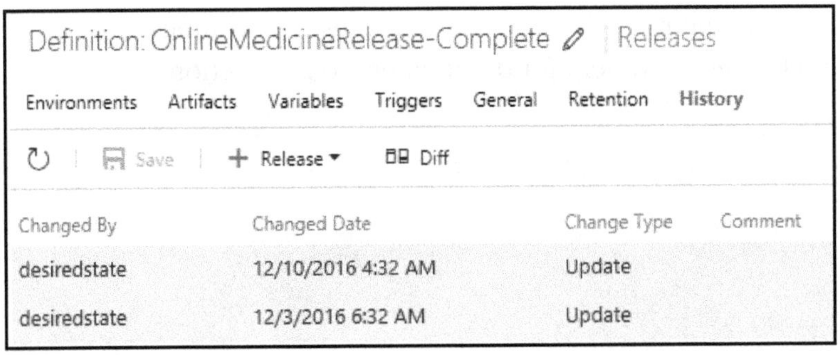

Figure 13: History tab of build definition

Release environments

This is a core and major part of the release definition, comprising of multiple environments. The release definition can be viewed as a container with metadata and hosts multiple environment definitions. The metadata includes global variable declarations, linking of artifacts, and release management-related activities such as starting a release, and defining release names. They affect the overall working of a release definition and they are available to every environment. The environments are free to override or use the default values of variables. Each environment definition consists of multiple tasks. It is these tasks that are executed when a release pipeline is executed. These tasks are executed in sequence, and each task is responsible for performing a single function. When a release is created from a release definition, it is responsible for orchestrating the execution of each environment depending on its configuration.

It is to be noted that VSTS allows the same tasks to be used in build as well as release definitions. An activity can be placed within a build definition as well as in a release definition. We have already witnessed the common properties of every task in the previous chapter while we discussed build definitions.

It is important to note that in continuous deployment configuration, a new release is created with the availability of new artifacts. The new release, in turn, executes the environments based on their deployment condition configuration. The details about deployment condition configuration are discussed in depth while discussing individual environments later.

Figure 14 shows the release definition for the *Online Medicine* application. It comprises three discrete environments:

- Preparation environment to upload scripts, templates, and packages to the Azure Blob storage
- Test environment for deployment to the test environment
- Production environment for deployment to production

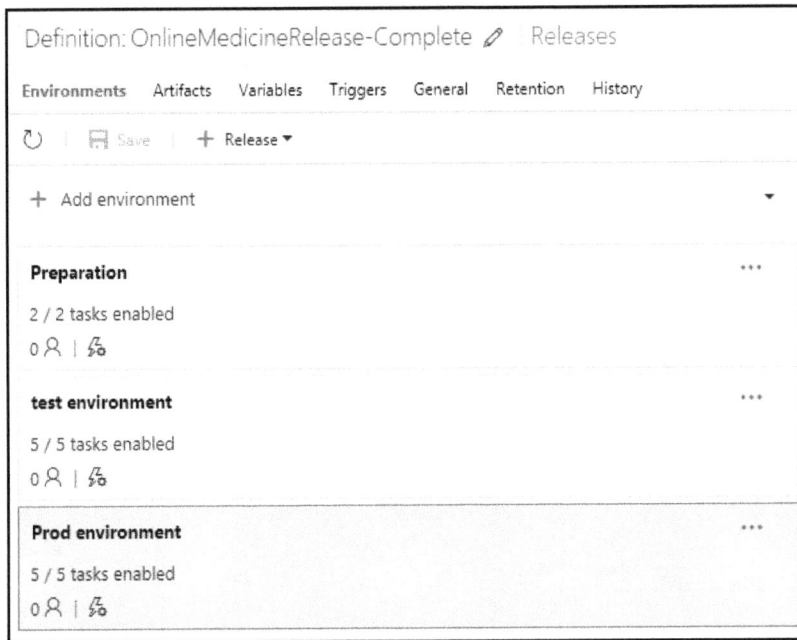

Figure 14: The Online Medicine release definition

Let's dig deeper into each of these environment configurations and the tasks comprising them.

Preparation environment

Preparation environment is not a deployment environment like other environments. Its sole responsibility is to upload `webdeploy` packages, PowerShell scripts, DSC configuration, SQL scripts, and Docker templates to the Azure Blob storage. This activity could have also been executed in a build pipeline instead of a release pipeline. The objective of putting this activity in the release definition was to ensure that the build pipeline remains as lean as possible and is able to provide feedback to developers immediately. If readers feel that these should be part of the build definition, they are free to include them, and in doing so, they will not violate any build best practices. Moreover, uploading of the files was kept in a separate environment definition configured to execute as the first environment to ensure that other environments dependent on these files can download them from a centralized location. Another reason to put this activity in the release pipeline was because the execution of the release pipeline is less frequent compared with the build pipeline.

Figure 15 shows the tasks that comprise the preparation environment. It comprises of two activities. Again, the uploading of scripts and templates could have been done through a single activity; however, to demonstrate the usage of multiple activities, the upload of files to the Azure Blob storage has been divided into two steps.

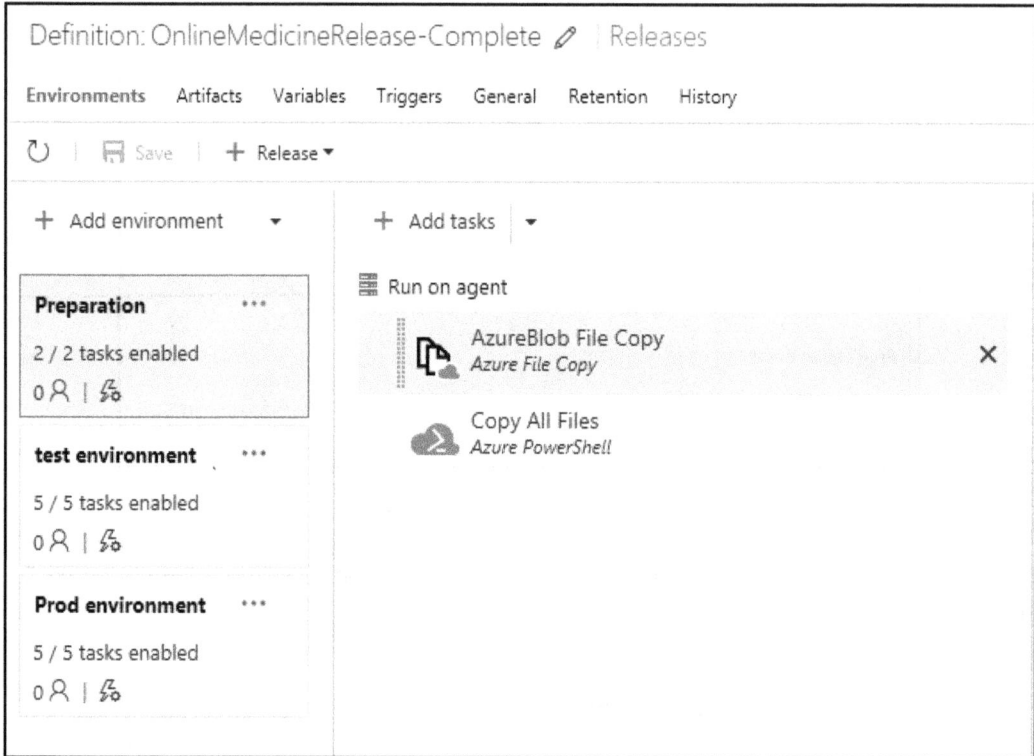

Figure 15: The preparation environment definition

This environment does not declare environment-specific variables, and its deployment condition is configured to execute automatically on the creation of a new release. This environment uses global variables declared at the release level. The approval for both pre- and post-deployment is also set to automatic for this task. Clicking on the ellipse button against each environment opens the configuration for that environment. The configuration for the preparation environment is shown in *Figure 16*.

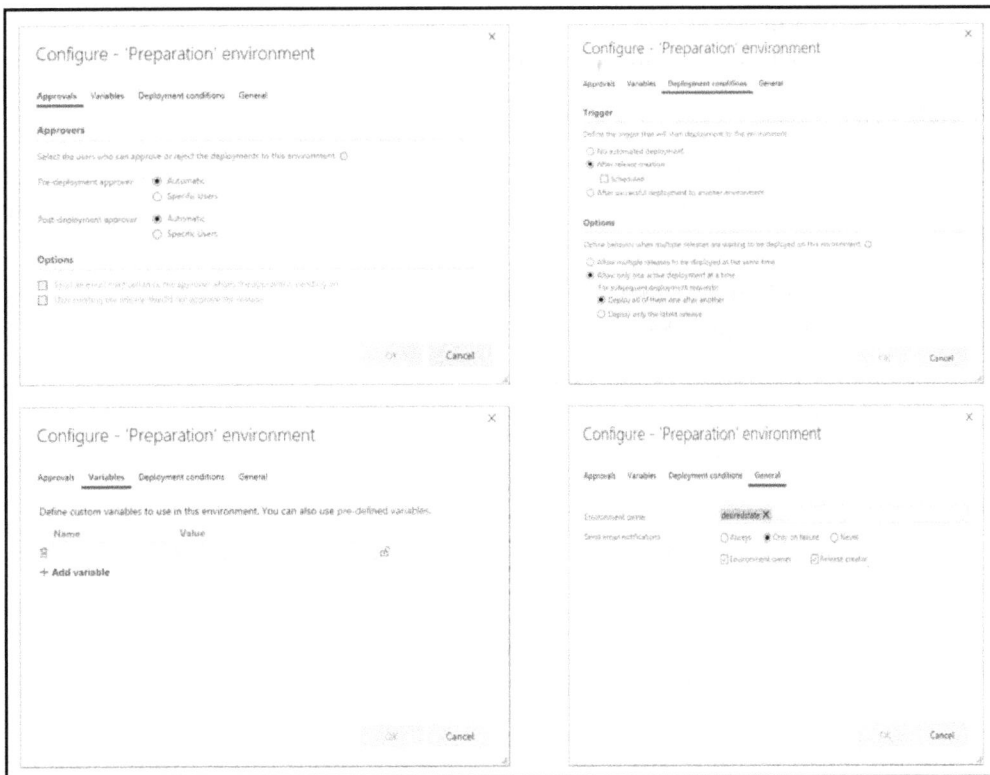

Figure 16: The preparation environment definition configuration

The details of each task in the preparation environment is discussed next.

Azure file copy task

This task is responsible for uploading the `webdeploy` package to the Azure storage account. If you recount, in `Chapter 9`, *Continuous Integration,* the build pipeline generated the `webdeploy` package while compiling the *Online Medicine* project and named it as `Deployment.zip`.

In *Figure 17,* the **Source** path is configured as **$(System.DefaultWorkingDirectory)/OnlineMedicine/Drop/OnlinePharmacy/Deployment.zip**.

Azure Connection Type is configured with **Azure Resource Manager** because all the examples in this book uses **Azure Resource Manager** as the preferred choice.

Azure RM Subscription is configured to use already and is created by the **ARM Connection** ARM service endpoint.

Destination Type is **Azure Blob**.

RM Storage Account is configured with the variable, **$(StorageAccountName)**. This syntax represents usage of variables. If you recollect, this variable was defined as the global release variable.

Container Name is configured as **$(ContainerName)** and **Storage Container SAS Token** is configured with the **$(StorageSAS)** variable.

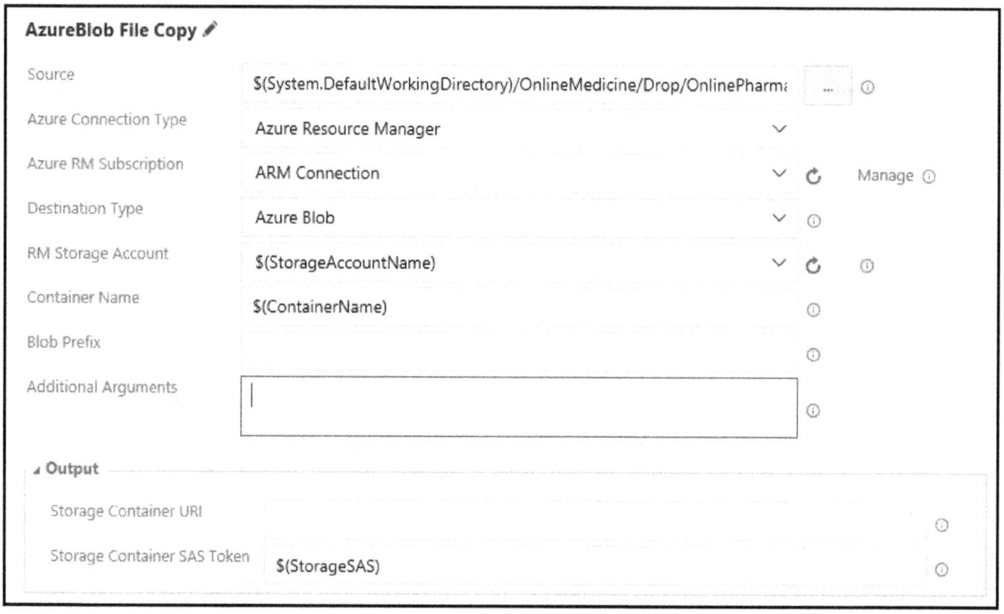

AzureBlob File Copy 🖉	
Source	$(System.DefaultWorkingDirectory)/OnlineMedicine/Drop/OnlinePharma ... ⓘ
Azure Connection Type	Azure Resource Manager ⌄
Azure RM Subscription	ARM Connection ⌄ ↻ Manage ⓘ
Destination Type	Azure Blob ⌄ ⓘ
RM Storage Account	$(StorageAccountName) ⌄ ↻ ⓘ
Container Name	$(ContainerName) ⓘ
Blob Prefix	ⓘ
Additional Arguments	ⓘ
⊿ **Output**	
Storage Container URI	ⓘ
Storage Container SAS Token	$(StorageSAS) ⓘ

Figure 17: PowerShell task for copying files to Azure blob storage

Azure PowerShell

Although Azure file copy is specifically designed to copy files to the Azure storage account, there is a more generic activity named Azure PowerShell. It can perform any activity on Azure that is possible using Azure SDK and PowerShell. This task is responsible to the Azure Blob storage for the following:

- Copy `PullServer.ps1` PowerShell script
- Copy `IISInstall.ps1` PowerShell script

- Copy `ContainConfig.ps1` PowerShell script
- Copy `ChangeConnectionString.ps1` PowerShell script
- Copy `lcm.ps1` PowerShell script
- Copy `dockerfile` Docker template
- Copy `OnlinePharmacy.sql` SQL script

In *Figure 18*, **Azure Connection Type** is configured with **Azure Resource Manager.**

Azure RM Subscription is configured to use already and is created by the **ARM Connection** ARM service endpoint.

Script Path is configured as $(System.DefaultWorkingDirectory)/OnlineMedicine/Drop/OnlinePharmacy.Configuration/PSScripts/UploadScriptFiles.ps1.

Script Arguments is configured as **-sqlFilePath "$(System.DefaultWorkingDirectory)/OnlineMedicine/Drop/OnlinePharmacy/OnlinePharmacy.sql" -scriptsFilePath "$(System.DefaultWorkingDirectory)/OnlineMedicine/Drop/OnlinePharmacy.Configuration" -containerName $(ContainerName) -resourceGroupName $(resourceGroupName) -storageAccountName $(StorageAccountName).**

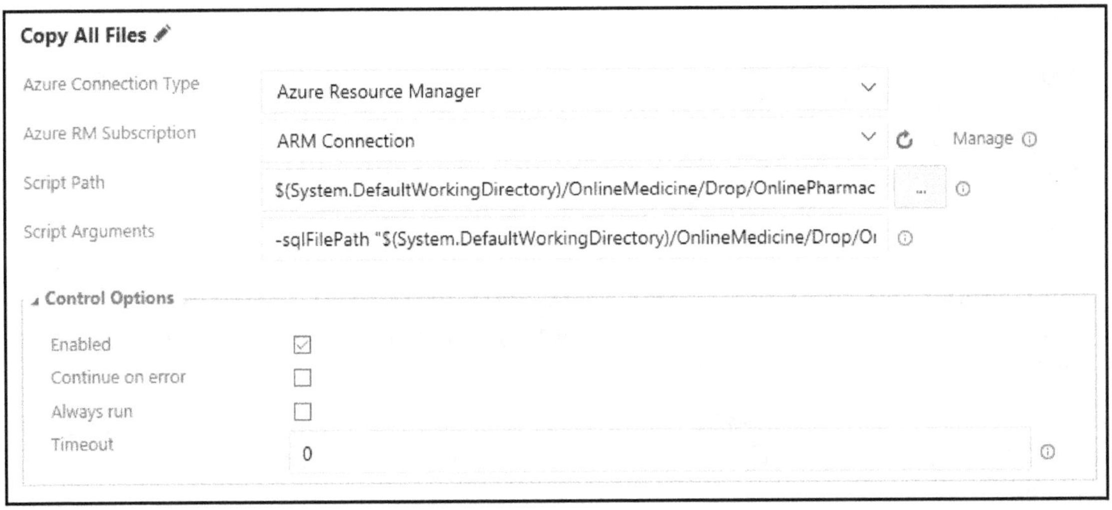

Copy All Files 🖉	
Azure Connection Type	Azure Resource Manager
Azure RM Subscription	ARM Connection
Script Path	$(System.DefaultWorkingDirectory)/OnlineMedicine/Drop/OnlinePharmac...
Script Arguments	-sqlFilePath "$(System.DefaultWorkingDirectory)/OnlineMedicine/Drop/O...

Control Options

Enabled	☑
Continue on error	☐
Always run	☐
Timeout	0

Figure 18: Azure PowerShell to copy files to Azure Blob storage

Test environment

The test environment is the first environment that conducts an actual deployment. It reuses and executes the scripts and templates uploaded to the Azure Blob storage and so is dependent on the preparation environment. It conducts deployment by executing a series of activities in its pipeline. The environment definitions are used as an orchestrator whose primary responsibility is to invoke scripts. The scripts have the bulk of logic implemented for provisioning, configuration, and testing of both the environment and application. The environment definition provides the execution model and ensures that tasks are executed one after another and provides feedback through audits and logs.

This environment declares environment-specific variables. They include the **ResourceGroupName**, **OMSWorkspaceName**, **skuName**, **deployLocation**, and **regKey**.

The preparation environment uploads the scripts in a storage account in a resource group that can be accessed by any deployment. The deployments execute in separate resource groups and reuse the scripts from the common storage account. Each environment creates its own resource group so that all deployments related to the test environment happens in that resource group.

The OMS workspace is needed to install agents on virtual machines and connect them to itself. The operational management suite was created in the chapter related to configuration management, and the agents were provisioned in virtual machines using ARM templates. In the next chapter, we will see how to configure the OMS workspace.

Every deployment in Azure should be uniquely named for easier identification There are resources in Azure that should be named uniquely across the Internet. This includes resources such as the storage account name and DNS names for IP addresses. The **skuName** acts a qualifier and is added to every resource to uniquely name them. For the test environment, the value for **skuName** is **test**, while for the production environment, it is **prod**. Readers are free to provide any name for this variable.

deployLocation denotes the location where the Azure resource group, and its related resources are provisioned. This makes the templates and scripts generic and can be provisioned on any location provided as a value to this variable.

regKey refers to the registration key of the Desired State Configuration. In general, this key should be static. Both the DSC Pull Server and its node should have this shared key with them to identify each other.

The deployment condition is configured to execute automatically on the successful completion of the preparation environment. The approval for both pre- and post-deployment is also set to automatic for this task. The configuration for the test environment is shown in *Figure 19*.

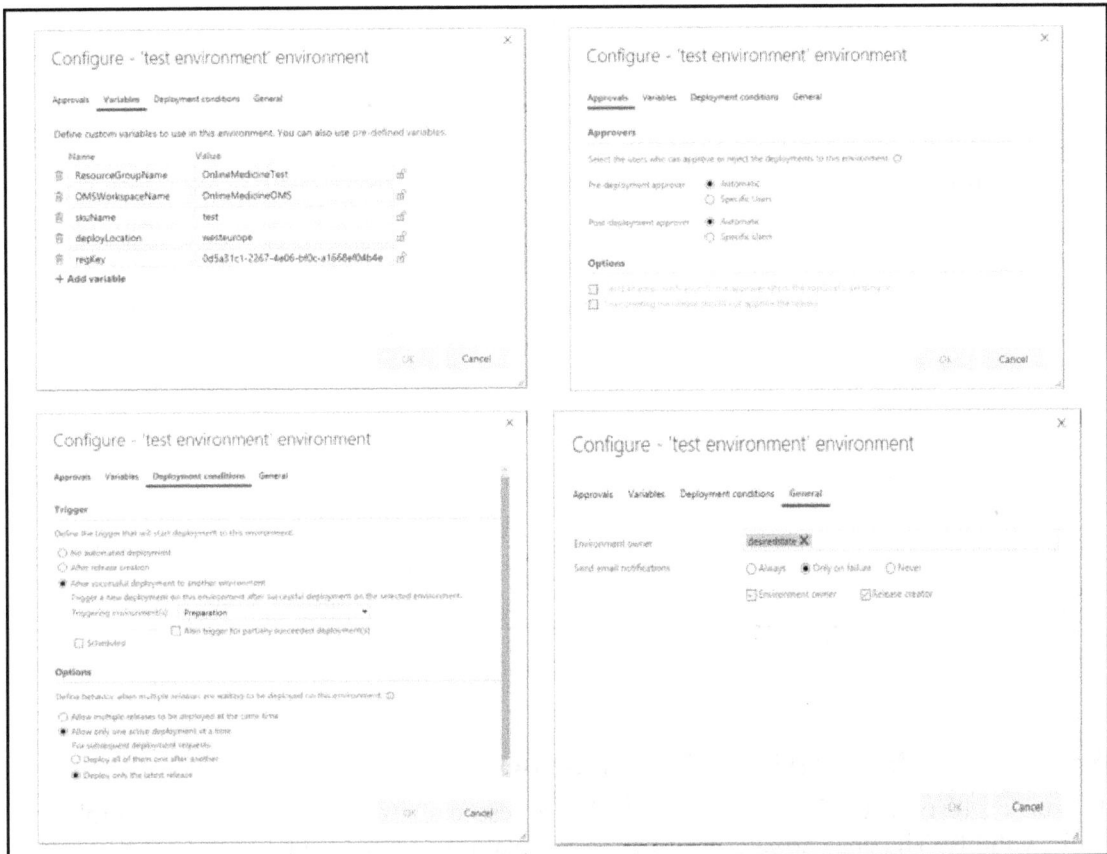

Figure 19: Test environment configuration

The details of the test environment definition are discussed next and shown in *Figure 20*.

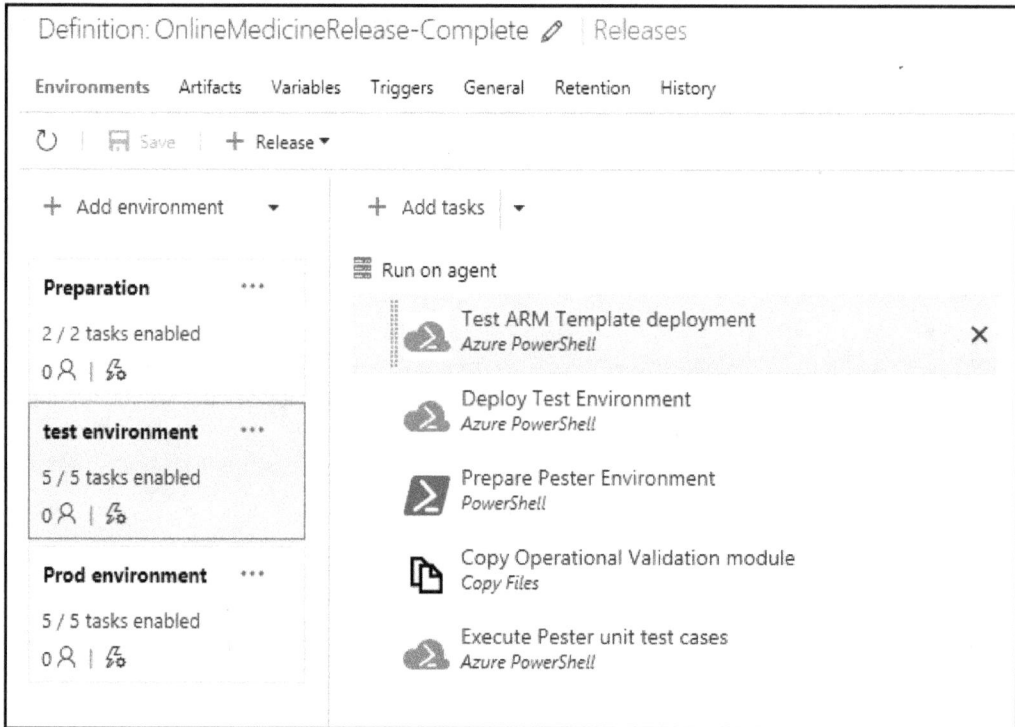

Figure 20: Test environment definition

Azure PowerShell – test ARM template deployment

This task is responsible for creating a new Azure resource group and testing the template for its validity. The `OnlineMedicine.json` template is passed as a parameter to this script for the `TemplatePath` variable. It executes a script `Test-ARMTemplate.ps1` that in turn uses `New-AzureRmResourceGroup` cmdlet to create a new resource group based on parameters passed for the resource group name and deploy location and `Test-AzureRMResourceGroupDeployment` to test the templates. The template and its parameter file paths are sent as argument to this script. It also passes the sku name and OMS workspace name as arguments.

In *Figure 21*, **Azure Connection Type** is configured with **Azure Resource Manager**.

Azure RM Subscription is configured to use already and is created by the **ARM Connection** ARM service endpoint.

Script Path is configured as **$(System.DefaultWorkingDirectory)/OnlineMedicine/Drop/OnlinePharmacy.Configuration/PSScripts/Test-ARMTemplate.ps1.**

Script Arguments is configured as **-ARMTemplatePath $(System.DefaultWorkingDirectory)/OnlineMedicine/Drop/OnlinePharmacy.Configuration/Templates/OnlineMedicine.json -ARMTemplateParametersPath $(System.DefaultWorkingDirectory)/OnlineMedicine/Drop/OnlinePharmacy.Configuration/Templates/OnlineMedicine.parameters.json -resourceGroupName $(ResourceGroupName) -OMSWorkspaceName $(OMSWorkspaceName) -deployLocation $(deployLocation) -pullserverRegKey $(regKey).**

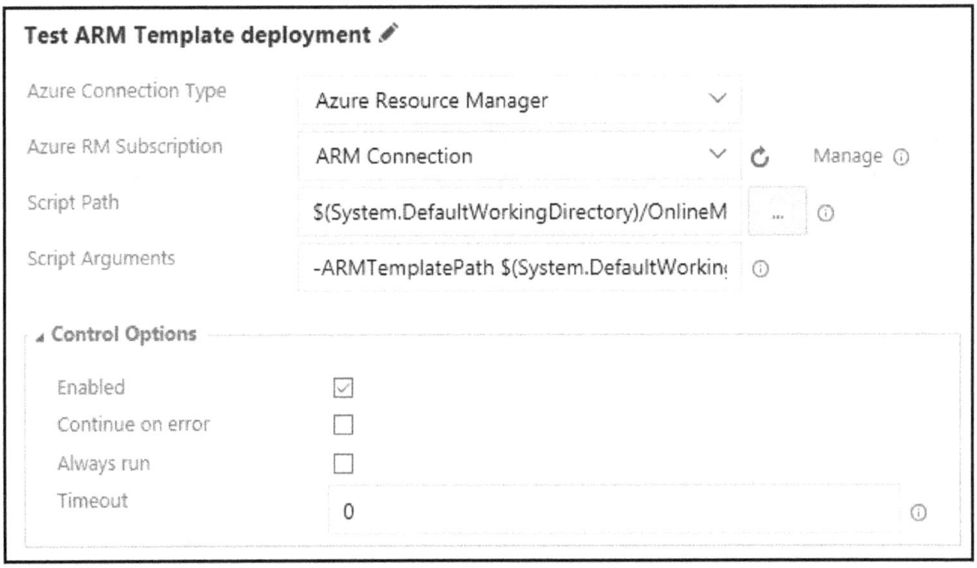

Figure 21: Creating resource group and testing deployment

Azure PowerShell – deploy test environment

This task is responsible for new deployment within previously created resource groups using the **Azure Resource Manager** template and its parameter file. It also provides values for **skuName**, **OMSWorkspaceName**, DSC Pull Server registration key values while executing the script `New-Templatedeployment.ps1`, that in turn uses the `New-AzureRmResourceGroupDeployment` cmdlet to create a new resource group with the provided parameters.

In Figure 22, **Azure Connection Type** is configured with **Azure Resource Manager**.

Azure RM Subscription is configured to use already and is created by the **ARM Connection** ARM service endpoint.

Script Path is configured as **$(System.DefaultWorkingDirectory)/OnlineMedicine/Drop/OnlinePharmacy.Configuration/PSScripts/New-TemplateDeployment.ps1**.

Script Arguments is configured as -ARMTemplatePath **$(System.DefaultWorkingDirectory)/OnlineMedicine/Drop/OnlinePharmacy.Configuration/Templates/OnlineMedicine.json -ARMTemplateParametersPath $(System.DefaultWorkingDirectory)/OnlineMedicine/Drop/OnlinePharmacy.Configuration/Templates/OnlineMedicine.parameters.json -resourceGroupName $(ResourceGroupName) -OMSWorkspaceName $(OMSWorkspaceName) -skuName $(skuName) -deploymentName $(RELEASE.RELEASENAME) -deployLocation $(deployLocation) -pullserverRegKey $(regKey).**

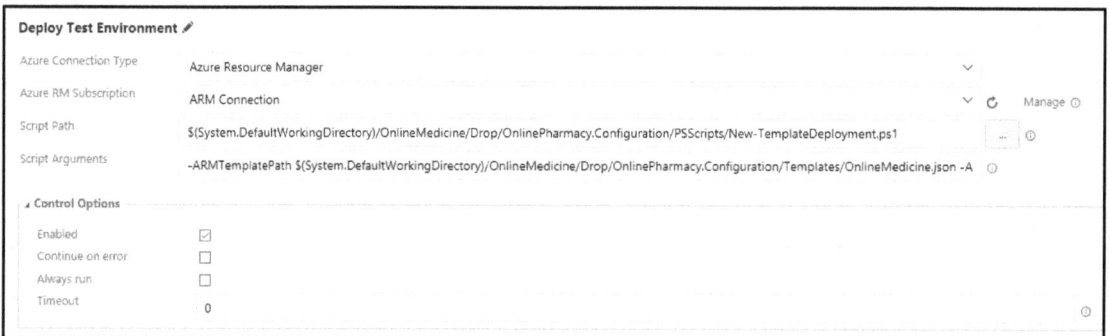

Deploy Test Environment ✏			
Azure Connection Type	Azure Resource Manager	∨	
Azure RM Subscription	ARM Connection	∨ ↻	Manage ⓘ
Script Path	$(System.DefaultWorkingDirectory)/OnlineMedicine/Drop/OnlinePharmacy.Configuration/PSScripts/New-TemplateDeployment.ps1	...	ⓘ
Script Arguments	-ARMTemplatePath $(System.DefaultWorkingDirectory)/OnlineMedicine/Drop/OnlinePharmacy.Configuration/Templates/OnlineMedicine.json -A	ⓘ	
⊿ Control Options			
Enabled	☑		
Continue on error	☐		
Always run	☐		
Timeout	0		ⓘ

Figure 22: Deploy test environment

PowerShell – prepare Pester environment

The release pipeline is configured to run on hosted release servers. Every time a release runs, it will potentially run on a new server. This activity is responsible for preparing the release server by installing it with dependencies, specifically Pester binaries and operational validation modules. This is a PowerShell activity that invokes the `PreparePesterEnvironment.ps1` PowerShell script. In this script, `Nuget` and `Chocolatey` are added as the package source and provider. They install Pester and the operation validation module needed for the execution of Pester unit test cases and operational validation scripts.

In *Figure 23*, **Type** is configured with **File Path**.

Script Path is configured as
$(System.DefaultWorkingDirectory)/OnlineMedicine/Drop/OnlinePharmacy.Configuration/PSScripts/PreparePesterEnvironment.ps1.

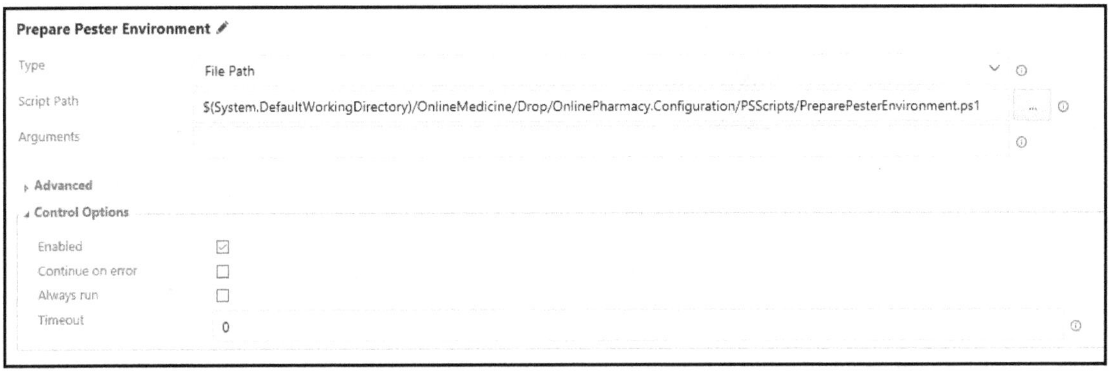

Figure 23: Preparing Pester environment

Copy files – copy operational validation module

This task copies the operational validation module from the artifacts source to the release server so that it can be executed from there. This is an optional activity used in the environment definition for the purpose of demonstration. Pester is capable of executing both Pester and operational validation test cases. Instead of using the operational validation module, Pester is used to execute both the test types. It is difficult to send parameters to the operations validation module, so for an example in this book, we are sending parameters to the test cases. It is for this reason that Pester is chosen over the operations validation module for running the tests. The configuration copies the `OnlineMedicine` and all its sub-files and folders to the `Modules` folder on release server.

In *Figure 24*, **Source Folder** path is configured as **$(System.DefaultWorkingDirectory)/OnlineMedicine/Drop/OnlinePharmacy.Configuration/Tests/OperationalValidation/OnlineMedicine**.

Contents is configured with ******.

Target Folder is configured as **$(USERPROFILE)\Documents\WindowsPowerShell\Modules**.

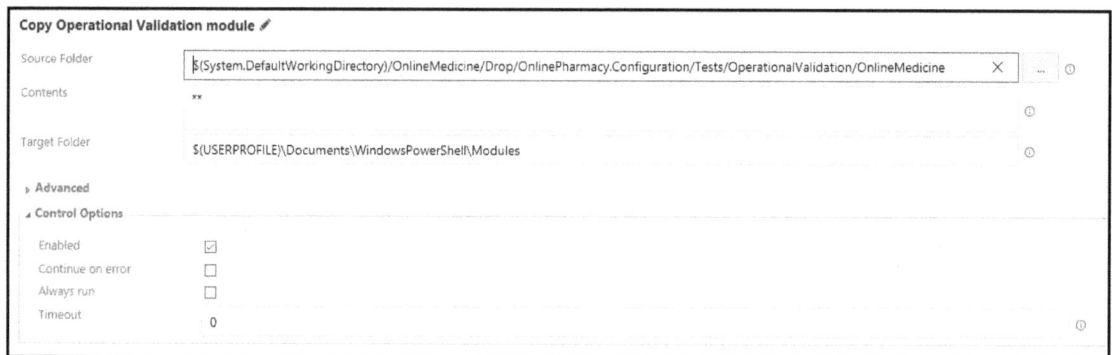

Figure 24: Copy operational validation test case module

Azure PowerShell – execute Pester and operational validation tests

This task is responsible for executing Pester and operational validation tests by executing the `Execute-Pester.ps1` PowerShell script. The script uses `Invoke-Pester` to execute Pester as well as operational validation test cases.

In *Figure 25*, **Azure Connection Type** is configured with **Azure Resource Manager**.

Azure RM Subscription is configured to use already and is created by the **ARM Connection** ARM service endpoint.

Script Path is configured as **$(System.DefaultWorkingDirectory)/OnlineMedicine/Drop/OnlinePharmacy.Configuration/PSScripts/Execute-Pester.ps1**.

Script Arguments is configured as **-testScriptPath "$(System.DefaultWorkingDirectory)\OnlineMedicine\Drop\OnlinePharmacy.Configuration\Tests\UnitTests" -releaseName "$(RELEASE.RELEASENAME)" -resourceGroupName "$(ResourceGroupName)" -operationTestsPath "$(System.DefaultWorkingDirectory)\OnlineMedicine\Drop\OnlinePharmacy.Configuration\Tests\OperationalValidation\OnlineMedicine\Diagnostics\Comprehensive"**.

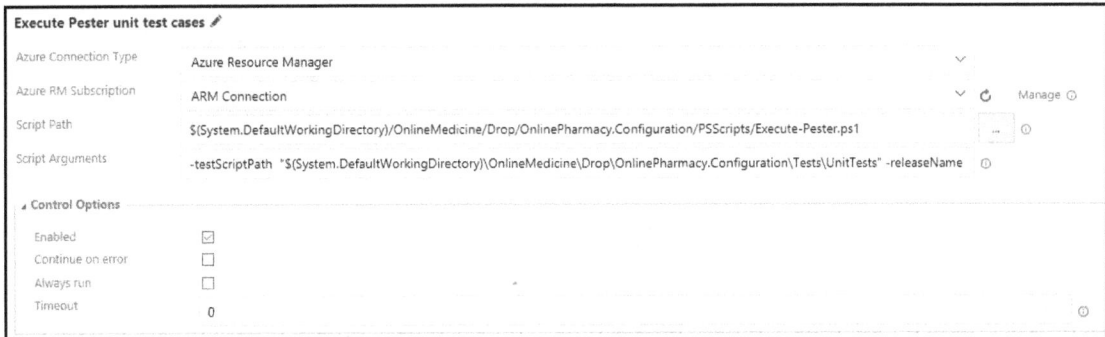

Figure 25: Execute Pester and operational validation test cases

Production environment

This environment is similar to the test environment. However, it is configured to execute after the successful deployment of the test environment and automatic approval. It declares the same variables as the test environment; however, the values are different compared with the test environment. It reuses and executes the scripts and templates uploaded to the Azure Blob storage and so is dependent on the preparation environment to be executed first. The approval for both pre- and post-deployment is also set automatic for this task. The configuration for the production environment is shown in *Figure 26*.

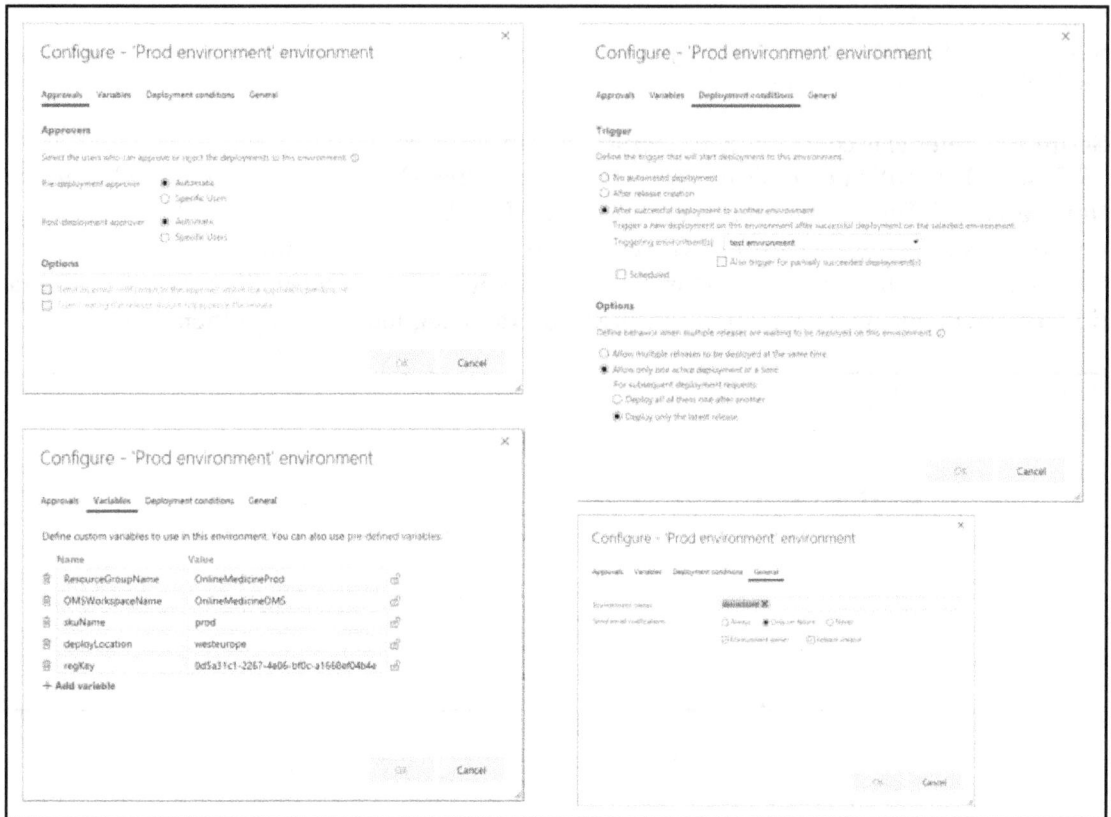

Figure 26: Production environment configuration

The details of the production environment definition are discussed next and shown in *Figure 27*.

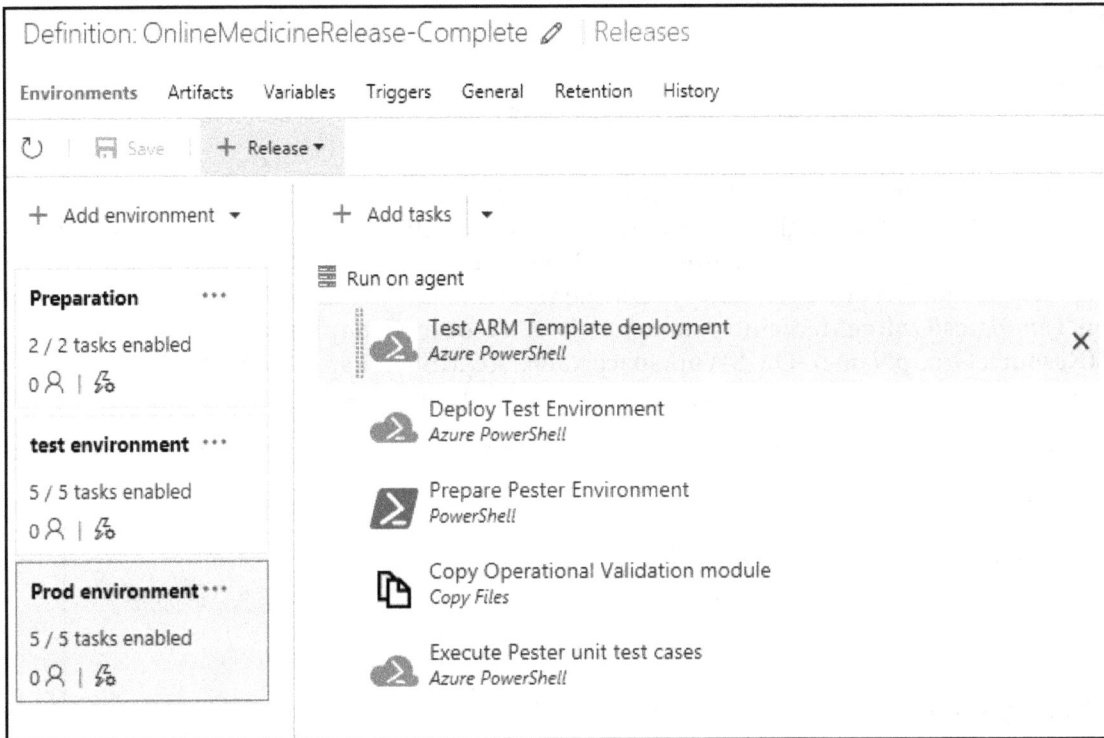

Figure 27: Production environment definition

Azure PowerShell – test ARM template deployment

This task is responsible for creating a new Azure resource group and testing the template for its validity. It uses the same template, `OnlineMedicine.json`, even for deployment to the production environment. It executes the same script, `Test-ARMTemplate`, as the test environment with different parameters.

In *Figure 28*, **Azure Connection Type** is configured with **Azure Resource Manager**.

Azure RM Subscription is configured to use already and is created by the **ARM Connection** ARM service endpoint.

Script Path is configured as **$(System.DefaultWorkingDirectory)/OnlineMedicine/Drop/OnlinePharmacy.Configuration/PSScripts/Test-ARMTemplate.ps1**.

Script Arguments is configured as **-ARMTemplatePath $(System.DefaultWorkingDirectory)/OnlineMedicine/Drop/OnlinePharmacy.Configuration/Templates/OnlineMedicine.json -ARMTemplateParametersPath $(System.DefaultWorkingDirectory)/OnlineMedicine/Drop/OnlinePharmacy.Configuration/Templates/OnlineMedicine.parameters.json -resourceGroupName $(ResourceGroupName) -OMSWorkspaceName $(OMSWorkspaceName) -deployLocation $(deployLocation) -pullserverRegKey $(regKey)**.

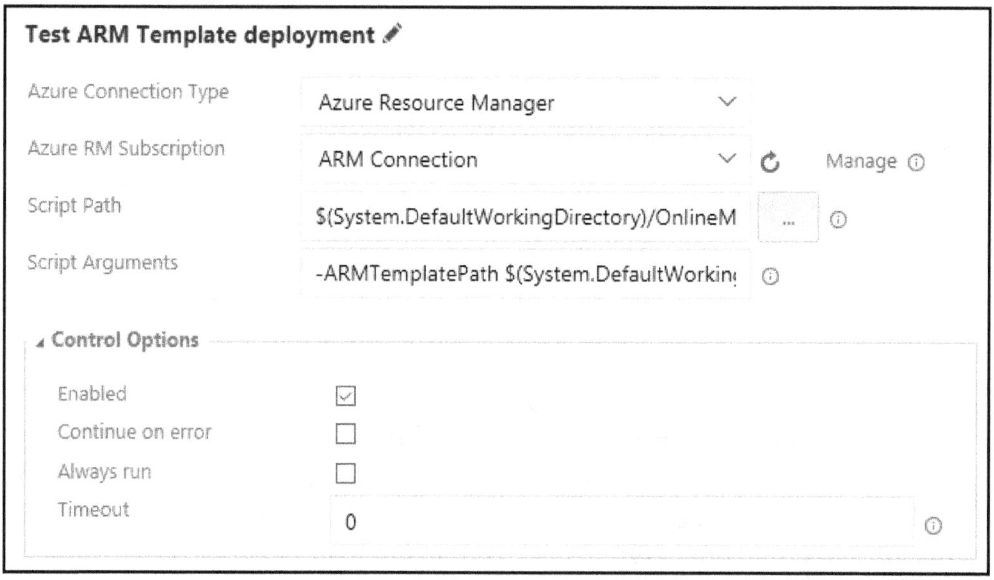

Figure 28: Creating resource group and testing deployment

Azure PowerShell – deploy test environment

This task is responsible for new deployments using the Azure Resource Manager template and its parameter file. It also provides the values for **skuName**, **OMSworkspaceName**, and DSC Pull Server registration key values while executing the script `New-Templatedeployment`.

In *Figure 29*, **Azure Connection Type** is configured with **Azure Resource Manager**.

Azure RM Subscription is configured to use already and is created by the **ARM Connection** ARM service endpoint.

Script Path is configured as **$(System.DefaultWorkingDirectory)/OnlineMedicine/Drop/OnlinePharmacy.Configuration/PSScripts/New-TemplateDeployment.ps1**.

Script Arguments is configured as **-ARMTemplatePath $(System.DefaultWorkingDirectory)/OnlineMedicine/Drop/OnlinePharmacy.Configuration/Templates/OnlineMedicine.json -ARMTemplateParametersPath $(System.DefaultWorkingDirectory)/OnlineMedicine/Drop/OnlinePharmacy.Configuration/Templates/OnlineMedicine.parameters.json -resourceGroupName $(ResourceGroupName) -OMSWorkspaceName $(OMSWorkspaceName) -skuName $(skuName) -deploymentName $(RELEASE.RELEASENAME) -deployLocation $(deployLocation) -pullserverRegKey $(regKey)**.

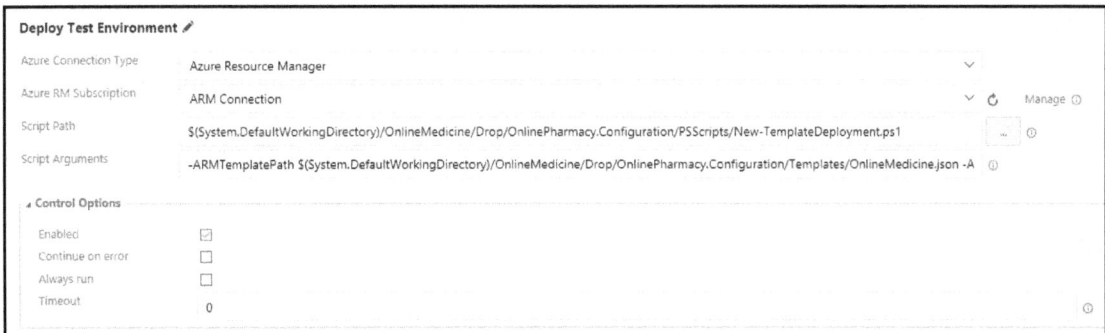

Figure 29: Deploy production environment

PowerShell – prepare Pester environment

This is again similar to the test environment, and it uses the same script.

In *Figure 30,* **Type** is configured with **File Path**.

Script Path is configured as
$(System.DefaultWorkingDirectory)/OnlineMedicine/Drop/OnlinePharmacy.Configurati on/PSScripts/PreparePesterEnvironment.ps1.

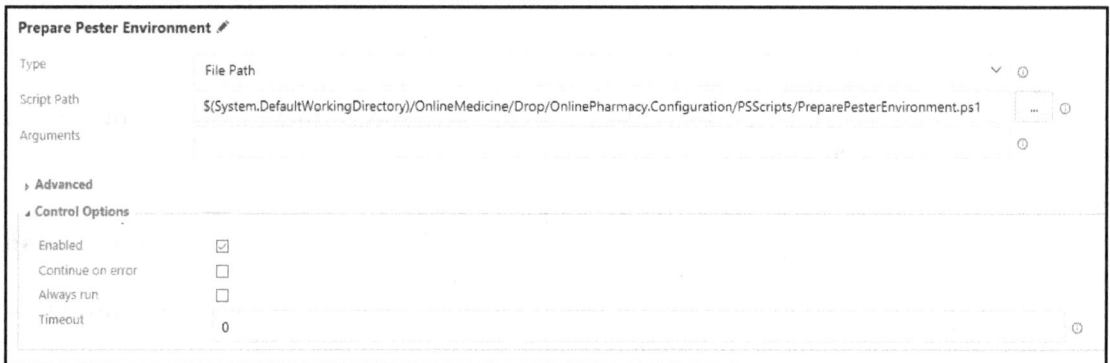

Figure 30: Preparing Pester environment

Copy Files – copy operational validation module

This is again the same as the test environment and uses the same configuration.

In *Figure 31,* the **Source Folder** path is configured as
$(System.DefaultWorkingDirectory)/OnlineMedicine/Drop/OnlinePharmacy.Configurati on/Tests/OperationalValidation/OnlineMedicine.

Contents is configured with ******.

Target Folder is configured as
$(USERPROFILE)\Documents\WindowsPowerShell\Modules.

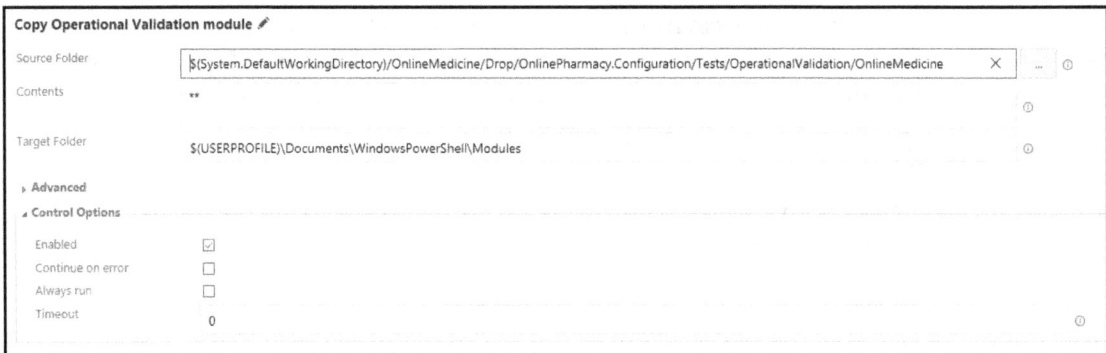

Copy Operational Validation module 🖊				
Source Folder	$(System.DefaultWorkingDirectory)/OnlineMedicine/Drop/OnlinePharmacy.Configuration/Tests/OperationalValidation/OnlineMedicine	✕	...	ⓘ
Contents	**			ⓘ
Target Folder	$(USERPROFILE)\Documents\WindowsPowerShell\Modules			ⓘ
▸ Advanced				
▲ Control Options				
Enabled	☑			
Continue on error	☐			
Always run	☐			
Timeout	0			ⓘ

Figure 31: Copy operational validation test cases module

Azure PowerShell – execute Pester and operational validation tests

This task is responsible for executing Pester and operational validation tests by executing the `Execute-Pester.ps1` PowerShell script. The script uses `Invoke-Pester` to execute Pester as well as the operational validation test cases.

In *Figure 32*, **Azure Connection Type** is configured with **Azure Resource Manager**.

Azure RM Subscription is configured to use already and is created by the **ARM Connection** ARM service endpoint.

Script Path is configured as
$(System.DefaultWorkingDirectory)/OnlineMedicine/Drop/OnlinePharmacy.Configuration/PSScripts/Execute-Pester.ps1.

Script Arguments is configured as **-testScriptPath
"$(System.DefaultWorkingDirectory)\OnlineMedicine\Drop\OnlinePharmacy.Configura
tion\Tests\UnitTests" -releaseName "$(RELEASE.RELEASENAME)" -
resourceGroupName "$(ResourceGroupName)" -operationTestsPath
"$(System.DefaultWorkingDirectory)\OnlineMedicine\Drop\OnlinePharmacy.Configura
tion\Tests\OperationalValidation\OnlineMedicine\Diagnostics\Comprehensive"**.

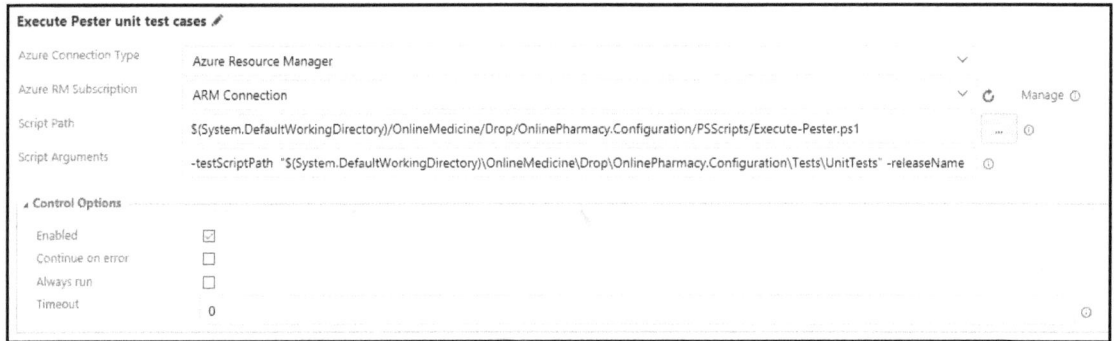

Figure 32: Executing Pester and operational validation test cases

Release pipeline execution

There are multiple places from where release definitions can be executed manually in VSTS.

Release definitions can be executed using the context menu available against each release definition as shown in *Figure 33*.

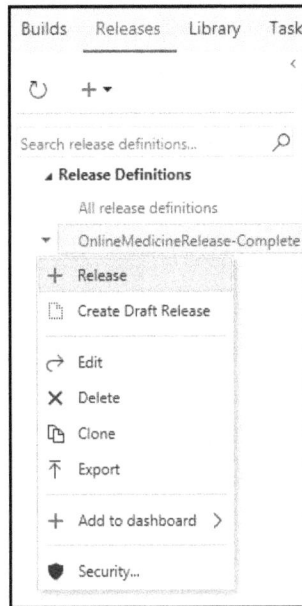

Figure 33: Queuing a release definition manually

If the release definition is in the edit mode, it can be executed by clicking on the **Create Release** button on the menu as shown in *Figure 34*.

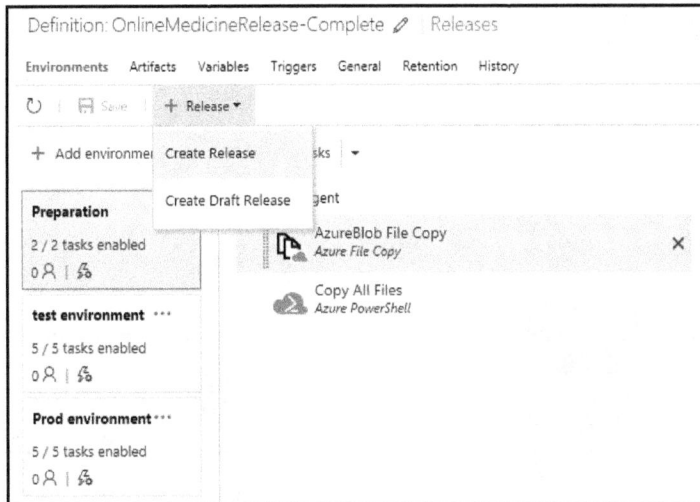

Figure 34: Another way to queue release definition manually

The release progress can be viewed from the console window. Clicking on the **Releases** link takes to window containing the details of all the release executions. This is shown in *Figure 35*.

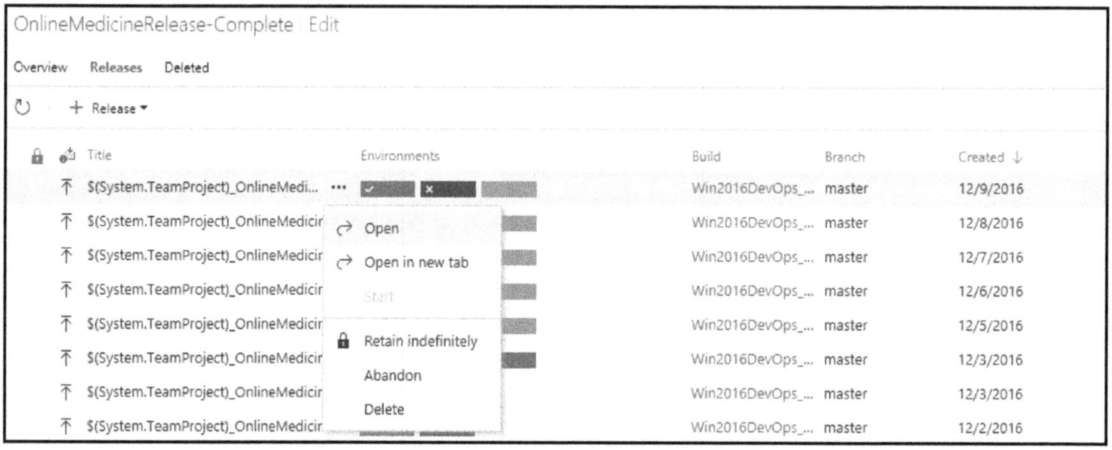

Figure 35: List of releases

Clicking on **Open** shows a dashboard containing all the details about the release executions including artifacts and logs. This is shown in *Figure 36*.

Figure 36: Release dashboard

Clicking on the logs menu items shows the log entries for each activity in each environment as shown in *Figure 37*.

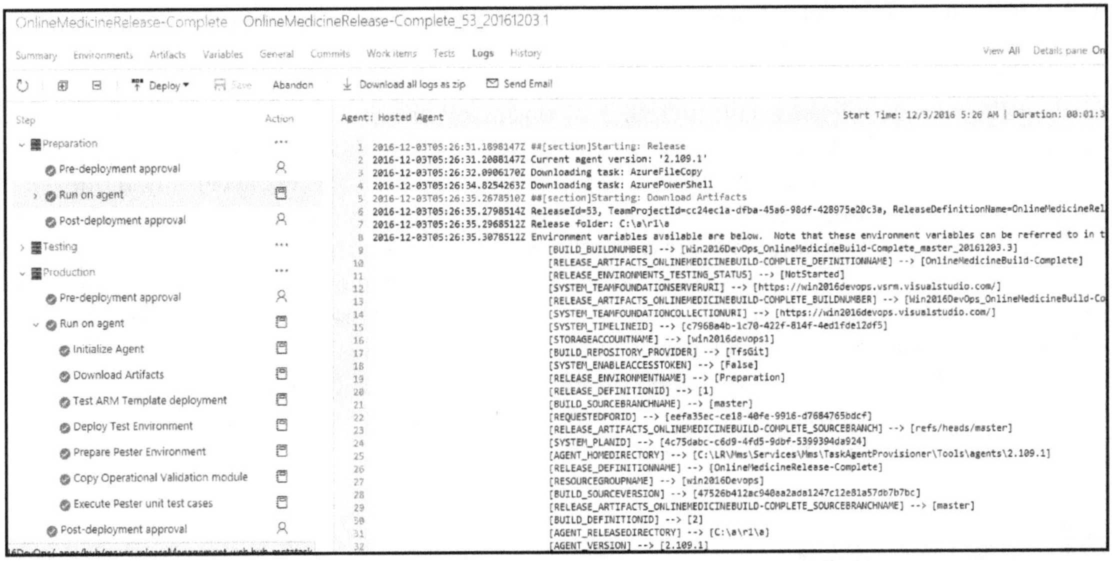

Figure 37: Release execution progress and logs

Release pipeline strategies

Release pipelines are used for deployment to environments such as development, testing, staging, and production; however, they can also be used for multiple other purposes as well. Some of them are mentioned next.

A/B testing

A/B testing is experimental testing of the application at the user interface level. It tries to mix and change the user interface to evaluate the adaptability, usage, and the consumption of the service. Multiple smaller releases can be made to change the UI aspect of the application and understand the best combination of UI that can lead to the best experience and performance from a usage point of view.

Blue/Green deployments

Blue/Green deployments are used to reduce risks in continuous deployment where two sets of production environments are maintained. One is referred to as the Blue environment, and the other is known as the Green environment. At any point of time, only one environment serves requests on production. The other environment is kept on a standby mode. When a new release is conducted, it is conducted on the servers that is in standby mode. Once complete rigorous testing including operation validation is successfully executed, the standby servers becomes the primary production servers accepting requests while the original primary servers are converted into standby mode. The swap ensures that there is minimum downtime and it is done during off-peak hours. It is to be noted that this is an expensive solution as two sets of redundant servers are maintained; however, only one set is used to serve requests on the production environment. However, this reduces the risks of the release and eliminates the need for rollback of a release on a production server. If the release does not work as expected on the standby servers, the release can be abandoned and can be tried again in future without disturbing the availability of the production environment to end users.

Canary releases

A canary release refer to the release of a smaller functionality to a smaller subset of users to check that it is working before making a fuller release. A host of smaller canary releases are done in sequence, and rigorous testing is conducted after each small release.

Summary

This chapter introduced both continuous deployment and delivery. There is a small difference between these concepts. In fact, achieving continuous delivery automatically will lead to continuous deployment. If you are doing continuous deployment with heavy automation, you are already doing continuous delivery. Continuous delivery is the first step toward continuous deployment. We looked in detail why at both continuous deployment and delivery are important and considered their benefits, and we discussed some of their important principles. They are a mature evolution from executing manual deployment processes to the automated delivery of code and deployment to multiple environments. It's a mechanism to tell developers about issues arising out of deployment and helps in failing earlier than later. These concepts are not complete without the discussion of release definitions and pipelines. Release pipelines are the automation of deployment processes on multiple environments using an approval workflow and environment definitions.

Tasks inside these environments are the main workhorse for getting the job of continuous delivery and deployment. VSTS is the set of core platform services used in this chapter and book for continuous delivery and deployment. The next chapter will focus on monitoring environments and applications by gathering telemetry information so that appropriate corrective action and improvements can be incorporated into both environments and applications. This will ensure that end users get a high-quality reliable, available, and performance-centric service.

11
Monitoring and Measuring

"If you can't measure it, you can't improve it" – Lord Kelvin

Wonderful! If you have reached here, trust me that you know quite a lot about DevOps both from an understanding and implementation perspective. This is the last chapter of this book, and we have covered all the major pillars of DevOps. We have covered the concepts and activities essential for the DevOps implementation and to make it work effectively and efficiently. There are other activities such as automated testing and coded UI tests, that were not covered in this book. They have been amply covered elsewhere on the Internet.

This chapter will discuss at length the concepts and implementation related to monitoring and measuring the different aspects of applications and environments on the production environment. Monitoring and measuring is an important activity within the DevOps life cycle as it helps in capturing the telemetry in real time about the status of the production environment and application. From raw telemetry data, appropriate information is derived and sent to a development team as feedback in order to improve the overall application quality and enhance its features. The same information is useful for the operations team to take proactive and reactive actions to keep the application operational, which is also named *keeping the lights on*. The telemetry information is also consumed by management stakeholders for effective decision making and in order to prioritize the next set of features from the implementation perspective.

Continuous monitoring is one of the main pillars of DevOps and deals with capturing information from the application and environments, storing it for a period of time, conducting an analysis on it, generating information, and making decisions based on it. This chapter will discuss technologies that help in conducting monitoring and measuring for both the application as well as the infrastructure environments.

Azure provides two services–Application Insights to monitor the application and Operational Insights to monitor the infrastructure environment. We will look at both in this chapter.

Application Insights

As the name suggests, Azure Application Insights provides insights about the health of an application. The insights relevant for a web application would include the incoming number of requests per second, requests failed per second, CPU utilization, memory availability, and much more. Application Insights provides a dashboard, reports, and charts to view various metrics related to the application's health. This helps in viewing and understanding the trends in terms of usage of the application, its availability, and usage to take both precautionary as well as reactive actions on the application. Trends information can be used to find out things not working in favor of the application and things working in its favor over a period of time.

The first step in working with Application Insights is to provision this service on Azure within a resource group. We will provision this service in the same resource group that contains shared resources consumed by all the applications. If you can recall, we had created a similar resource group named **Win2016DevOps** that contains all common shared services such as Azure Key Vault, Operational Insights, and a storage account to hold scripts and templates used across environments and applications.

Provisioning

As mentioned before, the first step in consuming Application Insights services is to provision it on Azure.

Application Insights can be provisioned either manually using the Azure portal or through automation using Azure REST APIs, PowerShell, and Azure Resource Manager templates. In this chapter, Application Insights will be created manually in the Win2016DevOps resource group using the Azure portal. Readers should by now be adapt at writing the resources in Azure Resource Manager templates and should add the Application Insights resource in the `GeneralServices.json` file to provision it through automation as an exercise.

If you have been following all the steps mentioned so far in this book, log on to your Azure portal and subscription using the appropriate credentials and navigate to the **win2016devops** resource group. Click on the **Add** button, as shown in *Figure 1*:

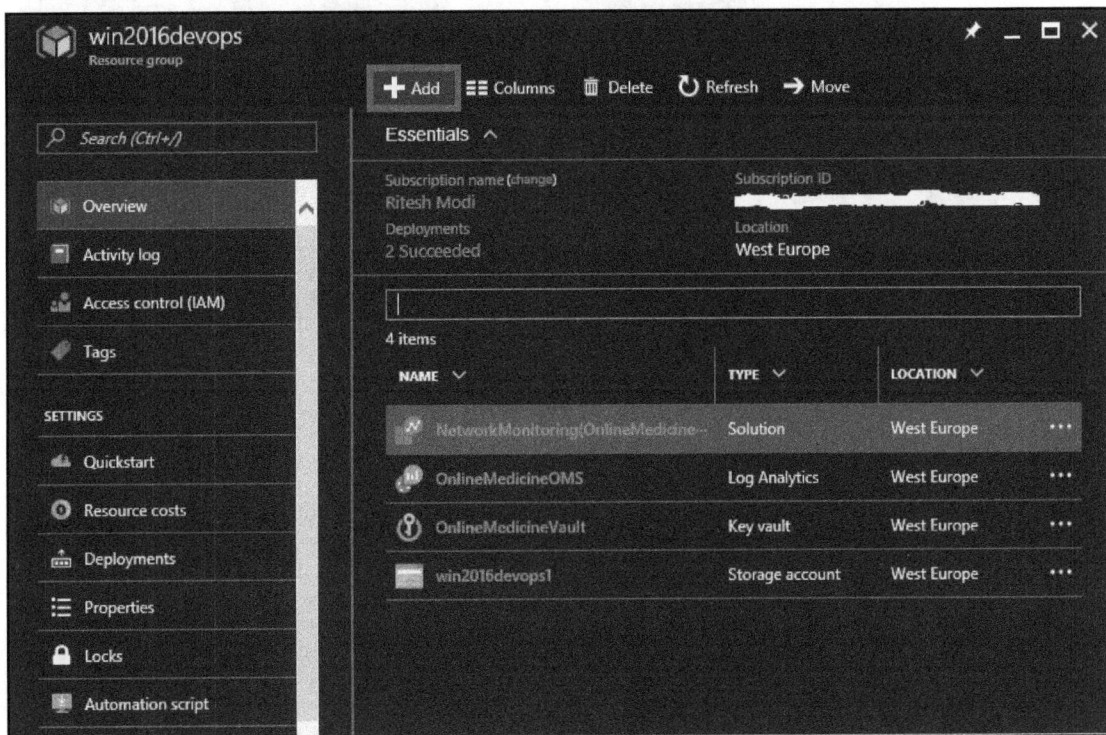

Figure 1: Azure resource group blade

Type **Application Insights** in the search box of the resultant blade; the first link should refer to **Application Insights**. Click on it to create a new **Application Insights** service instance as shown in *Figure 2*. Click on the **Create** button to get started.

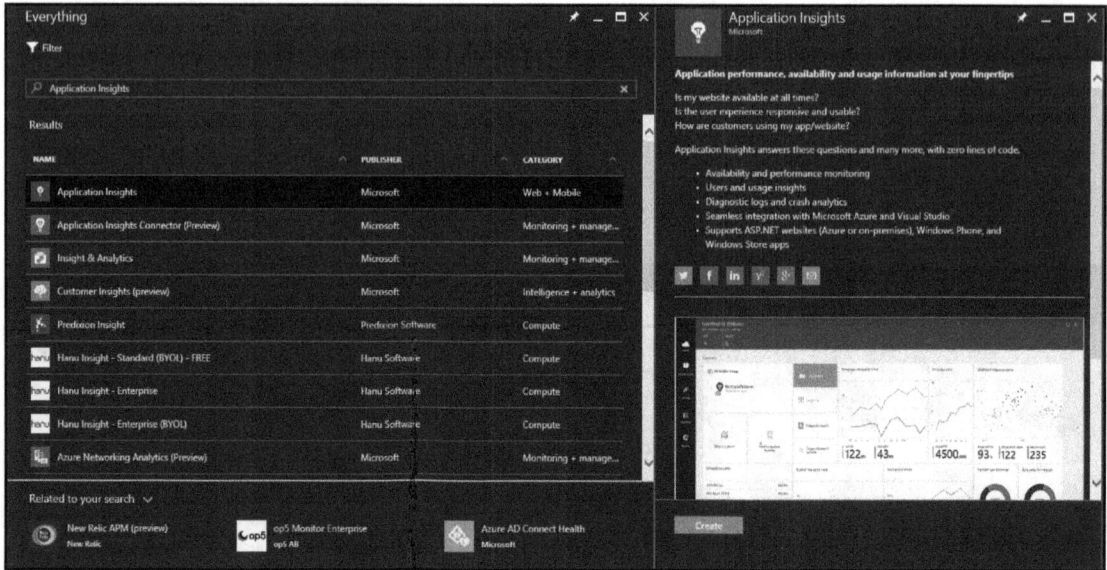

Figure 2: Add Application Insights service

The resultant blade will ask for the **Application Insights** service instance name, the type of application, subscription name, resource group name, and location of the service. Provide the details as appropriate and shown in *Figure 3* and click on the **Create** button. This will provision the service.

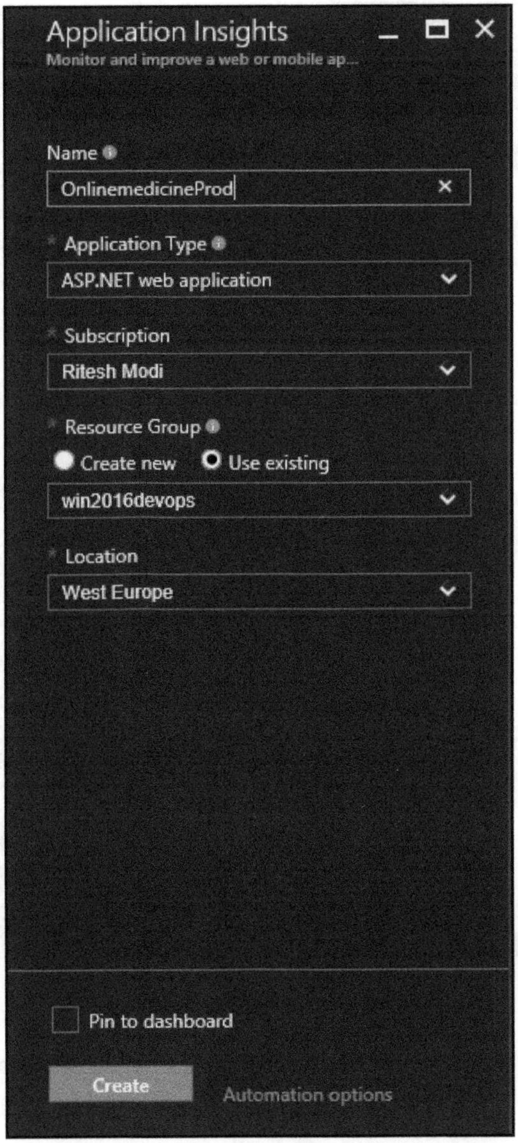

Figure 3: Application Insights inputs

Now, navigating to the service shows the essential properties such as its **Instrumentation Key**, as highlighted in *Figure 4*. The key will be different for every instance and should be copied for later use within Visual Studio. Please note that some of the information has been masked out due to security reasons.

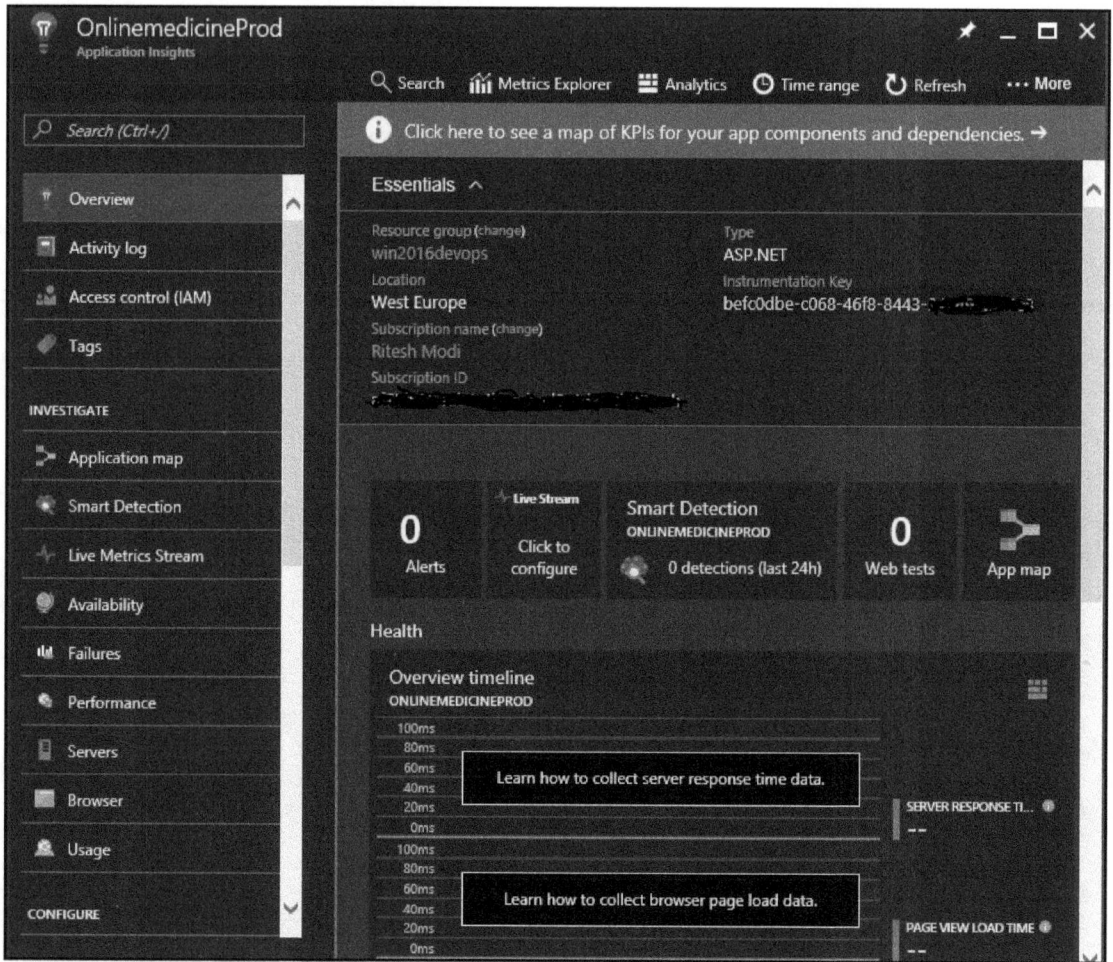

Figure 4: Application Insights instrumentation key

Next, changes should be made to the `OnlineMedicine` web application to start using the Application Insights service and send its telemetry information to it.

Changes to sample application

Open the **OnlinePharmacy** solution in Visual Studio and right-click on the
OnlinePharmacy web application project in solution explore. Select **ManageNuget** from the
Packages menu item from the context menu. It should open the **Nuget** window. Click on
the **Browse** menu and type **application insights** in the search box. It should show all
packages related to Application Insights. This is shown in *Figure 5*. Click on
the **Microsoft.ApplicationInsights.Web** and **Microsoft.ApplicationInsights** list items and
click on the **Install** button on the right to install the Application Insights assemblies within
the project. This needs to be done one after another as Nuget allows the installation of a
single package at a time. These assemblies can be viewed from within the references section
of the project. If it asks for a licence agreement confirmation, click on **I agree** to proceed
further.

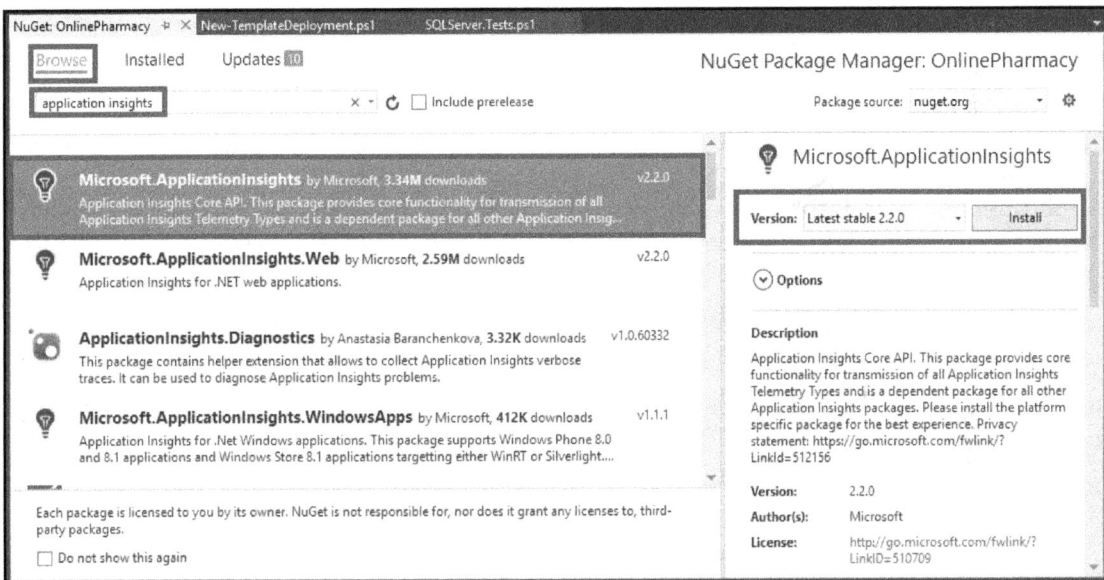

Figure 5: Installing Application Insights package through Nuget

A new `applicationInsights.config` file is generated. This file should be edited and the **Instrumentation Key** copied earlier should be added to it. This will ensure that the application starts using and sending telemetry to the Application Insights service on Azure.

The instrumentation key should be added within the `ApplicationInsights` XML element, as shown in *Figure 6*.

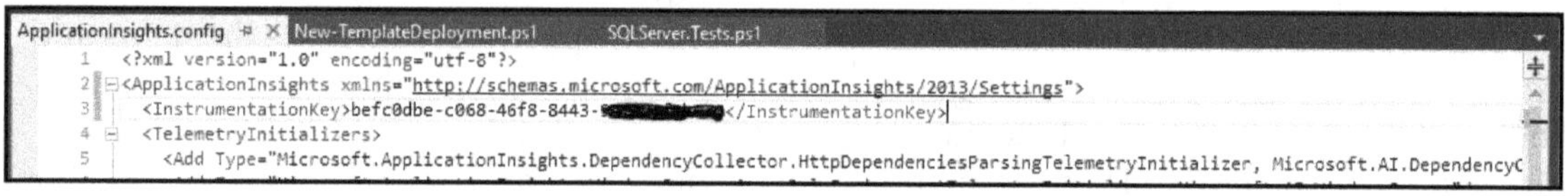

```xml
ApplicationInsights.config  ⇄ ×  New-TemplateDeployment.ps1        SQLServer.Tests.ps1
  1     <?xml version="1.0" encoding="utf-8"?>
  2   □ <ApplicationInsights xmlns="http://schemas.microsoft.com/ApplicationInsights/2013/Settings">
  3       <InstrumentationKey>befc0dbe-c068-46f8-8443-████████</InstrumentationKey>
  4   □   <TelemetryInitializers>
  5         <Add Type="Microsoft.ApplicationInsights.DependencyCollector.HttpDependenciesParsingTelemetryInitializer, Microsoft.AI.DependencyC
```

Figure 6: Adding the instrumentation key to the config file

Application Insights dashboard

Click on the **Live Metrics Stream** button on the Application Insights management dashboard in the Azure portal. Run the application on the local development box and keep refreshing the resulting page in the browser to generate requests. The live stream Application Insights dashboard should start showing information captured and sent to it by the web application. This is shown in *Figure 7*.

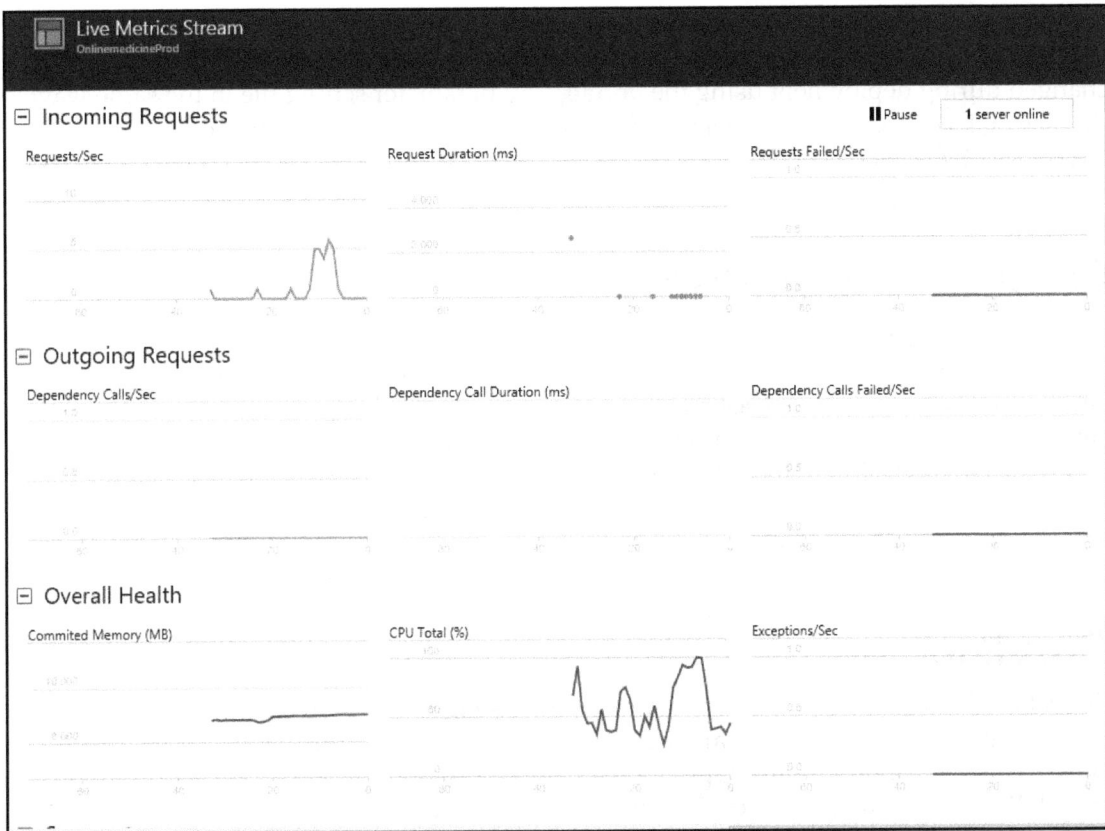

Figure 7: Application Insights live stream dashboard

The changes to the project should be checked in to the repository. It is important to note that developers may opt for a different Application Insights service for each environment or just provision an instance for the production environment instead of every environment or provision a single instance for all environments apart from the production environment and a dedicated instance for the production environment.

Readers should review their solution requirements and adopt a strategy that best suits them to identify the number of Application Insights services within the continuous integration and continuous deployment process.

Another approach in using this instrumentation key is to store it in the **Settings** section of the `web.config` file and read the same imperatively through the code. This key can be changed during deployment using the `webdeploy` parameter setting file in the same way that the SQL connection string was changed in `Chapter 8`, *Configuration Management and Operational Validation*.

Operational Insights

Application Insights is used to monitor custom applications; however, it is equally important to monitor the environment on which they are deployed and hosted. The environments can involve infrastructure components such as virtual machines, networks, storage accounts, any many other resources. Operational Insights will provide information about the overall health of the infrastructure in terms of its usage, availability, changes, security, and many other areas that can help an operations person to take both proactive and reactive actions on the environments.

Provisioning

Operational Insights, also known as **Operations Management Suite** (**OMS**) must be provisioned on Azure before it can be consumed to monitor the virtual machines. Again, similar to Application Insights, Operational Insights can be provisioned through Azure portal, PowerShell, REST API, or Resource Group Manager templates. For the purpose of this book, the Azure Resource Group Manager templates approach is used to provision the Operational Insights workspace. An Operational Insights workspace is a security boundary that can be allowed to be accessed by certain users. Multiple workspaces should be created for the isolation of users and their corresponding access to the environment telemetry data.

The JSON script used in `GeneralServices.json` to provision an Operational Insights workspace is shown here:

```
{
    "apiVersion": "2015-11-01-preview",
    "type": "Microsoft.OperationalInsights/workspaces",
    "name": "[parameters('workspaceName')]",
    "location": "[parameters('deployLocation')]",
    "properties": {
        "sku": {
            "Name": "[parameters('serviceTier')]"
        }
    }
}
```

The name, location, and sku information is needed to provision a workspace, and values for them are provided using parameters. The name of the workspace for the purpose of this book is **OnlineMedicineOMS** deployed at the **West Europe** location.

The workspace after provisioning is shown in *Figure 8*.

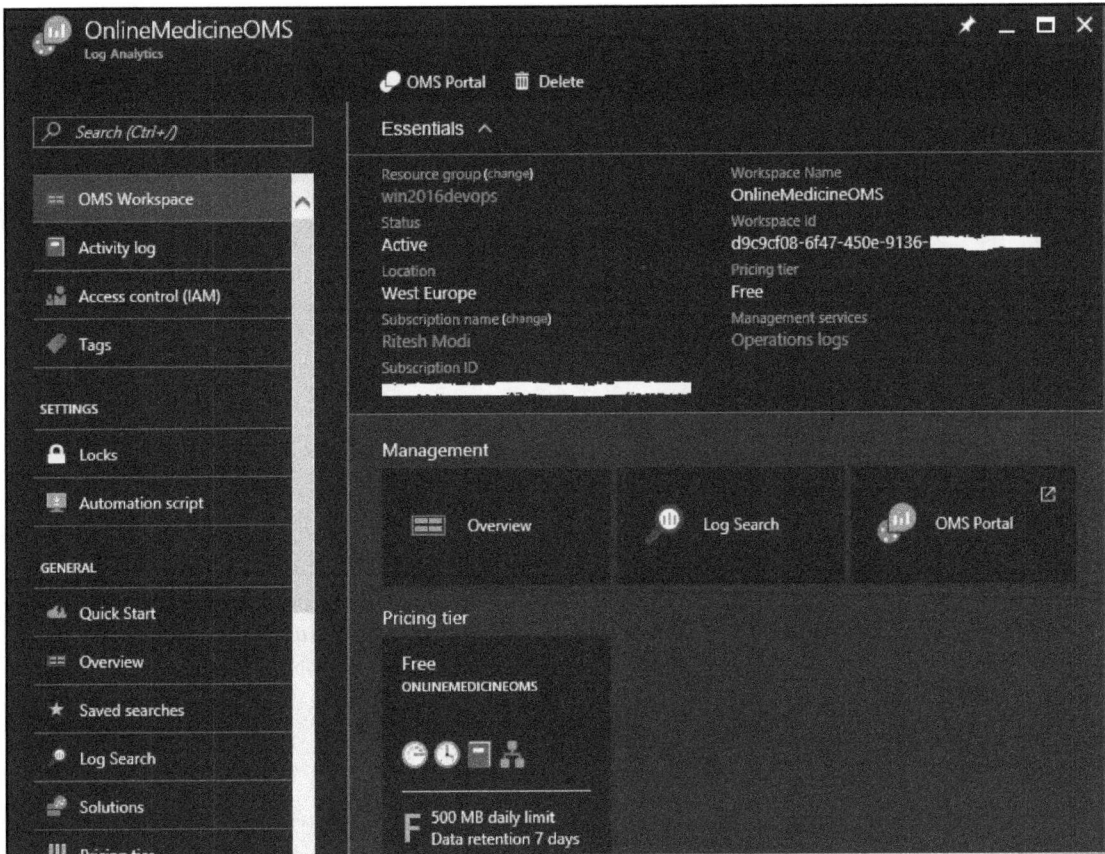

Figure 8: The Operational Insights management dashboard

Click on the **OMS Portal** section to open the workspace portal. This portal is used to view all telemetry information captured by Operational Insights, in configuring Operational Insights, and provides dashboard features and functionality.

The home screen of Operational Insights is shown in *Figure 9*.

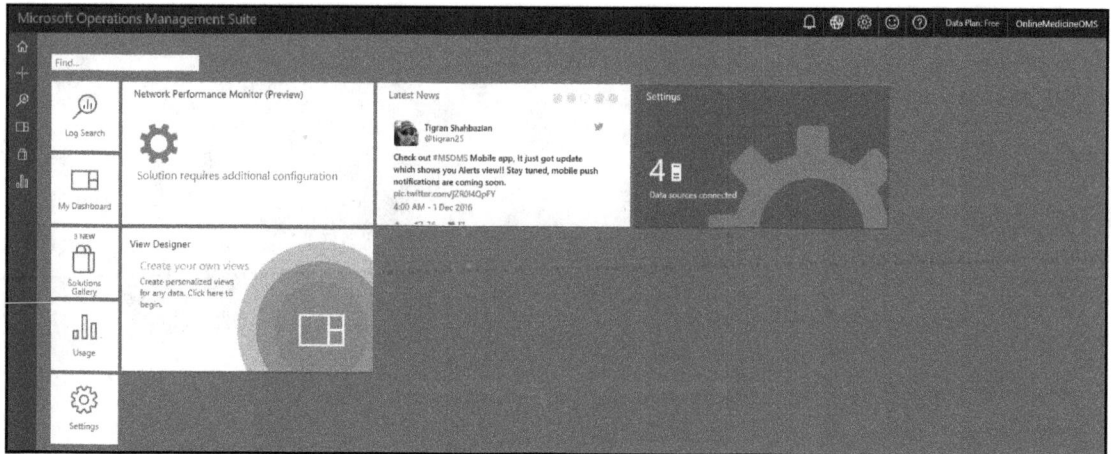

Figure 9: The Operational Insights workspace dashboard

The **Settings** section shows that four data sources are connected. These are four virtual machines connected to the workspace. Two virtual machines from each test and production environment are connected. A different strategy of having a separate workspace for each environment can be adopted, and readers should decide the best for their applications and solutions. Operational Insights can be configured using the **Settings** tile, as shown in *Figure 10*.

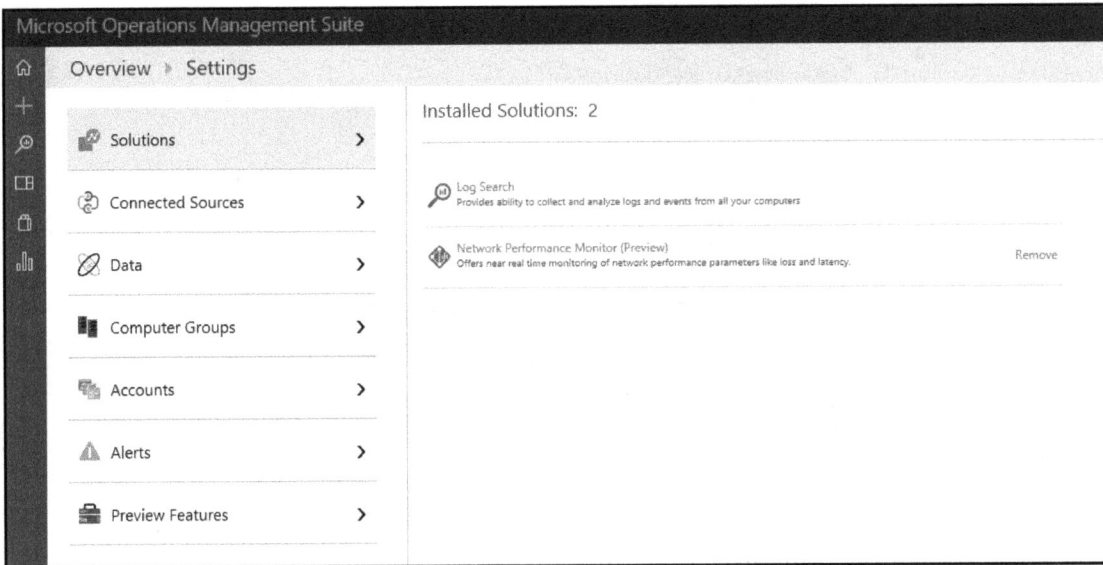

Figure 10: Operational Insights settings

OMS agents

If you may have noticed, no assembly or code changes are done to the application for consuming Operational Insights. Operational Insights depends on the installation of an agent on the virtual machines. These agents keep collecting telemetry data on these hosts and send them to the Azure Operational Insights workspace where they are stored for a specified period depending on the plan (sku) chosen while provisioning it. These agents can be installed manually on virtual machines. This book uses the Azure Resource Management virtual machine extensions to install agents automatically immediately after provisioning the virtual machines. The JSON code for provisioning an agent on a virtual machine is shown here:

```
{
        "apiVersion": "2015-06-15",
        "type": "Microsoft.Compute/virtualMachines/extensions",
        "name": "[concat(variables('vmName'),copyIndex(1),'/omsscript')]",
        "location": "[resourceGroup().location]",
        "dependsOn": [
"[concat('Microsoft.Compute/virtualMachines/',variables('vmName'),copyIndex
(1))]",
        "[resourceId('Microsoft.Compute/virtualMachines/extensions',
        concat(variables('vmName'),copyIndex(1)),'powershellscript')]"
```

```
        ],
        "copy": {
        "count": "[parameters('countVMs')]",
        "name": "omsloop"
        },
    "properties": {
        "publisher": "Microsoft.EnterpriseCloud.Monitoring",
        "type": "MicrosoftMonitoringAgent",
        "typeHandlerVersion": "1.0",
        "settings": {
          "workspaceId": "[parameters('WorkspaceID')]"
        },
        "protectedSettings": {
          "workspaceKey": "[listKeys(variables('accountid'),'2015-11-01-
preview').primarySharedKey]"
        }
    }
  }
}
```

The workspace ID and primary shared key is available from the **Settings** tile of the OMS workspace and a copy element is used to deploy agents on to multiple virtual machines. This resource is a child resource of the virtual machine resource ensuring that this extension is executed after provisioning of a virtual machine.

Figure 11 shows the configuration related to workspace ID and workspace key. The primary key of the OMS workspace is used to configure the agents using ARM templates.

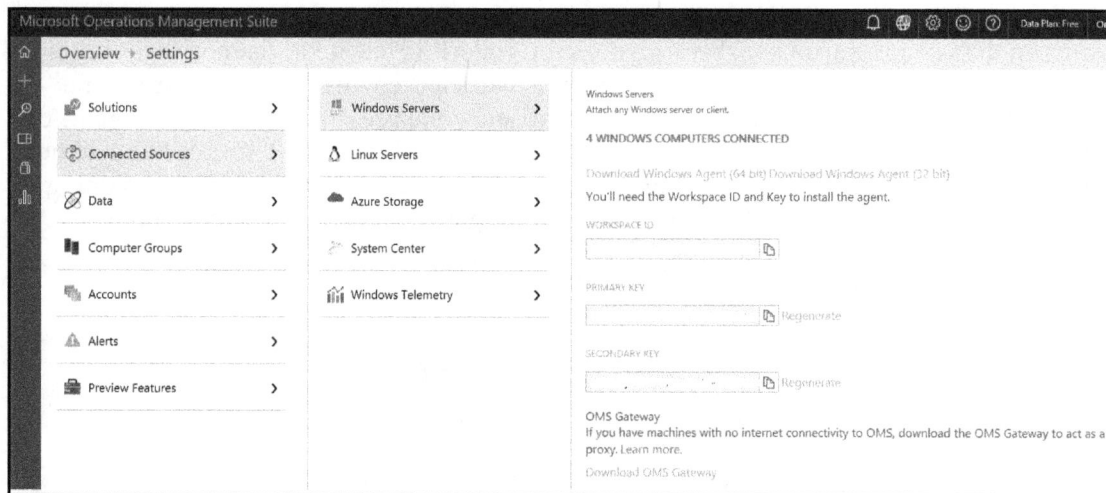

Figure 11: Operational Insights connected sources settings

Search

The OMS workspace provides advance search capabilities through the **Log Search** tile. It provides the capability to search log entries and helps in the export of telemetry data in multiple data formats including Excel and PowerBI.

Figure 12 shows the search screen:

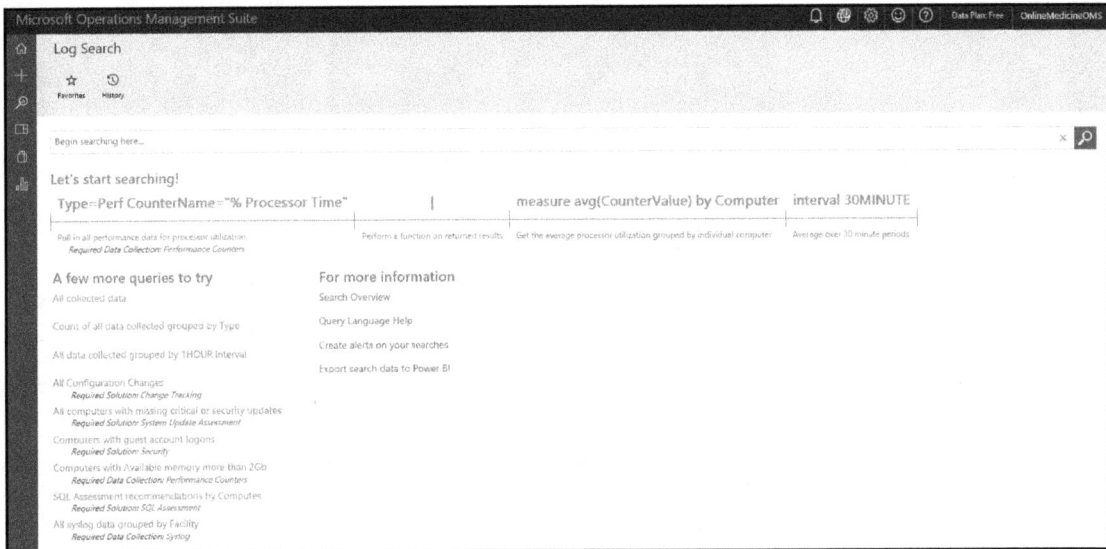

Figure 12: Operational Insights search blade

Solutions

Solutions in OMS are additional capabilities that can be added to the workspace capturing additional telemetry data that are not captured by default. When these solutions are added to the workspace, appropriate management packs are sent to all the agents connected to the workspace so that they can start capturing and sending solution-specific data from virtual machines to the OMS workspace.

Figure 13 shows the solution gallery on the OMS workspace. Clicking on any solution and subsequently clicking on the **Add** button adds the solution in context to the workspace.

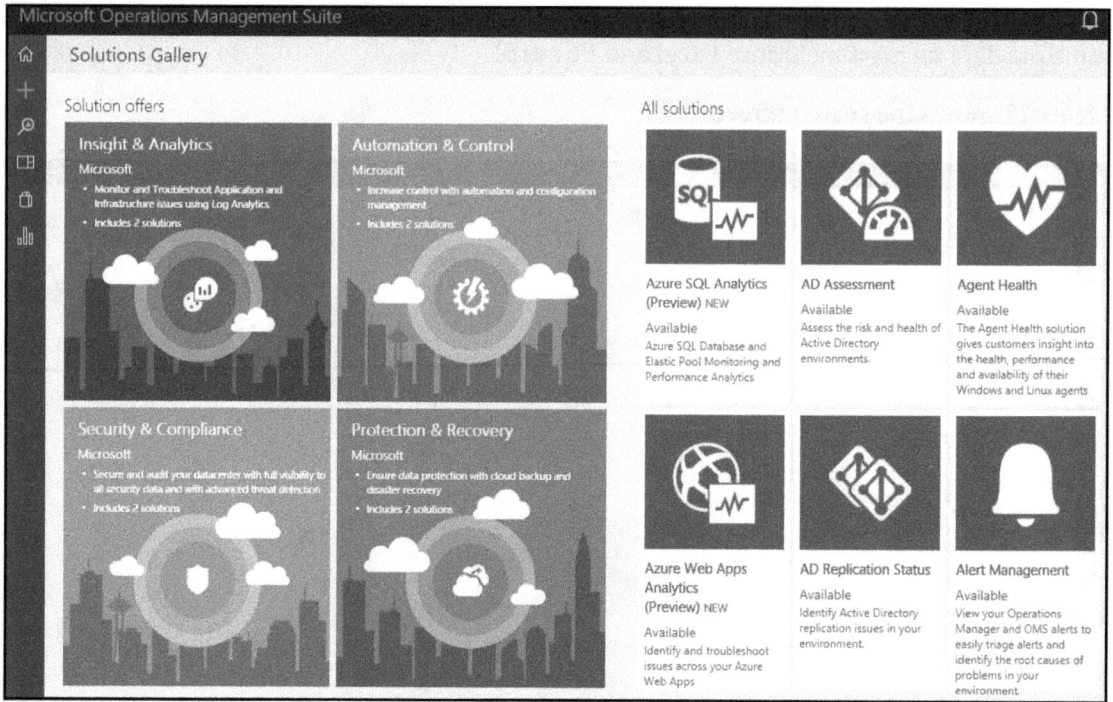

Figure 13: Operational Insights solution blade

In *Figure 14*, the capacity and performance solution is added to the workspace.

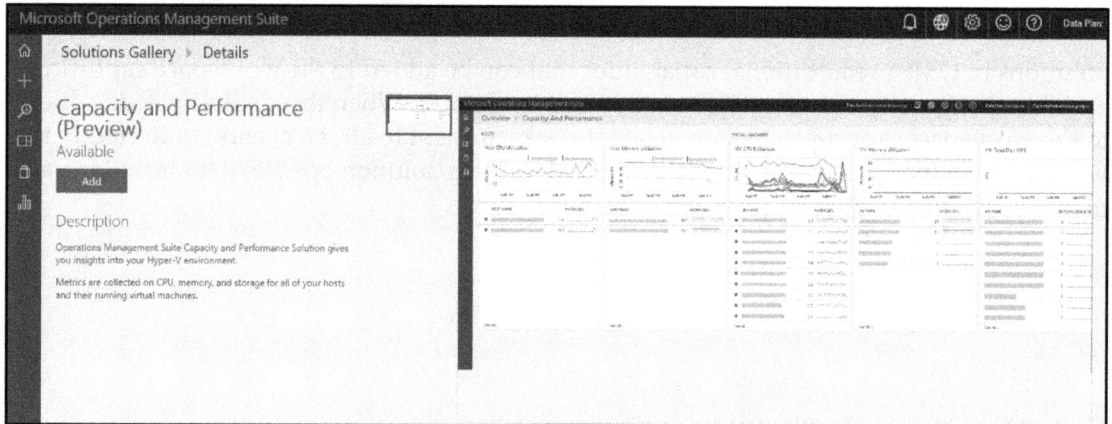

Figure 14: The Operational Insights solution blade

In order to capture enough telemetry information to ensure that environments are monitored well and to proactively find issues and risks, the following solutions should be added to the workspace:

- Capacity and performance
- Agent health
- Change tracking
- Containers
- Security and audit
- Update management
- Network performance monitoring

Although these solutions are not added through Azure Resource Manager templates, readers are advised to modify the template to add them. This will ensure that these solutions are provisioned every time these templates are executed.

Summary

This was the last chapter of the book and a very important chapter from a DevOps perspective. DevOps will not be effective and efficient without implementing adequate monitoring and measuring. The DevOps feedback loop and chain is incomplete in the absence of monitoring and measuring capabilities. Although monitoring and measuring can be done manually, their true benefits are realized using services such as Application Insights and Operational Insights. Azure provides Application Insights to monitor the availability, reliability, scalability, and performance of applications while Operational Insights helps the same way for environments.

With this, we come to the end of this chapter and book. It is hoped that you were able to comprehend, digest, and implement DevOps concepts, principles, and practices and were able to achieve the benefits to reach out to your customer faster, better, and cheaper with utmost quality. Let's signing off this book with the assumption that you would be able to build more, deploy and release more, fail fast, and fix early to provide a quality product and solution to your customer each and every time.

Index

www.ingramcontent.com/pod-product-compliance
Lightning Source LLC
Chambersburg PA
CBHW060949210326

41598CB00031B/4769

9 781786 468550